GLENN BROWN'S
HISTORY OF THE
UNITED STATES CAPITOL

Aerial view of the United States Capitol today.

GLENN BROWN'S
HISTORY OF THE
UNITED STATES CAPITOL

Introduction and Annotations
by
William B. Bushong

Annotated Edition in Commemoration of
The Bicentennial of the United States Capitol

Prepared by the Architect of the Capitol for
The United States Capitol Preservation Commission

108th Congress, 2nd Session

House Document 108–240

Printed pursuant to H. Con. Res. 358

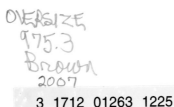

Brown, Glenn, 1854–1932.
    Glenn Brown's History of the United States Capitol / introduction
and annotations by William B. Bushong; prepared by the Architect of the
Capitol.—Annotated ed. in commemoration of the Bicentennial of the
United States Capitol.
        p. cm.
    Includes bibliographical references and index.
    1. United States Capitol (Washington, D.C.)—History.
I. Bushong, William. II. United States. Architect of the Capitol.
III. Title.
F204.C2B79 1998
975.3—dc21
                             97–50309
                                  CIP

Collection Credits

Collection credits are given in the captions only for objects from collections outside the United States Capitol. Architectural drawings are in the records of the Architect of the Capitol unless otherwise indicated in the caption. Current locations of works of art and contemporary room numbers are provided in many of the caption comments. In general, most of the works of art on the Senate side of the building are considered to be part of the United States Senate Collection under the Senate Commission on Art and those on the House side are in the United States House of Representatives Collection under the jurisdiction of the House Fine Arts Board. Works of art in the Rotunda and Crypt and the National Statuary Hall Collection are among those under the jurisdiction of the Joint Committee on the Library. In the case of prints, of which multiple impressions exist, a current outside collection is given where known for the reader's convenience.

Photographic Credits

Most black-and-white photographs in this book have been scanned from the plates produced from Frances Benjamin Johnston's negatives published in 1900 and 1903. In some cases, her turn-of-the-century views of some important rooms are contrasted with modern color photographs showing their present appearance. Modern color photographs of many paintings and drawings have been substituted for her black-and-white plates to enhance the reader's appreciation of them as works of art. In the case of architectural drawings, Brown often chose to show details or sections; in this edition the full drawing is shown if available.

American Architect and Building News	figure 4
American Competitions	figures 6, 7
Architectural Review	figure 9
Architect of the Capitol	figures 12, 13, 14, 15, 17, 18, 19, Frontispiece vol. I, 21, 22, 23, 24, 25, 26, 27
William B. Bushong	figures 2, 3, 5
Colonial Williamsburg Foundation	Plate 135
Corcoran Gallery of Art	Plate 99
Frances Benjamin Johnston (for Glenn Brown)	Plates 1, 2, 3, 7, 8, 9, 12, 13, 14, 23, 25, 28, 32, 33, 35, 36, 37, 38, 39, 53, 55, 56, 59, 60, 62, 67, 69, 71, 73, 74, 75, 76, 77, 78, 79, 80, 81, 82, 83, 86, 87, 88, 89, 91, 92, 93, 94, 95, 96, 97, 98, 100, 101, 101a, 102, 103, 104, 105, 106, 107, 112, 113, 114, 115, 116, 117, 118, 118a, 133, 134, 136, Frontispiece vol. II, 137, 155, 164, 165, 166, 167, 168, 171, 177, 178, 180, 183a, 185, 189, 199, 212, 219, 220, 221, 222, 223, 224, 225, 225a, 226, 227, 228, 229, 230, 231, 232, 233, 234, 235, 236, 237, 238, 239, 240, 241, 242, 243, 244, 245, 246, 247, 248, 249, 250, 251, 252, 253, 253a, 258, 259, 260, 261, 262, 263, 264, 265, 266, 267, 268, 269, 269a, 270, 271, 273, 275, 276, 277, 278, 279, 280, 282, 283, 284, 285, 286, 287, 288, 289, 290, 291, 292, 293, 294, 295, 296, 297, 298, 311, 312, 315, 316, 317, 318, 319, 320, 321, 322, Keys to paintings
Journal of the American Institute of Architects	figures 8a, 8b
Library of Congress	figures 1, 16
	Plates 15, 16, 17, 18, 19, 19a, 19b, 20, 21, 22, 24, 29, 30, 31, 34, 40, 41, 42, 43, 44, 45, 46, 47, 48, 49, 50, 51, 52, 61, 63, 64, 65, 66, 68, 70, 70a, 72, 90
Maryland Historical Society	Plates 4, 5, 6, 10, 11, 26, 27
Papers Relating to the Improvement of the City of Washington, District of Columbia	figure 10
Smithsonian American Art Museum, Smithsonian Institution	Plates 303, 304
The Kiplinger Washington Collection	Plates 58
The Octagon Museum, The American Architectural Foundation	figures 11, 20
The United States Patent and Trademark Office	Plate 130
United States Senate Commission on Art	Plates 128, 301, 305, 306, 307, 313, 314

(The box at the top of the page lists: Plates 54, 57, 84, 85, 108, 109, 110, 111, 119, 120, 121, 122, 123, 124, 125, 126, 127, 129, 131, 132, 138, 139, 140, 141, 142, 143, 144, 145, 146, 147, 148, 149, 150, 151, 152, 153, 154, 156, 157, 158, 159, 160, 161, 162, 163, 169, 170, 172, 173, 174, 175, 176, 179, 181, 182, 183, 184, 186, 186a, 187, 188, 190, 191, 192, 193, 194, 195, 196, 197, 198, 200, 201, 202, 203, 204, 205, 206, 206a, 207, 208, 209, 210, 211, 213, 214, 215, 216, 217, 218, 254, 255, 256, 257, 272, 273a, 274, 281, 299, 300, 302, 308, 309, 310, 311a, 311b)

For sale by the Superintendent of Documents, U.S. Government Printing Office
Internet: bookstore.gpo.gov Phone: toll free (866) 512–1800; DC area (202) 512–1800
Fax: (202) 512–2104 Mail: Stop IDCC, Washington, DC 20402–0001

ISBN 978-0-16-075368-8

PREFACE

The United States Capitol Preservation Commission has been pleased to support the preparation of this new annotated edition of Glenn Brown's *History of the United States Capitol* as part of its mission to provide for the preservation of the Capitol. In addition to preserving and enhancing the building and the art collection, this mission includes preserving knowledge about the history of the Capitol and encouraging understanding of the building through research and publications.

The publication of this book is part of the celebration of the Bicentennial of the United States Capitol. The bicentennial period extended from 1993, the anniversary of the laying of the first cornerstone of the Capitol by President George Washington on September 18, 1793, to the year 2000, the two-hundredth anniversary of the year the Congress moved to the new national capital on the banks of the Potomac River.

The annotated edition of Glenn Brown's *History* follows a series of publications sponsored by Congress on the history of the Capitol. These include *The United States Capitol: A Brief Architectural History*, first published in 1990 and reprinted in 1994; *The Dome of the United States Capitol: An Architectural History*, 1992; *"In the Greatest Solemn Dignity": The Capitol's Four Cornerstones*, 1994; Barbara Wolanin's *Constantino Burmidi: Artist of the Capitol*, 1998; and William C. Allen's *History of the United States Capitol A Chronicle of Design, Construction, and Politics*, 2001. The Commission cooperated in the preparation of *The United States Capitol*, 1993, with outstanding photographs of the building by Fred J. Maroon. *Capitol Builder: The Shorthand Journals of Montgomery C. Meigs, 1853–1859, 1861*, edited by Wendy Wolff, 2001, was a collaborative effort. We commend the Architect of the Capitol for preparing these much-needed and informative publications for the use of the Congress and the American people.

PRESIDENT PRO TEMPORE,
U.S. SENATE

SPEAKER,
U.S. HOUSE OF REPRESENTATIVES

CO-CHAIRMEN, U.S. CAPITOL PRESERVATION COMMISSION

FOREWORD

One of the most important publications about the United States Capitol is Glenn Brown's *History of the United States Capitol,* published in two volumes by the U.S. Government in 1900 and 1903. These beautifully designed volumes are treasured by those interested in the history of the Capitol, and, despite being over 100 years old, they still provide important information on the building and its art collection. The plates documenting the appearance of the Capitol at the turn of the century often provide clues vital to both historical research and modern restoration projects. Now, as the Capitol enters its third century, it is fitting that we recognize and re-examine this important study.

In this new one-volume edition, William Bushong sets the original publication in context by the introductory essay on Glenn Brown and his place in the story of the Capitol and the city of Washington. Extensive annotations provide the reader with information regarding Brown's sources and offer valuable perspective on his viewpoints and limitations. They also note twentieth-century publications on topics that Brown discussed. Many of the drawings that Brown published are preserved in the records of the Architect of the Capitol and newly photographed for this edition.

While the *History of the United States Capitol* is today considered a pioneering work of architectural history, it was also crafted by Brown to be helpful in two of his favorite crusades. He used the *History* to promote the restoration of the capital city's original plan along the lines of Pierre L'Enfant's 1791 design (as interpreted by the emerging "City Beautiful" aesthetic). Deviations from the plan and Victorian intrusions had, Brown believed, done untold harm to the beauty of Washington. Brown also credited George Washington and Thomas Jefferson with recognizing and appreciating the excellence of the city plan and the original design of the Capitol, an example worthy of emulation by modern political leaders; they should become patrons of the fine arts and, like Washington and Jefferson before them, insist that only the best American architects and artists work on the federal buildings in the capital. Through this work, Brown was able to make history a powerful force in his determination to improve the nation's capital.

The use of history as a force is, of course, a fascinating study in its own right, and the present volume is an excellent illustration of the way in which history seems to work. No matter how exhaustively researched and meticulously crafted, no study is truly definitive--there will always be room for reinterpretation, reconsideration, and revision as new information comes to light. William Bushong's work in this book exemplifies the value of the process, and as a result of his efforts we now have the benefit of Glenn Brown's knowledge and point of view but also that of a modern scholar's perspective on them.

The modern Capitol represents the work of generations of architects, engineers, artists, and builders. It also embodies the commitment of generations of Americans to our way of government. The publications and other educational projects undertaken by this office as part of the Congressional commemoration of the Capitol's bicentennial period are intended to increase the nation's and the world's awareness of how the Capitol has come to be the building that it is today. This book is a unique and important element of our overall program. In addition to its own documentary significance, it affords an understanding of the way in which the Capitol's history has been told.

Our office has been pleased to make possible William Bushong's research on Glenn Brown and the *History of the United States Capitol* through the United States Capitol Historical Society Fellowship program and by bringing the proposed publication to the attention of the United States Capitol Preservation Commission, which has funded its preparation. I am confident that the reappearance of Brown's *History* will be welcomed by the American public.

ALAN M. HANTMAN, FAIA
ARCHITECT OF THE CAPITOL

CONTENTS

VOLUME II: HISTORY OF THE UNITED STATES CAPITOL

LIST OF FIGURES AND PLATES

VOLUME I
PLATES

VOLUME I
PLATES

VOLUME I
PLATES

VOLUME II
PLATES

VOLUME II
PLATES

VOLUME II
PLATES

ACKNOWLEDGMENTS

THE United States Capitol is revered by Americans because it manifests the contributions of successive generations who have built, ornamented, remodeled, restored, or preserved a monument that symbolizes the growth and evolution of our representative form of government. It was the desire to understand this historic character of the building's architecture that inspired Glenn Brown to research and to produce a two-volume *History of the United States Capitol* (1900 and 1903). Through his research into the history of the Capitol, Brown became absorbed in the modern planning and development of Washington. His scholarship renewed public appreciation of Pierre Charles L'Enfant's 1791 plan for the city of Washington and would ultimately inspire its revival in new urban plans for the capital. Initially published as a Senate document, the *History* was a sumptuous book, the product of the Progressive era in which the United States emerged as a major nation-state and was seeking symbols to commemorate its status as a world power.

The purpose of this annotated edition is to revive a classic work of American architectural history that not only provides important information on the development of the Capitol but also is a remarkable visual record of the building and the art collection at the turn of the century. The publication is not intended to substitute for a new architectural history of the Capitol, nor is it a simple facsimile of the original book. In 1970 the Da Capo Press of New York published a smaller one-volume reprint of the *History,* which has long been out of print. The present book has been designed as a new critical edition of Glenn Brown's architectural history. I explore the author's background, biases, and achievements in an introductory profile and provide annotations to the text when necessary to correct errors, identify sources, describe controversial issues, or point readers to further modern published versions of cited documents or information on selected topics. Misspellings or factual errors and inconsistencies in Brown's original text, including those in the table of contents, list of plates, captions, and tables, have not been altered.

Brown largely reproduced drawings and works of art from the collections of the Library of Congress and the Architect of the Capitol, but he also copied prints in the collections of prominent Washingtonians. In the present edition, contemporary high-quality color or black-and-white photographs of architectural drawings, prints, and paintings have been used in place of the original black-and-white plates; entire images have been used in place of cropped versions. Special care has been taken to reproduce the book's original photographic views, which are invaluable images of the building at the turn of the century and represent a major body of architectural photography produced by master photographer Frances Benjamin Johnston. Johnston's photographs of architectural views have been scanned.

Research on this volume was completed in 1993, at the beginning of the bicentennial period. Additional major works concerning the Capitol published since that time are not reflected in the footnotes but are listed in the bibliography. These include Charles E. Brownell and Jeffrey Cohen's *The Architectural Drawings of Benjamin Henry Latrobe,* Pamela Scott's *Temple of Liberty: Building the Capitol for a New Nation,* Barbara A. Wolanin's *Constantino Brumidi: Artist of the Capitol,* William C. Allen's *History of the United States Capitol: A Chronicle of Design, Construction, and Politics,* and William Kloss and Diane K. Skvarla's *United States Senate Catalogue of Fine Art.*

The research and the preparation of the draft manuscript for this new edition of Brown's *History* was made possible by a fellowship program funded by the United States Capitol Historical Society and jointly administered by the Architect of the Capitol. Research conducted with this support led to the completion of my 1988 dissertation for the George Washington University, entitled "Glenn Brown, the American Institute of Architects, and the Development of the Civic Core of Washington, D.C.," and to the preparation of the draft manuscript for this work. I wish to thank the United States Capitol Historical Society, which supported this project from its inception. Society president Fred Schwengel had a keen interest in Glenn Brown and provided unfailing support of this project before his death in 1993. I am also indebted to his successors, who have continued and expanded the Society's mission and have strongly backed scholarly work related to the Capitol.

The preparation for publication of this new edition of Brown's architectural history was made possible by funding from the United States Capitol Preservation Commission beginning in 1991. The proposal for the book was presented to the commission by the Architect of the Capitol, who has been responsible for managing the project. I am grateful for the support given to the proposal by then Secretary of the Senate Walter J. Stewart; Richard Baker, Historian, U.S. Senate; James Ketcham, then Curator of Art, U.S. Senate; and Raymond Smock, then Historian, U.S. House of Representatives. The printing of the book was authorized by the Congress with the support of the commission. For his support and interest in the revival of this classic book and the outstanding administrative support that I received while working on this edition, I am indebted to then Architect of the Capitol George M. White. I would also like to thank the staff of the Architect of the Capitol's office, including Curator Barbara Wolanin, who not only inspired me to research and produce this monograph on Glenn Brown's *History* but also has been crucial to sustaining the endeavor. Architectural historian William C. Allen generously shared his extensive knowledge of the Capitol's architectural history and suggested numerous contributions that greatly improved the content of the final manuscript. Archivists John Hackett and Sarah Turner were my guides to the records of the Architect of the Capitol and deserve thanks for their advice and assistance in locating significant correspondence,

drawings, scrapbooks, and reports. Florian Thayn was most helpful at the beginning of this project. Eric Paff provided valuable advice. Pamela Violante McConnell was a constant source of cheer and efficiency in the search for documents, photographs, prints, and architectural drawings for reproduction in this book. Ann Kenny assisted with numerous revisions to prepare the book for publication. Photographer Wayne Firth's skill in preparing the photographs for hundreds of Brown's plates and a series of modern comparative views of the Capitol's interior spaces was vital to the appearance of this book; other Photography Branch Staff also contributed images. I would like to convey special thanks to Joel Treese for his research advice and assistance.

I am also indebted to numerous archivists, reference librarians, architectural historians, and historians who have shared their insights and knowledge of the history of Congress, Washington, D.C., or the Capitol over the years, including Howard Gillette, James Goode, C. M. Harris, Don A. Hawkins, Cornelius Heine, Donald Kennon, Antoinette J. Lee, Richard Longstreth, Jon Peterson, David Rabasca, Pamela Scott, Diane Skvarla, Farar Elliott, and Tony P. Wrenn. Rodney Ross, Richard Fusick, and Maryellen Trautman of the National Archives and Records Administration provided invaluable assistance in locating pre-serial-set congressional documents cited by Brown related to the construction of the Capitol. I am also grateful for the expert editorial work of Frank Rives Millikan, who contributed to the organization and overall readability of the book. Mary Kinnecome also deserves praise for her efficient word processing and research assistance. I would also like to thank Janice Sterling, designer from the Government Printing Office, for her boundless patience and invaluable assistance. My wife Rebecca receives my heartfelt gratitude for her constant encouragement, research, and editorial assistance throughout this project. Finally, I wish to dedicate my work on this project to the memory of Alan S. Rogers, M.D.

WILLIAM B. BUSHONG

LIST OF ABBREVIATIONS

AIA . . . . American Institute of Architects

AOC . . . . Architect of the Capitol

DCC . . . . Records of the Commissioners for the District of Columbia, 1791–1925

DHC . . . . House Commission on Construction of House Office Building, *Documentary History of the Construction and Development of the United States Capitol Buildings and Grounds* (Washington: Government Printing Office, 1904)

LC . . . . Library of Congress

MHS . . . . . . Maryland Historical Society

NARA . . . . . National Archives and Records Administration

RG . . . . Record Group

Annotator's Note

This annotation focuses on Glenn Brown's original text for volumes I and II and does not include Charles Moore's introduction. The data in the tables in both volumes stands as Brown published it. It has not been annotated or corrected because of the voluminous and numerous footnotes that would have made the tables confusing to read. Brown derived the data in the tables from a variety of official and popular publications and records, and it is not always possible to determine the source of his information. The printed sources used by Brown are cited in the bibliography in this annotated edition. This updated bibliography and the reference files in the Architect of the Capitol Curator's Office and the Senate Curator's Office should be consulted to verify the information in Brown's tables. Glenn Brown's captions are shown in capital letters as in the original volumes. Annotations providing current information appear below the original captions in mixed-case type.

GLENN BROWN AND THE UNITED STATES CAPITOL

BY WILLIAM B. BUSHONG

T HE most important legacy of Washington architect Glenn Brown's prolific writing career was his two-volume *History of the United States Capitol* (1900 and 1903). Brown's *History* created a remarkable graphic record and comprehensive account of the architecture and art of the nation's most revered public building. His research, in a period in which few architectural books provided substantive historical text, established Brown as a national authority on government architecture and elicited acclaim from European architectural societies. The *History* also played a significant role in shaping the monumental core of Washington, in effect serving as what Charles Moore called the "textbook" for the McMillan Commission of 1901–02.[1]

Brown's family background supplied the blend of political awareness and professionalism that inspired the *History*. His great grandfather, Peter Lenox, supervised construction of the original Capitol Building from 1817 until its completion in 1829. His grandfather, Bedford Brown, served two terms in Washington, D.C., as a senator from North Carolina (1829–1842) and counted among his personal friends Andrew Jackson, Martin Van Buren, Franklin Pierce, and James

Figure 1. Glenn Brown, secretary of the American Institute of Architects, at the Octagon in 1907. *Prints and Photographs Division, LC.*

[1] Charles Moore (1855–1942), chief aide to Senator James McMillan (R–MI) and secretary to the now famous Senate Park Commission of 1901–02, commonly referred to today as the McMillan Commission, made vital contributions to the administration and editing of the influential 1902 planning report that subsequently shaped the twentieth-century development of the civic core of Washington, D.C. Moore later became chairman of the United States Commission of Fine Arts from 1910 until his retirement in 1937. For Moore's discussion of the importance of Brown's *History* to Washington's planners, see Charles Moore, "Glenn Brown: A Memoir," *Royal Institute of British Architects Journal* 39 (October 15, 1932): 858.

Buchanan. Brown's most influential role model was his father, Bedford Brown II. An 1850 graduate of Jefferson Medical College in Philadelphia, Dr. Brown established his practice at Yanceyville in Caswell County, North Carolina, while living at his father's plantation, "Rose Hill." He later served as a Confederate brigade surgeon and hospital inspector during the Civil War. Due to the state's depressed postwar economy, he moved from North Carolina to Alexandria, Virginia, where he achieved prominence as a physician and as a leading proponent of the professional licensing of medical practitioners.[2]

Born in 1854 in Fauquier County, Virginia, where his father briefly practiced medicine, Glenn Brown was raised at "Rose Hill" in North Carolina. He completed two years of study at Washington and Lee University in 1873 and returned to Alexandria to serve as his father's apprentice. To supplement a small allowance, he studied mechanical drafting and began producing drawings for patent attorneys. Through this drafting experience Brown discovered his aptitude for architecture. In 1875 he attended the architecture school at the Massachusetts Institute of Technology, then located in Boston, where he studied under the department's founder, William R. Ware. Brown later recalled that his mentor had instilled in him "the highest ideals in the profession, striving, no matter against what odds, for the best."[3]

After completing his studies at MIT, Brown obtained employment on Henry Hobson Richardson's Cheney Building in Hartford, Connecticut, as a draftsman and paymaster for the Norcross Brothers. Soon after marrying Mary Ella Chapman of Staunton, Virginia, a grandniece of President James Madison, Brown returned to Alexandria, Virginia, and obtained work as a draftsman for the Baltimore and Ohio Railroad in 1877. In 1880, he opened an independent office in Washington, D.C., and soon became a leading advocate of modern domestic architecture and sanitation, offering his clients workmanlike Richardsonian designs with advanced household plumbing systems.

Richardson's Romanesque Revival designs continued to influence Brown's practice into the 1890s as was evident in his commercial and residential design between 1884 and 1894. These structures strongly reflected the balance of picturesque composition and rational planning characteristic of Richardson's architecture. But just as Washington embraced Richardson's Romanesque as a new "American style" for its public buildings, Brown's design inspiration shifted to late eighteenth- and early nineteenth-century Georgian and Federal architectural landmarks in Alexandria and Washington, such as Gadsby's Tavern, the Carlyle Mansion, and the Octagon.[4] Brown's interest in early American architecture and its revival as a design source for public buildings began and deepened with his study of the United States Capitol between 1890 and 1900. He recognized the urban planning potential of neoclassical public architecture during his visit to the 1893 Columbian Exposition in Chicago. Although Brown had expected to be disappointed by "sham classical structures," he left Chicago deeply impressed by the beauty and grandeur of "noble buildings, nobly and harmoniously grouped."[5]

---

[2] See William B. Bushong, "Glenn Brown, the American Institute of Architects, and the Development of the Civic Core of Washington, D.C." (Ph.D. Dissertation, George Washington University, 1988).

[3] Glenn Brown, *Memories, 1860–1930: A Winning Crusade to Revive George Washington's Vision of a Capital City* (Washington: W. F. Roberts, 1931), 18–21.

[4] For a discussion of the influence of Richardson's architecture on the design of both Washington's public and private buildings and the perception locally that it would be the "American style," see Appleton P. Clark, "History of Architecture in Washington," 500–502, in John C. Proctor, ed., *Washington Past and Present: A History,* vol. 2 (New York: Lewis Historical Publishing Company, 1930).

[5] Brown, *Memories,* 345.

Figures 2 and 3. The T. P. Simpson residence at 1301 Rhode Island Avenue, N.W., completed in 1886, is a bold wedge-shaped Richardsonian Romanesque Revival house adapted to an unusual triangular lot facing Logan Circle.

Brown's personal conversion to neoclassicism became increasingly evident in his practice after 1893, and by 1900 he designed almost exclusively in this idiom. During the 1890s he became one of Washington's leading advocates of the Colonial Revival movement. Along with several other prominent local firms, notably Hornblower and Marshall and Harvey L. Page, he began drawing inspiration from historic buildings for the design of door and window surrounds, cornices, and mantels of new residences to "imbibe the spirit of the old work without literally copying it."[6] Brown had extensively promoted the appreciation

[6] For Brown's quotation and a discussion of the inception of the Colonial Revival movement in Washington, D.C., see Brown, "Domestic Architecture in Washington City," *Engineering Magazine* 7 (June 1896): 454–460.

THE NATIONAL UNION INSURANCE COMPANY'S NEW BUILDING   918 F STREET N.W.

Figure 4. The Romanesque Revival National Union Insurance Company Building at 918 F Street, N.W., completed in 1890, was the location of Brown's office between 1891 and 1905. *American Architect and Building News,* September 20, 1890.

Figure 5. The residence of Mrs. Joseph Beale at 2301 Massachusetts Avenue, N.W., completed in 1907.

4

of the region's historic buildings in his publications in the 1880s and later directed a restoration of Christ Church in Alexandria (1891), which included a new Colonial Revival pulpit that would be featured in *The Georgian Period* (1898).[7] The church's interior appearance today reflects both Brown's pioneering interest in historic preservation and his influential contribution to the Colonial Revival movement in the region. While working in 1901–1902 as historical adviser and construction superintendent for McKim, Mead, and White's renovation of the White House, Brown formed a warm friendship with Charles F. McKim and developed an admiration for the firm's eclectic neoclassicism. Brown's 1907 residence for Mrs. Joseph Beale on Sheridan Circle (now, the Embassy of Egypt) was a notable building erected at the peak of this influence. Two unexecuted projects, developed during his partnership with his son Bedford Brown IV, illustrate the firm's mastery of the then fashionable Beaux Arts style: a competition scheme for a capitol in Puerto Rico (1908) that was "conservative and dignified in treatment . . . and suitable to the tropical climate" and preliminary plans for the construction of a new AIA headquarters and library (1912). The AIA project was especially interesting in its development of a design

that complemented Thornton's Octagon. It appeared that Brown's interest in Thornton's lost competition design for the west front of the Capitol inspired his domical entrance for the new headquarters sited to the rear of the Octagon.[8]

By the time the first volume of the *History of the United States Capitol* was published in 1900, Brown had developed a clear vision for rebuilding and expanding the core of Washington based on the revival of the 1791 L'Enfant plan. Brown promoted his vision—which included the construction of a federal enclave that would echo the neoclassical architecture of Washington's early federal buildings—through his work as an organizer and lobbyist for the architectural profession. In his first national campaign as director of the Washington chapter of the American Institute of Architects, which he had founded in 1887, Brown supported an intensive AIA lobbying effort led by Chicago architect Daniel Burnham, to implement key provisions of the 1893 Tarsney Act. This law eventually opened commissions for major federal buildings to private architects. In 1895 Brown both conceived and organized the Public Art League, a national fine arts lobby formed to advocate the establishment of an expert commission of architects and artists to advise the government on its patronage of architecture, art, and

[7] See Brown, "Old Colonial Work in Virginia and Maryland," *American Architect and Building News* 22 (October 22, 1887): 198–199; "Old Colonial Work in the South," 22 (November 19, 26, 1887): 242–243 and 253–254; and "The Tayloe Mansion, the Octagon House, Washington, D.C.," 23 (January 7, 1888): 6–7. Brown's drawings along with others in this series became part of an influential source book for the Colonial Revival movement. See William R. Ware, comp., *The Georgian Period* (Boston: American Architect and Building News, 1899–1902), subsequently enhanced and published as *The Georgian Period* [Student Edition] (Boston: American Architect, 1904) and *The Georgian Period* (New York: U.P.C. Book, Inc., 1923). For a discussion of the importance of these early measured drawings, see William B. Rhoads, *The Colonial Revival*, 2 vols. (New York and London: Garland Publishing Co., 1977), 77 and 608 n. 8. For information on Brown's interior restoration of Christ Church, see John Milner Associates, "The Historic Structure Report for Christ Church, Alexandria, Virginia," unpublished manuscript submitted to the Vestry of Christ Church, copy on file at Lloyd House, Alexandria Public Library, Alexandria, Virginia.

[8] For the design competition program for the Puerto Rico Capitol, see Adin B. Lacey, comp., *American Competitions* (Philadelphia: T Square Club, 1908), vol. 2, xxiv. Compare Brown's drawing for the domical recess of the AIA headquarters to Plate 32 in *History of the United States Capitol,* vol 1. In 1912 Brown and his son and then-partner Bedford Brown prepared preliminary designs for the headquarters "in order that the members of the Institute may offer suggestions for or approval of a general scheme, and that a systematic effort may be made to secure the money to make the improvement." The proposal was ambitious and would have required $300,000 to build a Colonial Revival crescent-shaped structure. Bedford Brown directed the design project, but this alternative sketch indicated his father's strong influence. The AIA did not build an addition until 1939–1940. That Colonial Revival building, designed by Eggers and Higgins, was demolished to make way for the present headquarters in the 1970s.

ELEVATION OF FRONT

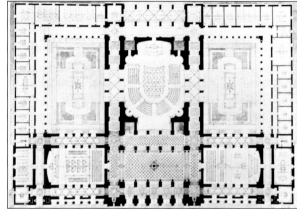

PLAN OF FIRST FLOOR

TRANSVERSE SECTION

ELEVATION OF SIDE

Figures 6 and 7. Four competition drawings for a capitol in Puerto Rico by Glenn and Bedford Brown. *American Competitions*, vol. II, 1908.

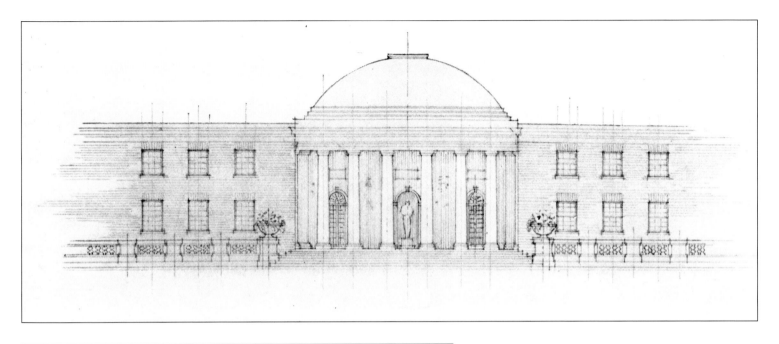

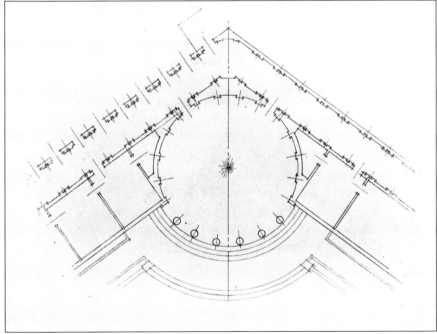

Figures 8a and 8b. These 1911 sketches of the elevation and plan for a domed recessed entrance to a planned AIA headquarters was largely based on Brown's interpretation of Thornton's design of the Capitol's west front (see Plate 32). *Journal of the American Institute of Architects*, Vol. 1, January—December, 1913.

sculpture. Brown's efforts on behalf of legislation for such a commission, introduced in the Senate by Francis G. Newlands (D-NV) in 1897 but never put to a vote, established his national professional prominence and resulted in his election as AIA secretary in 1898.

Once installed as a national AIA officer, Brown implemented an ambitious program to relocate the Institute's headquarters from New York City to Washington, to establish an archives and library as well as a professional journal, and to increase the organization's membership and its political influence. During his tenure as secretary, Brown so widely and effectively promoted the AIA that by 1913 it had attained recognition in Congress on par with that of the American Bar and Medical Associations.[9]

---

[9] Bushong, *A Centennial History of the American Institute of Architects* (Washington, D.C.: Washington Architectural Foundation Press, 1987), chapters 1 and 2.

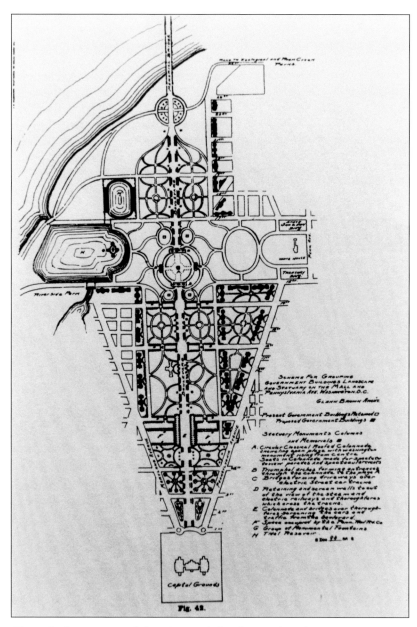

Figure 9. Brown prepared this "Proposed Plan for a Boulevard" in 1900 to promote professional oversight of a revival of L'Enfant's 1791 plan for central Washington. *Architectural Review, 1900.*

Figure 10. This 1899 photograph, "Vista at Fontainebleau," illustrated Brown's concept of the width necessary to create the expansive vista of L'Enfant's tree-lined Mall avenue. *Papers Relating to the Improvement of the City of Washington, District of Columbia (1901).*

Brown exerted additional influence through his writings. During his career he wrote or edited more than 80 articles and a dozen books, which usually became vehicles to promote the professional status of the architectural profession or to affect the government's patronage of public architecture and city planning.[10] Brown's "Selection of Sites for Federal Buildings" launched his crusade to base development of the national capital on a revival of the 1791 L'Enfant plan. He pointed to the mistakes of the past and described how the improper siting of the Library of Congress and the Treasury Building had blocked vistas to the Capitol from Pennsylvania Avenue, S. E., and to the White House from the Capitol, conspicuously marring the beauty of the plan. For Brown the essential element of the L'Enfant plan was "reciprocity of sight" between its cardinal points, the sites of the White House, United

---

[10] For a discussion of Brown's extensive writing career, see Bushong, "Glenn Brown," Chapter 2.

States Capitol, and the Washington Monument. Further mistakes, he argued, could be avoided if a Bureau of Fine Arts, composed of "cultivated architects and landscape artists," rendered decisions on the design and placement of public buildings and sculpture.[11]

In 1896 Brown produced a monograph on physician William Thornton in which he argued that Thornton deserved major credit for the original design of the Old Capitol (completed with significant revisions by Benjamin Henry Latrobe and Charles Bulfinch in 1826). Published in the *Architectural Record,* Brown's monograph contended that earlier historians underestimated Thornton's contribution to the design of the Capitol as well as his importance to Washington's early architectural development. Thornton's work as an architect, Brown asserted, "compares favorably with the best of the period in design and construction." He responded to Thornton's numerous nineteenth-century critics, who had dismissed the doctor as an untrained amateur, by maintaining that anyone who could have accomplished so much with "so little study must have been a truly remarkable man."[12]

Brown's case for Thornton became a cause in the "History of the United States Capitol," a series that appeared in the *American Architect and Building News* in 1896 and 1897. The articles provided the first history of the design competition for the Capitol and chronicled the Old Capitol's design and construction to 1829. These articles would be reprinted with minor revisions in volume one of the *History.* Brown established Thornton, Benjamin Henry Latrobe, and Charles Bulfinch as the architects of the Old Capitol. He depicted French architect Stephen Hallet and other early Thornton critics as jealous and petty rivals who attempted to destroy the integrity of the winning design. Brown even interpreted Benjamin Henry Latrobe's influence on the Capitol's development as detrimental to Thornton's design intent, although he generally praised Latrobe's work in rebuilding the Capitol after it had been burned by the British in 1814. The concluding articles described the completion of the building's central section and development of Charles Bulfinch's dome with a brief discussion of the landscape, paintings, and sculpture adorning the building before 1850. Brown's overriding theme in these articles was the wisdom of early government officials in selecting designers like Thornton, Latrobe, and Bulfinch, which resulted in the high quality of the Capitol's architecture.[13]

Brown's first volume of the *History* reflects an unswerving bias toward Thornton in his interpretations of the numerous conflicts and controversies that surrounded the early design and building of the Capitol. Today Latrobe is considered the designer who improved Thornton's exterior design and defined the overall interior architectural character of the Capitol before 1829. Brown's *History* was considered

[11] Brown, "The Selection of Sites for Federal Buildings," *Architectural Review* 3 (August 1894): 28. Brown failed to explain that L'Enfant's original intent for a memorial to Washington was an equestrian statue and that the Washington Monument as built was a far more dominant presence on the Mall.

[12] Brown, "Dr. William Thornton, Architect," *Architectural Record* 6 (July 1896): 52–70. His interpretation specifically challenged works by historians George A. Townsend and James Q. Howard, who promoted French architect Etienne (Stephen) Hallet as the building's principal designer. Late-nineteenth-century authorities on the architecture of the Capitol, such as Adolph Cluss and John H. B. Latrobe, also advanced this position. See also George A. Townsend, *Washington Outside and Inside* (Hartford: James Betts and Company, 1874); James Q. Howard, "The Architects of the American Capitol," *International Review* 1 (November–December 1874): 736–753; Adolph Cluss, "Architects and Architecture of the United States," *Proceedings of the Tenth Annual Convention of the American Institute of Architects* (Boston: Franklin Press, 1876); and John H. B. Latrobe, "The Capitol and Washington at the Beginning of the Present Century" [An Address before the American Institute of Architects in Washington, D.C., November 16, 1881], (Baltimore: W. K. Boyle, 1881).

[13] Brown, "History of the United States Capitol," *American Architect and Building News,* 52–55 (May 9, 1896): 51–54; (May 23, 1896): 75–77; (June 13, 1896): 99–102; (July 4, 1896): 3–5; (July 25, 1896): 27–30; (September 5, 1896): 75–78; (October 3, 1896): 3–6; (October 24, 1896): 27–29; (December 5, 1896): 81–83; (January 2, 1897): 3–6; (February 20, 1897): 59–60.

the authoritative source on the building until his objectivity and accuracy were seriously challenged by Wells Bennett and Fiske Kimball in a series of articles published between 1916 and 1923. Today Brown's discussion of the first competition for the Capitol and the early history of the building is considered flawed not only by his strong bias toward Thornton but also by inconsistencies and errors, including the

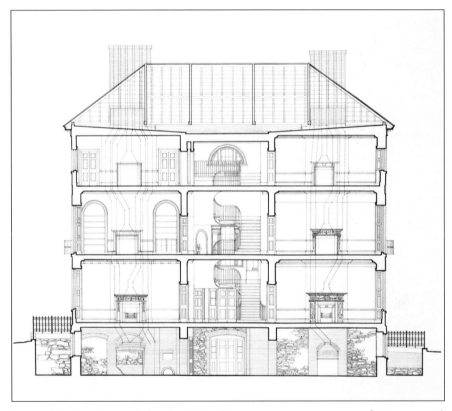

Figure 11. Commissioned by the AIA, this cross section was one of 30 measured drawings of the Octagon prepared under Brown's direction in 1913–1914. *Prints & Drawings Collection, The Octagon Museum, The American Architectural Foundation, Washington, D.C.*

misidentification of drawings, the omission of passages from key documents, and the hasty transcription of quotations.[14]

Brown's zealous promotion of Thornton as the "outstanding architect of his time" was related to his plan to have the AIA acquire and preserve Thornton's Octagon as its headquarters, an action which has since linked the public's recognition of the professional organization to this architectural landmark. If Thornton had been portrayed simply as an opportunistic gentleman architect with little practical knowledge of the field, Brown could hardly have convinced his colleagues to lease and later purchase the building. His promotion of Thornton's genius as a designer and the first Architect of the Capitol was motivated in part by a determination to preserve and adapt the Octagon as the AIA headquarters. Anticipating the reuse of the building for offices, a library, and a museum, Brown pressed for the building's purchase immediately after he became AIA secretary in 1899. The Institute purchased the Octagon in 1902 at a time when the preservation of historic buildings, except for houses associated with major historic figures, was a novel idea.[15]

---

[14] See Wells Bennett, "Stephen Hallet and His Designs for the National Capitol, 1791–94," reprinted from the *Journal of the American Institute of Architects* (July, August, September, October, 1916) [Harrisburg, Pa., 1916]. Fiske Kimball and Wells Bennett, "The Competition for the Federal Buildings," *Journal of the American Institute of Architects* 7 (January, March, May, August, December, 1919): 8–12, 98–102, 202–210, 355–361, 521–528; and Kimball and Bennett, "William Thornton and the Design of the United States Capitol," *Art Studies* I (1923): 76–92. See also Bennett's critique of Brown's *History*, printed as a letter to the editor in *The Nation* 102 (January 13, 1916): 43–44.

[15] In a gesture of gratitude for his loyal service to the organization, the AIA appointed Brown architect of the Octagon in 1914 to survey the building and administer repairs. Brown directed the preparation of a complete visual record of the building with photographs and measured drawings. Architectural photographer Frank Cousens, who published several books on Colonial Revival architecture, provided the illustrations. With the aid of his son and partner, Bedford Brown, and draftsmen Beverley Harris and William B. Cash, Brown produced thirty plates of elaborate measured drawings. The drawings and photographs were published in *The Octagon* (1915) and were his last tribute to Thornton.

Brown's intensive study of the Capitol's architecture made him the natural choice of Architect of the Capitol Edward Clark to assess damage to the building caused by a gas explosion in the basement in 1898. Brown produced a descriptive essay, six sheets of drawings, and numerous photographs illustrating the blast's impact on the lower levels of the building. The report also included plans of the existing condition of the sewer system and conduits for water, gas, steam, and other service needs. Brown offered several major recommendations: to reconstruct the central section of the Capitol roof with fireproof materials, to modernize the building's physical plant, and to erect a separate structure to house a power plant and store flammable materials such as wood, coal, documents, and books that had been stored in the Capitol basement. Brown suggested that a new building be erected to house power production and storage facilities. The proposed structure was to be connected to the Capitol by a subway to ferry coal, wood, and freight and to route all lines for gas, steam, and water, as well as electric, telephone, and telegraph wires.[16]

Impressed by the report, Clark asked Brown to prepare preliminary sketches in order to persuade members of Congress to appropriate funds for the project. Clark also promised to reward Brown with the commission for his preliminary design services. The sketches, titled "Building for Machinery, Storage, and Offices" and developed in 1900, illustrated Brown's solution to house the Capitol's power plant and presented a contextual design for a multipurpose structure that would provide the House of Representatives with additional space for offices and committee rooms. Brown developed a neoclassical exterior design that complemented the original building's historic architecture.

Meanwhile, Charles Moore convinced Senator James McMillan (R-MI), for whom Moore served as political aide, to sponsor publication of Brown's serial history of the U.S. Capitol as a Senate document. In December 1899, McMillan requested and obtained a Senate resolution to publish the history to commemorate the 1900 centennial of the removal of the seat of government to Washington. The Senate passed a motion to print 200 clothbound copies of the history for the use of the

Figure 12. Brown inspecting damage to the Capitol's west wall after the 1898 gas explosion.

---

[16] Brown, "Report on the Effects of an Explosion in the United States Capitol, November 6, 1898," in *Annual Report of the Architect of the Capitol* (Washington: Government Printing Office, 1899).

Committee on the District of Columbia.[17] Brown accepted the offer under the condition that he be allowed to design the book and supervise its production by the Government Printing Office. Brown personally selected the paper and type and designed the cover using the frieze of a mantel in the robing room adjoining the Old Supreme Court as a decorative motif. Charles Moore agreed to write the introduction, and the first volume appeared in December 1900.[18]

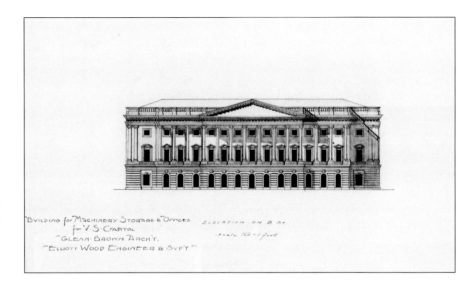

[17] "History of the Capitol," *Congressional Record* Senate, 56th Cong., 1st sess., vol. 33, December 15, 1899 (Washington, D.C.: Government Printing Office, 1900), 439. The book was not referred to the Committee on Printing because McMillan assured his colleagues it would not exceed the $500 cost limit on publications taken from the Senate contingency fund.

[18] The mantel was destroyed by the gas explosion of November 6, 1898. See Brown, *Memories*, 43.

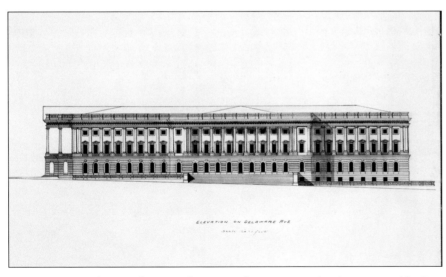

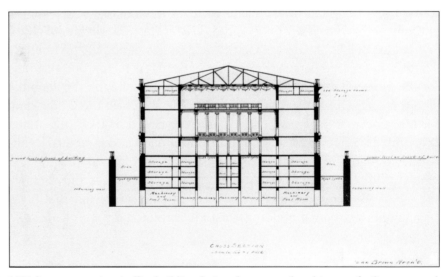

Figures 13, 14, and 15. Preliminary elevation and cross section drawings prepared by Brown in 1901 for a congressional office building designed, among other things, to facilitate removal of machinery and storage from the Capitol's basement.

Figure 16. Frances Benjamin Johnston in a portrait taken in 1903. *Prints and Photographs Division, LC.*

A few months after its publication, the *New York Times* weekly book review supplement printed a letter charging that the book was a lavish waste of government money and that only the author would profit from its sale. The newspaper concurrently ran an article informing readers that Brown's *History* had a small and limited run and that most of the volumes had been given to Senators and Representatives or donated to major public libraries. The *Times* praised the book and could see "nothing but credit to everybody who had anything to do with it, and to the Government which has issued it."[19]

As the *Times* suggested and as Moore noted in the introduction, the special value of Brown's work lay in its voluminous illustrations. An indication of the author's intent for a special visual quality was his creative collaboration with Frances Benjamin Johnston, recognized today as a master architectural photographer. Brown commissioned her to record the appearance of the building and to reproduce early maps of Washington and numerous paintings, prints, and drawings of the Capitol. The work was extensive and may have prompted a barter of services as Brown designed an addition for Johnston's V Street studio in 1902.[20]

The *History* included 322 plates representing a vast collection of large-scale plates of drawings, maps, paintings, sculpture, architectural

---

[19] *New York Times* (Saturday Review of Books Supplement, April 27, 1901), 298.

[20] Johnston had provided photographs for Brown's serial history of the Capitol in 1896–1897 as well as illustrations for his 1896 articles on William Thornton and domestic architecture in Washington. After Brown became AIA secretary in 1898, Johnston became the organization's unofficial photographer. She photographed the Octagon when the AIA purchased the building, documented the appearance of the White House before and after the McKim, Mead, and White renovation that Brown superintended, and made portraits of the organization's presidents during the first decade of the twentieth century. For background on her career, see Pete Daniel and Raymond Smock, *A Talent for Detail: The Photographs of Miss Frances Benjamin Johnston, 1899–1910* (New York: Harmony Books, 1974), 3–34. There are a number of letters in Brown's papers that discuss Johnston's preparation of the illustrations for the author's articles and books. See Johnston to Glenn Brown, January 25 and February 14, 1898; William Rotch Ware to Brown, March 16, September 26, November 18, December 1, 14, 19, 22, 26, 1896, and January 26, February 4, 10, 1897. See also Heliotype Printing Company (Boston) to Brown, June 19, 1900, forwarding proofs for the *History of the United States Capitol*, and Irving T. Guild to Brown, July 2, 1900. All of the above letters are located in the Brown Papers, RG 804, Ser. 5, AIA Archives. See also Herbert Wise to Frances B. Johnston, February 15, 1902, Johnston Papers, Manuscript Division, LC. The letters indicated that Brown usually obtained the negatives from Johnston, and then sent them to the publishers at their request. A survey of Johnston's negative proofs at the Prints and Photographs Division of the Library of Congress reveals that a number of negatives in that collection were produced for Brown's publications. However, the plates in the *History of the United States Capitol* do not match the proofs in Johnston's collection and may be extra project negatives.

photographs, and overall views of the grounds that with the text created a visual and descriptive catalog of the architectural evolution of the Capitol and its physical state at the turn of the century. Another impressive feature was the extensive original research, albeit without footnotes and flawed by Brown's bias in favor of Thornton. The second volume, based largely on the reports of the Architect of the Capitol, is more objective and included an annotated bibliography of the author's major sources.

Brown located and examined manuscripts, drawings, and maps deposited throughout the city at the State, Treasury, and Interior departments as well as public documents in the possession of the Superintendent of Buildings and Grounds, the Office of the Chief of Engineers, and the Office of the Architect of the Capitol. He also traveled to Baltimore to examine the first competition drawings for the Capitol at the Maryland Historical Society and consulted collections of papers or drawings of Latrobe's superintendent John Lenthall, Thornton, and Thomas U. Walter (then privately owned respectively by their descendants, William S. Abert, J. Henley Smith, and Olivia and Ada Walter). In addition, Brown drew on an extensive collection of published pamphlets, articles, and books at the Library of Congress bearing on the history of the building. The Latrobe papers were not then available to researchers.[21]

Brown's research was no easy task given the unorganized nature of the collections and the resistance of government bureaucrats to providing access to official files. Brown recalled that he had particular trouble seeing the early records of the District of Columbia, then located in the Office of Public Buildings and Grounds. Captain John Stewart, custodian of the records, had spent more than twenty years organizing and indexing the collection, which had been transferred to the jurisdiction of the Chief Engineer of the U.S. Army after Congress mandated in 1867 that public works and improvements in the capital be superintended by the Army engineers. Brown described Stewart as an "old Scotchman...who looked upon the records as private property upon which no one should encroach." Stewart performed meritorious service in cataloging the records because the Army was able to ascertain and locate missing and stolen documents and maps that belonged in the collection. Ultimately, the collection contained many documents and maps that proved invaluable to Brown's study, especially the original 1791 L'Enfant map and a wealth of other manuscripts and maps related to the early history of the city.[22]

Brown's *History* was calculated to instill pride in the origins of the national capital. George Washington emerged as a heroic figure whose vision of a new federal city and whose wisdom in selecting architects and engineers of talent and ability provided a model for contemporary political leaders. Brown relished Washington's comments on disputes surrounding the plans for the Capitol, quoting the first president: "I profess to have no knowledge of architecture, and think we should, to avoid criticism, be governed by the established rules which are laid

---

[21] Brown discussed his research in *Memories,* 37–42. He indicated that he had copied four boxes of Thornton's papers, which he described as containing "little that did not concern the history of the District and Government Buildings." At that time the papers were in the possession of Mrs. Bayard Smith. J. Henley Smith, after his mother's death, burned many of the letters despite Brown's pleas to donate them to the Library of Congress. Brown's copies of Thornton's papers have not been located. Brown noted that Mrs. Smith was a neighbor of the Latrobes in Baltimore and apparently did not request access to Benjamin Henry Latrobe's papers even though many of the architect's journals, letterbooks, and sketchbooks were in the family's possession at this time.

[22] See Brown, *Memories,* 40–42. For background on Stewart and the Army's care of the city's early records, see John M. Wilson to Brown, December 1, 1896, Brown Papers, RG 804, Ser. 5, AIA Archives; and Colonel Theodore Bingham, "Report on Senate 2725, 56/1, March 6, 1900," Correspondence 1899–1906, Office of Public Buildings and Grounds, Lot 441, RG 42, NARA. Senate 2725 was a bill introduced by Senator James McMillan that called for the transfer of these historical maps and documents from the Office of Public Buildings and Grounds to the city surveyor's office. Bingham's unfavorable report on the bill provides an extensive history of the agency's care and preservation of these materials since 1867.

down by the professors of the art."[23] Brown thought that this statement provided historical justification for expert control over the selection of plans for government architecture and the acquisition of fine arts. He applauded Washington for "far-seeing vision" that produced a plan for a capital city of a million inhabitants at a time when the national population was approximately only three million.[24]

Brown purposely opened the 1900 AIA convention on December 13, coinciding with the day President Washington transmitted the L'Enfant plan to Congress in 1791. With the development of the city's monumental core as its theme, the convention proved a resounding success. Papers presented by Frederick Law Olmsted, Jr., and other experts soon eclipsed other planning and public works proposals prepared for Washington's centennial. The AIA convention papers, published as a Senate document in 1901, comprised an important body of professional thought concerning the future planning of Washington and provided the Senate Park Commission with a framework for developing their own plan.[25]

[23] Brown, *History of the United States Capitol,* vol. 1, 54.

[24] Brown, *Memories,* 37–46.

[25] There is a large body of scholarly literature that discusses the origins of the McMillan commission's 1902 plan. Major works include Frederick Gutheim, *Worthy of the Nation: The History of Planning for the National Capital* (Washington, D.C.: Smithsonian Institution Press, 1977); Jon A. Peterson, "The Nation's First Comprehensive Plan," *American Planning Association Journal* (Spring 1985): 134–150; John Reps, *Monumental Washington: The Planning and Development of the Capital Center* (Princeton, N. J. : Princeton University Press, 1967); and Reps, *Washington on View: The Nation's Capital Since 1791* (Chapel Hill, N. C.: University of North Carolina Press, 1991). See also Richard Longstreth, ed., *The Mall in Washington, 1791–1991* (Hanover and London: University Press of New England, 1991); Bushong, "Glenn Brown," chapter 4; Brown, "A Suggestion for Grouping Government Buildings, Landscape, Monuments and Statuary", *Architectural Review* (August 1900): 89–94; Brown, comp., *Papers Relating to the Improvement of Washington City, District of Columbia* (Washington: 56th Cong., 2nd sess., S. Doc. 94).

Figure 17. Vista overlooking the Mall and Pennsylvania Avenue from the Capitol's dome (taken about 1900).

Brown's *History* provided the Senate Park Commission with an understanding of the city's historic design and influenced its decision to take the 1791 L'Enfant plan as a starting point for its own famous 1901–1902 comprehensive plan for the capital. Brown asserted that the city's design, as depicted and described on L'Enfant's 1791 manuscript map, had been retained in Andrew Ellicott's 1792 printed map of

Washington and that the modifications suggested by President George Washington were important.[26] According to Brown, the sites of the Capitol, White House, and Washington Monument formed an integral triangular relationship with the Mall, with each site intended as a focal point of a series of vistas. Brown suggested that "haphazard" siting of government buildings had mutilated this design and unplanned development had destroyed the vista from the Capitol to the Washington Monument. The root of the evil, in Brown's view, was that "no general system is being followed; no man or men seem to have studied the question as a whole. The development of the original and wise plan seems to have been forgotten." Brown called for a concerted effort to revive the L'Enfant plan and vigorously promoted the design concept for an open Mall vista.[27]

Brown's study, imbued with his own professional values and personal architectural and artistic biases, also singled out the men whom he believed had contributed most to its design and thus deserved the title of Architect of the Capitol. Brown considered Thornton, Latrobe, Bulfinch, Walter, and the incumbent Edward Clark as a successive line of Architects of the Capitol. This interpretation emerged as the official history for the origins and development of this office, created by Congress in 1867 to superintend the Capitol. Brown had dismissed as "superintendents" architects such as Stephen Hallet, George Hadfield, James Hoban, and Robert Mills, who contributed their share of design ideas, revisions, and working drawings. He largely ignored the Commissioners of Public Buildings and other federal officials who had administered the design, construction, and maintenance of the Capitol before 1867.[28]

Brown's choices revealed his underlying motive to develop a strong parallel between the evolution of the American architectural profession and the Office of the Architect of the Capitol. He considered Thornton a pioneer of the profession, while he saw Latrobe, the first true professional architect working in the United States, as embodying the architect as masterbuilder. He admired Bulfinch, the nation's first native-born professional architect, for expressing an American variation of the neoclassical designs of British architects Robert Adam and William Chambers; Bulfinch exhibited a "refinement in his work and capacity to simplify" that often was lacking in the European architecture of the period. Finally, Brown saw Walter, a founder and second president of the AIA,

---

[26] Brown, *History of the United States Capitol*, vol. 1, 34. In 1913 Brown made an interesting statement about his interpretation of the two maps: "I would not for a moment detract from Captain Ellicott's merit. Himself a surveyor, he modified or followed the suggestions of modifications desired in the plans after L'Enfant had proposed them; but the evidence goes to show that the great originality in the plan was L'Enfant's, that where ideas in the design were original they were L'Enfant's. It is those original ideas that the board of artists who have designed the future development of Washington have taken, and do not claim even to have improved upon." See Brown to William Howard Taft, undated, Taft Papers, Reel 415, Case No. 1291, Manuscript Division, LC. The letter was probably written in relation to Taft's research for his illustrated article, "Washington: Its Beginning, Its Growth, and Its Future," *National Geographic* 27 (March 1915): 221–292.

[27] Charles Moore, who became the commission's secretary and, later, biographer of commission members Daniel Burnham and Charles McKim, believed the fundamental importance of Brown's book was that it gave planners a necessary grounding on the history of the Capitol and the Mall for their work in Washington. Moore, "Glenn Brown," 832. William T. Partridge, the chief draftsman responsible for organizing the work of redesigning the Mall and public buildings connected with the monumental core under McKim's direction, considered Brown's *History* of "inestimable value" to the commission and that the author's vision of the transformation of the plans into reality was vital to the City Beautiful movement in Washington. "Personal Recollection of the McMillan Commission," by William T. Partridge. National Capital Planning Commission, Historical Data File, 1929–1949, RG 328, NARA.

[28] See George M. White's synopsis of the history of the Office of the Architect of the Capitol in the foreword to Jeanne F. Butler, "Competition 1792: Designing a Nation's Capital," *Capitol Studies* 4 (Special Issue 1976): 11–13. The Architect of the U.S. Capitol is an agent of Congress, appointed by the President, and is responsible for all design, construction, and maintenance of the U.S. Capitol complex.

as the dean of the American architectural profession.[29] Only Frederick Law Olmsted shared equal status with these four architects. Brown praised Olmsted's plan for the grounds and his design of the west terraces, emphasizing the government's wisdom in selecting "the one capable man, probably, in the country at that date" as the Capitol's landscape designer.[30]

Brown's *History*, despite its impression on official Washington, did not result in his appointment as Architect of the Capitol, a position he

[29] See Brown, *History of the United States Capitol*, vol. 2, chapter 12.

[30] Ibid., vol. 2, 466–467.

Figure 18. One of several House Office Building design proposals developed by Elliott Woods and rendered by Raymond Squier in 1902.

long coveted. The incumbent Edward Clark had held the post since 1865 and earned respect for his long and useful service. After Clark became gravely ill in 1898, Congress appointed as the acting Architect of the Capitol Elliott Woods, an employee of the office since 1885 who had risen through the ranks to become Clark's chief assistant. The choice was logical because of Woods's loyal service and experience as well as his cordial relations with many members of Congress.[31]

From Brown's perspective, Woods, a self-trained woodcarver, would be a disastrous choice for Architect of the Capitol. As a designer Brown considered him a rank amateur and totally unfit to be the custodian of a national monument. Brown's prejudice against Woods developed between 1898 and 1901, a period in which Brown was actively involved in preparing his *History* as well as working as a consultant on plans for a new House Office Building and the restoration of the Supreme Court Chamber. Woods emerged as the congressional choice for Architect in 1901 but felt threatened by Brown's proposed plans for the new multipurpose power plant, storage, and office building. After his appointment as Architect, Woods set forth his own ideas for an office building. In his first annual report (1902), he presented striking renderings for a new House Office Building prepared by artist Raymond Squier.[32] Angered by Woods's snub and motivated by his own ambition to design the House Office Building, Brown spearheaded an AIA lobbying campaign against Woods's design. Eventually Woods appeased his professional critics by arranging for the design of the new House Office Building to be prepared by the New York firm of Carrére and Hastings, both

[31] For biographical data on Edward Clark and Elliott Woods and for background on the appointment controversy, see Architect of the Capitol Scrapbook, vol. 1, 1836–1909, 34–37, Curator's Office, AOC.

[32] For an explanation of Woods's plans, see *Annual Report of the Superintendent of the Capitol* (Washington: Government Printing Office, 1902), 47–55.

prominent AIA members, and for the construction to be superintended by his office.

Brown also interfered with Woods's project to replace the roof structure of the Capitol's original north and south wings with fireproof materials after the 1898 gas explosion. Woods extensively photographed the old ceilings before demolition and then expected his contractors to replicate the historic ceilings from these images after installation of the new steel structural roof members.[33] Burgess and

---

[33] See Brown, *Memories,* 58.

Figure 19. Workmen rebuilding the roof of the Supreme Court ceiling (Old Senate Chamber) in 1901.

Richardson, a Washington contracting firm employed by Woods to reproduce the plasterwork in the Supreme Court Chamber, became concerned about the feasibility of this plan. They realized that Latrobe's intricate coffered plaster ceiling in the Old Supreme Court (originally the Senate Chamber from 1810 to 1859) could not be replicated from photographs and that its suspension by steel rods from the roof frame, as Woods proposed, would not hold it in place. The contractors, who had built several of Brown's residential and commercial buildings, hired him as a consultant on a per diem basis. Brown immediately stopped the workmen and made measured drawings of the Supreme Court ceiling's extant ribs, coffers, and circular skylights and then made a complete set of working drawings, which had not been provided to the contractors by Woods.[34]

Brown himself sought to be appointed Architect of the Capitol in 1902 and obtained the backing of the AIA and its president, Charles F. McKim. But his candidacy faced the opposition of Representative Joseph Cannon (R-IL), the powerful chairman of the House Committee on Appropriations. Cannon knew Brown as the leading crusader for the Senate Park Commission, which he vehemently opposed because it was

---

[34] Brown, *Memories,* 55–56. Brown's working drawings for this project have been lost, but one of the extant measured drawings is in the AIA's drawing collection. In 1919 the Mazer Acoustic Tile Company of Philadelphia installed a facsimile of the 1902 plaster ceiling built after Brown's drawings with an "acoustic membrane" made of "fireproofed unbleached cotton." See Florian H. Thayn, "Composite Report of the Research for the Proposed Restoration of the Old Senate Chamber and the Old Supreme Court Chamber," unpublished paper for a report of the Architect of the Capitol, Curator's Office, AOC. For information on the acoustic refitting, see Jacob Mazer to Elliott Woods, July 2, 1919, "Old Senate Chamber," RG 40, Subject Files, Curator's Office, AOC; *Report of the Superintendent of the United States Capitol Building and Grounds,* June 30, 1920 (Washington: Government Printing Office, 1920), 4. The present Old Senate Chamber was restored as a bicentennial project in 1976 under the direction of George M. White and the Senate Commission on Art and Antiquities.

formed without the consent of the House. After hearing of the AIA's promotion of Brown's candidacy, Cannon engineered a petition from House members and the Senate leadership calling for Woods's appointment, and several delegations of congressmen visited President Theodore Roosevelt to press their support of Woods.[35] Roosevelt, who had endorsed the 1902 McMillan plan and had cordial relations with the

leaders of the architectural profession, chose to compromise. He appointed Woods on the condition that Congress change the title from "Architect" to "Superintendent" of the Capitol but let the duties and responsibilities of the office remain the same.[36]

After his defeat, Brown remained a major figure in Washington and stayed at the forefront of public controversy over the implementation of the McMillan plan after 1903. For the next decade, he continued to rally the architectural profession and fine arts organizations throughout the country to defend the plan and to promote professional architects as arbiters of the federal government's fine arts patronage. Brown's agenda was dominated by his successful campaign to establish the U.S. Commission of Fine Arts in 1910. This body has advised the government on federal building projects in Washington for over seventy-five years and has had a profound influence on the aesthetic development of the city.[37]

After 1910 Brown devoted his energy to a political struggle over the siting of the Lincoln Memorial, spearheading opposition to congressional proposals for a monument between Union Station and the Capitol or for a memorial highway from Washington to Gettysburg, Pennsylvania. Shortly after legislation enacted in December 1913 ensured that the Lincoln Memorial would be sited on the Mall, Brown was deposed as AIA secretary. Younger architects wanted to restructure the Institute's operations to reduce the decision making authority of its secretary and to disperse responsibilities within a new corporate organization.

---

[35] President Roosevelt had been advised of Brown's suitability for the position by the chairman of the Civil Service Commission, J. R. Proctor. A close friend of the president, Proctor greatly admired the first volume of the *History*. He was so confident of Brown's appointment that he had the papers prepared for the president's signature. For Brown's version of the controversy, see *Memories*, 56–57. For newspaper coverage of Cannon's actions and the text of the petition, see Architect of the Capitol Scrapbook, vol. 1, 1836–1909, 34–37, Office of the Curator, AOC.

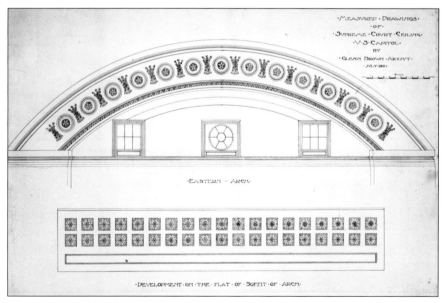

Figure 20. Brown's 1901 measured drawing of the Supreme Court Chamber ceiling (Old Senate Chamber). *Prints & Drawings Collection, The Octagon Museum, The American Architectural Foundation, Washington, DC.*

---

[36] Resolution of the struggle came swiftly because Cannon added an amendment to the 1902 appropriations bill, which changed the title of the office and cleared the president's appointment of his candidate. See "The Appointment of the Architect of the Capitol," *Inland Architect and News Record* 37 (March 1902): 13; "Employment, Duties, and Compensation of Employees of the House," 58th Cong., 1st Sess., *Congressional Record*, vol. 35 (Washington: Government Printing Office, 1902), 7675–7676; and Brown to Robert S. Peabody, January 7, 1902, Secretary Outgoing Correspondence, RG 801, Ser. 1.1, AIA Archives.

[37] See Bushong, "Glenn Brown," chapters 3 and 4.

Although Brown made efforts to maintain his professional influence in Washington, the loss of his AIA post sharply reduced his effectiveness. In addition, the Progressive public spirit that had pervaded the city at the turn of the century was all but dead by the end of World War I. Temporary government buildings erected during the war clogged the Mall and the area from Union Station to the Senate Office Building. Even worse, the twin stacks of a power station now interrupted the planned Mall vista. Disconsolate, Brown retired from his involvement in political and public affairs in 1919 to concentrate on his writing and architectural practice.[38]

Brown's later years were marked by a crusader's preoccupation with what he saw as the unfinished business of his career. He wrote many articles and editorials condemning the Institute's loss of influence with the federal government and its lackluster opposition to deviations from the McMillan plan. When Elliott Woods died in 1923, Brown, at age 69, again attempted to obtain appointment as Architect of the Capitol, seeing this as his last opportunity to influence federal design policy. He sought former President and then Chief Justice William Howard Taft's support. Taft informed Brown that although he was a deserving applicant, the appointment of Woods's chief engineer, David Lynn, was inevitable.[39]

When Brown pressed the AIA to support his nomination, Milton Medary, an active member of AIA committees concerned with the planning of Washington, sought Charles Moore's advice on what to do about "dear old Glenn Brown." Moore, although supportive of Brown's appointment twenty years before, had in the interim developed cordial working relations with Woods and his heir apparent, Lynn. The old wound regarding the slighting of Woods's professional status also had been fully healed in 1921, when Congress reinstituted his title as Architect of the Capitol. In his reply to Medary, Moore revealed impatience with Brown's persistent quest: "I have expressed the highest appreciation of Glenn Brown's long, intelligent, painstaking and effective work for the development of Washington... but his insistence on his appointment as Architect of the Capitol has been a constant embarrassment to the Commission in its relations with Congress." Moore advised Medary not to repeat the mistakes of 1902, but instead to leave the appointment as a "family matter" for Congress to decide. President Calvin Coolidge appointed Lynn in 1923.[40]

Brown took up residence at Corcoran Courts in 1925 and began work on his autobiography. His health grew worse, prompting frequent automobile trips to the Virginia shore and to the mountains to restore his constitution. Brown continued to write when he felt well enough. Propped up in his bed, he maintained a lifelong habit of heavy cigarette smoking as he scribbled reflections of his career onto small yellow note pads.[41] His son Bedford had this handwritten material typed, and the last

---

[38] For a discussion of changes in attitudes concerning civic causes in Washington after World War I, see Constance M. Green, *Washington: A History of the Capital, 1800–1950,* vol. 2 (Princeton: Princeton University Press, 1976), 257; 312–336.

[39] Brown to William Howard Taft, June 2, 1923, and Taft to Brown, June 4, 1923, Taft Papers, Reel 254, Ser. 3, Manuscript Division, LC.

[40] Cass Gilbert was particularly supportive of Brown's nomination and wrote Charles Moore to use his influence with the president. The rift between the American Institute of Architects and the Office of the Architect of the Capitol had been healed by the efforts of Thomas Hastings and Henry Bacon, who successfully advocated Woods's honorary membership in the Institute. See Cass Gilbert to Charles Moore, May 29 and June 4, 1923; Milton A. Medary to Moore, June 11, 1923; Moore to Medary (telegram), June 18, 1923, and July 6, 1923. Also see copies of letters sent to Moore in reference to Brown's appointment: Brown to William Faville (AIA president), June 4, 1923; Medary to Faville, June 11, 1923; Brown to Harry Cunningham (Washington chapter president), June 21, 1923; E. C. Kemper to Faville, June 29, 1923. All of the letters cited above are located in General Records, Architect of the Capitol, Commission of Fine Arts, RG 66, NARA.

[41] Interview with Elizabeth Downing, December 1, 1986. Ms. Downing is Brown's grandniece; her mother, Willis Williams Walker, was Brown's niece and adopted daughter. These recollections were drawn from many visits with her mother to see Brown in the last years of his life. Bushong, "Glenn Brown," chapter 7.

book of Brown's prolific writing career took shape. *Memories: A Winning Crusade to Revive George Washington's Vision of a Capital City* was released in a limited private printing of 300 copies in January 1931. Largely a reprint of Brown's many articles, his memoirs documented a life's work and contained many perceptive essays on the historical events that shaped the monumental core of Washington. It also contained valuable personal observations of colleagues and contemporary artists, architects, and public officials. The next year Brown died in Buxton Hospital in Newport News, Virginia, after a long battle with respiratory disease.

Charles Moore, at his retirement dinner in 1937, delivered a speech that recalled how the planning movement that shaped Washington began at the 1900 AIA convention and noted that in Brown "the spirit of L'Enfant was incarnate." [42] The observation underscored the passion with which Brown pursued his historical research and presented his findings. Brown's *History of the United States Capitol* was a call to the nation to revive an ignored architectural and planning heritage. The ideas and concepts presented in the book—including the revival of the L'Enfant plan, recognition of Thornton's role in the design of the Capitol, a simplified lineage of the Office of the Architect of the Capitol, and the formation of a commission of fine arts—reverberate to the present day. Brown's *History of the United States Capitol*, despite its pronounced bias, endures as a classic in American architectural history.

---

[42] "Address by Honorable Charles Moore, Given at the Mayflower Hotel on February 18, 1937," Charles Moore Papers, Commission of Fine Arts, RG 66, NARA.

HISTORY

OF THE

UNITED STATES CAPITOL

BY

GLENN BROWN

FELLOW OF THE AMERICAN INSTITUTE OF ARCHITECTS

VOLUME I

THE OLD CAPITOL—1792–1850

We have built no temple but the Capitol;
We consult no common oracle but the Constitution
—RUFUS CHOATE

VIEW OF THE OLD CAPITOL FROM THE EXECUTIVE MANSION.

W. H. Bartlett, ca. 1839.

I take pleasure in dedicating these volumes to Mr. James Rush Marshall and Mr. Robert Stead in recognition of their constant sympathy and interest during the collection and preparation of the material for publication.

AUTHOR'S PREFACE

THE Capitol having been under the jurisdiction of the District Commissioners, the special commissioners, and the State, Interior, and War Departments, as well as under the direct charge of Congressional committees and Architects, the Government records bearing upon its history are in various depositories. The controversies at different periods between the Architects, the superintendents, and the Departments in charge of the Capitol ended in many instances by the Architects taking possession of drawings and papers which should have been retained among the documents of the Government.

To obtain data for a clear understanding of the subject I have found it necessary to examine material available in the hands of the Government and of descendants of the Architects and superintendents. Many of the most valuable documents are in the possession of private individuals, who have come into such possession by inheritance or gift from descendants of those who were in charge of the building.

For the privilege of examining and making notes, extracts, and photographic copies I wish to thank the following Government officials: Hon. Daniel Lamont when Secretary of War; Hon. David J. Hill, Assistant Secretary of State; Mr. Edward Clark, Architect of the Capitol; his assistant, Mr. Elliott Wood, and Mr. Herbert Putnam, Librarian of Congress.

To the following private individuals I wish to tender my thanks: To Mrs. J. H. Bayard Smith for material relating to Thornton; to Mr. W. Stone Abert for data on Latrobe and Lenthal; to Misses Olivia and Ida Walter for the privilege of photographing numerous drawings made by Thomas U. Walter, as well as to Mr. W. B. Bryan and Mr. James F. Hood for the use of their collections of material relating to the District of Columbia and the reproduction of old prints in their possession. I am indebted to the papers of Miss Ellen Bulfinch for data relating to Bulfinch.

The Maryland Historical Society was also kind enough to allow me to reproduce the old competitive drawings now in their possession. I wish also to acknowledge my indebtedness to my wife, Mary Ella Brown, for her unceasing assistance in the preparation of the history.

After a long and laborious search I have been unable to secure the competitive drawings for the Capitol extension, this being the only material point on which I have been unable to secure data to make a comprehensive treatment of the subject.

The material for the work I have gathered during the past ten years, and portions of the matter have been published in the American Architect and Building News, the Architectural Review, of Boston, and the Architectural Record, of New York.

The plates giving reproductions of old drawings and prints, as well as photographs of the existing building, have all been made especially for this work. Only original documents have been used in the preparation of the work, and old drawings have been reproduced as they exist today without any effort being made to work them over so as to produce more pleasing results.

GLENN BROWN.

COSMOS CLUB, WASHINGTON, D. C.

INTRODUCTION

BY CHARLES MOORE, PH.D.

HISTORICALLY the Capitol at Washington is the most important structure in the United States. Other buildings, such as the Old South Church in Boston and Independence Hall in Philadelphia, are connected with important episodes in the history of this country. The Capitol is unique in that it both typifies the beginning and also marks the growth of the nation. Like the great Gothic cathedrals of Europe, its surpassing merit is not its completeness, but its aspirations. Like them, too, the Capitol is not a creation, but a growth, and its highest value lies in the fact that it never was, and it never will be, finished.

They misread history who see in the location of the seat of government at Washington only the clever bargain of scheming politicians. The great centralizing forces that found expression in the adoption of the Constitution, the assumption of the State debts, and the creation of a national bank, had their chief support in the commercial North; whereas the agricultural South, fearing an oligarchy of wealth only less than the monarchy so lately cast off, found in the removal of the national capital to the banks of the Potomac a promise that the legislators of the new nation would be removed from the domination of the commercial spirit so powerful in the business centers of New York and Philadelphia.

Washington, having thrown his great influence on the side of a strong central Government, gave to the location of the Federal City his personal attention, even to small details; and after the site was selected and the city was laid out his chief concern was the construction of the Capitol on a scale that would comport with the dignity of the great and powerful nation that he confidently expected the United States would become. Much has been written of the magnificence of the plans made by the founders of the District of Columbia, and so sober an historian as Hildreth speaks with quiet sarcasm of laying out a city for a million people. As a matter of fact, within two generations after the removal of the seat of government to the District of Columbia fewer than a quarter of a million people had not only occupied L'Enfant's city, but had also spread themselves beyond the city boundaries, creating ill-arranged subdivisions that must mar the beauty and symmetry of Washington for generations yet to come. However magnificent the plans of the founders may have seemed, time has proved that they were not extensive enough.

During the closing years of the eighteenth century the time had come for building a great edifice as the home of the National Legislature. The forces making for disintegration had spent themselves in a vain opposition to the adoption of the Constitution, and were not set in motion again until after the Government had become so firmly established as to enable it to resist all attacks on the supremacy of the nation above the States. From a vague abstraction the nation had grown to be a concrete fact. True, the actual accomplishment was but meager when compared with the ideal that existed in the minds of the fathers, and there were those among the wise who feared that the goal would prove to be a New World monarchy. Still, throughout the land the idea prevailed that a permanent government had been established; that progress was assured; that law would be enforced and property be safe. Thus permanence of material interests, the primal condition of all great building, had become an accomplished fact.

Then, too, the American mind had expanded. The Revolution had made neighbors of the colonies; and the very delay over the adoption of the Articles of Confederation had fostered the national idea. Maryland having refused to assent to the compact until those States which claimed title to western lands should make surrender of their title to the nation, actually forced such sessions; and when the treaty of 1783 gave to the United States as common property an empire beyond the Ohio, the people began to feel that national pride which always seeks expression in worthy monuments. Before work on the Capitol began, the American settler had established himself not only north of the Ohio, but also in foreign territory beyond the Mississippi, and a continental nation was clearly foreshadowed. The prophetic utterances of European statesmen at the time when the independence of the United States was acknowledged by England were fast being realized, and the historic consciousness of our people was ready to manifest itself.

It is true that the cost of the Capitol and other public buildings was to be paid in large part from the proceeds of lots sold in the Federal City; but these lots were sold not only to people in various States, but also to foreigners, all of whom had faith in the future greatness of the capital of the new Republic, and who realized that the money so received was to be expended in public buildings of a permanent character.

In the plans for and the construction of the Capitol Washington exercised a determining influence. The structure was to be essentially the great building of the nation. The President's House and the Department buildings might await a fuller treasury, and even the Capitol itself might be constructed one part at a time, but a sufficient portion properly to house the Congress must be completed by the time set for the transfer of the seat of government to its permanent location. "It may be relied on," writes Washington to the Commissioners, "it is the progress of that building that is to inspire or depress public confidence;" and he required—such is his word—that they carry out his ideas in this matter.

It appears from the records that the selection of a plan for the Capitol was a matter of great concern to the two laymen who were at that time perhaps best qualified to judge the merits of the sketches presented—Washington and Jefferson. Washington indeed professed to have no knowledge of architecture, and was ready to be governed by "the rules laid down by the professors of the art." What he sought, however, were the essential qualities in all good architecture—a combination of grandeur, simplicity, and convenience. That is to say, while he professed no knowledge of the processes by which results were reached, his natural good taste enabled him to select from among many plans the one that combined those qualities which a truly great building must possess. So, too, Jefferson approved Dr. Thornton's plan because it was "simple, noble, beautiful." It is interesting to note that both of these great men recognized the element of simplicity as of first consideration; for the chief source of weakness in American architecture during the period covered by our rapid commercial development has been the absence of this quality, just as the great hope for future architectural excellence is found in the gradual return to it.

Thornton, the architect of the Capitol, was by birth a West Indian, as was also Alexander Hamilton; and this nation owes to those islands a debt of gratitude that will endure while the Capitol stands and while our financial system remains essentially unchanged. When and where Thornton studied architecture is unknown; but we do know that imitative drawing was one of his early accomplishments and that wide travel in Europe enriched a mind peculiarly versatile and of remarkable power in mastering the details of intricate subjects. It has been said that he studied architecture less than a year. Probably he was a life-long student of this greatest among the arts, and it has been demonstrated that he had an intuitive sense as to its essentials.

Dr. Thornton's plan was well adapted to find favor with those most interested in the selection of a suitable design for the nation's Capitol. When Rome borrowed from Greece and adapted to her own larger purposes and more varied needs the most beautiful of architectural forms, succeeding ages gained a common medium of expression in building. The problem that presented itself to the architect became one of proportion, of harmony, of perfection of workmanship. Pediment and entablature, column and pilaster, even triglyph and scamillus had their laws derived from that most perfect of buildings, the Parthenon at Athens. The charm of simplicity, the beauty of line, the harmony of the parts, all subject to established and recognized laws, were the common language of architecture the world over.

These forms appealed to the spirit of the time in which the Capitol was built. Men of education and culture in those days were trained in the literature and political ideas of Greece and Rome. The strength and the weakness of their institutions pointed every moral and adorned every tale. Roman names were given to new towns springing up in the wilderness, the sites of colleges were named Athens, and the public square was known as the Campus Martius. Life in the cities was simple, but stately; form and ceremony were observed even among those who principles were most strongly republican. Equality of man was equality before the law, not familiarity among persons differing radically from one another in manners, education, and modes of thought.

Originality beyond such as arose from an adaptation of the building to its situation and the uses for which it was designed was not thought of by Dr. Thornton; and indeed had the idea of attempting to originate a style of architecture been suggested to his trained mind, he must have rejected it as surely as he would have rejected the idea of inventing a new language in which to express his thoughts. Even the eye untrained to architectural niceties fails not at a glance to see how immeasurably Thornton's plans are superior to the others submitted in the competition. From its very beginning the Capitol has been an imposing structure. None of the departures from the original designs have interfered seriously with the simplicity and dignity of the building, and within its walls beauty of form and richness of execution are

manifest, so that to this day mantels of rare beauty, moldings exquisitely executed, and columns of satisfactory proportions and with charmingly ornamented capitals reward the searcher into the dim and almost neglected portions of the original building. Those persons most appreciate the Capitol who are daily called on to thread its labyrinths, to learn the history of its various rooms, and to familiarize themselves with the adaptations which the growth of the country and of the public business have brought about.

The Capitol has ever been the peculiar charge of the President of the United States. Jefferson, who had been associated with Washington in the selection of the original plans, took a keen personal interest in the completion of the north wing. With none of the modesty that his illustrious predecessor had professed as to a knowledge of architecture, Jefferson undertook to say which one of the Grecian buildings should serve as a model for the builders; and he also watched over Thornton's plans to save them from serious change at the hands of zealous superintendents eager to magnify their office and to put the impress of their importance on the designs. The idea of building the Capitol from the proceeds of the sale of District of Columbia lands was early abandoned, and Congress began to place in the hands of the President sums of money to spend upon the extension and completion of the building.

The burning of the Capitol by the British during the war of 1812 was deeply resented by the American people, as an outrage against those laws of civilized warfare which protect public edifices as monuments of the arts. From the date of the destruction of the building, in August, 1814, until December, 1819, Congress occupied other quarters. Happily the strong walls withstood the effects of the fire, and, thanks to President Madison, Thornton's plans were not materially altered either in the rebuilding or in the construction of the central portion, begun in 1818, under the superintendence of Charles Bulfinch.

The idea of making the Rotunda of the Capitol a mausoleum of Washington met with the favor of Congress; a resolution was passed to carry out the plan, and the consent of the Washington family was obtained. In his first message President John Quincy Adams called the attention of Congress to the fact that "a spot has been reserved within the walls where you are deliberating for the benefit of this and future ages, in which the mortal remains may deposited of him whose spirit hovers over you and listens with delight to every act of the representatives of his nation which can tend to exalt his and their country." Much to President Adams's disappointment, however, Virginia protested against the removal of Washington's remains from Mount Vernon, and in 1832 the owner of that estate withdrew the family consent.

In 1850, when the President of the United States had placed at his command the sum of $100,000 for the extension of the Capitol according to such plan as he might approve and by such architect as he should appoint, competition again failed to yield satisfactory results, and a combination and adaptation of the various plans was decided upon. "It was desirable," wisely says President Fillmore, "not to mar the harmony and beauty of the present building, which as a specimen of architecture is so universally admired. Keeping these objects in view, I concluded to make the additions by wings detached from the present building, yet connected with it by corridors. This mode of enlargement will leave the present Capitol uninjured." These simple words of President Fillmore give no hint of what actually took place at a crisis in the history of the Capitol. Congress, having placed the charge of the extension in the hands of the Chief Magistrate, undertook, through one of its committees, to obtain plans for the work; but President Fillmore, ignoring the legislative branch of the Government, set himself resolutely to the task Congress itself had imposed upon him. Fortunately he selected as the architect Thomas U. Walter, a man who proved great enough to design the wings in conformity with the central building.

Thornton himself, had he lived long enough to do the work, could not have carried out his own plans in greater perfection of detail. As a result the Capitol stands today an architectural unit.

When the time came to lay the corner stone of the addition to the Capitol, the day selected was the Fourth of July, in the year 1851, and the orator named by President Fillmore was Daniel Webster, then Secretary of State. "Who does not feel," exclaimed Mr. Webster, "that when President Washington laid his hand on the foundation of the first Capitol, he performed a great work of perpetuation of the Union and the Constitution." To the prophetic vision of the orator the great storm, then a decade in the future, loomed dark and ominous; and with all the great eloquence at his command, he used the natal day of the Republic and the building of the Capitol as texts of an impassioned appeal for the stability of the Union of the States. As he closed his address, he turned to the President with these words: "President Fillmore, it is your singularly good fortune to perform an act such as that which the earliest of your predecessors performed fifty-eight years ago. You stand where he stood; you lay your hand on the corner stone of a building designed greatly to extend that whose corner stone he laid. Changed, changed is everything around. The same sun indeed shone on his head that now shines on yours. The same broad river rolled at his feet, and bathes his last resting place, that now rolls at yours. But the site of the city was then mainly an open field. Streets and avenues have since been laid out and completed, squares and public grounds inclosed and ornamented, until the city which bears his name, although comparatively inconsiderable in numbers and wealth, has become quite fit to be the seat of government of a great and united people. Sir, may the consequences of the duty you perform so auspiciously to-day equal those which flowed from his act."[1]

---

[1] Webster's Works, Vol. II, p. 620.

It is told of President Lincoln that during the civil war he required that work on the new Dome should not cease, so that in the continued progress of this crowning feature of the Capitol all might see typified the continued unity and strength of the United States. He knew that he could calculate on the affectionate regard of the people for their historic building. How strong this regard was, even at the South, is well illustrated by an incident that Charles Sumner has related in one of his letters to John Bright. At the conclusion of the historic conference that took place at Hampton Roads, February 3, 1865, between President Lincoln and Secretary Seward on one side, and Alexander H. Stephens, R. M. T. Hunter, and John A. Campbell on the other, Mr. Hunter, who had spent nearly all his life in Washington,[2] said to Mr. Seward: "Governor, how is the Capitol? Is it finished?" "This," writes Sumner, "gave Seward an opportunity of picturing the present admired state of the works, with the Dome completed, and the whole constituting one of the magnificent edifices of the world."[3]

Of all the statesmen who have learned to love and venerate the Capitol, perhaps none was more competent than Senator Sumner to pass judgment upon it. He spoke from daily familiarity with its Chambers, its corridors, its committee rooms; day after day he had watched the winter sun, shining from a cloudless sky, strike full upon the noble pile, as dazzling as the marbles of Greece; his cultivated eye had reveled in the play of light and shade upon portico and column; to his historic sense painting, bust, and statue appealed, even though their artistic value might be small; and from a bed of torture in a foreign land memory had recalled the sacred walls that inclosed his seat, kept vacant by an outraged Commonwealth. In a speech in the Senate, uttered in unavailing protest at the proposed desecration of the Capitol by placing in it an unworthy statue of Lincoln, Mr. Sumner said:

"Surely this National Capitol, so beautiful and interesting, and already historic, should not be opened to the rude experiment of untried talent. Only the finished artist should be admitted here. Sir, I doubt if you consider enough the edifice in which we are assembled. Possessing the advantage of an incomparable situation, it is among the first-class structures of the world. Surrounded by an amphitheater of hills, with the Potomac at its feet, it may remind you of the Capitol in Rome, with the Alban and Sabine hills in sight, and with the Tiber at its feet. But the situation is grander than that of the Roman Capitol. The edifice itself is not unworthy of the situation. It has beauty of form and sublimity in proportion, even if it lacks originality in conception. In itself it is a work of art. It should not receive in the way of ornamentation anything which is not a work of art. Unhappily, this rule is too often forgotten, or there would not be so few pictures and marbles about us which we are glad to recognize. But bad pictures and ordinary marbles warn us against adding to their number."

"Pardon me if I call attention for one moment to the few works of art in the Capitol which we might care to preserve. Beginning with the Vice-President's room, we find an excellent and finished portrait of Washington by Peale. This is much less known than the familiar portrait by Stuart, but it is well worthy to be cherished. I never enter that room without feeling its presence. Traversing the corridors, we find ourselves in the spacious Rotunda, where are four pictures by Trumbull, truly historic in character, by which great scenes live again before us. These works have a merit of their own which will always justify the place they occupy. Mr. Randolph, with ignorant levity, once characterized that which represents the signing of the Declaration of Independence as a 'shin piece.' He should have known that there is probably no

---

[2] Robert Mercer Taliaferro Hunter was a member of Congress from Virginia from 1837 to 1843, and Speaker of the House from 1839 to 1841; he was a United States Senator from 1847 to 1861; then was successively the Confederate Secretary of State and a Confederate Senator. In 1877 he was treasurer of Virginia.

[3] Pierce's Memoir and Letters of Charles Sumner, Vol. IV, p. 205.

picture having so many portraits less obnoxious to the gibe. If these pictures do not belong to the highest art, they can never fail in interest to the patriotic citizen, while the artist will not be indifferent to them. One other picture in the Rotunda is not without merit. I refer to the Landing of the Pilgrims, by Weir, where there is a certain beauty of color and a religious sentiment; but this picture has always seemed to me exaggerated rather than natural. Passing from the Rotunda to the House of Representatives, we stand before a picture which, as a work of art, is perhaps the choicest of all in the Capitol. It is a portrait of Lafayette by that consummate artist who was one of the glories of France, Ary Scheffer. He sympathized with our institutions, and this portrait of the early friend of our country was a present from the artist to the people of the United States. Few who look at it by the side of the Speaker's chair are aware that it is the production of the rare genius which gave to mankind the Christus Consolator and the Francesca da Rimini.

"Turning from painting to sculpture, we find further reason for caution. The lesson is taught especially by the work of the Italian, Persico, on the steps of the Capitol, called by him Columbus, but called by others 'a man rolling nine pins;' for the attitude and the ball he holds suggests this game. Near to this is a remarkable group by Greenough, where the early settler is struggling with the savage; while opposite, in the yard, is the statue of Washington by the same artist, which has found little favor because it is nude, but which shows a mastery of art. There also are the works of Crawford—the *alto-rilievo* which fills the pediment over the great door of the Senate Chamber, and the Statue of Liberty which looks down from the top of the Dome, attesting a genius which must always command admiration. There are other statues by a living artist. There are also the bronze doors by Rogers, on which he labored long and well. They belong to a class of which there are only a few specimens in the world, and I have sometimes thought they might vie with those famous doors at Florence which Michael Angelo hailed

as worthy to be the gates of Paradise. Our artist has pictured the whole life of Columbus in bronze, while portraits of contemporary princes and of great authors who have illustrated the life of the great discoverer add to the completeness of this artistic work." [4]

It has been said that the Capitol is not a creation, but a growth. The same is true of the city of Washington. The evolution of both city and building was accomplished through long and trying years. The scale which now seems too small then seemed too great. The history of the first half-century of Washington is a tale of inconveniences. Historian and traveler vie with each other in comparing the opulence of promise with the poverty of performance, and it is only since the civil war that the dream of the founders has begun to be realized. In 1808 the House of Representatives seriously debated the question of escaping the inconveniences of a miserable straggling village and a hall ill adapted to either speakers or hearers by a return of the seat of government to Philadelphia; but political considerations caused the defeat of the proposition by a small majority. The present Senate Chamber, which when first occupied seemed so large as compared with the small room in which the oratory of Webster and his associates added rich stores to the literature of statesmanship, is to-day none too extensive for the transaction of public business for forty-five States; and the time will soon come when the House of Representatives must change radically the present theory that a legislative chamber can also be made to serve as the place of business of the individual member. Even as these words are being written the sound of the workman's hammer breaks the vacation stillness, as the transformation into committee rooms of the space long used for the Library of Congress is being accomplished.

The story of the building of the Capitol and of its adornment, as related by Mr. Glenn Brown in the following pages, has never before

---

[4] Sumner's Works, Vol. X, p. 543.

been told with any degree of fullness or of accuracy. For a decade he has been gathering the plans and illustrations; his search has been both keen and unremitting, and it has been prosecuted as a labor of love and of inherited attachment for the Capitol. The photographs and prints herein reproduced have commanded the attention of architects throughout the country, who have known something of them through exhibitions of a portion of them in several cities and by the more or less satisfactory reproduction of some of them in architectural journals; and it is a matter of satisfaction, not only to students of architecture and of the history of the fine arts in America, but also to the public generally, that he has freely placed in this permanent form a collection of drawings possessing so great an architectural value and appealing so strongly to the historic consciousness of our people. Those who, by reason of long association with the Capitol, have learned to appreciate the appeal it makes to the American mind and heart will best understand the obligation under which the author has placed his readers.

CHARLES MOORE.

Chapter I

The Selection of Sites for Federal Buildings

WASHINGTON has an advantage over the modern cities of the world, with possibly the one exception of St. Petersburg, in having been designed and laid out as the capital city of a great nation.[1] Congress, after much discussion, located the Federal City on the Potomac River by act of Congress, which was approved by President Washington July 16, 1790. The first map of Washington was authorized by an act of Congress July, 1790.[2] As the first step in the preparation of the map Peter Charles L'Enfant wrote to Jefferson April 4, 1791, requesting maps and data concerning London, Madrid, Paris, Amsterdam, Naples, Venice, and Florence.[3] He states that he wishes to obtain this data not that he might copy any one of the maps, but that he might have suggestions for a variety of ideas. Streets, parks, and the sites for the President's House and the Capitol are all shown on the map made by L'Enfant in 1791 practically as they exist to-day. L'Enfant's draft was altered, and the map was completed under the direction of General Washington, who, with a clear understanding of the situation, gave close and painstaking personal attention to everything that related to the District of Columbia or the Federal City.[4] This accurate knowledge of details and interest of the President is clearly shown by letters to the Commissioners and others in authority at that time.[5] The streets were arranged so as to give quick communication between the buildings and other points of interest, as well as a reciprocity of sight between the buildings and other objects of art which were to be located in the capital city.[6]

Most important for the future beauty and artistic effect of the city was the selection and location of building, statuary, and monument sites. Washington, L'Enfant, and Ellicott, who was doing the field work,

---

[1] For an earlier version of this chapter, see Glenn Brown, "The Selection of Sites for Federal Buildings," *Architectural Review* 3 (August 1894): 27–29.

[2] Act of July 16, 1790, *United States Statutes at Large*, c. 28, 2 Stat. 130.

[3] See Saul K. Padover, ed., *Thomas Jefferson and the National Capital, 1783–1818* (Washington: Government Printing Office, 1946), 56–57. Jefferson had only two of the plans requested by L'Enfant. On L'Enfant's sources for his design, see J. L. Sibley Jennings, Jr., "Artistry as Design: L'Enfant's Extraordinary City," *Quarterly Journal of the Library of Congress* 36 (Summer 1979): 225–278. See also John Reps, *Washington on View: The Nation's Capital Since 1790* (Chapel Hill and London: University of North Carolina Press, 1991) and Pamela Scott, " 'This Vast Empire': The Iconography of the Mall, 1791–1848," in Richard Longstreth, ed., *The Mall in Washington, 1791–1991* (Hanover and London: National Gallery of Art, 1991), 37–60.

[4] Brown held that the design concepts of L'Enfant's 1791 map had been essentially retained in the engraved 1792 map by Andrew Ellicott, as modified under the direction of George Washington. See Jennings, "Artistry as Design," 226, for a discussion of the case that the differences between the plans have been underestimated by architects, historians, and planners.

[5] Washington appointed city commissioners by authority of the 1790 Residence Act to direct improvements for the new capital. The first commissioners were Dr. David Stuart of Alexandria, Thomas Johnson of Frederick, and Representative Daniel Carroll of Rock Creek. On the political background of the founding of the nation's capital, see Kenneth R. Bowling, *Creating the Federal City, 1774–1800: Potomac Fever* (Washington: American Institute of Architects Press, 1988); see also Bowling's *The Creation of Washington, D. C.: The Idea and Location of the American Capital* (Fairfax, Va.: George Mason University Press, 1991). For biographical information on the early commissioners, see William C. di Giacomantino, "All the President's Men: George Washington's Federal City Commissioners," *Washington History* 3 (Summer 1991): 53–75.

[6] For Brown's study of the vistas of the L'Enfant plan, see "A Suggestion for Grouping Government Buildings, Landscapes, Monuments and Statuary," *Architectural Review* 8 (August 1900): 89–94.

went over the ground together, and "carefully," as a note on the margin of the map informs us, "selected the sites of the 'grand edifices' where they would command the greatest prospect, and be susceptible of the greatest improvement." It will be seen from L'Enfant's map [Plate 1] that the Capitol is placed on the center line of four avenues, North, South, and East Capitol streets, and what was to have been the boulevard, thus giving sixteen pleasing and continuous vistas as one approaches the building from different directions.[7] There are few more pleasing effects than those produced by the Capitol ending the vista of the principal avenues. Similar views were intended of the President's House. The selection of the site for the Capitol was peculiarly happy in the beauty of the effects produced by distant views of the building. It is difficult to realize the pleasure produced by the sight of the building as seen from the hills of the District, Maryland, and Virginia. The Dome is constantly peeping out through the trees down the valleys in the most unexpected places as one drives or wanders through the country. These glimpses are always enjoyable because the Dome in itself is beautiful in all phases of the atmosphere and the surrounding landscape.

Although the most prominent feature in the landscape, the hill on which the Capitol is built is not of sufficient height to lift the building entirely above its surroundings. This gives the background of hills which, in connection with the sky and the changing colors which the foliage undergoes with the seasons, adds to the charm of this white pile. It is rarely that you lose sight of this beautiful object during more than a few minutes in riding or walking in the city of Washington or the surrounding country. The views of the city and the surrounding country from the Capitol are the most pleasing to be found in Washington. The

wisdom displayed in the selection of a site for the "Congress House," as the Capitol is designated on L'Enfant's first map [Plate 1], drawn in 1791, has been abundantly proven when we consider the never-failing pleasure produced by the finished result. The President's House was located so as to form the vista at the end of seven streets, the southern front facing the Washington Monument. The view also of the President's House from the river and hills of Virginia is very effective. The "grand edifices" were to be located in the center of parks, in which landscape artists could use their skill to enhance or emphasize the beauty of the building, and make it the crowning feature of the whole. Under such conditions the buildings could be seen, and if beautiful enjoyed. The Mall, extending from the Capitol to the Washington Monument, was to have been traversed by a grand avenue 400 feet wide. On both sides of this avenue parks were to have been laid out, ending against a background of public buildings. These sites allowed room for the growth of the Government business. The engraved map published in 1792 [Plate 2] shows sites for buildings as well as monuments, columns, and statuary, located so as to be viewed down the different avenues, the end in view being, L'Enfant says, "to preserve through the whole a reciprocity of sight" between the important points of the city.[8]

How has this really wise and artistic scheme been carried out? The Capitol and President's House are on the ground originally selected for them. The wisdom of the choice has been proved by the pleasure derived from the completed structures. The effectiveness of the White House has been marred by the erection of the Treasury and of the State, War, and Navy Department buildings. In this way a sight of it is cut off from Pennsylvania avenue on the east, and New York avenue on the west. The Congressional Library is the first structure to bring an antagonistic element

[7] Brown's Plate 1 was a detail photograph of the U.S. Coast and Geodetic Survey's 1887 facsimile of the L'Enfant plan. For a discussion of the history of the map's curatorial care, see Richard W. Stephenson, "Delineation of a Grand Plan," *Quarterly Journal of the Library of Congress* 36 (Summer 1979): 218–221.

[8] Quotation taken from "Observations Explanatory of the Plan," listed both on the 1791 L'Enfant manuscript plan and the 1792 Ellicott engraved plan. "Congress House" was changed by Thomas Jefferson to "Capitol" in his review of L'Enfant's plans.

in conjunction with the Capitol.[9] The Library has been built across Pennsylvania avenue on the east. Down this street for miles a fine view of the Capitol could formerly be obtained. Now the Dome of the Capitol rising over the Library, and seen in connection with the dome or central feature of the Library, produces a decided discord. In later years the selection of sites for public buildings seems to have been purely a haphazard one. No general system is being followed; no man or men seem to have studied the question as a whole. The development of the original and wise plan seems to have been forgotten.

It is to be regretted that we have no bureau of fine arts composed of cultivated architects and landscape artists. Such a board could study jointly the question of grouping as a whole and in detail. They could select intelligently designs for buildings as well as sculpture. If we are aiming at the beautiful, the building and its surroundings must be in harmony.

The most notable suggestion for building sites on the map of L'Enfant is the line which forms the north and south boundary of the parks between the Capitol and the Monument. Naturally, the first thought would be to keep the parks free from buildings, as they are the people's breathing spaces.

The more the scheme laid out by Washington and L'Enfant is studied, the more forcibly it strikes one as the best. It is easy to imagine the magnificence of a boulevard 400 feet wide, beginning at the Capitol and ending with the Monument, a distance of nearly a mile and a half, bounded on both sides by parks 600 feet wide, laid out by a skilled landscape architect and adorned by the work of capable artists. Looking from the boulevard across the park a continuous line of beautiful buildings was to have formed the background. They were not to have been deep enough to curtail either the natural or artistic beauties of the park, or to encroach upon the people's right to an air space. By this time such an avenue would have acquired a world-wide reputation, if it had been carried out by competent architects, landscape artists, and sculptors consulting and working in harmony with each other. The parked portion of the Champs Elysées, which is approximately 1,300 feet wide and three-quarters of a mile long, would not have compared with it in magnitude or grandeur.

The original plan can be commended for other reasons than those of beauty. It has every advantage in point of economy in maintenance, repairs, supervision, inter-communication, transportation, and accessibility of the Departments to each other and to the public. To carry out the original plan, or one closely allied thereto, in the erection of future Government buildings, is feasible, but the probability of such wise action without a competent bureau of fine arts is infinitesimal.

---

[9] Brown is referring to what today is called the Thomas Jefferson Building of the Library of Congress.

MAP OF WASHINGTON CITY BY PETER CHARLES L'ENFANT, PLATE I

NOTES COPIED FROM THE MARGIN OF L'ENFANT'S MAP.

Plan of the City, intended for the Permanent Seat of the Government of the United States. Projected agreeable to the PRESIDENT of the UNITED STATES, in pursuance of an ACT of CONGRESS passed the sixteenth day of July MDCCXC, "establishing the Permanent Seat on the bank of the Potomac." By Peter Charles L'Enfant.

OBSERVATIONS EXPLANATORY OF THE PLAN.

I.   The positions of the different grand edifices and for the several grand squares or areas of different shape as they are laid down were first determined on the most advantageous ground commanding the most extensive prospects, and the better susceptible of such improvements as the various intents of the several objects may require.

II.   Lines or avenues of direct communication have been devised to connect the separate and most distant objects with the principal, and to preserve through the whole a reciprocity of sight at the same time. Attention has been paid to the passing of those leading avenues over the most favorable ground for prospect and convenience.

III.   North and south lines, intersected by others running due east and west, make the distribution of the city into streets, squares, etc., and those lines have been so combined as to meet at certain given points with those divergent avenues, so as to form on the spaces "first determined" the different squares or areas, which are all proportioned in magnitude to the number of avenues leading to them.

REFERENCES.

A.   The equestrian figure of George Washington, a monument voted in 1783 by the late Continental Congress.

B.   An historic column. Also intended for a mile or itinerary column, from whose station (a mile from the Federal house) all distances or places through the continent are to be calculated.

C.   A naval itinerary column, proposed to be erected to celebrate the first rise of Navy and to stand a ready monument to consecrate its progress and achievements.

D.   This church is intended for national purposes, such as public prayer, thanks-givings, funeral orations, etc., likewise a proper shelter for such monuments as were voted by the late Continental Congress for those heroes who fell in the cause of liberty and for such others as may hereafter be decreed by the voice of a grateful nation.

E.   For grand fountains, intended with a constant spout of water. N. B. There are within the limits of the city above twenty-five good springs of excellent water, abundantly supplied in the driest season of the year.

F.   Grand cascade, formed of the water from the sources of the Tiber.

G.   Public walk, being a square of 1,200 feet, through which carriages may ascend to the upper square of the Federal house.

H.   Grand avenue, 400 feet in breadth and about a mile in length, bordered with gardens, ending in a slope from the houses on each side. The avenue leads to the monument A and connects the Congress Garden with the

I.   President's park and the

K.   Well-improved field, being a part of the walk from the President's house, of about 1,800 feet in breadth and three-fourths of a mile in length. Every lot deep-colored red, with green plots, designates some of the situations which command the most agreeable prospects and which are the best calculated for spacious houses and gardens, such as may accommodate foreign ministers, etc.

L.   Around the square and all along the

M.   Avenue from the two bridges to the Federal house the pavement on each side will pass under an arched way, under whose cover shops will be most conveniently and agreeably situated. This street is 160 feet in breadth and a mile long.

PLATE 1

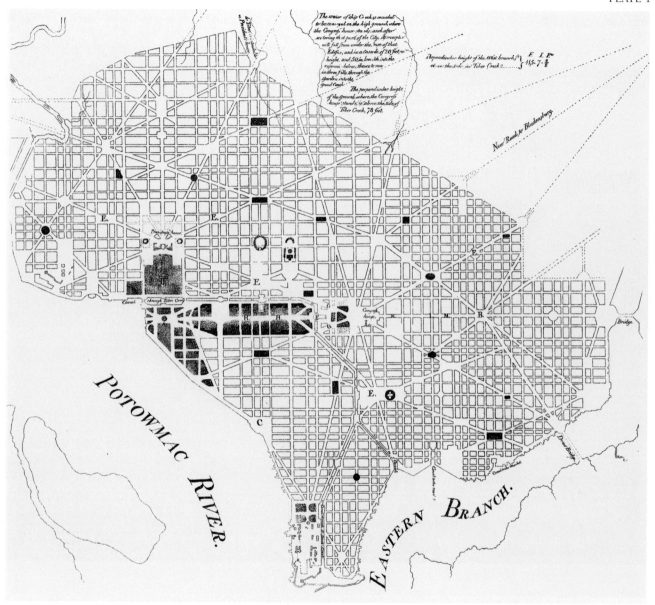

MAP OF PETER CHARLES L'ENFANT, 1791.

Cropped facsimile reproduction of the 1791 L'Enfant plan for Washington City, U.S. Coast and Geodetic Survey, 1887.
Geography and Map Division, LC.

PLATE 2

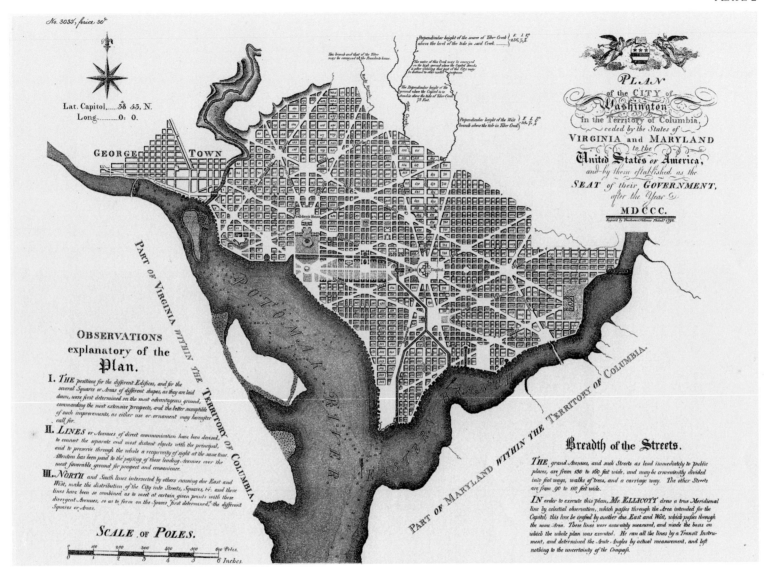

FIRST ENGRAVED MAP, 1792.

This engraving of the L'Enfant plan was considered the first "official" map of the city.
(The first large engraving of the L'Enfant plan was actually the Samuel Hill version of the plan published in Boston in 1792.)
This map was prepared by Andrew Ellicott and engraved by Thackara and Vallance, Philadelphia, 1792. *Geography and Map Division, LC.*

CHAPTER II

THE COMPETITION FOR A DESIGN

T HE history of what has transpired in the Capitol would be the history of the country from 1800 to the present day. All matters of import to our nation have been considered, weighed, and acted upon in this building, whether they related to war, finance, commerce, the making or the interpretation of law. All the Presidents and most prominent statesmen, warriors, and jurists of the country since the adoption of the Constitution have been intimately associated with this building. The histories of the distinguished men who have frequented its halls have been written by many able hands. In the following pages I propose to give a history of the structure in which the history of the country has been made.[1]

Thomas Johnson, David Stuart, and Daniel Carroll, the commissioners in charge of laying out the Federal City, in a letter to President Washington, October 21, 1791, say: "We have requested him [L'Enfant] to prepare a draft of the public buildings for our inspection, and he has

promised to enter on it as soon as he finds himself disengaged. He can have recourse to books in Philadelphia and can not have it here."[2]

L'Enfant made studies for the buildings in connection with the preparation of his map, but Washington and Jefferson do not seem to have at any time contemplated making use of his architectural ideas. Several years later L'Enfant made a claim for compensation for planning and conducting the erection of public buildings. This claim was evidently made with reference to work which he thought he was entitled to do in the future, as the letters of the period show that he never made the plans which the commissioners requested him to draw. L'Enfant was discharged February 27, 1792, before the public competitions for the Capitol and White House, and had nothing to do with any work in the city after that date.[3]

The act of Congress which established the city upon its present site also required that buildings should be erected to accommodate the

---

[1] For an earlier version of this chapter, see Glenn Brown, "History of the United States Capitol," *The American Architect and Building News* 52 (May 9, 1896): 51–54 and (May 23, 1896): 75–77, where drawings from the 1792 design competition for the Capitol were published for the first time. Brown's interpretation of this competition and his claim that Thornton was the primary architect of the old Capitol were widely accepted as authoritative until Fiske Kimball and Wells Bennett published their research between 1916 and 1923 on Stephen Hallet, William Thornton, and the design competition for the Capitol. See Wells Bennett, "Stephen Hallet and His Designs for the National Capitol, 1791–94," reprinted from the *Journal of the American Institute of Architects* (July, August, September, October, 1916): 1–31. Fiske Kimball and Wells Bennett, "The Competition for the Federal Buildings," *Journal of the American Institute of Architects* 7 (January, March, May, August, December, 1919): 8–12, 98–102, 202–210, 355–361, 521–528; and "William Thornton and the Design of the United States Capitol," *Art Studies* 1 (1923): 76–92. See also Wells Bennett's critique of Brown in a letter to the editor in the *Nation* 102 (January 13, 1916): 43–44.

[2] Commissioners of the District of Columbia to President George Washington, October 21, 1791, RG 42, DCC, NARA.

[3] For a modern and more speculative account of the importance of L'Enfant's influence on George Washington and for a discussion of L'Enfant's claims to Congress for professional compensation, see Bates Lowry, *Building a National Image: Architectural Drawings for the American Democracy, 1789–1912* (Washington: National Building Museum, 1985), 16–19; 226. Lowry contends that L'Enfant's drawings or studies for the Capitol may have provided a model that inspired both the Hallet and Thornton designs. He sees striking similarities between their designs and L'Enfant's ground plan for the Capitol, depicted in his 1791 manuscript plan. The only biography of L'Enfant is Hans Paul Caemmerer, *The Life of Pierre Charles L'Enfant, Planner of the City Beautiful* (Washington: National Republic Printing Co., 1950; reprint New York: Da Capo Press, 1970). See also the documentary work of Elizabeth Kite, *L'Enfant and Washington, 1791–92* (Baltimore: Johns Hopkins Press, 1929; reprint New York: Arno Press, 1972).

several branches of the Government, which were to be ready for occupancy by the year 1800. Commissioners Thomas Johnson, David Stuart, and Daniel Carroll were appointed to see that the laws of Congress in reference to the Federal City were properly executed, and one of their earliest duties was to obtain plans for the new buildings. As there were no buildings in this country of magnitude equal to the contemplated ones, it was difficult to select an architect, by judging of the work he had already accomplished, without selecting one from the Old World. So, after mature deliberation, the commissioners, acting on the recommendation of President Washington and Secretary of State Thomas Jefferson, decided to have a public competition for the Capitol and the President's House. March 6, 1792, Thomas Jefferson wrote to the commissioners: "It is necessary to advertise immediately for plans for the Capitol and the President's House." At the same time he returned the draft of an advertisement which the commissioners had sent him, revised by Washington and himself.[4] The commissioners were directed to send the advertisement, when finally correct, for insertion in Philadelphia and other papers. Probably this was the first architectural competition inaugurated in this country. Certainly the first Government competition soliciting plans was made by this advertisement. At the present day we would not consider the conditions of this competition model ones, and it is a matter of surprise that they should have produced such successful results.[5] The following is the form of the advertisement as it appeared in the papers of the period:

A PREMIUM

of a lot in the city, to be designated by impartial judges, and $500, or a medal of that value, at the option of the party, will be given by the Commissioners of Federal Buildings to persons who, before the 15th day of July, 1792, shall produce them the most approved plan, if adopted by them, for a Capitol to be erected in the city, and $250 or a medal for the plan deemed next in merit to the one they shall adopt; the building to be of brick and to contain the following compartments to wit:

A conference room. ⎤ To contain 300 ⎤
A room for Representatives. ⎦ persons each. ⎥
A lobby or antechamber to the latter. ⎥ These rooms to be
A Senate room of 1,200 square feet of area. ⎥ of full elevation.
An antechamber and lobby to the latter. ⎦

Twelve rooms of 600 square feet area each for committee rooms and clerks to be of half the elevation of the former.

Drawings will be expected of the ground plats, elevations of each front, and sections through the building in such directions as may be necessary to explain the material, structure, and an estimate of the cubic feet of the brick work composing the whole mass of the wall.

THOS. JOHNSON,
DD. STUART,
DANL. CARROLL,
Commissioners.

MARCH 14, 1792.[6]

---

[4] This letter and the draft advertisements for competitions for the design of the Capitol and President's House, with revisions and notes by Jefferson and Washington, are published in Charles T. Cullen, ed., *The Papers of Thomas Jefferson* (Princeton, N.J.: Princeton University Press, 1990), vol. 23, 224–228.

[5] At the time Brown was directly involved in the American Institute of Architects's legislative efforts to open commissions for federal government buildings to private architects and to establish a uniform method of conducting design competitions for federal projects. Brown sketched the background of this legislation and provided an exaggerated account of its success in "The Tarsney Act," *Brickbuilder* (May 1908): 5–12.

---

[6] See *Gazette of the United States* [Philadelphia], March 24, 1792. The competition announcement was published after its approval by the commissioners.

Jefferson sent the commissioners clippings of this advertisement on March 21, 1792, from several Philadelphia papers, at the same time advising them to advertise in other newspapers and to procure a superintendent.[7] In answer to this advertisement, plans were received from architects, contractors, and amateurs. The competitors who are mentioned in the records, old letters, or on drawings were Stephen Hallet, Judge Turner, Samuel Blodgett, Lamphiere, S. M. McIntire, Jacob Small, James Diamond, Charles Winter Smith, Andrew Mayo, Philip Hart, Abram Farris, Collen Williamson, Carstairs, and Hasborough.[8] The plans submitted were, with few exceptions, peculiarly indifferent. The larger number of the drawings were made by amateurs or contractors who did not have the first idea as to what constituted either good draftsmanship or design or what were the necessary requisites of a Congressional hall or a President's mansion. Quite a number of these rejected plans are in possession of the Maryland Historical Society. I have selected some of the poorest as well as the best for illustration. [See Plates 3 to 14.]

It is difficult to imagine anyone earnestly submitting designs such as are shown in Plates 4 to 9 with the idea of meeting the approval of an intelligent committee. Several competitors of a similar caliber protested against the award, as they considered the selected design inferior to the ones which they presented.

President Washington went to the new Federal City on July 15, 1792. The competition was closed on this date, and the commissioners had been duly notified by Thomas Jefferson, July 5, to hold all the drawings for the President's inspection.[9] James Hoban's design for the "President's Palace" was selected without hesitation. No one sent in drawings for the Capitol that were satisfactory. The only plans that appear to have received consideration were those of Lamphiere, Hallet, and Turner. Turner's plan was not received, judging by letter of notice, until July 19.[10]

On July 17, 1792, the commissioners wrote to Stephen Hallet, stating that his plan had been submitted to the President, and further saying: "Style of architecture of yours has attracted; the distribution of parts is not thought sufficiently convenient." The commissioners suggest additional rooms and recommend Hallet to come to Washington City and examine the site. "We wish you to visit us as soon as you can and have a free and full communication of ideas with us. Your design may perhaps be improved into approbation. In all events, we will liberally indemnify you for your expenses."[11] This letter was sent in the care of the Secretary of State in Philadelphia, showing that Hallet was at the time a resident of the Quaker City. July 19 the commissioners wrote to President Washington, saying they had determined to give Lamphiere's plan no further consideration, at the same time forwarding the drawings of Judge Turner and telling the President of their invitation to Hallet. Their letter ends in these words: "Still hope a little time may give you an opportunity of making a choice to your satisfaction."[12] It is well

[7] Thomas Jefferson to the Commissioners of the District of Columbia, March 21, 1792, in Cullen, ed., *The Papers of Thomas Jefferson*, vol. 23, 320–321.

[8] For a description and illustration of all known competition drawings, with biographical sketches of the entrants, see Jeanne F. Butler, *Competition 1792: Designing a Nation's Capitol* (special issue), *Capitol Studies* 4 (1976). Butler found no direct evidence to confirm that Andrew Mayo, John Collins, Thomas Carstairs, and Collen Williamson were competitors. Brown may have confused Andrew Mayo with Andrew Mayfield Carshore. Brown misspelled Robert Goin Lanphiere's name as Lamphiere, Collen Williamson's name as Colin, and Leonard Harbaugh's name as Hasborough, and he also misspelled Blodget. Judge Turner's first name was George.

[9] Saul K. Padover, ed., *Thomas Jefferson and the National Capital* (Washington: Government Printing Office, 1946), 152. Published from the Commissioner's letterbooks, 1791–93, RG 42, DCC, NARA.

[10] Commissioners to George Turner, July 19, 1792, RG 42, DCC, NARA.

[11] Commissioners to Stephen Hallet, July 17, 1792, RG 42, DCC, NARA.

[12] Commissioners to President George Washington, July 19, 1792, RG 42, DCC, NARA.

PLATE 3

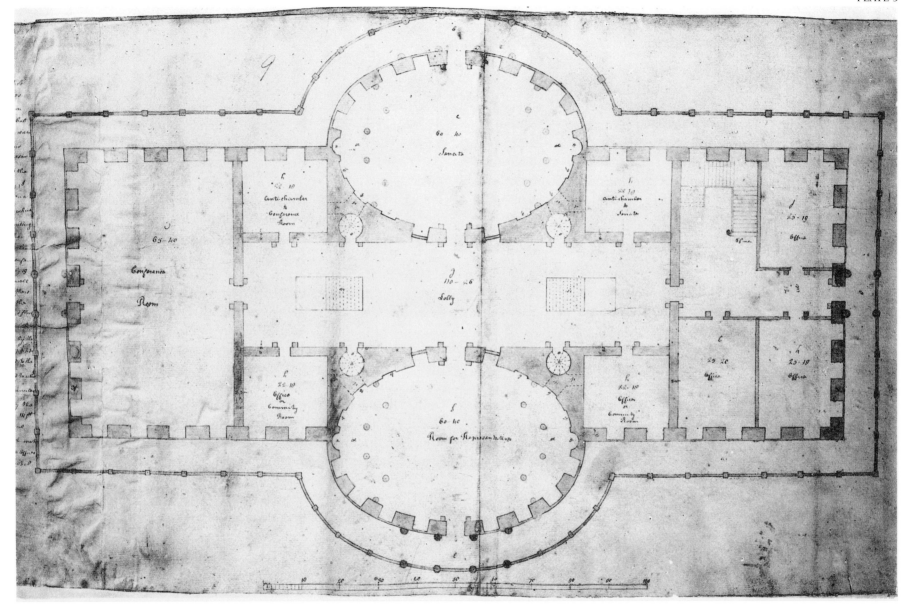

GROUND PLAN OF LAMPHIER'S COMPETITIVE DESIGN.

Cropped image of Robert Lanphier's "Second Floor" plan for the Capitol. Brown misspelled Lanphier's name and mislabeled the drawing. *MHS*.

PLATE 4

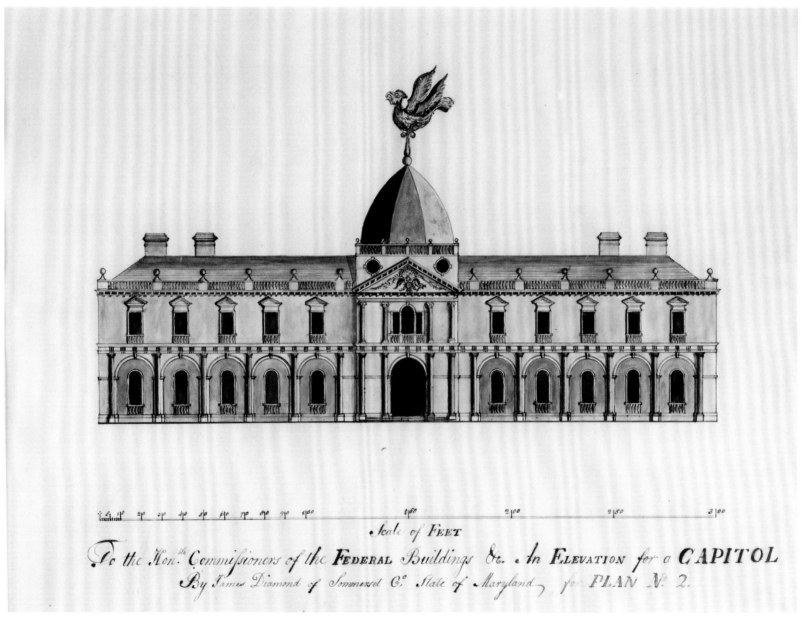

Scale of FEET

To the Hon.ble Commissioners of the FEDERAL Buildings &c. An ELEVATION for a CAPITOL
By James Diamond of Sommerset Co. State of Maryland, for PLAN No. 2.

ELEVATION OF JAMES DIAMOND'S COMPETITIVE DESIGN.
Elevation for plan no. 2. *MHS.*

PLATE 5

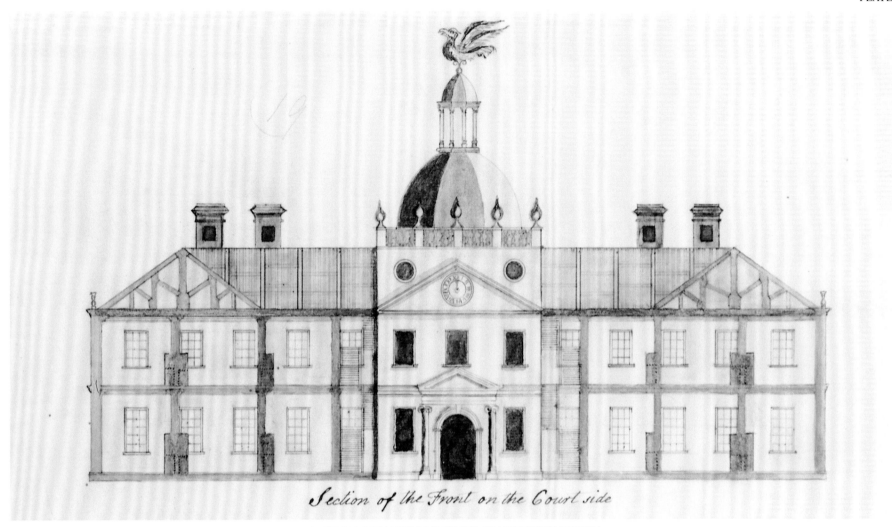

Section of the Front on the Court side

SECTION OF JAMES DIAMOND'S COMPETITIVE DESIGN.
Detail from the section and floor plan of "the Front on the Court Side, No. 1" for the Capitol. *MHS.*

PLATE 6

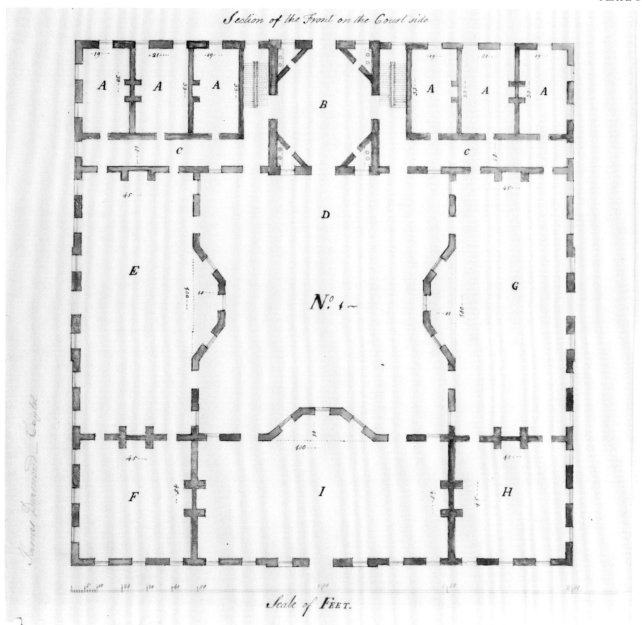

PLAN OF JAMES DIAMOND'S COMPETITIVE DESIGN.

Detail from the section and floor plan of "the Front on the Court Side, No. 1" for the Capitol. *MHS.*

PLATE 7

FRONT ELEVATION OF PHILIP HART'S COMPETITIVE DESIGN.

Front view of the Capitol "B." *MHS.*

PLATE 8

END ELEVATION OF PHILIP HART'S COMPETITIVE DESIGN.

"C" end elevation of the Capitol. *MHS.*

PLATE 9

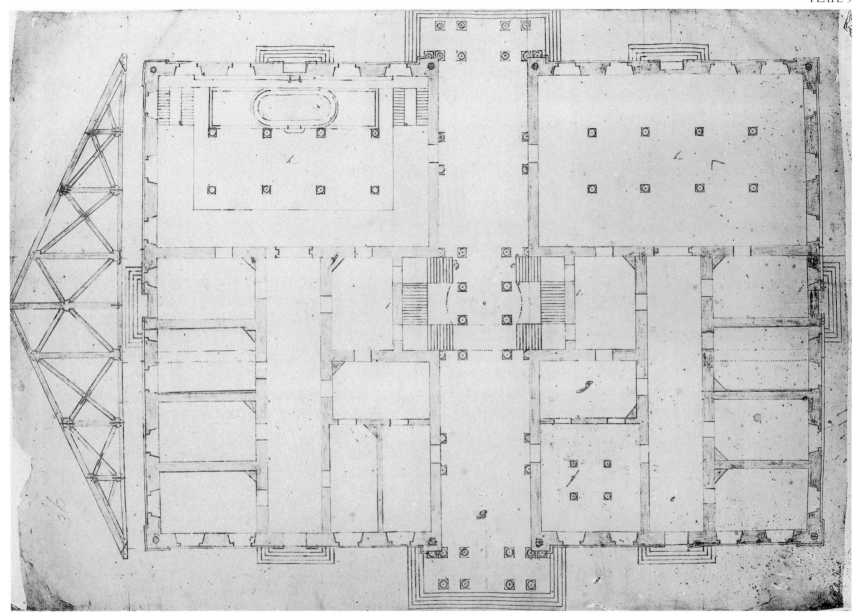

PLAN OF PHILIP HART'S COMPETITIVE DESIGN.
Floor plan and roof framing detail for the Capitol. *MHS.*

PLATE 10

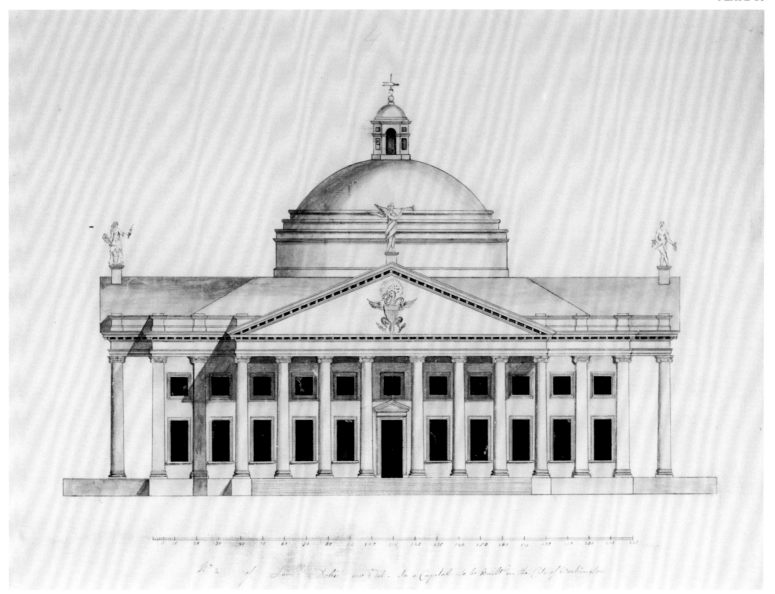

ELEVATION OF SAMUEL DOBIE'S COMPETITIVE DESIGN.
Elevation, no. 2. *MHS.*

PLATE 11

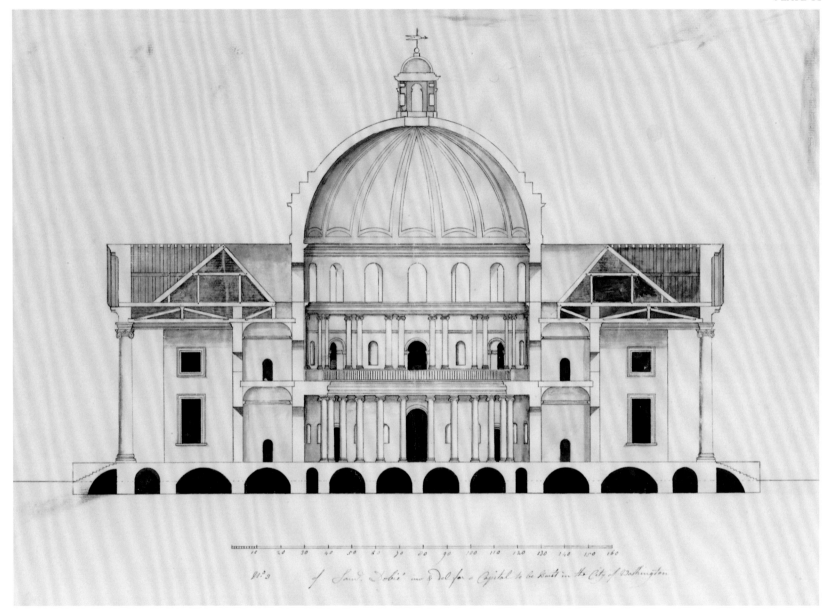

SECTION OF SAMUEL DOBIE'S COMPETITIVE DESIGN.

Section, no. 3. *MHS.*

PLATE 12

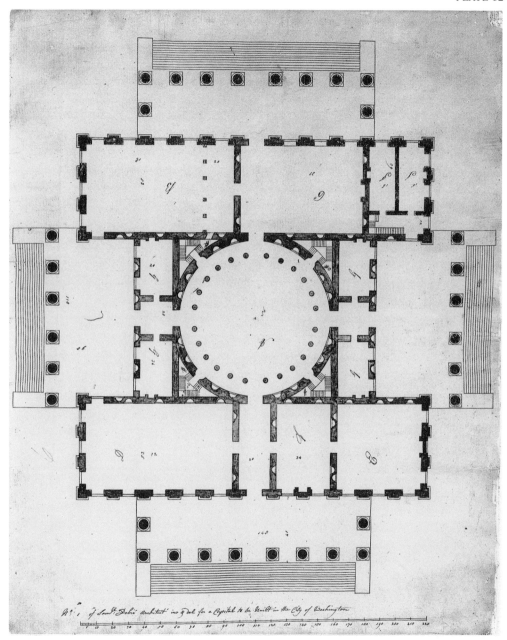

PLAN OF SAMUEL DOBIE'S COMPETITIVE DESIGN.

Floor plan, no. 1. *MHS.*

PLATE 13

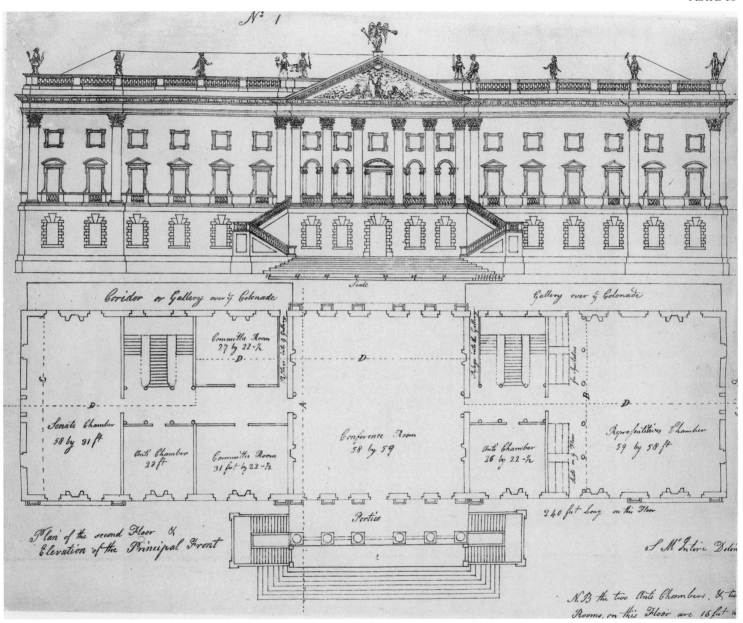

PLAN AND ELEVATION OF S. M. McINTIRE'S COMPETITIVE PLAN.
No. 1 "Plan of the second Floor & Elevation of the Principal Front." *MHS.*

PLATE 14

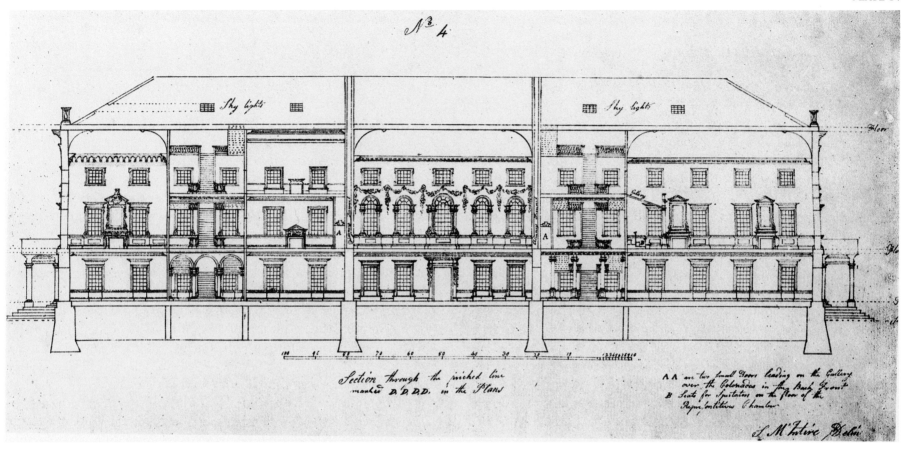

SECTION OF S. M. McINTIRE'S COMPETITIVE PLAN.

No. 4 "Section Through the pricked line marked D, D, D, D in the Plans." *MHS.*

to note the personal interest which President Washington took in the selection of the design. In fact, the decision seems to have rested almost entirely with him. On July 23, 1792, Washington wrote to the commissioners and commended Turner's plans as pleasing him better than any that had been so far submitted, but noting the same defects that existed in the other designs—the want of Executive Departments. Washington seems to have been particularly struck with the beauty and grandeur of the dome in the center. He thinks that if this plan should be adopted, the "pilastrade" ought to be carried around the semicircular projections at the ends. He suggests a location for the library and queries if Turner's plan could be surrounded by a colonnade like Hallet's. ["The roof of Hallet's, I must confess, is not to my taste."] "If it were not too expensive, it would, in my judgment, be a noble and desirable structure; but I would have it understood, in this instance and always when I am hazarding a sentiment on these buildings, that I profess to have no knowledge of architecture, and think we should, to avoid criticism, be governed by the established rules which are laid down by the professors of the art."[13]

As late as August 29, 1792, by a communication of the commissioners, it is shown that Samuel Blodgett and Hasborough submitted drawings. Although there were points to be commended in Blodgett's, Turner's, and Hallet's, none was found suitable for adoption. So they submitted to the last-named competitors a revised schedule, in which they say: "Though limited in means, we want a plan a credit to the age in design and taste."[14] The commissioners of the District show throughout the correspondence a decided preference for Hallet and his plans. On September 1, 1792, they write to him, praising the drawings, and stating that they have "strong expectations that they may, with mutual satisfaction, form lasting engagements, but present views may be crossed and nothing can be done until a plan of the Capitol is fixed."[15] November 2 Turner's drawings, probably those of the revised or second competition, were returned as not answering the purpose.[16]

October, 1792, Dr. William Thornton, of the island of Tortola, West Indies, wrote to the commissioners, requesting permission to submit drawings according to the first advertisement. November 15 the commissioners wrote to him stating that they would be pleased to look at his plans of the Capitol, and at the same time informing him of the fact that the premium for the architectural work on the President's House had been awarded to James Hoban. On December 4 of the same year they wrote Dr. Thornton another letter saying: "Your letter of the 9th is before us. Have to inform you that as none of the plans for the Capitol met with our entire approbation, Mr. Hallet, a French architect, was engaged to prepare one, which he tells us will be ready by the first of next month. As we shall then forward it immediately to the President, we think it will be best for you to lodge your plan with the Secretary of State for the President's inspection, who, when he returns Mr. Hallet's plans, will also send us yours."[17] Thornton had not presented his plan on December 13, 1792. On January 5, 1793, Hallet requested three more weeks in which to complete his drawings. The commissioners make a note of the fact that Hallet loses nothing in their estimation by failing to have his drawings completed in the time which he had specified. February 7, 1793, the fact was duly recorded that the

---

[13] George Washington to the District of Columbia Commissioners, July 23, 1792, in John C. Fitzpatrick, ed., *The Writings of George Washington from the Original Manuscript Sources, 1745–1799* (Washington: Government Printing Office, 1939), vol. 32, 93–95.

[14] Commissioners to Samuel Blodgett [Blodget], August 29, 1792, RG 42, DCC, NARA.

[15] Commissioners to Stephen Hallet, September 1, 1792, RG 42, DCC, NARA.

[16] Commissioners to George Turner, November 2, 1792, RG 42, DCC, NARA.

[17] William Thornton first wrote to the Commissioners from Tortola on July 12, 1792. Daniel Carroll to William Thornton, November 15, 1792; Daniel Carroll and David Stuart to William Thornton, December 4, 1792, William Thornton Papers, vol. 1, 135 (microfilm), Manuscript Division, LC.

commissioners and others were generally satisfied with Thornton's plans for the Capitol, and note the sorrow they feel for Hallet, but think they will be able to employ him usefully, notwithstanding.[18] March 3 Thornton came to Washington with an introduction from President Washington to the commissioners. In this letter Washington says of Thornton's plan: "Grandeur, simplicity, and convenience appear to be so well combined in this plan of Dr. Thornton's." Washington felt sure that it would meet the approbation of the commissioners, as it had been approved by all the best judges. As to the funds, "It should be considered that the external of the building will be the only immediate expense to be incurred; the internal work and many of the ornamental [parts] without may be finished gradually."[19]

Thomas Jefferson, Secretary of State, about this period says of this plan: "The grandeur, simplicity, and beauty of the exterior, the propriety with which the apartments are distributed, and the economy in the mass of the whole structure recommend this plan." A short time after, he says: "Thornton's plan had captivated the eyes and the judgment of all. It is simple, noble, beautiful, excellently arranged, and moderate in size.... Among its admirers none are more decided than he whose decision is most important."[20] The commissioners wrote to Washington March 11, after a thorough examination of Thornton's plan, that "the rooms for the different branches of Congress and the conference room are much to our satisfaction, and its outward appearance will be

striking and pleasing."[21] They criticise the unnecessary number of small rooms, fear lack of light, and advocate reducing the number of rooms. They commend a grand scale for the building, but fear expense and debt will affect their standing before the world; at the same time are willing to leave it to the President's ideas of propriety.

The merits of the plans were practically settled March 13, for on this date the commissioners express their regrets to Hallet, and, as his plan was the most meritorious in the first competition, state that it was "our hope and wishes that you would carry the prize in the second competition. Our opinion has preferred Dr. Thornton's, and expect the President will confirm our choice." [Judging from letter of March 3, they might have felt assured of the fact.] "Neither could demand the prize under the terms of the competition. We determine to give Thornton $500 and a lot worth £100. You certainly rank next."[22]

The following letter explains itself:

GEORGETOWN, *April 5, 1793.*

SIR: The President has given his formal approbation of your plan.

You will therefore be pleased to grant powers or put the business in a way to be closed on the acknowledgments your success entitles you.

As soon as the nature of the work and your convenience will permit, we wish to be in possession of your explanations with the plan, for we wish to mark out the ground, make preparations, and even lay out the foundations this fall.

We are etc.,   T. JOHNSON.
                                                          DD. STUART.
                                                          DANL. CARROLL.[23]

DR. WM. THORNTON, *Philadelphia.*

---

[18] Proceedings, January 5 and February 7, 1793, RG 42, DCC, NARA.

[19] George Washington to the Commissioners of the District of Columbia, March 3, 1793, in Fitzpatrick, *The Writings of George Washington*, vol. 32, 370–373.

[20] Thomas Jefferson to Mr. Carroll, February 1, 1793, in Padover, *Thomas Jefferson and the National Capital*, 171. Originally published in H. A. Washington, ed., *The Writings of Thomas Jefferson*, vol. 3 (Washington, 1853–54), 508.

[21] Commissioners to George Washington, March 11, 1793, RG 42, DCC, NARA.

[22] Commissioners to Stephen Hallet, March 13, 1793, RG 42, DCC, NARA.

[23] Commissioners to William Thornton, April 5, 1793, RG 42, DCC, NARA.

One fact is to be noted in connection with the competitions for the Capitol—the evident desire of the commissioners to employ Hallet in some way, so they could remunerate him for the time spent on the plans at their request. In the second competition he was practically working under the commissioners' personal instruction and supervision for six months, from July, 1792, to February, 1793, with a guaranty of expenses and liberal indemnity [July 17, 1792]. Nothing gives stronger evidence of the exceptional merit of Thornton's plan than its power to overcome the personal equation and interest of the commissioners in the plan of Hallet. Unfortunately, neither Thornton's nor Hallet's first plan, so far as I have been able to discover, is in existence, so we can not pass judgment upon their merits or demerits. There is a plan of Hallet's made in July, 1793, which, judging from one of Washington's letters, is closely on the lines of Hallet's competitive design [Plate 18] and numerous letters assert that later plans of Thornton were mere modifications of Thornton's original scheme [Plates 28 to 31]. From these designs it can be easily seen that Hallet's capacity in both planning and designing was far inferior to the ideas of Thornton both in utility, proportion, and refinement of details.[24]

By one of Thornton's letters we learn that he was offered the position of superintendent of this work, but declined.[25] The commissioners expected the superintendent to devote his entire time to this object.

The commissioners at this point (April 10, 1793) in the history of the building made the serious error of appointing Hallet (as payment to him for the time and trouble he had given to working on the Capitol) to make an estimate of the cost and study of Thornton's plan of the Capitol. We can easily imagine the avidity with which Thornton's principal competitor studied the drawings to find the minutest defects, and he, as was probably expected, made out a list of insuperable objections to its execution.

Hallet, Blodgett, Williamson, and Carstairs, all competitors, seemed to have combined, being on the spot, and urged the rejection of Thornton's plan. Soon after the above date, Hallet was employed to superintend the erection of the building. Instead of doing this, he seems to have spent his time in searching for defects and proposing alterations of the adopted plan. George Alfred Townsend, in his book Washington Inside and Out, published in 1873, takes decided grounds, giving Hallet the credit for designing the old Capitol. He mentions several drawings of Hallet's which are in the possession of the Congressional Library. A great number, if not all, of these drawings were made when Hallet was employed, after the selection of Thornton's plan, in a persistent effort to induce Washington and the commissioners to accept some of Hallet's ideas.[26]

---

[24] Brown incorrectly dates this drawing [Plate 18], relying on the original notation on the back of the drawing which read "A1 Plan of the Ground and Principal Floor of the Federal Capitol Sent to Philadelphia to the Board July 1793. S. Hallet." Correspondence indicated the drawing was in fact Hallet's first competition plan, "A," forwarded to the Commissioners by Jefferson, July 11, 1792. The error was first noted in Wells Bennett's discussion of the dating of Hallet's drawings in "Stephen Hallet and His Designs for the National Capitol, 1791–1797," 327–330. See also Alexandra Cushing Howard, "Stephen Hallet and William Thornton at the U.S. Capitol, 1791–1797" (Master's thesis, University of Virginia, 1974), 144–145. Both Bennett and Howard challenge Brown's opinion of Hallet's ability and his contributions to the design of the Capitol. Howard provides a valuable inventory of the Hallet and Thornton drawings in an appendix to her thesis. For a more recent study of Hallet's design contribution to the Capitol, see Pamela Scott, "Stephen Hallet's Designs for the United States Capitol," Winterthur Portfolio 27 (Summer/Autumn 1992): 145–170.

[25] William Thornton made this assertion in a printed letter to the Members of the House of Representatives, January 1, 1805, vols. 3–4, William Thornton Papers, Manuscript Division, LC.

[26] George Alfred Townsend, Washington Outside and Inside: A Picture and a Narrative of the Origin, Growth, Excellences, Abuses, Beauties, and Personages of Our Governing City (Hartford, Conn.: James Betts and Company, 1873), 56–74. This work, although containing several significant errors in its account of the design authorship of the Capitol, became a standard source for other writers. See, for instance, James Q. Howard, "Architects of the

Because a note on one of the drawings says Thornton sent for the elevation and plan, according to Townsend, Edward Clark, the present Architect of the Capitol, assumed that Thornton copied this drawing and turned it out as his own. They seem to have overlooked the fact that Thornton prepared his drawings in the West Indies, and at the period that this drawing of Hallet's was made Thornton's design was the accepted one, and he was most anxious to prevent its being modified.[27]

Hallet, in a footnote, says: "The President having seen this accidentally in September, 1793, agreed with the commissioners to have the Capitol planned in imitation thereof." All the documentary evidence is contradictory of this assertion, and proves that Washington was always in favor of the Thornton plan, a modification of which will be shown later [Plates 28 to 31].

The following letter from President Washington gives a very clear account of the condition of affairs at this date. The commissioners, on June 22, were awaiting this letter from Washington, showing that they were aware of the importunity of Hallet and others:

MOUNT VERNON, *June 30, 1793.*

DEAR SIR: You will find by inclosed letter from the commisioners that Mr. Hallet reports unfavorably of Dr. Thornton's plan "on the great points of practicability, time, and expense," and that I am referred to Mr. Blodgett, Hoban, and Hallet, whose verbal information will be better than any we can give you on which to form ultimate instructions. Mr. Blodgett I met at Baltimore at the moment I was about to leave it, consequently I had little conversation with him on the subject referred to; but Mr. Hallet is of opinion that the execution of Thornton's plan (independent of the cost, which would far exceed our means and the time allowed for the accomplishment of the building) is impracticable; would not in some parts answer the ends proposed. Mr. Hoban seemed

---

American Capitol," *International Review* 1 (November–December 1874): 736–753. The discovery of such errors encouraged Brown to revive the case for Thornton as the original designer of the Capitol.

[27] Brown's discussion of the "Tortola scheme" was first published in 1896 in his article, "Dr. William Thornton, Architect," *Architectural Record* 6 (July 1896): 53–70. Brown identified a drawing loaned to him by Architect of the Capitol Edward Clark as Thornton's competition design for the President's House. He based his conclusion on a letter dated July 12, 1792, written by Thornton from Tortola, British Virgin Islands, which stated that he had made competition plans for both the President's House and the Capitol. Brown also assumed that the strong resemblance of the drawing to a British country residence precluded it from being Thornton's first Capitol design. He explained in the article that it was "difficult to understand the plan from the elevations." Brown was thus unaware of two unsigned floor plans that correlated to this elevation then in the possession of Thornton heir J. Henley Smith. The plans were later discovered by Fiske Kimball and Wells Bennett in the Thornton papers, donated to the Library of Congress in 1903 (see their 1923 article, "William Thornton and the Design of the Capitol," 76–92). Kimball and Wells mistakenly believed Brown had obtained the elevations from a Thornton descendant. Since this discovery the elevation drawings have been commonly identified by architectural historians as Thornton's "Tortola scheme." These elevations were never actually submitted to the commissioners. It is not known how Edward Clark came into possession of the drawings or why he did not deposit the drawings in the Library of Congress as he did with the Hallet drawings received from B. H. Latrobe, Jr., in 1871.

A sampling of guidebooks of the nation's capital from the 1830s to the 1870s indicates that confusion long existed over the identity of the original designer of the Capitol. Jonathan Elliot noted in 1830 that Hallet was the first architect and did not mention Thornton. Robert Mills, who was a student and assistant of Latrobe from 1803 to 1808, credited Thornton with the original design, but claimed Hallet, whom he mistakenly identified as an Englishman, "modified it in some of its parts." Bohn's 1856 guidebook cited Hallet while an 1872 guidebook cited Thornton. See Jonathan Elliot, *Historical Sketches of the Ten Miles Square Forming the District of Columbia* (Washington: Printed by J. Elliot, Jr., 1830), 107; Robert Mills, *Guide to the Capitol of the United States Embracing Every Information Useful to the Visitor Whether Business or Pleasure* (Washington: privately printed, 1834), 58; *Bohn's Handbook of Washington Beautifully Illustrated With Steel Engravings of All the Public Buildings and Government Statuary* (Washington: Cashmir Bohn, 1856), 12; *The National Capital Explained and Illustrated, A Convenient Guide to All Points of Interest in the City of Washington* (Washington: Devlin and Company, 1872), 14.

to concur in this, and Mr. Blodgett, as far as I could come at his sentiments in the short time I was with him, approved the alterations in it which have been proposed by Mr. Hallet.

It is unlucky that this investigation of Dr. Thornton's plan and estimate of the cost had not preceded the adoption of it, but knowing the impatience of the Carrollsburg interest and the anxiety of the public to see both buildings progressing, and supposing the plan to be correct, it was adjudged best to avoid delay. It is better, however, to correct the error, though late, than to proceed in a ruinous measure, in the adoption of which I do not hesitate to confess that I was governed by the beauty of the exterior and the distribution of the apartments, declaring then, as I do now, that I had no knowledge in the rules of or principles of architecture, and was equally unable to count the cost. But if there be such material defects as are represented and such immense time and cost to complete the building, it would be folly in the extreme to proceed on the plan which has been adopted.

It has appeared to me proper, however, before it is laid aside, and justice and respect to Dr. Thornton require, that the objections should be made known to him, and an opportunity afforded to explain and obviate them if he can.

For this reason, and because Mr. Blodgett is in Philadelphia, and it might not be convenient for Dr. Thornton to leave it, I requested Mr. Hallet and Mr. Hoban to repair without delay to Philadelphia with all the plans and documents which are necessary to elucidate the subject, and do pray you to get all the parties herein named together and, after hearing the objections and explanations, report your opinion on the case and the plan which ought to have been executed. Nothing can be done to the foundation until a final decision is had, and this decision ought not to be delayed one moment that can be avoided, because time is wasting fast, because the public expectation is alive, and because the demon of jealousy may be at work in the lower town, when one building is seen to progress rapidly and a plan for the other not yet decided on. Whether it be practicable [even at an expense] to call in the aid of any other scientific character in Philadelphia to assist in deciding this point, or whether there be any there, is more than I can tell. Your own knowledge of this and judgment will decide.

The case is important. A plan must be adopted and, good or bad, it must be entered upon.

With great regard, I am, dear sir, your affectionate and obedient servant,

GEORGE WASHINGTON.[28]

To Secretary of State THOMAS JEFFERSON.

By order of the commissioners, acting on President Washington's letter, a commission was appointed July 17, 1793, to examine and report upon objections to the adopted plans.

In the meantime Hallet had drawn what he considered proper modifications of Thornton's design. [Plates 15, 16, 17.] The following are the objections which he raised:

1. Intercolumniation of western and central peristyle too wide for supports of stone; so are those of door and wing.

2. Colonnade in middle of conference room objectionable; if taken away, room too large for roof span.

3. The floor of central peristyle too wide to support itself.

4. Stairways on each side of conference room want headroom.

5. Windows in some important instances masked by the galleries.

6. Many parts of the building want light and air.

[28] George Washington to Thomas Jefferson, June 30, 1793, in Padover, *Thomas Jefferson and the National Capital*, 181–183.

On this board were Thornton, Hoban, Hallet, Williamson, and Carstairs [the three latter were competitors of Thornton's].[29]

Thomas Jefferson writes to Washington that the board reported that they considered the objections insurmountable without alteration of the plans. The necessary alterations were shown in the drawings made by Mr. Hallet [presumably between April 10 and July 17], "wherein he has preserved the most valuable ideas of the original and rendered them acceptable of execution, so that it is considered Dr. Thornton's plan rendered into practical form. Those persons consulted agreed that in the reformed plan the objections were entirely remedied and it was a work of great merit," and would cost about half of the first one. Plates 15, 16, and 17 show Hallet's modification of Thornton's design.[30]

In remedying objection 6, Hallet suppressed the portico on the eastern front. Commissioners thought this should be restored as in the original plan and overruled Hallet's change. Hallet's remedy for objection 5, i.e., placing windows on different levels, was overruled.

Colonel Williamson, undertaker [the old term for builder], after thorough consideration agreed with Thornton that all objections were removable without any alterations in the plans.[31]

July 25 Washington agrees with the action of the commissioners, but insists strenuously on retaining the eastern portico.

Washington on same date says: "The recess which Mr. Hallet proposes in that front strikes everyone that has viewed the plan unpleasantly...and it has been intimated that the reason of his proposing the recess, instead of the portico, is to make it in one essential feature different from Dr. Thornton's plan."[32]

Only four of the original objections remained; three of these had reference to size and would probably have been easily surmountable by an engineer of that or this day, as Thornton asserted. The judges were

---

[29] These objections had not been raised by Hallet alone as Brown implies. The opening of Jefferson's letter, which Brown does not quote, is important: "According [to] the desire expressed in your letter of June 30, I called together Doctr. Thornton, Mr. Hallet, Mr. Hoben [sic], and a judicious undertaker of this place, Mr. Carstairs, chosen by Dr. Thornton as a competent judge of the objections made to this plan of the Capitol for the city of Washington." Jefferson to Washington, July 17, 1793, in Padover, *Thomas Jefferson and the National Capital,* 184–186.

[30] Brown is mistaken in identifying this group as Hallet's modification of Thornton's design. The drawings were Hallet's design "E," so called because of the notation on the section: "No. 5...E$_6$ Section of Plan E$_1$, S. Hallet." The drawings, dating from January to March 1793, are important to the design history of the early Capitol because they contain many of the elements that appear in Hallet's "conference plan" as well as Thornton's later designs. Most scholars agree that the "E" design group was developed independently by Hallet and not derived from Thornton's competition scheme as Brown contends here. Yet there remains some skepticism about the originality of the design because of radical changes from Hallet's past designs. See Howard, "Stephen Hallet and William Thornton at the U.S. Capitol, 1791–1797," 153–155; and Don Alexander Hawkins, "William Thornton's Lost Design of the United States Capitol: A Study and Reconstruction," unpublished paper on file at the Curator's Office, AOC, 105.

[31] This was not Williams's [Brown calls him Williamson] first reaction, and Brown has been justly criticized for omitting a key passage in this letter and shading the interpretation to minimize contemporary objective criticism of Thornton's plans. The letter also stated: "I need not repeat to you the opinions of Col. Williams an undertaker also produced by Dr. Thornton, who on seeing the plans and hearing the objections proposed, thought some of them removable, others not so, and on the whole that the reformed plan was the best. This part in your presence, and with a declaration at the same time from Col. Williams that he wished no stress be laid on opinions so suddenly given but he called on me the day after, told me he had considered and conferred with Dr. Thornton on the objections, and thought all of them could be removed but the want of light and air in some cases." Col. Williams was Philadelphia contractor William Williams (ca. 1749–1794). Sandra L. Tatman and Roger W. Moss, *Biographical Dictionary of Philadelphia Architects: 1700–1930* (Boston, Mass.: G. K. Hall & Co., 1985), 854–856.

[32] George Washington to the Commissioners of the District of Columbia, July 25, 1793, in Fitzpatrick, *The Writings of George Washington,* vol. 33, 29–30. Brown omits Washington's statement in this letter that "after a candid discussion, it was found that the objections stated, were considered as valid by both the persons chosen by Doctor Thornton as practical Architects and competent judges of things of this kind."

two biased builders and two biased architects.[33] Objection 4 could certainly have been remedied without material alteration of the plans. Hallet's so-called "modification" of this plan seems to have ended simply in a proportionate reduction of the size of the building. Nowhere is it even hinted that the changes were made on the lines of Hallet's original or second plan, which he was unable to make satisfactory, with all the assistance he had from the commissioners.

Hallet made persistent and determined efforts to secure authority for a radical change in the design of the Capitol, as he submitted scheme after scheme, making elaborate drawings for a greater part of the year. July, 1793, he submitted to the commissioners a plan which, judging from description, must have been very similar to his competitive design [Plate 18]. October, 1793, he submitted a totally different scheme, with elevations, sections, and plan [Plates 19, 20, and 21]. As late as January, 1794, he submitted still another set of drawings for approval [Plates 22, 23, and 24].[34]

The transactions and letters of the commissioners and of President Washington do not even indicate that these several schemes were requested or desired; they simply show an earnest desire on the part of Hallet to introduce a design which he might claim as his own.

---

[33] Brown's charge of bias is exaggerated since only Thomas Carstairs was connected to the Capitol competition. William Williams had no interest in the Capitol other than his critique of the conference plan. Both men were Thornton's choices as judges. James Hoban was not a competitor and had no ambitions to design the Capitol. Hallet was the only person with a strong motive to replace Thornton's design.

[34] Brown's interpretation of Hallet's attempts to supplant Thornton may have been fueled by his misreading of the groupings and dating of Hallet's drawings. Brown's organization and dating of Hallet's proposed Capitol plan, section, and elevation drawings [19, 19a, 19b, 20, 21, 22, 23, and 24] were demonstrated to be in error by Wells Bennett, "Stephen Hallet and His Designs for the National Capitol, 1791–1794," 327–330. Brown's errors in identifying Hallet's drawings were for the most part due to his reliance on Hallet's inscriptions on the drawings, which Bennett proved through his documentary research to be dated late by one year. For a description and analysis of the Hallet drawings, see Howard, "Stephen Hallet and William Thornton at the U.S. Capitol, 1791–1797," 113; 141–166.

PLATE 15

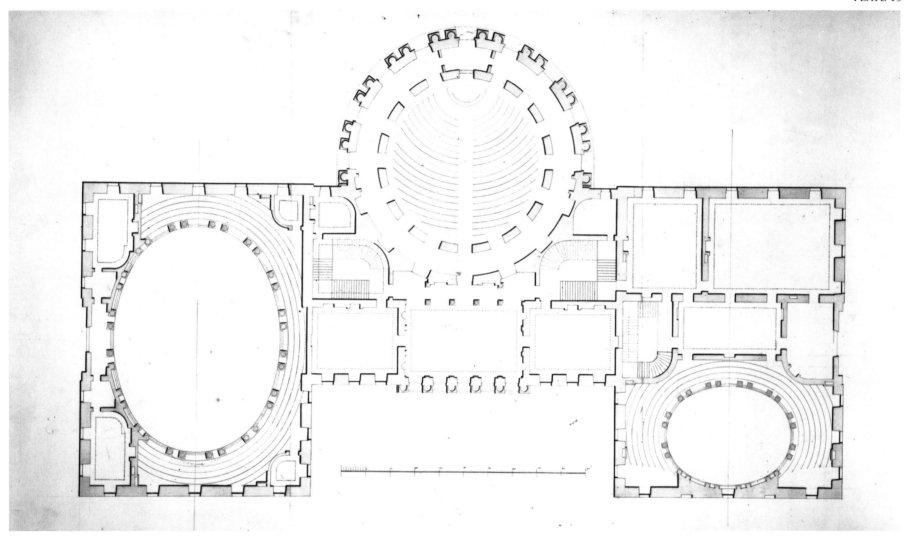

HALLET'S MODIFICATION OF THORNTON'S PLAN.

Ground plan, 1793, design "E." Scholarship undertaken since the 1970s documents that Hallet
is the sole author of the Capitol's ground plan, section and elevation illustrated in plates 15, 16, and 17.
Prints and Photographs Division, LC.

PLATE 16

HALLET'S MODIFICATION OF THORNTON'S DESIGN.
Cross section, undated (ca. 1793), Design "E6." *Prints and Photographs Division, LC.*

PLATE 17

ELEVATION, HALLET'S MODIFICATION OF THORNTON'S DESIGN.

Rear elevation, 1793, Hallet's design "E" for the Capitol. *Prints and Photographs Division, LC.*

CHAPTER III

THE WORK OF DR. WM. THORNTON, ARCHITECT

THE execution of the modified plan of Dr. Thornton began immediately after the letter of Washington, July 25, as on September 2 the commissioners write that the Capitol was progressing favorably, and say: "The southeast is yet kept vacant for the corner stone which is to be laid on the 18th instant." [1,2] At this period the building was under the superintendence of James Hoban. The contract allowed the commissioners to employ him in superintending any work on which they needed his services, and on September 23, 1793, he was officially appointed superintendent. During Hoban's rule as superintendent, with Hallet as assistant superintendent and draftsman, the corner stone was laid, September 18, 1793. This was done with considerable ceremony, as described in the History of the Alexandria Washington Lodge of Masons, from which I take the following quotations:

"The next important event of this kind was the laying of the corner stone of the United States Capitol, at the city of Washington, on the 18th day of September, 1793. The Masonic ceremonies were conducted by His Excellency General Washington, President of the United States, a past master of this lodge, which was present and holding the post of honor. Dr. Dick, elected worshipful master in 1789, still in office,

invited Washington to act as master on this occasion, in accordance with his own wishes and those of the public. The stone was deposited in the southeast corner of the building, instead of the northeast, as is now the custom. The inscription on the plate stated that Alexandria Lodge, No. 22, of Virginia, was present and participated in the ceremonies. The apron and sash worn by Washington on this occasion were the handiwork of Mrs. General Lafayette, and are now the property of this lodge." [3]

The following account of the ceremonies was published in the newspapers of that day [4]: "On Wednesday, one of the grandest Masonic processions took place, for the purpose of laying the corner-stone of the Capitol of the United States, which, perhaps, was ever exhibited on the like important occasion. About ten o'clock Lodge No. 9 was visited by that congregation so graceful to the craft, Lodge No. 22, of Virginia, with all their officers and regalia; and directly afterward appeared on the southern bank of the Grand River Potomack one of the finest companies of volunteer artillery that has been lately seen, parading to receive the President of the United States, who shortly came in sight with his suite, to whom the artillery paid their military honors; and His Excellency and suite crossed the Potomack, and was received in Maryland by the officers and brethren of No. 22, Virginia, and No. 9, Maryland, whom the President headed, preceded by a band of music; the rear brought up by the Alexandria Volunteer Artillery, with grand solemnity of march, proceeded to the President's Square, in the City of

---

[1] For the articles on which this chapter was based, see Glenn Brown, "History of the United States Capitol," *American Architect and Building News* 52 (May 23, 1896): 75–77 and (June 13, 1896): 99–102; and "The United States Capitol in 1800," *Records of the Columbia Historical Society* 4 (1901): 128–135. The later article was a public lecture delivered to the members of the Columbia Historical Society on April 2, 1900.

[2] Commissioners to President Washington, September 2, 1793, RG 42, DCC, NARA.

[3] *History of the Alexandria Lodge of Free Masons* (1896), quoted in Brown, "History of the Capitol," *American Architect and Building News* 52 (May 23, 1896): 76.

[4] *Columbian Mirror and Alexandria Gazette*, No. 89, vol. I, September 25, 1793.

PLATE 18

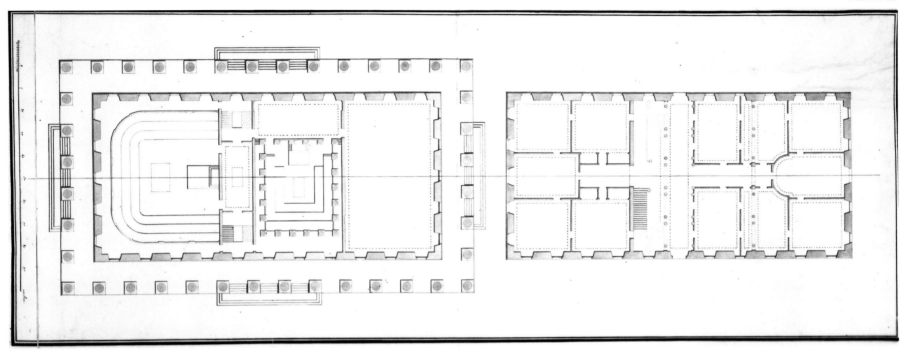

PLAN BY HALLET, SIMILAR TO HIS COMPETITIVE DESIGN.

Plan of the ground and principal floors of the Capitol, 1792. *Prints and Photographs Division, LC.*

PLATE 19

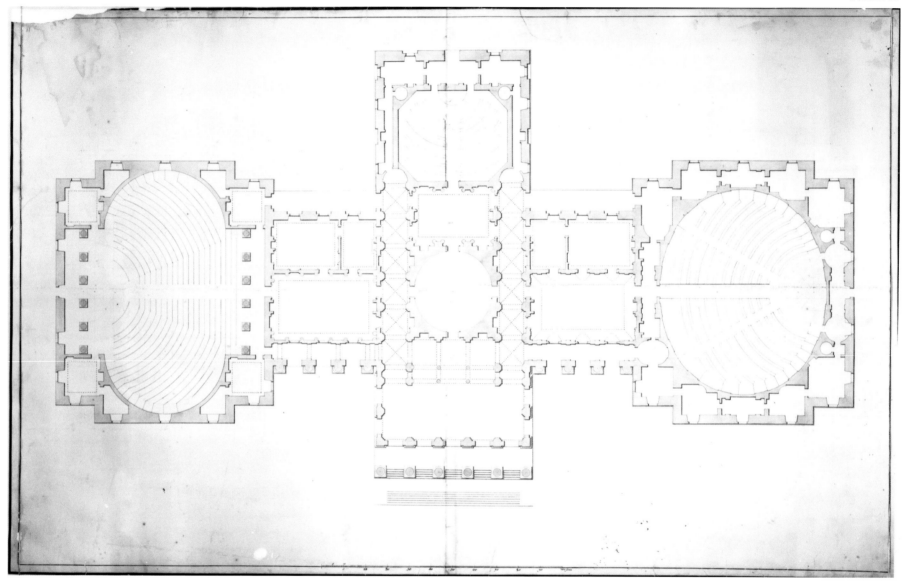

DESIGN OF HALLET 1793, PLAN.

Plan of the ground floor for the Capitol, 1793. *Prints and Photographs Division, LC.*

DESIGN OF HALLET 1793, SECTION.

Section of the Capitol, design C4, October 1792. Incorrectly dated by Brown. *Prints and Photographs Division, LC.*

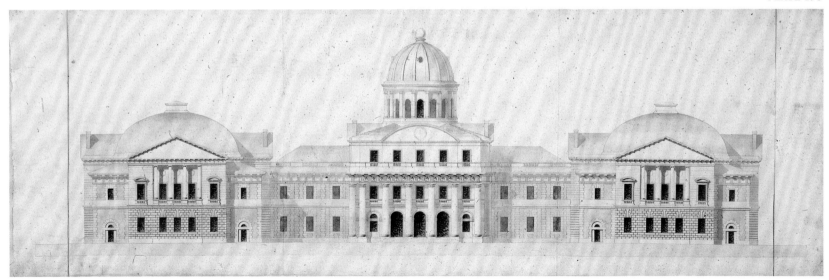

DESIGN OF HALLET 1793, ELEVATION.

Front elevation of the Capitol, design C3, October 1792. Incorrectly dated by Brown. *Prints and Photographs Division, LC.*

PLATE 20

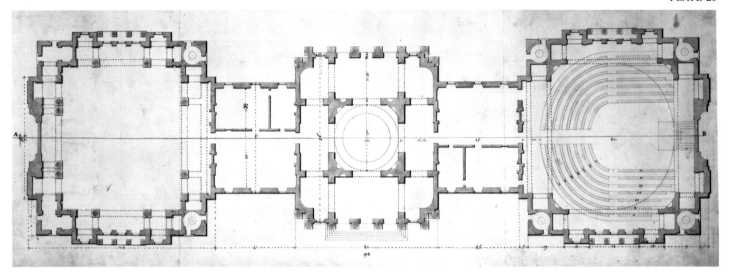

PLAN OF STEPHEN HALLET'S DESIGN 1793.

Plan of design C3 submitted to the District Commissioners, October 1792. Incorrectly dated by Brown. *Prints and Photographs Division, LC.*

PLATE 21

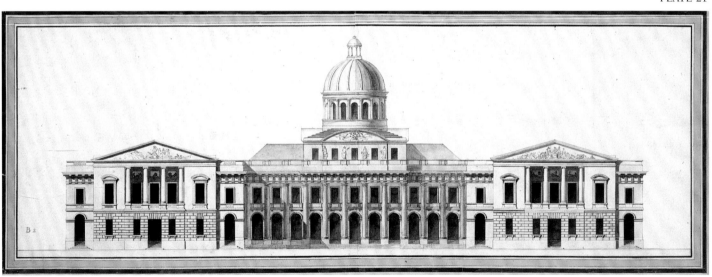

ELEVATION OF STEPHEN HALLET'S DESIGN 1793.

Front elevation of Hallet's 1791 pre-competition design for the Capitol, identified by the District Commissioners as the "fancy piece." Incorrectly dated by Brown. *Prints and Photographs Division, LC.*

PLATE 22

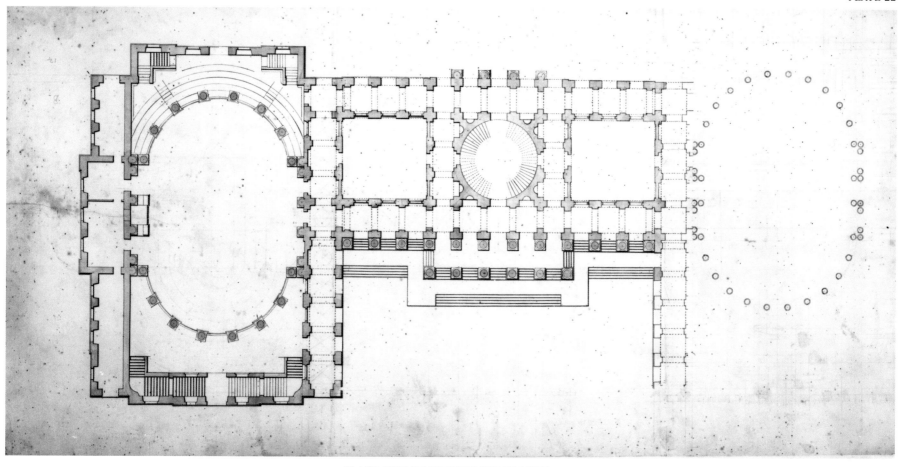

PLAN MADE BY STEPHEN HALLET 1793.

Plan of the 1791 ("fancy piece") pre-competition design for the Capitol. Incorrectly dated by Brown. *Prints and Photographs Division, LC.*

PLATE 23

SECTION, STEPHEN HALLET'S DESIGN 1794.

Section, design D2, January 1793. Incorrectly dated by Brown. *Prints and Photographs Division, LC.*

PLATE 24

ELEVATION OF STEPHEN HALLET'S DESIGN 1794.

Front elevation, design D2, January 1793. Incorrectly dated by Brown. *Prints and Photographs Division, LC.*

Washington, where they were met and saluted by No. 15, of the City of Washington, in all their elegant badges and clothing, headed by Bro. Joseph Clarke, R. W. Grand Master, *pro tem.*, and conducted to a large lodge, prepared for the purpose of their reception. After a short space of time, by the vigilance of Bro. Clotworthy Stephenson, Grand Marshal, *pro tem.*, the brotherhood and other bodies were disposed in a second order of procession, which took place amid a brilliant crowd of spectators of both sexes, according to the following arrangement, viz:

"The Surveying Department of the City of Washington.

"Mayor and Corporation of Georgetown.

"Virginia Artillery.

"Commissioners of the City of Washington, and their attendants.

"Stone-cutters, mechanics.

"The Sword-bearers.

"Masons of the First Degree.

"Bible, etc., on grand cushions.

"Deacons, with staffs of office.

"Masons of the Second Degree.

"Stewards, with wands.

"Masons of the Third Degree.

"Wardens, with truncheons.

"Secretaries, with tools of office.

"Past Masters, with their regalia.

"Treasurers, with their jewels.

"Band of music.

"Lodge No. 22, of Virginia, disposed in their own order.

"Corn, wine and oil.

"Grand Master, *pro tem.*, Brother George Washington, and Worshipful Master of No. 22, of Virginia.

"Grand Sword-bearer.

"The procession marched two abreast, in the greatest solemn dignity, with music playing, drums beating, colors flying and spectators rejoicing, from the President's Square to the Capitol, in the City of Washington, where the Grand Master ordered a halt, and directed each file in the procession to incline two steps, one to the right and one to the left, and face each other, which formed a hollow, oblong square through which the Grand Sword-bearer led the van, followed by the Grand Master, *pro tem.*, on the left, the President of the United States in the centre, and the Worshipful Master of No. 22, Virginia, on the right; all the other orders that composed the procession advanced in the reverse of their order of march from the President's Square to the southeast corner of the Capitol, and the artillery filed off to a destined ground to display their manoeuvers and discharge their cannon. The President of the United States, the Grand Master, *pro tem.*, and the Worshipful Master of No. 22, taking their stand to the east of a large stone, and all the craft forming a circle westward, stood a short time in solemn order. The artillery discharged a volley. The Grand Marshal delivered the Commissioners a large silver plate with an inscription thereon, which the Commissioners ordered to be read, and was as follows:

"This southeast corner-stone of the Capitol of the United States of America, in the City of Washington, was laid on the eighteenth day of September, 1793, in the thirteenth year of American Independence, in the first year of the second term of the presidency of George Washington, whose virtues in the civil administration of his country have been as conspicuous and beneficial as his military valor and prudence have been useful in establishing her liberties, and in the year of Masonry, 5793, by the President of the United States, in concert with the Grand Lodge of Maryland, several lodges under its jurisdiction, and Lodge No. 22, from Alexandria, Va., Thomas Johnson, David Steuart and Daniel Carroll, Commissioners; Joseph Clark, R. W. Grand Master, pro tem.; Joseph Hoban and Stephen Hallate, architects; Collin Williamson, master mason.'

"The artillery discharged a volley. The plate was then delivered to the President, who, attended by the Grand Master, *pro tem.*, and three most Worshipful Masters, descended to the cavazion trench and deposited the plate and laid it on the corner-stone of the Capitol of the United States of America, on which were deposited corn, wine and oil, when the whole congregation joined in reverential prayer, which was succeeded by Masonic chanting honors and a volley from the artillery.[5]

"The President of the United States and his attendant brethren ascended from the cavazion to the east of the corner-stone and there the Grand Master, *pro tem.*, elevated on a triple rostrum, delivered an oration fitting the occasion, which was received with brotherly love and commendation. At intervals during the delivery of the oration several volleys were discharged by the artillery. The ceremony ended in prayer, Masonic chanting honors, and a fifteen-volley from the artillery.

"The whole company retired to an extensive booth, where an ox of 500 pounds' weight was barbecued, of which the company generally partook, with every abundance of other recreation. The festival concluded with fifteen successive volleys from the artillery, whose military discipline and manoeuvers merit every commendation. Before dark the whole company departed with joyful hopes of the production of their labor."

From the above description, as well as from the records, it is clear that the corner stone was laid in the southeast corner of the portion of the building now occupied by the Supreme Court, as this was the old north wing.

The inference has been drawn from newspaper description that Hoban and Hallet were Architects of the Capitol; as already stated, the records show that Hoban was appointed superintendent, on November 21, 1793.[6] Stephen Hallet was appointed a superintendent as assistant to Hoban at the Capitol, with a salary of £400 a year, to be paid quarterly, payments to date from June, 1792. His services were supposed to have begun when he was put to work to dissect Thornton's plan. During this period Colin Williamson, another competitor, was made superintendent of stone cutters, at a salary of £400, Maryland money, per annum. Thus, apparently, Williamson's services were rated as equal to those of Hallet.[7]

The walls could not have been at any point above the ground on September 23, 1793, for on that date the commissioners resolved that the inner walls must be of hard brick and the facings of freestone.[8] The foundation work did not progress very rapidly, for Washington did not agree to this change until the latter part of June, 1794. All the work done during the fall, winter, and spring was below the surface of the ground.

Although Hoban was nominally in charge of the Capitol at this period, he seems, as a matter of fact, to have devoted his whole time to the work on the White House, of which he was both designer and superintendent. Hence Hallet appears to have been left to manage the laying of the foundations according to his own will, and he had the boldness, or foolishness, to change the plans as accepted by the commissioners and the President and lay the foundations of the central portion of the building square instead of circular in accordance with his own ideas [Plate 25].

---

[5] Brown misquotes the original news account, which said "deposited the plate and laid on it the cornerstone" and not "laid it on the cornerstone." His source may have been Duncan S. Walker, ed. and comp., *Celebration of the One Hundredth Anniversary of the Laying of the Cornerstone of the Capitol of the United States* (Washington: Government Printing Office, 1896), 121–123. This publication made the same error, which was important because it has created confusion over the years concerning the location of the original cornerstone, which had been presumed to be lost.

---

[6] The correct date is September 23, as Brown noted in the first paragraph of this chapter.

[7] Commissioners to Stephen Hallet, July 30, 1794, RG 42, DCC, NARA.

[8] Proceedings, September 23, 1793, RG 42, DCC, NARA.

Several times in June, 1794, the commissioners urge Hallet to complete working drawings and reprimand him for carelessness and changes in Thornton's plans.[9] The tone of their letters shows decided dissatisfaction and the drawings show a lack of appreciation, judging from the return to the original idea, of the good features of the plan and a total inability to grasp the refined design of the work given him for execution [Plates 25, 26, 27]. On June 26 the commissioners wrote a letter to Hallet which aptly describes the case at this period. This letter was in answer to a statement of Hallet's that he thought they had given him power to do as he saw fit. The commissioners say:

"In general, nothing has gone from us by which we intended or we believe you could infer that you had the chief direction of executing the work of the Capitol, or that you or anybody else were to introduce into the building any departures from Dr. Thornton's plan, without the President's or the commissioner's approbation.

"Mr. Hoban was employed here before our acquaintance began with you, more especially as chief over the President's House, of which he was fortunate enough to produce a plan which met with general, I may say almost universal, favor, and to extend his superintendence to any other public building we might require. We claimed his services as superior at the Capitol, and this was explained so fully last fall on the spot, with the addition that you were to communicate with him and be governed by his directions, that we flattered ourselves that the line of each was perfectly understood. It is painful to have these things to reiterate, and we do request that you will signify by letter your understanding of our agreement to this line, for we can not trust the same

piece of business to the direction of two heads capable of pursuing different wills. We shall soon separate. Hence a speedy answer will oblige.

> "THOS. JOHNSON,
> "DANL. CARROLL,
> "DD. STUART,
> *"Commissioners."* [10]

Hallet sent in his resignation because the commissioners insisted on his carrying out the adopted plans. This resignation was not accepted, although he seems to have ceased to perform his duties. Hallet refused to give up the drawings in his possession. November 15, 1794, Hallet was discharged because he laid parts of the foundations not in accordance with the accepted plans without the commissioners being able to get possession of the drawings. The last we hear of Hallet is the allowance of a small claim for services against the Government, June 10, 1795. [11]

There has been in recent years a persistent reiteration of the statement that Hallet, and not Thornton, was architect of the old Capitol. This statement can be traced to G. A. Townsend's book, Washington Inside and Out, and to an article in the International Review by J. Q. Howard, published 1874.[12] The foregoing history, taken directly from the official record, proves: First, that Hallet after exceptional opportunities could not produce a satisfactory design; that the alterations he was allowed to make in Thornton's work consisted in reducing the scale; that he was employed only as an assistant superintendent and draftsman, and because he attempted to overstep these bounds he was

---

[9] Commissioners to Hallet, June 24 and 26, 1794, RG 42, DCC, NARA. The commissioners did insist on Hallet's adherence to the agreed upon plan and on his subordination to Hoban, but Brown's charge of carelessness is exaggerated.

[10] Commissioners to Hallet, June 26, 1794, RG 42, DCC, NARA.

[11] Hallet's discharge is discussed in Proceedings, June 22–28, 1794, and July 29, 1794, RG 42, DCC, NARA.

[12] A reference to George A. Townsend's *Washington Outside and Inside* and James Q. Howard's "The Architects of the American Capitol."

PLATE 25

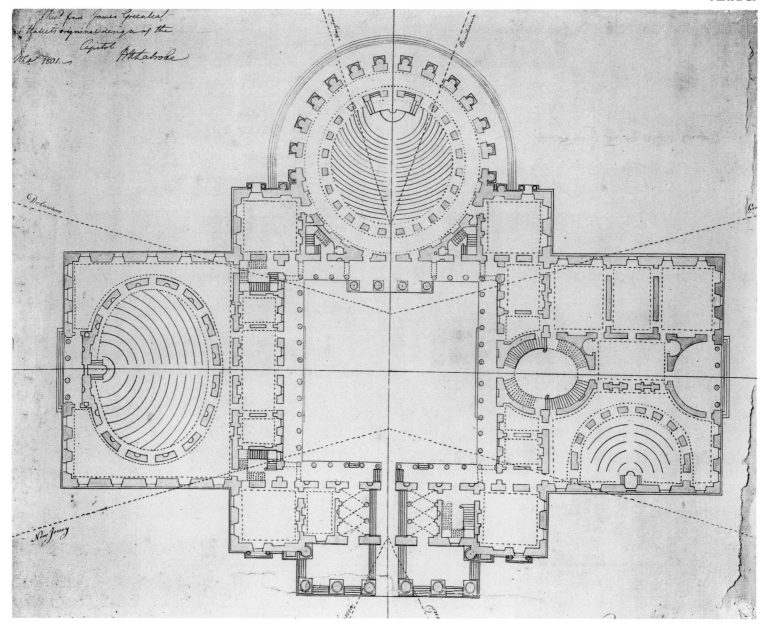

HALLET'S MODIFICATION OF THORNTON'S DESIGN, BY CHANGE IN CENTER PLAN.

Hallet's plan used for laying the foundation of the Capitol between August 1793 and June 1794. *Prints and Photographs Division, LC.*

PLATE 26

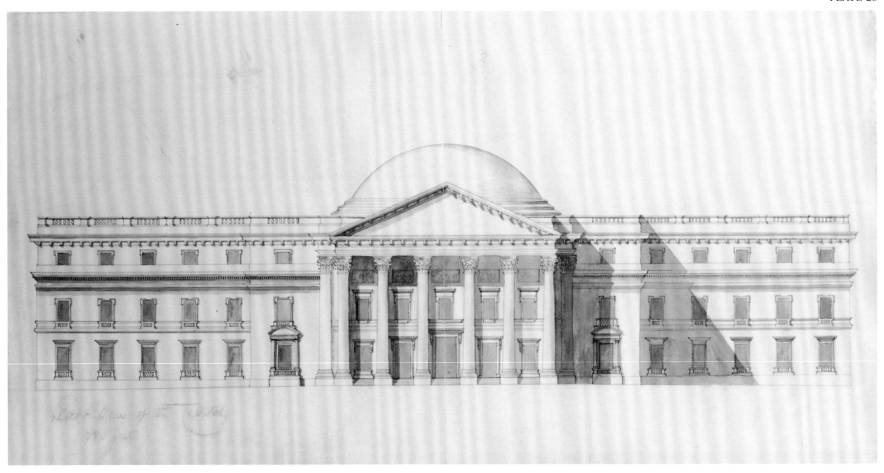

HALLET'S MODIFICATION OF THORNTON'S DESIGN, EAST ELEVATION.

Unsigned drawing, ca. 1795, sometimes attributed to Hadfield, of the east front of the Capitol. *MHS.*

PLATE 27

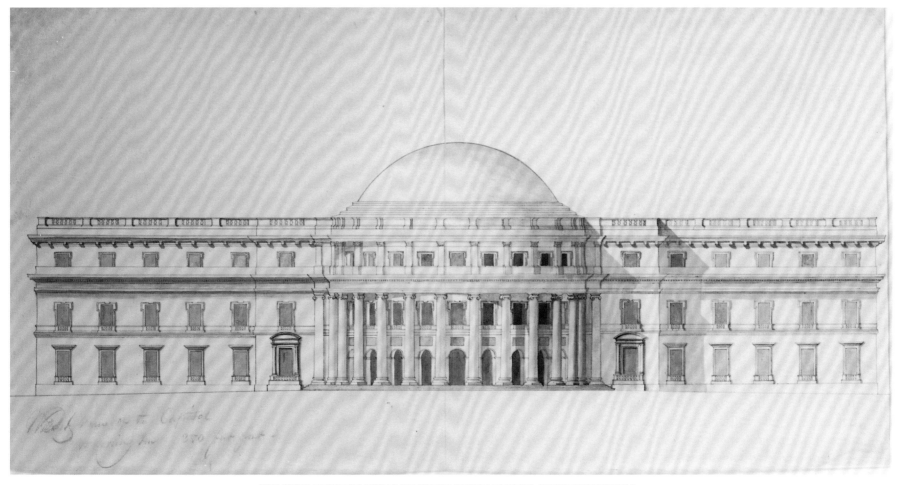

HALLET'S MODIFICATION OF THORNTON'S DESIGN, WEST ELEVATION.

Unsigned drawing, ca. 1795, sometimes attributed to Hadfield, of the west front of the Capitol. *MHS.*

discharged. Thornton, in a letter, gives Hallet the credit of offering some "judicious suggestions," which is more than the records show, "but in most of his attempts he did an injury." "He diminished the Senate Chamber, which is now too small. He laid square the foundation of the center building [see Fig. 25] excluding the Dome, and when General Washington saw the extent of the alterations he expressed his disapproval in a style of such warmth as his dignity seldom permitted." [13]

The President appointed Thornton to be one of the three commissioners in charge of the District of Columbia, September 12, 1794. At this period Andrew Ellicott, who was engineer in charge of laying out the streets and lots, congratulates Thornton and rejoices in the appointment, for the good of the streets and buildings, saying that the former commissioners were totally ignorant and easy prey. He warns Thornton to be on his guard. Washington when he made this appointment requested Thornton to restore the Capitol so that it would correspond with his original plan.

I have been fortunate enough to find several of Thornton's drawings which relate to this period of the building. These plans Thornton, Washington, and Jefferson considered the original design which won the competition, modified in scale so as to reduce the cost. [14] These drawings were given to Latrobe after he was appointed Architect and were not the working drawings, both Hallet and Hadfield when they

were discharged having taken the larger part of the working drawings with them. [15] The following indorsements were put on these drawings by Latrobe:

"Plans of Capitol received from Dr. Thornton [Plate 28].
"H. B. LATROBE.
"APRIL, 1804."

"Given to me by George Blagden as the only existing drawing of the Capitol [Plate 29].
"H. B. LATROBE.
"MAY 4, 1803."

When Thornton again took charge the work was below the ground. [16] He drew another elevation "presenting the general ideas, but making such alterations as the difference in dimensions of the ground plan rendered necessary. I improved the appearance and restored the Dome" [Plates 28 to 33]. [17]

A drawing showing Thornton's east elevation which belongs to these plans has been recently discovered in the Congressional Library [Plate 30], and one of the west front, on which Thornton was evidently

[13] William Thornton to the Members of the House of Representatives, January 1, 1805, vols. 3–4, William Thornton Papers, Manuscript Division, LC. This letter describes Thornton's involvement in the design of the Capitol. It was printed and circulated to the members of the House while Thornton was engaged in a dispute with Benjamin Henry Latrobe over major interior design changes.

[14] Brown's discovery and publication of Thornton's Capitol plans, developed between 1796 and 1802, was a major contribution. However, his comment that the difference in Thornton's original competition drawing, which was lost, and the modified plans actually built only applies to the design of the exterior walls of the Capitol's original wings is incorrect. Significant modifications of the plans had been contributed by Hallet and Hadfield.

[15] Correspondence between Thornton and his fellow commissioners concerning plans for the Capitol during James Hoban's superintendence indicated that he expected the superintendent to prepare the working drawings, such as the sections Hoban requested and any future "decorative drawings." See Gustavus Scott and Alexander White to William Thornton, April 17, 1799, and Thornton to Scott and White, April 17, 1799, William Thornton Papers, vols. 3–4, Manuscript Division, LC.

[16] The District commissioners were responsible for supervising construction of the Capitol, not Thornton alone as Brown implies. All decisions required the approval of at least two commissioners. See "An Act for Establishing the Temporary and Permanent Seat of the Government of the United States," 1 Stat. 130, July 17, 1790.

[17] William Thornton to the Members of the House of Representatives, January 1, 1805, vols. 3–4, William Thornton Papers, Manuscript Division, LC.

making an alternate scheme for a dome in place of the simple Greek dome shown on the other drawing, as well as omitting the windows shown on plans for the west projection [Plate 31]. The author has made a restoration of the west front showing the dome similar to the dome shown on the east, and inserting the pilasters and windows which are shown on the plans [Plate 32].[18]

The view [Plate 33] is taken from the margin of a map by Robert King, published about 1803, although the exact date is missing. "East front of the Capitol of the United States as originally designed by William Thornton and adopted by General Washington, President of the United States," is the title of this engraving.[19]

This statement is an error, as this is not a reproduction of the original or competitive drawing, but it is the design made by Thornton after Hallet was discharged.

Plate 34 is reproduction of an enlarged drawing of the Senate wing by Thornton. Among Thornton's papers I found the following notes in his handwriting on this modification of the competitive plan. The sizes mentioned show that it relates to the building as it was finally erected. The drawing referred to in the descriptions was colored:

"GROUND PLAN.

"A. Depository under Dome. [Thick wall.]
"B. Room under antechamber. H, R.
"C. Vestibule to Senate Chamber.
"D. Under. E, D.
"E, E, E, E. Offices, clerks' and committee rooms.
"Suggests covered carriage way.
"I, I, I. Platform. K, K. Stairs.
"L, L, L. Windows in M, M, M, water-closets.
"N, N. Niches. O, O. Fireplaces.
"Q, Q, Q. Passage [illumination by transoms].
"R. Recess.

Feet.
"The extreme length of plan is 352
"The extreme breadth of plan is 221
"Height of basement story 20

"PLAN NO. 2.

"A. Center of Dome. Dome supported by columns 30 feet high.
"All interior decorations should be of white marble. [No marble in this country yet of sufficiently good quality.] The very best workmanship and material should be used.
"B, B. Landing of east stairs.
"C. The Executive Department. [To be heated by two ornamental urns.]
"D, D. Passages.
"E, E. Closets.
"F. Water-closets.
"G, G. Great Conference room." [20]

---

[18] For an analysis and overview of past reconstructions of Thornton's Capitol design, see Don Alexander Hawkins, "William Thornton's Lost Design of the United States Capitol: A Study and Reconstruction," unpublished paper, Curator's Office, AOC. Based on an analysis of drawings and records, Hawkins challenges the accuracy of Brown's reconstruction. Brown's major errors included changing Thornton's orders for the columns, adding pedestal blocks, and introducing doubled pilasters at the inside corners where the wings and pavilions met. Brown probably erred in his reference to a "Greek dome" since Thornton's inspiration for the Capitol design was clearly a Roman temple. See C. M. Harris, "Classical Themes Inspired Design for U.S. Capitol," *Capitol Dome* 24 (February 1989): 1–3.

[19] Brown was referring to Robert King's map of Washington, published in 1818, which included engraved views of the Capitol and the President's House. Engraved by C. Schwarz, Geography and Map Division, LC. The map is reproduced in John Reps, *Washington on View: The Nation's Capital Since 1790* (Chapel Hill and London: University of North Carolina Press, 1991), 67.

[20] Thornton to the Commissioners, 1793, vols. 3–4, William Thornton Papers, Manuscript Division, LC.

PLATE 28

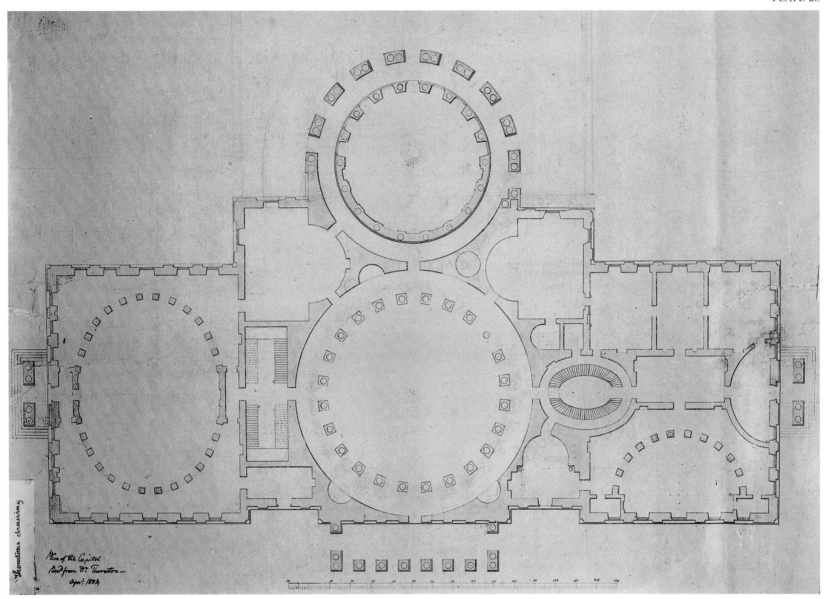

THORNTON'S MODIFIED PLAN.
Double column plan of the Capitol, ca. 1796. *Prints and Photographs Division, LC.*

PLATE 29

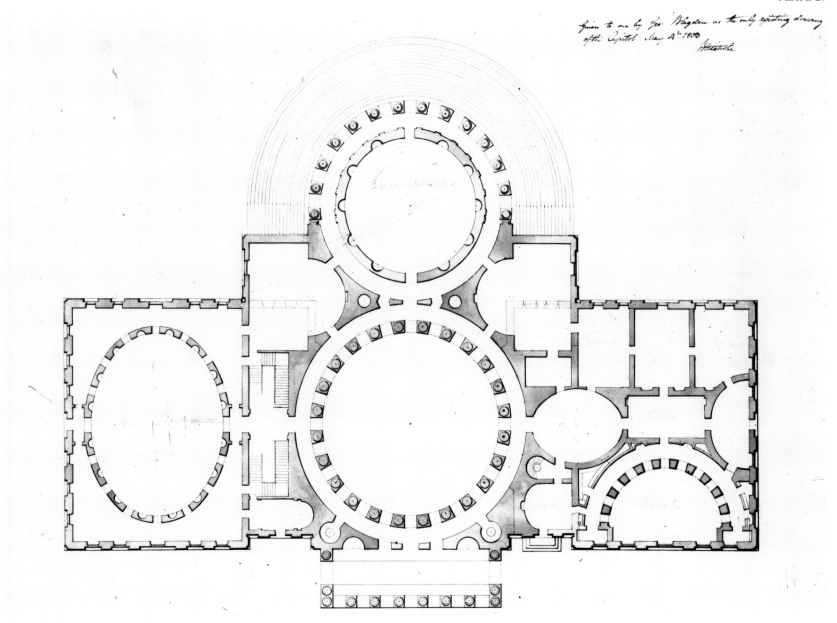

THORNTON'S MODIFIED PLAN.

Single column plan of the Capitol, ca. 1796. *Prints and Photographs Division, LC.*

PLATE 30

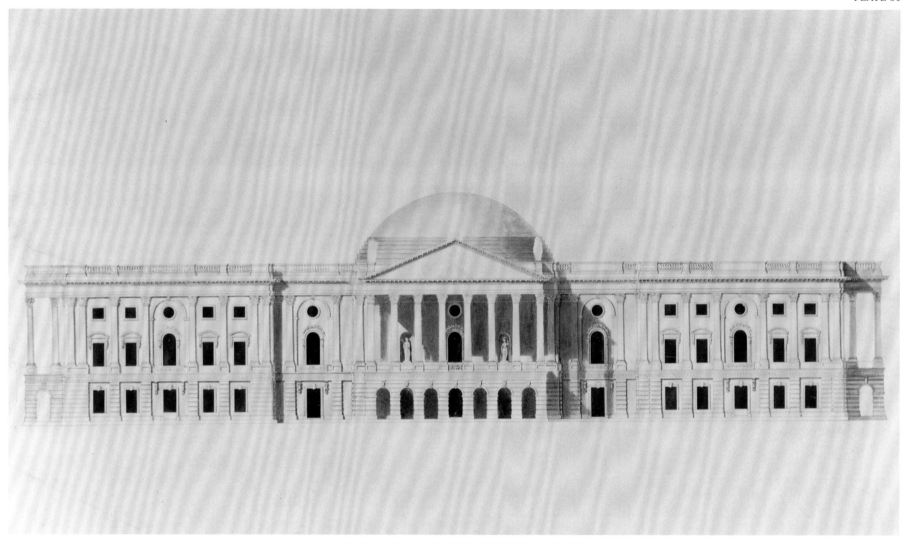

EAST ELEVATION, WM. THORNTON ARCHITECT.

Ca. 1796. *Prints and Photographs Division, LC.*

PLATE 31

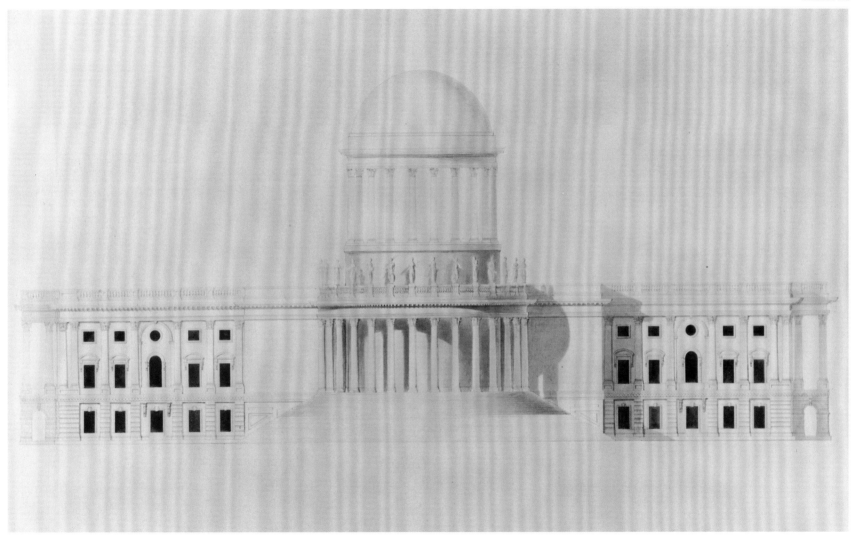

THORNTON'S WEST ELEVATION, SHOWING ALTERNATE DESIGN FOR DOME.

Ca. 1796. *Prints and Photographs Division, LC.*

PLATE 32

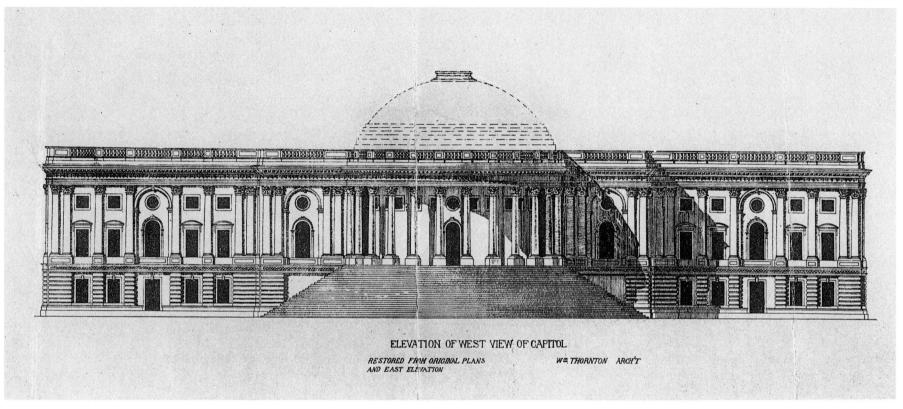

ELEVATION OF WEST VIEW OF CAPITOL

RESTORED FROM ORIGINAL PLANS   Wᵐ THORNTON ARCH'T
AND EAST ELEVATION

WEST ELEVATION, THORNTON'S DESIGN.

Drawing of William Thornton's intended design for the west front by Glenn Brown, 1900. *Location unknown.*

PLATE 33

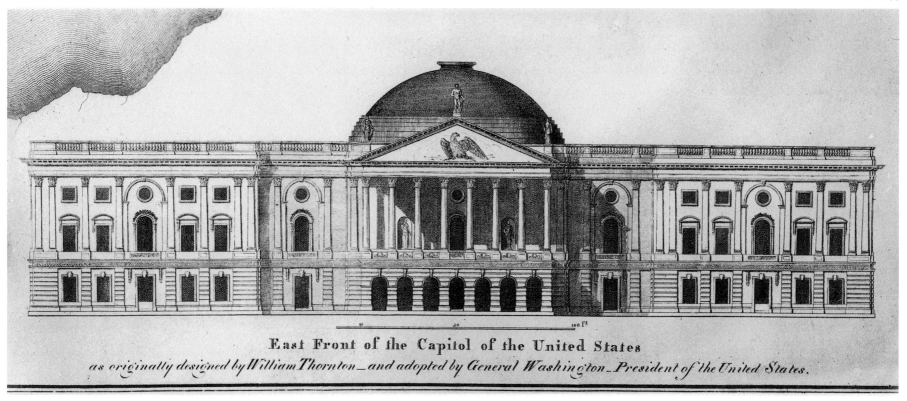

East Front of the Capitol of the United States

as originally designed by William Thornton _ and adopted by General Washington _ President of the United States.

EAST ELEVATION, BY WM. THORNTON.

Detail from a map of Washington, D.C., published by Robert King in 1818. *Geography and Map Division, LC.*

PLATE 34

THORNTON'S DRAWING FOR EAST FRONT OF SENATE WING.

East elevation of the north wing of the Capitol, ca. 1795–96. *Prints and Photographs Division, LC.*

The square foundation laid by Hallet in the center of the building was removed, portions of this foundation being left as a base for the temporary structure afterwards erected to accommodate the House of Representatives [Plate 25]. In this way the last of Hallet's changes were obliterated.[21]

Under the management of Thornton as a commissioner of Federal buildings and Hoban as superintendent, the work progressed rapidly and satisfactorily. December, 1794, James Reid, James Smith, and George Walker contracted to furnish stone and James Dobson made a contract to lay the stone.[22] In March, 1795, Thornton's fellow commissioners desired him to go to the President, "with whom he had many conferences with reference to this subject," and get a decision from him in reference to the cost and material to be used, their determination being to push the Capitol this season (1795) beyond other measures.[23] Hoban became restive under the continual calls made upon him for additional service without extra compensation. His letters and actions had always shown that he thought the commissioners were requiring too much in having him superintend both the President's House and Capitol. Consequently, on April 30, 1795, the following agreement was made: "The commissioners agree with James Hoban to take upon himself the superintendence of the said building [the Capitol] for the

whole of the present building season unless sooner discharged by the consent of the board. They also agree to allow said James Hoban 25 guineas per month extra wages for his attention to the Capitol, his wages to commence from this day."[24] June 3, 1795, Colin Williamson, master mason, was dismissed for inefficiency. In the autumn of 1795 the basement, or first story above the ground, of the north wing was about complete.

John Trumbull, United States minister to England, wrote to the commissioners, September 13, 1794, when he heard of Hallet's resignation, recommending George Hadfield as an architect of great merit. January 2, 1795, the commissioners—Thornton at this time being one of the board—offered Hadfield, through Minister John Trumbull, £300 and traveling expenses for his services "as superintendent of the Capitol." In this letter they state that "the conduct of Mr. Hallet was capricious and obstinate; his refusal to deliver up such sections of the Capitol as are wanting obliged the late commissioners to discharge him."[25] March 9, 1795, Trumbull gave Hadfield a letter of introduction to Thornton, in which he says: "I had before understood that your design had been generally adopted. I am glad to learn that I was rightly informed, as I should have been mortified to have known that so noble a plan had been passed by... I have known him [Hadfield] at least ten years and have seen in him nothing to diminish my esteem. He is modest, unassuming, and correct in his taste and judgment, and should any difficulties occur in the executive part of the plan he will state them with candor."[26] Developments in Hadfield's career show that Trumbull

---

[21] The square foundation, laid for the central section of the building, was not used for the south [House] wing foundation as Brown implies. Both the "Oven," a temporary brick structure erected in 1801 as a meeting room for the House of Representatives, and a wooden passage 145 feet long connecting the temporary House Chamber to the north wing were razed in 1804 to clear the site for the construction of Latrobe's south wing. See Allen, *The United States Capitol: A Brief Architectural History* (Washington: Government Printing Office, 1991), 5.

[22] Proceedings, December 20, 1794, RG 42, DCC, NARA.

[23] Commissioners to Edmund Randolph, March 20, 1795, RG 42, DCC, NARA.

---

[24] Proceedings, April 27, 1795, RG 42, DCC, NARA.

[25] The quoted letter is to George Washington and not George Hadfield as Brown implies. See Commissioners to George Hadfield, January 2, 1795; Commissioners to President George Washington, January 29, 1795, RG 42, DCC, NARA.

[26] Trumbull to Commissioners, March 9, 1795, RG 42, DCC, NARA.

was sadly mistaken in his estimate of his friend's character. George Hadfield received his appointment October 15, 1795, as superintendent of the Capitol, and he had no sooner taken his place than he recommended numerous alterations and additions, among them being the addition of an attic story to the building.[27] November 18, 1795, Dr. Thornton and James Hoban opposed Hadfield's suggestions as impractical, and the matter was referred to the President.[28] Hadfield waited upon Washington, who received the suggestions with so little favor that Hadfield resigned. He soon reconsidered his resignation and was reappointed, a special stipulation being made "that he was engaged to superintend the execution of the plan without alteration." Hoban's services, except when called in consultation, ceased upon the appointment of Hadfield, Hoban acting as superintendent of the President's House and Hadfield as superintendent of the Capitol. Judging from orders, letters, and reports, they were considered to have positions of equal importance. Each had a salary of $1,400 a year, paid in quarterly installments.

During the year 1795 the question as to the proper treatment of the terrace was under discussion, and Thornton recommended a flight of circular steps, conforming with his circular portico on this front of the Capitol.

May 31, 1796, the commissioners wrote that they can not guard against imposition, as they are not able at present, on account of lack of houses, to live in Washington; therefore they must depend upon the superintendent and "undertaker" or builder.[29] Hadfield's early experience does not seem to have taught him discretion. On June 29 he informed the commissioners that he would quit the public service at the end of the three months' notice required by his contract. The commissioners seem to have been quite independent at this period, for they informed Hadfield that he could quit as soon as he pleased, and that they would pay him a sum equal to his passage to Europe.[30] Upon the receipt of this determined reply Hadfield withdrew his notice and agreed to attend to the Capitol according to methods approved by the President. The commissioners allowed him to stay on sufferance, retaining the advantage which he had given them by his serving three months' notice. From this time until the end of his service everything seems to have run with comparative smoothness. Orders and letters indicate simply an inspection of materials and workmanship and the making of reports, contracts, and estimates of the work as it progressed.

Contracts were made early in January, 1797, with Middleton, Belt, Bennett, Fenwick, and Marshall Waring to furnish brick and Alan Wiley to do all brickwork for the season. We also learn that brickwork in this year was discontinued as early as November.[31]

The commissioners determined to omit the ventilating flues for the galleries of the Senate, and Thornton records his dissent June 30, 1797.[32] January, 1798, Thornton puts on record the following protest against the workmanship of the cornice, north front (this is in the

---

[27] Brown implies that Hadfield intended to make the Capitol a four-story building. In fact, Hadfield attempted to solve the design problem of Thornton's plan for locating the House and Senate Chambers on the ground level by adding an attic story and lowering the exterior architectural order to begin at the first floor. This gave the ground level first floor greater prominence. George Hadfield, Curator's Office, AOC.

[28] Commissioners to the President of the United States, November 18, 1795, RG 42, DCC, NARA.

[29] Commissioners to the President of the United States, May 31, 1796, RG 42, DCC, NARA.

[30] Commissioners to the President of the United States, June 29, 1796, RG 42, DCC, NARA.

[31] Proceedings, January 25, 1797, RG 42, DCC, NARA.

[32] Brown uses the term "ventilating flues" for fireplace chimneys. Proceedings, June 20, 1797, RG 42, DCC, NARA.

portion of the building where the present Supreme Court room is situated), "which includes the modillions, and which are now worked, but not put up—be rejected and worked anew on account of the irregularity of the present work, it being not in order but deviating from the true proportion, and, the board having given a negative to the same, I do hereby enter my protest against their proceeding, because this imperfection will remain a disgrace to the building, because it can be substituted without any loss of time, . . . and, finally, because it can never be renewed or corrected, but will forever remain a laughingstock to architects." [33] Thornton was overruled in this as well as in another protest which he made, against the use of pine for doors—he desired mahogany. Thornton was always the advocate of good construction and material, but his confrères did not always uphold him when his plans caused an increase in the first cost. The errors against which Thornton protested were undoubtedly caused by the inefficiency or carelessness of Hadfield. [34]

On May 10, 1798, the commissioners gave Hadfield another three months' notice that they would discharge him. [35] He did not apparently wait for his three months to expire, for on May 28 the following letter was sent to Hoban: "Ordered that James Hoban take upon himself the superintendence of the Capitol, and that he remove to reside there as soon as possible, and, until possession can be had of the house now occupied by Mr. Hadfield, that the board will pay the rent of any house he may engage near the building." They gave Hoban a double salary until June 9, "and until roof is on President's House he is to receive in addition to the $1,400 for Capitol superintendence 100 guineas per annum for directing operations at the President's House." [36] Hadfield's official discharge was made June, 1798. The reason given was that he refused to give up the drawings of the Executive offices. [37]

In the latter part of 1798 the minor rooms in the old north wing were ready for plastering and the work in the principal rooms was progressing rapidly.

We constantly see it mentioned that Hadfield was one of the architects of the Capitol, but the records show explicitly that he was only employed to superintend the erection of Thornton's design and plan, and although he made suggestions, none of them were adopted. Hadfield was, furthermore, inefficient as a superintendent. Among Thornton's papers is a statement saying that Hadfield acknowledged that he had never superintended either a public or private building before his employment on the Capitol. [38] Thornton states that he (Hadfield) was entirely incompetent from a practical point of view. Some years later, when Latrobe wished to prove that Thornton's plan had been materially changed, he wrote as follows to Hadfield: "If you could go over your drawings and ascertain what is his [Thornton's] in the plan now said to be the original plan, I should be infinitely obliged to you, . . . if in any

---

[33] Proceedings, January 10, 1798, RG 42, DCC, NARA. Thornton's criticism reflected a minor change in the design of the caissons between the modillions.

[34] Hadfield had no control over the funds for the building. Moreover, Brown attaches far more importance to Thornton's criticism than seems warranted.

[35] Brown misdated this letter. Commissioners to Hadfield, May 18, 1798, RG 42, DCC, NARA.

[36] Commissioners to Hoban, May 28, 1798, and Commissioners to Secretary of State, June 25, 1798, RG 42, DCC, NARA. The tone of the letter to Secretary of State Thomas Jefferson was undoubtedly influenced by Thornton: "We believe Mr. Hadfield to be a young man of taste, but we have found him extremely deficient in practical knowledge as an architect so much so, that we have often been obliged to interpose with respect to his mode of carrying on the Building, and to spend much time in dispensing the measures which we deemed exceptionable."

[37] Commissioners to Hadfield, June 1798, RG 42, DCC, NARA.

[38] Brown may be referring to an undated draft letter of 1798 in which Thornton wrote: "I asked if he [Hadfield] had ever undertaken any building, public or private, he answered no." Vols. 1–2, William Thornton Papers (Microfilm Reel 1), Manuscript Division, LC.

way it can lead to the removal of the load of calumny with which you have been treated."[39]

What more advantageous opportunity could Hadfield have desired to present his claims? That there is no foundation for such assertions is proved by the fact that neither specific claims nor proofs were presented at this time. In the portions of a pamphlet published by Hadfield in 1819, which I have seen, he makes no claim in reference to having any of his own ideas incorporated in the plan or design of the building.[40] From this period until the office of commissioners was abolished the work progressed rapidly and satisfactorily.

April, 1799, Hoban called on Thornton for sections of the Capitol. All drawings in the hands of the commissioners were turned over to Hoban, and we learn from a letter of a later date that other drawings were made for him by Thornton. This proves that at this date, even while acting as commissioner, Thornton was still expected to make drawings for the building when the data were not sufficiently clear.[41] There are records of several contracts being made at this period by men who in after years took a more or less active share in the completion of the old Capitol.[42] January 23, 1799, George Blagden made a contract to finish stonework of Capitol (this evidently referred to the nearly completed north wing) for the sum of £510 13s. 9d. January 12 Wilson Bryan was made superintendent of carpenters. In the same year Lewis Clephane entered into a contract for painting the Capitol. John Kearney was the plasterer. The above contracts refer to the completion of the north wing. In September, 1799, Clephane was ordered to give an additional coat of sand paint to the roof, and in May Peter Lenox, Wilson Bryan, and Harbaugh were requested to examine and report upon the roof of both the Capitol (north wing) and the President's House, "because they leak." [43] In February, 1800, James Hoban was ordered to make details of the Capitol to "conform with drawings given John Kearney by Dr. Thornton, in the ancient Ionic style, but with volutes like the modern Ionic for the Senate Chamber." The roof of the Capitol at this period was made of shingles and gave considerable trouble by leaking.[44]

In 1797 President Washington, who had taken such an active personal interest in the Capitol, retired from the Presidency, dying two years later. John Adams, who succeeded him, did not, judging from his correspondence, take a similar interest in the building.

The year 1800 was fixed by law for the Government to take its permanent seat in Washington City. Accordingly, in that year, the latter part of May, the President and his Cabinet, with the different Executive Departments and the documents and other material of both Houses of Congress, were moved from Philadelphia to the Federal City.

From the data in my possession I have drawn plans of the building on an 8-inch scale, showing its condition in 1800 [Plates 35 and

---

[39] Benjamin Henry Latrobe to George Hadfield, April 28, 1804, *Papers of Benjamin Henry Latrobe,* microfiche edition.

[40] Brown may be referring to a petition to Congress printed in a report made by a Mr. Wood. *Journal of the House,* January 19, 1821, 150.

[41] Thornton was asked by fellow commissioners Gustavus Scott and Alexander White for these sections of the building at Hoban's request, but he failed to produce them and in his response said that any "practical Architect" should be able to prepare what was needed from his instructions. Thornton to Scott and White, April 17, 1799, vols. 1–2, William Thornton Papers (Microfilm Reel 1), Manuscript Division, LC.

[42] Proceedings, January 12 and 23, September 1799, RG 42, DCC, NARA.

[43] Proceedings, September 12, 1799, RG 42, DCC, NARA.

[44] Thornton's reference to drawings given to John Kearney may have been plates from architectural books. Proceedings, February 10, 1800, RG 42, DCC, NARA.

PLATE 35

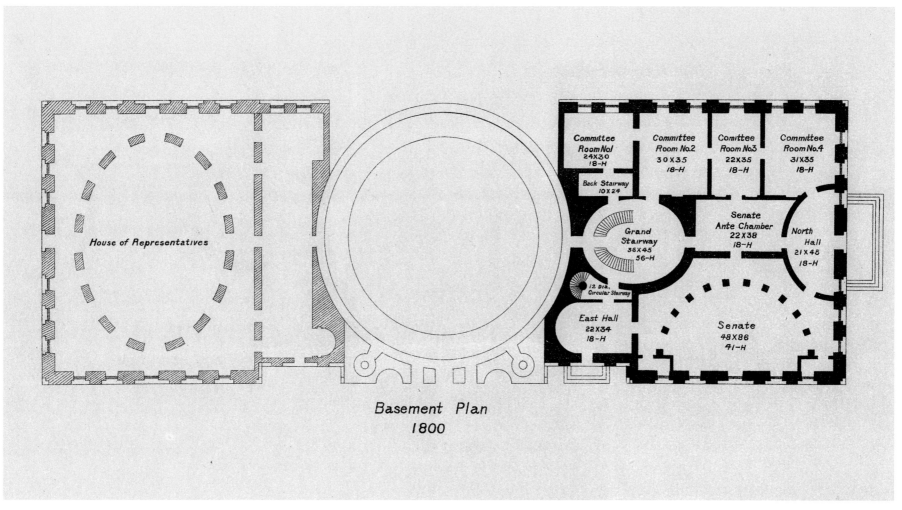

Committee
Room No1
24X30
18-H

Committee
Room No.2
30X35
18-H

Comittee
Room No3
22X35
18-H

Committee
Room No.4
31X35
18-H

Back Stairway
10 X 24

House of Representatives

Grand
Stairway
36X45
56-H

Senate
Ante Chamber
22X38
18-H

North
Hall
21X45
18-H

12 Dia.
Circular Stairway

East Hall
22X34
18-H

Senate
48X86
41-H

Basement Plan
1800

PLAN IN BLACK, SHOWING PORTION FIRST OCCUPIED BY CONGRESS, 1800.

Conjectural floor plan of the Capitol in 1800 by Glenn Brown, 1900. *Location unknown.*

PLATE 36

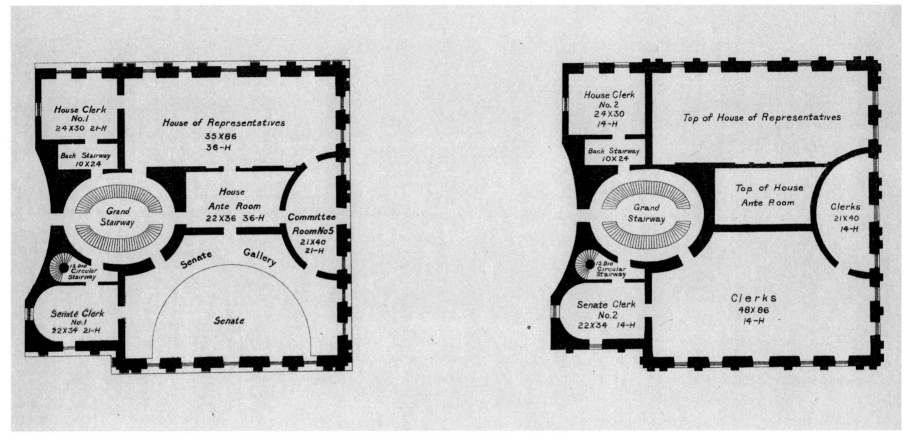

PRINCIPAL STORY.   CAPITOL IN 1800. AS FIRST OCCUPIED BY CONGRESS.   ATTIC STORY.

Conjectural floor plans of north wing of the Capitol in 1800 by Glenn Brown, 1900. *Location unknown.*

36].[45] The north or Senate wing, now occupied by the Supreme Court, and ready for its Congressional tenants November 17, 1800, was finished. The minor partitions, floors, and roof were of wooden construction. It had a basement, first and second story. Portions of the foundations of the central portion of the Rotunda were in place, Thornton having removed the foundations for the square central court which Hallet had had the temerity to put in, and for which he was discharged by Washington.[46] The basement or first story above ground of the House wing, now Statuary Hall, was in process of construction.

Judging from the relative height of windows, as shown on the exterior, and allowing for thickness of floors, the basement should have been about 18 feet high, the first story from 20 to 22 feet, and the second story 14 or 15 feet. The total size of the completed structure was 126 feet by 121 feet 6 inches.

After making the enlarged plans of the basement and principal stories, on which are shown the arrangements of the walls, the shape and size of the rooms, the next step was to take the report of James Hoban, which the Commissioners of the District of Columbia, William Thornton and Alex. White, sent in 1799 to the Sixth Congress, then holding their first session in Philadelphia. This report gives the dimensions, in many instances the shape and character of finish, for the different rooms in the building, as well as mentioning the purpose for which

they were to be used. This report does not give the stories on which the rooms are placed or position in which they are located except in three instances. It is only by taking the floor dimensions and heights and locating the rooms where they will fit into the plan that we are able to tell with accuracy the position they occupied in the building.[47] First taking the basement plan shown [Plate 35].

A room 48 by 86 by 41 feet was provided for the Senate. The dimensions of the old Senate Chamber, or the present Supreme Court room, were found to fit these floor dimensions, and the height mentioned would carry the room through the basement and first story. We have felt assured that the Senate met in this room, as Thornton marked it on his early plan as the Senate Chamber, but this corroborative testimony fixes the meeting of this branch of Congress in the portion of the building assigned to it. While Thornton's plan shows only twelve columns, Hoban mentions sixteen. This increase was doubtless made in preparing the working drawings.

One point has developed in this investigation which I think is unknown at the present time. It has been assumed that the floor of the old Senate was on the principal or first floor—in other words, where the floor of the Supreme Court is at the present time. Three points— the height of the Chamber, the location and height of the Senate lobby, and the exterior steps, which are shown as leading up to the Senate floor on Thornton's plan, indicated at a distance of about 2 feet from the ground—when taken in connection with the dimensions of rooms as given by Hoban, show that the Senate floor was in the basement of the Capitol. I have three letters bearing upon this subject, one by Latrobe in 1802, criticizing the fact that the Senate was placed on the

---

[45] Brown probably based his conjectural drawings on James Hoban's construction report of November 1799, which was included in the third annual address of President John Adams, December 3, 1799. See DCC, 87–89. Brown's drawings were first presented and interpreted in a public lecture, probably accompanied by lantern slides, for the members of the Columbia Historical Society on April 2, 1900. See Glenn Brown, "The United States Capitol in 1800," *Records of the Columbia Historical Society* 4 (1901): 128–135. Brown frequently lectured on the plan of Washington and its major public buildings; he also prepared a traveling lantern slide show for the use of American Institute of Architects chapters.

[46] There was no stonework built above the foundation at this time. Brown was referring to Hallet's construction of the south wing that was abandoned in 1796.

[47] Commissioners Scott, Thornton, and White, *Report on the City of Washington*, December 5, 1799. Ex. docs., 6th Cong., 1st sess. [American Imprint Collection, Rare Book Division, LC, #34869].

ground floor, but commending the beauty of the design, and one from Jefferson in 1805 in reference to raising the floor level of the Senate. The third letter is one of Jefferson to Latrobe, July 25, 1808, in which he says: "Lay the floors [of the Senate Chamber] where the gallery floor now is to be the floor of the future Senate Chamber, open it above to the roof to give it elevation enough, leaving the present columns uninjured until we see that everything else being done and paid for, there remains enough to make these columns of stone." [48] The columns were made of wood covered by a plaster stucco.

Plate 37 shows a section of this Chamber restored by the author from drawings and descriptions.

Two compartments in the basement are easily located, the north hall, which Hoban says was semielliptical and 21 by 45 feet, 18 feet high, and the east hall, 22 by 34 feet, 18 feet high, which are fixed by the point of the compass as well as their floor dimensions and height, and the first one also by the form mentioned.

The antechamber of the Senate is given as 22 by 38 feet, 18 feet high, and the fact is mentioned that the room is lighted from above. We find a room with no windows just west of the Senate Chamber which fits these dimensions, and being in the most natural position for a lobby, it was undoubtedly the Senate lobby or antechamber. Taking the other rooms, which Hoban states were 18 feet high, and marked "Committee rooms," we find the dimensions are similar to the sizes of the rooms Nos. 1, 2, 3, and 4.

The halls and stairways on this floor are easily placed when we compare the plans and descriptions. First, the principal stairway, as shown on the plan, is in accordance with Hoban's description, elliptical, and 36 by 45 by 56 feet in dimensions. The back stairway is 10 by 24 feet. The only space which approximates this dimension is on the west of the elliptical stairway, and the same space was afterwards, and is today, used for that purpose, although Thornton does not indicate a stairway on his plan. This stairway gave a private entrance for the members of the House of Representatives and their clerks. On the east of the principal staircase Thornton shows a circular one, and Hoban says the completed circular stairway was 12 feet in diameter. This diameter agrees with the dimensions of the plan. In a later report Hoban mentions these stairways as being in the southeast and southwest portions of the building, where we find them on Thornton's plan. He also mentions that the circular one leads to the offices of the Senate clerks in the stories above. This allotment occupies the space shown on the basement plan. As the south wing of the building intended for the House of Representatives was only a few feet above ground, it was necessary to locate the House in temporary quarters.

The principal story plan must now be considered [Plate 36].

Hoban says the room prepared for the House was 86 by 35 feet, 36 feet high, with cove ceiling [Plate 37]. The only space where such a room could be placed is, as is shown by the plan, on the west front of the wing. This space was found, on scaling the plan, to be exactly 35 feet wide and a little over 86 feet long. By a more careful scaling of the original it was found to be within a few inches of 86 feet, and must, according to its height, have taken in the first and second stories. This room had a gallery, probably on the lines of the gallery used in the same room when it was changed to a library. As corroborative testimony, Congress, on December 18, 1801, after the House had moved into the "oven," as it was called—a temporary structure erected in the south wing—passed a resolution to use the room occupied by the House during the second

[48] Thomas Jefferson to Benjamin Henry Latrobe, April 26, 1808, in Formwalt, ed., *The Papers of Benjamin Henry Latrobe*, vol. 2, 612. Brown erred in dating this letter July 25. For a discussion of how this letter reflected Jefferson's misunderstanding of Latrobe's design, see Talbot Hamlin, *Benjamin Henry Latrobe* (New York: Oxford University Press, 1955), 288.

PLATE 37

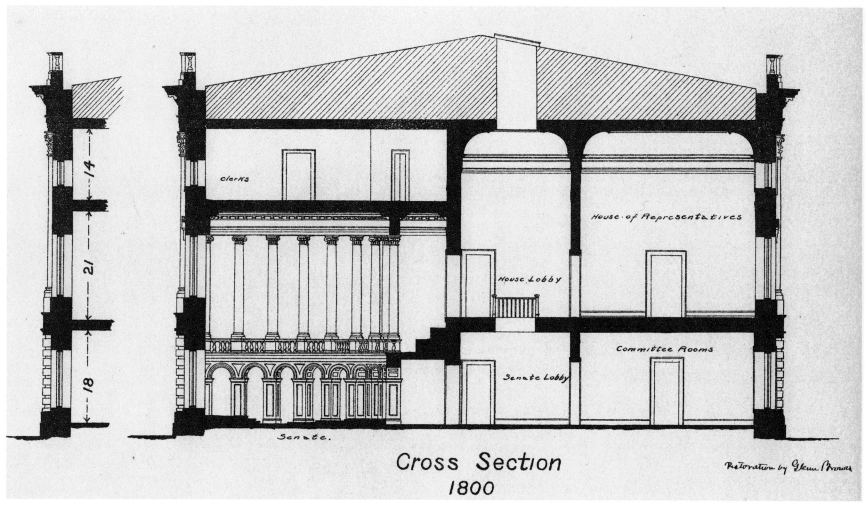

SECTION OF THE SENATE WING 1800.

Conjectural drawing of the north wing of the Capitol in 1800 by Glenn Brown, 1900. *Location unknown.*

PLATE 38

VIEW OF CAPITOL WHEN FIRST OCCUPIED BY CONGRESS 1800—THORNTON ARCHITECT.

Conjectural perspective view of the north wing of the Capitol in 1800 by Glenn Brown, 1900. *Location unknown.*

session of the Sixth Congress as a library, and we have the plan of Latrobe for fitting this room up as the First Library of Congress.[49]

The letter of Latrobe, 1802, gives a sketch showing the room occupied by the House where I have located it on the plan. The House antechamber is mentioned by Hoban as 22 by 38 by 36 feet. We find a room just this width and length over the Senate antechamber. The fact that this space was lighted by a skylight, which also lighted the antechamber of the Senate, proves that one was above the other, the lower being lighted by a well, around which Hoban mentions putting a railing. The other rooms on the principal floor are easily developed from the description. Committee room No. 5, 21 by 40 by 21 feet, over the north hall, is given as the same as the hall, but a little less in length. As this is the only space which approximates the size of this committee room, we must assume, and it is the only instance where it has been necessary to make an assumption, that the elliptical shape of this room was squared up by wooden furring to make the wall surfaces more suitable for committee purposes.[50] One of the rooms for the Secretary of the Senate, 24 by 30 by 21 feet, fits in over the east hall, and one of the rooms for the Clerk of the House fits in over committee room No. I. The staircase halls continue through this story and open on an entrance to the Senate gallery, which is an amphitheater 110 feet in circumference, the exact dimensions given by Hoban. On the third or attic floor [Plate 36] the clerks of the Senate and House have rooms over and of the same size as the rooms on the principal floor, except in height, which is 14 feet, and a large room for clerks, 48 by 86 feet by 14 feet

high, which could only be over the Senate Chamber.[51] This was the room which Jefferson ordered removed when the floor of the Senate was raised to the principal floor, so as to carry the ceiling of the modified Chamber up to the roof line. Another room was provided for clerks on this floor over committee room No. 5. The above rooms account for all space which the building contained except the cellar.

From the different descriptions I have been able to make a drawing [Plate 37] showing the interior of the Senate Chamber. It was a room of dignity and refinement, consisting of an arcade encircling the Senate seats on the ground floor, with panel piers and molded caps and bases. On this arcade rested the gallery. The front of the gallery was treated as a semielliptical, almost semicircular colonnade of ancient Ionic columns, sixteen in number, surmounted by an appropriate classical entablature.

Nothing is given of the character of the gallery in the House, as it was at the time a temporary expedient. It was probably not in any way elaborate. The section shows the heights of the different stories, and how the Senate and House each were two stories high. The exterior of the building and the portion executed was a simple, refined, and dignified structure, being a very good example of Italian Renaissance. The building showed the north wing completed, three sides of it being built of Aquia Creek sandstone, while the south side had a combination of temporary brick walls, and a portion of the permanent walls for the Dome. The south wing was several feet above ground, and the foundations were laid for the Dome, as has been mentioned.[52] The perspective

---

[49] Although Congress passed this resolution, the room was not used as a library but was temporarily occupied by the House as its hall. A reconstruction drawing of the "Oven" is in Allen's *The United States Capitol*, 5.

[50] Brown did not illustrate this change on his plan [Plate 36]. The semi-elliptical room over the north entrance was squared off on the west so that the library would not have an unsightly bulge in its northeast corner. Senate wing, RG 40, Subject Files, Curator's Office, AOC.

[51] The room for clerks above the Senate Chamber was not finished; it was used for storage of building materials until it was torn out to accommodate Latrobe's 1808 plans. Senate Chamber, RG 40, Subject Files, Curator's Office, AOC.

[52] Brown was mistaken because the foundation for the dome was not begun until Charles Bulfinch's employment in 1818; in 1800 the south wing was not above ground. Allen, *The United States Capitol*, 4–12.

shows the condition and appearance of the exterior when it was first occupied by Congress [Plate 38].

The second session of the Sixth Congress convened November 17, 1800, in the north wing. The first meeting did not have a quorum and Congress did not take formal possession of the building until November 21, on which occasion, in his opening speech, President John Adams said:

"I congratulate the people of the United States on the assembling of Congress at the permanent seat of their Government, and I congratulate you, gentlemen, on the prospect of a residence not to be exchanged. It would be unbecoming the representatives of this nation to assemble for the first time in this solemn temple without looking up to the Supreme Ruler of the universe and imploring his blessing. It is with you, gentlemen, to consider whether the local powers over the District of Columbia, vested by the Constitution in Congress of the United States, shall be immediately exercised. If, in your opinion, this important trust ought now be executed, you can not fail, while performing it, to take into view the future probable situation of the territory, for the happiness of which you are about to provide. You will consider it as the capital of a great nation, advancing with unexampled rapidity in arts, in commerce, in wealth, and in population, and possessing within itself those resources which, if not thrown away or lamentably misdirected, will secure to it a long course of prosperity and self-government." [53]

The Supreme Court did not meet in Washington in the year 1800. Its first session in the Capitol was held in 1801, in the room marked No. 1 [Plate 36].[54]

The House of Representatives evidently found its quarters too limited, for on May 28, 1801, Hoban was directed to make an estimate for a temporary chamber, to be located in the south wing of the Capitol, for the accommodation of the House of Representatives. This building or room was to be so arranged that the arcades and other work of the completed structure would not be interfered with, the Commissioners stating, "As much as possible of this building is to be so made as to form a part of the finished structure." June 10 bids were asked for this elliptical room, which was to be built of brick and to be completed by December 1, 1801. Lovering & Dwyer were awarded the contract. They were to complete the room before November 1, 1801, for the sum of $4,780, in accordance with plan and bill of particulars filed with the Commissioners.[55]

Hoban reports, December 14, 1801, that this structure was ready for the meeting of the first session of the Seventh Congress. It was an elliptical brick structure whose axes were 70 and 94 feet and walls a little more than 18 feet high. Its interior consisted of sixteen niches and sixteen arches, which together formed an elliptical arcade. It also contained a semielliptical gallery. This room was connected with the Senate wing by a covered way 145 feet long, in which were two flights of steps that probably led to the gallery in the temporary House.

Thomas Jefferson was elected President in 1801. He felt a lively interest in the whole subject of architecture and a particular interest in the Capitol, as he was Secretary of State when the design was selected and during the early progress of the building, and upon taking his seat

---

[53] "Address of John Adams to the Senate and the House of Representatives, 22 November, 1800," in *Annals of the Congress of the United States: Sixth Congress* (Washington: Gales and Seaton, 1851), 723–724. Adams delivered the address on November 22, not on November 21, as Brown states.

[54] The Supreme Court first met in Room No. 2, depicted on Plate 35.

[55] Proceedings, December 1, 1801, RG 42, DCC, NARA.

as President he immediately showed an active and interfering interest in the work. The next step of importance in connection with the Capitol was the abolition of the offices of the Commissioners of the District of Columbia by act of Congress, May, 1802.[56]

Mr. Thomas Munroe was appointed as superintendent, to perform such duties of the Commissioners as did not devolve upon the General Government. He received $1,200 as superintendent, at the same time acting as postmaster for Washington City, with an additional salary. From the account it is not clear whether he received $2,000 in all or $2,000 in addition to his salary as superintendent, but presumably the former amount.[57] With the end of his term as commissioner, Thornton's supervision and Hoban's superintendence of the Capitol practically ceased, although both were called in consultation in reference to the work at subsequent periods. Just before his retirement Thornton informed Jefferson that certain changes the President wished to make "would not be in consonance with his [Thornton's] plans." There is nothing to show whether this caused his further services in connection with the Capitol to be dispensed with. No further work apparently was done on the Capitol in 1802. James Hoban is always mentioned as one of the architects of the Capitol. The records show that he acted only as superintendent in times of emergency. He made no effort to incorporate any of his own ideas as to plan or design in the construction of the building. He and Thornton remained friends during the period of ten years in which they were thrown together in work connected with the Capitol. Hoban was first made superintendent, with Hallet as assistant. Hallet received $1,066 per annum, Hoban receiving his salary as super-

intendent of the President's House. Hadfield and Hoban held equal positions, one as superintendent of the Capitol, the other as superintendent of the President's House, each receiving $1,400 per annum. Finally Hoban was given $1,866.66 by special contract to superintend the Capitol and President's House. The records simply give him the title of superintendent. June 24, 1801, Hoban received the title of inspector of Government works, at a salary of 300 guineas per annum, "to continue as long as his services were needed."[58] The duties of this position included inspection of roads, bridges, and buildings. This office was abolished with the dissolution of the board of commissioners. Thomas Jefferson mentions him in his letters of later date as surveyor of public buildings, at a salary of $1,700 per annum. Neither of these titles indicates a designer, but from them one would infer that Hoban executed other men's designs. It is clearly shown by the records that he never made designs for any of the public buildings except the President's House.

From the beginning to this period in the history of the Capitol, it will be clearly seen that Thornton had been the only architect—the man who originated in design and plan. The other so-called architects or assistants had been merely draftsmen or superintendents. Although Hallet in the second competition worked directly under the instruction of the commissioners, and he had a second and third trial, still Thornton's first plan was so meritorious that it immediately commended itself to President Washington, Secretary Jefferson, and the Commissioners of the District as the best one submitted. To reduce the expense, this plan was made smaller by changing the scale, not the arrangement nor the design. Soon after Hallet was discharged Thornton threw out the changes Hallet had attempted to introduce and brought the plans back to their original shape. In making these changes Thornton drew new elevations incorporating some improvements. When Thornton retired

---

[56] Act of May 1, 1802, c. 41, 3 Stat. 175.

[57] Thomas Munroe was postmaster in Washington, D.C., from 1799 to 1829. See Wilhelmus B. Bryan, *A History of the National Capital*, vol. 1 (New York: Macmillan Company, 1914), 345–346. His total salary for both positions was $2,000. RG 40, Subject Files, Commissioners and Superintendents, Curator's Office, AOC.

[58] Proceedings, June 24, 1801, RG 42, DCC, NARA.

the north wing was complete (this is the portion now occupied by the Supreme Court), the foundation for the central Rotunda and Dome was in place, and the foundation and basement story of the south wing were partially built.[59] The exterior of these portions of the building is still in the form designed by Thornton. The plan of the north wing, or Supreme Court portion of the Capitol, is in practically the same form as it was when left by Thornton's hands. Parts of it have been replaced by brick and stone where it was originally wood, and the interior of the old Senate Chamber was altered, the original being in the form shown in Plate 37. A comparison of Thornton's designs and plans with others in this article will show the changes made from the original. Thornton's design made after Hallet's dismissal is shown in Plates 28 to 34.[60]

All through the transactions of the commissioners we find Thornton on record as desiring greater magnitude and better and more ornamental material than he was allowed to use. He wished the exterior and the principal portions of the interior to be of marble, and he went to the extent of saying it should be imported marble. He protested against reducing the size and number of rooms. He wanted mahogany doors and fittings. In fact, he appreciated the future wants and needs of the American people more fully than did many of his contemporaries. Upon retiring from his position of commissioner, Thornton was placed

in charge of issuing patents. In this position he remained until his death. Three papers read before the American Institute of Architects by P. B. Wight, Adolf Cluss, and J. H. B. Latrobe, the article before referred to by Mr. Howard, and G. A. Townsend, in his book on Washington, do not give Thornton the credit to which the records and letters of such shrewd men as Washington, Jefferson, and contemporary writers show him to be entitled.[61] These articles make him simply a dilettante, who endeavored to use others' ideas for his own advantage, and one who was constantly maneuvering to throw worthy men out of their positions. The records show that he made no protest until the different superintendents endeavored to misuse his plans. Thornton declined the position of superintendent, but accepted the commissionership, so that he could have a supervision of the building. Hallet was discharged because he insisted on changing Thornton's plan. This was before Thornton became commissioner. Hadfield was appointed directly through Thornton's influence, and was discharged because of his inefficiency as a superintendent. Hoban and Thornton remained friends from their earliest connection with the Capitol until the act abolished the office of the commissioners, when both ceased their services on this building.

---

[59] The foundation for the central Rotunda and dome and basement story of the south wing were not in place until 1818. Only the "Oven" was there at this time. See Allen, *The United States Capitol,* 4–12.

[60] Brown's interpretation that Thornton alone deserves credit for the design of the Capitol is no longer accepted. Scholarly writing on the history of the Capitol since the 1920s has developed a much more complex analysis of the design evolution of the building and the contributions of the early architects.

[61] Peter B. Wight, "Government Architecture and Government Architects," *American Architect and Building News* 1 (1876): 83–85; Adolf Cluss, "Architecture and Architects at the Capitol of the United States from its Foundation until 1875," in *Tenth Annual Proceedings of the American Institute of Architects* (Boston: Franklin Press, 1876); John H. B. Latrobe, "The Capitol at Washington at the Beginning of the Present Century," in *An Address by John H. B. Latrobe Before the American Institute of Architects* (Baltimore: William K. Boyle, 1881).

CHAPTER IV

THE WORK OF BENJAMIN HENRY LATROBE, ARCHITECT

T HE PLAT of the city made by Robert King in 1803 [Plate 39] gives an idea of the proposed arrangement of the grounds at this period of the Capitol's history. [1,2]

The following letters from Thomas Jefferson give the particulars of Benj. H. Latrobe's appointment as "Director of public works" or "Surveyor of public buildings," the position formerly held by James Hoban:

WASHINGTON, D.C., *March 6, 1803.*

SIR: Congress has appropriated a sum of $50,000, to be applied to the public buildings under my direction. This falls, of course, under the immediate business of the superintendent, Mr. Munroe, whose office is substituted for that of the board of commissioners. The former post of surveyor of the public buildings, which Mr. Hoban held until the dissolution of the board at [$1,700 a year], will be revived.

If you choose to accept it, you will be appointed to it, and would be expected to come on by the 1st of April. Indeed, if you could make a flying trip here to set contractors at work immediately in raising freestone, it would be extremely important, because it is now late to have to engage laborers, and the quantity of freestone which can be raised, delivered, and cut in the season is the only thing that will limit the extent of our operations this year.

I set out to-morrow for Monticello, and shall be absent three weeks, but shall be glad to receive there your answer to this.

Accept my friendly salutations and regards,

TH. JEFFERSON.

P. S.—On the raising of freestone be pleased to consult Col. D. H. Brent, who can give you better information and advice on the subject than any other person whatever, having been much concerned in the business himself.

MARCH 6, 1803. [3]

DEAR SIR: The letter in which this is inclosed being a public one, and to be produced whenever necessary as a voucher, I have thought that it would be useful to add a word in one of a private and friendly nature. From the sum of $50,000 we shall take between $5,000 and $10,000 for covering the north wing of the Capitol and the President's House.

The residue of $40,000 to $45,000 will be employed in building the south wing, as far as it will go. I think it will raise the external walls as far as the uppermost window sills, being those of the entresols, and I have no doubt Congress at their next session will give another $50,000, which will complete that wing inside and out in the year 1804. . . . Should you think proper to undertake it, if you come on here on a flying trip, as suggested in my other letter, you can advise with Mr.

---

[1] For the series of articles on which this chapter was based, see Glenn Brown, "History of the United States Capitol," *The American Architect and Building News* 52 (July 4, 1896): 3–5 ; 52 (July 25, 1896): 27–30; and (September 5, 1896): 75–78.

[2] Brown is referring to a set of plat maps compiled by Robert King and his two sons Nicholas and Robert King, Jr., between 1802 and 1804, known as the King plats. For a history of the surveyor's office in this period, see Ralph E. Ehrenberg, "Mapping the Nation's Capital: The Surveyor's Office, 1791–1828," *The Quarterly Journal of the Library of Congress* 36 (Summer 1979): 279–319.

[3] Thomas Jefferson to Benjamin Henry Latrobe, March 6, 1803, in John C. Van Horne and Lee W. Formwalt, eds., *The Correspondence and Miscellaneous Papers of Benjamin Henry Latrobe,* vol. 1 (New Haven, Conn.: Yale University Press, 1984), 260–261.

PLATE 39

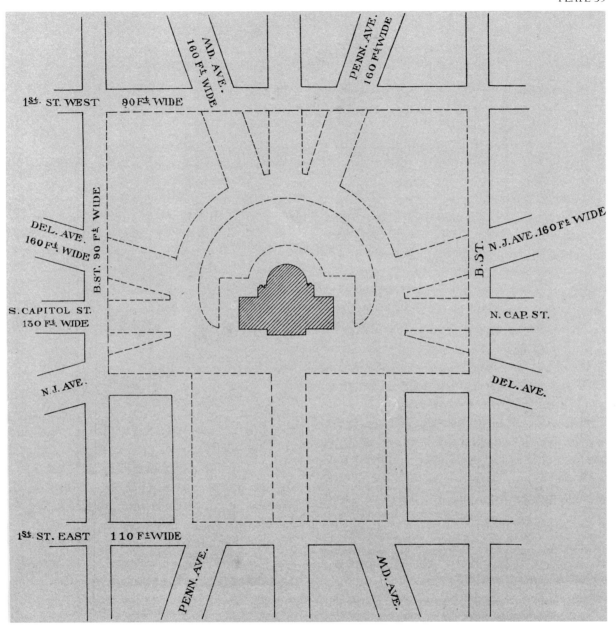

PLAT OF GROUNDS, 1803.

Site map based on the Robert King plats of Washington, D.C., by Glenn Brown, 1900. *Location unknown.*

Munroe, who will set into motion whatever you may desire, and if you can be here finally the first week in April you will find me here, and everything may be put under full sail for the season.

Accept my best wishes and respects,

TH. JEFFERSON.

P. S.—I think a great deal of sheet iron will be wanting.[4]

Latrobe accepted this appointment and took charge of the work immediately. April 7, 1803, he appointed John Lenthall clerk of works, giving him the following authority:

"I have to inform you that it is clearly understood by the President of the United States and the superintendent of the city that you are to be the sole judge of the merits of the workmen.... You are also the sole judge in my absence of the fidelity with which contracts are fulfilled...no money will be paid without your certificate; you will thereby obtain complete control over the conduct of every man employed."[5]

Although Latrobe was appointed to superintend the completion of the Capitol according to Thornton's designs, his first thought upon taking the work seems to have been upon changes he could suggest, and after the experience with Hallet and Hadfield this naturally provoked Thornton. Latrobe, after eight or nine months' study, made his suggestions to Jefferson, who referred him to Thornton. Latrobe's letter (February 27, 1804) to Jefferson gives the result of the interview:

"DEAR SIR: I judged very ill in going to Dr. Thornton. In a few peremptory words he, in fact, told me that no difficulties existed in his plan but such as were made by those who were too ignorant to remove them, and, though those were not exactly his words, his expressions, his tones, his manners, and his absolute refusal to discuss the subject spoke his meaning more strongly and offensively than I have expressed."[6]

President Jefferson replied on the following day:

"DEAR SIR: I am very sorry the explanations attempted between Dr. Thornton and yourself on the manner of finishing the House of Representatives have not succeeded."[7]

Latrobe carried on his crusade against Thornton's design and plans vigorously and persistently until he partially accomplished his purpose. To his own mind, as well as to that of others in authority, he justified his changes of the accepted plan. In efforts to accomplish his purpose, Latrobe had personal interviews with the President, and used his early reports to Congress with effect. His reports, many letters to Jefferson, and a pamphlet of 32 pages, entitled A Private Letter to Individual Members of Congress on the Subject of the Public Buildings of the United States (November 28, 1806), are on record.[8] In his criticisms Latrobe was sharp, sarcastic, in many cases unreasonable, and unjust,

---

[4] Jefferson to Latrobe, March 6, 1803, in Van Horne and Formwalt, *Papers of Benjamin Henry Latrobe,* vol. 1, 262.

[5] Latrobe to John Lenthall, March 6, 1803, in Van Horne and Formwalt, *Papers of Benjamin Henry Latrobe,* vol. 1, 284–286.

[6] Latrobe to Jefferson, February 27, 1804, in Van Horne and Formwalt, *Papers of Benjamin Henry Latrobe,* vol. 1, 437. Brown cites only the first few lines of the letter and omits Latrobe's account of his frustrating encounter with Thornton and his seeming inability to understand the plan's "practical difficulties in execution which twenty years' experience creates in the mind of a professional man."

[7] Jefferson to Latrobe, February 28, 1804, in Van Horne and Formwalt, *Papers of Benjamin Henry Latrobe,* vol. 1, 439–440. Strangely, Brown quotes only the first line of the reply. Later in the same letter, Jefferson praised the existing plan for the House of Representatives as "more handsome and commodious than anything which can now be proposed on the same area."

[8] Latrobe's reports and letters to Jefferson between 1804 and 1806 were compiled in Saul K. Padover, *Thomas Jefferson and the National Capital* (Washington: Government Printing Office, 1946), 335–380. See also Benjamin Henry Latrobe, *A Private Letter to the Individual Members of Congress on the Subject of the Public Buildings of the United States at Washington* (Washington: S. H. Smith, Printer, 1806).

judging from the records, his letters, drawings, and pamphlets. It is entirely natural Dr. Thornton should have been dissatisfied, and from the nature and ability of the man that he should return criticism of equal sharpness. Latrobe's letter to the President and reports state that the open space inclosed by the elliptical hall becomes a dark cellar when the Legislative Hall is raised to the story above. "Therefore the doors leading into it are useless if not absurd." "No fireplaces can be carried up except on outer walls and this would be difficult on account of hardness of brickwork. No staircases could be built behind the Speaker's chair in elliptical inclosure." [9]

Latrobe, although objecting to the plan made by Thornton for the House of Representatives and "which is said to be the plan approved by General Washington," writes, February 28, 1804, that he is determined to carry it out, elliptical room, colonnade, and all, provided he can raise the floor to the level of the principal floor.[10] Following this determination Latrobe submitted to the President, March 29, 1804, plans suggesting slight modifications of the original scheme, in which he proposed to rectify these errors, according to his ideas, by changing the elliptical form of the Chamber, and substituting "two semicircles abutting on a parallelogram." He further took the liberty to alter the whole of Thornton's plan where "a spacious stairway ran only to a gallery and a room 50 feet square with one window."[11] If Latrobe could have seen the present requirements of a gallery he would have seen that a spacious stairway was necessary. Latrobe seriously objected both in his letters and printed documents to the design with which he was compelled to conform, because of the portions of the building already erected.

The drawings submitted show a change in the plan of the form from an ellipse to two semicircles abutting on parallel sides, and change of floor level from the basement to the principal floor [Plates 40 to 42]. The illustrations show a plan and section through the north and south, and east and west. Latrobe in the drawings submits an alternate scheme for the order of the colonnades. Jefferson selected the most ornate one, which was taken from the Temple of the Winds at Athens. At Jefferson's request Thornton submitted a sketch showing how he would arrange office rooms in the basement if it was determined to raise the floor in the House and Senate [Plate 43]. The following indorsement is written on this drawing by Latrobe:

"Mr. Jefferson in putting this into my hands stated that he had communicated with Dr. Thornton on the plan submitted by me for putting a story of offices under the Hall of Representatives and that Dr. Thornton had, in consequence, given him this plan as showing how the projection might be effected, but at that time my plan was already in progress [Plate 43].

"B. H. LATROBE.

"FEBRUARY 1, 1805." [12]

To defend himself and his design before Congress and the people, Thornton addressed a letter to Congress in answer to Latrobe's report. The document is a very clear statement of the case, and all the facts as stated are confirmed by the records or contemporary documents. For

[9] Benjamin Henry Latrobe to Thomas Jefferson, March 29, 1804, in Edward C. Carter II, editor in chief and Thomas E. Jeffrey, microfiche editor, *The Papers of Benjamin Henry Latrobe* (microtext edition) (Clifton, N.J.: James T. White and Co., 1976). Brown fails to mention that these critical remarks were addressed toward a plan by Thornton for an office story for the south wing of the Capitol. See Plate 43.

[10] Latrobe to Jefferson, February 28, 1804, in Van Horne and Formwalt, *Papers of Benjamin Henry Latrobe*, vol. 1, 441–443.

[11] Latrobe to Jefferson, March 29, 1804, in Van Horne and Formwalt, *Papers of Benjamin Henry Latrobe*, vol. 1, 466–472.

[12] Thornton's original undated sketch plan bearing Latrobe's February 1, 1805, inscription is located in the Prints and Photographs Division, LC. Comparing Thornton's sketch with Benjamin Henry Latrobe's ground floor plans illustrates Latrobe's superior professional skill.

PLATE 40

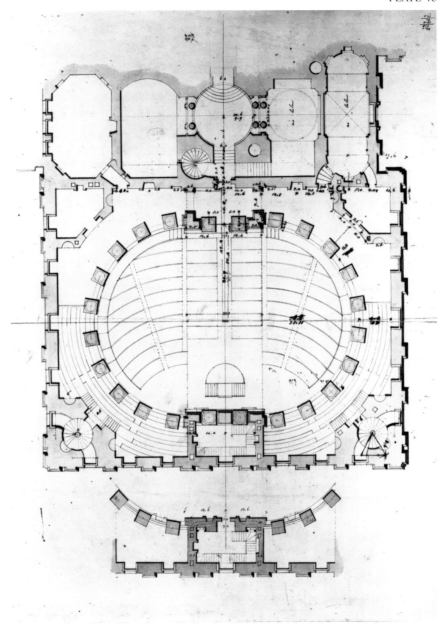

PLAN, LATROBE'S MODIFICATION OF THORNTON'S PLAN. HOUSE OF REPRESENTATIVES.

Plan of the principal floor of the south wing, as built under Benjamin Henry Latrobe's supervision before 1811. *Prints and Photographs Division, LC.*

PLATE 41

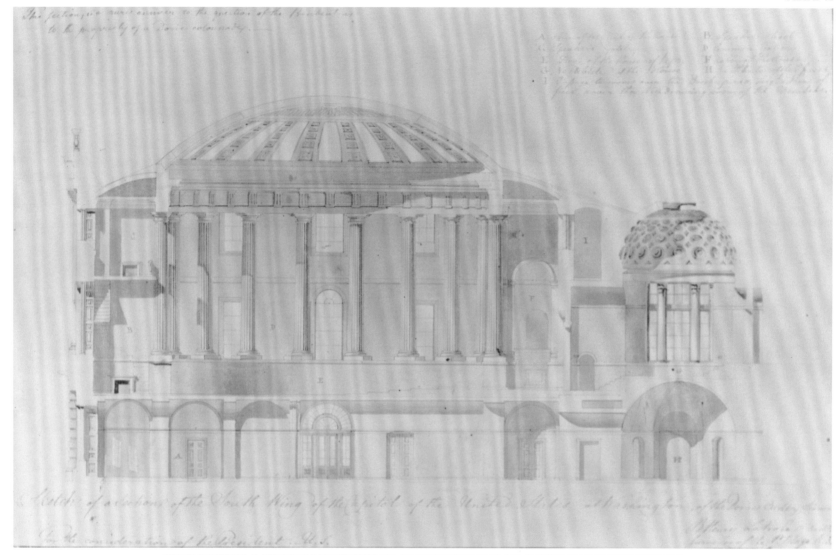

CROSS SECTION, LATROBE'S MODIFICATION OF THORNTON'S PLAN, HOUSE OF REPRESENTATIVES.

Section of the south wing (looking west), ca. 1804. *Prints and Photographs Division, LC.*

PLATE 42

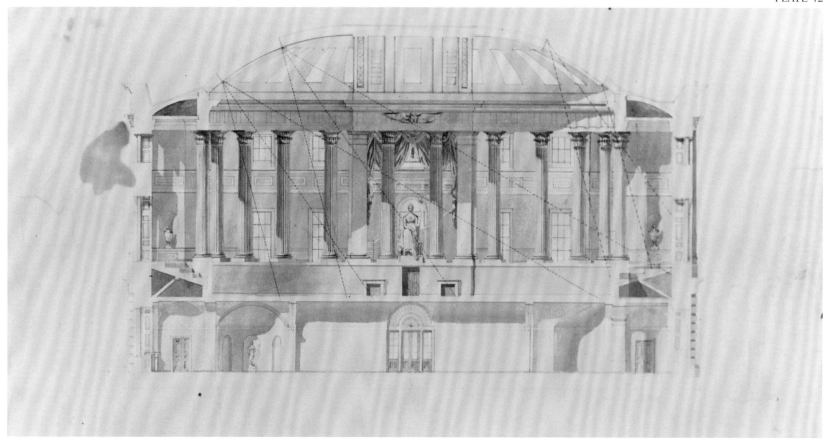

LONGITUDINAL SECTION, LATROBE'S MODIFICATION OF THORNTON'S PLAN FOR THE HOUSE OF REPRESENTATIVES.

Section of the south wing (looking south) through ground and principal floors, ca. 1804. *Prints and Photographs Division, LC.*

PLATE 43

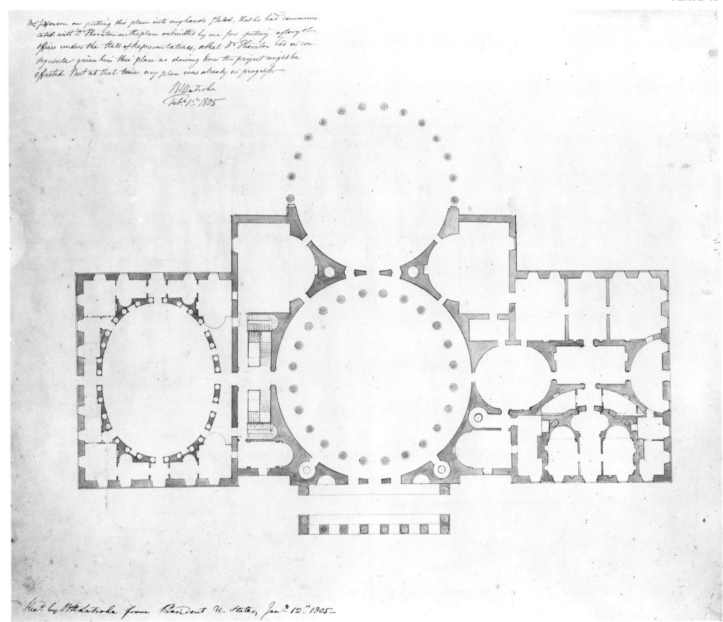

THORNTON'S SKETCH FOR BASEMENT ROOMS.

Plan of first floor of the Capitol, date unknown. *Prints and Photographs Division, LC.*

this reason I quote liberally from this letter of January 1, 1805. He says: "Previous to Mr. Latrobe's appointment, when he came to report on dry docks suggested by the President, he often complimented me on the plan of the Capitol, a ground plan and elevation of which I had shown him, and he declared in the presence of the superintendent [probably James Hoban at that time] that he never saw any other plan of a building besides his own that he would deign to execute. I must own I can not easily conceive why previous to this appointment I should hear nothing but approbation of my plan and after his appointment nothing but condemnation. In the commencement of his report he mentions the approval of my plan by General Washington. . . . Mr. Hallet was appointed to execute it, but not until after I had refused to superintend its execution. . . . Mr. Hallet was desirous of altering not merely what might be improved, but even what was most approved."[13] At this point he describes Hallet's attempted changes, an account of which I have given in previous pages. After describing the removal of the foundations laid by Hallet for his square central space instead of a dome, Thornton continues:

"A portion of what I intended to remove was directed by the board of commissioners to remain, in order to erect thereon a temporary building of brick for the accommodation of Congress until more committee rooms could be prepared by the further progress of the building. On the opposite side, the walls built by Mr. Hallet between the Dome and the Representatives' Chamber still remain, which may in some way account for the difference mentioned by Mr. Latrobe between the plan as laid down and the drawing. Mr. Hallet was not in the public service when I was appointed commissioner, September 12, 1794." Then he describes Hadfield's connection with the Capitol, an account of which

I have already given. After the statement of facts in reference to his design, which I have found fully proved by the public records, he continues: "Mr. Latrobe must have been exceedingly misinformed when he speaks of the various styles of each architect showing themselves in the work, one having been out of public employ before the present elevation was drawn and before a single freestone was laid, and the other having taken his discharge because he was not allowed to make any material alterations. They are both [Hallet and Hadfield], however, men of genius, which I acknowledge with pleasure.

"Mr. Latrobe's observation respecting the want of agreement in the plan and foundation is already answered; but if I could be surprised at any observation made by Mr. Latrobe after reading his report it would be at his stating the author furnished him only a ground plan. It may be true I did not give him drawings, but I informed him what was intended in completing the south wing, and to show that he understood we need only his description—tenth page of the committee's report." It must be remembered that it was only the south wing that was under discussion, and the exterior of the south wing was to be an exact duplicate of the north wing, which was completed when Latrobe took charge, and, further, that the drawings had never been in Thornton's possession since the commencement of the work. "He [Latrobe] speaks of the impracticability of the plan of the south wing. It has been deemed practicable by very skillful and practical architects, and I never heard it disputed by other than himself. He told me that he could not execute it as it was intended. To support a coved ceiling formed in the manner of the Hal au Blé at Paris of the extent contemplated on columns of wood [it will be remembered that Thornton's original idea was to make the interior work of marble] can not in the conception of an architect be difficult; and I believe it will be generally admitted that the grandeur of the room contemplated would far exceed the appearance of the one intended by him and at much less expense. The stability of the work

---

[13] William Thornton, *To the Members of the House of Representatives, January 1, 1805,* vols. 3–4, William Thornton Papers, Manuscript Division, LC.

could not be an objection, when it is remembered how many hundred years Westminster Hall has stood.

"It is astonishing what evidence is considered sufficient to establish facts to a mind that I am sorry to say appears preoccupied by a desire to condemn [Dr. Thornton here quotes from Latrobe]: 'The most indisputable evidence was brought before me to prove [a negation] that no sections or detail drawings of the building had ever existed excepting those that were made from time to time by Messrs. Hallet and Hadfield for their own use in the direction of the work.'" [Page 10 of Report.] "It will be remembered that one of these gentlemen never superintended the laying of a single stone of the elevation. The other did not make a single section that I ever heard of, but required sections of me, which I drew, and of which Mr. Munroe told me he had informed Mr. Latrobe.

"The whole area of the south wing of the Capitol might be conceived by some as too extensive for a Chamber of Representatives, but if we consider the rapid increase of the American people, and that 500 Representatives may be required, neither the space allotted for the members nor the gallery for the audience will be considered too large. To lessen either would therefore, in my judgment, be a very important objection.

"Mr. Latrobe mentions the want of committee and other rooms. The President [Mr. Jefferson] of the United States had, some months before Mr. Latrobe's appointment, spoken to me on the subject, and asked if they could be formed in the basement story with convenience, under the Representatives' Chamber. Approving much the idea on many accounts, independent of its restoring the building to a greater conformity with my original designs for the south wing raised, with committee rooms under the galleries, the President's idea was carried further, for I drew a plan of the Senate Room [present Supreme Court] raised within a few feet of the base of the columns and with two good rooms beneath, one on each side, besides two smaller for paper, etc., and a passage from a door in the external center to the lobby [Plate 43].

This would much improve the proportion of the Senate Room, the arcade of which is too high for the columns. A coved ceiling might be thrown from the entablature so as to give any desired elevation. These alterations were laid before the President [Jefferson] many months before Mr. Latrobe's report was written, and if Mr. Latrobe had extended his alterations only to the committee and other rooms, however they might have differed from mine in form, size, or appropriateness, I should not have considered them of sufficient importance to call forth my objections; but under a sincere conviction that the Representatives' Chamber will be irreparably [marred] by the alterations now in execution I am compelled by a sense of duty, but with great reluctance on other accounts, to express my disapprobation of the measure.

"I have seen Mr. Latrobe's report of December last and find much stress is laid on the imperfections of the foundation of the south wing, which required to be taken down. Six feet [in height] of the foundation had been built by a contractor, during whose absence the work was ill conducted by those in whom he had confided. The work was directed to be examined and was condemned by the commissioners. The correspondent part of the north wing was taken down and good bond stones intermingled throughout the new work, by which it was rendered completely solid; and as that and the stonework of the elevation were well executed, if any defect can be hereafter discovered it must depend upon injuries received by piercing so many large holes through it, or on defects in the lower part of the foundation which was laid before I was in office. It was a query at the time of its execution whether it would not be better to lay the foundation with inverted arches, but it was thought more expensive and not better than by good bond stones in the more usual manner, and I imagine that those who pierced the foundations of the north wing, thereby injuring it by cutting loose many of the bonds, found it to be exceptional work; but I think it might have been perfectly aired by tubes at a trifling expense without risking any injury whatever. The roof has been justly condemned. It is next to impossible to put any elevated covering that shall resist the ingress of water when the gutters are filled with snow or deluged with rain. I object to the roof as now executed not solely on that account. By rising so high, the balustrade is darkened until the beholder advances so near the building as to lose the general view; it is thus rendered heavy in appearance. I proposed a flat roof made with a composition that has since been found to answer perfectly by Mr. Foxall, and by varying the ingredients a little he has formed a variety of excellent cements. It is made in imitation of a terraced roof, though greatly superior."

This was the last public effort of Thornton in defense of his plan. The alterations advised by Latrobe were executed, and I think few will contend that they were improvements. [See Plates 40 to 46.][14]

Although Dr. Thornton made no further efforts to preserve the integrity of his plan, Latrobe still found he did not have an easy time contending with Jefferson, Congress, and the newspapers. Jefferson had individual ideas on architecture, Congress considered the cost, and were slow in making and gave but little in their appropriations; at the same time they were disposed to take exception to the time of erection and cost of construction. The newspapers complained of the slow progress, character of the work, and of Latrobe's frequent absence from the city in connection with his private business. Thornton likewise prodded him on his deficiencies, in private and published letters. As a general answer to these parties, Latrobe on November 28, 1806, issued a pamphlet entitled "A Private Letter to the Individual Members of

Congress on the Subject of the Public Buildings of the United States."[15] In this letter he gives as his excuse for the slow progress of the work the uncertainty of Government appropriations and the difficulties of quarrying stone. He makes a plea for changing the method of making appropriations. From this he passes into criticisms of Thornton's design, and states that the method of choosing a design by competition was a mistake and certain of defeating its own end. He refers to the design of the north wing which he was compelled to follow in the south wing [the present Supreme Court and Statuary Hall]. "I frankly confess that, excepting a few of the details, all my ideas of good taste and even good sense in architecture were shocked by the style of the building. I am well aware that in what I shall say in this I am in the minority. All books for the last three or four hundred years are against me. But as the arts continue to improve, simplicity gains more admirers daily....

"But with the actual shape and appearance of the building little could be done but adhere to the style of the exterior and to add all the conveniences of the offices which were required for the transaction of the business of the House." At this point Latrobe describes quite minutely the changes which he claimed to have made in the original plan. As these points are treated fully in other portions of this treatise, I will not quote them here.

He compliments Jefferson in the following glowing terms: "The warm interest which the President has taken in everything that relates to the design, arrangement, and management of the work, and to that impulse which a mind by whom no field of art or science has been unexplored gives to all the agents he employs, more is due than delicacy permits me to express. On the intelligent activity and integrity of the clerk of works, Mr. Lenthall, it is impossible to bestow too much

[14] Modern works since the 1950s praise Latrobe's alterations and acknowledge his superior skill. See, for example, Talbot F. Hamlin, *Benjamin Henry Latrobe* (New York: Oxford University Press, 1955); Paul F. Norton, *Latrobe, Jefferson, and the National Capitol* (New York: Garland Publishers, 1977); for a survey of American architectural history that reflects this view, see William H. Pierson, Jr., *American Buildings and Their Architects: The Colonial and Neo-Classical Styles* (Garden City, N.Y.: Anchor Books, 1976), 398–402.

[15] Benjamin Henry Latrobe, *A Private Letter to the Individual Members of Congress on the Subject of the Public Buildings of the United States at Washington* (Washington: S. H. Smith, Printer, 1806).

PLATE 44

West Elevation of the Capitol U.S. Washington

LATROBE'S DESIGN FOR DOME AND CENTER BUILDING, WEST VIEW.

West elevation of a partially executed design for the Capitol, 1811. *Prints and Photographs Division, LC.*

PLATE 45

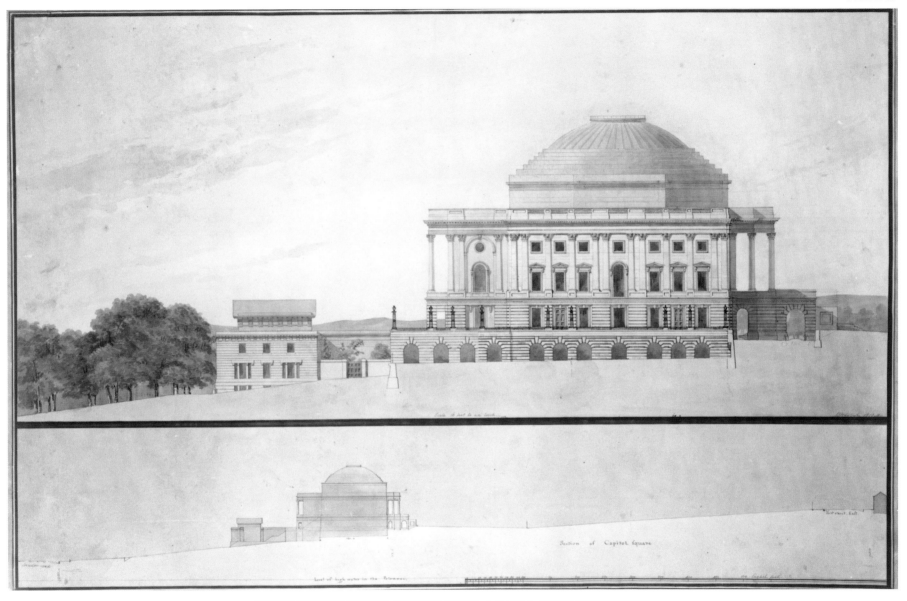

SOUTH VIEW SHOWING LATROBE'S DOME, & EAST & WEST PROJECTIONS.

South elevation of a partially executed design for the Capitol, 1810–11. *Prints and Photographs Division, LC.*

PLATE 46

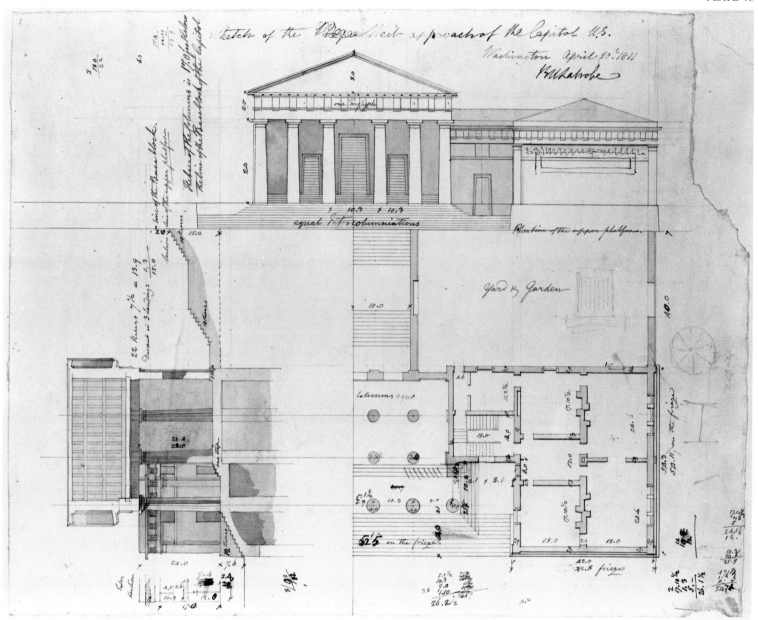

PROPOSED WEST ENTRANCE, BY LATROBE.

West approach of an unexecuted design for the Capitol, 1811. *Prints and Photographs Division, LC.*

commendation." Thornton published a sharp and sarcastic answer to this pamphlet, which is interesting in its local hits and comments, but as it simply covers facts which have been mentioned before I will not quote from it. From this period until the work ceased on the Capitol, in 1811, Latrobe appears to have been untrammeled except by the restrictions of President Jefferson. Munroe, who assumed a part of the duties belonging to the board of commissioners, either did not keep a record of the work or such record has been lost; the limited number of letters in reference to the subject in possession of the Government are in the State Department among the manuscript letters to and from Jefferson. The data from which information must be drawn are letters of Latrobe in the possession of the family; a volume from Latrobe to John Lenthall, clerk of works, in possession of Mr. W. S. Abert, a grandson of Lenthall; Latrobe's report to Congress, and Jefferson's published correspondence.[16] Unfortunately this matter covers only one side of the issue. In reference to all points before this date we have the regularly recorded transactions of the commissioners and letters covering both sides of every question. To arrive at a clear understanding of B. H. Latrobe's work on the Capitol it is necessary to compare his drawings with Thornton's and his letters and reports with documents of earlier date, showing what had been contemplated before he took charge.

I have already mentioned the changes which Latrobe proposed in connection with the south wing (present Statuary Hall) [Plates 40 to 42]. These changes were carried out, and Latrobe took great credit for the alteration of a very gracefully formed elliptical room into a badly formed one, with two short sides and semicircular ends, decreasing the size and changing the form of the staircase to the galleries, and placing committee rooms under galleries. Thornton had previously made a plan for this purpose [see Plate 43]. It will be seen at a glance, by comparing the plan of Thornton with the one of Latrobe, that the changes were simply modifications in form, size, and detail. Thornton's original scheme still remained, so changed as to destroy much of its beauty and utility, but the broad principles of his plan for this portion of the building were still intact.

The Hall of Representatives was considered upon its completion a very magnificent room. The British officer who burned it said it was a "pity to burn anything so beautiful," and Mr. Jefferson, in a letter from Monticello, April 14, 1811, says: "I declare, on many and all occasions, that I considered you [B. H. Latrobe] the only person in the United States who could have executed the Representative Chamber or who could execute the middle building on any of the plans proposed;"[17] and July, 1812: "The Representative Chamber will remain a durable monument to your talents as an architect."[18] It is easy for an architect to take the suggestion of Thornton's plan and imagine or realize how much more effective a hall reared on its lines would have been than the one built on the lines shown by Latrobe's plan. Jefferson's instructions or interference in the plan and design of the Capitol appears to have been,

[16] William S. Abert (1858–1921), the grandson of John Lenthall, was a Washington lawyer who had commissioned Brown to design his house (1892) and a commercial building (1896). Latrobe's sons, John H. B. Latrobe (1803–91) and Benjamin Henry Latrobe, Jr. (1806–78), inherited and preserved the bulk of their father's papers, which were acquired in the 1960s by the Maryland Historical Society from Latrobe descendant Mrs. Ferdinand Latrobe. Brown did not use this major collection for the preparation of the *History*. For Jefferson's correspondence Brown consulted either Paul Leicester Ford, *The Writings of Thomas Jefferson*, 10 vols. (New York: G. P. Putnam's Sons, 1892–1899), or Henry Augustus Washington, *The Writings of Thomas Jefferson: Being His Autobiography, Correspondence, Reports, Messages, Addresses, and Other Writings, Official and Private*, 9 vols. (Philadelphia: J. B. Lippincott and Company, 1869–71).

[17] Jefferson quoted in "The Capitol and Washington at the Beginning of the Present Century," in *An Address Delivered by John H. B. Latrobe Before the American Institute of Architects* (Baltimore: William K. Boyle, 1881).

[18] Jefferson to Latrobe, July [12?], 1812, in Van Horne, *Papers of Benjamin Henry Latrobe*, vol. 3, 329, n. 6.

judging from his letters, usually suggestive and not mandatory. These recommendations usually appear to have been in reference to detail; his idea, as we learn from hints all the way through the correspondence, was to follow Thornton's plan, with which he was familiar from its first appearance in the competition. Latrobe says, in the pamphlet above referred to (1806): "That he [Jefferson] directed I should deviate as little as possible from the plan approved by General Washington." [19]

Jefferson told Dr. Thornton no alterations should be permitted, when Latrobe was appointed, without allowing Thornton an opportunity of giving his judgment upon the changes. In Latrobe's letters to Lenthall he describes his troubles in obtaining the President's consent to change the form of the House of Representatives, and freely criticises the President and Congress. The majority of the suggestions made by Jefferson were approved by Latrobe. Sometimes Mr. Jefferson insisted on points against which Latrobe protested. From the sources mentioned above the progress and character of the work during this portion of Latrobe's incumbency can be readily described. The roof covering was one of the first parts of the building to which Jefferson called his attention, being anxious to have Latrobe cover both the Capitol and President's House with sheet iron, as the President was having a roof of this character placed on Monticello; and he expresses his surprise, September 5, 1803, that Latrobe had not already commenced his work. July 31, 1804, the exterior of the south wing was completed to the height of the principal floor and the foundations were ready for the interior work. After the adjournment of Congress in 1804 the temporary elliptical room was removed, and the House of Representatives again held its sessions in the room first occupied by them. This was done because Latrobe thought that the interior and exterior walls should go up simultaneously. January 16, 1805, Jefferson authorized Latrobe to order from Bordeaux, France, hexagon paving tiles for the floors of the Senate, House of Representatives, clerks' and committee rooms. August 31, 1805, the exterior walls were finished to the height of the cornice and the wall on which the colonnade encircling the House of Representatives was to rest was completed. At this period Jefferson determined that the windows in the roof of the hall should form panels in the ceiling coinciding with the curve of the ceiling, while Latrobe wished to put in segment windows. During the year 1806 the columns in the house were set and a large part of the cornice was in place. The eagle was on the frieze. Latrobe, August 27, 1806, says: "Not in ancient or modern sculpture is there an eagle head which is in dignity, spirit, and drawing superior to Franzoni's." [20] The office story was ready for the plastering and the walls were ready for the roof September 27, and later the roof was sheathed in. Latrobe framed the roof for ceiling lights, but at the same time put in framing for a lantern "in case the other lights failed." During the year 1807 the roof (it was found necessary to purchase the glass for the ceiling in England), plastering, and painting were completed. August 13, 1807, Latrobe was engaged in making drawings for the alterations in the north wing, which had been approved by Jefferson and by Congress in the session of 1806–1807. The model of a Statue of Liberty by Franzoni was put in place in August and the capitals around the House were being carved. [21]

Latrobe removed the portions of the roof on the north wing over the lobby and some of the valleys where the leakage had caused the timbers to rot, and replaced them with sound timbers. He first suggested grouping the chimneys and carrying them up through a cupola.

[19] Latrobe, *A Private Letter to the Individual Members of Congress on the Subject of the Public Buildings of the United States at Washington.*

[20] Latrobe to Jefferson, August 27, 1806, in Van Horne, *Papers of Benjamin Henry Latrobe,* vol. 2, 269–270.

[21] Latrobe to Jefferson, September 11 and November 18, 1808, in Padover, *Thomas Jefferson and the National Capital,* 434; 445–452.

Jefferson did not approve this scheme, but after the destruction of the interior with fire by the British a similar scheme was executed. He states that the House ceiling will be finished in September, and that much of the furniture is on hand for fitting up the room.[22]

In March, 1808, the woodwork of the south wing was complete, ready for the painting. The twenty-four Corinthian columns in the House of Representatives progressed slowly, as only two were finished, eight partly finished, and fourteen only roughed out. The trouble with stoves or furnaces in the basement and the echo are discussed by Latrobe at great length in this report. In the north wing the wooden skylight and cove over the main staircase hall was taken down and replaced by a brick cupola, 35 by 45 feet, crowned by a lantern.[23] In 1809 other portions of the wooden construction in the north wing were replaced by brick. The House first met in their new Chamber October 26, 1807. A letter from Mr. Latrobe to the Secretary of the Navy, in 1811, published in the appendix to Dunlap's History of the Rise and Progress of the Arts of Design in the United States, refers to Jefferson's positive orders, "that I should introduce Corinthian columns into the House of Representatives, and put one hundred lights of plate glass into the ceiling, contrary to my declared judgment, urgent entreaties, and representations. In other respects, however, the honor which the friendship of the great man has done me obliterates all feeling of dissatisfaction on account of those errors of a vitiated taste and an imperfect attention to the practical effect of his architectural projects."[24] Latrobe

wanted to make the capitals of the columns on the model of the Clepsydra at Athens, or the Roman Doric as exhibited in the Theater of Marcellus, at Rome [see Plates 41 and 42]. In his letter, which accompanied the drawings from which the latter plates are made, he suggests that the bells of the capitals be cast in iron in one piece, with the upper row of plain leaves, while the others may be cast separately and riveted on. Jefferson first recommended burnt-brick columns with hewn-stone capitals and bases, but insisted on the capitals being modeled from the Choragic Monument of Lysicrates. The columns were made of free-stone on this latter model. In reference to the skylight, Mr. Jefferson insisted "that the alternate panels in the alternate rows of panels into which the ceiling was divided should be of plate glass." Latrobe objected, because of cross lights, leakage, and condensation, and he was having the work done without the glass when Lenthall received the following letter from Jefferson:

WASHINGTON, D. C., *October 21, 1806.*

DEAR SIR: The skylights in the dome of the House of Representatives' Chamber were a part of the plan as settled and communicated to Mr. Latrobe; that the preparation for them has not been made and the building now to be stopped for them has been wrong; to correct that wrong now they must be immediately prepared, and that the building may be delayed as short a time as possible as many hands as possible should be employed in preparing them.

Accept my salutations and best wishes,

TH. JEFFERSON.

Mr. LENTHALL.[25]

[22] Latrobe to Jefferson, September 23, 1808, in Padover, *Thomas Jefferson and the National Capital*, 436–438.

[23] "Report of the Surveyor of the Public Buildings of the United States at Washington, March 23, 1808," in *Documentary History*, 131. See also Padover, *Thomas Jefferson and the National Capitol*, 399–413.

[24] Brown may be mistaken about the date of the letter. According to Dunlap, the letter was "written by Mr. Latrobe to Wm. Jones, Esq., then Secretary of the Navy." William Jones

of Pennsylvania was Secretary of the Navy from January 1813 to December 1814. See William Dunlap, *History of the Rise and Progress of the Arts of Design in the United States* (New York: George P. Scott and Co., Printers, 1834), vol. 2, 473–474.

[25] Jefferson to Lenthall, October 21, 1808, in Padover, *Thomas Jefferson and the National Capital*, 371–372.

The ceiling when finished was decorated by George Bridgport, a prominent decorative painter of the day. It was considered successful as a decorative element, but was open to the practical objections Latrobe had urged against it. Latrobe's letters to Lenthall throw light on the everyday troubles in the progress of the building during this period. August 12, 1805, in answer to a criticism calling attention to a lack of drawings for the cornices and entablatures, Latrobe quotes from former letters in which he has told Lenthall to follow Sir William Chambers: "Now, you have William Chambers' book and I have not. I choose rather to refer you to it than involve you in the possibilities of a mistake of mine which might have occurred by rendering the feet and inches of Stuart or Desgodetz into parts of a module; and ten minutes would suffice you, who have these things at your fingers ends, to have become master of the whole subject." [26]

Lenthall constantly urged the necessity for Latrobe's permanent residence in Washington, and Latrobe as constantly deferred the matter and simply made visits at long intervals. Latrobe lived in Newcastle, Wilmington, Philadelphia, and other towns, wherever he found it most convenient for his private work on the Delaware and Chesapeake Canal. The greater part of his supervision of the Capitol was performed through correspondence with Lenthall. March 3, 1806, Latrobe mentions the arrival from Italy of Giuseppe Franzoni and Giovanni Andrei, with the following comments: "Franzoni is a most excellent sculptor, and capable of cutting our figure of Liberty, and Andrei excels more in decoration. I wish they would seek clay for modeling and then model one of our capitals." [27] Latrobe found considerable difficulty in keeping the arched ceilings from falling. In answer to one of Lenthall's letters, December 31, 1806, he says: "I am sorry the arches have fallen, but I have had these accidents before on a larger scale, and must, therefore, grin and bear it." [28] Thornton twitted Latrobe on his vaults falling in Richmond, the Treasury, and the Capitol because of insufficient abutment or no tie-rods.

July 16, 1808, one of the larger arches in the staircase hall showed evidence of giving way, and quite a number of letters passed between Latrobe and Lenthall in reference to the subject. In September, 1808, Lenthall was killed by the falling of this arch. [29] The acoustic qualities of the new Hall of Representatives were very defective. A contemporary says that Randolph, of Roanoke, declared the Chamber was "handsome and fit for anything but the use intended." Thornton's advice was asked as to the best method of correcting the echo, and he recommended hanging curtains behind the columns. He at the same time called attention to the fact that if his plan had been strictly adhered to this echo would not have occurred. Latrobe informed Jefferson, January 28, 1808, that by direction of the committee, he had purchased curtains to be hung just back of the columns so as to enhance the beauty of the colonnade, and to experiment with their effect upon the acoustics of the Hall. J. H. B. Latrobe, the son of the architect, says that he can recall, as a recollection of his boyhood, the old Hall of Representatives: "I can see the heavy crimson drapery that hung in massive folds between the tall fluted Corinthian columns to within a short distance of their base; and I remember, or think I remember, the low gilded railing that ran

---

[26] Latrobe to Lenthall, August 9/12, 1805, in Carter, *Papers of Benjamin Henry Latrobe* (microtext edition).

[27] Latrobe to Lenthall, March 3, 1806, in Carter, *Papers of Benjamin Henry Latrobe* (microtext edition).

[28] Latrobe to Lenthall, December 31, 1806, in Van Horne, *Papers of Benjamin Henry Latrobe*, vol. 2, 346.

[29] Lenthall prematurely removed the centering of the Supreme Court vault. For an account of the accident and a discussion of the relationship between Lenthall and Latrobe, see Hamlin, *Benjamin H. Latrobe*, 260–61; 275–77.

from base to base, and over which the spectators in the gallery looked down upon the members on the floor. I seem to see even now the Speaker's chair, with its rich surroundings, and the great stone eagle with outspread wings projecting from the frieze, as though it were hovering over and protecting those below." [30]

Latrobe made an examination into the condition of the timbers and framework of the north wing of the Capitol in the latter part of 1805. He found the joists and beams much affected by dry rot and the plastering badly cracked. The floors of the room occupied by the House were sagging in the committee room No. 4 [Plate 35], and Latrobe reported, August 31, 1805, that the girder upon which the joists rested had decayed by dry rot, and he suggested placing a partition under this girder, thus dividing the room into two committee rooms.[31] This alteration was made. At a later date he says: "The tenons of the oak joists were entirely gone, and the only species of timber that has withstood decay was the pine and poplar of which the beams were made; all the white oak was seized with dry rot; almost all the plates and bond timbers which were partially buried in the walls were, on the interior, reduced to powder. Upon the damaged part of such timber the brick piers of the Senate Chamber stood. [Presumably this has reference to bond timbers let into the wall according to English methods. Both Hoban and Hadfield as superintendents would naturally have followed English precedents.] Independently of the general rottenness of the timber, the frequent alterations which the design had undergone in its original progress had so weakened the work and one of the heaviest walls had been so cut down in its lower part that whenever the timber had given way the top must have fallen in the Senate Chamber." [32] The letters which passed between Latrobe and Jefferson on this subject show the changes consisted in supporting the girder and replacing portions of the roof and addition of brick partitions instead of wooden partitions. It is easy to account for the decay through the leaky roof and dampness in the basement wall on which the girder rested.

Hadfield, who superintended the greater portion of the construction of this work, was, judging from documents on record, inefficient in the practical details of building superintendence. While a large part of the north wing was constructed under Hadfield's superintendence, the work was completed under the superintendence of James Hoban, and there is nothing to show that Hoban was not most skillful in the services he rendered to the Government. These services extended, with few intermissions, over a period of forty years. Although Latrobe altered the details in many places, it will be seen by a comparison of this portion of the building with the plans that Thornton's scheme was maintained.

Between the years 1807 and 1811 Latrobe made drawings for the exterior of the building, showing his idea for the treatment of the Dome and central portion of the Capitol [Plates 44 and 45], west entrance [Plate 46], and changes in the details of the Senate wing, among which is the Library [Plate 47], located on the west of the Senate Chamber [see Plate 35], as well as a design for a chair for the President of the Senate [Plate 48]. Latrobe made drawings for vaulting with brick the floors of the Senate wing, changing the level of the floors of the Senate Chamber [Plate 49], and providing a room for the Supreme Court in the basement beneath [Plate 50], and building the lobby [Plate 51] of the Senate in brick. In his report of December 11, 1809, Latrobe says

---

[30] John H. B. Latrobe, "The Capitol at Washington at the Beginning of the Present Century," in *An Address by John H. B. Latrobe Before the American Institute of Architects* (Baltimore: William K. Boyle, 1881).

[31] Benjamin Henry Latrobe to the President of the United States, August 31, 1805, in Carter and Jeffrey, *Benjamin Henry Latrobe Papers* (microtext edition).

[32] Latrobe to Jefferson, December 1, 1808, in Padover, *Thomas Jefferson and the National Capital,* 445–452.

PLATE 47

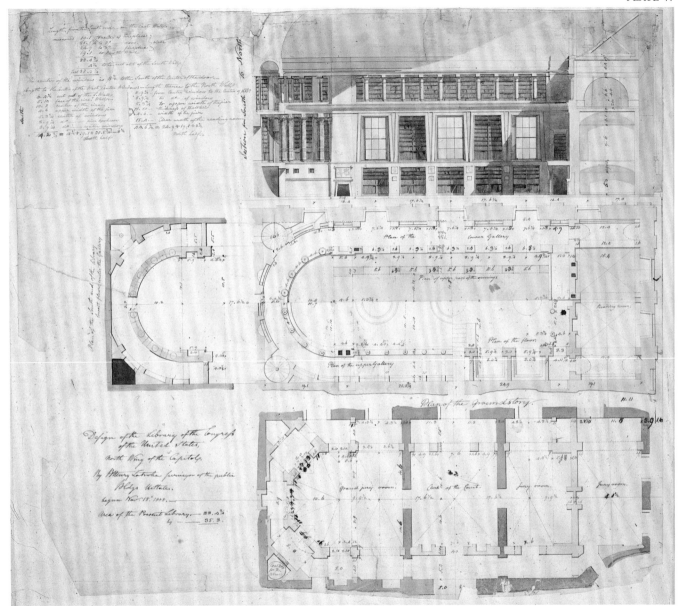

PLAN AND SECTION OF LIBRARY ON WEST OF SENATE, BY LATROBE.

An unexecuted design for the Congressional Library in the Capitol, ca. 1808.
This would have been the first Egyptian Revival style room in America. *Prints and Photographs Division, LC.*

PLATE 48

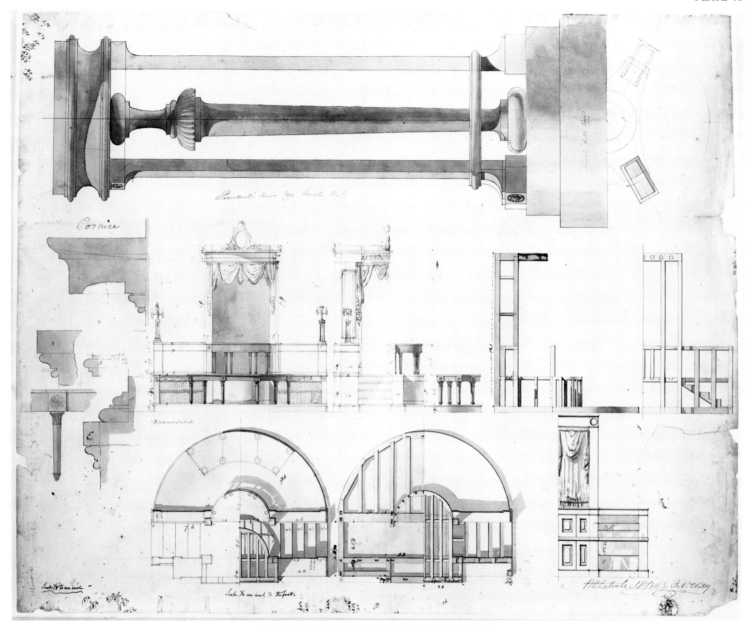

PRESIDENT'S CHAIR U.S. SENATE, LATROBE.

A drawing of furnishings for the Senate Chamber, Benjamin Henry Latrobe, 1809. *Prints and Photographs Division, LC.*

PLATE 49

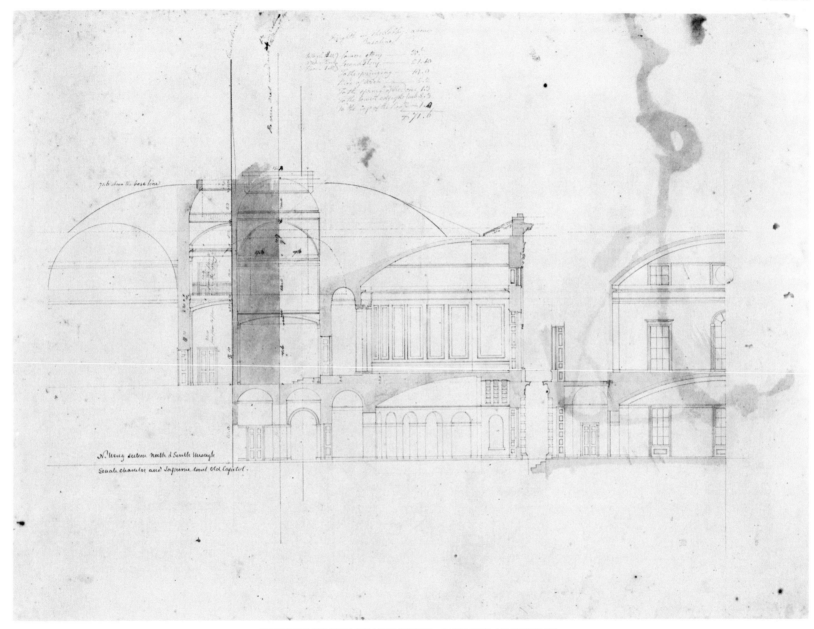

SECTION OF THE SENATE WING—LATROBE ARCHITECT.

Sections through ground and principal stories of the Capitol's north wing looking north and east, 1808. *Prints and Photographs Division, LC.*

PLATE 50

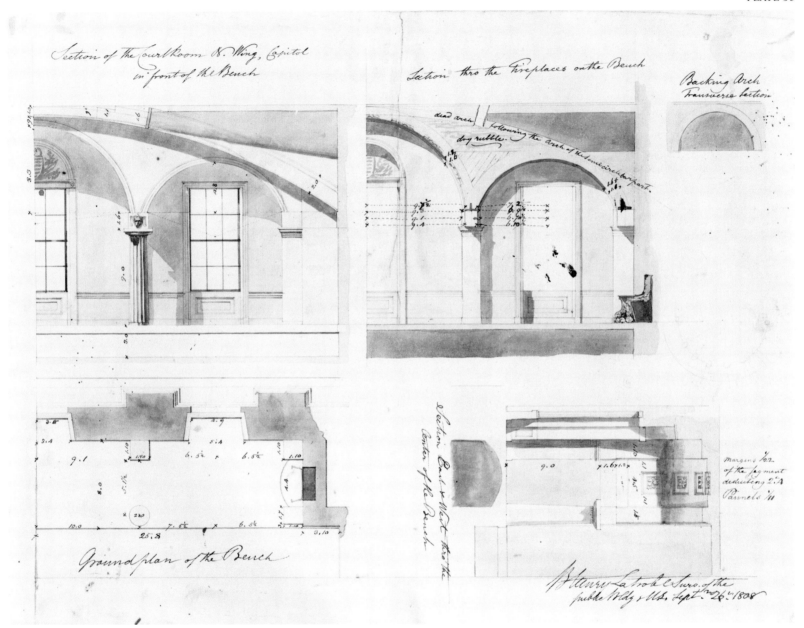

SUPREME COURT, PLAN AND SECTIONS OF BASEMENT—LATROBE ARCHITECT.

Design for Supreme Court room, 1808. *Prints and Photographs Division, LC.*

PLATE 51

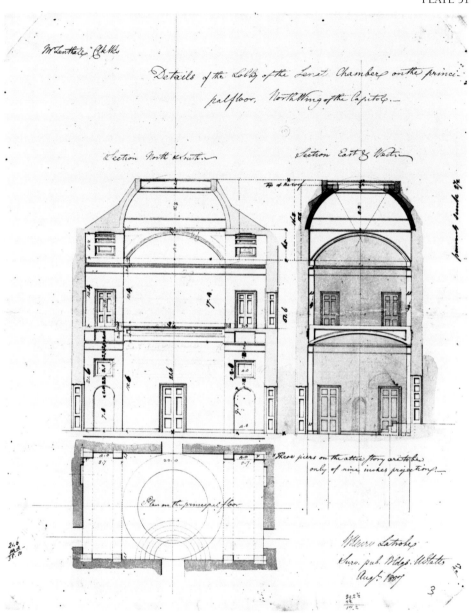

LOBBY OF OLD SENATE CHAMBER, LATROBE ARCHITECT.

Plan and sections of Senate Chamber lobby on the principal floor of the old Capitol's north wing, 1807. *Prints and Photographs Division, LC.*

PLATE 52

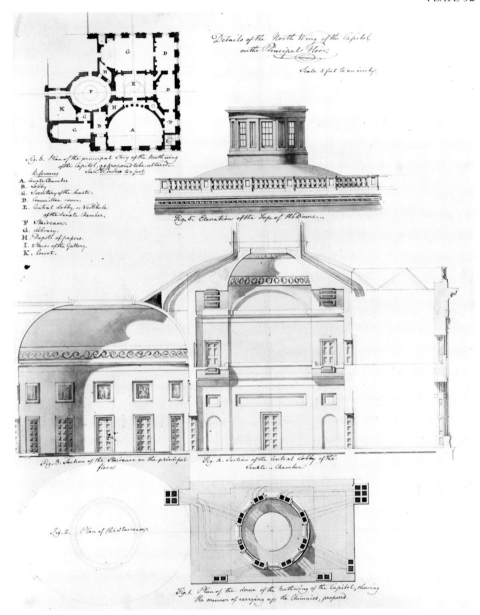

SECTION THROUGH LOBBY, NORTH WING, SHOWING GROUPING OF CHIMNEY FLUES.

Central lobby and staircase of the old north wing of the Capitol, Benjamin Henry Latrobe, 1807. *Prints and Photographs Division, LC.*

that the work of replacing the wooden construction of the old Senate Chamber, staircase, hall, and lobby was in progress. These changes consisted in raising the floor of the Senate to the principal floor, making a room for the Supreme Court beneath, and vaulting these compartments with brick. This work was completed by the year 1811. The wooden construction was retained on the west side of this wing.[33] The Senate from May 22, 1809, to January 1, 1810, occupied the room used for the Library or room first used by the House of Representatives [Plate 36] while these repairs were in operation, the House having taken up its quarters in the House wing. Plate 52 shows a scheme of Latrobe's to carry the chimneys over a broad arch and group them in a cupola over the Senate lobby; in this way no chimneys were apparent on the exterior of the building. This scheme was not carried out at this period, as the working drawing [Plate 51] shows a modification without the chimneys. After the fire a similar plan with chimneys and cupola was carried into execution.

One of the pieces of original design in the east basement vestibule, Senate wing, on which Latrobe prided himself were the capitals of the "American order," as it has been called.[34] The design of the capitals has been repeatedly attributed to Jefferson, but J. H. B. Latrobe quotes one of his father's letters which establishes the authorship. This letter, which was sent to Monticello August 28, 1809, would never have been written to Jefferson if the design had originated with the President:

"DEAR SIR: I have packed up and sent to Richmond to be forwarded to Monticello a box containing the model of the capital of the columns of the lower vestibule of the Senatorial department of the north wing of the Capitol, which is composed of maize, on a short frustum running about 4 feet from the ground. It may serve for a dial stand, and should you appropriate it for that use I will forward to you a horizontal dial in Pennsylvania marble of the proper size. These capitals during the summer session obtained me more applause from members of Congress than all the works of magnitude or difficulty that surrounded them. They christened them the 'Corn-cob capitals' whether for the sake of alliteration I can not tell, but certainly not very appropriately." [Plate 53.][35]

This capital made of freestone is now (1900) in the hall of Monticello. The central portion of the Capitol was not built for many years after Latrobe's connection with the work ceased, yet his drawings made in 1811 of the south and west elevations [Plates 44 and 45], and a perspective in a book of travels by D. B. Warden, published in Paris in 1816, made from Latrobe's drawings of that period [Plate 54], show what should be credited to him for work on the exterior central portions of the building.[36] Plate 55, from an old print published in 1808, shows the east front as it appeared at this period. The covered passageway between the wings, as the House wing was not in use, had been evidently removed. The basement, the proportions of the order, covering the principal story and attic, and the fenestration necessarily conformed with Thornton's wing. The eastern portico is a modification and enlargement of the one designed by Thornton [Plate 30]. The broad

[33] "The Report of the Surveyor of Public Buildings of the United States in the City of Washington, December 11, 1809," in *DHC,* 151–160.

[34] See Thomas U. Walter, "The Orders," *Journal of the Franklin Institute of the State of Pennsylvania and Mechanics Register,* 3rd. ser. I (1841): 194–196. Brown may be referring to the term coined by Walter for Benjamin Henry Latrobe's "American order" columns on the first floor vestibule near the Old Supreme Court Chamber.

[35] Latrobe to Jefferson, August 28, 1809, in Van Horne, *Papers of Benjamin Henry Latrobe,* vol. 2, 749–751.

[36] David Bailie Warden, *A Chorographical and Statistical Description of the District of Columbia* (Paris: 1816).

flight of steps from the principal story to the ground, east front, and the colonnade extending to the wings were additions by Latrobe, designed at this period, and finally executed [Plates 45 and 54]. It is constantly asserted in conversation and it has been reiterated again and again in written matter that the principal facade of the Capitol was made on the eastern front because the most important part of the city was expected to be built in that direction. It does not seem reasonable to suppose that the original projectors would have planned the larger portion of the city and parking system, with the President's House and other principal edifices, on the west of the Capitol, at the same time intending or thinking that the principal portion of the city would be on the east of that building. As a matter of fact, the most dignified and impressive front of the original design for the Capitol faced toward the President's House, or west. According to the original plan, the Capitol was visible from the President's House down Pennsylvania avenue. There is no doubt that the most pleasing effect was intended to be produced on this side. Thornton's design had a grand semicircular colonnade or portico in the center of the western front, with a broad sweep of circular steps running from the principal story to the ground [Plates 31 and 32], while he shows a portico on the east with a basement entrance [Plate 30]. Latrobe's drawings, made in 1811 [see Plate 54], show the west portico practically as it stands at the present time. For some reason Latrobe was allowed to change the original design so as to make the principal front on the east. It may have been because there was a tendency at this period (seventeen years after the first design was made) to build the principal residences on the hill.[37] The drawing of Latrobe shows [Plate 46] a very crude and peculiar entrance from the west. It is nothing

more nor less than a small Doric temple at the foot of the hill. The change in the western front indicated on the drawing [Plate 44] was executed, with modifications, by Bulfinch, which materially changed its appearance. The terrace temple was happily omitted. Neither Latrobe's nor Bulfinch's designs are happy alterations of the original. Latrobe modified Thornton's form of dome by increasing the height, but it was not executed on the lines he suggested. Several notes in one of Thornton's pamphlets would indicate that at one time Latrobe contemplated the omission of the central Dome and Rotunda which were features of the original design. He makes Latrobe say: "The entrance will be in the recess. It may seem contradictory when I say that he [Jefferson] directed that I should deviate as little as possible from the plan approved by General Washington," and that "he [Jefferson] approved of the present plan in which by this recess I block out the Dome [in another place he calls it the principal dome, to distinguish it from the dome which Hallet proposed placing over the circular portico], which the General [Washington] directed should be restored when left out by Mr. Hallet. [See Plates 28 and 29.] But if you consider what use this was intended for after his death was announced to a Federal Congress, you will not blame me."[38]

After Washington's death Congress proposed to place a statue of him under the Dome. This plan to omit the Dome does not appear to have been seriously considered, as it was probably opposed by those in authority. The country in 1811 was on unfriendly terms with Great Britain and a war was impending. The Congress sitting in that year ceased to make appropriations for public buildings. The Capitol at this period consisted of two wings, connected by a corridor made of rough boards. [See Plate 56.] The greater part of the foundation of the central

[37] See Glenn Brown, "The Plan of the City and Its Expected Growth," *Records of the Columbia Historical Society* 7 (1904): 114–117. Brown took part in a discussion of "Why the City Went Westward," which was published in the same volume.

[38] William Thornton, *To the Members of the House of Representatives, January 1, 1805,* vols. 3–4, William Thornton Papers, Manuscript Division, LC.

PLATE 53

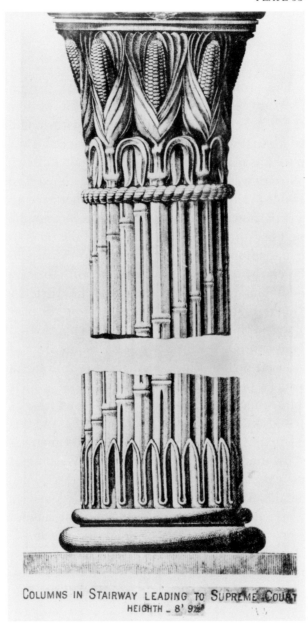

COLUMNS IN STAIRWAY LEADING TO SUPREME COURT
HEIGHTH – 8' 9½"

INDIAN CORN COLUMN AND CAPITAL, LATROBE.

Photograph of an engraving reproduced in the Capitol Extension and New Dome Photographic Books ca. 1860. *Location unknown.*

PLATE 54

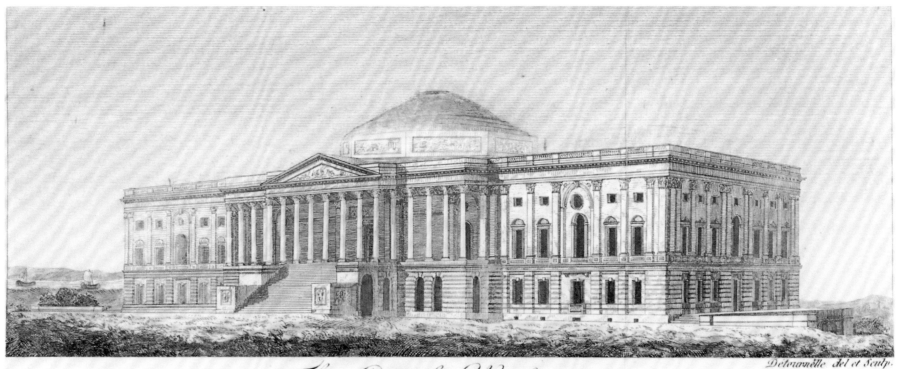

The Capitol - Washington.

Detournelle del et Sculp.

EXTERIOR VIEW FROM LATROBE'S DRAWINGS.

Engraving published in D. B. Warden, *A Chorographical and Statistical Description of the District of Columbia*, Paris, 1816.

PLATE 55

EAST VIEW 1807.

Engraved title page of William Birch's *County Seats of North America* (1808). *Rare Book and Special Collection, LC.*

PLATE 56

WEST ELEVATION, 1811 TO 1814.

Conjectural drawing of the appearance of the Capitol from 1811 to 1814 by Glenn Brown, 1900. It is now known that the connecting passage
was raised to two stories in 1810. This depiction also shows the two recesses (the six-windowed structures at the ends of the connecting passageway)
as being the same size; in fact, the south recess (on the right) was only half-built during this period. *Location unknown.*

portion was in place.[39] The surroundings of the Capitol at this time must have been truly forlorn; the grounds and apparently the sidewalks and driveways uncared for, even if they had ever been made. The chairman of the Committee on Public Buildings and Grounds wrote to Latrobe, February 8, 1811, suggesting the importance of leveling an area of 60 feet wide in front for carriages, "which ought to be 100 feet wide," and carrying a permanent platform on the south wing as far as the gallery door on the southeast corner and on the north to the north door, to facilitate an entrance to the court room. "Except for motives of economy, he would advise the extension of platforms to the western angles of both wings."[40]

J. H. B. Latrobe (son of the architect), who had a personal recollection of the city at that time, says: "Pennsylvania avenue was little better than a common country road. On either side were two rows of Lombardy poplars, between which was a ditch, often filled with stagnant water, with crossing places at the intersecting streets. Outside of the poplars was a narrow footway, on which carriages often intruded to deposit their occupants at the brick pavements on which the few houses scattered along the avenue abutted. In dry weather the avenue was all dust; in wet weather, all mud.... The Capitol itself stood on a steep declivity, clothed with old oaks and seamed with numerous gullies. Between it and the navy-yard were few buildings, here and there, over an arid common. Following the amphitheater of hills from the southeast around to the heights of Georgetown, houses few and far

between indicated the beginning of the present city. The Patent and Post Offices, in one huge, unornamental, barn-like, brick edifice, occupied the place of their successors [this was Blodgett's Hotel on E and Eighth streets], and at the other end of the avenue the White House had become a conspicuous object, with the adjacent public offices. Still following the amphitheater around, the eye caught a glimpse of Alexandria and rested upon the broad expanse of water where the Eastern Branch joined the Potomac."[41]

In the month of August, 1814, the British captured Washington, and on August 24 the Capitol and White House were burned. The British intended the complete destruction of these buildings. Happily their efforts were only partially successful. The greater part of the exterior and the principal divisions of the interior resisted their efforts. The soldiers piled the interior of the Senate and House Chambers, as well as the wooden corridor between the wings, with inflammable material and made a great blaze. The wooden floors and roofs were destroyed. The stone columns in the House of Representatives and in the Senate were so badly damaged that it was necessary to take them down. The cornice and balustrade on the exterior were more or less damaged. In this way the interior of the south wing was practically destroyed, as well as the interior of the west side of the Senate wing.[42] The brick vaults over the Senate, court room, and the halls in the north wing resisted the action of the fire. Andrei, one of the sculptors on the Capitol when the work stopped, made a very interesting drawing, showing the effect of the fire on the sandstone columns in the Hall of Representatives. A reproduction can not do justice to the delicacy of the original, which is in pencil,

---

[39] Brown is in error. The central foundation was not put in place until Bulfinch took charge of the work in 1818.

[40] The letter Brown cites has not been identified. There was no Committee on Public Buildings and Grounds in 1811. Brown may be referring to the House Select Committee on the Expenditure of Monies appropriated for the Capitol, which existed from January 19 to February 6, 1811. This committee was chaired by Joseph Lewis, Jr. (1772–1834), a Federalist representative from Virginia.

[41] John H. B. Latrobe, "The Capitol at Washington at the Beginning of the Present Century." *An Address by John H. B. Latrobe Before the American Institute of Architects* (Baltimore: William K. Boyle, 1881).

[42] The first-floor offices, the small House rotunda, and the octagonal vestibule all survived the fire. See "Burning of the Capitol," RG 40, Subject Files, Curator's Office, AOC.

emphasized wherever necessary by a delicate wash. The workmen, in repairing or pulling down, were afraid to work until the most dangerous portions of this part of the building were shored up. This drawing indicates the method adopted for shoring, as well as the damage done to the stonework [Plate 57]. At this period Mr. Chittenden, a miniature painter, was in Washington, and he made interesting colored drawings of both the Capitol and President's House, showing the damage caused by the fire on the exterior of the buildings. Plate 58 shows a reproduction of this drawing.

Latrobe gives the following graphic description of the effect of the fire: "In the Hall of Representatives the devastation has been dreadful. There was no want of materials for the conflagration, for when the number of members of Congress was increased the old platform was left in its place and another raised over it, giving an additional quantity of dry and loose timber. All the stages and seats of the galleries were of timber and yellow pine. The mahogany desks, tables, and chairs were in their places. At first rockets were fired through the roof, but they did not set fire to it. They sent men on it, but it was covered with sheet iron. At last they made a great pile in the center of the room of the furniture and, retiring, set fire to a quantity of rocket stuff in the middle. The whole was soon in a blaze, and so intense was the flame that the glass of the lights was melted, and I have now lumps weighing many pounds run into a mass. The stone is, like most freestone, unable to resist the force of flame, and I believe no known material would have been able to resist so sudden and intense a heat. The exterior of the columns and entablature scaled off, and not a vestige of sculpture or fluting remained." [43] [Plate 57.]

The damage done by the fire was not investigated until the war with Great Britain was at an end.[44] The burning of the Capitol left Congress and the Supreme Court no suitable place for the transaction of business. The Thirteenth Congress met September 19, 1814, in a building erected for a hotel on the corner of Eighth and E streets (the site of the United States Post-Office) by Samuel Blodgett, which in 1814 was used as the Government Patent and Post Office. This building was saved by Dr. William Thornton's exertions, he having been able to persuade the British officers, Ross and Cockburn, that science would sustain a serious loss by the destruction of the patent models and records, which were at this time in his charge. This was the only available building, but the accommodation it afforded was inadequate. The prominent citizens of the District, for fear that Congress might leave the city, organized a stock company known as the "Capitol Hotel Company," to erect a building for the temporary accommodation of Congress. This structure was commenced July 4, 1815, and occupied by Congress from December, 1815, to 1819, while the Capitol was being rebuilt. This building, which is on the corner of A and First streets northeast, has since that period been called the "Old Capitol." It again became noted during the civil war as a prison for Southern sympathizers.[45]

After the fire it was doubtful for some time whether the Federal buildings would be repaired or be rebuilt on some other site or in another city. Many Congressmen thought this a favorable time to remove the seat of government to some city in which they and their constituents were personally interested. Others proposed a change of

[43] Latrobe's description of the fire in the Hall of Representatives is found in a letter to Jefferson, July 12, 1815, in Van Horne, *Papers of Benjamin Henry Latrobe*, vol. 3, 670–671.

[44] Brown may be referring to Latrobe's professional survey report in 1815. See "Burning of the Capitol," Curator's Office, AOC.

[45] For a historical photograph and sketch of this once famous Washington landmark, see James Goode, *Capital Losses: A Cultural History of Washington's Destroyed Buildings* (Washington: Smithsonian Institution Press, 1979), 290–292. The structure, razed in the nineteenth century, was replaced by a block of rowhouses on the site of the Supreme Court Building.

PLATE 57

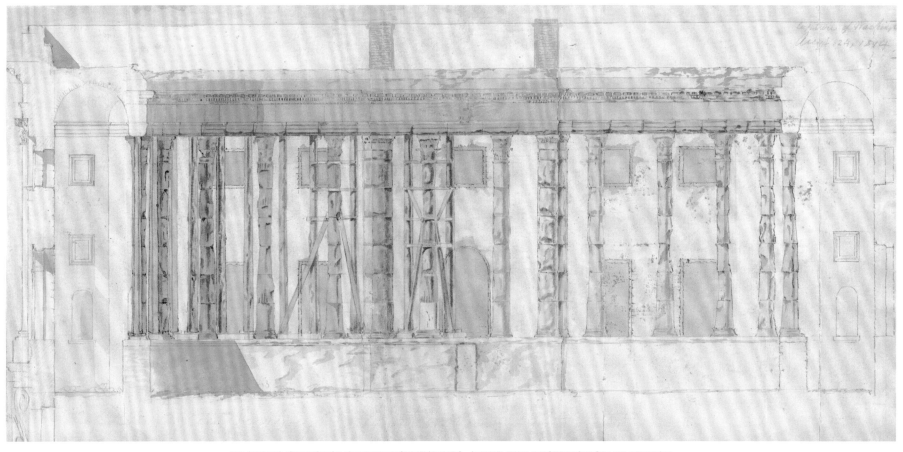

DRAWING OF HOUSE OF REPRESENTATIVES, AFTER THE DESTRUCTION BY BRITISH.

Drawing attributed to Giovanni Andrei after the 1814 fire.

PLATE 58

EXTERIOR AFTER THE FIRE, FROM DRAWING OF CHITTENDEN 1814.

George Munger, Watercolor, 1814. *Kiplinger Washington Collection.*

site in Washington for both the Capitol and the President's House. A committee was appointed by Congress to consider these questions, and on November 21, 1814, this committee reported in favor of repairing the old buildings, because it would be cheaper, while to remove them would be an injustice to the property owners who had bought lots in the vicinity of these buildings with the idea of their being permanently located.[46] February 15, 1815, Congress authorized the President (Madison) to borrow $500,000 to rebuild the public buildings. On the same date Madison appointed three commissioners, John P. Van Ness, T. Ringgold, and Richard Bland Lee, at a salary of $1,600 each, to superintend their restoration.[47] March 14, 1815, B. H. Latrobe was requested to call on the new commissioners in reference to retaining the place as principal architectural adviser, which he had held when the work stopped in 1811. When the work ceased on the Capitol Latrobe had gone to Pittsburg, where he was engaged in introducing steamboats on Western rivers, and it is a little strange that Thornton had entered into the same enterprise as early as 1789, when steamboats were not in a sufficiently advanced state for him to make the venture successful. Latrobe's private enterprise, however, prevented his going to Washington to answer the summons of the commissioners as quickly as they thought he should, and on March 31 they wrote a strong protest against further delay.[48] Latrobe arrived in Washington April 20, 1815, and was

appointed to undertake the repairs of the Capitol. On May 16 the commissioners wrote to President Madison: "We have employed Mr. Latrobe as architect or surveyor of the Capitol." In the same letter they state that Latrobe had made a preliminary report on the Capitol, and thought the south wing could be completed before 1816. This letter contains the first suggestion for changing the form of the House of Representatives. A semicircular room, with a segment slightly greater than a semicircle, with committee rooms beneath the galleries, was recommended by the commissioners, and plans on that form were submitted to President Madison for his approval.

After a preliminary investigation Latrobe returned to Pittsburg for six weeks, so as to settle his private enterprises and to bring his family to Washington.

June 29, 1815, Latrobe was requested by the committee in charge to furnish Congress with an accurate statement concerning the labor and materials needed to finish the House of Representatives by December, 1816. This and other committees were doomed to much disappointment, as this portion of the building was not finished for many years.

August 8, 1815, Andrei was sent to Italy, with orders to purchase twenty-four Corinthian capitals for the House of Representatives and four Ionic capitals for columns, with two pilaster capitals for the Senate Chamber, for all of which Latrobe furnished the necessary drawings. These capitals were all to be of the best statuary marble. Andrei was promised an increase in his salary to $1,500 per annum when he returned to the United States. He was also authorized to engage a sculptor who was proficient in making or modeling figures, and to make arrangements to bring over the sculptor's family. It was about this period (August 26, 1815) that the first mention is made of the columns used in the present Statuary Hall. It was suggested that variegated marble from Frederick County, Md., should be used. In December, 1815, Latrobe made a plat for the grounds surrounding the Capitol, introducing the

---

[46] The Select Committee on Rebuilding the Public Buildings in the City of Washington Operated from October 20 to November 21, 1814. "Burning of the Capitol," Curator's Office, AOC.

[47] An Act Making Appropriations for Repairing or Rebuilding the Public Buildings within the City of Washington. [*United States Statutes at Large*, vol. 3, 205.] In *DHC*, 185.

[48] Commissioners of the Public Buildings to Latrobe, March 14, 1815, and Protest from the Commissioners of Public Buildings to Latrobe, March 31, 1815, in Van Horne, *Papers of Benjamin Henry Latrobe*, vol. 2, 634 and 635, n. 3.

landscape effects which he thought desirable in connection with the building, and showing his proposed disposition of the Tiber Creek and the canal, both of which ran near the Capitol [Plate 59].

In the latter part of December, 1815, Latrobe made a request for an architectural assistant, to be paid by the Government. On December 29 the commissioners replied: "It never having been mentioned or even alluded to in the interviews we have had with you, we fairly assumed that it was not anticipated," and consequently they declined to appoint an assistant, but increased Latrobe's salary $500, making it $2,500 per annum.[49]

From November, 1815, until Latrobe severed his connection with the Capitol the records show many protests from the commissioners against the slow progress of the work and against his giving too much attention to private matters, for Latrobe had many private interests and enterprises which he was endeavoring to manage contemporaneously with his work on the Capitol. Both he and the commissioners were fretting, the first because he felt under too much restraint, and the latter because Latrobe gave, according to their ideas, too little time and attention to the public work. One of the principal causes of delay was the difficulty found in obtaining the marble columns from the Potomac, and Latrobe suggested sandstone in the place of marble. In a letter of February 26, 1816, the commissioners objected to this change.[50]

Latrobe's plans for the reconstruction of the House wing made at this period are in the possession of the Congressional Library, selections from which are shown in Plates 60 to 64. The drawings show a complete change in the form, design, and details of the interior of this wing of the Capitol. Plate 62 shows Latrobe's idea of a masonry vault, the erection of which Madison overruled. Plate 63 shows a framing

plan of the roof as it was finally constructed. Judging from the plan, elevation [Plate 61], and details [Plate 64], this wing was completed strictly according to Latrobe's drawings. Plate 65 shows Latrobe's drawing for the central portion of the west front.

April 24, 1816, Congress abolished the commission of three who had been put in charge of Government buildings, and authorized the appointment of a single commissioner at a salary of $2,000 per annum, Samuel Lane, of Virginia, being appointed to fill this position.[51] Congress by the same act gave President Madison power to make any changes that he might think proper in the plans of the Government buildings.

At this period Hoban, in charge of the President's House, and Latrobe, in charge of the Capitol, were requested to give their opinion as to the best material for covering the public buildings. Latrobe named, placing them in the order he considered most meritorious, marble, freestone, zinc, iron, copper. Hoban placed copper first. Madison agreed with Hoban, and copper was selected as the covering. The whole interior of the west side of the north wing having been constructed of timber, and the old shingle roof being over the greater part of the wing, this section of the building was completely destroyed. The columns in the Senate Chamber were burned to lime and everything of freestone was cracked, but the brick dome of the Senate Chamber was entire, while the vaults in the lobby, stairway hall, and Supreme Court were more or less damaged. Latrobe's report to Congress, November, 1816, gives a clear idea of the state of the building at this period.[52] In the south wing no progress had been made on the interior, because of the

---

[49] Commissioners to Latrobe, December 29, 1815, DCC, NARA.

[50] Commissioners to Latrobe, February 26, 1816, DCC, NARA.

[51] See "Act to . . . Abolish the Office of Commissioners of the Public Buildings, and of Superintendent, and for the Appointment of One Commissioner for the Public Buildings." [*United States Statutes at Large*, vol. 3, 325]. In *DHC*, 189. The act was approved on April 29, 1816, not on April 24.

[52] "Report on the United States Capitol," November 28, 1816, reprinted in Van Horne, *Papers of Benjamin Henry Latrobe*, vol. 3, 831–835.

PLATE 59

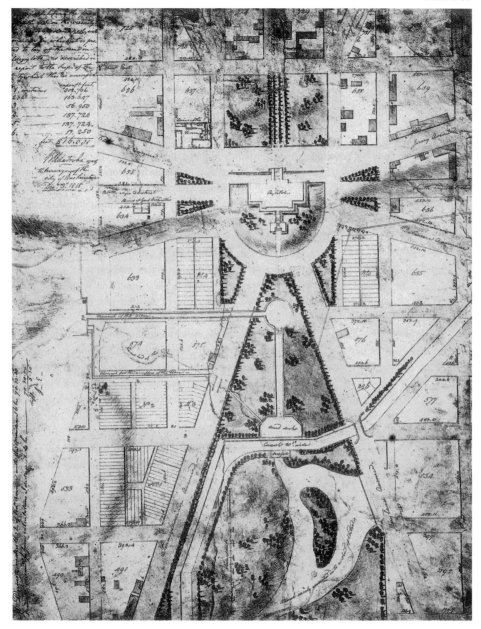

PLAT OF GROUNDS 1815.

Map of grounds and city surrounding the Capitol, Benjamin Henry Latrobe. *Geography and Map Division, LC.*

PLATE 60

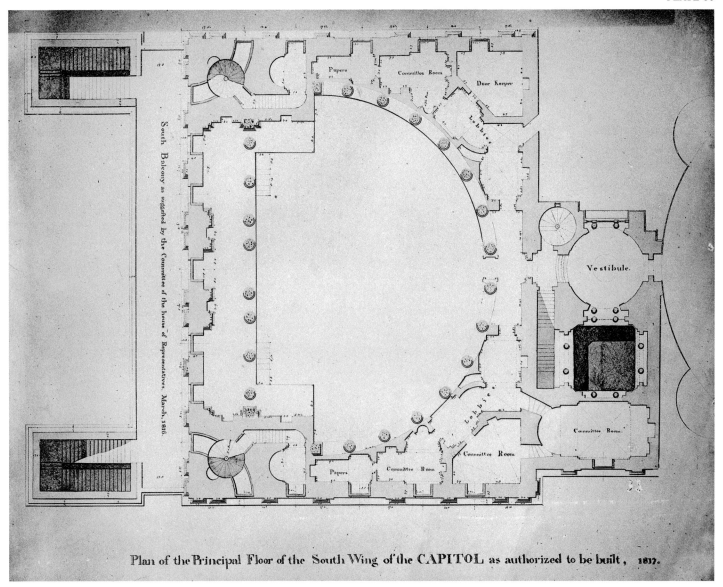

Plan of the Principal Floor of the South Wing of the CAPITOL as authorized to be built, 1817.

PLAN OF HOUSE OF REPRESENTATIVES AFTER THE FIRE, LATROBE.

Principal floor plan of the south wing of the Capitol, as reconstructed according to the design of Benjamin Henry Latrobe. Drawn by Washington Blanchard, June 1817. *Prints and Photographs Division, LC.*

PLATE 61

COLONNADE, HOUSE OF REPRESENTATIVES AFTER THE FIRE, LATROBE.

Drawing of the proposed reconstruction of the Hall of the House of Representatives, 1815. *Prints and Photographs Division, LC.*

PLATE 62

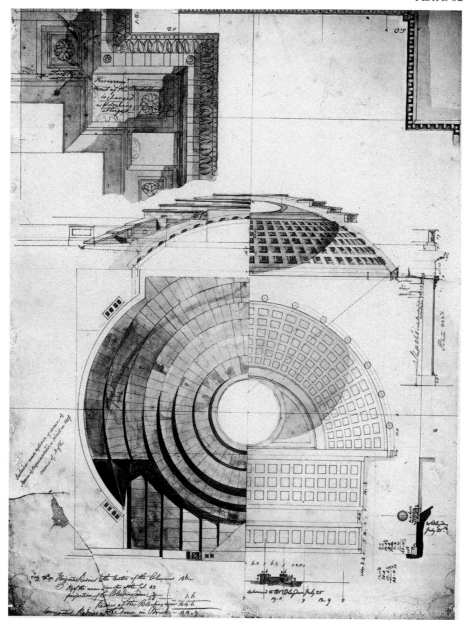

DRAWING FOR A MASONRY DOME OVER HOUSE OF REPRESENTATIVES, LATROBE.

Drawing of an unexecuted masonry dome, ca. 1817. *Prints and Photographs Division, LC.*

PLATE 63

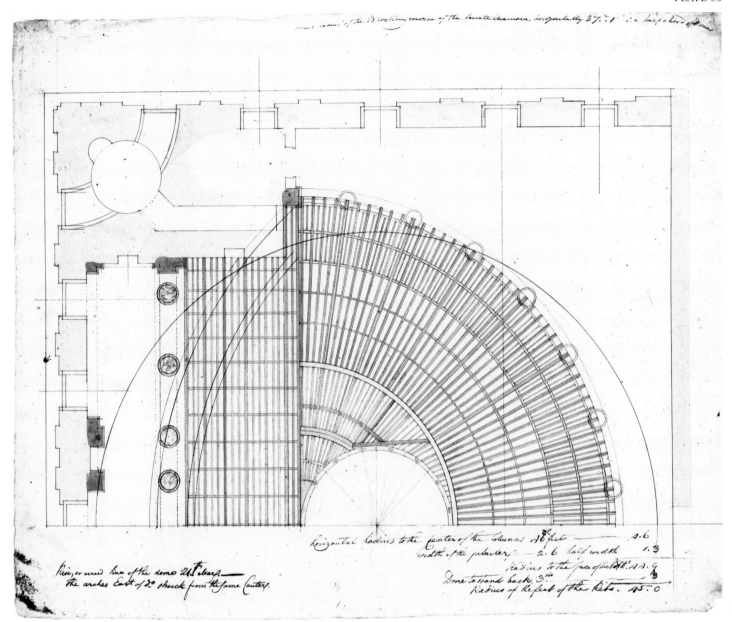

mean radius of the 33 cocking course of the lunate chamber, horizontally 37..1 : i.e. half chord of dome

Horizontal Radius to the center of the Columns 48 feet ——— 2.6
width of the pilaster — 2.6 half width 1.3
Radius to the face of the Pilr. 4 1. 9
Dome to stand back. 3 in.
Radius of the feet of the Ribs. 45. 0

Rise, or versed line of the dome 21. clear.
The arches East of D° struck from the same Centers.

FRAMING PLAN WOODEN DOME, OLD HOUSE OF REPRESENTATIVES.

Latrobe's drawing for the framing, ca. 1817. *Prints and Photographs Division, LC.*

PLATE 64

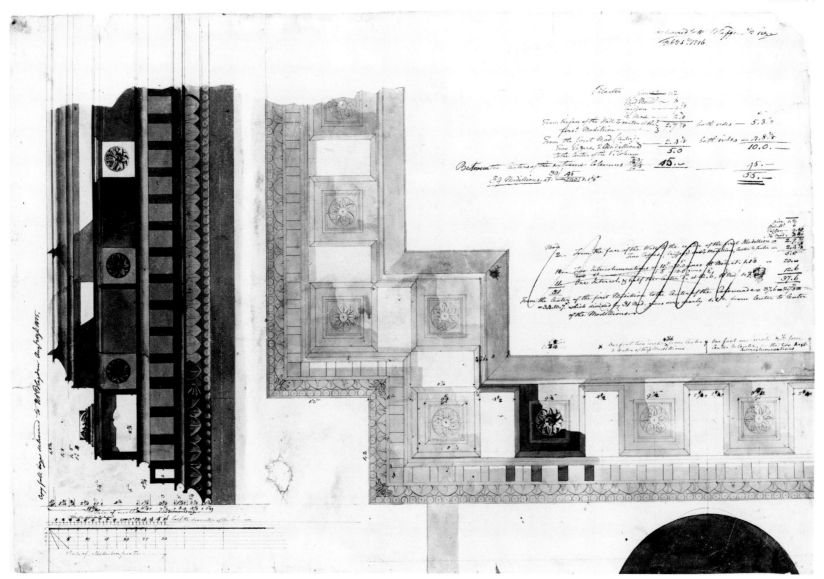

DETAILS OF CORNICE, OLD HOUSE OF REPRESENTATIVES.

Latrobe's drawing as executed, 1815. *Prints and Photographs Division, LC.*

PLATE 65

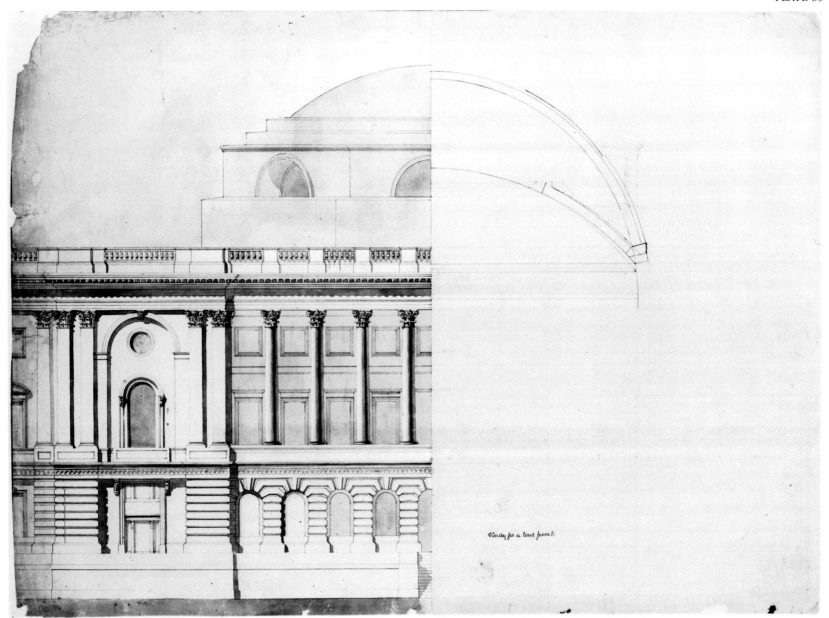

HALF OF CENTRAL PORTION WEST FRONT, LATROBE.
Study drawing, 1810–11. *Prints and Photographs Division, LC.*

PLATE 66

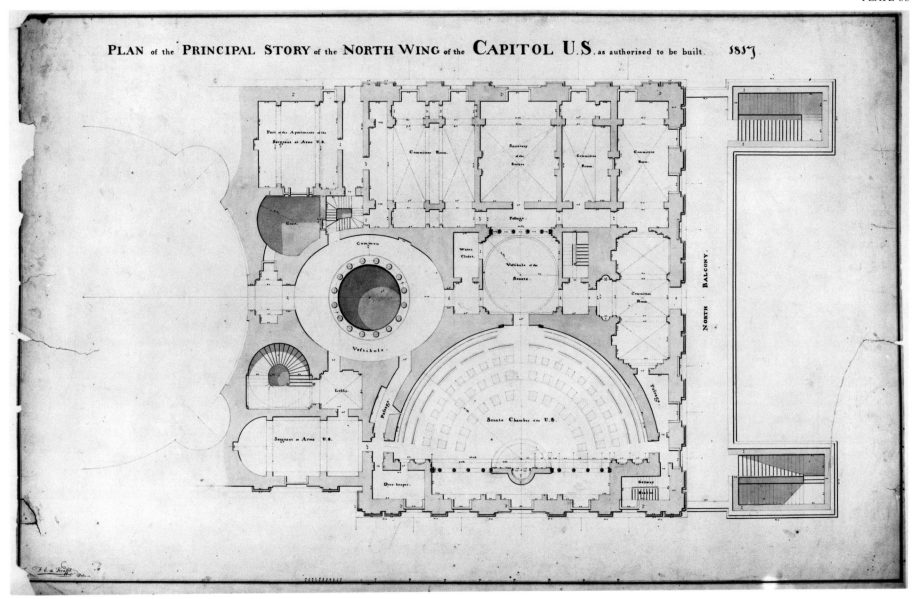

PLAN OF SENATE WING AFTER FIRE, LATROBE.

Plan for the reconstruction of the second story of the Senate wing, 1817. F. C. DeKrafft, delineator. *Prints and Photographs Division, LC.*

PLATE 67

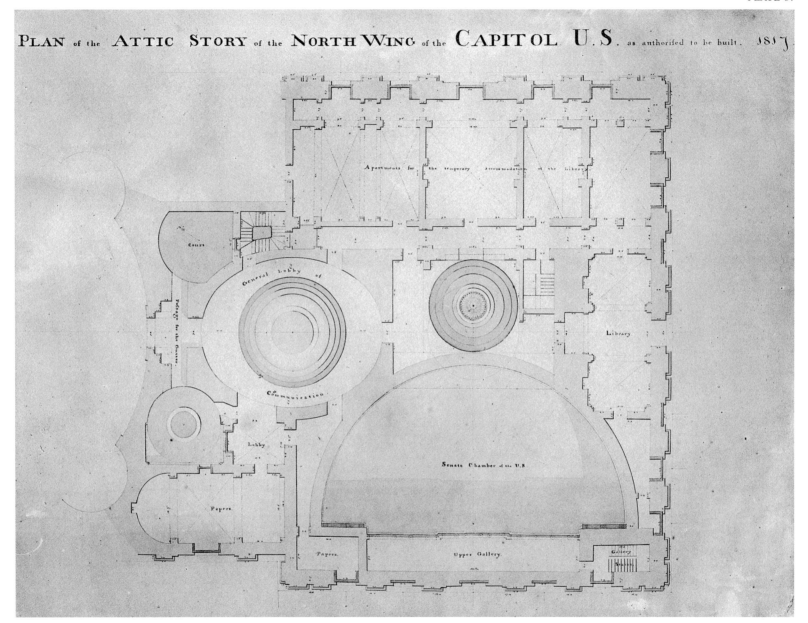

ATTIC PLAN NORTH WING 1817—LATROBE.

Plan for the attic story of the Senate wing. F. C. DeKrafft, delineator. *Prints and Photographs Division, LC.*

PLATE 68

SMALL ROTUNDA, SENATE WING, LATROBE.

Ca. 1815. *Prints and Photographs Division, LC.*

PLATE 69

TOBACCO CAPITAL, LATROBE.

Photograph of an engraving included in the Capitol Extension and New Dome Photographic Books, ca. 1860. *Location unknown.*

difficulty in getting stone, but externally all damage done by the fire had been repaired. Just before retiring, the three commissioners adopted alterations in the north wing suggested by Latrobe. One of the alterations consisted in the enlargement of the Senate wing so that it would encroach upon the central space. It will be remembered that this was one of Latrobe's suggestions against which Thornton protested early in 1800. August 22, 1816, President James Madison recorded his objection to this part of the alteration. The Senate and President finally agreed upon an enlargement of the Senate Chamber itself without enlarging the wing so as to interfere with the central space. September 19, 1816, Samuel Lane, the commissioner of public buildings, directed Latrobe to proceed with an enlargement of the Senate Chamber. It will be remembered that this was a point Thornton advocated with persistence at the beginning of the work.

Latrobe says in a report, 1816: "In pursuance of the order, it was necessary to take down the vaults which had been constructed on the west of the house [Senate wing] and raise them to the principal floor.... The ruinous state of the building further required that the dome of the center vestibule, the colonnade, and all the vaulting of the court room and the dome of the great stairs, with all the walls as far as they were injured, should be taken down. The enlargement of the Senate Chamber required the great dome of the apartment and its semicircular wall to be entirely removed, and the arches and walls of the two committee rooms and the lobby adjoining the Chamber could also be demolished."[53] Madison took an active interest in the construction of the Capitol and did not hesitate to express his opinion on matters of

design and construction. August 29 he objected to Mr. Latrobe's idea of a brick dome over the Senate Chamber, because the former arch had pressed out the walls 3½ inches. Madison was justified in such opposition by the trouble Latrobe had previously had with similar but much smaller arches. Mr. George Blagden also felt certain that the walls would not hold such an arch. All interior work in the Senate wing (except the roof and ceiling of Senate Chamber) was ordered replaced by solid masonry. Latrobe's drawings for the north wing [Plates 66 to 69] show that the interior of the wing of the building was reconstructed from them on the lines of Thornton's original plan. The plans [Plates 66 and 67] show this portion of the building as it stands to-day with very slight alteration. Plate 68 is a section through the light shaft or small rotunda where Thornton placed the principal staircase in the hall of the Senate wing. It is on these columns that Latrobe introduced his tobacco-plant capitals [Plate 69]. In a letter of February 16, 1817, explaining the reasons for delay on the work and the increased cost of the undertaking, Latrobe describes the following alterations: "Very extensive improvements of the Senate Chamber were suggested by the Senate and ordered carried out by the President [Madison]. To carry out the order it was not only necessary to take down work which had been constructed the preceding season, but the enlargement of the Senate Chamber required that the great dome of that apartment and its semicircular wall should be taken down, and that the arches and walls of the committee rooms and the lobby adjoining the Chamber should be entirely abolished, and much additional strength and solidity given to the whole structure. This produced the loss of one season's work on the north wing and took another season in undoing what had already been done."[54] The Capitol had been heated by stoves and furnaces, and

[53] United States Congress, House Committee on the Public Buildings, "City of Washington: Progress Made in Rebuilding the Public Edifices," in *American State Papers: Miscellaneous*, vol. 2, 426–438. Brown quotes Latrobe's report of November 28, 1816, describing the Capitol's north and south wings after the fire of 1814 and reporting the progress on their reconstruction. Van Horne, *Papers of Benjamin Henry Latrobe*, vol. 3, 834.

[54] Commissioner Samuel Lane to Samuel Condict, chair of the Committee on Expenditures on Public Buildings, February 15, 1817, published in *DHC*, 196. Brown misdated the letter and misidentified its author.

there are several letters inquiring into the merits of different kinds of stoves. It was April 2, 1817, before the order was issued that the domes over both the House of Representatives and the Senate Chamber of the Capitol should be of wood.

April 5 President Madison authorized the employment of two skilled draftsmen to assist Latrobe, with the hope that in this way the work would progress more rapidly.[55]

During the spring and summer the work progressed slowly, according to the opinion of Congress and other interested parties. From early in April until the fall Latrobe made a weekly report to President Madison, showing the number of men at work at the end of each week. The number employed varied from ninety to a hundred. The columns of Brescia, secured from quarries on the Potomac in Loudoun County, Va., and Montgomery County, Md., in the House of Representatives, now Statuary Hall, seem to have given Latrobe considerable trouble, because of the difficulty he found in getting them quarried and cut. September 24, 1817, the north wing was still without its roof covering, the entablature was not complete for the House of Representatives, the columns in the Senate were not up, and the doors and woodwork were still unordered. Samuel Lane, on October 31, 1817, made Capt. Peter Lenox clerk of works of the Capitol. Lenox was transferred from a similar position at the President's House, and Charles Davis, who occupied the position at this time on the Capitol, was sent to the President's House. Latrobe, in a letter to Lenthall, 1806, stated that Thomas Jefferson favored Lenox's appointment to this position in 1803, but allowed Latrobe to make his own selection at that time.

Latrobe protested against the removal of Davis, but Commissioner Lane insisted, as he thought for the sake of expediency and economy the change was necessary. He accuses Latrobe of often recommending men in every way unsuitable for the work, and he transferred Captain Lenox from the Executive Mansion to the Capitol "from a conviction of his abilities in every branch of the business which he would have to perform, and the proof he has lately furnished of activity and success in the prosecution of the work at the President's House. My anxious desire is to accelerate, not retard, the work at the Capitol. Knowing my duties, I shall scrupulously perform them. All I wish of you is attention to your own."[56] The appointment of Peter Lenox against the protest of Latrobe was the cause of Latrobe's sending in his resignation to President Madison, who does not seem to have raised any objection to this action, but referred it to the commissioner, through whom it should have come.[57]

The commissioner answered as follows:

NOVEMBER 24, 1817.

B. H. LATROBE.

SIR: Having seen your letter to the President of the United States, resigning the appointment of Architect of the Capitol, I have to inform you that your resignation is accepted and to request that you will deliver to Captain Lenox all the books, plans, instruments, etc., belonging to the public in your possession.

Yours,   SAMUEL LANE,
          Commissioner of Public Buildings.[58]

Latrobe had nothing further to do with the supervision of the Capitol, although the larger portion of his designs in reference to

---

[55] James Monroe to Samuel Lane, April 4, 1817, in *DHC*, 198–199. Brown mistakenly identified Madison as the correspondent.

[56] Samuel Lane to Latrobe, October 31, 1817, in Van Horne, *Papers of Benjamin Henry Latrobe,* vol. 3, 962–963.

[57] James Monroe became President in March 1817. Brown often confused Madison with Monroe in this chapter.

[58] Samuel Lane to Benjamin Henry Latrobe, November 24, 1817, in Carter and Jeffrey, *Papers of Benjamin Henry Latrobe* (microtext edition).

interior work were carried out with but little change. Latrobe left his personal impress on the work as a designer as well as a superintendent. He made the original design for the reconstruction of the interior of the south wing or old Hall of Representatives and the Senate Chamber. He changed the western front of the central building and modified the portico on the east, as I have previously mentioned [Plates 45, 54, and 70].

He added the domical roof with cupolas over each wing. Plate 70 gives a plan of the principal floor of the building as he proposed (1817) to have it completed.

William Strickland and Robert Mills, both of whom afterwards became prominent architects, worked on the Capitol as draftsmen for Latrobe.

CHAPTER V

THE WORK OF CHARLES BULFINCH, ARCHITECT

THE resignation of Latrobe placed the position of Architect of the Capitol at the disposal of the Commissioner of Public Buildings and Grounds.[1] President Monroe, who was now in the White House, became acquainted with Charles Bulfinch when on a visit to Boston, July, 1817. On this occasion Bulfinch was chairman of selectmen, as well as of the reception committee which received the President.

Miss Ellen S. Bulfinch, in the life of her grandfather, Charles Bulfinch, which was recently published, gives several letters and other data, from which I have taken extracts throwing light upon this period in the history of the Capitol.

Bulfinch, in his brief manuscript autobiography, says:

"About November, 1817, following the visit of the President, I received a letter from William Lee, esq., one of the auditors at Washington, and in the confidence of the President, stating the probability of the removal of Mr. Latrobe, the Architect of the Capitol, and proposing that I should apply for the place. I declined making any application that might lead to Mr. Latrobe's removal, but before the end of the year disagreements between him and the commissioner became so serious that he determined to resign, and his resignation was immediately accepted. On receiving information of this in another letter from Mr. Lee I made regular application through J. Q. A. [John Quincy Adams], Secretary of State, and by return of post received notice from him of my

appointment, with a salary of $2,500 and expenses paid of removal of family and furniture."[2]

The letter of Mr. William Lee, referred to by Bulfinch, shows that the friction between Latrobe, the commissioner, and the President was at the point of rupture before September, 1817. He says: "I am sorry for Latrobe, who is an amiable man, possesses genius and a large family, but in addition to the President not being satisfied with him, there is an unaccountable and I think unjust prejudice against him by many members of the Government, Senate, and Congress." Bulfinch says that although he would be pleased to have the situation, "I have always endeavored to avoid unpleasant competition with others, that by opposing their interests would excite enmity and ill will. I should much regret being the instrument of depriving a man of undoubted talents of employment which places him at the head of the profession."[3] The President on his return appointed a commission, consisting of General Mason, Mr. Graham, and Colonel Bomford, to examine and report upon the state of the Capitol.

Mr. Lee wrote to Bulfinch that either Commissioner Lane or Latrobe must go out, and he thought the commissioner would be retained, as he had more friends than the architect. The three commissioners reported in favor of retaining Latrobe. William Lee still urged Bulfinch to apply for the place, telling him that with the assistance of his friends he would

---

[1] For an earlier version of this chapter, see Glenn Brown, "History of the United States Capitol," *American Architect and Building News* 54 (October 3, 1896): 3–6; (October 24, 1896): 27–29.

[2] See Ellen Susan Bulfinch, ed., *The Life and Letters of Charles Bulfinch, Architect, with Other Family Papers* (Boston: Houghton, Mifflin and Company, 1896), 199–200. The William Lee letter to which Bulfinch refers was dated September 14, 1817.

[3] Charles Bulfinch to William Lee, November 15, 1817, in Bulfinch, *Life and Letters of Charles Bulfinch*, 200–201.

PLATE 70

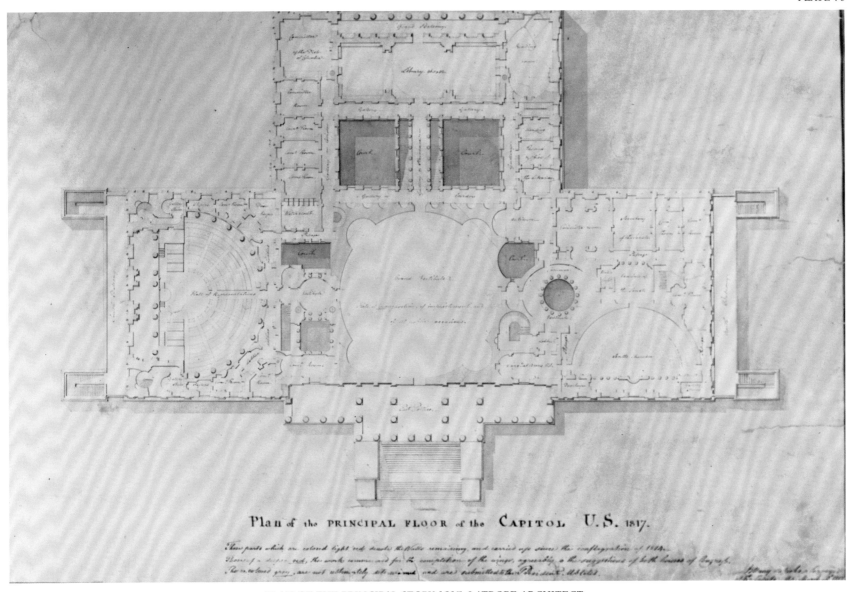

PLAN OF THE PRINCIPAL STORY 1817, LATROBE ARCHITECT.

Proposed plan for the second floor of the Capitol showing Latrobe's design for the Central Building, 1817. *Prints and Photographs Division, LC.*

157

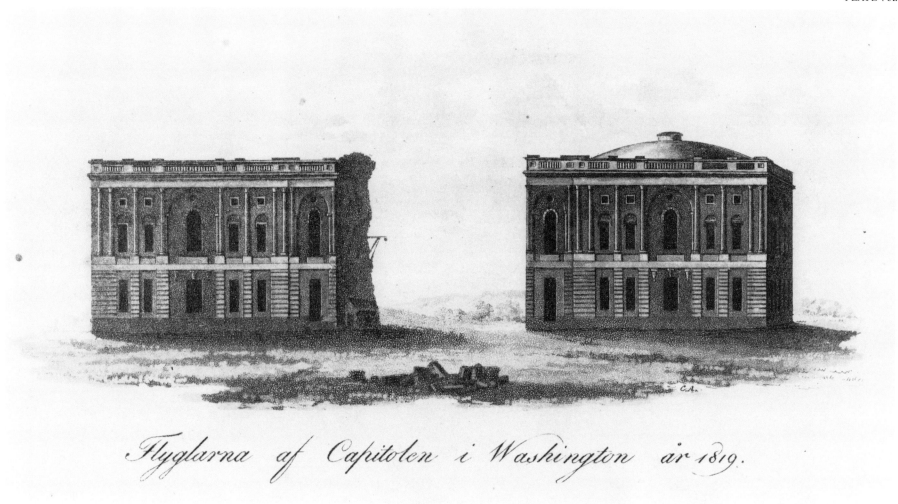

Flyglarna af Capitolen i Washington år 1819.

WEST VIEW OF BUILDING 1818.

Brown incorrectly identifies a view of the east front by Klinckowstrom, published in 1824. *Prints and Photographs Division, LC.*

undoubtedly be appointed. But after the report in favor of Latrobe, Bulfinch declined to make an effort, writing a letter to that effect November 15.[4] Latrobe's resignation, two days later, left the position open. Bulfinch's friends, William Lee, H. G. Otis, and J. Q. Adams, urged the appointment of Bulfinch. Monroe said to Mr. Otis, "Sir, we are looking to him [Bulfinch], but Mr. Latrobe is a great loss and it will require two persons to supply his place, and we think also of a Mr. Macomb [architect of the city hall, New York]."[5] Several letters passed between Bulfinch and his friends bearing upon the salary, expenses, and climate of Washington.

He was tendered the position at $2,500 per annum, and in addition to his salary and traveling expenses he was allowed $500 a year for a draftsman. Through John Quincy Adams Bulfinch informed the authorities that he would not be able to remove to Washington before January, 1818.

His official appointment was made out January, 1818:

To Charles Bulfinch, Esq.

Sir: Having entire confidence in your professional talents and integrity, I have appointed you Architect of the Capitol of the United States, to discharge all the duties and to receive the emoluments attached to this appointment.

Your salary to commence the 11th day of December last past.

Given under my hand at the city of Washington, the 8th day of January, 1818.[6]

Samuel Lane,
Commissioner of Public Buildings.

A letter of Bulfinch's, in his granddaughter's book, gives an interesting description of his feelings and what he found upon taking possession of his office:

"I have received from Colonel Lane a great number of drawings, exhibiting the work already done and other parts proposed but not decided upon. At the first view of these drawings, my courage almost failed me—they are beautifully executed, and the design is in the boldest style. After long study I feel better satisfied and more confidence in meeting public expectation. There are certainly faults enough in Latrobe's designs to justify the opposition to him. His style is calculated for display in the greater parts, but I think his staircases in general are crowded and not easy of access, and the passages are intricate and dark. Indeed the whole interior, except the two great rooms, has a somber appearance. I feel the responsibility resting on me, and should have no resolution to proceed if the work was not so far commenced as to make it necessary to follow the plans already prepared for the wings; as to the center building, a general conformity to the other parts must be maintained. I shall not have credit for invention, but must be content to follow in the prescribed path; as my employers have experienced so much uneasiness of late, they are disposed to view me and my efforts with complacency."[7] The first report Bulfinch made gives a clear statement of the condition of the work when he took charge, as he had spent his time between arrival and writing his report in viewing the building and studying the original plans and designs for work.

"Great progress has been made toward rebuilding the north and south wings. It will be necessary to complete them according to the designs already adopted and on the foundations already made. I have

---

[4] Ibid., 206–207.

[5] Harrison Gray Otis to Charles Bulfinch, December 2, 1817, in Bulfinch, *Life and Letters of Charles Bulfinch*, 207.

[6] Samuel Lane to Charles Bulfinch, January 8, 1818, in Bulfinch, *Life and Letters of Charles Bulfinch*, 211.

[7] Charles Bulfinch to Hannah Bulfinch, January 7, 1818, in Bulfinch, *Life and Letters of Charles Bulfinch*, 212–216.

been engaged in preparing several designs for the central portion, from which the President may choose one." [8]

It is strange that none of Bulfinch's drawings of the Capitol have been preserved.

C. A. Busby, an English architect, made drawings in 1819 (a short time after Latrobe retired) and published them in 1822, from measurements and drawings obtained on the spot. As this elevation and plan show a different treatment from those of Latrobe, we can assume that they present one of the designs made by Bulfinch. The plan and elevation have been carefully executed, although the points of the compass have been transposed on the original engraving [Plates 71 and 72]. This plan shows a circular opening and stairway in the Rotunda from the principal story to the crypt or basement story below, in addition to the alteration in the designs of the east and west porticoes made by Bulfinch. The west portico was executed according to the plan of Bulfinch, while the design of Latrobe for the east portico was retained. [9]

To better explain his ideas to the President and Congress, Bulfinch had a model made of the Capitol: "I have been engaged the past week, and still continue so, in giving directions to a young man from Boston, Mr. Willard, who is making a model of our great building. He works in my room. I hope this will prove a satisfactory mode of conveying clear ideas of the several plans for finishing the center,

and enable the President and the committees of Congress to select the one that on all considerations shall promise best." [10]

When Bulfinch took charge a large amount of stone had been accumulated for the Hall of Representatives and marble for the stairways of the north wing. Only three of the columns and two pilasters for the House of Representatives were complete, while the others were in various stages of progress. Fifty mantels [Plates 73 to 76], marble doorways for the Senate and House, all window frames, sashes, and parts of doors were completed. As the mantels were on hand when Bulfinch took charge the credit must be given to Latrobe for either designing or selecting them. [11]

Bulfinch in this report mentions a portico on the north and south ends which Latrobe had proposed. The elevations of Thornton [Plates 30 and 31] show porticoes on the north and south sides. Although these porticoes were not built on the old Capitol, it is interesting to note that they are similar to the ones afterwards erected on the north and south of the new wings under T. U. Walter.

One of the first problems Bulfinch had to solve was to discover the cause of the accident to the brick arch which was intended to carry the cupola over the flat dome on the Senate wing. May 1, 1818, he made a report on the accident, saying that, having confidence in his predecessor, he instructed the workmen to complete the arch as directed by Latrobe. On loosening the center "the arch moved 4 inches, the workmen left in alarm, and the clerk of works [Lenox] informed me of the fact, and I immediately went to the roof to view it, with the clerk, the principal of the stone department [Blagden], and the master mason." The arch was 40 feet in span, running from north to south, and 30 feet in width. It was to support a stone cupola intended to light the space

---

[8] Architect of the United States Capitol to the Commissioners of the Public Buildings, November 21, 1818, in *Message from the President of the United States, Transmitting a Report of the Commissioner of the Public Buildings,* H. doc. 8 (15–2), Serial 17 (Washington: Printed by E. De Krafft, 1818), 8–13.

[9] Bulfinch's drawings of the Capitol dome and stove designs for the Library of Congress were acquired by the Library of Congress.

[10] Charles Bulfinch to Hannah Bulfinch, March 16, 1818, in Bulfinch, *Life and Letters of Charles Bulfinch,* 225.

[11] Architect of the United States Capitol to the Commissioners of the Public Buildings, November 21, 1818, in *Message from the President of the United States.*

PLATE 71

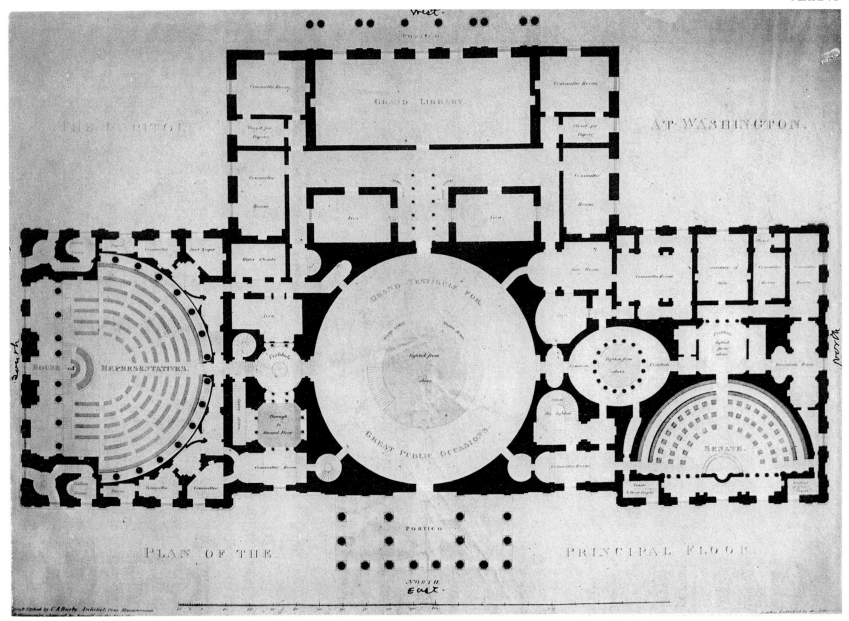

PLAN SHOWING CHANGES BY CHAS. BULFINCH.

Plan by C. A. Busby, showing Bulfinch's design for the central building, 1819. *Location unknown.*

PLATE 72

EAST ELEVATION, SHOWING SUGGESTED CHANGES BY BULFINCH.
Elevation by C. A. Busby, 1819. *Geography and Map Division, LC.*

PLATE 73

MANTEL IN OLD SENATE CHAMBER.

Mantel under the north end of the east gallery in the Old Senate Chamber, S–228.

PLATE 74

MANTEL IN OLD SENATE CHAMBER.

Mantel under the south end of the east gallery in the Old Senate Chamber, S–228.

PLATE 75

MANTEL, SERGEANT AT ARM'S OLD OFFICE.

Typical of marble mantels imported from Italy for the restoration of the Capitol after the fire of 1814.
This mantel, located in S–229, was destroyed in the gas explosion of 1898.

PLATE 76

MANTEL IN THE OLD ROOM OF THE VICE PRESIDENT.

Mantel in S–231, a room currently occupied by the Republican Leader.

beneath. The piers between the windows were intended to contain eighteen flues, twelve of which were carried over the arch from the west, three from the south, and three from the north to this outlet. Plate 52 shows a drawing made by Latrobe before the British invasion for a similar treatment of the chimneys, although the spans were not as great and a smaller number of flues were conducted up through the cupola. Bulfinch attributed the failure of the arch, first, to the location of the 15-foot opening 10 feet nearer one side of the arch than it was to the other, also to the unequal distribution of loads produced by the chimneys. General Swift and Colonel Bomford, engineers, were called in consultation. They agreed with Bulfinch that the arch would not bear any additional weight, and approved of his method of using a brick cone as a foundation for a cupola. This report of Bulfinch's on the arch was not published until he sent in his report to Congress in the latter part of November, 1818.[12] Latrobe wrote an elaborate reply in December, 1818. He states that the arch was not begun when he resigned, but from his interest in the matter he examined the stone and directed the beginning of the work. The change from a vaulted ceiling to a wooden roof in the Senate Chamber made the arch necessary to support the cupola which was required to light the vestibule of the Senate and attic stairway, and to conceal the numerous chimneys which it was necessary to carry above the roof. Although Latrobe thought the changes in the Senate made this arch necessary, Bulfinch seems to have contrived a simpler method. Latrobe attributes the failure of the arch to improper haunches, or lack of any loading, and the error of the workmen in not putting any hoop around the circular opening, which he had uniformly undone in

similar cases. He justifies the use of iron by quoting its use in the domes of St. Paul's, Ste. Geneviève, and the Cathedral of Baltimore.[13]

The question of the location, he justly says, could have had nothing to do with the problem if, as he says, the weakest side was ample to support the cupola. The report of Bulfinch, November 21, 1818, gives an idea of the progress on the Capitol at that date. On the north wing the stone balustrade over the cornice, on the east and west sides, the attic on the north, and the stone cupola were complete. The roof was covered with copper. On the interior the marble staircase was laid to the principal floor. The colonnade to the vestibule or small rotunda [Plate 68] and part of the east gallery of the Senate Chamber were completed. The apartments of the attic story and the committee rooms and offices on the principal floor were plastered and paved, and the carpenter work finished. It was expected that the court room would be finished in December. The Senate room was delayed by the difficulty in getting the marble work. On the south wing the balustrade on the roof was nearly complete [Plate 70]. On the interior the columns of Brescia were completed and in place, and the entablature and stone inclosure for the gallery were built. The ribs of the domed ceiling were raised and secured and the exterior roof was completed. In the center, excavation had been completed for the "new work on the west of center" [Plate 71]. The foundations were laid and the cellar carried up to the level of the ground-floor arches. The external walls of the basement were commenced.[14] The report of Mr. Cobb, Member of Congress, February 16, 1820, states that everything in the north and south wings was completed with the exception of painting and a few changes desired by Congress.[15] The first appropriation for the purpose of commencing the

---

12 "Report of the State of the Arch in the Roof of the North Wing, May 1, 1818," in *DHC*, 209–210.

13 "Memorial to Congress in Vindication of His Professional Skill," in Van Horne, *Papers of Benjamin Henry Latrobe*, vol. 3, 1010–1018.

14 Architect of the United States Capitol to the Commissioners of the Public Buildings, November 21, 1818, in *Message from the President of the United States.*

15 Thomas Willis Cobb, "Additional Report of the Committee on Public Buildings," in *DHC*, 225–227.

central portion was made April 20, 1818. "Upon the request of a former committee of the House, the plan of the central portion has been changed from the design of the late architect, Mr. Latrobe [Plate 70], so as to afford more convenience and a greater number of necessary rooms. This alteration has been approved by the President [Monroe], and it is believed that it will not affect either the beauty or increase the cost of the erection, inasmuch as its external is substantially preserved and its size diminished." [16]

Congress held its sessions in the new Hall of Representatives in December, 1819. At this period we find members complaining of the acoustic properties of the Hall. April 13, 1820, the House sent the following questions to Bulfinch in reference to preventing echo:

1. Whether it can be remedied without total alteration?

2. Whether anything can be added without destroying the beauty of the hall?

3. Would partial benefit justify the expense?

I have not been able to find the answer of Bulfinch to these questions, but the presumption is that no change was advocated unless it was a total change.

During the same year (1820) Dr. Thornton was called on for advice on the same subject. He a second time advised hangings, and took the opportunity to call the attention of Congress to the deviations from his original scheme and to state how they had affected both the utility and beauty of the building. Three old engravings give a good idea of the appearance of the Hall of Representatives at this period, showing the semicircular colonnade galleries and curtains hanging behind the columns [Plates 77, 78, and 79]. Plate 79 shows the space

under the gallery open, while Plates 77 and 78 show this space inclosed by a solid partition concentric with the columns, which was not put in until 1836, when Robert Mills was in charge. [17]

During the year 1821 the number of mechanics employed on the central portion of the building varied from 80 in December to 229 in July. About this period Samuel Lane was replaced by Joseph Elgar as Commissioner of Public Buildings, who, to effect an economy, proposed to reduce the salary of the Architect. Miss Bulfinch gives the correspondence between Bulfinch and his friends in reference to this proposed reduction:

OFFICE OF COMMISSIONER OF PUBLIC BUILDINGS,
Washington, D.C., September 30, 1822.

SIR: I have a painful duty to perform. It is that of announcing a general reduction of salaries, to take place at the end of the present year.

Subsequently to that period yours will be $2,000 per annum.

Very respectfully, your most obedient servant,

J. ELGAR,
Commissioner of Public Buildings.

TO CHARLES BULFINCH. [18]

Bulfinch protested through John Quincy Adams, making the claim that his salary was fixed by contract. President Monroe referred the question to Attorney-General Wirt, who decided in favor of Bulfinch:

[President Monroe to Attorney-General Wirt.]

JANUARY 31, 1823.

---

[17] Brown has confused the room's original lower stone wall below the gallery, designed by Benjamin Henry Latrobe, with a wood and plaster wall built by Robert Mills behind the gallery. The space below the gallery was never open. See "House of Representatives," RG 40, Subject Files, Curator's Office, AOC.

[18] Joseph Elgar to Charles Bulfinch, September 30, 1822, in Bulfinch, *Life and Letters of Charles Bulfinch,* 245.

---

[16] "Act making appropriations for the public buildings, and for furnishing the Capitol and President's House." [Stats. at Large, vol. 3, 458] in *DHC,* 206.

DEAR SIR: I send you a paper, the claim of Mr. Bulfinch, which will not require five minutes' attention. The question involved in it is whether the invitation to him to come here at a given salary formed a contract not to be altered, supposing his conduct to be correct, until the Capitol should be finished?

I wish an immediate answer, as I promised one on my part this morning.

J. M.[19]

[Attorney-General Wirt to President Monroe.]

JANUARY 31, 1823.

SIR: I am of the opinion that Mr. Adams' letter of 4th December, 1817, and Mr. Bulfinch's answer thereto, make a contract between the Government and that individual which is unalterable by the mere will of either party, as if it had been, instead of a salary, a contract for a fixed sum to be paid for the whole work.

I have the honor to remain, sir, very respectfully, your obedient servant,

WM. WIRT.[20]

The report of Bulfinch in 1823 gives a clear synopsis of the state of the building at this period:

WASHINGTON, D. C., *December 9, 1822.*
JOSEPH ELGAR, ESQ.,
Commissioner of Public Buildings.

SIR: The season for continuing the external work on the Capitol being near its close, I present a statement of the progress made thereon during the past year.

The exterior of the western projection [central portion] has been completed by finishing the copper covering, painting the walls, and inserting the window frames and sashes; the scaffolding is removed, and this front of the building exhibits the appearance it is intended to retain, being deficient only in the iron railings between the columns of the loggia, which are in forwardness and will soon be executed. The two principal stories of committee rooms, with their extensive passage or corridors, are plastered, and a great portion of the carpenters' work is finished. The principal labor of the season has been devoted to raising the dome of the center. For this purpose the interior walls of the Rotunda were continued. As soon as appropriations were made in the spring they were raised to the full height and covered with entablature and blocking course. The exterior walls were carried up with stone, formed into large panels, and crowned with a cornice and four receding gradines. About two-thirds of the interior dome is built of stone and brick and the summit of wood. The whole is covered with a wooden dome of more lofty elevation, serving as a roof [Plate 80]. It is hoped that a few days of favorable weather will enable the workmen to sheath it securely, when it will be in readiness for the copper covering. It will be finally crowned with a balustrade, to surround a skylight of 24 feet diameter, intended to admit light into the great Rotunda. This work has required a great effort to complete it, from the mass of stone and other materials employed in it, and raised and secured at so great a height. I can not omit this occasion to mention the ingenuity and persevering diligence of the superintendents of each branch of the work and cheerful and unremitted exertions of the workmen in their endeavors to execute their orders and to bring this part of their labors to a close. I sincerely hope that the effects of our joint efforts will meet the approbation of the President of the United States and the Representatives of the nation.

Respectfully submitted.

CHARLES BULFINCH,[21]
Architect of the Capitol of the United States.

---

[19] James Monroe to William Wirt, January 31, 1823, in Bulfinch, *Life and Letters of Charles Bulfinch*, 246–247.

[20] William Wirt to James Monroe, January 31, 1823, in Bulfinch, *Life and Letters of Charles Bulfinch* , 247.

[21] Bulfinch's report to Joseph Elgar on the progress of the Capitol, December 9, 1822, in *DHC*, 206.

PLATE 77

OLD HOUSE OF REPRESENTATIVES, FROM FRENCH PRINT.

Historical Society of Washington, D.C.

PLATE 78

OLD HOUSE OF REPRESENTATIVES, NORTH VIEW.

Engraving published in *Penny Magazine*, October 10, 1835. *Historical Society of Washington, D.C.*

PLATE 79

HOUSE OF REPRESENTATIVES, SOUTHWEST VIEW.

Color lithograph published by Goupil, Vibert, & Co. Lithography by Deroy. *Prints and Photographs Division, LC.*

PLATE 80

EXTERIOR OF BULFINCH DOME.

Photograph of a drawing by Thomas U. Walter, ca. 1854,
reproduced in the Capitol Extension and New Dome Photographic Books, 1860. *Location unknown*

We find Bulfinch requesting a guard and guides as the Capitol approaches completion. On December 10, 1824, the fact is recorded that the interior of the Capitol is finished, with the exception of some painting on the stonework, "which is not sufficiently seasoned to receive it." The colonnade of the east portico was incomplete.[22]

Bulfinch was employed during 1826 and 1827 in charge of what is called new work and in landscape work on the grounds. The latter had reference to designs for the steps and approaches made necessary by the hill on which the Capitol stands. Plates 81 and 82 show the gate lodge and a section of the fence, which were removed in 1873 and set up in the Monument lot. The sculptors were actively at work.

June 4, 1826, while Bulfinch was away from the city, the commissioner wrote to him, saying: "We have met with an irreparable loss—Mr. Blagden was killed last evening at the falling of the bank at the south angle of the Capitol."[23]

We learn from Robert Mills that the original design for the Senate Chamber had an upper gallery on the east, supported by an attic colonnade. But because this obstructed the light, it was removed in 1828 and a light circular gallery on the west was erected [Plate 83].[24]

Although an act was passed May 2, 1828, abolishing the office of Architect of the Capitol, Bulfinch held his position until the end of June, 1829.[25]

[From Joseph Elgar to Charles Bulfinch.]

WASHINGTON, D.C., *June 25, 1829.*

SIR: I am directed by the President to inform you that the office of Architect of the Capitol will terminate with the present month.

Respectfully, I remain your faithful and obedient servant,

J. ELGAR.[26]

Bulfinch sent a memorial to President Jackson, saying that the building was not in a condition to leave it without the supervision of an architect. He inferred from the act of Congress (March, 1829) and the statement of the Congressional committee that he would be retained until the work was complete, which he thought would be sometime in September, 1829.

He ends his memorial as follows:

"I most respectfully suggest that if the President should think proper to recall his orders, and continue my employment for another quarter, it would insure the right execution of the work; it would gratify my feelings, in closing my labors, with satisfaction, and my time would be at the command of the Government to visit the navy hospital at Norfolk, if the public services should seem to require it, and to make inquiry into its actual situation, and report of the proceedings there as might lead to more correct prosecution of the distant works in future.

"The above is respectfully submitted to the consideration of the President of the United States by one who feels a pride in his profession and who would regret the appearance of censure more than the loss of the emoluments of office.

"With great respect,　　　　CHARLES BULFINCH,
"Architect of Capitol of the United States.

"JUNE 27, 1829."[27]

President Jackson answered as follows:

"WASHINGTON, *June 27, 1829.*

---

[22] DHC, 265.

[23] For correspondence and information concerning the accident, see "George Blagden," RG 40, Subject Files, Curator's Office, AOC.

[24] Robert Mills, *Guide to the Capitol of the United States* (Washington: n.p., 1834), 44.

[25] Act of May 2, 1828, c. 45, 4 Stat. 265.

[26] Joseph Elgar to Charles Bulfinch, June 25, 1829, in Bulfinch, *Life and Letters of Charles Bulfinch*, 262.

[27] Charles Bulfinch to Andrew Jackson, June 27, 1829 ["Memorial to President Jackson, On Close of My Services"], in Bulfinch, *Life and Letters of Charles Bulfinch*, 262–263.

"Sir: Your note of this morning has been received. As the law under which you have been employed makes the period of your services depend upon your necessity, it became the duty of the President, as soon as he was advised that the public buildings had so far advanced as no longer to require them, to notify you accordingly. But it was far from his intention in so doing to manifest the slightest disapprobation of the manner in which you have discharged your duties. The superintendent of the buildings had reported that they were so far advanced as not to require the employment of the Architect. Of course, the President, whose duty it is to guard against a wasteful expenditure of the public money, was bound to direct his discharge.

"Your suggestion in regard to the work at Norfolk will receive the most respectful consideration.

"Your obedient servant,

ANDREW JACKSON." [28]

After his connection with the Capitol ceased Charles Bulfinch evidently remained in Washington about a year. Ashton R. Willard, in the New England Magazine (1890), quotes from a letter of Bulfinch in the possession of a member of his family, written June 3, 1830: "I date from this place [Washington] for the last time. We have taken places on the stage and leave for Baltimore at 2 o'clock. We have not time to regret at leaving friends . . . and a place which has given us a pleasant and respectable home for twelve years, and where we leave memorials of us which we trust will long endure." [29]

Charles Bulfinch designed and planned the modified form of the western extension of the building as finished [Plate 71]; made slight alterations in the interior arrangements of the wings, the galleries in the Senate Chamber being one of the changes. Otherwise he carried out Latrobe's ideas according to the drawings. He altered the form of the Dome, making it much higher than it had been indicated on either Thornton's or Latrobe's drawings [Plate 80]. [30]

An old water-color drawing, made about this period, shows the east front as completed [Plate 84]. George Strickland made a perspective drawing of the building as it was completed. This drawing is reproduced in Plate 85. Robert King made a drawing showing the exterior from the west. This drawing was evidently made before the terraces and entrance steps were put in place [Plate 86].

The three men who deserve credit for the rebuilding of the old Capitol, as assistants to the Architect, were Peter Lenox, clerk of works; George Blagden, superintendent of stonework and quarries, and Giovanni Andrei, in charge of the carvers and sculptors. In 1822 each received a salary of $1,500 per annum. Blagden was killed in 1826. Andrei died in December, 1824, on which occasion Bulfinch paid a high tribute to his merit. Congress allowed $400 to send Andrei's family back to Italy, according to agreement. Francis Iardella, who came from Italy to work on the Capitol in 1816, succeeded Andrei April 25, 1825, at $1,250 per annum.

It seems proper to give here a recapitulation of the facts in reference to the men in charge and result of their work in the building. That a structure as interesting and harmonious as the old Capitol proved to be should have been produced, when we consider the various hands through which it has passed, is remarkable. This was due both to the

[28] Andrew Jackson to Charles Bulfinch, June 27, 1829, in Bulfinch, Life and Letters of Charles Bulfinch, 263–264.

[29] Ashton R. Willard, "Charles Bulfinch, The Architect," New England Magazine 3 (November 1890): 284.

[30] The height of the dome was determined by President Monroe and his cabinet. Bulfinch prepared alternative designs of different heights and preferred a scheme higher than Latrobe's but lower than the one selected by the Monroe administration. For a history of the design and construction of the Capitol dome, see William Allen, The Dome of the United States Capitol: An Architectural History (Washington: Government Printing Office, 1992).

PLATE 81

ENTRANCE OR GATE LODGE.

Bulfinch Gate Lodge from the west grounds, which was relocated to Constitution Avenue near 15th Street, N.W. in 1874.

PLATE 82

GATE POST AND FENCE OF OLD CAPITOL GROUNDS.

Bulfinch gateposts, which were relocated to the corner of 17th Street and Constitution Avenue, N.W., and to the National Arboretum in northeast Washington.

PLATE 83

SENATE CHAMBER, SHOWING WESTERN GALLERY.

Engraving by Thomas Doney, 1842.

skill of the architects employed and the determination of the many Presidents who took a personal interest in the work to see it executed, if not in strict conformity, at least in harmony, with the original design. Hallet and Hadfield were both discharged by order of General Washington because they persisted in attempting to introduce changes in Thornton's scheme. No changes were allowed until Latrobe's entrance into office, and the only material change he made in the plans or elevations was on the eastern and western central porticoes, Jefferson insisting that everything should agree with the original design. After the destruction of the building by the British, in 1814, Latrobe changed completely the interior of the south wing, or old Hall of Representatives, but over this Madison held a restraining hand. Bulfinch can only be credited with planning and designing the western central portico and the earth terraces and landscape work, as shown in the steps leading up the hill. The result produced is to be attributed to the employment of the most skillful architects that could be obtained in the country, combined with the good conservative judgment and personal interest of such cultivated men as Washington, Jefferson, Madison, Adams, and Monroe.

Thornton, Latrobe, and Bulfinch deserve the distinction of being the architects of the building. Each designed and planned. Of the three, Thornton deserves the greatest praise, as the originator; Latrobe next, doing much original work in detail as well as planning and general arrangement of the interior. Bulfinch executed Latrobe's drawing, with the exception of the western portico, as noted above. Hallet, Hadfield, and Hoban were simply employed as and were called "superintendents,"

and deserve probably less credit than Lenthall and Lenox, who were called in the documents of the day "clerks of work" or "principal surveyors." Thornton showed an appreciation of the needs of the American people and a confidence in the growth of the country which his contemporaries did not appreciate, and his original plan was materially curtailed in scale and material under his direction.

Latrobe, when he was employed, made changes which could not be considered as satisfactory as the original design. He left out the grand semicircular portico on the west, and changed the form of the Hall of Representatives from an ellipse to a room with semicircular ends with parallel connecting lines, and omitted the grand staircases which were in prominent view, relegating them to out-of-the-way corners, where only those familiar with the building could find them. His curtailment of the number and size of entrances to the Rotunda was also unfortunate. While he made the eastern portico more imposing, it is a question whether it is as thoroughly in harmony with the building as the original portico, shown on Thornton's elevation. This change made the eastern the principal front, whereas the most imposing design should have been toward the west, where it shows from the river and city, and overlooks the broad expanse of country toward the President's House and Potomac River. Bulfinch by his alteration gave a better plan for the central western part of the building, without improving on Latrobe's design. Bulfinch made the projection of the central portion less, decreased the size of the courts or light wells, and increased the size of the halls [Plates 70 and 71].

PLATE 84

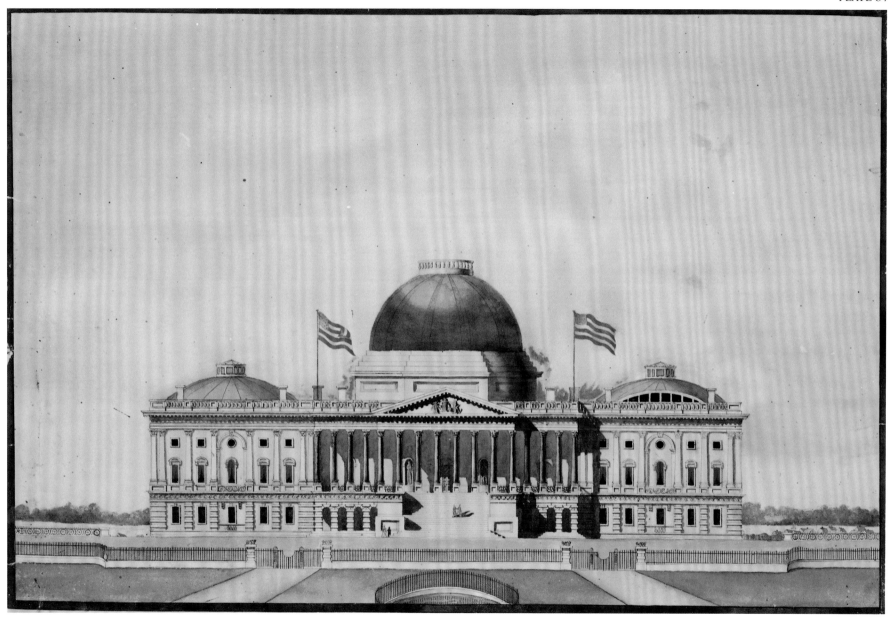

DRAWING OF LATROBE FOR EAST FRONT.

Watercolor now attributed to Alexander J. Davis, ca. 1832–34. *Prints and Photographs Division, LC.*

PLATE 85

PERSPECTIVE VIEW DRAWN BY GEO. STRICKLAND.

Drawing attributed to George Strickland, 1830–40.

PLATE 86

WEST VIEW OF CAPITOL. ABOUT 1830, DRAWING BY ROBERT KING.

Bermed terraces, begun in 1826, were not shown in this view. *NARA*.

CHAPTER VI

THE OLD CAPITOL AS COMPLETED

THE old Capitol was situated in a park of 22½ acres [Plate 87], inclosed by an iron railing.[1] There were nine entrances to the grounds, two each from the north and south for carriages, two on the east and three on the west for pedestrians. The western entrances at the foot of the hill were flanked by two ornamental gate or watch houses [Plate 81]. The fence was of iron, taller than the head of an ordinary man, firmly set in an Aquia Creek sandstone coping, which covered a low wall [Plate 82].

On entering the grounds by the western gates, passing by a fountain, one ascended two flights of steps to the "Grand Terrace" [Plate 88].

Upon the first terrace was the Naval Monument, erected to those who fell in the battle of Tripoli. This was a white marble column, decorated with beaks of vessels and anchors grouped in various positions. On and around the column and base were allegorical figures [Plate 89]. On the socle were the names of those who fell in the battle: Somers, Caldwell, Decatur, Wadsworth, Dorsey, and Israel. The monument rose out of a basin of "water, supplied from the contiguous fountain." This monument is now at Annapolis. There was an entrance into the sub-basement of the Capitol from the first terrace. Under the archway leading into this entrance was a marble fountain, with water from Smith's Spring. The second flight of steps landed on the main terrace a few feet below the level of the basement entrance.[2]

The eastern entrance, according to Mills, had spacious gravel walks, through a "dense verdant inclosure of beautiful shrubs and trees, circumscribed by an iron palisade."[3] An old print, made from a drawing by Wm. A. Pratt, a rural architect and surveyor in 1839, gives a clear idea of the eastern front of the building and its surroundings at this period [Plate 90].

The old Capitol building covered 67,220 square feet of ground. The front was 351 feet 4 inches long. The depth of the wings was 131 feet 6 inches; the central eastern projection, including the steps, 86 feet; the western projection, 83 feet; the height of wings to the top of balustrade, 70 feet; to top of Dome in center, 145 feet. The portico on the east is 160 feet wide, composed of a double row of Corinthian columns, elevated on a rustic basement.

With the exception of the Dome, the central portion of the present Capitol is the old building unchanged on the exterior. The basement of rusticated stonework is surmounted by the Corinthian order. Between the pilasters and columns two stories are grouped. The top of the building is surrounded by a stone balustrade. Over each wing is a low dome, surmounted by a cupola. The central Dome was considered high because it reached a greater altitude than the domes shown on the plans of Thornton and Latrobe, Bulfinch having materially increased its height. The whole exterior walls and porticoes were of Aquia Creek

---

[1] For an earlier version of this chapter, see Glenn Brown, "History of the United States Capitol," *American Architect and Building News* 54 (December 5, 1896): 81–83; 55 (January 2, 1897): 3–6; 55 (February 20, 1897): 59–60.

[2] The Naval Monument, erected in 1803 at the Navy Yard in southeast Washington, was moved to the Capitol's western grounds in 1831 and later transferred to the Naval

Academy at Annapolis, Maryland, in 1860. *Art in the United States Capitol* (Washington: Government Printing Office, 1978), 409.

[3] Robert Mills, *Guide to the Capitol of the United States, Embracing Every Information Useful to the Visitor Whether Business or Pleasure* (Washington: privately printed, 1834), 13.

sandstone, painted white. The roof of the building, including the Dome, was of wood, covered with copper. The subbasement, under the western portion of the central building, was utilized for committee rooms. The north side was used by the Senate and the south side by the House. On the east of the subbasement were the storerooms and "refectory," or restaurant.

From the western entrance of the subbasement a stairway leads to the basement story above. On both sides of this stairway a hall leads to the chamber prepared to receive the sarcophagus of George Washington, beneath the center of the crypt.

Plans of the building drawn by Robert Mills in 1846 show the arrangement of the building as it was at this period, with possibly a few slight modifications.[4]

The basement story [Plate 91] was a few feet above the street level on the east and the same distance above the principal terrace on the west. This floor of the Capitol had several entrances on the south, north, east, and west, where they would afford readiest access to the different portions of the building. An arcaded passageway ran under the principal eastern portion. At the north and south ends of this passageway were the vestibule entrances leading to the main stairways of the Senate and House [Plate 92].

The rooms in the north half of the Capitol, except on the third floor and Supreme Court room, were appropriated to the use of the Senate and its committees, while the rooms in the south part were appropriated to the House and its committees, clerks, and other officials.

The central portion of the basement is the crypt—a circular room beneath the Rotunda. The floor of the apartment above is supported on groined arches resting upon Doric columns modeled after those of the

Temple of Paestum [Plate 93]. Leading north from the crypt is a passageway to a central hall lighted from above. This was originally intended for the stairway. The brickwork surrounding it has remained through all the changes. Latrobe removed the stairway which led to the Senate above and placed it in the hall to the east, in a particularly out-of-the-way position, where only those familiar with the plan can find it. From this confined hall one doorway led into the Supreme Court, the other into the marshal's office. On the west side of the elliptical passageway was a door leading to the Law Library. Farther north, on the west side, were the entrances to the apartments of the clerk of the Supreme Court. Near the north entrance were the rooms of the Attorney-General and judges, west and east of the hall, respectively. The entrances to the court room were from the Senate stairway hall and from the lobby in the center of the building. This room is semicircular in plan, with an arched recess on the west, through which an arcaded passageway ran, and on which the groined-arch ceiling, which covered the whole room, rested. On the east of the room is a colonnade, through which the chamber is lighted [Plate 94]. At the present time the room is used as the Supreme Court library. The columns were modeled on the Doric order. The construction of the walls and supports is particularly massive, as the first domed ceiling of the room failed for want of proper abutments. Complaints were made of the lack of light and ventilation in this room. The floor, as late as 1847, was below the general level. On the south of the crypt a passageway led directly to the southern entrance. The stairway to the House of Representatives is a little to the west of this hall; the space was occupied by committee rooms.[5] A furnace room was in the cellar below for heating the House. The principal story [Plate 95] of the Capitol was reached by the broad

---

[4] Brown is referring to the plans published in Robert Mills, *Guide to the Capitol and the National Executive Offices of the United States* (Washington: Wm. Greer, Printer, 1847–48).

[5] The stairway to the House Chamber was east and not west of the hall Brown described, and it was unlikely that committee rooms were located in a stairway.

flight of steps of the eastern portico, or through the basement from the stairway [Plate 96] in the western projection or by the two circular stairways on the north and south of the crypt. The direct exterior entrances to the Senate and House of Representatives were from the eastern portico. The principal eastern and western entrances opened directly into the Rotunda, which was 96 feet in diameter and 96 feet high [Plate 97].[6] The frescoes shown in the illustration above the second cornice are modern. The circular walls of this apartment, which still remain, are divided by Grecian pilasters into panels. The pilasters are surmounted by a bold entablature ornamented by olive wreaths. Rising from the cornice was a hemispherical dome divided into sunken panels. The panels on the circular wall are appropriated to paintings and bas-reliefs of historical subjects.

The other panels have floral wreaths, in which are placed the heads of Columbus, Sir Walter Raleigh, La Salle, and Cabot [Plate 98].

The north door in the Rotunda opens into the small circular hall in which are the "tobacco capitals" [Plates 68, 101] designed by Latrobe. The south door led directly into the vestibule of the House. A door on the west of the vestibule led into the hall of the principal stairway, which runs from the basement to the roof, giving access to the gentlemen's galleries. The entrances to the ladies' gallery were in the lobby south of the hall. The circular vestibule south of the Rotunda gave access directly to the lobby of the old House of Representatives [Plate 100]. On the east was a stairway leading to the Library of the House. The Speaker's, clerks', and other rooms surrounded the hall. The Hall of Representatives, at the time of its construction and for many years afterwards, was considered by enthusiastic Americans the "most elegant legislative hall in the world" [Plate 99]. The room is a

semicircle with a diameter of 96 feet, with a parallelogram on its south side, 73 by 35 feet. The height to the top of entablature is 35 feet, and to the apex of the domed ceiling is 57 feet. The circular colonnade is composed of fourteen columns and two antes. The shafts of breccia from the Potomac are in solid blocks. The capitals are of Italian marble, modeled from those of the monument of Lysicrates. From the entablature springs the dome, decorated by a young Italian painter, named Bonani, who died soon after the completion of this work. Plate 101 shows the old Hall of Representatives in its present condition, now called Statuary Hall.

The apex of the dome is crowned by a lantern, through which abundant light reaches the chamber below. The colonnade of the south is composed of eight columns and three antes, similar to the others. An arch of 72 feet chord springs over the colonnade. In the center of this arch is a plaster cast of a statue of Liberty, on the right of which is an altar entwined by a serpent; at her feet reposes an eagle. Robert Mills commends this group as one of the best pieces by Causici, who died before he was allowed to put it into marble. Under the statue of Liberty, on the frieze of the entablature, is a spread eagle carved in stone by Valaperti, an Italian sculptor.[7]

The ladies' gallery was on the south, and the public gallery was back of the circular row of columns.[8] The former accommodated two hundred and the latter five hundred people. The space between the columns was draped with crimson curtains, those back of the Speaker's chair being made of crimson silk, "flowing down as from a center from the top of the capitals of the columns."[9]

---

[6] Brown was mistaken in thinking there were direct entrances to the House and Senate Chambers from the east portico.

[7] Mills, *Guide to the Capitol of the United States*, 33–34.

[8] The ladies' gallery was removed in 1880. "Rotunda," RG 40, Subject Files, Curator's Office, AOC.

[9] Mills, *Guide to the Capitol of the United States*, 35.

Opposite the Speaker's desk, between the draped curtains, was a clock, on which History sits in the winged car of Time.

The appearance of the House as finished and furnished was striking. The Speaker's chair was placed on a platform 4 feet above the level of the hall. This was inclosed by a rich fluted bronze balustrade, surmounted by an impost and brass railing. There were desks on each side for the Speaker. Three feet below the Speaker, on a marble base, was the Clerk's desk, "a rich mahogany table," inclosed below with beautiful curtains of damask silk and above with a dwarf brass railing. Between the columns were sofas on which the members could lounge. Reporters had boxes between the columns, ten spaces being allotted to them. Each member had a desk; the desks were of mahogany and numbered. The floor inclined, rising from the Clerk's desk to the outer wall. On the last row of seats was a bronzed iron railing, with curtains inclosing the space occupied by the members. In the old hall was a painting of Lafayette by a French artist, and one of Washington by Vanderlyn.

The doorway on the north of the Rotunda led through the small elliptical rotunda to the Senate Chamber and its committee rooms. A doorway on the east side of this elliptical apartment led to the main stairway. This marble stairway also gave access to the galleries of the Senate.[10] The western door from the elliptical room led into a hall opening on a toilet and folding rooms, and on a stone stairway that runs from the basement to the roof. From the north the halls passes by the stairway of the ladies' gallery to the vestibule of the Senate, "a quadrangular room lighted from above," with a screen of marble columns on the west, and the entrance to the Senate Chamber on the east [Plate 102].[11]

Back of the colonnade is a hall that gave access to the rooms of the President and Secretary and the other officers of the Senate.

Mills describes the Senate Chamber [Plate 83] as a large semicircular room covered with a dome and richly ornamented with deep sunken panels and circular apertures to admit light from above. Across the chord of the semicircle a screen of columns stretches on each side of the President of the Senate's chair, which was placed in a niche on an elevated platform, in front of which are the desks of the Secretary and Chief Clerk. "The columns are Grecian-Ionic, the shafts being of breccia and the caps of statuary marble. A gallery was supported on the entablature of these columns."[12] In front is another lighter gallery running around the circle of the room, supported by reeded bronzed iron columns surmounted by a rich gilt iron balustrade. Plate 103 shows the condition of the old Senate Chamber in 1900, the semicircular gallery having been removed and the interior fitted up and occupied by the Supreme Court. In this room was a picture of Washington by Rembrandt Peale, which Mills considered the best portrait of Washington in existence. The desks, placed in circles, were of mahogany, each Senator having a desk. "They were on platforms, each row being above the other." Having plain walls and a flat dome, the Senate was a good room in which to speak. Diameter, 75 feet; 45 feet greatest width; 45 feet high. Jonathan Elliott (1830), William Elliott (1837), and Robert Mills (1847) say: "The principal staircases and entrances to the two Houses of Congress are all unworthy of the rooms they communicate with, being confined, dark, and difficult to be found by strangers."[13]

The western door from the Rotunda, passing around both sides of the principal western staircase, leads to the Library [Plate 104], which is situated in the western projection, at the entrance of which are two

[10] This extant stairway did not provide access to the Senate galleries.

[11] Mills, *Guide to the Capitol of the United States*, 35.

[12] Ibid., 43.

[13] Quotation from Mills, *Guide to the Capitol of the United States*, 43. See also Jonathan Elliot, *Historical Sketches of the Ten-Miles Square Forming the District of Columbia* (Washington: J. Elliot, Jr., 1830) and William Elliot, *The Washington Guide* (Washington: Franck Taylor, 1837).

PLATE 87

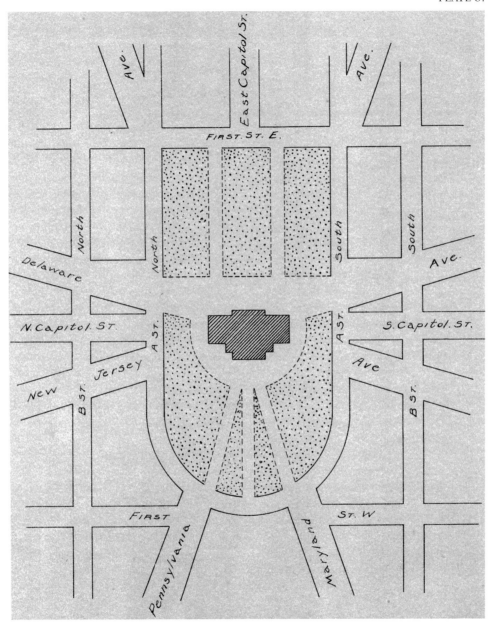

PLAT OF GROUNDS, 1830.

Brown based this 1896 conjectural drawing on the King plat maps. *Location unknown.*

PLATE 88

ASCENT TO THE CAPITOL, WASHINGTON.

ENTRÉE DU CAPITOLE, À WASHINGTON.   DER WEG DAS CAPITOL HINAUF, ZU WASHINGTON.

LONDON,
PUBLISHED BY GEORGE VIRTUE, 26, IVY LANE.

STEPS AND ENTRANCE TO WEST FRONT OF OLD CAPITOL.

Engraving published by George Virtue, ca. 1840.

PLATE 89

TRIPOLI NAVAL MONUMENT.

Photograph taken during construction of the Capitol extension.
The monument was relocated in 1860 to the U.S. Naval Academy Grounds in Annapolis, Maryland.

PLATE 90

EAST FRONT OF CAPITOL, FROM LITHOGRAPH, 1830.

"Elevation of the Eastern Front of the Capitol of the United States," drawn by William A. Pratt, ca. 1832. The reservoir was built about 1832. *Prints and Photographs Division, LC.*

PLATE 91

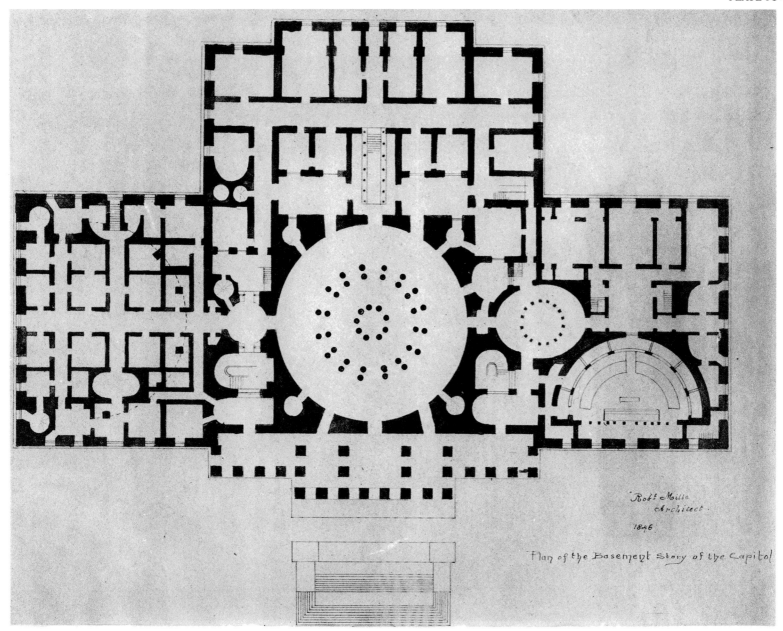

BASEMENT OF OLD CAPITOL, DRAWN BY ROBERT MILLS.
Signed and dated, 1846. *NARA.*

PLATE 92

VESTIBULE BASEMENT, NORTH WING.

The exterior door became an interior door when the east front extension was built between 1958 and 1962.

PLATE 93

THE CRYPT, OLD CAPITOL.

The crypt, which now houses exhibitions and sculpture, was once an informal storage space where bicycles were parked.

PLATE 94

OLD SUPREME COURT ROOM, 1900 A. D. SUPREME COURT LAW LIBRARY.

This rare photograph shows the room's turn-of-the-century use as a library.

FIGURE 21

The restored Old Supreme Court Chamber, which was opened to the public in 1975, is managed by the U.S. Senate Commission on Art.

PLATE 95

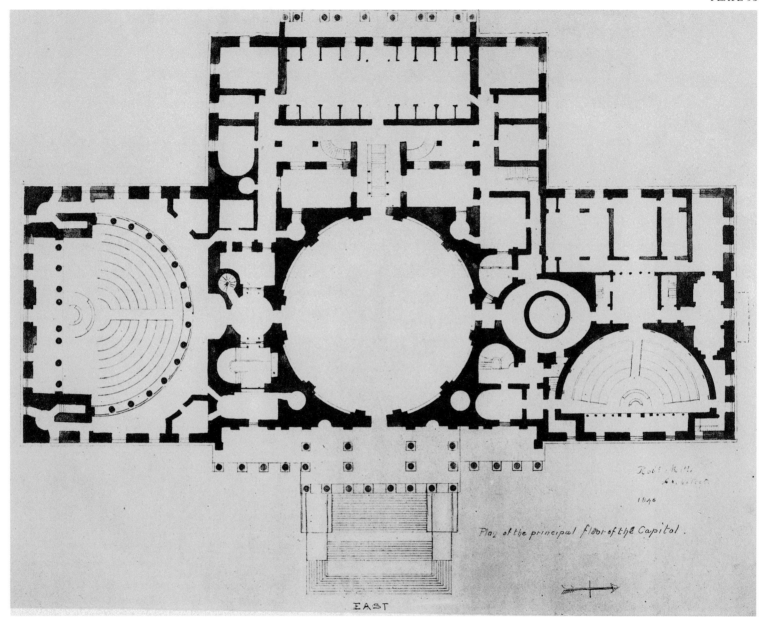

PRINCIPAL FLOOR OF OLD CAPITOL, DRAWN BY ROBERT MILLS.

Signed and dated, 1846. *NARA.*

PLATE 96

PRINCIPAL STAIRWAY, CENTRAL PART OF OLD CAPITOL.

The door at the head of the stairs is the west door of the Rotunda.

PLATE 97

THE ROTUNDA.

View looking northeast to the former location of Robert Weir's *Embarkation of the Pilgrims.*
The painting was moved to its present position in the Rotunda in 1979.

PLATE 98

PANEL OVER DOOR, EASTERN PORTICO.

Fame and Peace Crowning George Washington,
Antonio Capellano, ca. 1827.

PANEL IN ROTUNDA.

Untitled decorative panel, Francisco Iardella, ca. 1827.

PANEL IN ROTUNDA.

Christopher Columbus, attributed to Francisco Iardella, 1827.

PLATE 99

HOUSE OF REPRESENTATIVES, FROM PAINTING BY SAMUEL FINLEY BREEZE MORSE.

Oil on canvas, 1822. *Corcoran Gallery of Art, Washington, D.C. Museum Purchase, Gallery Fund.*

PLATE 100

LOBBY VESTIBULE, TO OLD HALL OF REPRESENTATIVES.

This is the oldest surviving space designed in the Greek Revival style in the U.S.A.

PLATE 101

VIEW OF OLD HALL OF REPRESENTATIVES, 1900 A. D. HALL OF STATUARY.

Photograph showing the gallery fitted with shelves for books and documents.
The wooden ceiling, painted to appear coffered, was removed in 1901.

FIGURE 22

Statuary Hall (Old Hall of the House of Representatives). The fireproof ceiling installed in 1901 was recently restored.

SMALL ROTUNDA, SENATE WING.
View documenting the small rotunda with columns painted white.

PLATE 102

SENATE LOBBY, 1900, SUPREME COURT ENTRANCE.

This view depicts the entrance to S–233, which is now the Office of the Republican Leader.

PLATE 103

OLD SENATE CHAMBER 1900 A. D., SUPREME COURT.

Photograph depicting the appearance of the space during its use as the Supreme Court between 1860 and 1935.

FIGURE 23

The restored Old Senate Chamber, opened to the public in 1976, is managed by the U.S. Senate Commission on Art.

PLATE 104

ENTRANCE TO OLD CONGRESSIONAL LIBRARY.

This entrance is no longer extant. The Library of Congress space on the west central side of the
Capitol was rebuilt into office space in 1900.

PLATE 105

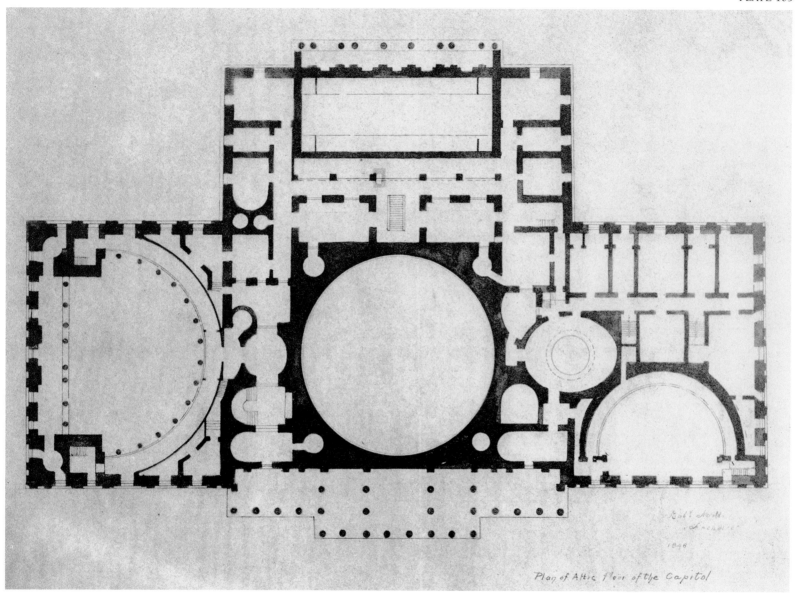

Plan of Attic floor of the Capitol

PLAN OF ATTIC STORY, DRAWN BY ROBERT MILLS.
Signed and dated, 1846. *NARA.*

marble columns modeled from the Octagon Tower in Athens. There are similar columns at the door opening out on the western colonnade. The original Library occupied only the front portion of the building, and was without the two rooms on the north and south which are familiar to visitors at the present time.

The old portion of the room was 92 feet long, 34 feet wide, and 36 feet high. Extending the whole length of the room was (I say was, for the interior has been changed) a series of alcoves ornamented in front with fluted pilasters which, with their entablature, supported two galleries, divided as below into twelve shelved recesses. Above these sprung the great arch forming the ceiling, decorated with enriched panels, borders, and wreaths of flowers, and pierced with three circular ornamented apertures, which admitted the light and ventilated the room. "A table and chair were in each alcove." The cases were glazed and labeled. This room was heated by furnace from below. The stairway to the north of the Rotunda led to the third story, occupied by committee rooms. The stairway continued to the roof, thence on the exterior of and over the roof to the top of the Dome. The House of Representatives, Senate, and Library in height occupied the space of two stories or extended from the principal floor to the roof. The other portions of the attic story were used by the Houses of Congress [Plate 105].[14]

The echoes in the House of Representatives produced such disagreeable results that there was from 1820 to 1836 a continued discussion as to a feasible method of rectifying the trouble.

Bulfinch, in his review upon the subject, says: "Upon Congress being reinstated in the Capitol in 1820, it was found that a difficulty existed both in speaking and hearing in the House of Representatives."[15]

This was attributed to the resonances and echoes occasioned by the unfinished state of the Hall and the dampness of the new work. To remedy these defects draperies were suspended in front of the galleries and between the columns of the prostyle, and carpets were spread in the galleries. In 1821 a committee was appointed "to inquire into the practicability of making such alterations in the present structure of the Hall of the House of Representatives as shall better adapt it to the purposes of a deliberative assembly."[16] This committee consulted Bulfinch, as well as other architects and scientists. Many contradictory theories and reports were the result of these consultations. Bulfinch, in his report of 1821, says that the three following methods had been proposed as a remedy: "(1) To raise the floor; (2) to contract the space by a screen; (3) to form a level ceiling at the foot of the dome."[17] He advocates the last method, although he regrets the effect that it would have upon the appearance of the room. Nothing was done, and another committee was appointed, and a new report was sent in 1822 by Bulfinch, discussing the question, in which he refers to Saunders on Theaters as the best work on the subject, and recommends that a flat ceiling of cloth be stretched over the room as an experiment. Acting on this suggestion canvas was stretched over the whole Hall at the height of the blocking course above the columns. This ceiling put a stop to echoes, but seemed to absorb the whole volume of sound and obstructed the light. It was removed after a few days' service. Another experiment was tried at the next session by putting up a wooden partition between the columns. This was removed after one week's trial.[18]

---

[14] Mills, *Guide to the Capitol of the United States,* 46–47.

[15] *Memorial of Charles Bulfinch on the Subject of the Hall of the House of Representatives,* H. report 123 (21–1), Serial 199.

[16] *Report on Alterations in the Hall of Representatives,* February 13, 1823, Committee Report 90 (17–2), Serial 87.

[17] Charles Bulfinch to Silas Wood, January 10, 1821, in *DHC,* 236–237.

[18] Architect of the United States Capitol to the Commissioners of the Public Buildings, January 4, 1822, in *Message from the President of the United States, Transmitting the Annual Report of the Commissioner of Public Buildings,* H. doc. 26 (17–1), Serial 64.

In 1826 William Strickland, of Philadelphia, was employed to act in conjunction with Bulfinch for "devising a plan for improving the Hall so as to make it better suited for the purposes of a deliberative assembly." [19] A board, consisting of the Secretaries of State and War and the Attorney-General, was authorized to have the scheme which might be recommended by Bulfinch and Strickland, if it met their approval, carried into execution. Strickland visited Washington several times to consult with Bulfinch and the board. He recommended the breaking up of the plain surface of the dome by "numerous deeply sunken panels, bounded by raised styles or margins," instead of the painted panels which were and are on this surface. As an alternative he suggests a lath-and-plaster flat ceiling above the columns. [20] The matter rested from this time until 1828, when decided objection was raised to the lack of ventilation as well as the deficiency in the acoustic properties of the Hall. Bulfinch reported on this January 24, 1830, recommending a reduction of the height of the galleries so as to get direct communication with windows in the rear, and again insisted on the insertion of the flat plaster ceiling. [21]

January 14, 1830, Robert Mills, who had been one of Latrobe's assistants, sent a memorial to Congress repeating the views upon the subject which were contained in a memorial from him dated October 22, 1826. [22] He attributed the principal trouble to the walls in the rear of the columns running at different angles, which tended to produce an infinite variety of echoes, saying: "The fundamental error in the plan of this hall consists in breaking the curve line behind the columns of the gallery and disposing of the walls there in irregular surfaces. To correct this evil it will be absolutely necessary to perfect the curve line, making it parallel to that formed by the semicircular colonnade." [See Plate 101.] In this suggestion Mills is careful to state that he assumes the ceiling to be built so that it reflects the sound at a proper angle to prevent echoes. Mills recommended a permanent screen parallel with the colonnade, and put on record his positive objection to a flat ceiling, which had been recommended. In a footnote to this memorial Mills calls attention to his ignorance at the time of writing of the fact that another architect had been called in to make a report on the same subject, and states that his scheme could not with propriety be considered until the result of the first one had been ascertained. The report alluded to was made by Charles Bulfinch, January 25, 1830.

February 4, 1832, Robert Mills made a report to the select committee of the House, repeating his former recommendations. In this he asserts that the center of the curved ceiling being about on a level with or above the ear of a man standing in the Hall, all sounds are reflected back to the ear.

The committee in charge recommended: "(1) That the floor be raised to the level of the foot of the columns surrounding the Hall; (2) that the chair of the Speaker be placed near where the principal entrance now is and that the seats of the members be turned so as to preserve their relative positions to the chair; (3) a circular wall to be built back of the third row of seats in the gallery." "Resolved, That the Committee on Public Buildings cause the Hall of Representatives to be altered according to the plan of Robert Mills, and the expense to be paid out of the contingent fund of the House." [23] The reports and investigations to

---

[19] "Letter from Henry Clay, Secretary of State, Transmitting a Report to the Board of Inspection, in Respect to Improvements of the Hall of Representatives, February 9, 1827," in *DHC*, 284–285.

[20] This painted wooden ceiling was removed and replaced with a superstructure of cast steel in 1901. *Annual Report of the Superintendent of the Capitol* (Washington: Government Printing Office, 1902).

[21] *The Hall of the House of Representatives*, January 25, 1830, H. report 123 (21–1), Serial 199.

[22] *Hall of the House of Representatives, U.S.: Memorial of Robert Mills, of South Carolina,* H. report 83 (21–1), Serial 199, reprinted in DHC, 304–307.

[23] *Alteration of the Hall House of Representatives: Report,* H. report 495 (22–1), in *DHC*, 319–325.

which I have referred, either ignored or tried in a temporary way as an experiment, were not found satisfactory.

After Bulfinch retired, in 1829, repairs to the building were made under the jurisdiction of William Noland as Commissioner of Public Buildings, with Pringle Slight acting as assistant superintendent. Reports to Congress show that water was brought into the Capitol from springs in the neighborhood in 1832. In January, 1834, the old copper roof on the Dome was replaced by a new copper covering.[24]

From 1829 until the appointment of Robert Mills there was no architect in the employment of the Government. Robert Mills applied for the position of Architect of Government Buildings, February 15, 1815, and from that date until his appointment frequently memorialized Congress on questions relating to this work: April 26, 1815, in relation to warming Capitol; October 22, 1822, in relation to acoustics of Capitol; October 11, 1833, in relation to water distribution in Capitol. April 26, 1838, the public buildings were placed under the jurisdiction of the Secretaries of State, Treasury, and War, John Forsyth, Levi Woodbury, and J. R. Poinsett being in office at that date. The following Commissioners of Public Buildings were in charge: William Noland, 1829–1846; Andrew Beaumont, 1846; Charles Douglas, 1847; Ignatius Mudd, 1847–1851; William Easby, appointed March 4, 1851.[25]

Under authority conferred upon him by the act of July 4, 1836, President Andrew Jackson appointed Robert Mills, on July 6, 1836, "architect to aid in forming the plans, making proper changes therein from time to time, and seeing to the erection of the new buildings [Treasury and Patent Office] in substantial conformity to the plans hereby adopted."[26] The salary of Mills was fixed at $1,800 per annum. On the 26th of October it was increased to $2,300. May 17, 1839, when the new Post-Office was authorized, his salary was increased to $2,400, and in October of the same year he was allowed $500 "for assistance in drawing and copying."[27] During the period from 1836 to 1851 all matters relating to changes in and the maintenance of the Capitol came under the supervision of Mills.[28] In this way he was able to carry out his suggestions in reference to the improvement of the acoustic properties of the Hall of Representatives. The floor was raised to the level of the floor in the Rotunda and a partition was placed in the rear of the colonnade concentric with it [Plate 95].

On April 5, 1840, Mills made a report on the expediency of lighting the public grounds with carbureted hydrogen as a substitute for oil. After an elaborate review of the subject, he concludes that it would be safer, more manageable, and economical. In 1841 experiments were made with gas-lighting apparatus by Robert Grant. Nothing further seems to have been done in this direction until 1847, when a thorough plan of lighting the building and grounds was begun. A mast over 100

[24] See *Public Buildings: Report of the Commissioner of the Public Buildings, of the Expenditure of Appropriations for the Improvement of the Capitol, etc., etc., etc., during the Year 1833*, H. doc. 19 (23–1), Serial 254; *Public Buildings: Report of the Commissioner of the Public Buildings, Transmitting Statements Exhibiting the Amount of Moneys Expended, etc.*, H. doc. 35 (23–2), Serial 272. Joseph Elgar was Commissioner of Public Buildings from 1822 to 1834; he was succeeded by William Noland. Pringle Slight was a carpenter who worked at the Capitol from 1825 until his death in 1860.

[25] Brown's dates of service for some of the commissioners were in error. The correct dates are: William Noland, 1834–1846; Charles Douglas, 1847–49; Ignatius Mudd, 1849–1851.

[26] For a discussion of Mills's appointment and salary, see Douglas E. Evelyn, "The Washington Years: The U.S. Patent Office," in John M. Bryan, ed., *Robert Mills, Architect* (Washington: The American Institute of Architects Press, 1989), 114.

[27] Ibid., 132.

[28] Brown was mistaken. The commissioners of public buildings, not Robert Mills, had authority over these matters. However, Mills was often consulted for advice and ideas by the commissioners concerning improvements at the Capitol.

feet high was raised on the Dome of the Capitol, on which was placed a lantern 6 feet in diameter. This was to contain the solar gaslight prepared by James Crutchet, giving a light equal to 30,000 candles, and capable, the inventor calculated, of extending its rays as far as Baltimore, 39 miles distant. The interiors of the Senate, House, and Rotunda were to be lighted in the same manner.[29]

The statues of War and Peace [Plate 117], by Luigi Persico, were ordered in 1832, and put in the niches on the western portico about 1837.[30] Statues of the same character are indicated on Thornton's design of 1794.

A few pieces of the old furniture used in the Capitol have been placed in the rooms of the Supreme Court. This furniture, and the present appearance of these rooms, which are used now in connection with the Supreme Court, are shown in Plates 106 and 107.

The Hall of the House was heated at this period (1847) by furnaces, with brass registers set in the floor. The air was first introduced into a mixing chamber, arched with brick, just beneath the floor. The whole floor was kept warm.[31] This was done when the floor was raised by Mills. Very interesting exterior views of the Capitol (1840) were made by Bartlett, an English painter. From these paintings steel engravings were made for the work of N. P. Willis, on American scenery. Plates 88, 108, 109, and 110 show reproductions of these views, one from Pennsylvania avenue looking east and west, another from the roof of the circular porch on the President's House, and a view of the exterior stairway. These illustrations, with a drawing made by W. A. Pratt, rural architect, 1839 [Plate 90], give an idea of the treatment of the grounds and surroundings.

[29] Robert Mills to the Commissioner of Public Buildings, April 5, 1840, in *Documents Relating to the Bill (S. 329) "to Provide for Lighting the Capitol and the President's Squares, and the Pennsylvania Avenue, with Carburetted Hydrogen Gas,* S. doc. 434 (26–1), Serial 359; Committee on the District of Columbia, *Robert Grant—Gas Lights: Report,* H. report 6 (27–1), Serial 393. Brown's information on the lighting plan may have been derived from plans prepared by Robert Mills in *Contingent Expenses of the House of Representatives, Transmitting Statements of the Expenditures of the Contigent Fund of Said House for the Year 1848,* H. misc. doc. 4 (30–2), Serial 544. For an account of Cruchett's efforts to light the Capitol and its grounds, see Robert R. Hershman, "Gas in Washington," *Records of the Columbia Historical Society* 50 (1948–50): 137–157.

[30] The statues were placed on the eastern portico. *Art in the United States Capitol* (Washington: Government Printing Office, 1978), 356.

[31] William Noland contracted with John Skirving to install warm-air furnaces in the Capitol in 1846. See *Report of the Commissioner of Public Buildings: Letter from the Commissioner of Public Buildings, Transmitting Copies of Contracts, etc.,* H. doc. 14 (29–2), Serial 499.

Chapter VII

Statuary and Paintings in the Old Capitol

THE need of ornamentation for the Capitol Building was appreciated by its designers from the beginning of the work.[1] Thornton indicated sculptural work on his earliest drawings, and advocated finishing or decorating the interior of the building with foreign marbles. Such treatment was beyond the pecuniary capacity of the Government at that period, but as the wings neared completion under Latrobe we find that he sought the assistance of sculptors to do the decorative carving and model the statuary which he thought appropriate to accentuate and ornament the building. Artists of this character had found no inducement to establish themselves in the United States, therefore it was necessary to obtain them from abroad. As the House of Representatives neared completion Latrobe sent to Italy for sculptors, securing the services of Giuseppe Franzoni and Giovanni Andrei, who arrived in this country March 3, 1806.[2] The former was skilled in modeling and chiseling figures, while the latter was more noted for decorative sculpture, making capitals, panels, and similar ornamental work. The first work of Franzoni was

the eagle on the frieze in the House of Representatives. This piece of work met with the hearty approval of Latrobe and others who were familiar with its appearance. August, 1807, a model of the Statue of Liberty by Franzoni was placed between two columns in the colonnade, over the Speaker's chair.[3]

Andrei's first work was on the capitals in the House of Representatives. All of the above-mentioned sculptural work was destroyed when the British burned the Capitol. When work was again commenced and the repairs of the building begun, Andrei was sent to Italy, in August, 1815, to secure capitals for the Halls of Congress, and at the same time he was authorized to engage sculptors who were proficient in modeling figures. Andrei probably engaged at this time Francisco Iardella, who came over in 1816, and Carlo Franzoni, the latter being a brother and the former a cousin of the first Franzoni.[4]

Giuseppe Franzoni made a model for the clock of the Hall of Representatives, to be placed over the north door and opposite the Speaker's desk, as indicated in Latrobe's drawing [Plate 61]. This clock consists of the figure of History, recording the events of the nation, passing in a winged car over the globe, on which are inscribed the signs of the zodiac in low relief. The exposed wheel of the car is utilized as the face of the clock [Plate 112]. The figure in this clock was modeled from Franzoni's daughter. He died in 1816, before its completion,

[1] For an earlier version of this chapter, see Glenn Brown, "History of the United States Capitol," *American Architect and Building News* 55 (January 2, 1897): 3–6; (February 20, 1897): 59–60.

[2] In a letter to John Lenthall dated March 3, 1806, Latrobe mentions that Franzoni (1779–1815) and Andrei (1770–1824) arrived in the United States the previous month. This letter and related correspondence concerning their employment as sculptors for the Capitol are reprinted in Charles Fairman, *Art and Artists of the Capitol of the United States* (Washington: Government Printing Office, 1927), 3–8. For information on the work of these and other Italian artists in the Capitol, see Vivian Green Fryd, "The Italian Presence in the United States Capitol," in Irma B. Jaffe, ed., *The Italian Presence in American Art, 1760–1860* (New York: Fordham University Press, 1989), 132–164.

[3] This statuary was destroyed by the 1814 fire. See AOC, *Art in the United States Capitol* (Washington: Government Printing Office, 1978), 412–413.

[4] See Fairman, *Art and Artists of the Capitol*, 27; Fryd, "The Italian Presence in the United States Capitol," 132–164.

and the work was completed by Francisco Iardella, who married Mrs. Franzoni.[5]

On the north side of the old Supreme Court room, facing what was formerly the judges' bench, is a group of figures in high relief, consisting of Justice in the center, with a winged figure on the right calling attention to the Constitution, a youth presumably typifying the young nation, and on the left an eagle guarding the Laws [Plate 113]. The figures in this group are very graceful and pleasing in their modeling and poses. This piece of sculpture was probably done by the Franzonis, but I have not been able to verify their authorship.[6]

As the Capitol neared completion a larger number of artists were needed, and again Italy was the country from which the principal supply was obtained. In 1823 Enrico Causici and Antonio Capellano, of Italy, and Nicholas Gevelot, of France, commenced work on the Capitol.[7] Capellano and Causici were pupils of Canova. Over the principal entrance doorways in the Rotunda are four panels with the figures in low relief. The efforts of the sculptors, who had been educated to produce on classic lines either in the nude or with flowing draperies, show their lack of skill when attempting these historical bits of sculpture, with the figures dressed according to the period which they depict. The figures and grouping are treated in a conventional manner, which shows the evident training of the sculptors, in an effort to make them simply a part of the decorative treatment of the Rotunda. They are suggestive of some of the classical sculpture which has been modeled on conventional lines, but the dress of the characters tends to mar the effect evidently intended by the sculptors. The early guidebooks as well as the majority of later writers usually refer to these panels with ridicule.[8]

Over the western entrance is represented the Preservation of Captain Smith by Pocahontas, by Capellano, a pupil of Canova; over the eastern entrance, the Landing of the Pilgrims on Plymouth Rock, by Causici, also a pupil of Canova; over the southern door is the Conflict between Daniel Boone and the Indians, by Causici, and over the northern entrance is Penn's Treaty with the Indians, by Gevelot, a Frenchman [Plate 114].

The other panels have floral wreaths, in which are placed the heads of Columbus, Sir Walter Raleigh, La Salle, and Cabot [Plate 98].

Another Italian sculptor, named Valaperti, a man of some prominence in his profession, according to statements of the period, came to this country during the year 1823 or 1824. He designed the eagle on the frieze of the south colonnade in the old Hall of Representatives (Statuary Hall) [Plate 115]. This work was ridiculed to such an extent that the author was supposed to have drowned himself in chagrin. He disappeared, and the eagle was the only piece of work he completed in America.[9]

---

[5] Carlo Franzoni, not Giuseppe, created the model for the clock of the Hall of Representatives. The statuary is located over the north entrance of Statuary Hall. For further description and historical background on Franzoni's *Car of History,* see Fairman, *Art and Artists of the Capitol,* 41–42; and AOC, *Art in the United States Capitol,* 367.

[6] The bas-relief has been documented as Carlo Franzoni's work and is still located in the Old Supreme Court Chamber (S–141). See AOC, *Art in the United States Capitol,* 291.

[7] For a discussion of the work of these sculptors at the Capitol, see Vivian Green Fryd, "The Italian Presence in the United States Capitol," 132–164; and Fryd, *Art and Empire: The Politics of Ethnicity in the United States Capitol,* 1815–1860 (New Haven: Yale University Press, 1992).

[8] For example, see Jonathan Elliot, *Historical Sketches of the Ten Miles Square Forming the District of Columbia* (Washington: Printed by J. Elliot, Jr., 1830), 115. Describing the *Preservation of Captain Smith by Pocahontas,* 1606, Elliot commented, "The face and head-dress of Pocahontas are somewhat Grecian, and the features of Powhatan are less like an Indian, than a European."

[9] Giuseppe Valaperti (or Valaperta) arrived in Washington, D.C., in 1815 and completed the sculptural relief eagle in 1816. Fairman, *Art and Artists of the Capitol,* 129, 452; AOC, *Art in the United States Capitol,* 368; I. T. Frary, *They Built the Capitol* (Richmond: Garrett and Massie, 1940), 125–126; see also RG 40, Subject Files, Curator's Office, AOC.

Above the eagle of Valaperti, resting upon the cornice of the colonnade and in the center of the arch, is a plaster cast of the Statue of Liberty [Plate 115], by Enrico Causici. On the right of the figure is an altar entwined with a serpent. The figure of Liberty is graceful and dignified, and the most satisfactory piece of work left by its sculptor Causici, who died before he was able to put this group in marble.

In May, 1825, it was determined to hold a competition for the figures in the pediment of the eastern or principal portico. A premium was offered, probably at the suggestion of President John Quincy Adams, for these pieces of sculpture.

The following extract from a letter of Bulfinch gives an idea of the method of and cause for the adoption of the present sculpture in the pediment of the central eastern portico [Plate 116]:

"Our work at the Capitol proceeds but slowly, owing to the delay of contractors in delivering the large blocks for columns. We have received only four this season, which are raised into their places, and must have seven more before the much-talked-of pediment can be commenced. With respect to the ornament proposed to decorate this the artists in general feel much disappointed. About thirty persons presented thirty-six designs, some well and others badly executed, but none answering the President's idea of a suitable decoration for a legislative building. He disclaimed all wish to exhibit triumphal cars and emblems of victory, and all allusions to heathen mythology, and thought that the duties of the nation or its legislators should be expressed in an obvious and intelligent manner. After several attempts the following has been agreed upon: A figure of 'America' occupies the center, her right arm resting on the shield, supported by an altar or pedestal bearing the inscription 'July 4, 1776,' her left hand pointing to the figure of 'Justice,' who, with unveiled face, is viewing the scales, and the right hand presenting an open scroll inscribed 'Constitution, March 4, 1789.' On the right hand of the principal figure is the eagle, and a fig-

ure of 'Hope' resting on her anchor, with face and right hand uplifted—the whole intended to convey that while we cultivate justice we may hope for success. The figures are bold, of 9 feet in height, and gracefully drawn by Mr. Luigi Persico, an Italian artist." [10] Luigi Persico came to this country in 1826, and, in addition to the pieces of sculpture in the pediment, modeled the heroic figures of Peace and War which stand in the niches on the eastern portico on each side of the entrance door to the Rotunda. These figures, which have great dignity and repose, as well as grace, were ordered March 3, 1829, completed March 2, 1833, but apparently not put in place until 1837. [11] In Thornton's elevation, made in 1794, he indicated figures of War and Peace in the niches on this portico, and it was evidently simply the completion of his design that was contemplated in having these figures placed in this position.

The first American to receive an order for a piece of sculpture for the Capitol was Horatio Greenough, of Boston, Mass. Congress gave him a commission for a statue of Washington in 1832. [12] February 10, 1840, Robert Mills made a report upon the foundation and location of this statue of Washington. He recommended an opening in the floor of the Rotunda, with a grand staircase from the crypt to the present Rotunda floor, and the introduction of light into the Rotunda at a lower level, so

[10] The Bulfinch letter was dated June 22, 1825. See Ellen Susan Bulfinch, ed., *The Life and Letters of Charles Bulfinch, Architect, with other Family Papers* (Boston: Houghton, Mifflin and Company, 1896), 249. The group was replicated in Vermont marble in 1958 when the east front of the Capitol was extended.

[11] Persico's *War* and *Peace* were removed from the niches of the east front portico during the 1958 extension of the east front of the Capitol. The deteriorated statues were mended and cast in plaster, copied in Vermont marble, and placed in the replicated niches. The original statuary is in storage, and the plaster models are located in the rotunda of the Cannon House Office Building on the subway level. RG 40, Subject Files, Curator's Office, AOC.

[12] Prior to Greenough, American pioneer-sculptor John Frazee (1790–1852) received a commission of $500 for his bust of John Jay in 1831. RG 40, Subject Files, Curator's Office, AOC.

that the statue could be seen to the best advantage. The act of Congress designated the center of the Rotunda as the location of the statue. It was placed in position on the floor level in 1841, a special foundation being prepared for it. In 1842 it was removed to the eastern park because of its unsatisfactory appearance in the Rotunda [Plate 118]. This statue caused much discussion among Congressmen and visitors to the Capitol, because of its pose and drapery. Greenough contended that the only method of treating a statue which was to last for generations was to treat it as a nude or with simple conventional drapery, as he considered fashions in clothes as changeable and liable to become in a short time ridiculous. He also desired to remove the statue from the Rotunda to the west front, but Congress determined to place it on the east front. Over the statue he wished a classical structure erected, which would be an ornament to the grounds, as he states it was not intended to be exposed to the weather.[13] At present day (1900) the statue is housed during the winter in a cumbersome wooden structure, which is a constant subject of ridicule. A classical structure might be readily devised to protect this work, which would improve its artistic qualities and at the same time be an ornament to the grounds.[14]

Congress made appropriations to commemorate the Chief Justices at a comparatively early date, ordering a bust of Chief Justice Ellsworth on June 30, 1834. This bust was completed by Mr. Augur, an American sculptor, in 1840. A marble bust of Chief Justice Marshall was ordered May 9, 1836, and completed in 1840. March 2, 1831, John Frazee was authorized to execute a bust of John Jay for the Supreme Court room. [Plate 118a.][15]

May 5, 1832, Congress authorized the Committee on Library to purchase from the executors a bust of Jefferson by Ceracci.[16]

The Tripoli naval monument was moved from the Navy-Yard and placed on the terrace in front of the western portico by act of March 2, 1831, and remained in this position until it was removed to Annapolis, Md. This monument was executed in Italy of Italian marble, and the base in this country of Maryland marble. The naval officers bore the expense of this memorial to their fellows who were killed in the battle of Tripoli, August 3, 1804. The monument consisted of a small Doric column crowned by an eagle in the act of flying. The shaft of the column was ornamented by the beaks of Turkish vessels. One face of the base on which the shaft rested was a sculptured basso-rilievo of Tripoli and its fortresses on the Mediterranean in the distance, and the American fleet in the foreground. The other sides of the base contain descriptions, one giving the names of the officers who fell in the battle—Somers, Caldwell, Decatur (brother of the Commodore), Wadsworth, Dorsey, and Israel—another the epitaph. On each angle of the base stood a marble figure, one representing America directing the attention of her children to History, who is recording the intrepid action of the Navy; another represented Fame with a wreath of laurel in one hand and a pen in the other, while a fourth represented Mercury as the genius of commerce, with his cornucopia and caduceus. [Plate 89.][17]

---

[13] Committee on the Library, *Removal of Greenough's Statue of Washington: Report [To Accompany Joint Resolution H.R. No. 43]*, H. report 219 (27–3), Serial 427. This report includes Greenough's letter requesting that Congress allow him to supervise the removal of his statue of Washington from the Rotunda to the Capitol grounds.

[14] Greenough's George Washington was transferred by the Architect of the Capitol to the Smithsonian Institution in 1908. It is now located at the National Museum of American History. The pedestal of the statue became the cornerstone for the Capitol Power Plant set in 1908. RG 40, Subject Files, Curator's Office, AOC.

[15] See AOC, *Art in the United States Capitol*, 209–210. Modern scholarship indicates that the busts of Ellsworth and Marshall were completed ca. 1837 and 1839, respectively.

[16] Giuseppe Ceracchi's bust of Jefferson was destroyed by a fire in the Library of Congress in 1851. See AOC, *Art in the United States Capitol*, 412–413.

[17] The *Tripoli* or *Peace Monument* by Charles Micali was originally placed in the Navy Yard, and later moved to the Capitol's west grounds in 1831. It was transferred to the United States Naval Academy in Annapolis, Maryland, in 1860. See AOC, *Art in the United States Capitol*, 409.

PLATE 106

OLD ROOM OF VICE PRESIDENTS, 1900 A. D., ROBING ROOM SUPREME COURT.

S–230, now used by the Republican Leader.

PLATE 107

OLD ROOM OF VICE PRESIDENT. 1900 A. D. ROBING ROOM SUPREME COURT.

The portraits of the Supreme Court Justices depicted in this view of S–231 were moved to the Supreme Court Building when it opened in 1935.

PLATE 108

NORTHWEST VIEW OF CAPITOL 1840.

View by W. H. Bartlett, published in N. P. Willis, *American Scenery* (London, 1840).

PLATE 109

SOUTHEAST VIEW, 1840.

Engraving by R. Brandard after the painting by W. H. Bartlett, published in N. P. Willis, *American Scenery* (1840).

PLATE 110

CAPITOL VIEW FROM PRESIDENT'S MANSION, 1840.

W. H. Bartlett, ca. 1839.

PLATE 111

SOUTHWEST VIEW 1840, FROM OLD PRINT.

View of the Capitol from the west front showing the original dome, J. & F. Tallis, 1831. This view did not include Bulfinch's earthen terraces. The central stair was never a part of the west front design. *Kiplinger Washington Collection.*

PLATE 112

CLOCK IN OLD HOUSE OF REPRESENTATIVES.

Carlo Franzoni, *Car of History,* marble, 1819.

PLATE 113

JUSTICE IN OLD SUPREME COURT. 1900 A. D. SUPREME COURT LIBRARY.

Carlo Franzoni, *Justice*, plaster, 1817. Once used as the Supreme Court Library, S–141 has been restored as the Old Supreme Court Chamber.

PLATE 114

CAPTAIN SMITH AND POCAHONTAS.

WM. PENN AND THE
INDIANS.

DANIEL BOONE AND
THE INDIANS.

LANDING OF THE PILGRIMS.

Antonio Capellano, *Preservation of Captain Smith by Pocahontas,*
sandstone, ca. 1826.
Located over west door.

Nicholas Gevelot, *William Penn's Treaty with the Indians,*
sandstone, 1826–1827.
Located over north door.

Enrico Causici, *Conflict of Daniel Boone and the Indians,*
sandstone, 1826–1827.
Located over south door.

Enrico Causici, *Landing of the Pilgrims,*
sandstone, 1825.
Located over the east door.

PANELS IN ROTUNDA.

PLATE 115

STATUE OF LIBERTY, OLD HOUSE OF REPRESENTATIVES

Enrico Causici, *Liberty and the Eagle,* plaster, 1817–1819, National Statuary Hall.

PLATE 116

EAST CENTRAL PORTICO, SHOWING STATUARY IN PEDIMENT.

Luigi Persico, pediment relief, *Genius of America*, sandstone, 1825–1828.
The pediment relief was reproduced in marble in 1959–60 as part of the east front extension project. The sculptures on the cheekblocks
(left: Luigi Persico, *Discovery of America*, marble, 1844; right: Horatio Greenough, *Rescue*, marble, 1853) were removed and have not been reproduced.

228

PLATE 117

FIGURES OF PEACE AND WAR, ON EAST PORTICO.

Luigi Persico, marble, placed in 1834. Brown's caption suggests incorrectly that the figure of *Peace* is on the left; in fact, *War* is on the left and *Peace* is on the right.
The present reproductions were carved in marble in 1958 after Persico.

PLATE 118

GEORGE WASHINGTON, BY GREENOUGH.

Horatio Greenough, marble, 1833–36. The statue was located on the east Capitol grounds until 1908, when it was transferred to the Smithsonian Institution, Washington, D.C. It can be viewed today at the National Museum of American History.

GROUP OF CHIEF JUSTICES, SUPREME COURT.

John Frazee, *John Jay,* 1831; Hiram Powers, *John Marshall,* 1839; Alexander Galt, *John Rutledge,* 1858; and Hezekiah Augur, *Oliver Ellsworth,* ca. 1837.
These marble busts are now located in the Old Supreme Court Chamber, S–141.

DECLARATION OF INDEPENDENCE
In Congress, at the Independence Hall, Philadelphia, July 4th 1776.

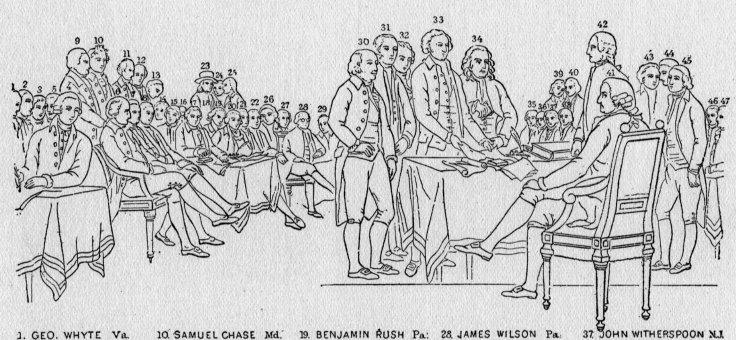

1. GEO. WHYTE Va.	10. SAMUEL CHASE Md.	19. BENJAMIN RUSH Pa.	28. JAMES WILSON Pa.	37. JOHN WITHERSPOON N.J.
2. WM. WHIPPLE N.H.	11. LEWIS MORRIS N.Y.	20. ELBRIDGE GERRY Mass.	29. FRANCIS HOPKINSON N.J.	38. SAM HUNTINGTON Con.
3. JOSIAH BARTLETT N.H.	12. WILLIAM FLOYD N.Y.	21. ROB. TREAT PAINE Mass.	30. JOHN ADAMS Mass.	39. WILLIAM WILLIAMS Con.
4. BENJ. HARRISON Va.	13. ARTHUR MIDDLETON S.C.	22. ABRAM CLARK N.J.	31. ROGER SHERMAN Con.	40. OLIVER WOLCOTT Con.
5. THOMAS LYNCH S.C.	14. THOMAS HAYWARD S.C.	23. STEPH HOPKINS R.I.	32. ROB. L. LIVINGSTON N.Y.	41. JOHN HANCOCK Mass.
6. RICHARD HENRY LEE Va.	15. CHAS. CARROLL Md.	24. WILLIAM ELLERY R.I.	33. THOMAS JEFFERSON Va.	42. CHAS THOMPSON Pa.
7. SAM. ADAMS Mass.	16. GEO. WALTON Ga.	25. GEO. CLYMER Pa.	34. BENJ. FRANKLIN Pa.	43. GEORGE READ Del.
8. GEO. CLINTON N.Y.	17. ROB. MORRIS Pa.	26. WILLIAM HOOPER N.C.	35. RICHARD STOCKTON N.J.	44. JOHN DICKINSON Pa.
9. WILLIAM PACA Md.	18. THOM. WILLING Pa.	27. JOSEPH HEWES N.C.	36. FRANCIS LEWIS N.Y.	45. EDW. RUTLEDGE S.C.

46. THOMAS McKEAN Pa.   47. PHILIP LIVINGSTON N.Y.

PLATE 119

THE DECLARATION OF INDEPENDENCE, ROTUNDA.
John Trumbull, oil on canvas, placed in the Rotunda in 1826.

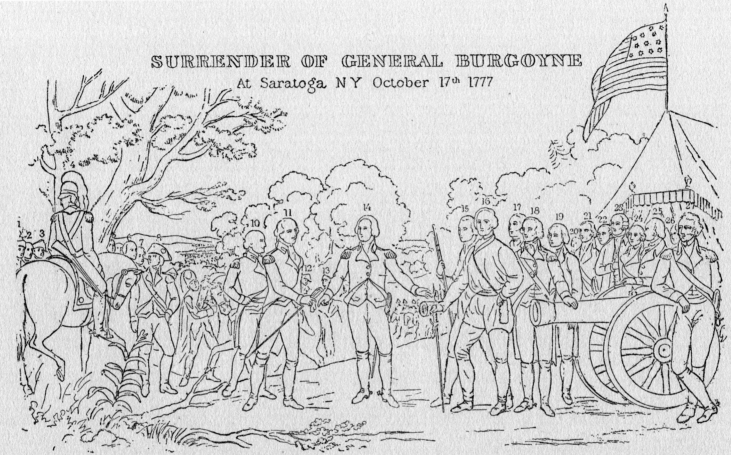

SURRENDER OF GENERAL BURGOYNE

At Saratoga NY October 17th 1777

1. Major LITHCOW Mass 2 Colonel CILLY N H   3. General STARK N.H   4 Capt SEYMOUR Con of Shelton's horse.
5 Major HULL Mass   6 Colonel GREATON Mass   7 Major DEARBORNE N H   8 Colonel SCAMMELL N H.
9. Colonel LEWIS Quartermaster General N H.   10. Major General PHILLIPS British   11. Lieut General BURGOYNE British.
12. General Baron RIEDESEL German   13. Colonel WILKINSON Deputy-Adjudant General, American   14 General GATES.
15. Colonel PRESCOTT Mass. Volunteers.   16. Colonel MORGAN Virginia Riflemen   17 Brigadier General RUFUS PUTNAM Mass.
18. Lieutenant Colonel JOHN BROOKS late Governor of Massachusetts.   19 Rev Mr HITCHCOCK Chaplain R.I
20. Major ROB. TROUP Aid de Camp N.Y.   21. Major HASKELL   22 Major ARMSTRONG.   23. Major Gen PH SCHUYLER Albany.
24. Brigadier General GLOVER Mass.   25 Brigadier Gen WHIPPLE N H Militia.   26. Major M CLARKSON Aid de Camp N Y
27. Major EBENEZER STEVENS Mass Commanding the Artillery

PLATE 120

SURRENDER OF BURGOYNE, ROTUNDA.

John Trumbull, oil on canvas, placed in the Rotunda in 1826.

SURRENDER OF LORD CORNWALLIS

At Yorktown Va. October 19th 1781.

The portraits of the French Officers were obtained in Paris 1787 and painted by Trumbull from the living men, in the house of Mr Jefferson then Minister to France from the United States.

1. Count DEUXPONTS *Colonel of French Infantry*. 2. Duke de LAVAL MONTMORENCY *Colonel of French Infantry*.

3. Count CUSTINE *Colonel of French Infantry*. 4. Duke de LAUZUN *Colonel of French Cavalry*.

5. General CHOIZY. 6. Viscount VIOMENIL. 7. Marquis de St SIMON. 8. Count FERSEN *Aid de Camp of Count Rochambeau*.

9. Count CHARLES DAMAS *Aid de Camp of Count Rochambeau*. 10. Marquis CHASTELLUX. 11. Baron VIOMENIL.

12. Count de BARRAS *Admiral*. 13. Count de GRASSE *Admiral*. 14. Count ROCHAMBEAU *General en Chef des Français*.

15. General LINCOLN. 16. Colonel E. STEVENS *of American Artillery*. 17. General WASHINGTON *Commander in Chief*.

18. THOM. NELSON *Gov. of Va*. 19. Marquis LA FAYETTE. 20. Baron STEUBEN. 21. Col. COBB *Aid de Camp to Gen. Washington*.

22. Colonel TRUMBULL *Secretary to Gen. Washington*. 23. Major General JAMES CLINTON N.Y. 24. General GIST Md.

25. Gen. ANTHONY WAYNE Pa. 26. General HAND Pa. *Adjutant General*. 27. General PETER MUHLENBERG. Pa.

28. Major Gen. HENRY KNOX *Commander of Artillery*. 29. Lieut. Col. E. HUNTINGTON *Acting Aid de Camp of Gen. Lincoln*

30. Colonel TIMOTHY PICKERING *Quartermaster General*. 31. Colonel ALEX. HAMILTON *Commanding light Infantry*

Col. JOHN LAURENS S.C. 33. Colonel WALTER STUART Phila. 34. Colonel NICHOLAS FISH N.Y.

PLATE 121

SURRENDER OF LORD CORNWALLIS, ROTUNDA.

John Trumbull, oil on canvas, placed in the Rotunda in 1826.

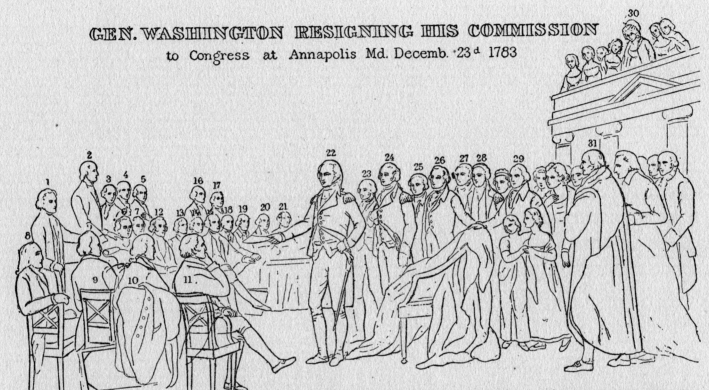

GEN. WASHINGTON RESIGNING HIS COMMISSION

to Congress at Annapolis Md. Decemb. 23ᵈ 1783

1 THOMAS MIFFLIN Pa. *President, Member of Congress* 2. CHAS THOMPSON Pa. *Member of Congress.* 3. ELBRIDGE GERRY Mass. *M.C.*
4 HUGH WILLIAMSON N.C. *M.C.* 5 SAMUEL OSGOOD Mass. *M.C.* 6. EDW McCOMB Del *M.C.* 7 GEO. PARTRIDGE Mass *M.C.*
8. EDWARD LLOYD Md. *M.C.* 9 R.D. SPAIGHT N.C. *M.C.* 10 BENJ. HAWKINS N.C. *M.C.* 11. A FOSTER N.H. *M.C.*
12. THOMAS JEFFERSON Va. *M.C.* 13 ARTHUR LEE Va. *M.C.* 14 DAVID HOWELL R.I. *M.C.* 15 JAMES MONROE Va. *M.C.*
16. JACOB REID S.C. *M.C.* 17 JAMES MADISON Va. *Spectator* 18. WILLIAM ELLERY R.I. *M.C.* 19. J TOWNLEY CHASE Md. *M.C.*
20 S. HARDY Va. *M.C.* 21 CHAS. MORRISS Pa. *M.C.* 22 General WASHINGTON 23 Colonel BENJ. WALKER *Aid de Camp.*
24. Col DAVID HUMPHRYS *Aid de Camp.* 25 Gen SMALLWOOD Md. *Spectator* 26. Gen. OTHO HOLLAND WILLIAMS Md *Spectr.*
27 Col SAMUEL SMITH Md. *Spectr* 28 Col. JOHN E. HOWARD Baltimore. *Spectr* 29 CHAS. CARROLL *and two daughters* Md.
30 Mrs WASHINGTON *and her three Grand-Children* 31. DANIEL of St JENNIFER Md *Spectator.*

PLATE 122

WASHINGTON RESIGNING HIS COMMISSION, ROTUNDA, BY JOHN TRUMBULL.

Oil on canvas, placed in the Rotunda in 1826.

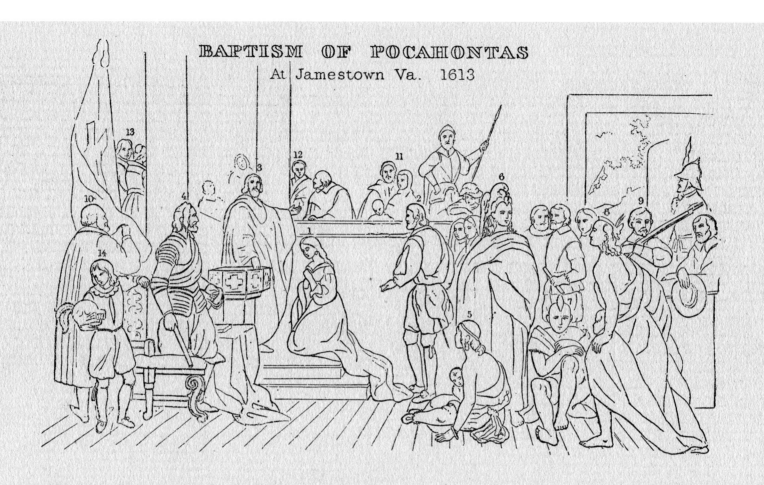

BAPTISM OF POCAHONTAS

At Jamestown Va. 1613

1. POCAHONTAS.   2. JOHN ROLFE.   3. ALEX. WHITEAKER   4 SIR THOMAS DALE.   5 SISTER to POCAHONTAS.
6. NANTEQUAUS *Brother to Pocahontas.* 7. OPECHANCANOUGH   8. OPACHISCO *Uncle to Pocahontas* 9. RICH. WYFFIN.
10. STANDARD BEARER.   11. Mr. & Mrs. FORREST   *the first gentlewoman who arrived in the colony.*   12. HENRY SPILMAN.
13. JOHN & ANNE LAYDON *the first persons married in the colony*   14. THE PAGE.

Entered according to Act of Congress in the year 1859 by F. & C. Metzeroth.

PLATE 123

BAPTISM OF POCAHONTAS, BY JOHN G. CHAPMAN.

Oil on canvas, placed in the Rotunda in 1840.

LANDING OF COLUMBUS

At the Island of Guanahani, West-Indies, October 12th 1492.

1. COLUMBUS. 2. MARTIN ALONZO PINZON. 3. VINCENT YANNEZ PINZON. 4. RODRIGO des ESCOBEDO or ESCOBAR *Notary of the Armament.*
5. RODERIGO SANCHEZ *Insp. of Armam.* 6. MUTINEER *in a suppliant Attitude.* 7. ALONZO de OJEDA. 8. CABIN BOY *in kneeling posture.*
9. SOLDIER *whose attention is partly diverted from the ceremony by the appearance of the awe striken natives in the forest.*
10. SAILOR *in attitude of veneration for the Admiral.* 11. FRIAR *bearing a cruzifix.*
In the distance groups express joy and hilarity on their landing. Two figures somewhat nearer are contending for glittering particles in the sand. The three vessels – the Santa Maria, Pinta and Ninna are seen in the distance.

PLATE 124

THE LANDING OF COLUMBUS, BY JOHN VANDERLYN.

Oil on canvas, placed in the Rotunda in 1847.

EMBARKATION OF THE PILGRIMS

At Delft Haven, Holland, July 22nd 1620.

1. Mr. ROBINSON *Pastor of the congregation* 2. Elder WM. BREWSTER. 3. Mrs. BREWSTER *and sick child.*
4. Gov. CARVER. 5. WM. BRADFORD 6. Mr & Mrs WHITE 7 Mr & Mrs WINSLOW. 8. Mr. & Mrs FULLER.
9. MILES STANDISH *and his wife Rose.* 10. Mrs BRADFORD, *she fell overboard the day the vessel came to anchor.*
11. Mrs CARVER *and child.* 12. Capt. REYNOLDS *and Sailor* 13 BOY *belonging to Carver and family.*
14 BOY *in charge of Mr. Winslow.* 15. BOY *belonging to Mrs. Winslow's family* 16 A NURSE *and child.*

PLATE 125

THE EMBARKATION OF THE PILGRIMS, BY ROBERT WIER.

Robert Weir, oil on canvas, placed in the Rotunda in 1843. Brown misspelled the artist's surname.

PLATE 126

PORTRAIT OF LAFAYETTE BY ARY SCHEFFER.

Oil on canvas, gift of the artist, 1824. The painting was located in the Old Hall of the House of Representatives until 1857, when it was moved to the new House Chamber.

PLATE 127

GEORGE WASHINGTON, BY VANDERLYN.

John Vanderlyn, oil on canvas, 1834, after Gilbert Stuart. The painting was commissioned in 1832 by the House of Representatives to commemorate the centennial of George Washington's birth. It hung in the Old Hall of the House until 1857, when it was moved to the new House Chamber.

PLATE 128

PORTRAIT OF WASHINGTON. BY PEALE.

Rembrandt Peale, oil on canavas, 1823. It was purchased in 1832 by the Senate to commemorate the centennial of George Washington's birth.
It hangs in the Old Senate Chamber, S–228.

The groups on the central eastern portico, one by Persico and the other by Greenough, although ordered March 3, 1837, were not completed for years—the one by Persico not until 1846, and the group by Greenough not until 1854. They were not set in place early enough to become identified with the old Capitol.

The paintings in the Capitol at this period were limited in number, the principal ones of interest being the historical ones in the Rotunda. Four of these paintings were made by Col. John Trumbull, who was Washington's aid-de-camp in the first year of the Revolutionary War, and was then Deputy Adjutant-General under General Gates. Trumbull studied painting in this country and Europe with the purpose of commemorating the historical events of the Revolution, being well acquainted with the events and the famous men who participated in the scenes. He came back to this country in 1789 and made portraits of the men and traveled through the country making sketches of the localities where the scenes which he wished to depict had occurred. February 6, 1817, Congress passed a resolution authorizing four paintings commemorating the most important events of the American Revolution. The price paid was $32,000.[18]

THE DECLARATION OF INDEPENDENCE.

The Declaration of Independence was the first. Trumbull consulted with Adams and Jefferson as to the parties who should be represented in this painting, and spared neither time nor expense in obtaining portraits of those who were living and of whom he had no portraits. Adams was painted in London, Jefferson in Paris, Hancock and Samuel Adams in Boston, Edward Rutledge in Charleston, Wythe in Williamsburg, Va.

The costumes are a faithful copy of those worn at the period, and the room is a painted reproduction of the interior in which Congress held their sessions. [Plate 119, with explanatory key.]

THE SURRENDER OF BURGOYNE.

After the battle at Bemis Heights, October 7, 1777, Burgoyne found his position so critical that he commenced a retreat toward Canada, but on account of bad roads, dismantled bridges, and the hostile Americans along the road he halted at Saratoga, and on October 17 surrendered his army to the American forces under General Gates. [Plate 120, with explanatory key.]

SURRENDER OF CORNWALLIS.

Cornwallis, after a successful campaign through the South and in Virginia, was finally hemmed in by the combined forces of Washington, the French allies from the North, and the French fleet and army under Count de Grasse from the West Indies, at Yorktown, Va., where he found it necessary to surrender on the 19th of October, 1781. The terms of surrender were arranged by General Lincoln.

The painting represents the principal officers of the British army, conducted by General Lincoln, passing the two groups of American and French generals and entering between the lines of the victorious armies. [Plate 121, with explanatory key.]

THE RESIGNATION OF GENERAL WASHINGTON.

After taking leave of his old comrades in New York, General Washington proceeded to Annapolis, where Congress was in session, and to that body handed his resignation as General of the Army. The Journal of Congress, December 23, 1783, gives the speech of Washington on this occasion, as well as the speech made by Thomas Mifflin, President of the Congress. Mifflin, who accepted his resignation, and

---

[18] *Expenditures in the District of Columbia: Report,* H. report 515 (18–1), Serial 446. This source includes the titles and dates of all bills appropriating money for the Capitol building between 1789 and 1843, including major works of art.

Trumbull, who painted the picture, were both aids-de-camp of Washington. [Plate 122, with explanatory key.]

Under a joint resolution of Congress of June 23, 1836, a committee was appointed to "contract with one or more competent American artists for the execution of four historical pictures upon subjects serving to illustrate the discovery of America, the settlement of the United States, the history of the Revolution, and the adoption of the Constitution, to be placed in the vacant panels of the Rotunda, the choice to be left to the artists, under the control of the committee." [19] The committee reported February 28, 1837, that they had selected John Vanderlyn, Henry Inman, Robert Wier, and John G. Chapman to undertake the execution of these paintings. The committee had made contracts with two of the artists mentioned and expected to close a contract with the other two for $10,000 each. Henry Inman died apparently without commencing his picture and the panel was given to William H. Powell March 3, 1847.[20] The final payment was made on the paintings, excepting the one executed by Powell, in the year 1847. The period at which they were put in place identifies only three of the paintings with the old building, and these three only with the latest period of its history. The painting by Powell was installed in the year 1855, when the Capitol extension was well advanced.

[19] F. C. Adams, *Art in the District of Columbia*, a report to the Commissioner of Education, ca. 1868, p. 729, bound in "Documentary History of Art Commissions, 1858–1911," Curator's Office, AOC.

[20] "Report of Mr. McKeon on choice of Chapman, Inman, Vanderlyn, and Weir (misspelled by Brown) as artists for paintings for the Rotunda, February 28, 1837," in *DHC*, 335.

"THE BAPTISM OF POCAHONTAS," BY JOHN G. CHAPMAN.

This scene is supposed to have taken place just prior to the marriage of Pocahontas, which occurred April, 1613. The picture gives idealized representations of Pocahontas, her brother and sister, as well as of Rolfe, Sir Thomas Dale, and other colonists and Indians. [Plate 123, with explanatory key.]

'THE LANDING OF COLUMBUS," BY JOHN VANDERLYN.

This painting is intended to represent the landing of the Spaniards on San Salvador in 1492. Columbus, in command of the Santa Maria, Nina, and Pinta, takes formal possession of this island with the fond idea that he had discovered a new passage to the East Indies. As this picture is not equal, according to critics, to the work of Vanderlyn shown in other paintings, particularly his marines, much of the actual execution is attributed to French painters who assisted him. [Plate 124, with explanatory key.]

"THE EMBARKATION OF THE PILGRIMS," BY ROBERT WIER.

The artist represents the Pilgrims on the Speedwell before she set sail from Delftshaven for Southampton, July 22, 1620. The Speedwell did not reach America, as she proved unseaworthy, and the larger part of her passengers were transferred to the Mayflower at Plymouth, England, before the latter vessel finally set sail, late in September, 1620. [Plate 125 with explanatory key.]

There were two paintings prominently placed in the old Hall of Representatives, one of George Washington by Vanderlyn, the other of Lafayette by Ary Scheffer, an eminent Dutch artist. The painting of Lafayette was executed by his order and presented to Congress by him on his second visit to the United States, in 1824. [Plate 126.]

The apparent necessity for a picture on the other side of the Speaker's chair was the cause of Congress ordering the portrait of

Washington. Vanderlyn, who had been a pupil of Gilbert Stuart, evidently used one of Stuart's paintings of Washington as his motive in the execution of this work. [Plate 127.] [21]

In the year 1832 Congress passed a resolution to purchase for $2,000 the painting of Washington by Rembrandt Peale. This portrait was painted from sketches of Washington made by the painter when a young man, combined with zealous study of the Houdon statue and existing portraits of Washington. The picture was much commented on by Washington's contemporaries as better depicting the character and appearance of the man than any other portrait of our first President. [Plate 128.] [22]

The committees in charge of selecting works of art for the old Capitol used good judgment in obtaining the most capable American sculptors of their period to execute the commissions which were awarded to them. After the employment of Greenough and Trumbull no commissions were given to either foreign sculptors or painters. Viewed from this standpoint, the work is valuable as an exhibition of the artistic history of the country. This fact, taken in connection with the fact that the larger number were made from the living personage and depict the character and details of costume and settings, makes them both very interesting and valuable.

---

[21] The House of Representatives commissioned this portrait to commemorate the centennial of Washington's birth. The artist used Gilbert Stuart's portrait of Washington as his model. Curator's Files, AOC.

[22] Report of the Secretary of the Senate, with the Annual Statement of Expenditures from the Contingent Fund, S. doc. 2 (22–2), Serial 230. The painting, purchased for the centennial of Washington's birth, is now located in S-228, Old Senate Chamber. See AOC, Art in the United States Capitol, 4.

CHAPTER VIII

HISTORY OF THE ARCHITECTS OF THE CAPITOL

D R. WILLIAM THORNTON, architect [Plate 129], a West Indian, was one of the first as well as one of the most interesting of the pioneers of the profession in this country.[1] His family were prominent among the Friends in England. His parents moved to the island of Tortola, in the West Indies, in 1761. Here Thornton was born, May 27 of the same year. At this period either Thornton's father or uncle was governor of the island.

When 5 years old Thornton was sent to England to be educated. He studied medicine under Dr. Feld, and with the noted Dr. Brown, of Edinburgh. In that city he graduated in medicine in 1784. His studies were continued in Paris, and there an intimate friendship was formed with the noted Countess Beauharnais, a relative of Empress Josephine's first husband. She was an authoress and held a famous salon. Thornton traveled extensively on the continent of Europe with Count Audriani, the naturalist, after which he came to this country and formed a temporary residence in Philadelphia. In 1790 he married the daughter of Mrs. Ann Brodeau, a successful school-teacher of Philadelphia. Mrs. Thornton, who was born in England, was a lady of culture, and an artist of some ability, which is proved by a miniature of her husband in the possession of Mrs. Kennon. After their marriage they returned to Tortola, where Thornton had an interest in the estate of his father. In 1793 he moved to Washington City, where he lived until his death, in 1828. He left no children. Upon his arrival in the city he found it necessary to take a house in Georgetown. Some years afterwards he moved to 1331 F Street, opposite the present Ebbitt House. At this place he and James Madison were neighbors for eight years. Benj. Ogle Tayloe says: "He had a well-earned reputation for letters and taste; . . . he was a wit, a painter, and a poet." Dunlap, whose work was published only a short time after Thornton's death, says: "He was a scholar and a gentleman, full of talent and eccentricity, a Quaker, by profession a painter, a poet, and well acquainted with the mechanics and arts; his company was a complete antidote to dullness." [2]

Thornton's duties brought him into close relation with such eminent men of his day as Washington, Madison, Jefferson, Randolph, L'Enfant, Adams, Hamilton, and Fulton. He was intimate socially with the Tayloes, Carrolls, Stuarts, Van Nesses, and others who were the features of political and social life at the Federal capital in those days. The acquaintance with Washington ripened into such an intimacy that his home was the President's familiar resort when in the Federal City.

The National Intelligencer of March 29, 1828, as well as the Columbian Institute and the Colonization Societies in memorials on his death, pay a high tribute to his ability, good-fellowship, and philanthropy. The American Philosophical Society conferred the Magellenic gold medal upon him in December, 1792, as a distinction for his book on the elements of written language, which was published in Philadelphia, in 1793, under the title of Cadmus. There is an extended review of Cadmus in the Monthly Review of the year of publication, as well as a note in reference to an article on teaching the dumb. He published

---

[1] A portion of this chapter was based on Brown's article, "Dr. William Thornton, Architect," *Architectural Record* 6 (July–September, 1896): 52–70.

[2] For quotations, see William Dunlap, *A History of the Rise and Progress of the Art of Design in the United States*, 3 vols. (Boston: C. E. Goodspeed & Co., 1918; new edition, with additions by Frank W. Bayley and Charles E. Goodspeed), vol. 2, 8.

papers on medicine, astronomy, philosophy, finance, government, and art, as well as on language.

According to the Science Record, in June, 1810, he published a long defense of Fitch as the inventor of the application of steam to navigation. This pamphlet was reprinted in the Patent Office Record in 1850, and is considered an official document of value. As an inventor he claimed, according to Tayloe, to be the first to apply steam to boat propulsion. He was associated with Fitch in his experiments on the Delaware before Fulton commenced his on the Hudson. Brissot describes Fitch running a boat from Philadelphia to Trenton in 1789 by steam, and notes the fact that thousands witnessed the event. In his pamphlet (1810) Thornton claims that Fulton was indebted to him for valuable suggestions, as Fulton saw Thornton's drawings when he visited the Patent Office in 1806. As early as 1788 Rumsey applied for a patent on steamboats, which conflicted with the invention of Fitch. This was proved by Fitch winning the case. Fulton's first patent was not issued until 1809. Thornton claimed that Fulton's death was due to worry caused by the strength of his pamphlet. While in America the first time Thornton was engaged to build steamboats to navigate the Mississippi (before 1790). This scheme fell through for lack of financial aid. Thornton seems to have had greater faith in the future of steamboats than Fulton, who offered to bet the former that a boat could never go more than 5 miles an hour, while Thornton expected a speed of 12 miles.

Another invention which has recently been revived was the conversion of sawdust into planks. Thornton received patents for improvements in steamboats, steam boilers, and condensers. Fernando Fairfax gave him £2,000 for a quarter interest in his patents and manufacturing companies.

As an artist Thornton was more than an amateur. Tayloe mentions a head of Jefferson by King as a copy of a painting by Thornton, and Mrs. Kennon, at present the owner of Tudor House, in Georgetown, who knew Thornton in her childhood, has a miniature of Washington painted by him. Mr. Charles Hoffman, of Frederick, Md., and Mrs. Miller, of Washington, have pieces of his work, among them being a portrait of the Countess of Beauharnais.

Thornton was noted for both philanthropy and bravery. Brissot says: "From conversations with Thornton, although his exterior denotes not the Quaker, yet he professes their principles and practices their morality." [3] Brissot gives quite a lengthy account of Thornton's efforts to colonize the negroes in Africa. He went to the expense of sending an agent to Africa to locate a colony. Unfortunately, this vast scheme was not accomplished. He became actively interested in negro colonization as early as 1789, and was until his death a member of the American Colonization Society.

When the British captured Washington, in 1814, an officer ordered a gun turned on the Patent Office building. Thornton rode up and jumped off his horse in front of the gun demanding: "Are you Englishmen or Goths and Vandals? This is the Patent Office, the depository of the inventive genius of America, in which the whole civilized world is concerned. Would you destroy it? If so, fire away and let the charge pass through my body." By this effort the patent records were saved. Thornton carried the Patent Office records to his farm in the country, so that none were lost. He also placed a guard at the Navy-Yard and Capitol during the evacuation. [4]

---

[3] J. P. Brissot de Warville, *New Travels in the United States of America in 1788* (1792; reprint ed., New York: Augustus Kelly, 1970), 167–168.

[4] This often repeated account first appeared in the diary of Mrs. (Anna Maria) Thornton. "Diary of Mrs. William Thornton: Capture of Washington by the British," *Records of the Columbia Historical Society* 19 (1916): 172–183.

PLATE 129

DR. WM. THORNTON, ARCHITECT.

Filippo Costaggini, oil on canvas, 1881, after a miniature in the possession of the Thornton family.

Several instances are on record where in attempting to protect a wife from a brutal husband he in turn found it necessary to defend himself against both wife and husband.

Among his papers are his commissions as lieutenant and captain in the war of 1812.

One of his most intimate friends was John Tayloe, the owner of the Octagon House, probably the most noted producer of race horses in this country. Thornton also kept and raised race horses. He imported fine animals from Barbary and England. His account books show quite a number of blooded stock that were valued at more than $2,000 apiece. By horses and benevolence he is said to have lost large sums of money.

There are three things that connect Thornton intimately with the history of Washington City and the country, and where the excellent character of his work places the people under obligation to him: First, for his artistic capacity and skill in producing the best scheme for a Capitol, which forms the nucleus of the present structure. Second, for his general culture, breadth, and capacity as one of the Commissioners of the District, which are shown in the execution of the magnificent ideas of Washington and L'Enfant as to streets, and his own and Hoban's ideas as to buildings and grounds. Third, for his mechanical knowledge and executive ability. The Patent Office, which has fostered and encouraged the inventive ability of the country, began under his management.

The Superintendent of Public Buildings and Grounds has quite a number of volumes, embracing early letters concerning the formation of the District of Columbia, the laying out of Washington City, and the erection of the Federal buildings, as well as a complete record of the proceedings of the Commissioners from 1792 to 1802. The history of Thornton's connection with the city and public buildings is to be found in these volumes and in letters in the possession of private parties. By act of Congress of January 4, 1790, the President was authorized to appoint a commission to survey the District, and to purchase, adopt,

and lay out a plan for the Federal City, and prior to the first Monday in December, 1800, they were to "provide suitable buildings for the accommodation of Congress, the President, and the public offices of the United States Government." All their work was subject to the approval of President Washington. The first commissioners, appointed January 22, 1791, were Thomas Johnson and David Carroll, of Maryland, and David Stuart, of Virginia.

On September 16, 1794, Thornton received this commission from President Washington: ... "I hereby appoint said William Thornton one of the commissioners for surveying the district of territory accepted ... for the permanent seat of the Government of the United States, ... with all authority to proceed according to law.

"Given this 12th day of September, 1794, of the Independence of the United States the nineteenth.

"GEORGE WASHINGTON,
"BY EDW. RANDOLPH."

There is nothing in the records to show the time that the commissioners were expected to devote to their duties. This matter was probably left to their own judgment, and they must have had considerable time to devote to private business.

The salary of a commissioner was $1,600 per annum. After Thornton became a member of the board of commissioners, a decided improvement is evident in their written proceedings and in the business forms and contracts which were introduced in connection with the streets, bridges, and buildings that were in their charge. As they appear in the records after his appointment, Thornton should have the credit for the improvement. The ability of Thornton was appreciated by his contemporaries. Andrew Ellicott, who was doing the field work in laying out the city, sent a letter rejoicing in Thornton's appointment for the good of the streets and buildings, saying: "The former commissioners were totally ignorant and an easy prey." He warns Thornton to be on his guard. Washington, before retiring from the Presidency, says: "I think the United States are interested in the continuance of you in the service; therefore I should regret if either of you [Thornton, Scott, or White] by resignation should deprive them of assistance which I believe you are able to give."

Thornton's education and disposition caused him to take an active part in all the duties of the commissioners, which consisted in supervising the surveys for the District boundary, and the streets of the city, the subdivision of the squares into lots, the location of Federal buildings, the preparation of maps and their reproduction, obtaining plans for the Federal and the arrangements for temporary buildings and bridges, laying out grounds, the opening of quarries, brick yards and kilns, and lime kilns, the cutting of lumber, and obtaining workmen for brickmaking, quarrying, and stone-cutting, as well as brick and stone masons, carpenters, and laborers. Workmen at this period were obtained by advertisement and negotiation from England, Scotland, France, and different parts of this country.

The commissioners let all contracts and supervised the foremen who obtained the material from the quarry, kiln, or forest, and who superintended the work on streets, buildings, or bridges. In all cases we find Thornton insisting on the necessary grandeur of scale. He puts himself frequently on record as opposed to some of the narrower views of other members of the board. The commissioners, on July 20, 1795, made building regulations for the city. It would be fair to assume that Thornton, being the architect on the board, was the prime mover and preparer of these regulations. The commissioners obtained and disbursed money, bills for even the most trifling objects being submitted for their approval. They attended to the sale and other negotiations in connection with transfers of lots. Thornton was delegated to negotiate a loan in Philadelphia, and another later on in England. In both cases he was successful.

In answer to a letter from Washington concerning a national university, two commissioners write, February 18, 1797: "Dr. Thornton has long had in contemplation to lay before the Executive such a one."

In 1801 the commissioners of the District became offended at some report of Congress which reflected upon their management. By request, a committee of Congress examined their accounts and it was proved that the commissioners had served with perfect integrity. An act, May 1, 1802, abolished the office of the commissioners, their principal work being completed, and the President appointed Thomas Monroe to perform a part of their duties.

Thornton early displayed a talent for drawing. When a lad at school in England, he showed his uncle two £5 notes, asking him to select the one which was best engraved; the selection proved to be one young Thornton had just copied in pen and ink. When or where he prosecuted his architectural studies is not recorded. It has been asserted by some writers that he was simply a dilettante in the profession. The only way in which we can judge of his attainments is by an examination of his work, and a knowledge of the estimation in which he was held by his contemporaries. His drawings show skill in draftsmanship, as well as education and refinement in design. His executed work compares favorably with the best of the period in design and construction. He was trusted in a professional capacity during long periods by such astute men as Washington, Jefferson, Madison, and many others. Adolf Cluss, in an address in 1869, calls him an amateur. J. H. B. Latrobe, in an address delivered before the American Institute of Architects in Washington in 1881, states that Thornton had only two weeks' study in the profession. Trumbull gives him the credit of having studied three months. To have accomplished so much with so little study, he must have been a truly remarkable man.

Washington erected a building on North Capitol street, between B and C streets, Washington, D. C., which at the present time is known as the Hotel Kenmore. Dr. Thornton was the architect and superintendent, as is shown by letters of Washington. The exterior of the building has been altered and additional stories have been added. Some of the interior work still remains intact and shows the skill and refinement of the architect in detail. An old sketch gives an idea of the exterior of this building as it appeared in 1793.

Montpelier, Orange County, Va., the country residence of James Madison, was another piece of Thornton's work, which in dignity, simplicity, and refinement compares favorably with some of the best modern residences. In a letter to Mrs. M. H. Smith, September, 1830, President Madison says: "The only drawing of my house is that by Dr. William Thornton. It is without the wings now making a part of it." [5] The interior of Montpelier has been remodeled out of all semblance to its original self.

The Octagon House, Washington City, one of the most interesting old residences in this section of the country, was built by John Tayloe and completed in 1801. George Washington took a lively interest in its erection, as it was by his advice that the owner of the Octagon selected Washington for his home. Thornton was the architect. This house is simple and dignified on the exterior, being built of brick, with sandstone trimmings. The entrance porch has columns with Ionic caps. The plan is peculiarly interesting. The interior work, such as mantels, cornices, pilasters, and doors, is rich, elaborate, refined, and thorough in construction. It is still in an excellent state of preservation, although the house has been indifferently cared for for many years. The doors of the first floor in this house are mahogany. The figures on the parlor mantel are so good that they must have been made by some of the noted sculptors of that day, possibly Canova or Thorwaldsen.[6] John Tayloe, being wealthy, could have indulged his taste in such things. This house is interesting also from its historical associations, Madison having occupied it after the White House was burned by the British in 1814.

The Tudor House, Georgetown, D. C., was built about 1810 by a Mr. Peter. Although an imposing old structure, the work does not compare with that shown in the Octagon House. The interest in this house centers in the fact that one of Thornton's original sketches for both plan and elevation is still in existence. The exterior of this house is very nearly in its original condition. In the plan is the elliptical form of room which Thornton first used in his plan of the Capitol. While the exterior of this house is an improvement on the sketch, the alterations in plan, probably to save money, are decidedly inferior to the original.

There are several of Thornton's sketches for private houses in my possession.

He made Jefferson a design for the mace of the State of Virginia, in which he used the rattlesnake as the principal feature, because it is peculiarly American, is peaceful until hurt or aroused for self-defense, and only strikes after giving warning.

He made an elaborate scheme for a Washington Monument, a description and rough sketch of which are among his private papers. The sketch shows a mound of massive natural bowlders, on and around which are grouped many typical and natural figures, Washington surmounting the whole.

Among the drawings of Thornton which Mr. Edward Clark presented to the American Institute of Architects is what was evidently his design for the President's House. Thornton wrote from Tortola to the commissioners at that date, 1792, stating that he had made designs in

---

[5] Thornton was not involved in the design of Montpelier as Brown implies.

[6] Tayloe ordered the mantels from Coade Manufactory, Lambeth, England. For a detailed history of the architectural development and construction of the Octagon, see Orlando Ridout V, *Building the Octagon* (Washington: American Institute of Architects, 1989).

conformity with the advertisements soliciting competitive plans for the President's House and the Capitol. In an answer to this letter, November 15, 1792, the commissioners state that the plan for the President's palace had already been selected. This design of Thornton's conforms with the requirements of the advertisement, which suggests a central building and wings, built of brick and stone. Knowing that Thornton made such a design, it will be readily seen that this could not have been prepared for any other purpose. This sketch shows a well-executed wash drawing of good proportion, dignified and simple in its treatment. The alternate flap suggests a decidedly improved form for the wings.

It is difficult to understand the plan of the building from the elevations, although it is clear that official, private, and social duties were each intended to have an apartment to themselves. It is difficult to compare this plan with that of the present structure, of which only the central portion has been erected. The central portion of Thornton's design will compare favorably with the structure as erected.

Thornton's work in connection with the Capitol has been fully described in previous pages of this history. When the board of commissioners was abolished, Thornton was placed in charge of issuing patents.

The first patent legislation occurred in 1790. The Secretaries of War and State and the Attorney-General were authorized to grant patents. It is stated that over the issue of the first patents Jefferson, Secretary of State, Knox, Secretary of War, and Randolph, Attorney-General, would hold special conferences. In 1793 this law was changed, putting the matter in the hands of the Secretary of State. In May, 1802, President Jefferson appointed William Thornton a clerk at $1,400 per year to take charge of patents. At one period he was given $2,000 a year as Superintendent of Patents, at the same time acting as justice of the peace (being entitled to certain fees), a commissioner of bankruptcy, and a member of levy court. He was the first to have charge of patents. His salary, with his income from other positions, was supposed to be $2,400.

Madison urged Congress to give him this amount for his Patent Office work. In 1810 Thornton moved models, records, etc., into Blodgett's Hotel. The Government had purchased this building, located on the north side of E street, between Seventh and Eighth streets. Into the east end of this building the Patent Office was moved. The United States Patent Office and Post-Office remained in this building until the fire of 1836. In the Blue Book of 1821 Thornton is recorded as Superintendent of Patents. Mr. Campbell says: "During many years of his superintendency, he freely exercised his discretion in issuing patents. In a communication to the Secretary of State, January 16, 1818, Thornton defined equities and limitations of a reissue as concisely and luminously as has ever been done by any court or text writer." From Thornton's practice grew the act of July 3, 1832, providing for the reissue of a defective patent. Thornton held this office until his death, March 28, 1828.

When the present Patent Office was being erected, Mrs. Thornton requested Robert Mills, the architect, to put either a niche or bracket in the building for the reception of a bust of Thornton, because he had done so much for the good of this department. No notice seems to have been taken of this request. In 1873 Mrs. Adelaide Talbot, a half niece of Thornton, presented to the Patent Office, a portrait of Thornton by Gilbert Stuart. It hangs in a place of honor in the Commissioner's room [Plate 130].

Thornton is buried in the Congressional Cemetery, under a tomb similar in form to those erected to Senators and Representatives. The President of the United States, members of the Cabinet and of Congress, followed his body to the grave. On his tomb is chiseled his motto, "Deo Spes Meo." [7]

---

[7] Ironically, his rival Benjamin Henry Latrobe designed Thornton's cenotaph. For modern studies of Thornton's life and work as an architect, see Ridout, *Building the Octagon;* Daniel D. Reiff, *Washington Architecture, 1791–1861: Problems in Development* (Washington: U.S. Commission of Fine Arts, 2d ed., 1977); and Elinor Stearns and David N. Yerkes, *William Thornton: A Renaissance Man in the Federal City* (Washington: American Institute of Architects, 1976).

BENJAMIN HENRY LATROBE, ARCHITECT.

Among the ancestors of Benjamin Henry Latrobe [Plate 131], were the noble family of Boneval, of Languedoc, France. John Henry de la Trobe, who was in the military service of the Prince of Orange, went with the prince to England when William took his seat upon the throne of Great Britain. La Trobe settled in Waterford. A son of his, named Benjamin Latrobe, was a minister and superintendent of the Moravian sect in England. He married Anna Margaretta Antes, a Moravian from Pennsylvania, in the United States, who was pursuing her studies in one of the English Moravian schools. Benjamin Henry Latrobe, the subject of this sketch, was one of three sons born of this marriage, being born May 1, 1764, at Fulme, in Yorkshire. At 12 years of age he was sent to a Moravian school in Saxony, where he remained until he went to the University of Leipzig. He left Leipzig in 1785, for the sake of adventure, and joined the Prussian army as a cornet of hussars. While in that command he participated in two severe engagements, being wounded in the second one. He resigned his commission, and after some time spent in travel on the Continent he returned to England in 1786. He first secured a place in the stamp office, but left this in a short time and entered the office of an architect of note, S. P. Cockerell, with whom he remained from 1786 to 1788.

At this period he commenced the practice of his profession on his own account. His first piece of work was Hammerwood Lodge, near East Grimstead, in Sussex, which was the cause of his receiving the commission for a house in Ashdown Park for Mr. Trayton Fuller. In a short time he obtained a good rural practice in Surrey and Sussex, as well as the arrangement of the police offices in the metropolis of London.

In 1790 he married Miss Lydia Sellon, who died in 1793. Some time after his wife's death, influenced largely by love of adventure as well as his interest in our democratic institutions, he determined to go to the United States. He was not induced to remain in England,

although Lord Barham offered him the surveyorship of the Crown, with a salary of £1,000 per year. He landed in Norfolk March 20, 1796. Soon after landing he met Col. Bushrod Washington, who procured him an introduction to the President. His first work was to improve the navigation of the James River, and his success in this obtained for him the appointment as engineer of the State of Virginia. Leaving Richmond, he went to Philadelphia, Pa., where he was made city engineer and directed the installation of a new water supply. The engine house for this service, which was placed in the center of the principal square, was built with monolithic columns 16 feet in height. He was also employed to repair and improve the works of defense on the coast line as well as to superintend the light-houses.

In 1800 he married a daughter of Isaac Hazelhurst, of Philadelphia. Among other pieces of engineering work he constructed the Chesapeake and Delaware Canal and took an active interest in placing steamboats on Western rivers between the years 1811 and 1815. In 1811 he obtained the exclusive privilege to supply the city of New Orleans, La., with water. When he took charge of the Capitol a second time, in 1815, his son, Henry Latrobe, was left in charge of the work, Latrobe returning to New Orleans in 1818, when he resigned his position on the Capitol.

The architectural work which Latrobe accomplished in this country shows a good education and appreciation of classical forms, but a want of refinement in detail.[8] Although his drawings show great care

---

[8] Latrobe is generally regarded by modern architectural historians as a master architect and engineer who studied every facet of a design. Major works discussing Latrobe's career include Talbot F. Hamlin, *Benjamin H. Latrobe* (New York: Oxford University Press, 1955); Paul F. Norton, *Latrobe, Jefferson, and the National Capitol* (New York: Garland, 1977); and John C. Van Horne and Lee W. Formwalt, eds., *The Correspondence and Miscellaneous Papers of Benjamin Henry Latrobe,* 3 vols. (New Haven, Conn.: Yale University Press, 1984–88).

PLATE 130

WM. THORNTON BY GILBERT STUART.
United States Patent and Trademark Office.

PLATE 131

BENJAMIN H. LATROBE, ARCHITECT.
Filippo Costaggini, oil on canvas, 1881, after Rembrandt Peale.

and exactness in execution, they at the same time show his fondness for construction rather than artistic feeling. His work in connection with the Capitol has already been described in these pages.

Among his notable pieces of work for individuals, States, or corporations may be mentioned the Bank of Pennsylvania, in Philadelphia, which was built of white marble and vaulted throughout. The roof consisted of large blocks of marble, six of which were from 21 to 25 feet long, 5 feet wide, and 1 foot thick. These blocks projected over and formed the cornice of the central attic portion of the building. Latrobe considered this his best piece of architectural work, and thought it gave tone to the architecture of Philadelphia and had its effect in changing the character of architectural work in the whole country. At the time of his death, 1820, the Bank of the United States was being erected in Philadelphia, from his designs, under the direction of William Strickland, a pupil and draftsman of his on the Capitol.[9] While in Washington he designed St. John's Church, which stands on the corner of Sixteenth and H streets, opposite Lafayette square. In 1812 he designed the Van Ness mansion, one of the notable private residences of the early days in Washington. It was the residence of J. P. Van Ness, a member of Congress from New York, and the son-in-law of Daniel Burns, one of the largest landholders in the new Federal City. He also designed Brentwood, a mansion of dignity and magnitude, in the suburbs of the city, and in 1818 the residence of Commodore Decatur, which is still standing on Lafayette square, but remodeled out of all semblance to its original appearance. The other residences mentioned still remain, but in a dilapidated and abandoned condition. He designed a residence of importance as far west as Cincinnati, and the penitentiary in Richmond,

Va. The Catholic Cathedral in Baltimore is also one of his designs. This is a massive structure with a classical colonnade and a low central dome, and is still used in its original form by the Catholic Church.

Latrobe was a linguist, speaking and writing several languages, and a clear and forcible writer; a man of unbounded confidence in his own capacity as a constructor and designer, and with little toleration for those who differed with him in such matters. He died from an attack of yellow fever while superintending the construction of the water supply of New Orleans, September 3, 1820.[10]

CHARLES BULFINCH, ARCHITECT.

The first one of the Bulfinch family to locate in this country was Aldino Bulfinch, who settled in Boston, Mass., in 1681, where he accumulated wealth and became a prominent citizen. Thomas, the son of Aldino, was educated as a physician in Paris, and practiced his profession with success in Boston. A second Thomas, a son of the one just mentioned, also selected medicine as his profession and was educated in Europe. The latter Thomas Bulfinch was the father of the architect. Charles Bulfinch [Plate 132] was born in 1763, attended school at Harvard, where he graduated when he was 18. He then went abroad to receive his professional training, studying in England. He returned to Boston early in 1786, and was soon enjoying an active practice.

When Bulfinch commenced the practice of architecture, the Adams brothers, and other architects in London, were discussing the treatment of streets as a mass, and this appears to have been among the early

[9] Strickland independently designed the Second Bank of the United States in 1818. See William H. Pierson, Jr., *American Buildings and Their Architects: The Colonial and Neo-Classical Styles* (Garden City, NY: Anchor Books Edition, 1976), 434–436.

[10] Brown's sources for his biographical sketch of Latrobe included *The Architectural Dictionary*, 8 vols. (London: Architectural Publication Society, 1852–1892); James Q. Howard, "The Architect of the American Capitol," *International Review* 1 (November–December, 1874): 736–753; and *Appleton's Cyclopedia of American Biography*, vol. 3 (New York: D. Appleton and Company, 1898), 626–628.

PLATE 132

CHARLES BULFINCH, ARCHITECT

Frontispiece portrait from Ellen Susan Bulfinch, ed., *The Life and Letters of Charles Bulfinch, Architect* (1896).

problems with which Bulfinch had to deal. He designed a long block of symmetrical buildings, called Franklin Crescent, making the whole street from Hawley to Devonshire streets a curve line, and treating the row as a mass and not as individual buildings. This row of buildings stood from 1793 to 1855, and, judging from descriptions and cuts, must have been very effective with its broad and sweeping curve in connection with the trees and shrubbery of its semioval park. At a later period Bulfinch erected a grouped row of buildings facing the Common.

A large number of churches, probably as great a number as ever fell to one man in this country, were designed and erected under Bulfinch's supervision. Among the more prominent ones I mention the following:

The first Catholic church built in Boston, the Church of the Holy Cross, on Franklin street, was dedicated September 29, 1803. While the erection of the Catholic church was in progress Bulfinch made designs for the "New North," on Hanover street. This church was dedicated May 2, 1804, and was standing in 1890. Neither of these churches had spires, but simple cupolas. In his methods of design he followed closely the style of design used during the same period in England. The church on Hanover street was the only known church of Bulfinch's design standing in Boston in 1890. The only attempt, as far as is known, of Bulfinch in Gothic design was a church on Federal street. The church which was considered the most beautiful in Boston, and which gave Bulfinch his greatest reputation in this line of design, was the New South Church, which stood from 1814 to 1868 on Summer street. It was the first church to be built in Boston of hammered granite. Bulfinch designed a number of churches outside of Boston, a brick one at Lancaster, Mass., and the Unitarian church on the corner of Sixth and D streets NW., Washington, D. C. This has been remodeled by the Government and is now utilized as a police court. The church at Lancaster was built in 1816, and is said to be one of the best examples of his church work which remains.

Bulfinch became most popular throughout New England with State and municipal authorities, and designed the county court-houses and capitols of many counties and States. In 1810 was built the Suffolk County court-house, which was for the latter part of its existence the Boston city hall, the county having provided a new habitation in 1836. It remained until 1862, when it was removed to make way for the new city hall. It is said to have been built of hammered granite and in style resembled the work done in England during the last century. The court-house in Worcester was commenced in 1801, from his designs, and a brick court-house, combined with a town hall, was built in 1805. The Middlesex County court-house, which is still standing in Cambridge, was "built in 1814, enlarged in 1848." The enlargement has so carefully carried out the original design that it is difficult to tell which is Bulfinch's or which the product of the architect who enlarged it, as there is no lack of harmony in the styles on the exterior.

In 1815 University Hall, one of the interesting old buildings of Harvard University, was commenced, under the direction of Bulfinch. He also built a chapel and library for Andover Theological Seminary, which was dedicated September 22, 1818. Another piece of work executed by Bulfinch was the Massachusetts General Hospital, the foundation stone of which was laid in 1818, and the building was opened in 1821. This building was built of granite, had a hexastyle Ionic portico, with pediment which extended two stories in height, and in the center was a low and, judging from illustrations, an inartistic dome. This building was, by some, considered superior in effect to the Massachusetts state capitol. He built the asylum at Somerville, the almshouse at Salem, and a State prison at Charlestown, Mass.

Two statehouses, one among Bulfinch's earlier pieces of work and the other his last, are interesting. The Massachusetts statehouse was finished in 1798, and at the time of its completion was the most imposing structure in the United States. The front portico and dome still stand as a monument to his skill and good taste. The Maine statehouse was first occupied in 1831. It is supposed to be the Boston statehouse reduced in size. While this was probably the intention, in massiveness and treatment of detail he evidently was influenced by the work which he had been conducting on the Capitol. His work in connection with the Capitol has been amply described in the foregoing pages. Bulfinch was called upon to remodel Faneuil Hall. In that work he appears to have had a veneration for the old work, and made as few alterations in the original design as possible. The first theater erected in Boston, 1794, designed by Bulfinch, was highly commended for its exterior design and interior arrangements. Besides the McLean Asylum, which was a work of considerable magnitude, Bulfinch designed a large number of banks and business buildings in Boston and its vicinity.

Bulfinch shows throughout his career as an architect good judgment and refinement in his work and a capacity to simplify and not overload with poor ornament. He always seems to have had a good eye for the proper proportion of the masses and a delicacy in treating his details. At the time he pursued his studies in England the followers of Wren were fast destroying and belittling the beauty of the style which Wren had introduced. Bulfinch seems to have had the good taste and

judgment to avoid the extravagances which were coming into vogue and adhere to the simpler and better models. He probably followed the Adams brothers and Chambers to a greater extent than other leaders.

Bulfinch served his native city from 1800 to 1816. He was chairman of the selectmen of the town of Boston, discharging these duties at the time in which he was actively engaged in the practice of his profession. He died in Boston on the 15th day of April, 1844.

I am indebted for most of the facts in relation to Bulfinch to the book of his granddaughter and to an article by Mr. Willard.[11]

---

[11] Brown's sources for his biographical sketch of Bulfinch included Ellen Susan Bulfinch, ed., *The Life and Letters of Charles Bulfinch, Architect* (Boston: Houghton, Mifflin, 1896); Ashton R. Willard, "Charles Bulfinch, the Architect," *New England Magazine* 3 (November 1890): 29; *Appleton's Cyclopedia of American Biography*, vol. 1, 444; *The Architectural Dictionary*; and Howard, "The Architect of the American Capitol," 736–753.

Major modern studies of Bulfinch's career include Harold Kirker, *The Architecture of Charles Bulfinch* (Cambridge, Mass.: Harvard University Press, 1969) and Harold Kirker and James Kirker, *Bulfinch's Boston* (New York: Oxford University Press, 1964). For Bulfinch's overall contribution to American architecture, see also Pierson, *American Buildings and Their Architects*.

Chapter IX

Principal Superintendents

JAMES HOBAN was born in Dublin, Ireland, about the year 1762. He was educated in Dublin and won the medal in his art studies from the Society of Arts in 1781. Not long after this period he came to the United States and settled in Charleston, S. C., where he quickly secured commissions as an architect, erecting the old statehouse at Columbia, S. C. This building, which was highly commended as an artistic production, has been destroyed by fire. He also designed a number of private structures in Charleston.

When the Government offered a premium for the best design for a Capitol and Executive Mansion, Hoban entered the competition. There is nothing in the record to show that he made plans for the Capitol; he apparently confined his efforts to the design for a President's palace. This competition was closed July 15, 1792, and Hoban's plan was selected immediately and without hesitation, after a view of the drawings which were submitted. They being similar in character to those illustrated in this book, which were sent in for the Capitol, there could have been no doubt as to the wisdom of the selection. He was highly recommended by Laurens and others from South Carolina.

Hoban's design contemplated a central building with wings. His original drawings of this building are not to be found; therefore his treatment of the building as a whole is open to conjecture. The central portion of the building was executed from his designs and under his supervision both before and after the damage to the building perpetrated by the British in 1814. The north portico was not completed until about 1829, but it was executed under Hoban's direction. Hoban, as has been stated before in this work, was placed in charge of the Capitol as principal superintendent when Thornton declined this position, and

according to a letter of Jefferson he had the title of surveyor or superintendent of public buildings from 1797 to 1803. Although he held this position, he seems to have confined his labors as architect or designer to the Executive Mansion. As far as I can discover, he did not design any other building after obtaining the President's House, either for the Government or private individuals. His work in connection with the Capitol has already been described in other portions of this history.

From the time he came to the city, in 1792, until his death, in 1832. Hoban was almost continuously employed in superintending work for the Government, such work extending to roadways and bridges as well as buildings. He apparently had no ambition for architectural designing other than that shown in the Executive Mansion. He was a man of even temper and on friendly terms with all the Architects and superintendents with whom he came in contact. Having dealings with Thornton, Hallet, Hadfield, and Latrobe, he never seemed to have at any time but the most pleasant relations with them. He was a good draftsman and a refined designer as well as a most successful superintendent, and his services were in demand until the time of his death.[1]

STEPHEN HALLET was born in France and educated in Paris. He established himself in Philadelphia, Howard, in a magazine article, says, before the Revolution, but I can not find any confirmation of this

---

[1] Brown's principal source for his sketch of Hoban came from James Hoban, *Eulogy Pronounced, March 6, 1806* (Washington: J. E. Norris, 1846). For major modern works discussing Hoban's architecture in Washington, see William Seale, *The President's House*, 2 vols. (Washington: White House Historical Association in cooperation with the National Geographic Society, 1986) and *The White House: The History of an Idea* (Washington: American Institute of Architects, 1992).

statement. At the time of the competition for the Capitol he had acquired considerable local reputation. Hallet, as shown by the records, left no traces of his designs behind him, although he labored zealously to induce the authorities to modify Thornton's designs and adopt in their place some of his own unsatisfactory efforts.[2] I can find no trace of other work which he performed or notice of him after his connection with the Capitol ceased, in 1794. He always occupied a position subordinate to Thornton and Hoban.[3]

GEORGE HADFIELD was born in England and educated in London. He received at the British Royal Academy of Art the first prize for excellence in architecture. This entitled him to four years' travel and study. Benjamin West, when he was president of the Royal Academy, thought that Hadfield possessed a knowledge of the theory of civil architecture superior to any young man in England at that time. When Hallet was discharged, John Trumbull, being in England, urged Thornton to appoint Hadfield superintendent of the Capitol, praising both his capacity and temperament highly. Hadfield was a man of no experience in superintendence when he took charge of this branch of work on the Capitol, as was proved by the results. He was a draftsman of considerable ability and a good and refined designer, having left work which is still standing in this city to prove his capacity in this line. He designed the old executive offices which were removed to make way for the present buildings of the Treasury and State, War, and Navy Departments. He designed the old city hall in Washington, which is standing to-day and used by the courts of the District of Columbia, a building of dignity and refinement. He also designed a tomb for the Van Ness family, which was built in the burial grounds of David Burns, the father-in-law of Van Ness. This tomb was removed to Oak Hill Cemetery and is now one of the most satisfactory mortuary structures in the cemetery. It is modeled from the Temple of Vesta. When his work on the Capitol terminated, in 1798, he remained in Washington, making plans for the other Government work mentioned, as well as conducting a private business. He died in 1826 and was buried in the Congressional Cemetery.[4]

JOHN LENTHAL [Plate 134] was born in England in 1762. He was a great-great-grandson of Sir John Lenthal, the fourth of the name, who was a member of Parliament, and whose father, Sir William Lenthal, was speaker of the House of Commons. Latrobe selected Lenthal as superintendent when he took charge of the work in 1803. He was called clerk of works and principal surveyor. A letter of Latrobe gives an idea of the duties which the clerk of works was expected to perform. He was to represent the Architect during his absence, act as judge on all materials and workmanship, employ and discharge men, and make detail drawings under the direction of the Architect. An arch on the staircase hall, constructed according to Latrobe's directions, fell in the month of September, 1808, and Lenthal was killed by the falling brick. Latrobe thought most highly of his ability and capacity, only a short time before his death telling him in a letter: "I gave you the office from no motive whatever but a conviction that in skill and integrity I should not find your superior—a conviction which experience has since verified."

Davis was the clerk of works who succeeded Lenthal. I have found no data in relation to him, but he does not appear to have proved satisfactory, as he was replaced on the Capitol by Peter Lenox because of what the commissioner of public buildings considered inefficient

---

[2] Many of Hallet's drawings of the Capitol are held by the Library of Congress. See Pamela Scott, "Stephen Hallet's Designs for the United States Capitol," *Winterthur Portfolio* 27 (Summer/Autumn 1992): 145–170.

[3] Brown's source for his discussion of Hallet was James Q. Howard, "The Architects of the American Capitol," *International Review* 1 (November–December, 1874): 736–753.

[4] Ibid. For a more recent biographical sketch, see George Hunsberger, "The Architectural Career of George Hadfield," *Records of the Columbia Historical Society* 51–52 (1951–52): 46–65.

conduct of the work. This change of clerks of the work was also the cause of Latrobe resigning his position.

PETER LENOX [Plate 135] was born in Williamsburg, Va., March, 1771. His ancestor on the Lenox side came from Scotland to the United States early in 1700 and settled in Williamsburg. His father, Walter Lenox, married a Miss Carter, of that town. Walter Lenox, who was a man of means in that section of Virginia, lost a large part of his property during the Revolution, and his son, Peter Lenox, came to Washington in 1792 to seek his fortune. He was made a foreman on the Executive Mansion and then clerk of works. This position he held before the building was partially destroyed by the British and during its reconstruction after the fire. In 1817 he was transferred to the Capitol and held this position until the work was completed, in 1829. He was commissioned a captain in the war of 1812. The duties of Lenox were similar to those performed by Lenthal. It appears from the record that parties in these positions were not required to give their entire time to the Government, as Lenox conducted an extensive lumber business and amassed for that day quite a fortune. Comparatively early in his career, in the early part of 1800, he had built and lived in a large four-story residence (which is still standing), on Maryland avenue, near the river, with its grounds extending to the river. This house is considered a handsome structure at the present day. He invested in real estate and became one of the active and prominent men of the Federal City, frequently serving in the city council before his death, in December, 1832. He was highly respected by all in the community.[5]

GEORGE BLAGDEN [Plate 133], who was superintendent of stonework and quarries, came to this country some time before 1794, at which date he was employed on the Capitol, and continued as superintendent until he was killed by the caving in of an embankment at the Capitol June 4, 1826. The commissioner at the time of this accident wrote to Bulfinch, who was in Boston: "We have met with an irreparable loss. Mr. Blagden was killed last evening at the falling of the bank at the south angle of the Capitol." Blagden was a man in whom all who were connected with the work—Thornton, Latrobe, Bulfinch, and the several commissioners—had the most implicit confidence, and on whom they frequently called for advice. He was also a thrifty man and accumulated a moderate fortune.[6]

ROBERT MILLS [Plate 136], when he was appointed architect of Government buildings by Andrew Jackson, in 1836, assumed the duties of superintendent of repairs and additions to the Capitol. He added nothing to the design or plan of the building, but performed many services in connection with repairs and alterations to add to the comfort of Congress, which are mentioned in previous pages of this history. He served in this capacity from 1836 to 1851.

Mills was born in the city of Charleston, S. C., August 12, 1781. He was the son of William Mills, of Dundee, Scotland, who came to Charleston in 1772. His mother was Anne Taylor, a great-granddaughter of Thomas Smith, who held the title of landgrave from the British

[5] Peter Lenox was Brown's maternal grandfather; Brown's information probably came from his grandmother, who Brown recalled "had many stories to tell about Hoban, Latrobe and Bulfinch, with whom she was acquainted with as a girl." Lenox's papers were destroyed in a fire sometime before 1850. See Glenn Brown, *Memories, 1860–1930: A Winning Crusade to Revive George Washington's Vision of a Capital City* (Washington: W. F. Roberts, 1931), 38 and 103; see also C. T. Coote, *Discourse Delivered at the Second Presbyterian Church, December 27, 1832, on the Death of Peter Lenox* (Washington: anon., 1883).

[6] Brown's information on Blagden came from a letter concerning the death of Blagden and progress on the work on the Capitol. See Joseph Elgar to the President, December 7, 1826, in *Public Buildings: Message of the President of the United States, Transmitting the Annual Statement of the Commissioner of the Public Buildings, of the Expenditure on the Same, and the Progress of the Said Buildings* (Washington: Printed by Gales and Seaton, 1826), 5–6. See also Curator's Files, AOC.

Crown, being one of five Carolinians to hold this title. Smith was also governor of Carolina from 1690 to 1694. Robert Mills died at his home on Capitol Hill, in Washington, March 3, 1855.

Mills studied first with Hoban and then with Latrobe, working as a draftsman for the latter on the Capitol. His practice was extensive. In Pennsylvania he designed the fireproof wings of Independence Hall, Philadelphia, the capitol at Harrisburg, and the single-arch bridge over the Schuylkill.[7] At a later date he designed several United States custom-houses and marine hospitals. In Virginia he designed the Monumental Church, and worked for Thomas Jefferson on his dwelling at Monticello. Letters in the possession of his family show that it was at least a cooperation with Jefferson that produced the effective work at the University of Virginia. He was architect for the well-known Washington monument in Richmond, Va. Another Washington monument in Baltimore, Md., a Doric column, simple and impressive, the custom-houses in New London and Middletown, Conn., New Bedford and Newburyport, Mass., and the marine hospitals in New Orleans and Charleston are also of his design.

While State engineer in South Carolina he constructed the Charleston and Hamburg Railroad, one of the first works of the kind projected and carried into execution.

After his appointment in 1836, as architect of public buildings in Washington he remained in this city until his death, in 1855, and in his position until 1851, designing while in this position the E Street front of the old Post-Office building, the F street front of the Patent Office, and the Fifteenth street front or long colonnade of the Treasury building, as well as making a design for the Washington Monument which was adopted by the association and which contemplated a shaft 600 feet high. This was to have been surrounded at the base by a pantheon in which it was contemplated to place statues to the illustrious dead. Of course, it is well known that this portion of the design was never executed and that the shaft as completed was not carried up to the contemplated height.

Mills, in the work which he executed, showed great ability as a designer, always producing simple and dignified buildings, with well-proportioned masses and refined details, in which he always followed the best classical examples, preferring Greek to Roman models. His buildings for the Government were vaulted in brick and of the best fireproof construction, with the exception of the roofs. He showed a high order of ability, both in design and construction.[8]

---

[7] Mills's design for the Pennsylvania capitol complex in Harrisburg was not erected. See John M. Bryan, ed., *Robert Mills, Architect* (Washington: American Institute of Architects, 1989).

[8] For early biographical works on Mills's career, see Helen Mar Pierce Gallagher, *Robert Mills, Architect of the Washington Monument, 1781–1855* (New York: Columbia University Press, 1935) and Gallagher, "Robert Mills, 1781–1855: America's First Native American Architect," *Architectural Record* 65 (1929): 387–393.

PLATE 133

GEO. BLAGDEN, SUPERINTENDENT.

Plaster bas-relief. *Location unknown.*

PLATE 134

JOHN LENTHAL, SUPERINTENDENT.

Bas-relief detail from Lenthall's monument at Rock Creek Cemetery, Washington, D.C. Brown misspelled Lenthall's name.

PLATE 135

PETER LENOX, SUPERINTENDENT.

Charles Bird King, oil on canvas, ca. 1820. Lenox was Glenn Brown's maternal grandfather. *Colonial Williamsburg Foundation*.

PLATE 136

ROBERT MILLS ARCHITECT.

This drawing was executed by Glenn Madison Brown, ca. 1900. *Location unknown.*

CHAPTER X

DATA CONCERNING MEN AND MATERIAL
CONNECTED WITH THE OLD CAPITOL

THE organization of the working forces, the division of labor, the responsibility of the different officials, the cost of labor and material, and the dimensions of the Capitol are all a part of its history. When the Government commenced operations, Washington was in existence only on paper—a small number of houses, and without population, except in Georgetown, a village with less than 3,000 inhabitants, about 2 miles from the Capitol. There were none of the facilities for conducting work usual to a city, no machinery, few mechanics or teams, only newly made dirt roads. Portions of the work were let out by contract, but by far the larger part was done by day labor. The quarrying of stone at Aquia Creek was at first done by contract, but afterwards by the Government by day labor. Brick were made in the city. After the fire in 1814 the marble caps for interior work were secured in Italy.

The architects and principal superintendents in the early work came from abroad—one from the West Indies, one from France, and four from England. Only three who had to do with the old Capitol were born in this country—Bulfinch, Lenox, and Mills.

The Presidents of the United States for the first forty years in our history took quite an active interest in the building operations of the Government, and directed the work personally in many instances, all urging a close adherence to the original design and insisting on classic models. Their instructions were carried into operation and details of administration were executed first through the District commissioners until 1802, when their duties in relation to Government buildings were assumed by a superintendent of public buildings until 1815, when

three commissioners were appointed to reconstruct the Federal buildings after the invasion by the British in 1814. They were replaced in 1816 by one commissioner of public buildings. This form of office continued in existence until the commencement of the present wings or Capitol extension, in 1851. The commissioner continued in charge of the central portion of the building until 1867.

Of the architects, clerks of works, and superintendents, it is not necessary to say that their duties were those usual to their positions.[1]

---

[1] The tables in Brown's volumes have been reprinted in this edition with his original footnotes. Brown obtained the data for his tables from a variety of sources, including statutes enacted by Congress establishing the names, salaries, and duties of the principal individuals in charge of the Capitol prior to the design and construction of the Capitol Extension. These laws, listed by Brown in his bibliography as laws governing the office of Commissioner of Public Buildings and Grounds, were passed on the following dates: July 16, 1790; May 6, 1796; April 18, 1798; May 1, 1802; May 27, 1804; February 13, 1815; April 19, 1816; May 15, 1820; March 3, 1823; May 26, 1824; May 2, 1828; March 3, 1829; May 1, 1832; May 2, 1832; March 2, 1833. See *United States Statutes at Large*.

For the period 1793–1800, Brown also used the various reports on the federal city submitted by the Commissioners of the District of Columbia between 1796 and 1799 and the messages of Thomas Jefferson relative to the affairs of the federal city, dated 1800 to 1803. See also the reports on public buildings made by Charles Bulfinch and Robert Mills between 1800 and 1838, and indexes of accounts located in the Office of the First Auditor, 1790–1838.

The *U.S. Statutes at Large* reprinted both public and private laws enacted by Congress relative to the construction, repair, furniture, lighting, and artwork in the Capitol over the time period covered in the first volume. Treasury Department records also contained records for warrants drawn for payment to certain individuals who worked on the Capitol. Most of the information gathered here was a matter of public record, such as salary information contained in the reports of the Architect of the Capitol.

NOTE: This table contains the information published by Glenn Brown, which has not been corrected or updated.

Table 1.   Names, salaries, and duties of the principal men in charge of the Capitol from 1793 to 1850.

Office	Name	Date of service	Salary per annum	Duties
Commissioners District of Columbia.[1]	Thos. Johnson ....1791-1794 David Stuart ....1791-1794 Daniel Carroll ....1791-1795 Wm. Thornton ......1794-1802 Gustavus Scott ......1794-1800 Alex. White ....1795-1802 Wm. Cranch ....1801-1802 T. Dalton 1801	..........$1,600.00 ....1,600.00 ....1,600.00 ....1,600.00 ....1,600.00 ....1,600.00 ....1,600.00 ....1,600.00	To put into operation the plans for the formation of the new city; laying out streets, parks, and sewers; selecting plans for buildings, architects, contractors, mechanics, and materials; their action subject to the approval of the President.
Superintendent of public buildings.	Thos. Monroe 1802-1815	...........1,200.00 [2]	Given powers in relation to Government buildings held by the commissioners.
Commissioners of public buildings.[3]	J.P. Van Ness ....1815-1816 T. Ringgold ....1815-1816 R. Bland Lee ....1815-1816 Samuel Lane ....1816-1822 James Elgar ....1822-1829 Wm. Noland ....1829-1846 And. Beaumont .....1846 Chas. Douglas ......1847 Ignatius Mudd ......1847-1851 Wm. Easby 1851	...........1,600.00 ....1,600.00 ....1,600.00 ....2,000.00 ....1,500.00 [4] ....2,000.00 ....2,000.00 ....2,000.00 ....2,000.00 ....2,000.00	"A general supervision of both buildings (Capitol and President's House); to procure such materials as may be called for; to invite proposals for contracts; to disburse moneys and settle accounts monthly."
Architects.	Dr. Wm. Thornton ....1793-1802 B.H. Latrobe ....1803-1817 Chas. Bulfinch ....1818-1829 Robert Mills 1836-1851	............(5) ....1,700.00 2,000.00 2,500.00 ....2,500.00 ....1,800.00 2,300.00 2,500.00	"It is the duty of the Architect to make out full sets of plans and sections for the workmen and such additional drawings during construction of the work as may be necessary; to make estimates of all the materials that may be required, and to see that the plans are faithfully executed."
Draftsmen and superintendents.	Stephen Hallet ....1793-1794 Geo. Hadfield ....1795-1798 James Hoban 1793-1794 1794-1795 1798-1802	...........1,066.00 ....1,400.00	Instructed to make detail drawings and superintend Capitol according to Thornton's drawings and directions.

[1] Form of government changed May, 1802.

[2] At same time $2,000 as postmaster.

[3] The first three served jointly. From 1816 to 1851 there was only one commissioner. In 1838 commissioner put under Secretaries of State, Treasury, and War.

[4] Received a similar amount from another office.

[5] Salary as commissioner.

NOTE: This table contains the information published by Glenn Brown, which has not been corrected or updated.

Table 1. (Continued)

Office	Name	Date of service	Salary per annum	Duties
Clerks of works.	John Lenthal	1803-1808	$4.00 [6]	"Sole judge of merits of workmen; sole judge in the Architect's absence of the fidelity with which contracts are fulfilled; money paid on their certificate." They also judged material and made working drawings.
	Shadrack Davis	1815-1817	4.00 [6]	
	Peter Lenox	1817-1829	1,500.00	
Draftsmen.	Robert Mills	1803-1811	(7)	Draftsmen for Latrobe.
	Wm. Strickland	1803-1811	(7)	
Superintendent of stonework and quarries.	Geo. Blagden	1793-1826	1,500.00	In charge of stone, stonework, and quarries.
Sculptors.	Giovanni Andrei	1806-1825	1,500.00	In charge of ornamental plaster and stone work and sculpture.
	Giuseppe Franzoni	1806-1816	1,500,00	
	Francisco Iardella	1816-1829	1,187.50 1,250.00	
	Carlo Franzoni	1816		Bas reliefs and figures.
	Enrico Causici	1823	(8)	
	Nicholas Gevelot	1823	(8)	
	Antonio Capellano	1823	(8)	
	Valaperti	1823	(8)	
	Luigi Persico	1826-1836	(8)	
	Hobentein Greniv	1832	(8)	

[6] Per day.
[7] Paid by Latrobe.
[8] Work done by contract for each piece, usually.

Many mechanics were secured by advertisement in other cities of this country, while others were obtained through agents in Europe.

From 1793 to 1814 mechanics and laborers worked from 6 to 6; after 1814 mechanics worked ten hours, except short winter days, when they worked from sun to sun, and laborers continued to work from sun to sun during the whole year until 1840, when they were put upon the ten-hour basis. Wages do not seem to have varied materially until after the war of 1812, when they were about doubled.

Negro mechanics were objectionable to the white mechanics and were only employed once as an experiment.

NOTE: *These tables contain the information published by Glenn Brown, which has not been corrected or updated.*

Table II.   Wages per day of mechanics and laborers, and cost of building materials.

Wages Per Day of Mechanics and Laborers.

	1793-1800.	1800-1812.	1815-1818.	1819.	1820.	1821.	1822.	1836.	1837.	1838.
Foreman of carpenters			$2.50				$2.25	$4.00		$4.00
Foreman of bricklayers			3.00				3.00	3.50		3.50
Foreman of stonecutters ...			3.75				3.25	3.50		3.50
Overseer of laborers			2.12½				2.12½	3.50		3.50
Bricklayers	$1.50–$1.75	$1.50–$1.75	2.00–2.25	$1.50–$1.75	$1.33–$1.50	$1.50	1.50		$1.75–$2.25	2.25
Carpenters	1.00–1.50	1.00–1.50	1.62–1.88	1.33–1.50	1.33–1.50	1.12½	1.00–1.12½		1.37½–2.25	1.75
Stonecutters	1.25–1.33	1.00–1.75	2.50–2.75	1.50–1.75	1.00–1.25	1.25–1.37			1.75–2.25	2.25
Carvers						1.50	1.37½–1.50			
Coppersmiths						1.12½	1.12½			
Laborers	.75	.75	1.00			.75	.70–.75		.87½	1.00
Horse and cart:										
Man driver									1.75	1.75
Boy driver									1.50	1.50

Cost of Building Materials.

	1793-1800.	1800-1812.	1815-1818.	1819.	1820.	1821.	1822.	1836.	1837.	1838.
Granite					(1)					$0.43½–$0.50 [1]
Freestone, per ton	$7.00–$8.00	$8.00–$9.00	$10.00–$12.00	$6.00–$10.00	(1)					
Brick, per thousand	7.00	7.50	9.00–9.50	7.50–8.50	(1)					
Plank, per foot	.04⅔	.04⅔	.07½	.04	(1)					
Inch clear	.01½–.02	.01½–.02	.04	.01½–.02	(1)					
Rough	.01	.01¼–.01½	.02	.01 –.01¼	(1)					
Marble					(1)					1.75 [1]

[1] No purchase of material in 1820; brick reduced.   [2] Per cubic foot.

The records do not give the rate of wages between 1822 and 1836, and as far as I can ascertain there seems to be no data on the subject.

Table III.   Dimensions of the Capitol from 1830 to 1851.

	Feet.
Length	352⅓
Depth of wings	121½
East projection.	65
West projection	83
Height of wings to top of balustrade	70
Height to center of Dome	145
Representatives' Room:	
Length	95
Height	60
Senate Chamber:	
Length	74
Height	42
Central Rotunda:	
Diameter	96
Height	96

Table IV.   Cost of the Capitol from 1794 to 1835.

Wings previous to destruction by British, 1814	$788,077.98
Rebuilding wings	687,126.00
Center portion	957,647.36
	2,432,851.34
Repairs to 1835	9,740.00
Conveying water to Capitol, 1832, and putting in fountain, 1834	41,022.00

If we omit the cost of repairing the building made necessary by the destruction by the British in 1814, the old Capitol cost about 42 cents per cubic foot.

Statement of appropriations and expenditures, from the National Treasury, relating to old Capitol.

General object (title of appropriation), and details and explanations.	Date of act making the appropriation.	References to the Statutes at Large.			Amount of annual appropriation.	Year of expenditure.	Expenditure by warrants.	Repayments.	Amount carried to the surplus fund.	Net expenditures.
		Volume.	Page.	Section.						
CAPITOL.										
OLD BUILDING.										
To be applied, under the direction of the President, in such repairs or alterations in the Capitol and other public buildings as may be necessary for the accommodation of Congress in their future sessions; and also for keeping in repair the highway between the Capitol and other public buildings.	Mar. 3, 1803	2	236	5	$50,000.00	1803	$40,000.00			$40,000.00
To be applied, under the direction of the President, in proceeding with the public buildings at the city of Washington, and in making such necessary improvements and repairs thereon as he shall deem expedient.	Mar. 27, 1804	2	298		50,000.00	1804	60,000.00			60,000.00
Toward completing the south wing of the Capitol.	Jan. 25, 1805	2	311	1	110,000.00	1805	83,000.00			83,000.00
To be applied, under the direction of the President, to such necessary alterations and repairs as he may deem requisite in the north wing of the Capitol and other public buildings.	do	2	311	2	20,000.00					
Toward completing the south wing of the Capitol.	Apr. 21, 1806	2	399	2	40,000.00	1806	87,000.00			87,000.00
For finishing the south wing of the Capitol.	Mar. 3, 1807	2	432		25,000.00					
For making a new roof and other repairs to the north wing of the Capitol.	do	2	432	1	25,000.00	1807	50,000.00			50,000.00
For making good the deficit of 1807, including the debt due from the public offices.	Apr. 25, 1808	2	499	1	46,096.24					
For carrying up in solid work the interior of the north wing, comprising the Senate Chamber.	do	2	499	1	25,000.00					
For executing the work deficient in the interior of the south wing, and for painting.	do	2	499	1	11,509.00	1808	82,596.24			82,596.24
For improvements and repairs of the House of Representatives.	Mar. 3, 1809	2	537	1	6,000.00					
For completing the work in the interior of the north wing, comprising the Senate Chamber, court room, etc.	do	2	537	1	20,000.00					
To defray the expenses of finishing and furnishing the permanent Senate Chamber, its committee rooms, lobbies, and other apartments.	June 28, 1809	2	552	1	15,000.00					
To defray the expense incurred in fitting up the temporary Senate Chamber and repairing and providing articles of furniture.	do	2	552	2	1,600.00	1809	42,600.00			42,600.00

Statement of appropriations and expenditures, from the National Treasury, relating to old Capitol. (*Continued*)

General object (title of appropriation), and details and explanations.	Date of act making the appropriation.	Volume.	Page.	Section.	Amount of annual appropriation.	Year of expenditure.	Expenditure by warrants.	Repayments.	Amount carried to the surplus fund.	Net expenditures.
CAPITOL. (Continued)										
For sculpture, and warming and ventilating the Chamber of the House of Representatives.	May 1, 1810	2	607	1	$7,500.00					
For defraying the expense of completing the court room and the offices of the judiciary on the east side, completing the Senate Chamber, and stopping the leaks in the roof of the north wing of the Capitol.	do	2	607	1	20,000.00	1810	$27,500.00			$27,500.00
The superintendent of the city of Washington authorized to contract for the completion of the sculpture in the south wing of the Capitol, under direction of the President.	July 5, 1812	2	775	3	4,000.00	1812 1813	1,000.00 3,000.00			1,000.00 3,000.00
For completing the sculpture and the work on the galleries of the Senate Chamber, the railing of the stairs, and minor works deficient in the east part of the north wing of the Capitol, and for temporary repairs to the roof.	do	2	775	4	4,000.00	1812 1813	3,000.00 1,000.00			3,000.00 1,000.00
To be applied, under the direction of the President, in such repairs or alterations in the Chamber of the House of Representatives as may be necessary for their accommodation in their future sessions, having in view as well the increased number of the members, as the better lighting, ventilating, and warming the Chamber.	Mar. 3, 1813	2	822	1	5,000.00	1813	5,000.00			5,000.00
To repair the roof of the Capitol.	do	2	822	2	500.00	1813	500.00			500.00
To be applied, under the direction of the President, to finishing the Senate Chamber and repairing the roof of the north wing of the Capitol.	July 26, 1813	3	48	1	9,500.00	1813 1815 1817 1819	7,000.00	$2,002.05	$2,500.00 2,002.05	4,997.95
Total					**495,696.24**		**493,196.24**	**2,002.05**	**4,502.05**	**491,194.19**
CENTER BUILDING.										
For procuring the materials, laying the foundation, and other preparations for the center building of the Capitol.	Apr. 20, 1818	3	458	1	$100,000.00	1818	$93,000.00			$93,000.00
For erecting the center building of the Capitol.	Mar. 3, 1819	3	516	1	136,644.00	1819	143,644.00			143,644.00
For finishing the wings of the Capitol, in addition to the sums already appropriated.	do	3	516	1	51,322.00	1819	51,332.00			51,322.00
For contingencies.	Apr. 20, 1818	3	458	1	437.00	1820	437.00			437.00

NOTE: This table contains the information published by Glenn Brown, which has not been corrected or updated.

Statement of appropriations and expenditures, from the National Treasury, relating to old Capitol. (*Continued*)

General object (title of appropriation), and details and explanations.	Date of act making the appropriation.	References to the Statutes at Large.			Amount of annual appropriation.	Year of expenditure.	Expenditure by warrants.	Repayments.	Amount carried to the surplus fund.	Net expenditures.
		Volume.	Page.	Section.						
CAPITOL. (Continued)										
For completing the repairs of the north and south wings of the Capitol.	Feb. 10, 1820	3	541	1	$75,000.00	1820	$75,000.00			$75,000.00
For continuing the work of the center building of the Capitol.	Apr. 11, 1820 Mar. 3, 1821	3 3	562 635	1 1	111,769.00 80,000.00	1820 1821	90,000.00 101,769.00			90,000.00 101,769.00
For painting the inside of the north and south wings of the Capitol, and providing for the expense of making such alterations therein as have been directed during the present session of Congress.	Apr. 11, 1820	3	562	1	2,867.00	1821	2,867.00			2,867.00
For making alterations and improvements in the Senate Chamber for the better accommodation of the Senate.	do	3	562	1	2,400.00	1821	2,400.00			2,400.00
For improvements in the Senate Chamber, in the Hall of the House of Representatives, and in the Library.	Mar. 3, 1821	3	635	1	700.00	1822	700.00			700.00
For continuing the work on the center building of the Capitol.	May 1, 1822	3	674	1	120,000.00	1822	120,000.00	$4,280.27		115,719.73
To pay William R. Maddox the sum of $170.30, being a part of his account of $474.83 for 67,833 brick delivered by him to the late commissioner for the public buildings in the year 1820.	May 7, 1822	6	275		170.30	1822	170.30			170.30
For making the necessary alterations in the Representatives' Hall for the accommodation of the Eighteenth Congress.	Mar. 3, 1823	3	784	1	1,200.00	1823	1,200.00			1,200.00
For carrying on the center building of the Capitol.	do	3	762	1	100,000.00	1823	90,000.00			90,000.00
For continuing the work on the center building.	Apr. 2, 1824	4	16	1	86,000.00	1824	100,280.27			100,280.17
For continuing the work on the Capitol.	May 22, 1826	4	194	1	100,000.00	1826 1827	80,000.00 20,000.00			80,000.00 20,000.00
For completing the work remaining to be done on and about the Capitol, the Capitol square and its inclosures, and for engine house: *Provided,* That no platform nor steps be extended from the top of the area wall to the building, nor any change whatever be made in the present arrangement of the room under the Library.	Mar. 2, 1827	4	218	1	83,985.05	1827	70,000.00			70,000.00
For completing the work remaining to be done on and about the public buildings.	May 2, 1828	4	265	1	56,400.08	1828	70,385.13			70,385.13
Total					**1,108,904.43**		**1,113,184.70**	**4,280.27**		**1,108,904.43**

NOTE: This table contains the information published by Glenn Brown, which has not been corrected or updated.

Statement of appropriations and expenditures, from the National Treasury, relating to old Capitol. (*Continued*)

General object (title of appropriation), and details and explanations.	Date of act making the appropriation.	References to the Statutes at Large.			Amount of annual appropriation.	Year of expenditure.	Expenditure by warrants.	Repayments.	Amount carried to the surplus fund.	Net expenditures.
		Volume.	Page.	Section.						
CAPITOL. (Continued) REBUILDING THE PUBLIC BUILDINGS.										
The act of February 13, 1815 (3 Stats., 205), provides that the President cause to be repaired or rebuilt forthwith the President's House, Capitol, and public offices on their present sites in the city of Washington, and that he be authorized to borrow, at an interest not exceeding 6 per cent per annum, from any bank or banks within the District of Columbia, or from any individual or individuals, a sum not exceeding $500,000, to be applied exclusively to that object.	Feb. 13, 1815	3	205	1	$500,000.00	1815 1816	$175,000.00 $179,932.44			$175,000.00 179,932.44
For the purpose of repairing the public buildings, to be applied by the commission under the direction of the President.	Mar. 3, 1817	3	389	1	100,000.00	1817	245,067.56			245,067.56
For the purpose of repairing the public buildings.	Jan. 27, 1818	3	405		200,000.00					
For the completion of the wings of the Capitol.	Apr. 20, 1818	3	458	1	80,000.00	1818 1819	270,000.00 10,000.00			270,000.00 10,000.00
For the public buildings in Washington City for the year 1825.	Feb. 25, 1825	4	90	1	80,000.00	1825	80,000.00			80,000.00
Total					**960,000.00**		**960,000.00**			**960,000.00**
REPAIRS.										
For repairs on the Capitol.	Mar. 2, 1827	4	218	1	500.00	1828	500.00			500.00
For an entrance and doorway into the Capitol from the top of the terrace on the western front.	May 2, 1828	4	266	1	3,121.10	1828	3,121.10			3,121.10
For repairs and other work necessary to be done on and about the Capitol and its inclosures.	Mar. 3, 1829	4	362	1	18,762.63	1829	18,762.63			18,762.63
To pay William R. Maddox for the balance of the price of 67,883 bricks.	do	6	401		304.53	1829	304.53			304.53
For completing the painting of the Capitol.	Mar. 2, 1831	4	474		3,760.00	1831	3,760.00			3,760.00
For alterations and repairs.	do May 5, 1832	4 4	474 507	1	500.00 500.00	1831 1832	500.00 500.00			500.00 500.00
For alterations in the Hall of the House of Representatives and other expenditures on the Capitol.	July 14, 1832	4	580	1	960.00	1833	960.00			960.00

NOTE: This table contains the information published by Glenn Brown, which has not been corrected or updated.

Statement of appropriations and expenditures, from the National Treasury, relating to old Capitol. (Continued)

General object (title of appropriation), and details and explanations.	Date of act making the appropriation.	References to the Statutes at Large.			Amount of annual appropriation.	Year of expenditure.	Expenditure by warrants.	Repayments.	Amount carried to the surplus fund.	Net expenditures.
		Volume.	Page.	Section.						
CAPITOL. (Continued)										
For alterations in the Representatives' Hall, to accommodate the twenty-third Congress, according to a plan recommended by a select committee of the House of Representatives of June 30, 1832.	Mar. 2, 1833	4	650	2	$13,000.00	1833	$13,000.00			$13,000.00
For alterations and repairs of the Capitol.	do do	4 4	627 650	1 2	500.00 1,000.00	1833	1,500.00			1,500.00
For compensation to Robert Mills, the architect employed by order of the House of Representatives to superintend the alterations in the Representatives' Hall, according to the plan of said Mills.	June 27, 1834	4	697	2	1,000.00	1834	1,000.00			1,000.00
For alterations and repairs of the Capitol, including the repairs of the roof.	June 30, 1834	4	722	1	6,292.00	1834	6,292.00			6,292.00
For alterations and repairs in the Capitol, including the domes of the chambers of the Senate and House of Representatives, replacing and renewing the copper of the same, and painting the ceiling of the Rotunda.	Mar. 3, 1835	4	770	1	12,500.00	1835	12,500.00			12,500.00
For preparing the niches for the reception of the statues at the east front of the Capitol.	do	4	770	1	460.00	1835	460.00			460.00
For alterations and repairs of the Capitol, including repairs of the roof over the principal stairway to the Representatives' Hall, and coppering the projecting steps and the surface of the cornice around the base of the Dome of the Rotunda.	July 4, 1836	5	114	4	6,318.75	1836	6,318.75			6,318.75
For enlarging the folding room of the House.	do	5	115	4	350.00	1836 1841	350.00	$2.54	$2.54	347.46
For alterations and repairs of the Capitol, and incidental expenses.	Mar. 3, 1857	5	172	1	3,600.00	1837	3,600.00			3,600.00
For improving the crypt of the Capitol by closing the openings on the east front with sash doors, making double doors to the outer entrances, and repairing furnaces.	do	5	174	1	1,150.00	1837 1841	1,150.00	71.00	71.00	1,079.00
For making the post-office, document, and folding rooms of the House of Representatives fireproof.	Mar. 3, 1837	5	174	1	3,150.00	1837	3,150			3,150.00
For alterations and repairs of the Capitol, and incidental expenses.	Apr. 6, 1838 Mar. 3, 1839 May 8, 1840	5 5 5	222 347 378	1 1	6,331.00 1,198.00 1,551.00	1838 1841 1839 1840	6,331.00 1,198.00 1,551.00	403.98	403.98	5,927.02 1,198.00 1,551.00

NOTE: This table contains the information published by Glenn Brown, which has not been corrected or updated.

Statement of appropriations and expenditures, from the National Treasury, relating to old Capitol. *(Continued)*

General object (title of appropriation), and details and explanations.	Date of act making the appropriation.	References to the Statutes at Large.			Amount of annual appropriation.	Year of expenditure.	Expenditure by warrants.	Repayments.	Amount carried to the surplus fund.	Net expenditures.
		Volume.	Page.	Section.						
CAPITOL. (Continued)										
For repairing two cupolas on the north wing of the Capitol.	July 21, 1840	6	815	8	$300.00	1840	$300.00			$77.03
						1841		$222.97	$222.97	
For three new cupolas over the Library of Congress.	Mar. 3, 1839	5	348	1	1,482.24	1839	1,482.24			1,430.19
						1841		52.05	52.05	
For removing two cupola sashes over the principal stairway and vestibule leading to the Hall of the House of Representatives.	July 21, 1840	6	815	8	392.00	1840	392.00			392.00
For repairing chimney stacks of the Capitol.	do	6	815	8	250.00	1840	250.00			108.10
						1841		141.90	141.90	
For the payment of expenses incurred, under the direction of the Joint Committee on the Library, in the erection of shelves and book-cases in the committee rooms of the Capitol for the reception of books and documents to be transferred from the Library to the several committee rooms.	July 20, 1840	5	406	1	1,250.00	1841	1,250.00			1,250.00
For annual repairs of the Capitol, attending furnaces, water-closets, lamplighting, oil, laborers on Capitol grounds, tools, etc.	Mar. 3, 1841	5	429	1	7,582.50	1841	7,582.50	3,709.28		3,873.22
	Aug. 26, 1842	5	532	22	7,458.50	1842	7,458.50			7,458.50
For altering the two passages and doorways of the roof, new steps, new doors, covering the wood with copper, removing the circular horizontal sash over the Hall of the House of Representatives and substituting a permanent roof covered with copper, and repairing the copper work of the roof.	Aug. 26, 1842	5	532	22	600.00	1842	600.00			600.00
For alterations and repairs and fixtures of the north wing of the Capitol.	do	5	532	22	1,853.46	1842	1,853.45			1,853.45
For annual repairs of the Capitol, attending furnaces and water-closets, lamplighting, oil, laborers, tools, etc.	Mar. 3, 1843	5	644	1	11,231.50	1843	1,800.00			1,800.00
						1844	9,431.50			9,431.50
For materials and work for bulkhead frames and doors and windows in the cellar of the Capitol.	Mar. 3, 1843	5	645		221.00	1843	221.00			221.00
For pay of James Kelley, amount allowed him by the commissioners under the resolution of Congress.	do	5	645	1	50.44	1843		50.44		50.44
For repairs of the Capitol, attending furnaces and water-closets, lamplighting, oil, laborers on the Capitol grounds, tools, keeping iron pipes and wooden fences in order, attending at the western gates, etc.	June 17, 1844	5	681	1	9,084.00					

NOTE: This table contains the information published by Glenn Brown, which has not been corrected or updated.

Statement of appropriations and expenditures, from the National Treasury, relating to old Capitol. (*Continued*)

General object (title of appropriation), and details and explanations.	Date of act making the appropriation.	References to the Statutes at Large.			Amount of annual appropriation.	Year of expenditure.	Expenditure by warrants.	Repayments.	Amount carried to the surplus fund.	Net expenditures.
		Volume.	Page.	Section.						
CAPITOL. (Continued)										
For digging out the crypt, excavating and making sufficient drains, paving points, and whitewashing lower story under the north wing, cutting out additional windows, etc.	do	5	682	1	$1,750.00	1845	$10,834.00	$588.40		$10,245.60
For repairs to windows, glass, and glazing, heretofore done by John Purdy.	do	5	681	1	150.25	1845	150.25			150.25
For repairing the figure in the tympanum of the Capitol.	do	5	682	1	200.00	1845	200.00			200.00
For repairs of the Capitol, lamplighters, oil for lamps, wick and repairs of lamps and lamp-posts, attending furnaces and water-closets, cleaning the Rotunda and crypt, laborers and cartage on the Capitol grounds, tools, wire, leather, etc.	Mar. 3, 1845	5	757	1	8,274.50	1846	6,776.95			6,776.95
For replacing platforms on the Dome and repairing baluster, repairing hatchway, door, and frame, furnishing and repairing stepladders and platforms on the different roofs, etc.	Aug. 10, 1846	9	93	1	490.75	1847	490.75			490.75
For annual repairs of the Capitol, lamplighters, oil for lamps, wicks and repairs of lamps and lamp-posts, attendance on furnaces of the crypt, attendance on water-closets, cleaning the Rotunda and crypt, brushes, and brooms, etc.	do Mar. 3, 1847	9 9	92 163	1 1	9,914.00 10,381.50	1847 1848	11,000.00 7,500.00		$146.97	11,000.00 7,500.00
For constructing six water-closets for the Senate and two for the Supreme Court, on the same floors, respectively.	Aug. 10, 1846	9	93	1	3,468.00	1847 1849	3,408.00		60.00	3,408.00
For taking up and relaying the floor of the Senate Chamber, to increase the number of seats, making flues, building fireproof and ventilating apparatus, and other work.	Mar. 3, 1847	9	164	1	4,876.00	1848	4,876.00			4,876.00
For annual repairs of the Capitol, attendance on furnaces in the crypt, attendance on water-closets, cleaning Rotunda, for public gardener and laborers and cartage on the Capitol grounds, tools, wire, twine, leather, nails, chains, etc.	Aug. 12, 1848	9	293	1	17,497.50	1849	14,647.89			14,647.89
For pay for removing the mast and lantern above the Dome of the Capitol.	do	9	293	1	323.00	1849	323.00			323.00
For painting the Capitol.	do	9	293	1	20,000.00	1849 1850 1851 1852	7,564.90 7,200.00 3,300.00	1,566.61	3,501.71[1]	7,564.90 7,200.00 1,733.39
For annual repairs of the Capitol and attendance on furnaces in the crypt, attendance on water-closets, for public gardener and laborers and cartage on the Capitol grounds, tools, wire, leather, nails, etc.	Mar. 3, 1849	9	362	1	17,000.00	1850	27,293.37			27,293.37

[1] Transferred to "Executive Mansion Repairs."

NOTE: This table contains the information published by Glenn Brown, which has not been corrected or updated.

Statement of appropriations and expenditures, from the National Treasury, relating to old Capitol. *(Continued)*

General object (title of appropriation), and details and explanations.	Date of act making the appropriation.	References to the Statutes at Large.			Amount of annual appropriation.	Year of expenditure.	Expenditure by warrants.	Repayments.	Amount carried to the surplus fund.	Net expenditures.
		Volume.	Page.	Section.						
CAPITOL. (Continued)										
For completing the room under the post-office of the Senate and the staircases and passages communicating therewith, and the circular room on the upper floor of the Capitol.	do	9	366	1	$4,000.00	1850	$4,000.00			$4,000.00
For annual repairs in the Capitol and attendance on furnaces in the crypt, attendance on water-closets, cleaning Rotunda, for public gardener and laborers, cartage, tools, wire, twine, etc.	Sept. 30, 1850	9	537	1	20,000.00	1851	20,000.00	$373.17		19,626.83
For the casual repairs of the Capitol, repairs of water-closets, cleaning furnaces, etc., repairing stables, and various other appendages to the Capitol.	Mar. 3, 1851	9	612	1	4,500.00	1852	4,873.17			4,873.17
FURNITURE.										
For the suitable accommodation of Congress at the city of Washington, the Secretaries of the four Executive Departments, or any three of them, shall be, and are hereby, authorized and directed to cause suitable furniture to be forthwith provided for the apartments which are to be occupied in the Capitol at said city by the two Houses respectively, and for the offices and committee rooms to be furnished in a suitable manner, so as to be ready for the reception of Congress on the day fixed by law for the removal of the Government to said city.	Apr. 24, 1800	2	55	3	9,000.00	1800	9,000.00			9,000.00
Payment for certain articles of furniture purchased for the accommodation of Congress and not provided for by former appropriations.	Mar. 3, 1801	2	117	1	1,000.00	1801	995.69	4.31[1]		995.69
For defraying the expense of new furniture provided for the House of Representatives.	May 1, 1802	2	184	1	1,244.85	1802 1803	1,244.85	2.32		1,242.53
For furniture for the House of Representatives, being an expense incurred in the year 1803.	Mar. 14, 1804	2	265	1	1,200.00	1804	1,200.00		2.32	1,200.00
For furnishing the same (south wing of the Capitol) for the accommodation of the House of Representatives.	Mar. 3, 1807	2	432	1	17,000.00	1807	14,000.00			14,000.00
For making good the deficit of 1807, including the debt due from the public offices.	Apr. 25, 1808	2	499	1	5,403.76	1808 1810	8,403.76	7.43	7.43	8,396.33
For furnishing the Representative Chamber and committee rooms.	Apr. 20, 1818	3	458	1	30,000.00	1818 1819 1820	15,000.00 11,000.00 4,000.00	5,092.63		15,000.00 9,907.37

[1] Transferred to "Contingent expenses of Congress."

NOTE: *This table contains the information published by Glenn Brown, which has not been corrected or updated.*

Statement of appropriations and expenditures, from the National Treasury, relating to old Capitol. *(Continued)*

General object (title of appropriation), and details and explanations.	Date of act making the appropriation.	References to the Statutes at Large.			Amount of annual appropriation.	Year of expenditure.	Expenditure by warrants.	Repayments.	Amount carried to the surplus fund.	Net expenditures.
		Volume.	Page.	Section.						
CAPITOL. (Continued)										
For furnishing the Senate Chamber and committee rooms.	Apr. 20, 1818	3	458	1	$20,000.00	1819 1822	$20,000.00		$5,092.63	$20,000.00
For furnishing the rooms in the center building of the Capitol, under the direction of the commissioner of public buildings.	May 26, 1824	4	60	3	3,289.50	1824	3,289.50			3,289.50
LIGHTING.										
For erecting 14 additional lamps in or around Capitol square.	Mar. 3, 1829	4	362	1	210.00					
For keeping lighted 24 lamps in or around said square.	do	4	362	1	605.00	1829	815.00			815.00
For lighting lamps in and around the square and erecting 24 new lamps.	Mar. 2, 1831	4	474		1,500.00	1831	1,500.00			1,500.00
For expense of lighting the lamps in the Capitol square.	May 5, 1832	4	512	1	750.00	1832	750.00			750.00
For improving the Capitol square, including the gardener's salary, and lighting the lamps.	Mar. 2, 1833	4	650		2,750.00	1833	2,750.00			2,750.00
For lighting lamps, keeping the grounds and walks in order, and planting in the Capitol square and adjacent public grounds.	June 30, 1834	4	722	1	4,826.00	1834	4,826.00			4,826.00
For lighting lamps and keeping the grounds and walks in order, including cost of trees and shrubs.	Mar. 3, 1835	4	770	1	4,500.00	1835	4,500.00			4,500.00
For lighting lamps and keeping the grounds and walks of the Capitol square in order, including the cost of trees and shrubs.	July 4, 1836	5	114	4	4,500.00	1836	4,500.00			4,500.00
For lighting lamps and superintendence of the public grounds around the Capitol.	Mar. 3, 1837 Apr. 6, 1838	5 5	172 222	1 1	5,164.00 5,976.00	1837 1838	5,164.00 5,976.00			5,164.00 5,976.00
For lighting lamps and keeping in order the public grounds around the Capitol, the iron water pipes, and wooden fences.	Mar. 3, 1839	5	347	1	6,306.00	1839	5,306.00			5,306.00
For lighting lamps, purchasing trees, shrubs, and compost, for keeping in order the public grounds around the Capitol, the iron water pipes, and wooden fences.	May 8, 1840	5	378		6,860.00	1840	7,860.00			7,860.00
To be expended under the direction of the commissioner of public buildings in erecting and lighting lamps on Pennsylvania avenue, between the Capitol and the President's square.	July 27, 1842	5	498		2,500.00	1842	1,100.00			1,100.00

NOTE: This table contains the information published by Glenn Brown, which has not been corrected or updated.

Statement of appropriations and expenditures, from the National Treasury, relating to old Capitol. *(Continued)*

General object (title of appropriation), and details and explanations.	Date of act making the appropriation.	References to the Statutes at Large.			Amount of annual appropriation.	Year of expenditure.	Expenditure by warrants.	Repayments.	Amount carried to the surplus fund.	Net expenditures.
		Volume.	Page.	Section.						
CAPITOL. (Continued)										
For repairing the flag footways at the Capitol and President's House and for repairing lamp-posts and lamps at the Capitol.	Aug. 26, 1842	5	532	22	$200.00	1842 1845 1846	$200.00	$1.38	$1.38	$198.62
For lighting Pennsylvania avenue.	Mar. 3, 1843	5	641	1	150.00	1844	1,550.00			1,550.00
For lighting Pennsylvania avenue during the session of Congress.	June 17, 1844	5	691	1	600.00	1845 1846	600.00	82.00	82.00	518.00
The Secretary of the Senate and Clerk of the House authorized and directed to contract with James Crutchett for lighting up the Capitol and the Capitol grounds with the solar gaslight: *Provided,* That such contract can be made upon terms deemed reasonable by the said Secretary and Clerk.	Mar. 3, 1847	9	207		17,500.00	1847	5,000.00			5,000.00
For paying James Crutchett for lighting the Capitol and grounds.	Mar. 27, 1848	9	217	1	3,000.10	1848 1849	15,490.80 9.30			15,490.80 9.30
For compensation to James Crutchett for extra work done in making the necessary fixtures for lighting the Capitol with gas.	Aug. 12, 1848	9	293	1	2,877.18	1849	2,877.18			2,877.18
For the purchase and erection of lamps and lamp-posts of iron and for the laying of gas pipes and other necessary fixtures for lighting the Capitol grounds with gas.	do	9	293	1	10,000.00	1849 1850 1852	4,958.70 5,041.29 .01			4,958.70 5,041.29 .01
For paying the Washington Gas Company for lighting the Capitol and Capitol grounds, including fixtures furnished, to the 31st of August, 1848.	Aug. 12, 1848	9	294	1	2,000.00	1849	2,000.00			2,000.00
For lighting Pennsylvania avenue from the Capitol square to the Treasury Department.	Mar. 3, 1847	9	162	1	775.00	1848	775.00			775.00
For laying gas pipes from the main gas pipe at the Capitol to the foot of Fifteenth street, on both sides of Pennsylvania avenue, and for 100 lamp-posts and lamps and other necessary fixtures, and for work and materials rendered and supplied in establishing the same, to be expended under the direction of the commissioner of public buildings; and it shall be the duty of the commissioner to have the pipes fully and sufficiently tested and proved before they are received.	Aug. 12, 1848	9	293	1	10,000.00	1849	10,000.00			10,000.00
For paying a balance due the contractors for laying gas pipes between the Capitol and Fifteenth street, within the Capitol and Capitol grounds, and for chandeliers and burners in the President's House, and for completing the branch pipes, lamps, etc., within the Capitol grounds.	Sept. 30, 1850	9	538	1	3,000.00	1851	3,000.00			3,000.00

NOTE: This table contains the information published by Glenn Brown, which has not been corrected or updated.

Statement of appropriations and expenditures, from the National Treasury, relating to old Capitol. *(Continued)*

General object (title of appropriation), and details and explanations.	Date of act making the appropriation.	References to the Statutes at Large.			Amount of annual appropriation.	Year of expenditure.	Expenditure by warrants.	Repayments.	Amount carried to the surplus fund.	Net expenditures.
		Volume.	Page.	Section.						
CAPITOL. (Continued)										
For lighting Pennsylvania avenue from the Capitol square to the Treasury Department, and for compensation for one lamplighter for the same, and for lighting the Capitol and Capitol grounds and President's House; to be expended under the direction of the commissioner of public buildings.	Aug. 12, 1848 / Mar. 3, 1849	9 / 9	293 / 362	1 / 1	$6,000.00 / 6,000.00	1849 / 1850	$2,514.00 / 9,486.00			$2,514.00 / 9,486.00
For deficiency in the appropriation for the present fiscal year for lighting the Capitol and Capitol grounds, Pennsylvania avenue, and the President's House.	May 15, 1850	9	427	1	6,000.00	1850	6,000.00			6,000.00
For lighting Pennsylvania avenue from Capitol square to the Treasury Department, and compensation of two lamplighters for the same, and for lighting the Capitol and Capitol grounds and President's House.	Sept. 30, 1850	9	536	1	11,000.00	1851	9,548.35			9,548.35
HEATING AND VENTILATING.										
For new stoves for warming and ventilating the Hall of the House of Representatives.	Mar. 2, 1831	4	474		800.00	1831	800.00			800.00
For attendants on the furnaces of the Rotunda during the recess.	July 4, 1836	5	114		150.00	1836	150.00			150.00
For taking down and removing the two furnaces beneath the Hall of the House of Representatives and building three new ones on the floor below the crypt, excavating a coal vault, constructing additional flues, etc.	Aug. 26, 1842	5	532	22	9,634.00	1842	9,634.00			9,634.00
For taking down the two old furnaces in the crypt under the Rotunda and building two new ones, cutting out the necessary flues, and doing other work connected therewith, according to a proposition of John Skirving, under date of February 1, 1843.	Mar. 3, 1843	5	644	1	1,454.00	1844	1,454.00			1,454.00
For constructing two furnaces under each end of the first story of the center of the Capitol, for warming the rooms and passages upon and above said first story, including the Congress Library room, according to the proposition of John Skirving.	Mar. 3, 1843	5	644	1	7,973.00	1844	7,973.00			7,973.00
For constructing seven furnaces for warming and drying the lower story, halls, and passages of the north wing of the Capitol.	Aug. 10, 1846	9	93	1	3,910.00	1847	3,910.00			3,910.00
For payment of bill of John Skirving for extra work done in the Capitol during the year 1846.	Mar. 3, 1847	9	164	1	321.82	1847	321.82			321.82
To enable the Clerk of the House to cause to be erected in the basement under the east entrance of the Capitol, nearest the House of Representatives, a suitable furnace for warming and excluding the dampness from that part of the building.	Mar. 3, 1851	9	612	1	500.00	1853			$500.00	

NOTE: This table contains the information published by Glenn Brown, which has not been corrected or updated.

Statement of appropriations and expenditures, from the National Treasury, relating to old Capitol. (*Continued*)

General object (title of appropriation), and details and explanations.	Date of act making the appropriation.	References to the Statutes at Large.			Amount of annual appropriation.	Year of expenditure.	Expenditure by warrants.	Repayments.	Amount carried to the surplus fund.	Net expenditures.
		Volume.	Page.	Section.						
CAPITOL. (Continued)										
IMPROVEMENT OF GROUNDS.										
To be applied, under the direction of the President, to inclosing and improving the public square east of the Capitol.	Apr. 29, 1816	3	324	1	$30,000.00	1816	$30,000.00			$30,000.00
For the purpose of completing the inclosure and improvement of the public square near the Capitol.	Mar. 3, 1817	3	389	2	38,658.00	1817	38,658.00			38,658.00
For graduating the ground round the Capitol and supplying the deficiency in former appropriations for inclosing and improving the Capitol square.	Apr. 11, 1820	3	562	1	5,591.00					
For graduating the Capitol square, putting the grounds in order, and planting trees within the same.	May 15, 1820	3	601	1	2,000.00	1820	7,591.00			7,591.00
For graduating and improving the ground around the Capitol.	Mar. 3, 1821	3	635	1	2,000.00	1821	2,000.00			2,000.00
For improving the grounds around the Capitol.	May 1, 1822 / Mar. 3, 1823	3 / 3	674 / 784	1 / 1	1,250.00 / 1,000.00	1822 / 1823	1,250.00 / 1,000.00			1,250.00 / 1,000.00
For improving the Capitol square and painting the railing round the same.	Apr. 2, 1824	4	16	1	2,000.00	1824	2,000.00			2,000.00
For improving the Capitol square.	Feb. 25, 1825	4	90	1	1,000.00	1826	1,000.00			1,000.00
For erecting an iron rail fence and central gate on that part of the public ground west of the Capitol which adjoins the circular walk.	Mar. 3, 1829	4	362	1	2,800.00	1829	2,800.00			2,800.00
For planting and improving the ground within the inclosure of the Capitol square, including the gardener's salary for 1830 and pay of laborers, 1831.	Mar. 2, 1831	4	474		3,000.00	1831	3,000.00			3,000.00
For purchasing Seneca-stone flagging for the terrace and walks adjoining the Capitol.	do	4	474		3,000.00	1831	3,000.00			3,000.00
To make good the deficiency in the estimates for the year 1829 for finishing gates and fences.	do	4	474		5,984.00	1831	5,984.00			5,984.00
For improving the grounds, including the gardener's salary.	May 5, 1832	4	507	1	2,000.00	1832	2,000.00			2,000.00
The commissioner of the public buildings authorized and directed to contract for the purchase, delivery, and laying of Seneca flagging on the walk from the western gate to the Capitol.	May 25, 1832	4	518	3	7,102.00	1833	7,102.00			7,102.00

NOTE: This table contains the information published by Glenn Brown, which has not been corrected or updated.

Statement of appropriations and expenditures, from the National Treasury, relating to old Capitol. *(Continued)*

General object (title of appropriation), and details and explanations.	Date of act making the appropriation.	References to the Statutes at Large. Volume.	Page.	Section.	Amount of annual appropriation.	Year of expenditure.	Expenditure by warrants.	Repayments.	Amount carried to the surplus fund.	Net expenditures.
CAPITOL. (Continued)										
For dressing and laying the stone procured for paving the terrace of the Capitol.	Mar. 2, 1833	4	649	2	$7,000.00	1833	$7,000.00			$7,000.00
For inclosing and improving the public ground north of the Capitol.	do	4	649	2	2,000.00	1833	2,000.00			2,000.00
For graveling the yard east of the Capitol.	July 4, 1836	5	114	4	2,000.00	1836	2,000.00			2,000.00
For extending the Capitol square and improving the grounds within and adjacent to the same as far west as the first street intersecting Pennsylvania avenue from the east.	do	5	114	4	25,000.00	1836	25,000.00			25,000.00
For completing the improvements commenced by extending the Capitol square west.	Mar. 3, 1837	5	172	1	40,000.00	1837	40,000.00			40,000.00
For extending Capitol square west and improving the same south of the center footway, according to the plan already in part executed under the provisions of an act of the last Congress.	Apr. 6, 1838	5	222	1	23,127.86	1838	23,127.86			23,127.86
TEMPORARY COMMITTEE ROOMS.										
For erecting a temporary building for a committee room near the Capitol.	Apr. 20, 1818	3	458	1	3,634.00	1819	3,634.00			3,634.00
TEMPORARY ACCOMMODATION OF CONGRESS.										
The President authorized to lease, in behalf of the United States, from the owners thereof, the new building on Capitol Hill, on square 728, with the adjoining buildings and appurtenances, for the term of one year next after the passing of this act, and from thence until the Capitol is in a state of readiness for the reception of Congress, at a rent not exceeding $1,650 per annum, to be paid half-yearly by the United States: *Provided always,* That any lease to be executed by virtue of this act shall and may be determinable at any time after the expiration of the first year, at the pleasure of Congress.	Dec. 5, 1815	3	251	1	1,650.00 1,650.00 1,650.00 1,650.00	1816 1817 1818 1819	1,650.00 1,650.00 1,650.00 1,650.00			
That so soon as the lease aforesaid shall have been duly executed it shall and may be lawful for the President to pay to the owners aforesaid the sum of $5,000 for fixtures and other extraordinary expenses incurred in fitting up the said buildings and otherwise preparing them for the better accommodation of Congress.	Dec. 8, 1815	3	251	2	5,000.00	1816	5,000.00			
To pay to Daniel Carroll, of Duddington, and others, proprietors of the building occupied by the Congress of the United States from the year 1816 to the year 1819, for repairing the same.	May 19, 1824	6	307		1,555.00	1824	1,555.00			
Total					**13,155.00**		**13,155.00**			**$13,155.00**

NOTE: This table contains the information published by Glenn Brown, which has not been corrected or updated.

Statement of appropriations and expenditures, from the National Treasury, relating to old Capitol. *(Continued)*

General object (title of appropriation), and details and explanations.	Date of act making the appropriation.	References to the Statutes at Large.			Amount of annual appropriation.	Year of expenditure.	Expenditure by warrants.	Repayments.	Amount carried to the surplus fund.	Net expenditures.
		Volume.	Page.	Section.						
CAPITOL. (Continued)										
REPAIRS.										
For defraying the expenses incidental to the dismantling the late library room of Congress and fitting it up for the accommodation of the House of Representatives at the ensuing session.	Mar. 1, 1805	2	317	1	$700.00	1805 1807	$689.23		$10.77	$689.23
For completing the staircase and providing temporary and adequate accommodations for the Library in the room now used for that purpose, and in the one in which the Senate now sit.	Mar. 3, 1809	2	537	1	5,000.00	1809	5,000.00			5,000.00
For repairing the roof, and fitting up a room in the west side of the north wing of the Capitol for the Library of Congress.	Feb. 20, 1811	2	643	1	600.00	1811	600.00			600.00
The President authorized to cause a proper apartment to be immediately selected and prepared for a library room, and to cause the library lately purchased from Thomas Jefferson to be placed therein during the ensuing recess of Congress.	Mar. 3, 1815 do	3 3	226 226	2 2	972.37 1,520.87	1815 1816	972.37 1,520.87			972.37 1,520.87
The accounting officers of the Treasury are authorized and required to investigate and settle the accounts against the Library of Congress exhibited by George Waterston, Daniel Rapine, and William Elliott.	Apr. 16, 1816	3	283	1	1,981.25	1816	1,981.25			1,981.25
The Joint Library Committee authorized to cause suitable apartments in the north wing of the Capitol to be fitted up and furnished for the temporary reception of the Library Congress, and to cause said Library to be removed and placed in the same.	Dec. 3, 1818 do	3 3	477 477	3 3	537.00 375.86	1819	912.86			912.86
For the purchase of furniture for the new Library.	May 26, 1824 Feb. 25, 1825	4 4	60 92	2 2	1,546.00 339.00	1824 1825	1,546.00 339.00			1,546.00 339.00
For defraying the expense for 2 stoves and 9 tons of coal for the use of the new Library of Congress.	Mar. 3, 1826	4	139	2	295.25	1826	295.25			295.25
For repairs and furniture for the Library of Congress.	Mar. 5, 1832	4	507	1	3,000.00	1832	3,000.00			3,000.00
For new articles of furniture for the Library of Congress.	Mar. 3, 1835	4	766		1,500.00	1835 1836	500.00 1,000.00			500.00 1,000.00
For laying the floor of principal library room with hydraulic cement.	Mar. 3, 1843	5	630	1	225.00	1844	225.00			225.00
For enlarging the law library, constructing a new stairway and other work, and the materials therefor, according to the plan of John Skirving, dated July 20, 1846.	Aug. 10, 1847	9	93	1	2,412.00	1847	2,412.00			2,412.00

Statement of appropriations and expenditures, from the National Treasury, relating to old Capitol. *(Continued)*

General object (title of appropriation), and details and explanations.	Date of act making the appropriation.	References to the Statutes at Large.			Amount of annual appropriation.	Year of expenditure.	Expenditure by warrants.	Repayments.	Amount carried to the surplus fund.	Net expenditures.
		Volume.	Page.	Section.						
WORKS OF ART.										
WASHINGTON STATUE.										
To enable the President of the United States to contract with a skillful artist to execute in marble a pedestrian statue of George Washington, to be placed in the center of the Rotunda of the Capitol.	July 14, 1832	4	581	1	$5,000.00	1833	$5,000.00			$5,000.00
For an additional payment for the statue of Washington.	Mar. 2, 1833	4	650	2	5,000.00	1834	5,000.00			5,000.00
For additional payment for the statue of Washington.	June 27, 1834 Mar. 3, 1835	4 4	697 768	1 1	5,000.00 5,000.00	1835 1836	5,000.00 5,000.00			5,000.00 5,000.00
For cost of preparing suitable foundation for supporting the colossal statue of Washington in the center of the Rotunda of the Capitol.	July 21, 1840	6	815	8	2,000.00	1840 1841 1842	2,000.00	$9.26	$9.26	1,990.74
That the accounts of Horatio Greenough, for expenses incurred in the execution of the pedestrian statue of Washington, authorized by a resolution of Congress February 13, 1832, and the accounts and charges for freight of the same to the United States, be settled, under the direction of the Secretary of State, according to the rights of the claimants under their several contracts liberally construed.	Sept. 9, 1841	5	460	1	6,500.00					
For the freight aforesaid and detention of the ship, and for an iron railing around the statue, including the sum of $1,500 assumed to be paid by the said Greenough in addition to the original contract as made by Commodore Hull, or so much thereof as may be necessary.	do	5	460	1	8,600.00	1841 1844	7,700.00 620.00		6,780.00	7,700.00 620.00
For the purpose of removing the said statue from the navy-yard at Washington and for erecting the same in such part of the Rotunda of the Capitol as may be deemed best adapted for the same by the Secretary of the Navy, in accordance with the joint resolution of Congress of May 27, 1840 (5 Stats., 409).	Sept. 9, 1841	5	460	2	5,000.00	1841 1842	1,000.00 4,000.00			1,000.00 4,000.00
For the removal of the statue of Washington, under the direction of a joint committee of both Houses of Congress, the account for which shall be audited and certified by said committee.	May, 1842	5	485	180	1,000.00	1842 1846	860.00		140.00	860.00

NOTE: This table contains the information published by Glenn Brown, which has not been corrected or updated.

Statement of appropriations and expenditures, from the National Treasury, relating to old Capitol. *(Continued)*

General object (title of appropriation), and details and explanations.	Date of act making the appropriation.	References to the Statutes at Large.			Amount of annual appropriation.	Year of expenditure.	Expenditure by warrants.	Repayments.	Amount carried to the surplus fund.	Net expenditures.
		Volume.	Page.	Section.						
WORKS OF ART. (Continued)										
For the removal of the statue of Washington from its present position and permanently placing the same on a proper pedestal and covering it temporarily in the inclosed and cultivated public grounds east of the Capitol, directly in front of the main entrance and steps of the east front of the Capitol, as suggested in the report of the Joint Committee on the Library and in the letter of Mr. Greenough dated February 3, 1843, referred to and reported by said committee in connection with the memorial of Horatio Greenough, under the direction and supervision of the said Greenough.	Mar. 3, 1843	5	642	1	$5,000.00	1843 1844 1851	$2,500.00 2,500.00 19.61	$19.61		$2,500.00 2,500.00
For the removal of the building over the statue of Washington and erecting an iron fence around the same.	Aug. 10, 1846	9	93	1	1,000.00	1847	1,000.00			1,000.00
Total					**49,100.00**		**42,199.61**	**28.87**	**6,929.26**	**42,170.74**
BUST OF CHIEF JUSTICE ELLSWORTH.										
The Joint Committee of the two Houses of Congress on the Library be, and they are hereby, authorized and required to contract with a suitable American artist for the execution in marble and delivery in the room of the Supreme Court of the United States, of a bust of the late Chief Justice Ellsworth.	June 30, 1834	4	717	1-2	800.00					
To Mr. Augur, for the bust of the late Chief Justice Ellsworth.	Mar. 3, 1837	5	173	1	400.00	1837 1838 1840 1844	1,100.00 100.00 145.00	479.75	334.75	865.25
Total					**1,200.00**		**1,345.00**	**479.75**	**334.75**	**865.25**
BUST OF CHIEF JUSTICE MARSHALL.										
For a marble bust of the late Chief Justice Marshall.	May 9, 1836 do	5 5	25 25	1 1	500.00 500.00	1838 1840	500.00		500.00	500.00
Total					**1,000.00**		**500.00**		**500.00**	**500.00**
BUST OF JOHN JAY.										
For employing John Frazee to execute a bust of John Jay for the Supreme Court room.	Mar. 2, 1831	4	474		400.00	1831	400.00			400.00

Statement of appropriations and expenditures, from the National Treasury, relating to old Capitol. *(Continued)*

General object (title of appropriation), and details and explanations.	Date of act making the appropriation.	References to the Statutes at Large.			Amount of annual appropriation.	Year of expenditure.	Expenditure by warrants.	Repayments.	Amount carried to the surplus fund.	Net expenditures.
		Volume.	Page.	Section.						
WORKS OF ART. (Continued)										
BUST OF THOMAS JEFFERSON.										
For the purchase of a bust of Thomas Jefferson, executed by Ceracci, now in the possession of Mr. Jefferson's executor, if so much be deemed necessary by the Committee on the Library.	May 5, 1832	4	513	1	$4,000.00	1833	$4,000.00			$4,000.00
PERSICO STATUES.										
To enable the President of the United States to contract with Luigi Persico to execute two statues in front of the Capitol.	Mar. 3, 1829	4	362	1	4,000.00	1829	4,000.00			4,000.00
For the second payment to Luigi Persico for statues for the Capitol.	Mar. 18, 1830	4	382		4,000.00	1830	4,000.00			4,000.00
For the third payment to Luigi Persico for statues for the Capitol.	Mar. 2, 1831	4	458		4,000.00	1831	4,000.00			4,000.00
For the fourth payment.	May 5, 1832	4	512	1	4,000.00	1832	4,000.00			4,000.00
For the fifth payment.	Mar. 2, 1833	4	625	1	4,000.00	1833	4,000.00			4,000.00
Total					**20,000.00**		**20,000.00**			**20,000.00**
PERSICO AND GREENOUGH STATUES.										
To enable the President of the United States to contract for two groups of statues to adorn the two blockings on the east front of the Capitol.	Mar. 3, 1837	5	173	1	8,000.00	1837 1838	4,000.00 4,000.00			4,000.00 4,000.00
For the second payment to Luigi Persico, according to the contract made with him, for a group of statues for the Capitol.	Apr. 6, 1838	5	223	1	4,000.00	1839	4,000.00			4,000.00
For the third payment.	Mar. 3, 1839	5	347	1	4,000.00	1841	4,000.00			4,000.00
For payment of Luigi Persico and Horatio Greenough for statues to adorn the two blockings, east front of the Capitol: *Provided,* That the work is in such state of progress as, in reference to the whole sum to be paid to the artists, respectively, for their execution, shall, in the opinion of President, render it proper to make such payments.	May 8, 1840 Mar. 3, 1841	5 5	378 428	1	8,000.00 8,000.00	1842 1843 1844 1845 1853	8,200.00 5,000.00 338.67 723.89	$1,737.44 [1]		8,200.00 5,000.00 338.67 723.89

[1] Transfer account.

NOTE: *This table contains the information published by Glenn Brown, which has not been corrected or updated.*

Statement of appropriations and expenditures, from the National Treasury, relating to old Capitol. *(Continued)*

General object (title of appropriation), and details and explanations.	Date of act making the appropriation.	References to the Statutes at Large.			Amount of annual appropriation.	Year of expenditure.	Expenditure by warrants.	Repayments.	Amount carried to the surplus fund.	Net expenditures.
		Volume.	Page.	Section.						
WORKS OF ART. (Continued)										
For payment to Horatio Greenough for statues for the east front of the Capitol.	June 17, 1844	5	690	1	$4,000.00					
For compensation to Luigi Persico for services rendered and expenses incurred in bringing the groups of statues made by him to this country and placing it on the pedestal, by direction of the Secretary of the Treasury.	June 17, 1844	5	690	1	4,000.00	1845	$4,000.00			$4,000.00
For removing Persico's statues from the navy-yard to the Capitol, preparing the pedestal, erecting the statues, and inclosing the same with an iron railing.	July 17, 1844	5	682	1	1,350.00	1845 1846	1,329.03		$20.97	1,329.03
For payment to Horatio Greenough for a group of statues to adorn the eastern portico of the Capitol: *Provided*, The work is in such state of progress as, in reference to the whole sum to be paid for its execution, shall, in the opinion of the President, render it proper to make such payment.	Aug. 10, 1846	9	92	1	8,000.00 1,737.44 [1]	1847 1853 1854 1856	7,500.00 5,830.00	$328.11	407.44 328.11	7,500.00 5,501.89
For freight and transportation of the group of statuary contracted for with Horatio Greenough from Leghorn to Washington, and for placing it upon the pedestal in front of the eastern portico of the Capitol.	Aug. 31, 1852	10	95	1	7,000.00	1854	7,000.00			7,000.00
Total					**58,087.44**		**55,921.59**	**328.11**	**2,493.96**	**55,593.48**
PAINTINGS BY JOHN TRUMBULL.										
Resolved, That the President of the United States be, and he is hereby, authorized to employ John Trumbull, of Connecticut, to compose and execute four paintings commemorative of the most important events of the American Revolution, to be placed, when finished, in the Capitol of the United States.	Feb. 6, 1817	3	400	J. R.						
On account of the paintings authorized by the resolution of Congress.	Mar. 3, 1817	3	358	1	8,000.00	1817	8,000.00			8,000.00
For the second payment to John Trumbull for paintings, agreeably to his contract with the Secretary of State, made in pursuance of a resolution of Congress of February 6, 1817 (as above).	Mar. 3, 1819	3	502	1	6,000.00	1819	6,000.00			6,000.00
For the third payment to John Trumbull.	Apr. 11, 1820	3	561	1	6,000.00	1820	6,000.00			6,000.00
For payment to John Trumbull for paintings commemorative of the most important events of the Revolution.	Apr. 30, 1822 Mar. 3, 1823	3 3	672 762	1 1	6,000.00 6,000.00	1822 1824	6,000.00 6,000.00			6,000.00 6,000.00
Total					**32,000.00**		**32,000.00**			**32,000.00**

[1] Transfer account.

NOTE: *This table contains the information published by Glenn Brown, which has not been corrected or updated.*

Statement of appropriations and expenditures, from the National Treasury, relating to old Capitol. *(Continued)*

General object (title of appropriation), and details and explanations.	Date of act making the appropriation.	References to the Statutes at Large.			Amount of annual appropriation.	Year of expenditure.	Expenditure by warrants.	Repayments.	Amount carried to the surplus fund.	Net expenditures.
		Volume.	Page.	Section.						
WORKS OF ART. (Continued)										
PAINTINGS BY VANDERLYN, WIER, AND CHAPMAN.										
For fulfilling the contracts made with John Vanderlyn, Henry Inman, Robert Wier, and John G. Chapman by the joint committee of Congress under the joint resolution of June 23, 1836 (5 Stats., 133), for the execution of four historical paintings for the vacant panels of the Rotunda of the Capitol.	Mar. 3, 1837	5	173	1	$8,000.00	1837	$8,000.00			$8,000.00
For the second payment to the artists engaged in executing paintings for the Rotunda of the Capitol, under the joint resolution of the two Houses.	Apr. 6, 1838	5	223	1	8,000.00	1838	8,000.00			8,000.00
For the third payment of the artists engaged.	Mar. 3, 1839	5	347	1	8,000.00	1839	8,000.00			8,000.00
For payment to the artists engaged: *Provided*, The paintings are in such a state of progress as, in reference to the whole sum to be paid to the artists respectively for their execution, shall, in the opinion of the President, render it proper to make such payment.	May 5, 1840 Mar. 3, 1841	5 5	378 428	1	8,000.00 8,000.00	1840 1841 1842 1844 1846 1847	6,000.00 2,000.00 600.00 2,000.00 600.00 800.00		$4,000.00 [1]	6,000.00 2,000.00 6,000.00 2,000.00 600.00 800.00
Total					**40,000.00**		**36,000.00**		**4,000.00**	**36,000.00**
MISCELLANEOUS.										
For balance of compensation to N. Gevelot for sculpture in the Capitol.	Mar. 3, 1829	4	362	1	750.00	1829	750.00			750.00
For compensation to Ferdinando Pettrich for models of statues for blocking to the western front of the Capitol.	July 7, 1838	5	267	7	600.00	1838	600.00			600.00
For preparing panels for the Rotunda with curtains for the reception of the paintings.	July 21, 1840	6	815	8	542.00	1840	542.00			542.00
NAVAL MONUMENT.										
For rebuilding and removing the monument erected in the navy-yard at Washington by the officers of the American Navy to the memory of those who fell in battle in the Tripolitan war.	Mar. 2, 1831	4	462		2,100.00	1831	2,100.00			2,100.00

[1] Transferred to "Painting by William H. Powell."

Statement of appropriations and expenditures, from the National Treasury, relating to old Capitol. (*Continued*)

General object (title of appropriation), and details and explanations.	Date of act making the appropriation.	References to the Statutes at Large.			Amount of annual appropriation.	Year of expenditure.	Expenditure by warrants.	Repayments.	Amount carried to the surplus fund.	Net expenditures.
		Volume.	Page.	Section.						
WORKS OF ART. (Continued)										
For the purpose of paying the workmen for renewing the inscriptions and giving uniformity of color to the naval monument, its ornaments and statues, recently removed from the Washington Navy-Yard to the Capitol square.	July 14, 1832	4	580		$200.00	1832	$200.00			$200.00
Total					**2,300.00**		**2,300.00**			
RELIEF OF P. C. L'ENFANT.										
To pay P. C. L'Enfant the sum of $666⅔ with legal interest from March 1, 1792, as a compensation for his services in laying out the plan of the city of Washington.	May 1, 1810	6	94		1,394.20	1810	1,394.20			1,394.20
RELIEF OF JAMES FRASER.										
Balance due him for 21 days' work done and performed for the Government in the city of Washington.	May 26, 1828	6	391		33.25	1828	33.25			33.25
RELIEF OF WIDOW OF GIOVANNI ANDREI.										
To defray the expenses of her return to Italy.	May 22, 1826	4	194	1	400.00	1826	400.00			400.00
RELIEF OF THE HEIRS OF GIUSEPPE FRANZONI.										
To Virginia Franzoni, as administratrix of Giuseppe Franzoni, as an allowance to close a contract with him to return his family to Italy, their native country.	Feb. 9, 1836	6	620	1	400.00	1836	400.00			400.00
RELIEF OF THE HEIRS OF FRANCIS IARDELLA.										
To Virginia Franzoni, as guardian of the children and heirs of Francis Iardella, being the amount due said Iardella for services on the Capitol in executing the ornamental fine carving and superintending the same, in addition to what he received in his lifetime.	do	6	621	2	1,050.00	1836	1,050.00			1,050.00
RELIEF OF ITALIAN SCULPTORS.										
For the purpose of enabling the President to return to their native country the two Italian sculptors lately employed on the public buildings, and to close the original contract made with them on behalf of the United States.	July 5, 1812	2	775	2	1,000.00	1814			$1,000.00	

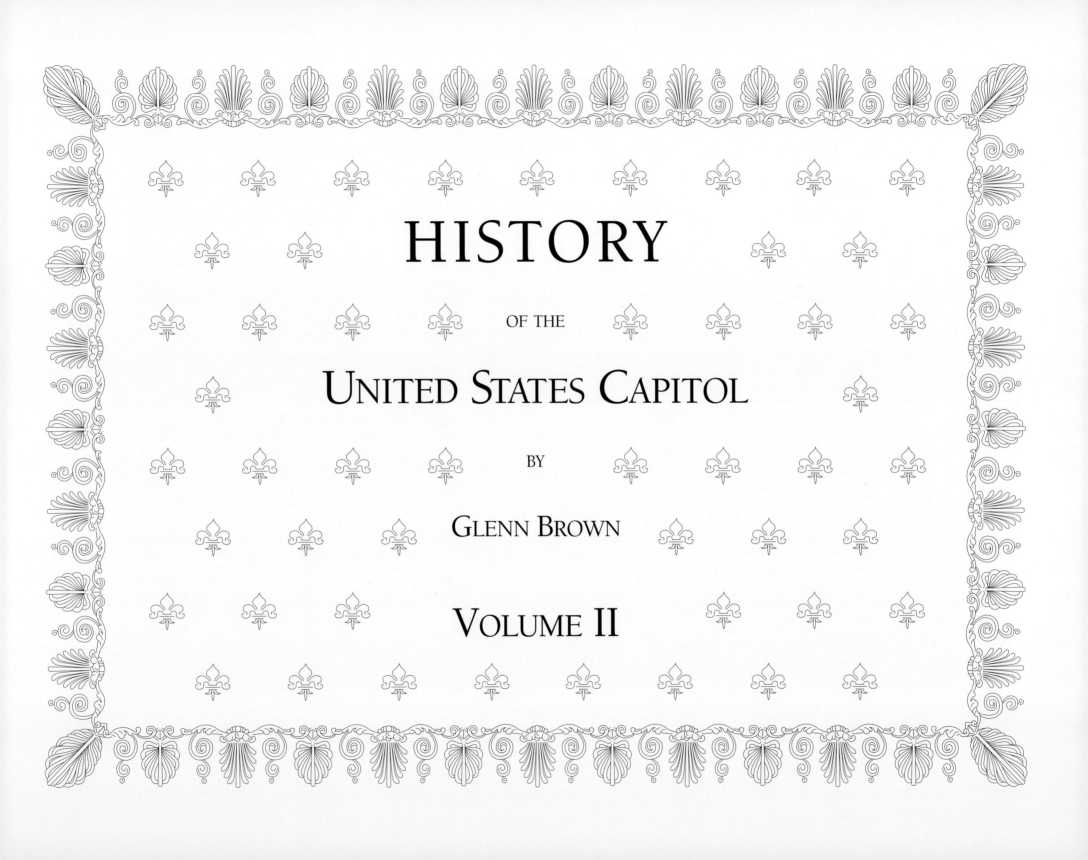

HISTORY

OF THE

UNITED STATES CAPITOL

BY

GLENN BROWN

VOLUME II

WEST VIEW OF CAPITOL.

West Front, 1900.

HISTORY

OF THE

UNITED STATES CAPITOL

BY

GLENN BROWN

FELLOW OF THE AMERICAN INSTITUTE OF ARCHITECTS; CORRESPONDING MEMBER OF THE
SOCIÉTÉ CENTRALE DES ARCHITECTES FRANÇAIS

VOLUME II

We have built no temple but the Capitol;
We consult no common oracle but the Constitution
—RUFUS CHOATE

CHAPTER XI

THE COMPETITION FOR THE EXTENSION OF THE CAPITOL

THE growth of the United States and the consequent increase in the membership of Congress, as well as the number of visitors to the Capitol, found the building inadequate for its purposes twenty years after it was completed. On May 28, 1850, the Committee on Public Buildings recommended an extension of the Capitol, in accordance with a report and drawings made by Robert Mills, who was at the time the Architect of Public Buildings.[1] Mills, in his description of the proposed extension by wings, states that each wing was planned to be 100 feet north and south by 200 feet east and west, forming projections 60 feet east and west from the line of the old building, divided or separated from the present building by a spacious court, so that the usefulness of the rooms of the old building would not be injured by the annexation of the wings. The space allotted in each wing for the two halls was in the center or on the axis of the old Capitol. The Senate Chamber was to accommodate one hundred Senators, and was to be nearly semicircular in form, with a semidomical ceiling flatter than the one used in the old Chamber. It was to be 90 feet wide by 60 feet deep, and with windows located on its north and south sides. The President's chair was to be located on the north, so that the members would face a northern light. In the rear of the President's chair an entrance was arranged for a portico with ten columns, forming the principal feature on the northern façade. On the east and west of the Chamber were grand stairways, together with sixteen rooms for the officers of the Senate. Below were twenty-eight committee rooms. The Senate wing was designed to have four entrances—a central entrance on the axis of the Capitol, with a corridor leading through the Rotunda from wing to wing; an eastern entrance through a colonnade on the eastern front, this colonnade to extend from wing to wing 360 feet long, with an entrance from each of the grand stairways on the east and west [Plate 137]. The south or House wing was arranged on a plan similar to the Senate wing, giving a larger audience chamber, while a House Library was to be obtained from the square spaces of the old Hall of Representatives. The Congressional Library was to have been enlarged so as to occupy the whole of the western projection of the old building. The old Hall of Representatives was to have been turned into an audience room, where works of art could be displayed with advantage. The old Senate Chamber was to be made into a Supreme Court room, while it was proposed to change the old Supreme Court into the Law Library. With this report Robert Mills presented drawings showing plans, sections, and elevations. I have been able to find only a section and an elevation of these drawings [Plates 138 and 139], although diligent search has been made through the Departments and among the descendants of the Architect for the missing drawings.[2]

---

[1] *Congressional Globe* (31–2), vol. 21, pt. 2, 1081. Mills identified himself as "Architect of Public Buildings" but did not hold the title officially. By 1850, he had been the architect or superintendent of many important public buildings in Washington, including the Treasury Department (1836–42), the Patent Office (1836–40), the Post Office (1839–42), and the Washington Monument (1848–1884). See John M. Bryan, ed., *Robert Mills* (Washington: American Institute of Architects, 1989).

[2] *Enlargement of the Capitol*, S. report 145 (31–1), Serial 565. The section and elevation drawings (Plates 138 and 139) of Mills's proposed 1850 design, submitted with his May report, are located in the Architect of the Capitol collection. In February, Mills addressed a memorial to both houses of Congress presenting drawings and a model of a proposed Capitol extension. These drawings and the model have been lost. See Pamela Scott, "Robert Mills: Unofficial Architect Designs Capitol Improvements and Extensions," *Capitol Dome* 24 (November 1989): 7–8.

In the description Mills says the different details of the architecture of the old building are carried out around the wings, with porticoes located on the north and south.

This scheme proposed a central dome similar in character to that of St. Peter's in Rome, St. Paul's in London, or the Invalides in Paris, in which the colonnade was to extend around and rest upon the base of the Dome of the old Capitol.

The Senate did not approve the report of the Committee on Public Buildings, and on September 26, 1850, passed the following resolution:

"*Resolved*, That the Committee on Public Buildings be authorized to invite plans, accompanied by estimates, for the extension of the Capitol, and to allow a premium of $500 for the plan which may be adopted by the Committees on Public Buildings (acting jointly) of the two Houses of Congress, to be paid out of the contingent fund of the Senate."[3]

The following general invitation was published in the National Intelligencer, of Washington, daily from September 30 to October 21, 1850:

"ENLARGEMENT OF THE CAPITOL.

"The Committee on Public Buildings of the Senate, having been authorized by a resolution of that body 'to invite plans, accompanied by estimates, for the extension of the Capitol, and to allow a premium of $500 for the plan which may be adopted by the Committees on Public Buildings (acting jointly) of the two Houses of Congress,' accordingly invite such plans and estimates, to be delivered to the Secretary of the Senate on or before the 1st day of December next.

"It is required that these plans and estimates shall provide for the extension of the Capitol, either by additional wings, to be placed on the north and south of the present building, or by the erection of a separate and distinct building within the inclosure to the east of the building.

"The committee do not desire to prescribe any conditions that may restrain the free exercise of architectural taste and judgment, but they would prefer that whatever plan may be proposed may have such reference to and correspondence with the present building as to preserve the general symmetry of the entire structure when complete. Although but one plan can be adopted, the committee reserve to themselves the right to form such plan by the adoption of parts of different plans submitted, *should such a course be found necessary*, in which event the committee also reserve to themselves the right to divide or proportion, according to their own judgment, the amount of premium to be awarded for the whole plan to those whose plans may in part be adopted, according to the relative importance and merit of each part adopted.

"R. M. T. Hunter,
"Jefferson Davis,
"John H. Clarke,
"*Committee of Senate on Public Buildings*.
"SENATE CHAMBER, *30 September, 1850*.

"N. B.—The several daily papers published at Washington will please insert the above daily for two weeks, and send their accounts to the Secretary of the Senate."[4]

The plans of the various competitors were examined by the committee, and they determined not to adopt any design as a whole, but selected the four sets which they considered the most meritorious, and

---

[3] *Congressional Globe* (31–1), vol. 21, pt. 2, 1081. Brown misdated the resolution, which was passed on September 25. See also "An Act Making Appropriations for the Civil and Diplomatic Expenses of the Government in the Year Ending the 30th of June, 1851, and for other Purposes," in *United States Statutes at Large*, vol. 9, 538.

[4] For an example of the general invitation, see *Daily National Intelligencer* [Washington, D.C.], October 11, 1850.

divided the premium of $500 between the four competitors.[5] Jefferson Davis submitted the report of the Committee on Public Buildings to the Senate February 8, 1851. This committee appears to have been careful and conscientious in the execution of their duties, as they say: "To answer the requirements of Congress without impairing the beauty or disturbing the harmony or diminishing the effect of the noble structure our fathers erected was a problem of extreme perplexity. It will be readily perceived that there must be greater difficulty in devising a plan for the enlargement of a building to which additions were not originally contemplated than in deciding upon one for an entirely new edifice."[6] Although I have been able to discover only the plans of a competitor who failed to put his name on the drawings [Plates 141 to 144] and two schemes by Thomas U. Walter, one a competitive plan and the other a modification of the same scheme [Plates 145 to 148], the wording of different reports gives a clear idea of the general arrangements which were under contemplation. The first was an extension of the building north and south, simply increasing the length. The second was a duplication of the old building, placing the new structure on the east. A third contemplated wings whose east and west axis was at right angles and whose north and south axis was coincident with that of the old building. A fourth contemplated wings extending much farther to the east than to the west of the old building [Plates 141 to 144].[7]

After mature deliberation, Robert Mills was instructed to draw a plan combining features from various sources, particularly utilizing the four sets of drawings which had been submitted in the competition. They recommended the addition of wings to the north and south ends of the old structure, the east and west axis of which were at right angles to the north and south axis of the old Capitol. The west front of the wings was to be placed on a line back of the west front of the building, and their east front was to extend far beyond the east front of the portion already built. While the drawings [Plates 141 to 144] show the general plan approved by the committee, discrepancies show that it is one of the original competitive plans, and the similarity is due to the fact that the general features were adopted by the committee. In the plan approved it was proposed to devote the whole of the west front to the Library, and special accommodations for the Supreme Court were arranged in the basement of the north wing. The committee state that "The exterior of the present [old] Capitol was changed from the original design by increasing the height of the principal Dome and adding two of a smaller size. It is proposed in the alterations to restore, as far as may be, the classic beauty and simplicity of the first plan by reducing the size of the principal Dome and removing the others, and to break the long horizontal line of the roof by an elevation over each wing through which the Chamber of the Senate and the Hall of Representatives may be lighted. The small domes [at present on old wings] may be replaced by any of the various methods of lighting from the roof without raising a prominent object above the building."[8]

Among the drawings of Thomas U. Walter I find a perspective made by the Corps of Topographical Engineers after this competition was closed [Plate 140].[9]

---

[5] Five competitors actually shared the premium, including William P. Elliot, Philip Harry, Robert Mills, Charles F. Anderson, and F. McClelland. See William C. Allen, *The Dome of the United States Capitol: An Architectural History* (Washington: Government Printing Office, 1992), 7.

[6] "Report on the Enlargement of the Capitol Building," in *Congressional Globe* (31–2), vol. 23, 475.

[7] Plates 141 to 144 were the composite drawings prepared by Robert Mills in 1851 combining the best features of the competition submittals. These drawings are located in the Architect of the Capitol collection.

[8] "Report on the Enlargement of the Capitol Building," 475.

[9] Philip Harry, not Walter, drew this perspective of the proposed Capitol extension (Plate 140). The drawing actually captured second place in the competition. See RG 40, Subject Files, Curator's Office, AOC.

PLATE 137

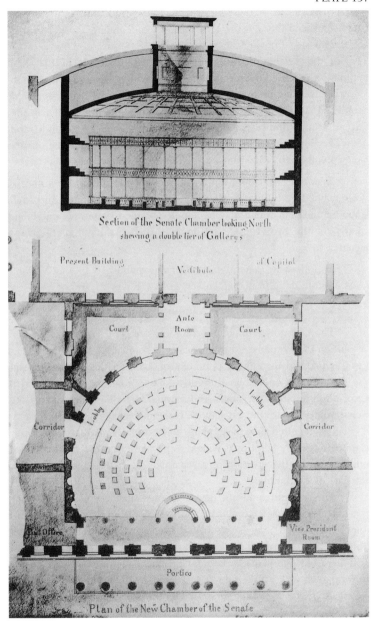

Section of the Senate Chamber looking North
shewing a double tier of Gallerys

Plan of the New Chamber of the Senate

PLAN NEW SENATE CHAMBER, BY ROBERT MILLS, ARCHITECT.
Section and plan of a proposed Senate Chamber, February 1850. *Location unknown.*

PLATE 138

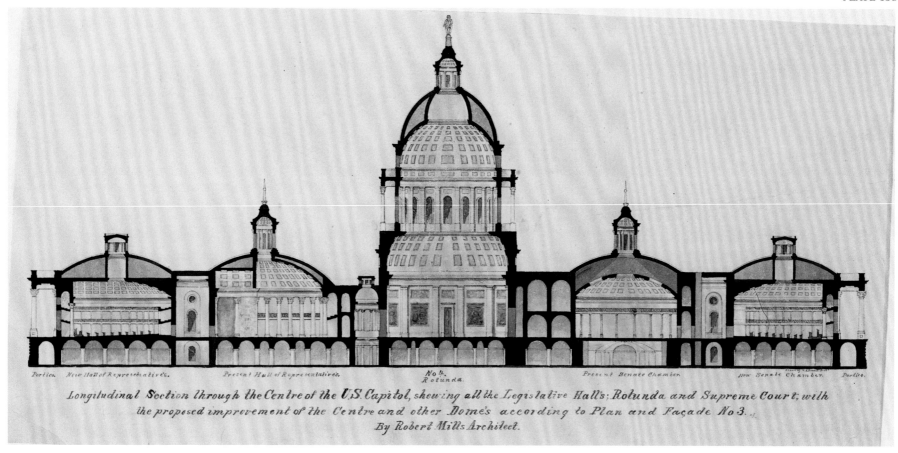

Longitudinal Section through the Centre of the U.S. Capitol, shewing all the Legislative Hall's; Rotunda and Supreme Court; with the proposed improvement of the Centre and other Dome's according to Plan and Façade No 3.
By Robert Mills Architect.

SECTION OF DESIGN BY ROBERT MILLS.

Longitudinal section of a proposed extension of the Capitol (facade no. 3), February 1850. Drawn by W. A. Powell. A figure of "Liberty" would have crowned Mills's dome.

PLATE 139

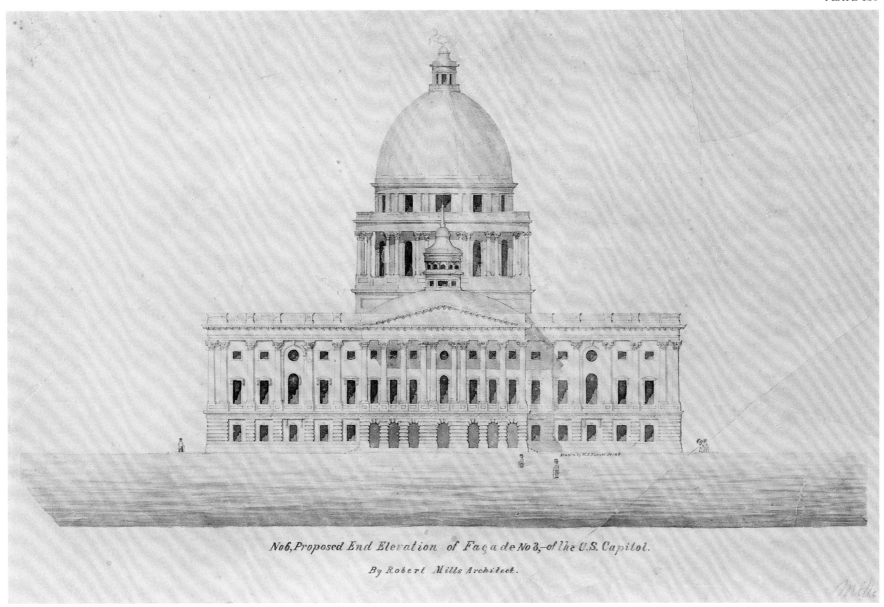

No 6, Proposed End Elevation of Façade No 3, of the U.S. Capitol.

By Robert Mills Architect.

NORTH OR SOUTH ELEVATION, DESIGN BY ROBERT MILLS.

End elevation of a proposed extension of the Capitol (facade no. 3), February 1850. Drawn by W. A. Powell.

PLATE 140

PERSPECTIVE VIEW OF THE EASTERN FACADE OF THE CAPITOL WITH PROPOSED ADDITIONS

as shown in Plan and Elevations Nº 3, from the Bureau of Topl. Engrs.

December 1850.

PERSPECTIVE FOR CAPITOL EXTENSION, BY BUREAU OF TOPOGRAPHICAL ENGINEERS.

Drawn by Philip Harry, December 1850. Harry placed second in the competition of 1850.

PLATE 141

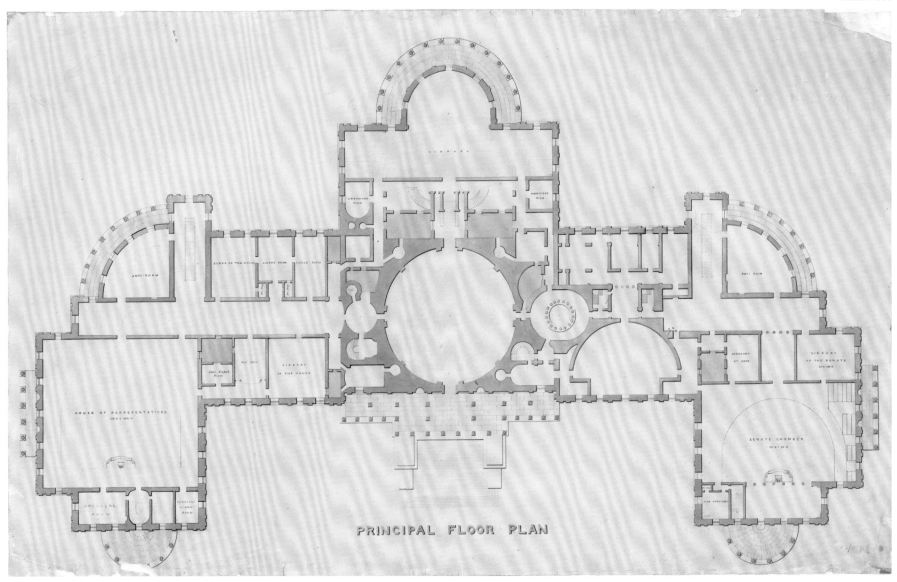

PRINCIPAL FLOOR PLAN

COMPETITIVE PLAN, AUTHOR UNIDENTIFIED
Principal floor plan of the Capitol by Robert Mills, 1851.

PLATE 142

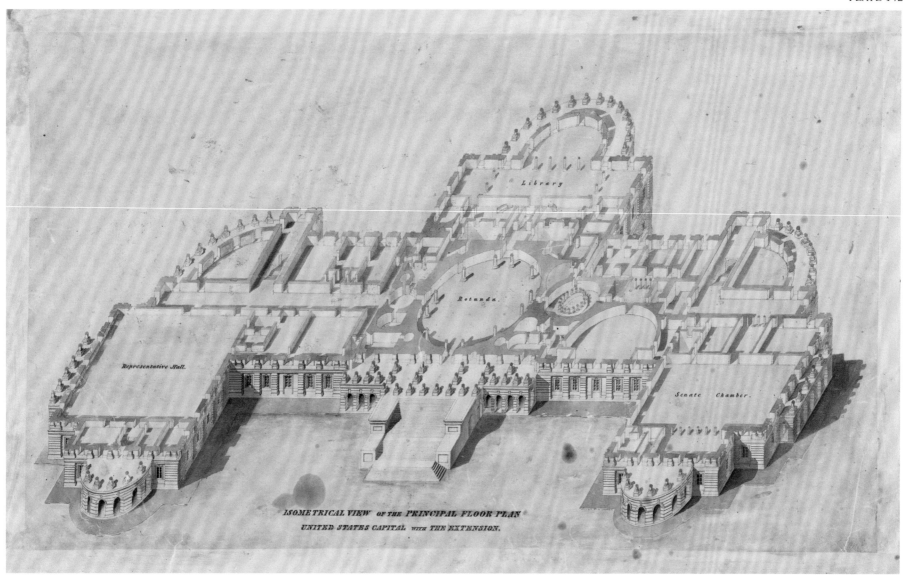

COMPETITIVE PLAN.

Isometric view of the principal floor plan (related drawing, plate 141) by Robert Mills, 1851.

PLATE 143

COMPETITIVE PLAN, WEST ELEVATION.

West front elevation for a Capitol extension by Robert Mills, 1851 (related plans, plates 141 and 142).

PLATE 144

COMPETITIVE PLAN, EAST ELEVATION.

East front elevation for a Capitol extension by Robert Mills, 1851 (related drawings, plates 141, 142, and 143).

PLATE 145

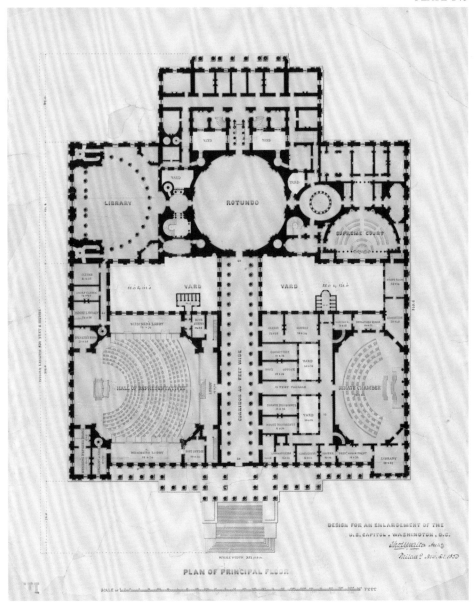

COMPETITIVE PLAN OF T. U. WALTER FOR CAPITOL EXTENSION 1850.

Floor plan for a proposed Capitol extension by Thomas Ustick Walter, November 1850. This plan was drawn to illustrate an extension of the east front, the approach favored by the House of Representatives.

313

PLATE 146

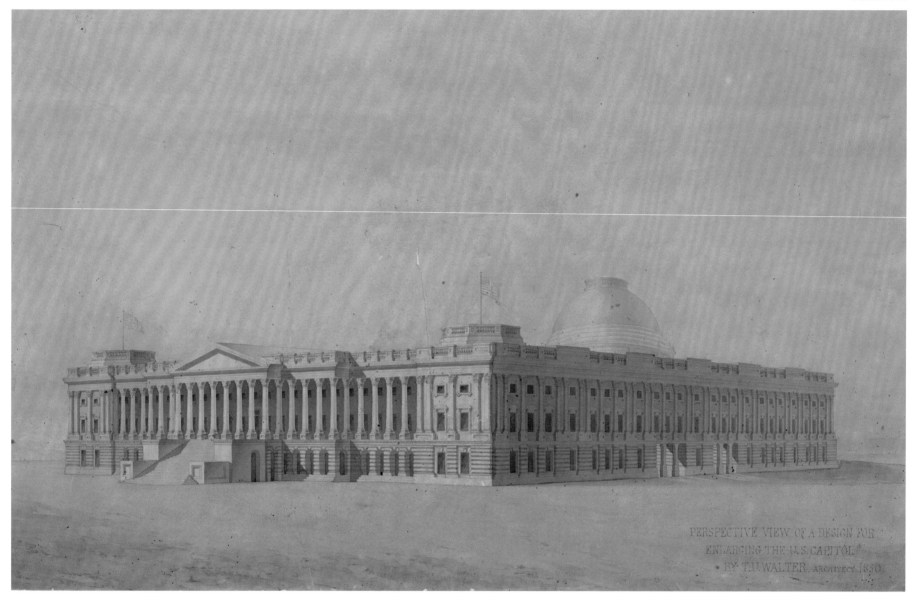

PERSPECTIVE VIEW COMPETITIVE DESIGN,—T. U. WALTER, ARCHITECT.

Perspective view from the northeast of a proposed extension of the Capitol by means of a large addition to the east front, November 1850.

PLATE 147

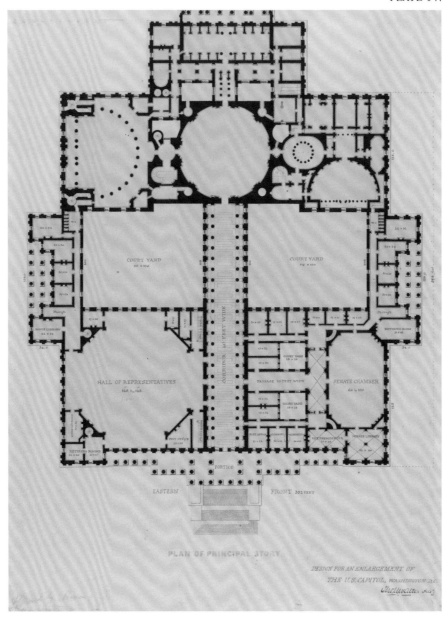

MODIFICATION WALTERS' COMPETITIVE PLAN.

Plan of the principal floor for a proposed extension of the Capitol by Thomas Ustick Walter, 1851. The plan shows a huge addition to the east front with a monumental central corridor lined by columns and flanked by large open courtyards to link the old and new sections of the building.

PLATE 148

PERSPECTIVE OF COMPETITIVE PLAN,—WALTER ARCHITECT.

Southeast perspective view of an 1851 revision of Walter's competition plan for a proposed extension of the Capitol (related plan, plate 147).

Chapter XII

The Work of Thomas U. Walter, Architect

PRESIDENT Millard Fillmore evidently considered the action of the Senate in authorizing a competition not within the law, as he states in his annual message of December, 1851, that an "act of Congress approved September 30, 1850, contained a provision for the extension of the Capitol according to such a plan as might be approved by the President, and appropriated $100,000 to be expended under his directions by such architect as he should appoint to execute the same."[1] Acting under this authority, President Fillmore appointed Thomas U. Walter Architect of the United States Capitol Extension, and on the 10th day of June, 1851, approved a general outline of the plan submitted by Walter. June 11 the following oath of office was administered:

"I, Thomas U. Walter, do solemnly swear that I will support the Constitution of the United States, and well and faithfully discharge the duties of Architect to execute the plan adopted by the President for the extension of the Capitol, as authorized by act of 30 September, 1850.

"Tho. U. Walter.

"Sworn to and subscribed before me this 11th day of June, A.D. 1851.

"T. Hartley Crawford, *Judge of Court, D.C.*"

---

[1] For President Fillmore's second annual message of December 2, 1851, see James D. Richardson, ed., *A Compilation of the Messages and Papers of the Presidents* (New York: Bureau of National Literature, Inc., 1897), vol. 6, 2672. See also "An Act making Appropriations for the Year ending the 30th of June, 1851," in *United States Statutes at Large*, vol. 9, 538. Fillmore did not consider the competition authorized by the Senate illegal. The competition and the law enacted by Congress for the extension of the Capitol were separate actions, and were not in conflict as Brown assumes.

Walter made several plans on this authority. Plates 149 and 150 show two of his suggested methods of treatment, and the third one, which was approved by the President, is illustrated by the following description and plates: This scheme for an extension contemplated two wing buildings placed on the north and south of the old Capitol and 44 feet from it, but connected with the old building by corridors.[2] The dimensions of each building as planned were 142 feet 8 inches from north to south and 238 feet 10 inches from east to west, exclusive of porticoes and steps. Plates 151, 152, 153, and 154 show the cellar, basement, and principal and third story plans of the Senate wing, while Plates 155, 156, 157, and 158 show the basement, and principal and third stories of the House wing.

The corridors consisted of passages leading from the center of the building to the wings, 21 feet 4 inches wide, with outside colonnades, making the entire width of each corridor 56 feet 8 inches. Plate 159 shows a design for the south and north fronts of the wings, made by Walter, but modified in the approved plan as shown in perspective [Plate 164]. The east front of the wings was to have porticoes similar to the one on the old building, extending across the whole front. Each portico had a central projection 10 feet 4 inches by 78 feet [Plate 160]. Porticoes were designed on the west fronts with 10 feet 6 inches projection by 105 feet 8 inches in width [Plate 161]. On the north and south fronts were similar porticoes 124 feet 4 inches wide. Plate 162 shows the character of design where the wings face the old building,

---

[2] Plates 149 and 150 were studies Walter made prior to his appointment. They were not alternative plans as Brown claimed.

and Plate 163 shows the design of the walls behind the porticoes. Walter, in his first report, dated December 23, 1851, says that "The architecture of the exterior is designed to correspond in its principal features to that of the present [old] building, and the disposition of the various parts is intended to present the appearance of one harmonious structure and to impart dignity to the present building rather than to interfere with its proportions or detract from its grandeur or beauty."[3]

The principal entrances were placed on the eastern porticoes, at the top of a long flight of steps leading from the ground up to the colonnade. The principal doorways opened into a vestibule 27 feet wide, and this vestibule opened on a hall 45 feet square, lighted from the roof. Galleries around this hall gave access to the offices in the second story. The gallery was supported on columns with entablature and balustrade. From the large halls vaulted passages 26 feet wide led to a corridor 23 feet wide, which connected the wings with the main building [Plates 153 and 157]. The Hall of Representatives and the Senate Chamber were placed in the western half of the south and north wings respectively, the Senate occupying only the northern portion of this part of the wing. The Hall of Representatives was to have been 130 feet by 97 feet 10 inches and 35 feet high. The Senate Chamber was 76 feet 6 inches by 97 feet 10 inches, with a ceiling 35 feet high. Both Houses were to have galleries on three sides, and to be lighted from the ceiling, as well as from windows in the exterior walls [Plates 153 and 157].

July 4, 1851, the corner stone of the Capitol extension was laid with elaborate civic and Masonic ceremonies. The President of the United States, Millard Fillmore, attended by Walter Lenox, mayor of Washington and son of Peter Lenox, clerk of works for thirteen years on the old building, heads of Departments, officers of the Army and Navy, George Washington Parke Custis, the clergy, Masonic orders, and civic organizations, formed a procession at the City Hall and marched to the Capitol. Thomas U. Walter, the Architect, deposited a sealed jar in the corner stone containing historical parchments, coins of the United States, a copy of the oration to be delivered by Daniel Webster, the Secretary of State, newspapers, and other memorials. President Millard Fillmore then laid the corner stone, and the Masonic ceremonies for such occasions were performed. B. B. French, grand master of the Masonic fraternity, made a short opening address, and Daniel Webster made an elaborate oration.

An excellent account of the proceedings of the day is given in the following portion of the address which Webster prepared and which was placed in the corner stone:

"On the morning of the first day of the seventy-sixth year of the independence of the United States of America, in the city of Washington, being the 4th day of July, 1851, this stone, designated as the corner stone of the extension of the Capitol, according to a plan approved by the President of the United States, in pursuance of an act of Congress, was laid by Millard Fillmore, President of the United States, assisted by the grand master of the Masonic lodges, in the presence of many members of Congress; of officers of the executive and judiciary departments, National, State, and District; of officers of the Army and Navy; the corporate authorities of this and other cities; many associations, civic, military, and Masonic; officers of the Smithsonian Institution and National Institute; professors of colleges and teachers of schools of the District of Columbia, with their students and pupils, and a vast concourse of people from places near and remote, including a few surviving gentlemen who witnessed the laying of the corner stone of the Capitol by President Washington on the 18th of September, 1793.

[3] Architect of the United States Capitol Extension to the Secretary of the Interior, December 23, 1851, in "Extension of the Capitol: Message from the President of the United States, Transmitting the Report of the Architect for the Extension of the Capitol," H. ex. doc. 60 (32–1), Serial 641.

"If, therefore, it shall hereafter be the will of God that this structure shall fall from its base, that its foundation be upturned and this deposit brought to the eyes of men, be it known that on this day the Union of the United States of America stands firm; that their Constitution still exists unimpaired and with all its original usefulness and glory, growing every day stronger and stronger in the affections of the great body of the American people, and attracting more and more the admiration of the world.

"And all here assembled, whether belonging to public or private life, with hearts devoutly thankful to Almighty God for the preservation of the liberty and happiness of the country, unite in sincere and fervent prayers that this deposit, and the walls and arches and domes and towers, the columns and entablatures, now to be erected over it may endure forever.

"God save the United States of America!

"DANIEL WEBSTER,
"Secretary of State of the United States."[4]

The work progressed rapidly after the corner stone was laid, and many contracts were let for both labor and materials.

Thomas U. Walter made the following contracts: August 1, 1851, with James S. Piper, quarryman, of Baltimore, Md., to furnish building stone for the foundation, for $2.25 per perch, measured in the wall; Samuel J. Seely, of New York, lime merchant, for wood-burned lime at $1.30 per barrel, with a reduction of 12½ cents for every barrel returned. August 12, with Aloysius N. Clements, Washington, D.C., dealer in building sand, for clean, sharp river sand, at 2¾ center per bushel (3 cents, November 28, 1851). August 22, with George Shafer, dealer in

cement, Funkstown, Md., for best hydraulic cement, in barrels, for $1.17, delivered. November 25, with Christopher Adams, brickmaker, Albany, N.Y., for 5,000,000 hard-burned brick, made of tempered clay, at $6.37 per thousand. November 28, with John Purdy, lumber merchant, of Washington, D.C., for cullings, at $14 per thousand; spruce scantling, $15 per thousand; white pine scantling, $16 per thousand. December 4, with Henry Exall, builder, of Richmond, Va., and M. G. Emery, granite cutter, of Washington, D.C., to furnish and set all granite work for $22,400. December 4, with Andrew Hoover, lime merchant, of Washington, D.C., for wood-burned lime, at 97 cents per barrel, 12½ cents deducted for returned barrels. December 19, with Alexander R. Boteler, dealer in cement, Shepherdstown, Va., for hydraulic cement, at $1.12½ for every barrel delivered, and deduction of 12½ cents for barrels returned. John Rice, John Baird, Charles Hubner, and Mathew Baird, all of Philadelphia, Pa., for all exterior marble work, to be procured from quarries at Lee, Mass., at the following rates: Blocks less than 30 cubic feet, 65 cents per cubic foot; over 30 cubic feet, $1.98 per cubic foot; contract made January 17, 1852. Contract made with Provest, Winter & Co., of Washington, D.C., marble masons, on July 12, 1852, at stipulated prices, which are laid down minutely in the contract, by piecework, for cutting and setting all the marble work.[5]

Neither the Senate nor the House seems to have been consulted as to the character of the arrangements in the building that was being erected for their comfort and convenience, as the Senate on March 16, 1852, directed the Committee on Public Buildings to make a thorough examination of the work which had been completed on the Capitol extension and to obtain the aid of the United States Topographical

[4] "Oration of Daniel Webster, Delivered July 4, 1851, At the Capitol, on the occasion of the Laying of the Cornerstone of the Extension of the Capitol," *Daily National Intelligencer,* July 8, 1851, 2.

[5] "Accounts Current from August 2, 1851, to March 27, 1852," in *Reports of the Commissioners of Public Buildings, 1850–1855,* bound volume, Curator's Office, AOC.

PLATE 149

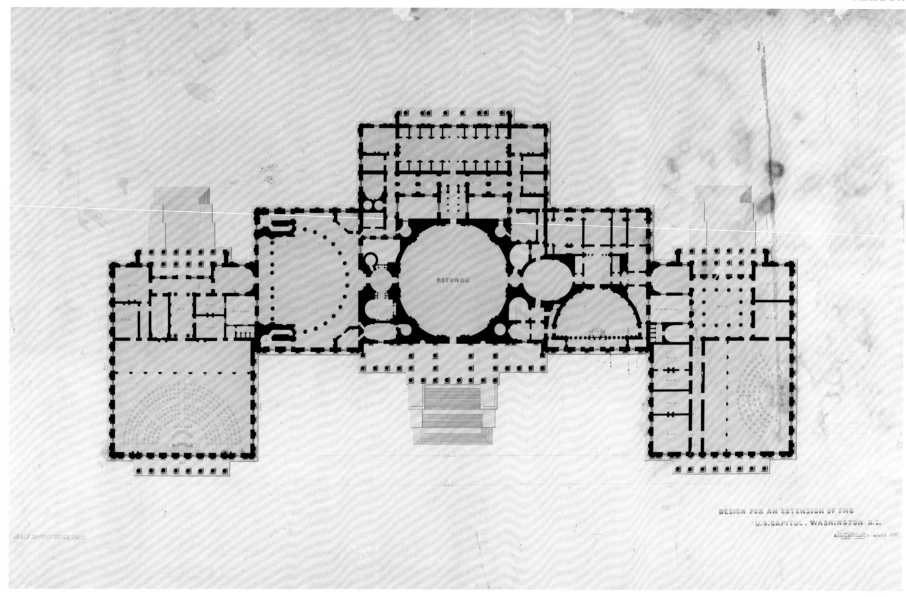

PROPOSED PLAN, AFTER COMPETITION,—WALTER ARCHITECT, 1851.

Principal floor plan for a proposed extension by wings extended eastward.
In this study, the chambers for the House of Representatives and the Senate are located in the eastern section of each wing.

PLATE 150

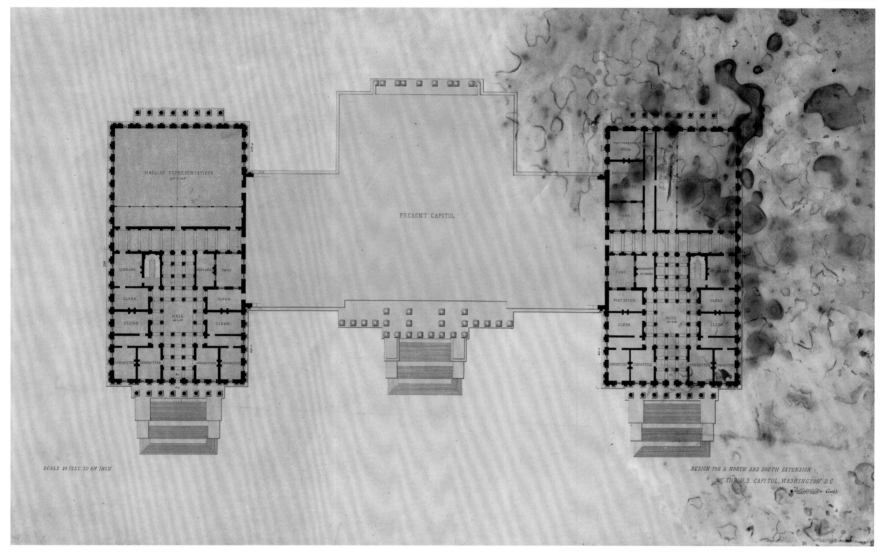

PLAN MADE BY WALTER AFTER THE COMPETITION.

Principal floor plan for a proposed extension by wings attached directly to the north and south elevations of the Capitol, 1851.
In this study, the chambers for the House of Representatives and the Senate are located in the western section of each wing.

PLATE 151

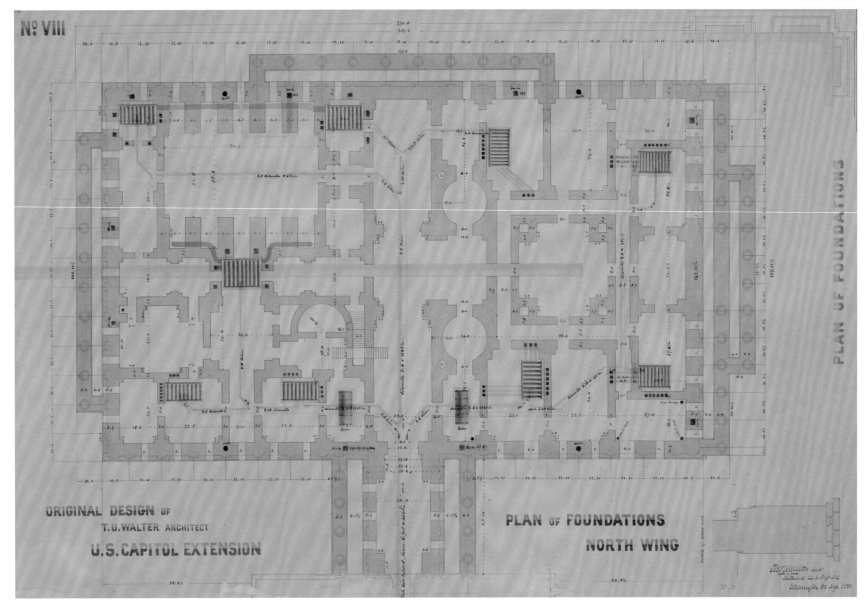

PLAN OF FOUNDATION 1851, NORTH WING,—T. U. WALTER ARCHITECT.

This plan shows the north wing as it would be executed, attached to the old building by a connecting corridor.

PLATE 152

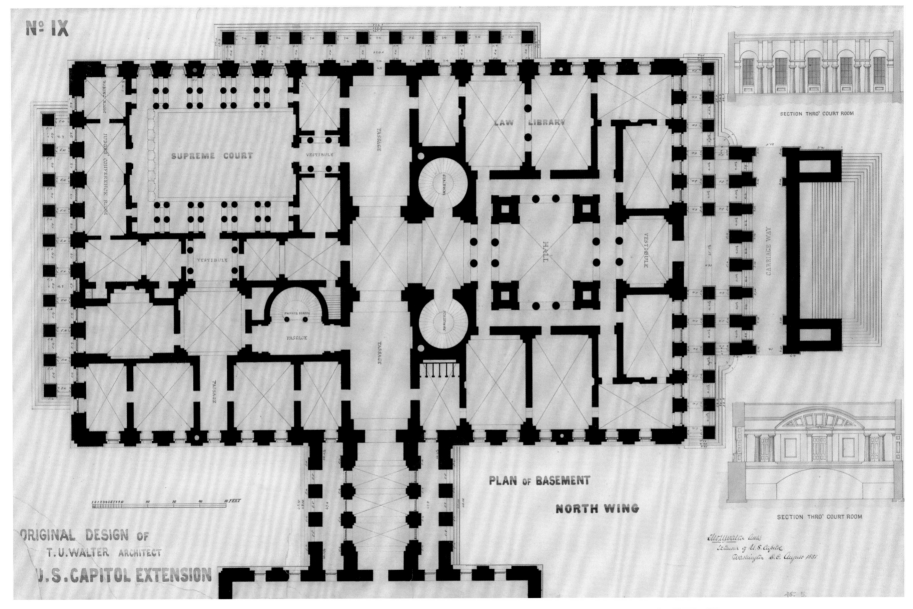

Nº IX

SUPREME COURT

VESTIBULE

JUDGES CONFERENCE ROOM

PASSAGE

LAW LIBRARY

HALL

VESTIBULE

PRIVATE STAIRS

PASSAGE

PASSAGE

PASSAGE

CARRIAGE WAY

SECTION THRO' COURT ROOM

SECTION THRO' COURT ROOM

PLAN of BASEMENT

NORTH WING

FEET

ORIGINAL DESIGN of
T. U. WALTER ARCHITECT

U. S. CAPITOL EXTENSION

BASEMENT PLAN NORTH WING, APPROVED BY PRESIDENT FILLMORE 1851—WALTER ARCHITECT.

Walter prepared drawings to illustrate ideas for the Supreme Court's accommodation in the Capitol's extension.
This design was not used, and the court moved into the Old Senate Chamber in 1860.

PLATE 153

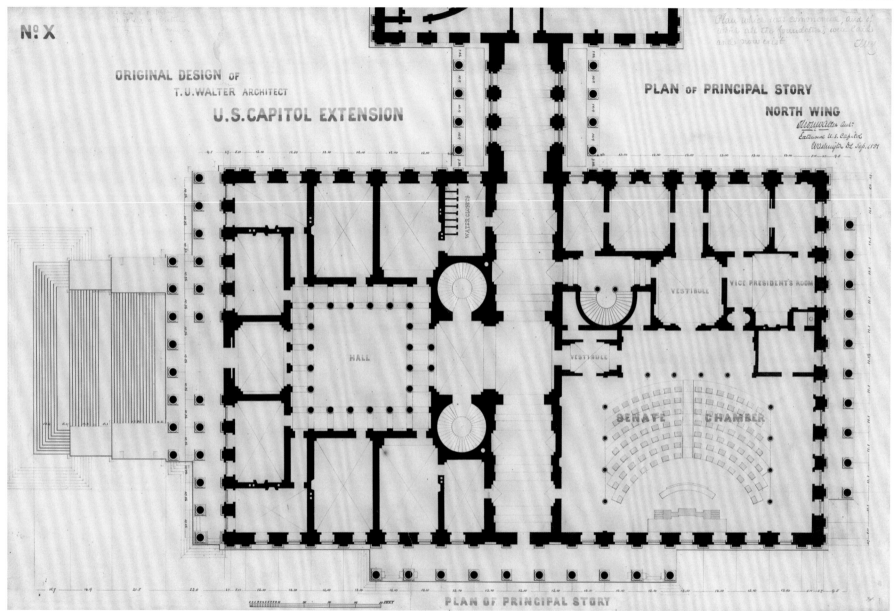

PRINCIPAL STORY PLAN, NORTH WING, APPROVED BY PRESIDENT FILLMORE 1851—WALTER ARCHITECT.

In this plan of the second floor, the Senate Chamber was to be placed in the western half of the north wing.

PLATE 154

Nº XI

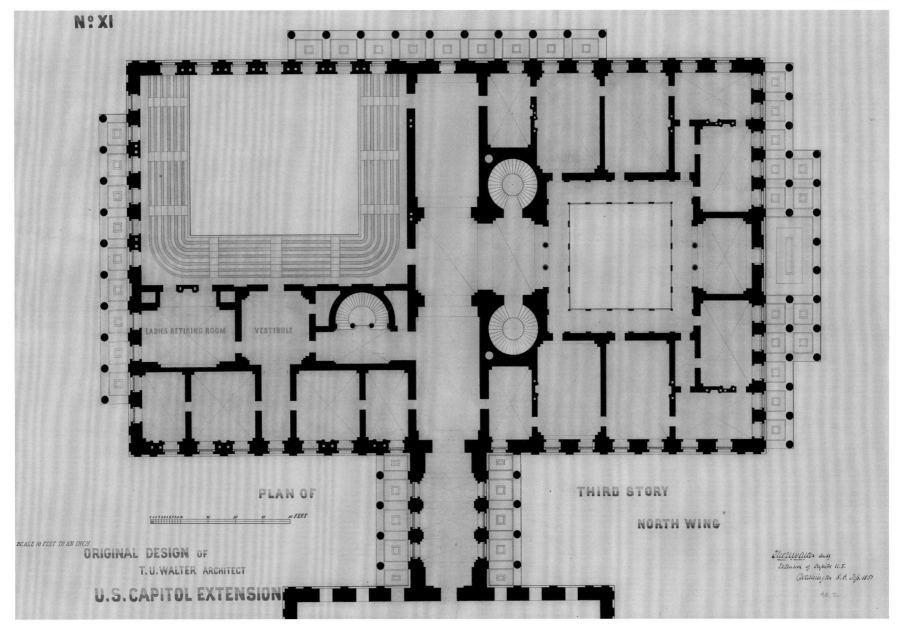

LADIES RETIRING ROOM   VESTIBULE

PLAN OF   THIRD STORY

NORTH WING

SCALE 10 FEET TO AN INCH

ORIGINAL DESIGN OF
T. U. WALTER ARCHITECT

U.S. CAPITOL EXTENSION

ATTIC STORY PLAN NORTH WING, APPROVED BY PRESIDENT FILLMORE 1851—WALTER ARCHITECT.

In Brown's time the third floor was called the attic story.

PLATE 155

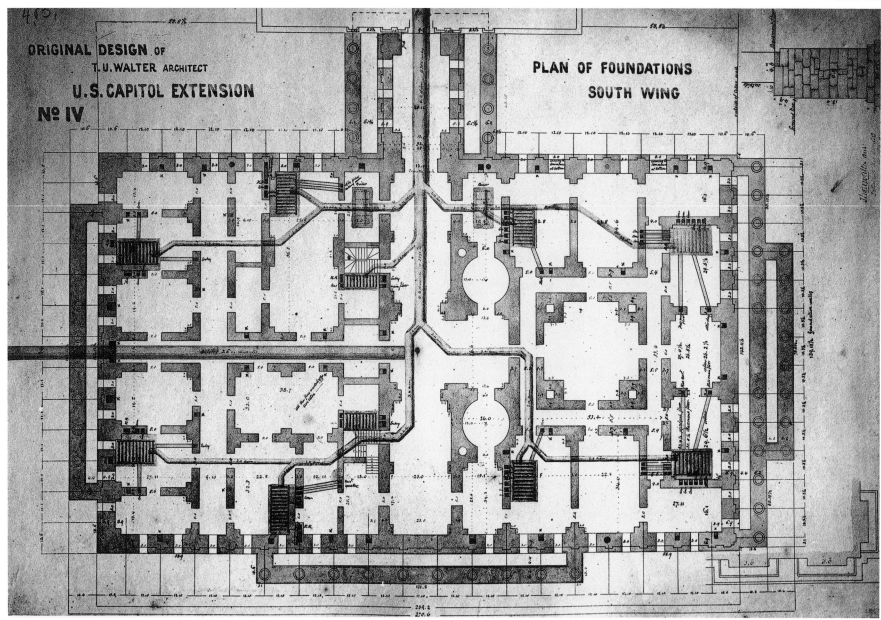

PLAN OF FOUNDATION 1851, SOUTH WING,—WALTER ARCHITECT.

PLATE 156

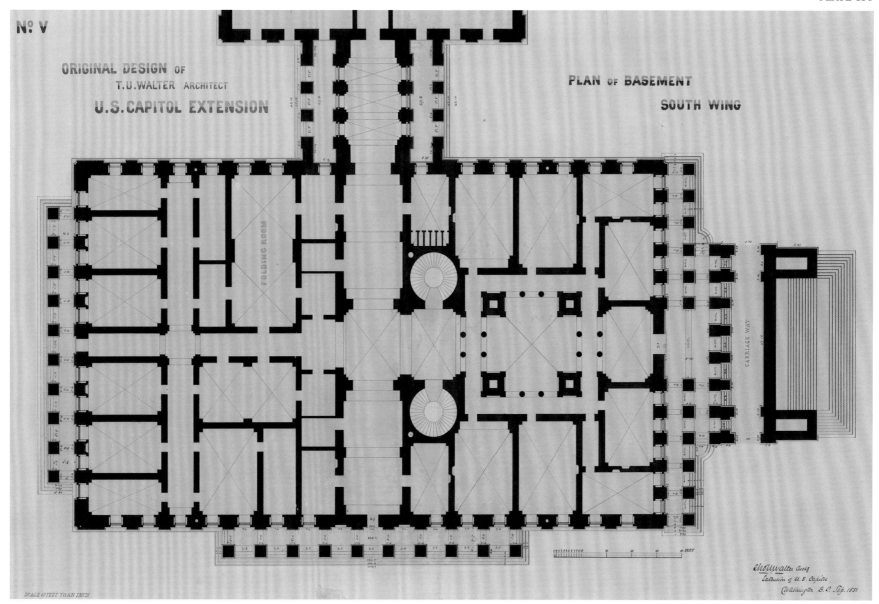

BASEMENT PLAN, SOUTH WING, APPROVED BY PRESIDENT FILLMORE 1851—WALTER ARCHITECT.

PLATE157

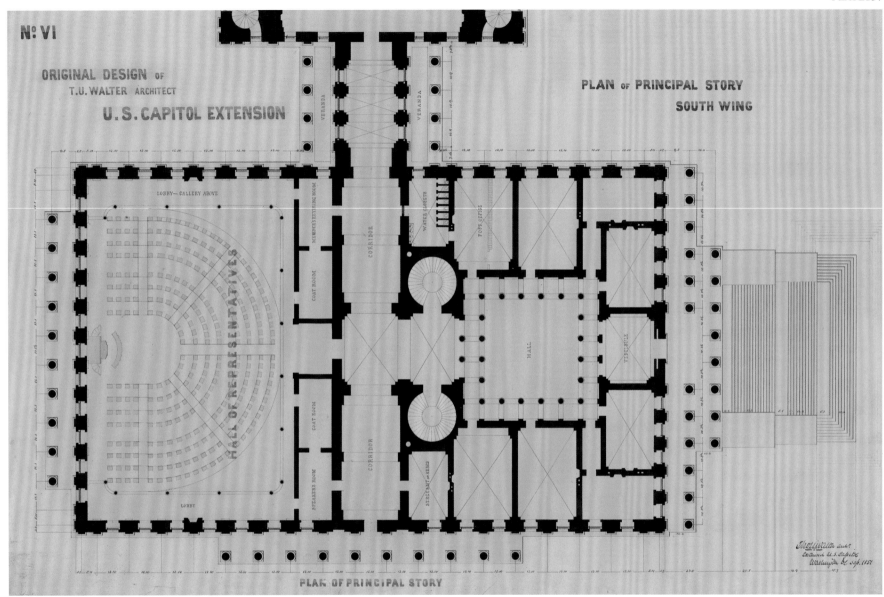

PLAN OF PRINCIPAL STORY

PRINCIPAL STORY PLAN, SOUTH WING, APPROVED BY PRESIDENT FILLMORE 1851—WALTER ARCHITECT.

The House of Representatives Chamber is located in the western half of this plan of the south wing.

PLATE 158

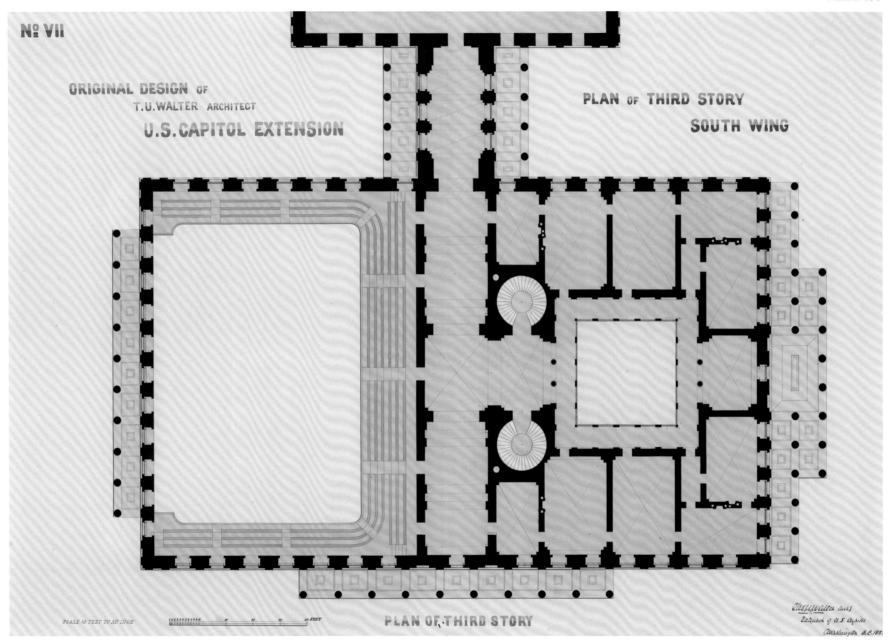

No VII

ORIGINAL DESIGN OF
T.U.WALTER ARCHITECT
U.S.CAPITOL EXTENSION

PLAN OF THIRD STORY
SOUTH WING

SCALE 10 FEET TO AN INCH

PLAN OF THIRD STORY

PLAN OF THIRD STORY, SOUTH WING, APPROVED BY PRESIDENT FILLMORE 1851,—WALTER ARCHITECT.

PLATE 159

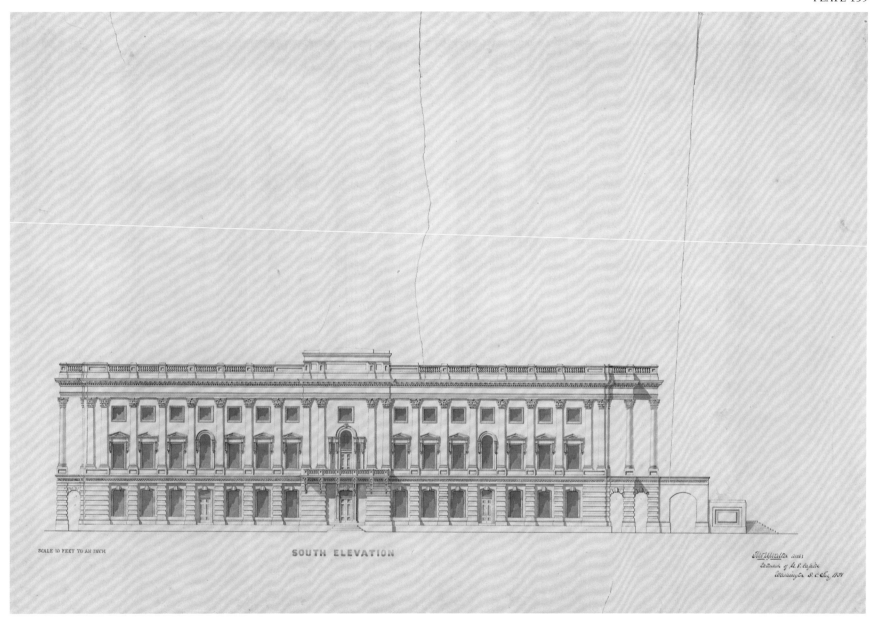

SOUTH ELEVATION

SCALE 10 FEET TO AN INCH

DESIGN FOR SOUTH ELEVATION 1851,—T. U. WALTER, ARCHITECT.

Design study illustrating the appearance of the Capitol without the end porticos that were eventually built.

PLATE 160

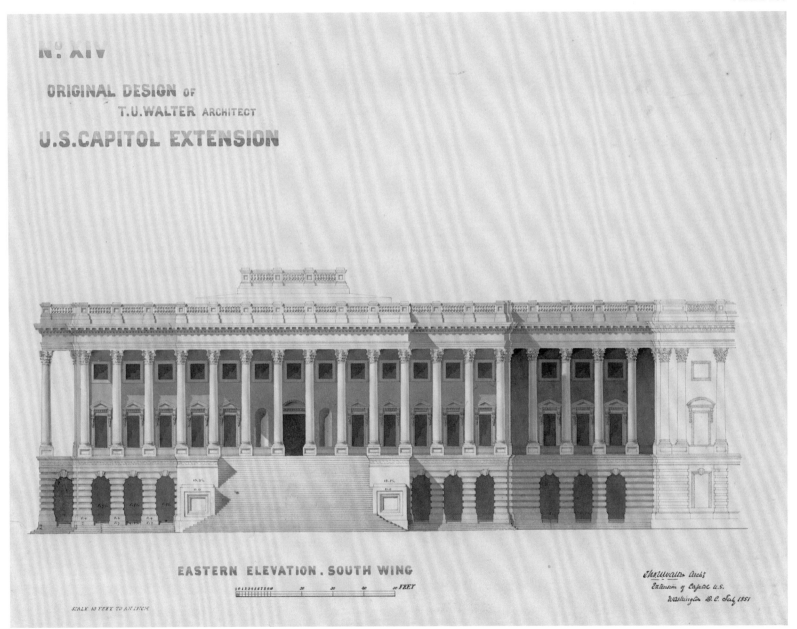

No. XIV

ORIGINAL DESIGN OF
T.U.WALTER ARCHITECT
U.S.CAPITOL EXTENSION

EASTERN ELEVATION. SOUTH WING

SCALE 10 FEET TO AN INCH

EAST ELEVATION, NORTH AND SOUTH WINGS SIMILAR, APPROVED BY PRESIDENT FILLMORE 1851,—WALTER ARCHITECT.

The original design of the east front did not include pediments, which were added in 1853 (related drawing, plate 182).

PLATE 161

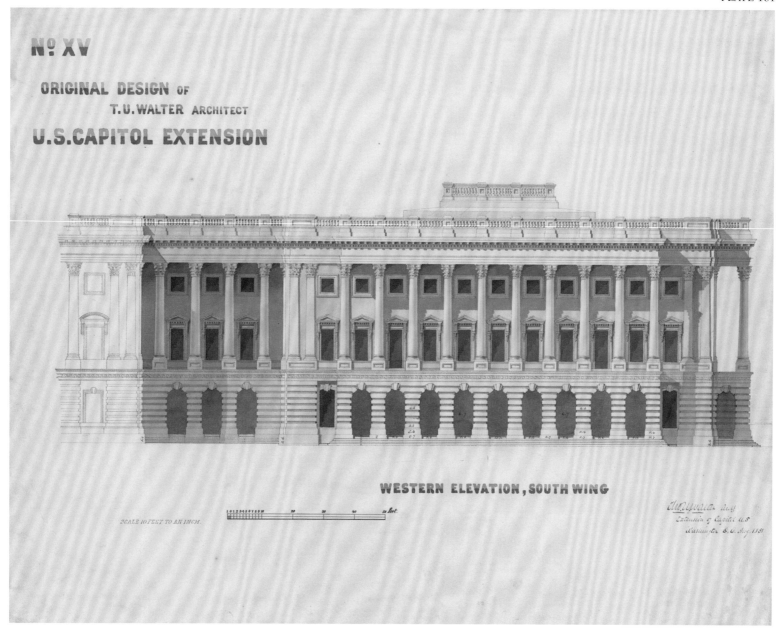

WEST ELEVATION, NORTH AND SOUTH WINGS OF SIMILAR DESIGN, APPROVED BY PRESIDENT FILLMORE 1851—WALTER ARCHITECT.

A later version of this design is illustrated in plate 183.

PLATE 162

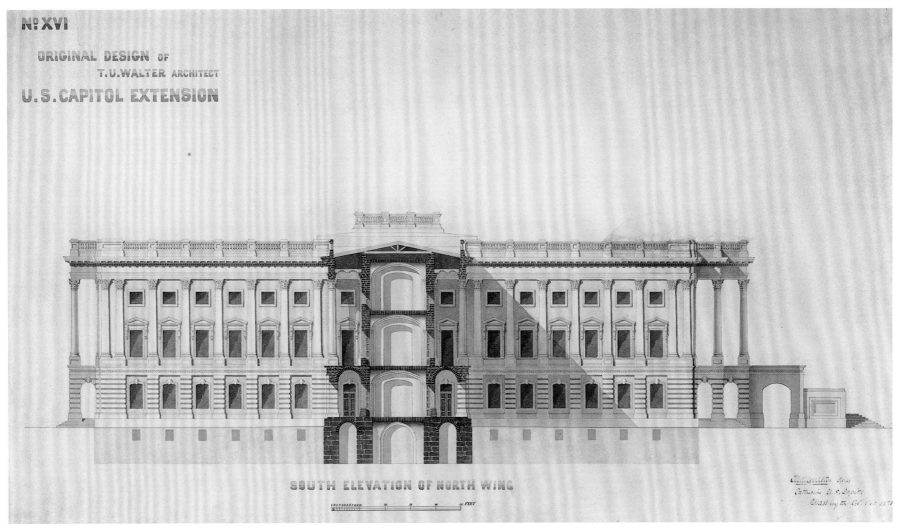

N° XVI

ORIGINAL DESIGN OF
T.U. WALTER ARCHITECT
U.S. CAPITOL EXTENSION

SOUTH ELEVATION OF NORTH WING

ELEVATION OF WINGS FACING OLD BUILDING, 1851,—WALTER ARCHITECT.

View of the Senate wing looking north.

PLATE 163

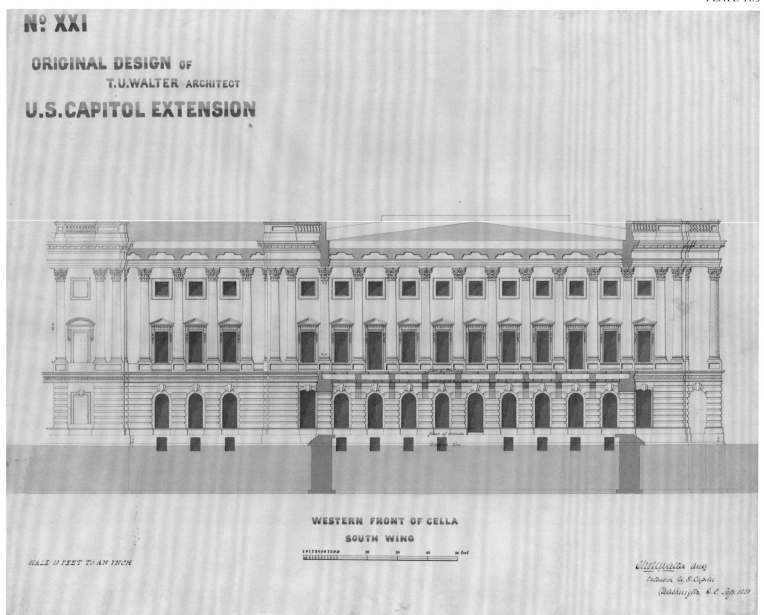

N⁰ XXI

ORIGINAL DESIGN OF
T.U.WALTER ARCHITECT
U.S.CAPITOL EXTENSION

WESTERN FRONT OF CELLA

SOUTH WING

SCALE 10 FEET TO AN INCH

ELEVATION REAR OF PORTICO 1851,—WALTER ARCHITECT.

Walter removed the portico for this western elevation to show the building's facade.

PLATE 166

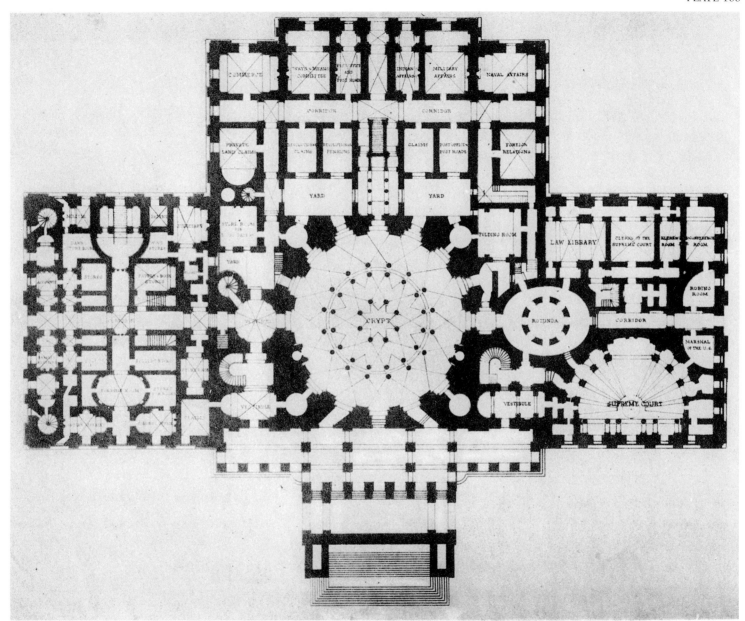

BASEMENT PLAN OF CENTRAL BUILDING 1852.

Location unknown.

PLATE 167

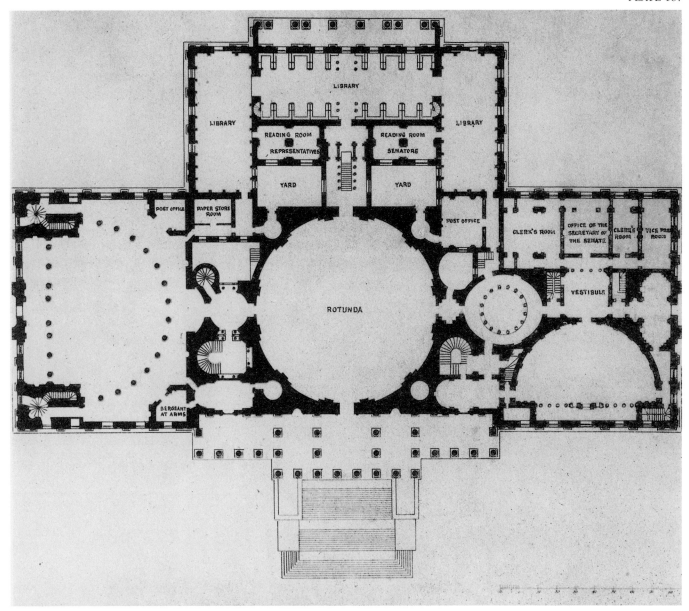

PRINCIPAL STORY PLAN, CENTRAL BUILDING 1852.

Construction on the Library of Congress extensions indicated in the plan did not begin until 1865. *Location unknown.*

PLATE 168

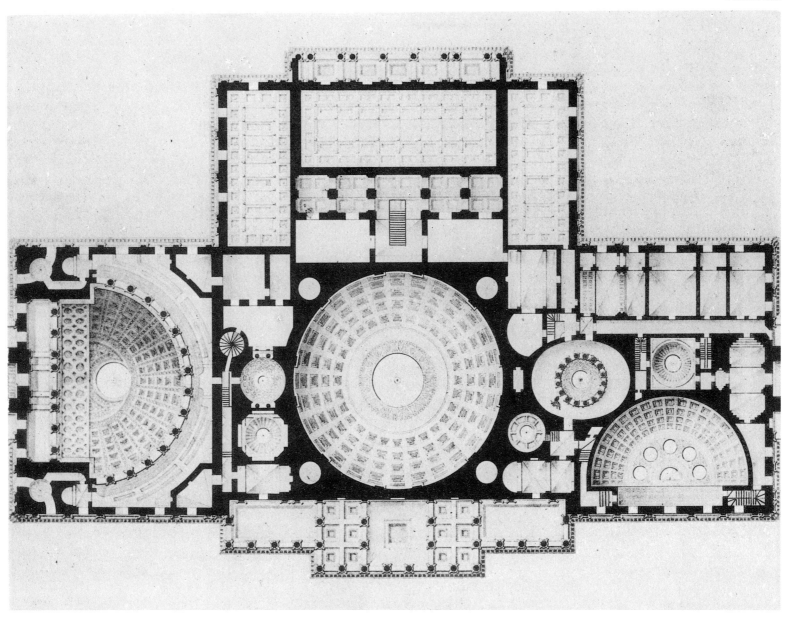

ATTIC PLAN, CENTRAL BUILDING 1852

This drawing records the reflected ceiling plan of the building. The 1865–66 Library of Congress extensions are also indicated. *Location unknown.*

Engineers and others whose assistance was considered valuable. [6] On March 24, 1852, the same body passed a resolution calling upon President Fillmore "to communicate to the Senate any plan which may have been adopted for the extension of the Capitol," "what, if any, plan had been adopted to secure the proper lighting, warming, and ventilating," and asking what construction had been approved to secure proper acoustics for the two Halls of Congress and the Supreme Court. [7] The last resolution was answered by the President's message of March 29, 1852, accompanied by a report from the Architect which contained the information desired.

The report of the Committee on Public Buildings, together with reports of several United States engineers, was made April 2, 1852. Another Senate resolution was passed August 26 asking for further information which Mr. Walter answered December 1, 1852, by abstracts from his annual report, stating that the cellars of both wings and the arches to support the basement floors were completed; all the foundations were laid, some of which were 40 feet and none of which were less than 15 feet below the ground line of the building. In connection with this report Mr. Walter gives a report of Prof. Walter R. Johnston on the stone used or proposed to be used in the building. The House of Representatives had shown its interest in the new structure by a special committee requesting that tests should be made by Professor Johnston of the stone which had been used in the foundations of the wings. [8] This stone came from the Potomac River, above Washington. Mr. Johnston informs us that the stone is midway in composition between true mica,

slate, gneiss, having quartz, mica, and feldspar in its composition. His test showed an ultimate average crushing strength of about 15,000 pounds per square inch. Before the marble was selected for the exterior of the building Alexander H. H. Stuart, Secretary of the Interior, who was in charge of public buildings, appointed a commission to test the samples of marble submitted from different quarries. This commission consisted of Joseph G. Totten, Joseph Henry, Thomas Ewbank, A. J. Downing, and Thomas U. Walter. The commission was appointed November 30, 1851, and made its report December 22, 1851. [9] The difficulties in making satisfactory tests and the results of the tests made by this commission are interesting. They first experimented with several testing machines and finally adopted one invented by Major Wade and used at the Navy-Yard for testing gun metal. "The instrument consisted of a compound lever, the several fulcra of which are knife-edges opposed to hardened-steel surfaces... the equilibrium of which was produced by 1 pound in opposition to 200 pounds." The specimens of marble were prepared in the forms of cubes with 1½-inch faces, and they were dressed and rubbed so that the faces were as nearly parallel as it was possible to make them. In carrying out the test the cubes were placed between steel plates, then pieces of sheet lead were inserted between the cubes and the steel plates, following the instructions as laid down by Remie in the Transactions of the Royal Society, so as to equalize the pressure on the face of the cube. Other tests were made without the lead sheets, and the commission was very much surprised to find that the cubes, when lead sheets were not interposed between the stone and the dies of the testing machine, required twice as much pressure to break them. The report says: "This remarkable fact was verified in a series of

[6] *Congressional Globe,* (32–1), vol. 24, pt. 1, 761.

[7] Ibid, pt. 2, 845. "To the Secretary of the Interior, 27 March 1852," in *Message from the President of the United States Communicating an Answer to a Resolution of the Senate, Calling for Information in Relation to the Extension of the Capitol, a Report of the Secretary of the Interior,* S. ex. doc. 52 (33–1), Serial 619.

[8] *Report on Public Buildings,* H. ex. doc. (32–2), Serial 673.

[9] Report of the Commission Appointed by the Department of the Interior, "To Test Several Specimens of Marble Offered for the Extension of the United States Capitol," H. doc. 1, Serial 673, 588–594.

experiments embracing samples of nearly all the marbles under trial, and in no case did a single exception occur to vary the result." After this fact was clearly proved, lead and all other intervening substances were discarded and the cubes were tested directly between the steel plates. Experiments were made to show the action of freezing and thawing on the different specimens submitted. These tests were made by alternate freezing and thawing by artificial cold and heat. The commission concluded that these latter tests proved but little. Marble from Lee, Mass., was selected for the building. It was found to require 22,702 pounds to crush a square inch, the marble had a specific gravity of 2.862, weighed 178.87 pounds per cubic foot, absorbed 103/10000 of an ounce of water, and lost by freezing 9/10000 of an ounce per cubic foot.

Plates 165 to 168, inclusive, show the plans of the cellar, basement, and principal and attic stories of the central portion of the building at this period. The two latter plates give Walter's modification of the central portion so as to increase the area of the old Library.

On December 24, 1851, the interior of the central portion of the west front of the old building, occupied by the Congressional Library, was destroyed by fire. Mr. Walter made an examination and recommendations for repairs. On January 27, 1852, he submitted plans for refitting the Library within its old limits, with suggestions for its enlargement. These plans were approved by the Senate Committee on Public Buildings, and an act was passed on March 19, 1852, authorizing the execution of the design and appropriating $72,000 for its execution, and the work was contracted for June 21.[10] The interior ornamental and structural work was to be of iron, including shelves and bookcases [Plates 169 and 170].

The work on the foundations of the wings progressed rapidly. The base was laid with an 8 foot 9 inch footing, and the cellar wall was built 6 feet 9 inches thick above the footings. While good natural ground was found on the east and west fronts, it was necessary to excavate to a depth of from 20 to 40 feet on the east.[11] December 4, 1852, the last report made by Thomas U. Walter before Captain Meigs was placed in charge shows that the foundations were complete for subbasement and the brick floor arches of basement turned and pavements laid ready for tiling, a large part of the cut granite finished, and portions of the basement story or marble work in progress, and the refitting of the Library nearly completed.[12] Samuel Strong acted as superintendent, the work being done by day labor. The Library iron work was contracted to Beebe & Co., New York. From the beginning of the work on the extension until March 23, 1853, the building was under the Interior Department, Alexander H. H. Stuart, Secretary, supervised by Thomas U. Walter. Fillmore, during his term of office, judging from the reports and messages of that period, was not swayed or influenced by Congressional action. He continued the execution of the work on the lines which he had first approved, in the face of many requests for information and protests, until he retired from the Presidency, March 4, 1853.

The Capitol was in charge of the Commissioner of Public Buildings and Grounds, but when the extension was commenced his jurisdiction over that portion ceased, and the Architect became responsible directly to the Secretary of the Interior (the Commissioner retained jurisdiction over the central or old Capitol). William Easby, the incumbent at this period, felt aggrieved at not having charge of the extension

[10]"An Act to Provide for the Repair of the Congressional Library Room, lately destroyed by fire," 19 March 1852, in *United States Statutes at Large,* vol. 10, 3. This tragedy influenced congressional approval of fireproof materials for the new wings. RG 40, Subject Files, Curator's Office, AOC.

[11]The east foundation had an excavated depth of 20 feet and the west 40 feet. RG 40, Subject Files, Curator's Office, AOC.

[12]Walter's last report was dated December 1, not December 4. See *Report on Public Buildings,* H. ex. doc. 1 (32–2), Serial 673.

and he soon made objection to the methods of work. August 28, 1852, he made charges of fraud in the employment of workmen, the method of letting contracts, and in the character and quality of materials as well as the method of measuring the material and completed work. After a searching investigation a House committee reported March 22, 1853, giving all the affidavits of the parties who testified. This testimony when carefully sifted shows that the allowance of 65 cents per cubic foot for marble in blocks under 30 cubic feet and $1.98 per cubic foot for blocks over 30 cubic feet was unnecessary, and that the contractor was allowed to furnish a greater proportion of large blocks than was necessary for the proper execution of the work. Mr. Walter's testimony shows that no more of the large blocks were used than were intended under the original estimate on which the award was made. While Walter wished to let out both workmanship and material under one contract for a specified sum, he was overruled by the President and the committee of Congress. Consequently the contracts were let separately. The stone contract, by the cubic foot, was always a fruitful source of trouble. It was found that Adams, a brick contractor, had assigned his contract to the superintendent, Samuel Strong, whose resignation was accepted January 13, 1852. The Architect wished to let out all parts of the work by contract, as the most desirable method next to a general contract, but he was again overruled by the committee, and large portions were done by the day. Many of the charges were that some of the work was done unnecessarily well, while other portions were imperfect in material and workmanship. In reference to the latter charges, Capt. F. H. Smith and Brevet Lieutenant-Colonel Mason, of the Engineer Corps, made a report on the questions submitted to them March 25, 1852, finding that the "natural foundation on which the building rests is of uniform incompressibility, and that there is no reason to apprehend a settlement of the walls from its giving way. The quality of stone used (gneiss) is excellent; probably no better could be obtained for

foundations. We would have used more cement in the lime mortar, but the introduction of cement in this country has been of quite recent date, and in many large and substantial structures not a particle has been employed. The character of the work and the mode of construction we consider excellent, with the exceptions alluded to [mortar], and in no part do we perceive deficiencies to warrant in us an apprehension as to the power of these foundations to resist the pressure of the superstructure." [13]

Lieut. Col. James Kearney and Capt. Thomas J. Lee, of the Topographical Engineers, made a similar report March 20, 1852. President Fillmore and Alexander H. H. Stuart, Secretary of the Interior, explained the reasons and methods of making the contracts and upheld Thomas U. Walter. Although the party who brought the charges was to a certain extent an interested party, and the witnesses against the building were nearly, if not all, unsuccessful bidders or discharged workmen, it probably had its effect in causing the new President, Franklin Pierce, to transfer the superintendence of the building to the War Department. [14]

President Franklin Pierce was apparently inclined to conciliate the Senate, as he issued the following order a short time after his inauguration:

"EXECUTIVE OFFICE, *March 23, 1853.*

"Believing that the public interest involved in the erection of the wings of the United States Capitol will be promoted by the exercise of the general supervision and control of the whole work by a skillful and competent officer of the Corps of Engineers or of the Topographical

---

[13] Fred. A. Smith, Captain Engineers, and J. L. Mason, Capt. Engineers, Bvt. Lt. Colonel to R. M. T. Hunter, Chairman of the Committee on Public Buildings, *In the Senate of the United States: Report*, S. report 1 (32–1), Serial 630.

[14] James Kearney, Lt. Col. Topographical Engineers, and Thomas J. Lee, Captain Topographical Engineers, to R. M. T. Hunter, Chairman of the Committee on Public Buildings, in Ibid.

Corps, and as those corps are more amenable to the Secretary of War, I hereby direct that the jurisdiction heretofore exercised over the said work by the Department of the Interior be transferred to the War Department, and request that the Secretary of War will designate to the President a suitable officer to take charge of the same.

"FRANKLIN PIERCE." [15]

Acting upon this order, the Secretary of War, Jefferson Davis, on March 29, detailed Capt. M. C. Meigs to act as superintendent. He was specially charged to examine the condition of the foundations which had been already completed, and to minutely inquire into the arrangements for warming, ventilating, and the acoustic properties for speaking and hearing. Captain Meigs did not consider the scheme for ventilation or the arrangements for acoustics satisfactory, and on May 20, 1853, Prof. A. D. Bache and Prof. Joseph Henry were commissioned to investigate these subjects in connection with the new extension.[16]

Captain Meigs immediately suggested radical changes in the interior arrangements of the wings, and these modifications were approved by the above-mentioned commission. All reports on the Capitol extension at this period were made by the Engineer officer or Superintendent to the Secretary of War. In his report of October 22, 1853, he states that "the [modified] plans were prepared by the accomplished Architect, Thomas U. Walter, and I am happy in being supported by his opinion that not only will the Legislative Halls be better adapted to their main purpose as rooms for debate, but that the architectural beauty and the convenience of the buildings will be increased by the changes which have been made." Upon the receipt of this report of May 23, President Pierce, on June 27, adopted the modified plans which had been prepared

for the south wing, and on July 5, 1853, adopted the modified plans for the north or Senate wing.[17] Plates 171 to 174 show cellar, basement, and principal and attic stories of the south wing. Plates 175 and 176 show longitudinal and transverse sections of these wings. Plates 177 to 180 show principal and attic stories of north wing. Plate 181 shows a cross section of north wing made on a broken line through the lobbies and halls. The change in the arrangement consisted in placing the Senate Chamber [Plate 179] and the Hall of Representatives [Plate 173] in the center of their respective wings instead of in one end of each wing, as was the case in the plan originally adopted by President Fillmore. Broad halls encircled the Chambers and gave access to the gallery and floor on all sides. Monumental stairways were located on the east and west of the Chambers. The ceiling was formed into panels by deep beams, and the panels were glazed. In this modified plan the Hall of Representatives was 137 feet long, 92 feet wide, and 30 feet high, and upon three sides was surrounded by a wide gallery capable of seating 1,200 people. Arranged in a semicircle on the House floor were 300 separate desks for the use of members. The ceiling was to be of iron suspended from iron trusses, with many panels filled with stained glass, through which the light for the Halls of Congress came. The position of the Hall of Representatives in the center of the wing gave an opportunity to group around it committee, retiring, conference, and other rooms for the convenience of the members. In addition to the Hall of Representatives, the principal floor contained a vestibule, corridors, stairways, two for the public and two private, and fourteen well-lighted rooms.

The second floor gave access to the public galleries through five doors, while a reporters' gallery with retiring and work rooms were provided on the third side.

[15] DHC, 585.

[16] H. doc. 1, 1853, Capitol Extension, October 22, 1853, 69–92.

[17] Captain of Engineers in Charge of the U. S. Capitol Extension, "Capitol Extension," in Report of the Secretary of War, S. ex. doc. 1 (33–1), Serial 691.

PLATE 169

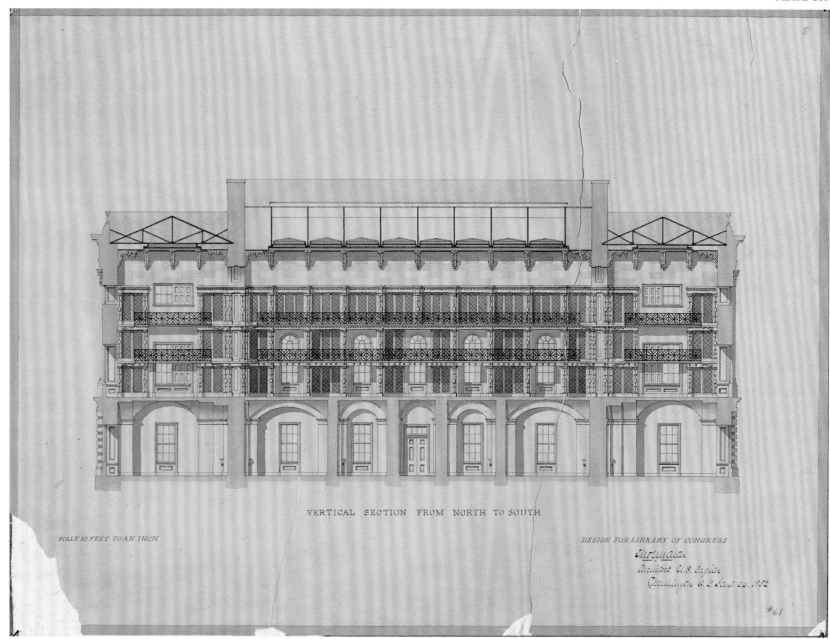

VERTICAL SECTION FROM NORTH TO SOUTH

SCALE 10 FEET TO AN INCH

DESIGN FOR LIBRARY OF CONGRESS

Architect U.S. Capitol

Washington D.C. Januy 24. 1852

#61

NORTH & SOUTH SECTION FOR REMODELLING, CONGRESSIONAL LIBRARY 1852,—WALTER ARCHITECT.

PLATE 170

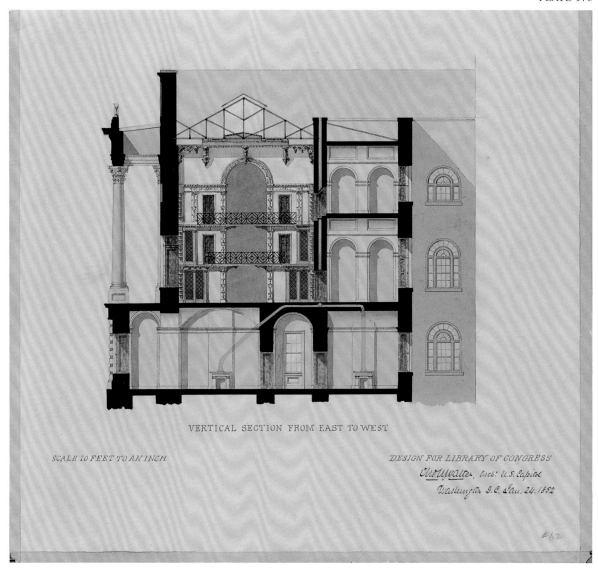

VERTICAL SECTION FROM EAST TO WEST

SCALE 10 FEET TO AN INCH

DESIGN FOR LIBRARY OF CONGRESS

Thos U Walter, Arch: U.S. Capitol

Washington D.C. Jan. 24.1852

EAST AND WEST SECTION OF CONGRESSIONAL LIBRARY, 1852—WALTER ARCHITECT.

Section looking north.

PLATE 171

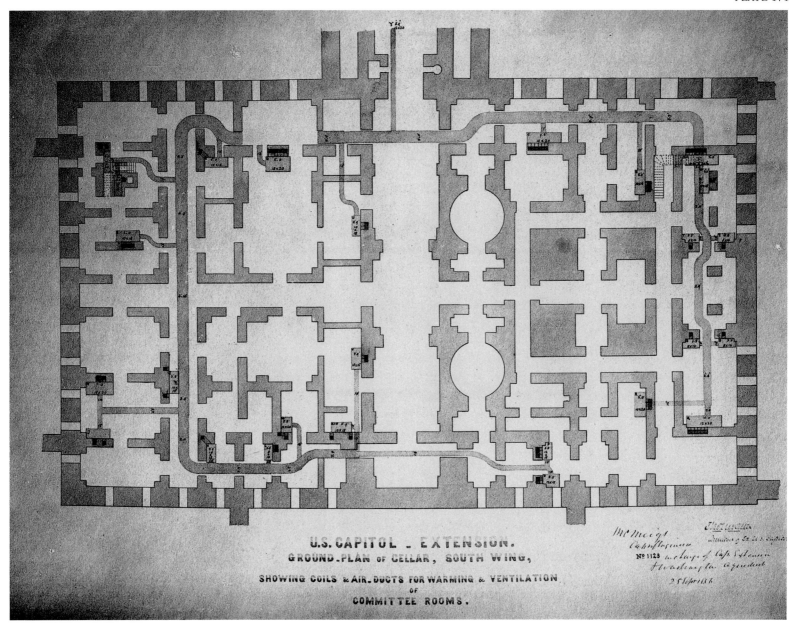

U.S. CAPITOL . EXTENSION.
GROUND.PLAN OF CELLAR, SOUTH WING,
SHOWING COILS & AIR.DUCTS FOR WARMING & VENTILATION
OF
COMMITTEE ROOMS.

CELLAR PLAN SOUTH WING 1853,—WALTER ARCHITECT.

Brown incorrectly dated this drawing, which was completed on September 25, 1856. *Location unknown.*

PLATE 172

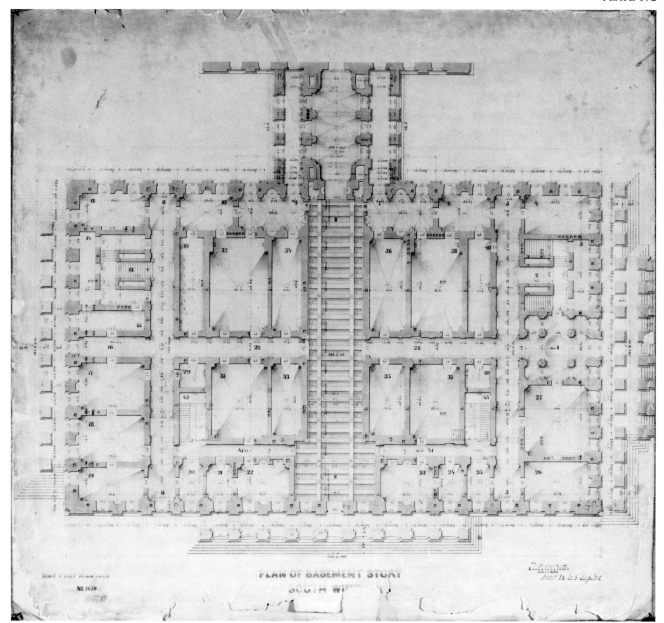

PLAN OF BASEMENT STORY

SOUTH WING

MODIFIED PLAN OF BASEMENT, SOUTH WING, 1853—WALTER ARCHITECT.

Brown incorrectly dated this drawing, which was completed on October 28, 1857.

PLATE 173

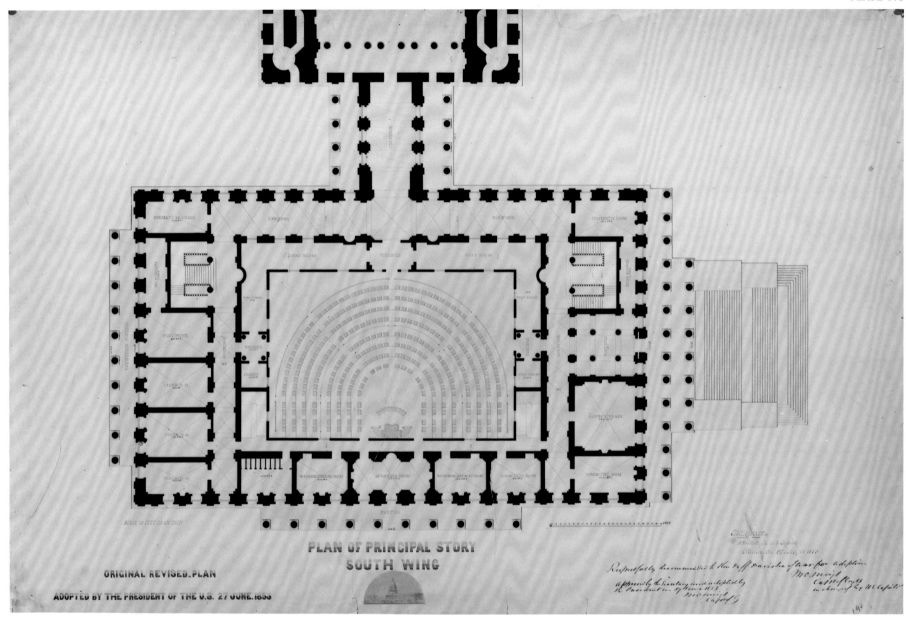

PLAN OF PRINCIPAL STORY
SOUTH WING

ORIGINAL REVISED PLAN

ADOPTED BY THE PRESIDENT OF THE U.S. 27 JUNE 1853

MODIFIED PLAN OF PRINCIPAL STORY, SOUTH WING, 1853—WALTER ARCHITECT.

PLATE 174

MODIFIED PLAN ATTIC STORY, SOUTH WING, 1853—WALTER ARCHITECT.

Brown incorrectly dated this drawing, which was completed on July 25, 1854.

PLATE 175

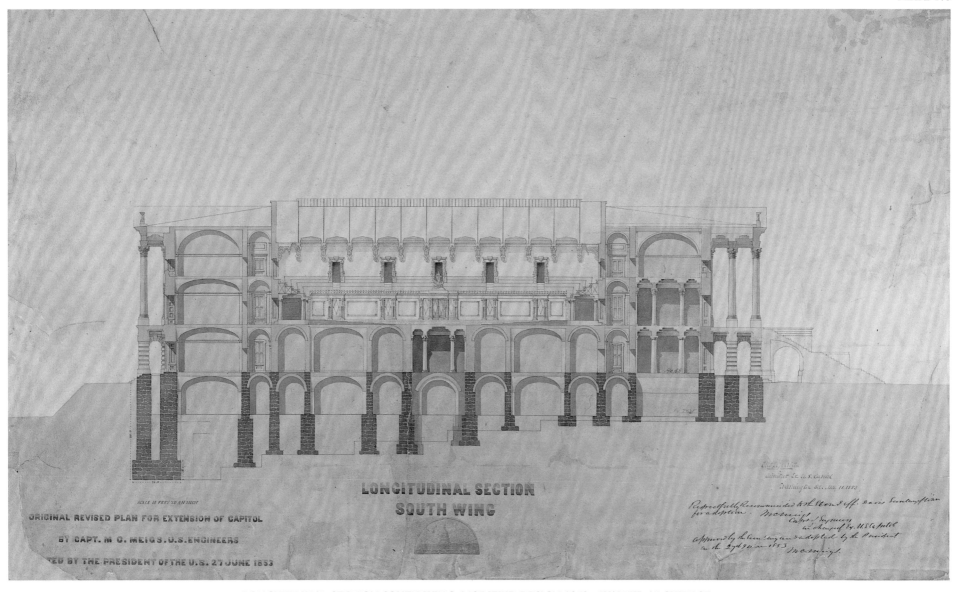

LONGITUDINAL SECTION SOUTH WING, MODIFIED DESIGN 1853—WALTER ARCHITECT.

Drawing relettered by Captain Meigs to assert his authority over Walter and to claim credit as the building's principal designer.

PLATE 176

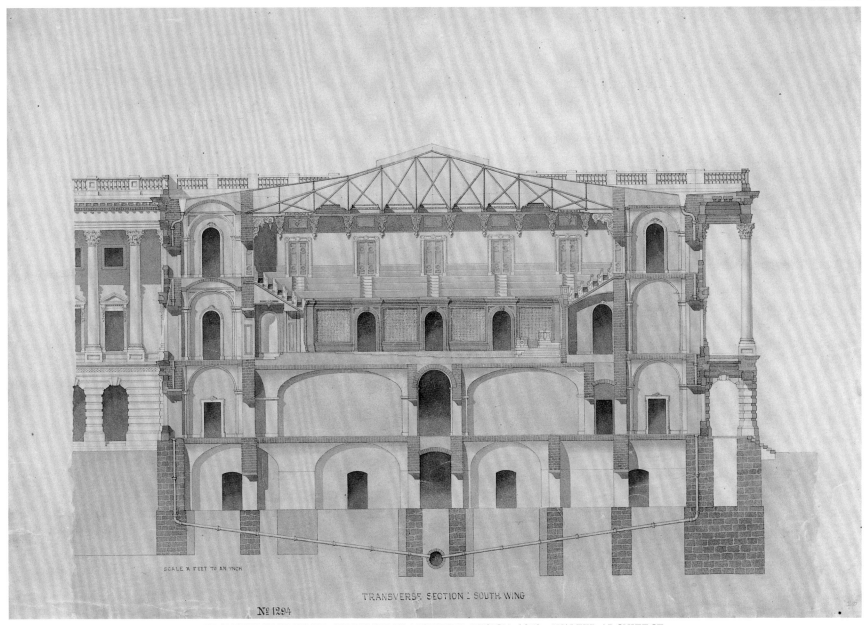

SCALE X FEET TO AN INCH

TRANSVERSE SECTION SOUTH WING

Nº 1294

TRANSVERSE SECTION, SOUTH WING, MODIFIED DESIGN, 1853—WALTER ARCHITECT.

Brown incorrectly dated this drawing, which was completed on February 17, 1857.

One of the most striking features of this wing was the entrance lobby, with its coupled Corinthian columns and marble ceiling.

The Hall of the Senate was smaller, but arranged on the same plan, being 82 by 112 feet. The size of this Hall gave an opportunity for larger retiring rooms and more imposing lobbies. The most important suite of apartments were the Senators' retiring room, the conference rooms, with the Vice-President's room, and their approaches. The western and northern porticoes were reserved for the use of Senators.

The design for the east portico was modified by introducing a pediment over the central projection [Plate 182], while the west portico was unchanged [Plate 183].

The Senate Committee on Public Buildings, on March 29, 1864, made an interesting report on a memorial of Charles F. Anderson, one of the competitors for the Capitol extension in 1850.[18] Anderson claimed compensation for the use of his design in the building as finally executed. From this report it appears that Anderson was the only competitor who located the Houses of Congress in the center of each wing. His stairway and committee rooms were not arranged like the executed drawings. In Anderson's plan the west front of the wings of the building was placed 80 feet east of the extreme western line of the old building, with the Halls of Congress in the center of each wing. Anderson's plan was one of the four schemes purchased under the competition held in 1850, from which Robert Mills was directed to take certain features in the preparation of his plan for the building. From the description of the

committee and the fact that the plan of Mills shows the wing extending far to the east it is probable that this general idea was taken from the plans submitted by Anderson. Thomas U. Walter, when he made the designs under the approval of President Fillmore, changed the position of the wings and placed the central axis north and south on the north and south axis of the old building, keeping the Halls of Congress in the east end of the wings, where they were located on the plans prepared by Mills. This committee says that Meigs had several interviews with Anderson, and as the Government at that time was in possession of Anderson's plans, they felt assured that it was these suggestions which caused Captain Meigs to propose the change of location of the halls which was adopted in the execution of the work, and finally that it was Anderson's plans of the interior which Meigs first submitted to the President for approval. Thomas U. Walter, while approving and adopting the general suggestion, so modified the interior as to make it his own. In matters of design and detail he seems to have been untrammeled, and it will be seen by a comparison that on the exterior he made but few changes from the design which received the approval of President Fillmore.[19] One of the first duties performed by Captain Meigs was to personally investigate the character of the work which had already been executed. He found the foundations ample to bear the weight which was to be imposed upon them, although he states that he would have used a greater proportion of hydraulic cement in the mortar. The foundation stone of Potomac blue gneiss was good in quality and of proper size, well laid, and the joints well filled. He could not find any evidence of recent settlement, and as the walls varied in height from 15 to 40 feet, this was a sign of a good natural foundation and workmanship,

---

[18] *Congressional Globe* (38–1), vol. 42, pt. 2, 1847. The Senate passed a private bill (S. No. 27) directing the Secretary of the Treasury to pay Anderson $7,500 for his work on the plans of the Capitol extension. Walter and Meigs vehemently denied that Anderson's plan influenced the eventual design of the Capitol. For discussions of Anderson's claims, see William Sener Rusk, "Thomas U. Walter and His Works," *Americana* 33 (1939): 151–179, and William Allen, *The Dome of the United States Capitol: An Architectural History* (Washington: Government Printing Office, 1992), 13.

---

[19] There were five plans purchased by the federal government from the competition of 1850 and not four as Brown noted. Before his appointment Walter had prepared a plan with the chambers on the east side, but President Fillmore wanted the chambers on the west side. RG 40, Subject Files, Curator's Office, AOC.

in both footings and walls. The question of the discoloration of the marble was submitted to a chemist, and he reported that the stains would disappear as the stone dried out. This was proved to be true by stone which had been under observation, and Captain Meigs concluded that after the walls dried out it would present the "most beautiful specimen of marble work in the United States.[20]"

The question of the validity of the contracts for furnishing, cutting, and laying the marble was referred to the Attorney-General, and he sustained their validity in an opinion dated May 6, 1853. These reports finally disposed of the complaints against the character of the work done under Walter's supervision. Contracts were made with Frederick A. Burch, December 29, 1852, to lay all brick, including arches and groined arches, but to furnish no material, for the sum of $2.49 per thousand, kiln count, and on April 23, 1853, with Cornelius Wendell, brickmaker, of Washington, D.C., to furnish 10,000,000 brick, at $5.85 per thousand. These contractors failed to carry out their contracts, both having taken the work at too low a figure. Because of this failure, early in 1853 the contractor for brickwork was relieved and the brickwork done by day labor. Captain Meigs purchased brick in Baltimore, Philadelphia, and New York, because the former contractor failed to deliver them as rapidly as his contract required, and the contractor and his bondsmen were held responsible for the difference in price. During the year 1853 the basement story was completed with the exception of the floor arches for the principal story, and during the year 1854 the masonry of the basement story in both wings was completed, the marble facing was carried up to the top of the window openings on the principal story, and the interior walls were built up to the roof or ceiling of the Halls of Congress. The stone was not delivered as rapidly as

could be desired. Being quarried in Berkshire, Mass., it was necessary to transport it 90 miles by rail to Bridgeport, Conn., and thence it was carried by water to Washington.[21]

April 4, 1855, just before adjournment, Congress authorized a change in the design of the old Dome, or rather the replacing of the old Dome, which was of wood covered with copper, by a dome of cast iron.[22] The drawings [Plates 184, 185, and 186] for this dome were made by Thomas U. Walter, the exterior showing an octagonal base which was to rest upon the walls of the old Dome, on which was placed a peristyle 124 feet in diameter composed of columns 27 feet in height. The entablature of the peristyle was to be 127 feet above the basement floor. From the entablature sprang an attic 44 feet high and 108 feet in diameter, and from the cornice of the attic arose a semiellipsoidal dome to a height of 228 feet. The dome was surmounted by a lantern 17 feet in diameter, 52 feet high, the whole to be capped with a bronze figure 16 feet 6 inches high and 300 feet above the basement floor. It was determined to leave the old Rotunda unchanged to the level of the stone cornice 44 feet above the Rotunda floor. It was the intention to carry the wall 9 feet above this cornice, recessing it so as to receive a continuous band of sculpture illustrating the history of the country from the landing of Columbus to the period of the work. Just above the cornice of this frieze was a corridor encircling the Rotunda, composed of a series of piers and attached columns, from the cornice of which the interior dome sprang. An opening 65 feet in diameter was left in the crown of the interior dome, through which could be seen a lighter colonnade ending at the base of the lantern. This work was commenced in 1855 by

---

[20] See "Capitol Extension," in *Report of the Secretary of War*, 1853, 69–72;

[21] See Captain of Engineers in Charge of the U. S. Capitol Extension, "Report on the Capitol Extension," in *Report of the Secretary of War*, H. ex. doc. 1 (33–2), Serial 778.

[22] This authorization was passed March 3, 1855. For a discussion of this authorizing legislation, see Allen, *The Dome of the United States Capitol*, 17–18.

erecting a temporary roof over the Rotunda and a partial removal of the old Dome. A scaffolding 100 feet high and 18 feet base was extended up through the eye of the old Dome to form a platform for a derrick. (Plate 187 shows scaffolding.) This derrick had a mast and boom each 80 feet, so that all the ironwork could be raised from the exterior by a boiler and an engine, which were placed on the roof of the old building. The columns for the peristyle were let to Poole & Hunt, of Baltimore, Md. The work on the Capitol progressed satisfactorily during the next few years. In October, 1855, the marble work was reported as being at an average height of the attic windows on the exterior. On the interior about half of the columns and pilasters of the grand corridor of the south wing were in place, and one of the grand stairways commenced in the same wing, the brick vaulting for the floors was leveled up for tiling, the roof trusses for the south wing were completed and a number of them erected, while the trusses for the Senate wing were ready for erection. The Tredegar Iron Works, of Richmond, Va., supplied tie-rods. All tensile members were subjected by hydraulic proving machine to a strain of 10,000 pounds per square inch. Cooper & Hewitt, of New York, furnished the rolled I beams weighing 30 pounds to the linear foot. Plastering was progressing in the basement story.[23]

In November, 1856, Captain Meigs reported that the exterior marble work was leveled up to the top of the architrave, and that in many places the cornice was finished. The principal corridor in the south wing was complete and work progressing rapidly on corridors in the north wing. The work was progressing on the principal and private stairways and brickwork for same completed; granite stairways to cellar and attic finished; tiling progressing rapidly on the floors; corrugated copper roofing and glass were all in place; the iron ceilings of both Houses of Congress were completed; the cast-iron door and window frames and the cast-iron trimmings in the basement were set, and many of the committee rooms and corridors were painted.[24] The work on the Dome was confined to completing the derricks, cranes, and other machinery and casting the columns for the peristyle, because Congress expressed an intention to have the designs which they had adopted changed. For this purpose Walter submitted a modified drawing of the Dome [Plate 188]. In 1860 a drawing was made showing suggestions for roof of Dome [Plate 189].[25]

During the session it was determined to adhere to the first design, and the old stone and brick work was removed down to the old exterior cornice, 64 feet above the Rotunda floor, and the brick lining was removed to the level of the interior cornice. Brickwork was relaid in cement as a foundation for the new Dome.

The corridors connecting the wings with the old building were the last portion of the new structure to be commenced. The excavations and a part of the foundations were put in during the year 1856. All vaulting under the pavements for the boilers, coal, and passageways was also completed during this year. Tilework and stairways were still in progress. In the report for November, 1857, Captain Meigs states that the House of Representatives was nearly ready for occupancy. The House at first questioned the propriety of meeting in the Chamber, as they feared ill effects from the dampness of the walls, and a special committee was appointed to investigate the condition of the Hall, and

[23] Captain of Engineers in Charge of the U. S. Capitol Extension, "Reports of Captain M. C. Meigs, Corps of Engineers, in Charge of the Capitol Extension, Reconstruction of Dome, and Post Office Extension," in *Report of the Secretary of War*, H. ex. doc. 1 (34–1), Serial 841, 111–112.

[24] Captain of Engineers in Charge of the U. S. Capitol Extension, "Reports on the Capitol Extension, Re-construction of the Dome, and Post Office Extension," in *Report of the Secretary of War*, S. ex. doc. 5 (34–3), Serial 876, 217–227.

[25] This design change in the Dome's proportions was prompted by the need to accommodate Thomas Crawford's statue of *Freedom*. For a discussion of the Dome's redesign, see Allen, *The Dome of the United States Capitol*, 42–49.

reported December 14 that the Hall was dry and everything ready for occupancy. The Hall was first used for divine worship, December 13, 1857, Rev. G. D. Cumming conducting the services. December 16, 1857, the House of Representatives took formal possession and held their first session in their new Hall.[26]

The detail drawings made for the House of Representatives by Walter show careful consideration of every particular. Plate 190 gives a detail section of this Hall, and Plate 191 shows a reproduction of the drawing for the desk of the Speaker and clerks. The ceiling was a carefully designed paneled work in iron and glass [Plate 192].

The delay in receiving ironwork for the Senate wing caused a delay in the completion of this portion of the building. During this year (1857) all woodwork was completed; plastering completed, with few exceptions; progress made on stairways, painting, and decorations; drainage for roof water, water-closets, wash basins, and other toilet fixtures were put in place. A 10-inch gas main connecting with the main of the gas company was put in place. This branched so as to give one 8-inch main for each wing. Although these mains were run, it was found that the gas company's plant was not large enough to supply the new demand until they could erect a new gasometer. The base for the ironwork on the Dome was built into place, consisting of the large brackets which were to carry the peristyle, with interior vertical framing.[27]

Work during the year 1858 consisted in the erection of the arcades on the basement story of the porticoes, and the cellar walls, of the connecting corridors on the exterior, and the completion of the marble work connected with the stairways on the interior. The Dome was completed as high as the cornice of the circular colonnade, and the cast-iron work for the outside shell was let to James Beebe & Co., of Baltimore, Md.[28]

December 23, 1858, the Senate passed a resolution directing that their new Hall should be ready for occupancy by January 4, 1859, and on that date the Senate first assembled in its new home. Plate 193 shows an enlarged drawing of a section of this room. The ceiling and an enlarged drawing of one of the panels are shown in Plates 194 and 195. In the latter part of 1859 the interior of the building was nearly complete, with exception of the iron and bronze work on stairways, and painting. In 1858 Congress passed a resolution prohibiting the use of any part of the current appropriation for decoration until a committee of artists should pass upon the character of decorations that should be most suitable for the building. The floors of all except a few rooms were laid with encaustic tile, from Minton, Stoke-upon-Trent, by Miller & Coates, of New York. The last of these floors was laid before the meeting of Congress in December, 1859.[29]

The interior construction of the wings of the Capitol is of solid brick masonry, all the ceilings and floors being composed of brick vaulting, with the exception of the ceilings over the Halls of Congress, which were made of cast iron with glazed panels on which are painted the coats of arms of the different States. The roofs are carried by trusses of rolled beams and iron rods and are covered by glass and copper laid on rolled-iron purlins.[30]

---

[26] Captain of Engineers in Charge of the U. S. Capitol Extension, "Report on the Capitol Extension, Re-construction of the Dome, and Post Office Extension," in *Report of the Secretary of War,* S. ex. doc. 11 (35–1), Serial 920, 40–47.

[27] "Report of the Architect of the United States Capitol Extension," in the *Report of the Secretary of War* (Washington: Government Printing Office, 1857), 750–751.

[28] The contract was let to Janes, Beebe & Co., of New York, not James Beebe of Baltimore. See Captain of Engineers in Charge of the U.S. Capitol Extension, "Report on the Capitol Extension, Re-construction of the Dome, and Post Office Extension," in *Report of the Secretary of War,* S. ex. doc. 11 (35–1), Serial 920, 40–47.

[29] *DHC,* 722.

[30] Trabeated marble ceilings of the landings were built as a part of the four main staircases, the Senator's Retiring Room (called the marble room) and two principal eastern entrance vestibules; there is a cast iron ceiling over the Hall of Columns and Members' Retiring Room in the House wing. In the Senate the glazed panels were emblems of industry and science and in the House Chamber they represented the state seals.

PLATE 177

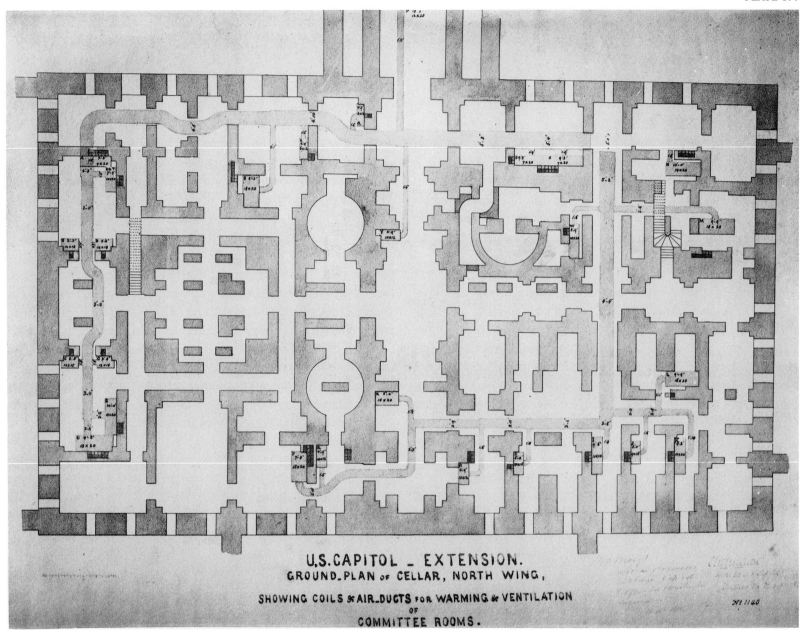

CELLAR PLAN, NORTH WING, 1853—WALTER ARCHITECT.

Brown incorrectly dated this drawing, which was completed on October 9, 1856. *Location unknown.*

PLATE 178

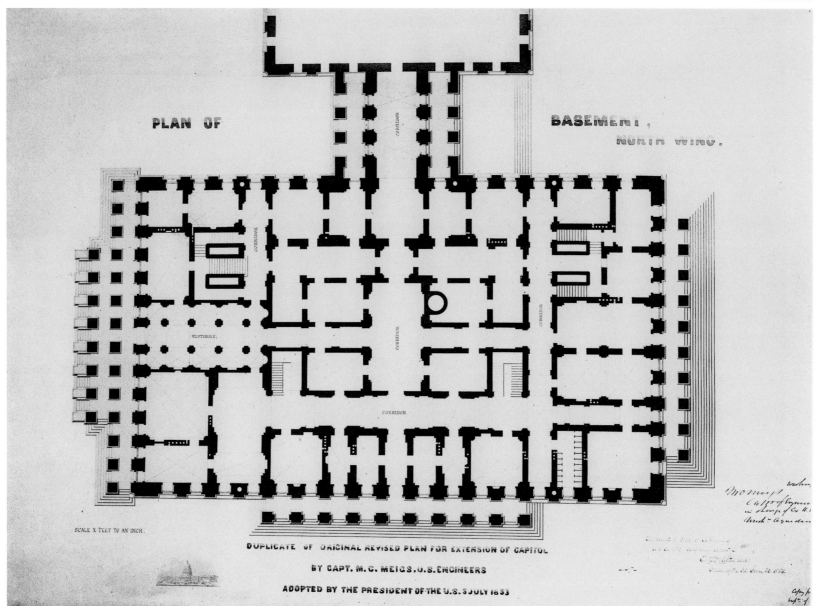

PLAN OF   BASEMENT,
                                            NORTH WING.

VESTIBULE.

CORRIDOR

SCALE X FEET TO AN INCH.

DUPLICATE OF ORIGINAL REVISED PLAN FOR EXTENSION OF CAPITOL

BY CAPT. M. C. MEIGS, U.S. ENGINEERS

ADOPTED BY THE PRESIDENT OF THE U.S. 5 JULY 1853

MODIFIED BASEMENT PLAN NORTH WING 1853,—WALTER ARCHITECT.
Brown incorrectly dated this drawing, which was completed on June 20, 1854.
Another drawing relettered by Meigs to support his claim for credit in the design of the extensions. *Location unknown.*

PLATE 179

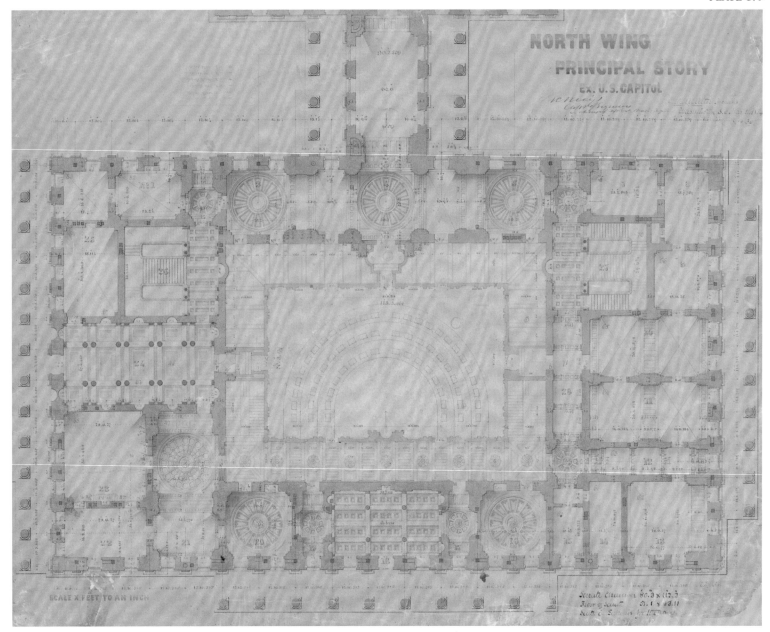

MODIFIED PRINCIPAL STORY PLAN, NORTH WING, 1853—WALTER ARCHITECT.

Brown incorrectly dated this drawing, which was completed on March 31, 1854.

PLATE 180

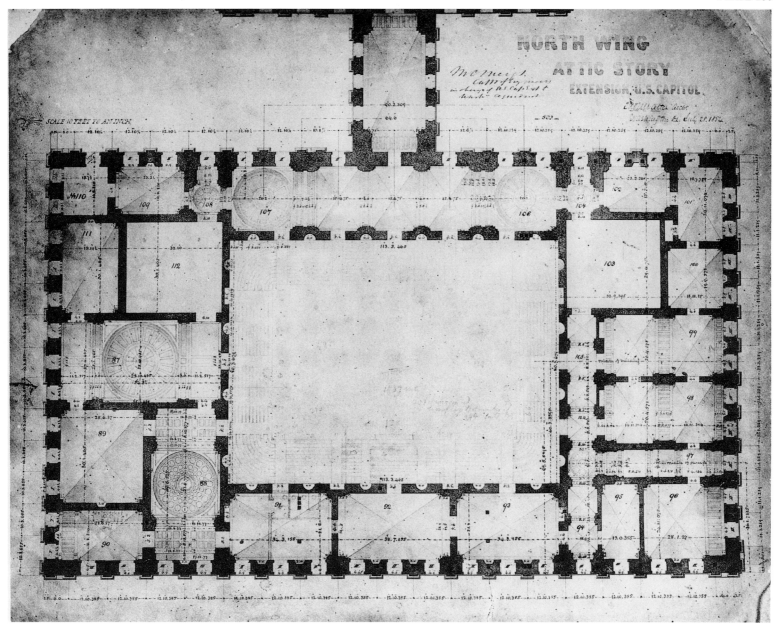

MODIFIED ATTIC PLAN, NORTH WING, 1853,—WALTER ARCHITECT.
Brown incorrectly dated this drawing, which was completed on July 28, 1854.

PLATE 181

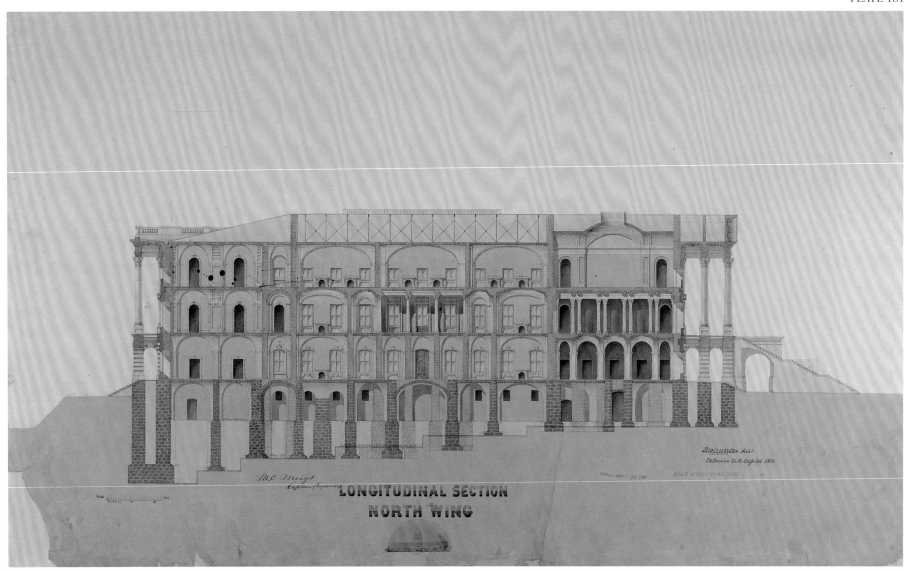

MODIFIED LONGITUDINAL SECTION, NORTH WING 1853,—WALTER ARCHITECT.

Brown incorrectly dated this drawing, which was completed on September 20, 1854.

PLATE 182

EAST PORTICO OF WINGS, 1853—WALTER ARCHITECT.

Compare to the earlier design of the east front porticos illustrated in plate 160.

PLATE 183

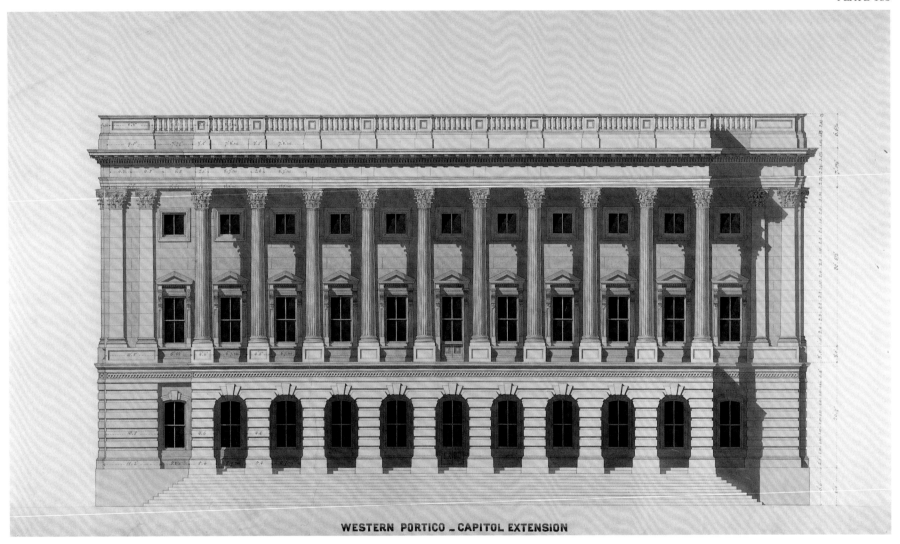

WESTERN PORTICO _ CAPITOL EXTENSION

WEST PORTICO OF WINGS, 1853—WALTER ARCHITECT.

Compare to the earlier design of the west front porticos illustrated in plate 161.

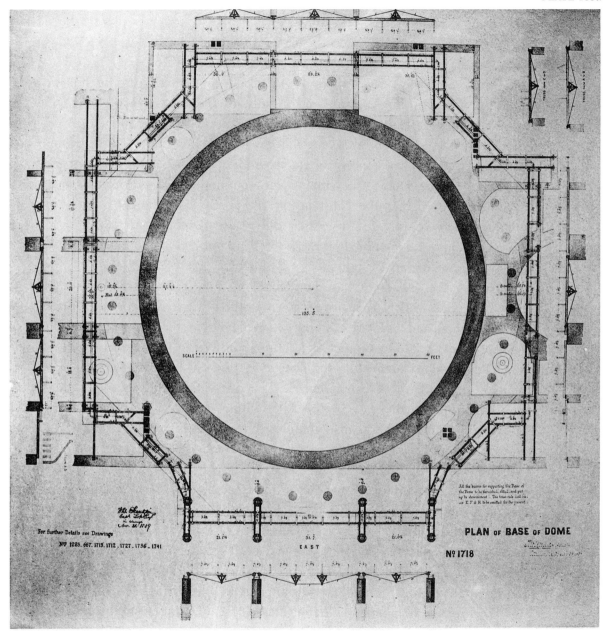

PLAN OF BASE OF DOME,—T. U. WALTER, ARCHITECT.

January 25, 1858. *Location unknown.*

PLATE 184

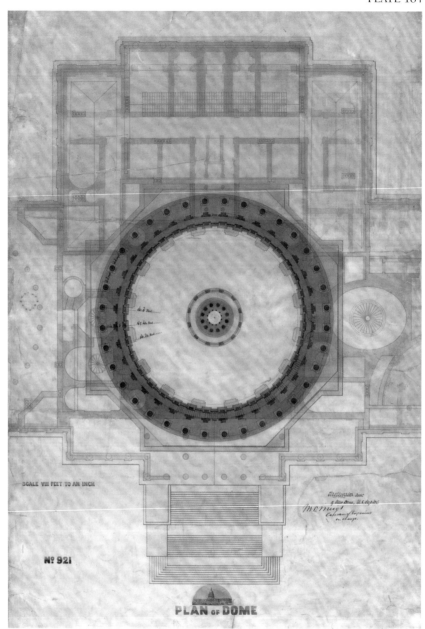

SCALE VIII FEET TO AN INCH

N° 921

PLAN of DOME

PLAN OF DOME,—WALTER, ARCHITECT.

March 25, 1856.

PLATE 185

ELEVATION OF NEW DOME 1855,—WALTER ARCHITECT.

PLATE 186

SECTION OF DOME,—WALTER ARCHITECT.

Revisions made in 1859 resulted in this double dome. Walter finished the drawing on July 21, 1859.

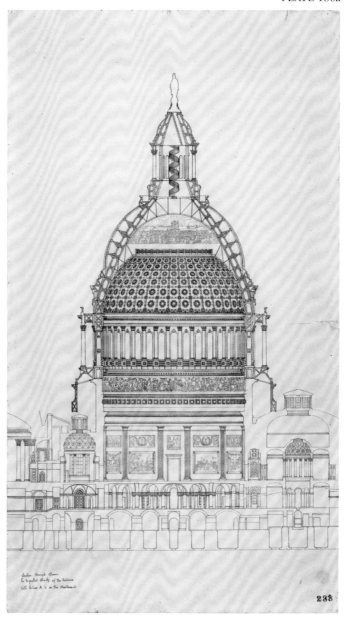

238

OUTLINE SECTION OF DOME SUGGESTING ALTERATIONS ABOVE THE PERISTYLE,—WALTER ARCHITECT.

1859 design study eliminating the dome's second story (related drawing, plate 188).

PLATE 187

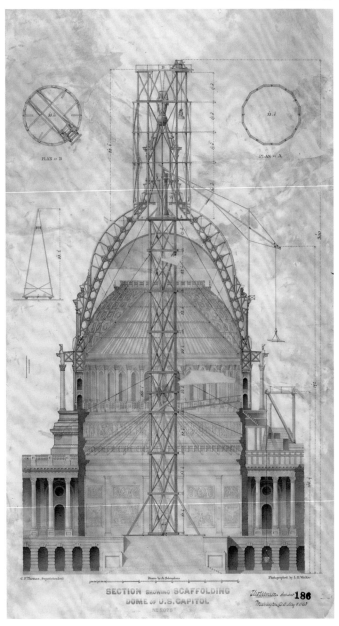

SECTION OF DOME SHOWING SCAFFOLDING AND TEMPORARY ROOF.

The head of the Statue of Freedom is shown being lifted into place.

PLATE 188

MODIFIED ELEVATION FOR DOME,—WALTER ARCHITECT. NOT EXECUTED.

1859 design study (related drawing, plate 186a).

PLATE 189

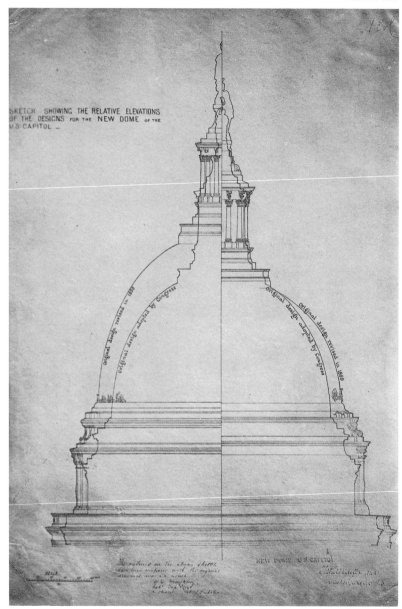

SUGGESTIONS FOR OUTLINE OF DOME.—WALTER ARCHITECT.

Drawing comparing the heights and profiles of the various dome designs. Signed and dated, February 25, 1860.
This drawing was included in the *Capitol Extension and New Dome Photographic Books*, ca. 1860. *Location unknown.*

The relative positions of those in charge of the Capitol extension is worthy of attention. Jefferson Davis, as chairman of the Committee on Public Buildings, first adopted the plans which were prepared by Robert Mills, using such features as the committee thought desirable in the drawings secured by the competition of September, 1850 [Plates 141 to 148].[31] President Fillmore fortunately took advantage of the power vested in him by the act authorizing the Capitol extension, and appointed Thomas U. Walter Architect, and adopted the plans and elevations which Walter had prepared [Plates 151 to 166].

Judging from the repeated requests made by the Senate that the President should give them information as to the progress of the work, as well as requests for information as to the arrangements of the plan which he proposed, the Senate was not satisfied with the action of the President. When President Fillmore retired from office one of the first steps taken by the new Executive, Franklin Pierce, was to again place the extensions of the building in charge of Jefferson Davis, who was Secretary of War. Mr. Davis detailed Capt. M. C. Meigs to look after the work of superintendence and finance, with the title of Engineer in Charge. Mr. Walter and Captain Meigs at first worked together amicably in their different departments. Captain Meigs adopted designs for the heating and ventilating apparatus, and attended to all matters of business and supervision. He was also the prime mover in altering the general arrangement of the interior, as he advocated the placing of the Halls of Congress in the center of each wing. Walter approved of this change and made all the plans and designs necessary to adapt the interior of the building to the new plan. Jefferson Davis, as long as he was Secretary of War, upheld Captain Meigs whenever a conflict of authority

occurred. When a new Administration (James Buchanan's) came into office and John B. Floyd was made Secretary of War, the conflict between the two in authority on the building became more bitter.[32] In January, 1858, the controversy reached such a stage that the question as to who should have charge of the drawings was submitted to the Secretary of War. On October 4, 1858, Meigs obtained an order from the Secretary directing Walter to give Captain Meigs "all drawings necessary to carry on the building under your [his] charge." In answer to this letter the Architect wrote to the Secretary saying: "I have reason to believe that the drawings you allude to in your order are such as are now required for the prosecution of the public work.... This I understand to be the intention of your order, and this I am not only willing but anxious to comply with. But you will observe that Captain Meigs does not limit his demands to these drawings. He calls upon me to deliver to his office, first, all the drawings connected with the Capitol extension that were made by me, and in my office, from the beginning of the work; second, all the original drawings of the post-office and Dome; third, all the drawings of all the public works made since he has been in charge of them. These three items cover every line made for the Capitol extension and Dome.... The Architect's office is unquestionably the place for all the drawings which are not actually in the hands of the workmen.... His allusion to my designs having been made under his directions plainly manifest the spirit that has given us all our trouble and hinders the prosecution of the public work.... I am exceedingly weary of the constant annoyances to which I am subjected by him and the difficulties he is constantly throwing in the way of the proper

---

[31] Senator Jefferson Davis was a member of the Committee on Public Buildings in 1850–51, but was not its chairman. He was an influential figure in the development of the Capitol because he chaired the Senate Committee on Military Affairs, which had oversight of the activities of army engineers.

[32] For a discussion of the Meigs-Walter controversy, see Allen, *History of the Dome of the United States Capitol*, 36–41; Russell F. Weigley, *Quartermaster General of the Union Army* (New York: Columbia University Press, 1959); and "Journals" (transcribed by William Mohr for the United States Bicentennial Commission), Montgomery C. Meigs Papers, Manuscript Division, LC.

discharge of my duties. . . . If it is your desire that Captain Meigs shall control the architecture of the public works, of which I am Architect, and you will so inform me, I will retire from them without a moment's delay; but if you wish the control of the architecture to rest with the Architect, and will issue such orders as will prevent any further interference with my professional rights, I will cheerfully continue to give my individual time and attention to these works as I have been doing for the last seven years. . . . If Captain Meigs is to have the control of the architecture, I shall take pleasure in retiring." [33] The location of the Architect's office was changed from time to time as the work in the Capitol progressed. After Captain Meigs's appointment it was first located in a room adjoining the one occupied by him in the south wing, then moved to the floor above, then to the north wing. Each move carried the Architect and Engineer farther apart. Captain Meigs says: "Being so far removed, I saw less of him and the draftsmen, and he [Walter] began to feel more independent." Finally Captain Meigs rented a house on A street north, and moved his office, at the same time directing Mr. Walter to transfer his offices to the same building, but instead of following these orders Mr. Walter moved his office, together with the drawings, into the attic story of the center building. This occurred in January, 1858, and Captain Meigs, in a letter to the Secretary, accused Mr. Walter of having abstracted the drawings from his (Meigs's) office. In another letter, August 23, 1859, to Acting Secretary of War William R. Drinkard, Meigs says: "I used the word abstracted advisedly. A harsher one would have been just, but respect for the Department prevented its use." In this letter Captain Meigs gives a review of his connection with the work, quoting letters from Jefferson Davis, when

Secretary of War, and one written by Davis at his request, January 23, 1858, to John B. Floyd. These letters state how Captain Meigs had been put in charge of the work, "with full authority to make all needful changes in the administration of the work; he was informed that upon him would rest the responsibility of a proper and economical execution of the buildings. . . . Upon the great scientific problems (ventilation and acoustics) involved in the principal objects of the extension it will be found that Captain Meigs was put in consultation with Professor Bache and Professor Henry." Mr. Davis says: "Even in matters of architectural style, a reference to the accompanying photographs will show how important will have been the modifications of the original design." He does not say that Captain Meigs made these important changes in architectural design, and the drawings made and approved before Meigs's appointment [Plates 151 to 168], when compared with those of the executed building [Plates 171 to 185], will show the changes. Captain Meigs says, in the letter above quoted: "When the drawings are restored and the disobedient and rebellious assistant dismissed, there will be no further difficulty." He continues to complain of the impossibility of doing the work without all of the original drawings. [34]

He calls attention to the fact that on September 16, 1858, he appealed to the President and was reproved by the Secretary for his act of official discourtesy. Captain Meigs says: "I am worn out with this distasteful work. . . . My subordinate has been allowed to set my authority at defiance and to interfere in all ways most mortifying and injurious to me." The above letter was answered by Mr. Walter in a communication to the Secretary of War August 30, 1859. In this letter Walter calls attention to the fact that his appointment as Architect approved by act of Congress September, 1850, had never been revoked, and that he performed the duties of an architect from that period, and "I have continued to be

---

[33] Brown's source for the quotations was "Papers Relating to the Heating and Apparatus of the Capitol Extension," in *Message of the President of the United States* (Washington: George Bowman, printer, 1860), 115–117; 160–180.

[34] Ibid., 162–180.

the Architect, and the only Architect, of the work to this day." He quotes many letters and reports from Captain Meigs in proof of his accepting the fact until about the time the open controversy arose. August 30, 1859, Captain Meigs again called the Department's attention to Mr. Walter's delinquencies and asked for an order to obtain possession of the drawings. In an answer to this letter, Acting Secretary W. R. Drinkard says: "In reference to the letter giving Captain Meigs authority to call upon the Architect for all drawings necessary to prosecute the work, it is proper for me, knowing the fact, to say that the Secretary did not intend by that letter of October, 1858, to give Captain Meigs authority permanently to remove from the possession of the Architect any of the drawings referred to, but simply to afford him every proper facility for consulting and using the drawings when rendered necessary by the work in hand. In other words, the Secretary deemed that the rooms in the Capitol occupied by the Architect were the proper depository for the drawings, and intended that they should remain there, and as the necessities of the work required, be seen and used, there or elsewhere, 'by Captain Meigs freely and without constraint.'" [35]

This letter was answered September 23, reiterating the charges against Walter and objecting to the Acting Secretary speaking for the Secretary, in the following manner: "I am as capable of understanding a written order of the Secretary as the chief clerk or Acting Secretary, and must act on my responsibility as an officer under orders as I understand them." Secretary of War John B. Floyd upon his return placed the following indorsement upon the letter of September 22 by Acting Secretary Drinkard: "The paper to which it is appended contains the opinions and views of the Secretary of War, which were then and are now deemed to be proper and correct. The conduct of Captain Meigs in thus interpolating the records in his possession with a paper manifesting

such flagrant insubordination and containing language both disrespectful and insulting to his superiors is reprehensible in the highest degree." After this correspondence one would naturally expect Captain Meigs to be relieved of further duty. He wrote the following letter to President James Buchanan November 1, 1859:

"SIR: It is commonly reported that an order has been written, if not already issued, relieving me from certain works.

"In justice to myself I ask that my last letters to the War Department be read before you decide the case.

"I have endeavored simply to do my duty, to protect the interests of the United States in all things under my charge, and, while expressing plainly my views, even when differing from the War Department, to give the Department no just cause for offense.

"I am, with grateful acknowledgments for kindness and courtesy received from you, with highest respect,

"Your obedient servant,

"M. C. MEIGS,
"*Captain of Engineers.*[36]

"The PRESIDENT OF THE UNITED STATES."

Captain Meigs was relieved from duty November 1, 1859, in connection with the public buildings, and Capt. W. B. Franklin, captain of Topographical Engineers, was detailed by the Secretary of War to fill his place, November 1, 1859.

Judging from the public documents, Captain Meigs's principal duty while in charge was to manage the business affairs of the work and superintend the constructive features, and special stress was laid upon his devising a scheme for heating and ventilating, and seeing that the Halls of Congress should have satisfactory acoustic properties. He

[35] Ibid.

[36] Ibid.

called upon Professor Bache and Professor Henry for scientific advice, and they made an elaborate report upon the subjects about which information was desired. The Congressional committee who were investigating the claims of Charles F. Anderson assert that the principles laid down by the scientists in reference to proper acoustic properties were not followed on the executed work. The first step taken in reference to heating and ventilating was a call made upon Joseph Nason, of Nason & Dodge, of New York, to prepare working plans and submit estimates for the work. Nason and Dodge delegated Robert Briggs, Jr., to take charge of the work. He made the plans for heating and ventilating, which were completed while Captain Meigs was sick and were afterwards modified by him in only a few slight details. Robert Briggs was for many years one of the prominent heating and ventilating engineers of the country, and should receive credit for designing the heating and ventilating apparatus. What is good or what has been found deficient in design of this apparatus should be attributed to him.

Captain Meigs was the prime mover in having the Halls of Congress changed from the ends of the wings to the center, but according to a committee report this was simply adopting a plan devised by Anderson in the first competition, after several conferences between Anderson and Meigs and using Anderson's plans in his interviews with the President, while Walter made all the actual plans, designs, and working drawings for this interior work. How far Captain Meigs assisted in the design of constructive features it is difficult to determine. All constructional drawings, except those for heating and ventilating, were made either by Walter himself or under his direct supervision, and as he was capable and skilled in such work there is no reason to think that he received assistance. Captain Meigs discharged duties in connection with superintendence of the work and the business details of letting contracts and disbursing funds. Work which progressed during Meigs's supervision commenced with the basement story, the wings

were completed except porches, and the Dome was about half finished when he was relieved. Capt. W. B. Franklin continued to perform duties similar to those of his predecessor, without in any way antagonizing the Architect of the building.[37]

No appropriation having been made for the building, the work was suspended from December 1, 1859, to July 1, 1860. August 18, 1860, a contract was made with Rice & Heebner to furnish thirty-four monolithic columns 25 feet 2⅛ inches high, with diameter 3 feet above base and 2 feet 6⅛ inches at the neck, for the porticoes. These monolithic blocks were to be obtained from Conolly's quarry, Baltimore County, Md.[38] In his first report on the progress of the work, November 6, 1860, Captain Franklin states that the arcades and platforms of all the porticoes were complete, ready for setting the pedestals for the columns; the stairways and other interior work completed, with the exception of decoration; the foundations for all steps laid, and the steps on the north and south fronts set. Captain Franklin had levels (July, 1860) taken on the granite base course and found that on the south wing it was 4½ inches lower on the west than it was on the east, while on the north wing the west side was 2⅞ inches lower than the east end. The levels were again taken in October, 1860, and no change had taken place. The Dome was raised to a height of 30 feet above the colonnade,

---

[37] Brown's interpretation of Meigs was biased by his leadership role in the architectural profession. Professional architects and Army engineers competed in Washington throughout the late nineteenth and early twentieth centuries to determine the federal government's policy toward architectural design and urban planning. Brown had no respect for Meigs's work as an architect and thought that his Pension Building (National Building Museum), built between 1882 and 1887, epitomized "the period of decline in Federal art." See Glenn Brown, "Art and the Federal Government," *Appleton's Magazine* 7 (February 1906): 240–247.

[38] Captain of Engineers in Charge of the U. S. Capitol Extension, "Letter from the Superintendent of the Capitol Extension, to the Chairman of the Committee on Public Buildings and Grounds, in Relation to the Dome and the Porticoes of the Capitol," S. misc. doc. 29 (36–1), Serial 1038.

and contracts were made for furnishing ironwork for the Dome at 7 cents per pound.[39] The Secretary of War, Joseph Holt, ordered Captain Meigs to resume charge of the Capitol February 27, 1861, but the latter was soon ordered to the Gulf of Mexico on service in connection with the civil war. The Secretary placed J. N. Macomb, Corps of Topographical Engineers, in charge of the work, but little work was done, and no appropriation was asked to carry it on for the ensuing year.[40] While the civil war caused the army officers to undertake duties more serious than the superintendence of buildings, it at the same time was the cause of giving the Capitol occupants which its designers had never contemplated. During the summer of 1861 the western portion of the old building was turned into a bakery for the soldiers, and the crypt was used as a storage room for flour. The following order was issued:

"SPECIAL ORDERS,

"No. 177. Headquarters Military District of Washington.
[Extract.]

"I. The following buildings and premises will be taken possession of forthwith for hospital purposes:

"The Capitol.

"By command of Brigadier-General Wadsworth:

JOHN P. SHERMAN,
"Assistant Adjutant-General."

Following this order 1,500 beds were placed in the building, occupying nearly all portions of it. The Commissioner of Public Buildings, who was in charge of the old building and the completed portions of

the new building, protested against this occupation, and finally by the order of President Lincoln the army occupation ceased, on October 15, in time to repair the damage and clean the building before the meeting of Congress.[41]

April 16, 1862, the following act of Congress was passed:

"That the supervision of the Capitol extension and the erection of the new Dome be, and is hereby, transferred from the War Department to the Department of the Interior; and all money which may be hereafter appropriated for either of the improvements heretofore mentioned shall be expended under the direction and supervision of the Secretary of the Interior: *Provided,* That no money heretofore appropriated shall be expended upon the Capitol until authorized by Congress, except so much as is necessary to protect the building from injury by the elements and to complete the Dome."[42] Thomas U. Walter was again put in charge, both as Architect and superintendent. Under this resolution work was resumed April 30, 1862; the steps and cheek blocks on the eastern porticoes were set and more than half completed, and all the columns of the connecting corridors were in place by November 1, 1862. The principal framework of the Dome was also erected [Plates 196, 197, 198].[43]

During the year 1863 the work on the porticoes and Dome was still in progress. Mr. Walter, in his report of November 1, 1863, calls

---

[39] Captain of Engineers in Charge of the U. S. Capitol Extension, "Report on the Capitol Extension," in *Report of the Secretary of War,* S. ex. doc. 1 (36–2), Serial 1079.

[40] Meigs was responsible for the appointment of J. N. Macomb, his brother-in-law. See Allen, *The Dome of the United States Capitol,* 54.

[41] Benjamin B. French, the Commissioner of Public Buildings, summarized the Capitol's role as a Civil War garrison, bakery, and infirmary in his 1862 report. See "Report of the Commissioner of Public Buildings," in *Report of the Secretary of the Interior* (Washington: Government Printing Office, 1862), 596–603. For information on the use of Capitol spaces for a bakery and hospital, see also RG 40, Subject Files, Curator's Office, AOC.

[42] "A Resolution Transferring the Supervision of the Capitol Extension and the Erection of the new Dome from the War Department to the Interior Department," in *United States Statutes at Large,* vol. 12, 617.

[43] Construction of the ironwork for the dome was continued during the year the contract was suspended (May 1861–May 1862), and the structure was finally completed in 1865. See Allen, *The Dome of the United States Capitol,* 50–65.

PLATE 190

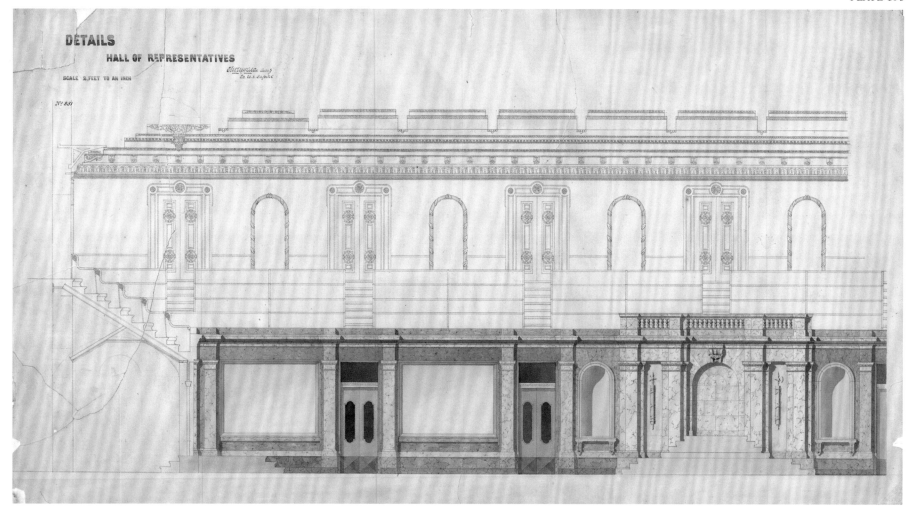

DETAILS
HALL OF REPRESENTATIVES

SCALE 2 FEET TO AN INCH

ENLARGED SECTION, HOUSE OF REPRESENTATIVES—WALTER ARCHITECT.

The term "enlarged" referred to a drawing that detailed elements in a room's design. March 29, 1854.

PLATE 191

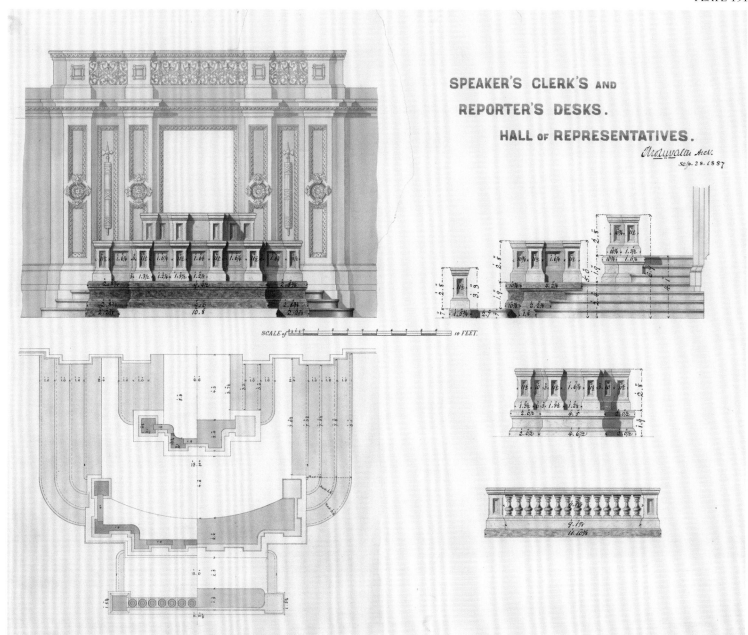

SPEAKER'S CLERK'S AND
REPORTER'S DESKS.
HALL OF REPRESENTATIVES.

SCALE of 10 FEET.

SPEAKER'S DESK, HOUSE OF REPRESENTATIVES—WALTER ARCHITECT.

PLATE 192

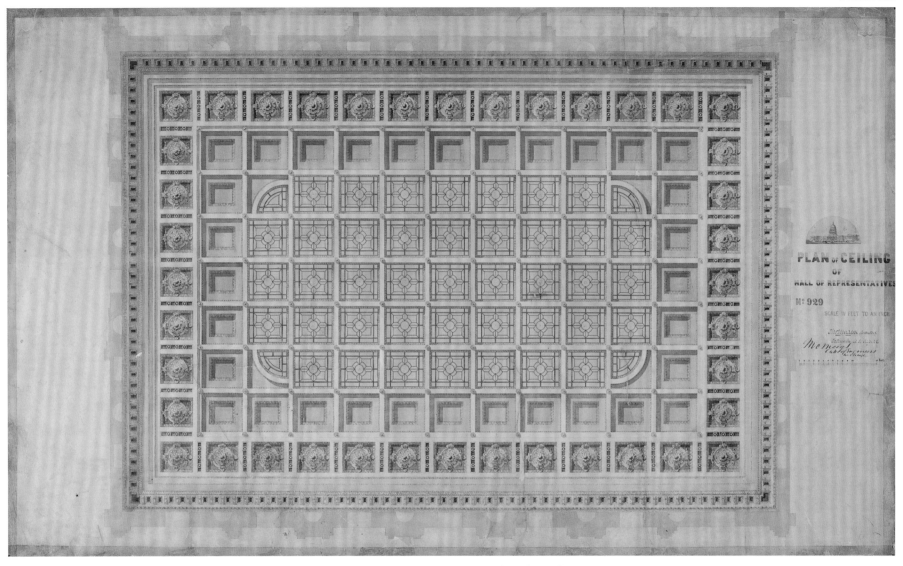

CEILING OF HOUSE OF REPRESENTATIVES.

The original ceiling and skylight were removed in 1949 as part of a renovation of the House of Representatives. Drawing dated March 28, 1856.

PLATE 193

DETAILS OF SENATE CHAMBER
U.S. CAPITOL EXTENSION

ENLARGED SECTION OF SENATE CHAMBER,—T. U. WALTER, ARCHITECT.

The term "enlarged" referred to a drawing that detailed elements in a room's design.

PLATE 194

CEILING OF SENATE CHAMBER—WALTER ARCHITECT.

The original ceiling and skylight were removed in 1949 as part of a renovation of the Senate Chamber.

PLATE 195

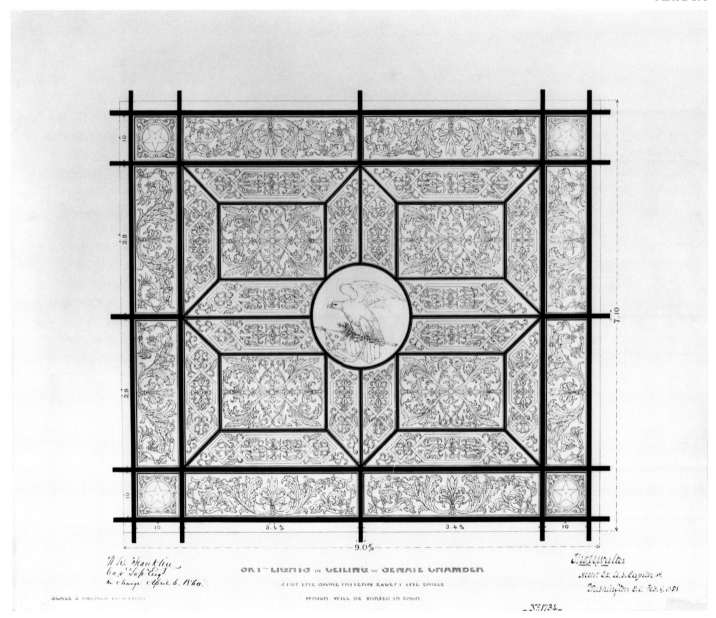

SKY-LIGHTS in CEILING of SENATE CHAMBER

ALL OF THE SAME PATTERN EXCEPT THE EAGLE

WHICH WILL BE VARIED IN EACH

PANEL, CEILING OF SENATE CHAMBER—WALTER ARCHITECT.

The skylights are no longer extant.

PLATE 196

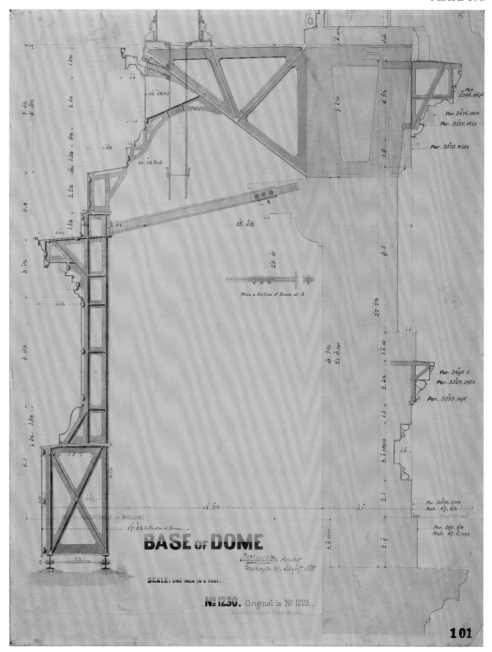

DETAILED BASE OF DOME,—WALTER ARCHITECT.

PLATE 197

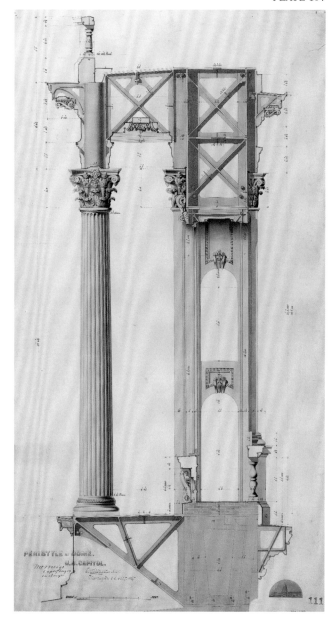

PERISTYLE OF DOME—WALTER ARCHITECT.

The drawing detailed how the peristyle columns would be
cantilevered beyond the old rotunda walls to provide a greater diameter for the new dome.

PLATE 198

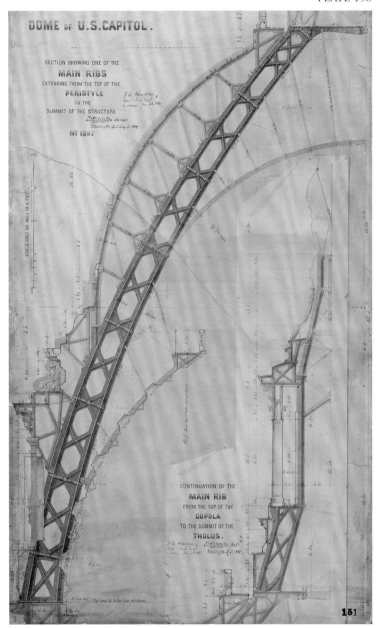

DETAILED SECTION OF TOP PORTION DOME,—WALTER ARCHITECT.

PLATE 199

STATUE OF FREEDOM, CRAWFORD SCULPTOR.

Thomas Crawford's photograph of his model for the third design for the statue of *Freedom*, 1856.

attention to the great difficulty in obtaining the marble promptly, because of the war. He also mentions the fact that the copper covering for the roof and the cast-iron gutters were not satisfactory, as the expansion and contraction in the metals opened the joints, with result of leakage. He caused the up-and-down joints to be riveted, and depended upon the corrugations of the metal providing for the expansion and contraction which would result from the difference in the temperature. The lapped and calked joints of the cast-iron gutters were covered with pitch. During this year arrangements were made for lighting the gas by Gardner's electro-magnetic gas-lighting apparatus.[44]

On December 2, 1863, the Statue of Freedom, by Crawford [Plate 199], was raised to its resting place on the top of the tholus which surmounted the Dome. This statue is 19 feet 6 inches high, and is made of bronze in five sections, bolted in place. On this occasion the following order was issued by the War Department:

"SPECIAL ORDERS,   "HEADQUARTERS DEPARTMENT OF WASHINGTON,
"No. 248.   "TWENTY-SECOND ARMY CORPS,
                     "*December 1, 1863.*

"3. At 12 m. on the 2d instant the Statue of Freedom, which crowns the Dome of the National Capitol, will be inaugurated. In commemoration of this event, and as an expression due from the Department of respect for this material symbol of the principle on which our Government is based, it is ordered—

"First. At the moment at which a flag is displayed from the statue a national salute of thirty-five guns will be fired from a field battery on Capitol Hill.

"Second. The last gun from the salute will be answered by a similar salute from Fort Stanton, which will be followed in succession from right to left by salutes from Forts Davis, Mahan, Lincoln, Bunker Hill, Totten, De Russy, Reno, Cameron, Corcoran, Albany, and Scott.

"Fourth. Brig. Gen. W. F. Barry will make the necessary arrangements for and superintend the firing from Capitol Hill, Brigadier-General De Russy from the works south, and Lieut. Col. J. A. Haskin from those north of the Potomac.

"By command of Major-General Augur:
                 "CARROLL H. POTTER,
                 "*Assistant Adjutant-General.*"

The head of the statue, being hoisted by the steam derrick, was started from the ground at 12 m., and in twenty minutes it was in place, the flag unfurled, and the salute fired.[45]

Mr. Walter in his report for November 1, 1864, states that the eastern portico of the north wing, together with steps and stairways, was completed with the exception of the caps for the cheek blocks. In this portico the column shafts are monoliths. Each base and pedestal is worked out of a single stone. The capitals are sculptured from the solid blocks, being two courses in height. The architraves over each intercolumniation and the panels of the ceiling are each made from a monolithic block, the latter being deeply paneled and richly carved. Work was stopped on all porticoes except the eastern portico on the south wing. Each year a limited amount of painting was done on the interior wall surfaces.[46]

[44] Architect of the United States Capitol Extension, "Report of the Architect of the Capitol Extension," in *Report of the Secretary of the Interior*, H. ex. doc. 1 (38–1), Serial 1182.

[45] Brown reprinted documents and orders first published in Walter's "Report of the Architect of the Capitol Extension," which contained an account of the ceremonies placing the statue of Freedom atop the dome. For a contemporary news account of the event, see "The Statue on the Capitol Dome," *Daily National Intelligencer*, December 3, 1863, 3. See also Robert L. Gale, *Thomas Crawford: American Sculptor* (Pittsburgh, Pa: University of Pittsburgh Press, 1964), 190.

[46] Architect of the United States Capitol Extension, "Report of the Architect of the Capitol Extension," in *"Report of the Secretary of the Interior,"* 38th Congress., 2d sess., H. ex. doc. 1 689–696. [Serial 1220]

Although work continued on the Capitol throughout the war, it was delayed by the increased prices in freight, and the difficulty of obtaining vessels at any price was so great that the delay caused dissatisfaction in Congress.

In February, 1863, the freight rate on stone was $1.75 per ton; before the end of the year it was $6 per ton. Vessels were in great demand as carriers of army supplies, and everything gave way to the demands and needs of the Army. But while work progressed slowly it progressed steadily. In the year 1865 Thomas U. Walter sent in the following resignation, which was accepted by the President, Andrew Johnson, and Edward Clark was appointed Architect of the Capitol.

"ARCHITECT'S OFFICE, U.S. CAPITOL,
"Washington, D.C., May 26, 1865.

"Hon. JAMES HARLAN,
    "Secretary of the Interior.

"SIR: I have the honor to acknowledge the receipt of your letter of yesterday inclosing a copy of a communication addressed by you to the contractor for the enlargement of the Library of Congress, in which you state that the contract entered into between myself, on the part of the Government, and Mr. Charles Fowler, the aforesaid contractor, 'is void,' and that 'no accounts or claims for service performed or materials furnished under it will be allowed.' You also state that 'the Commissioner of Public Buildings will be instructed to take the necessary action to prevent the further progress of said work under said supposed contract, and also to preserve the public buildings until the work can be legally resumed, after advertisement for bids.' This, of course, removes all jurisdiction of the work from me, which, it is proper for me to say, I do not at all regret.

"I may, however, be permitted to remark that I consider the stoppage of the work at this time as particularly unfortunate. The season has so far advanced that it is scarcely possible, under the most favorable circumstances, to bring it to such a state of forwardness before the assembling of Congress as will prevent it from interfering with the convenience of the members. It is also of the highest importance that accommodations should be obtained for the books at the earliest possible moment. In view of these facts, any delay in the prosecution of the work is greatly to be deplored.

"It occurs to me further to say, in this connection, that I regret that so important a movement as the abrogation of a contract, in which I stand as the representative of the Government by authority vested in me by one of its executive departments, should have been effected without any consultation whatever with me, and without the slightest intimation having been given me of the intention of the Department on the subject. And more particularly do I regret this action as I was the Architect of the work in question, acting under direct orders from the Secretary of the Interior.

"I have likewise received a letter from the Commissioner of Public Buildings and Grounds, inclosing a copy of a communication received by him from the Department of the Interior, under date of the 23d instant, in which you direct him to take immediate 'charge of all work on public buildings in the District of Columbia in course of construction, extension, or repair, and now in progress, that are legally subject to the control of the Secretary of the Interior.' This, of course, places me in a position subordinate to the aforesaid Commissioner of Public Buildings and Grounds.

"These changes, particularly the stoppage of the enlargement of the Library of Congress, suggest the present as the proper time for me to retire altogether from the charge of the public works. I therefore respectfully request you to accept this as my resignation as Architect of the United States Capitol Extension, the new Dome, the continuation of the Patent Office Building, the enlargement of the Library of

Congress, and the extension of the Government Printing Office. In order that time may be afforded for the proper arrangement of the drawings and papers in my office, I respectfully suggest that this resignation shall take effect on the 31st instant.

"In taking this step I am moved by considerations of self-respect as well as by the fact that the public buildings heretofore under my charge have so far approached completion as to render the services of an architect no longer absolutely necessary.

"I have completed all the designs and drawings for these works, and I have the satisfaction to say that the contractors and foremen who have thus far executed them understand all that relates to what remains to be done. They have proved themselves by years of trial to be skillful and faithful; I have therefore no hesitation in intrusting my reputation as the architect of these structures in their hands.

"I received my appointment as Architect of the Capitol Extension directly from the President on the 11th day of June, 1851, and I have thus far brought this work to completion. Nothing remains now to be done except a few stones on the eastern portico of the south wing, the caps of the cheek blocks, and the colonnades on the north, south, and west fronts, a large portion of the materials for which are already wrought.

"My design for the Dome on the Capitol was approved by Congress, and an appropriation made for commencing work, on the 3d of March, 1855. I have prosecuted this improvement ever since with all proper diligence, and I have now to say that the entire exterior is completed, and that nothing remains to be done to finish the interior except a portion of the stairways which are now in progress of construction, and the great fresco painting of Brumidi, which I trust will be finished before the assembling of Congress.

"The enlargement of the Library is part of my original design for that improvement which was adopted by Congress March 19, 1852. The center portion was immediately thereafter executed, and I believe that I am correct in saying that it is the first room ever constructed with a complete iron ceiling. The enlargement is simply the carrying out of my original design, with some modifications to increase the room for books.

"The remaining works which have heretofore been under my charge have been so placed from time to time by the Department of the Interior, and it is proper for me to say that I have received no compensation for any professional service I have ever performed upon them, or upon any other of the Government works, beyond my salary as Architect of the Capitol Extension.

"I shall turn the drawings, with all the records and Government property in my office, over to the Commissioner of Public Buildings and Grounds, in conformity with your order, which places all these works in his charge, and I have no doubt that he will be able to bring them to a proper conclusion without any further professional aid.

"I have the honor to be, sir, very respectfully, your obedient servant,
"THO. U. WALTER,
"*Architect.*"[47]

Mr. Walter was the architect of the north and south wings and the Dome and the interior of the old Congressional Library, having been connected with the work in that capacity from the beginning of the Capitol extension in 1851 until its practical completion in 1865. From the years 1853 to 1861, while the public buildings were in charge of the War Department, he was nominally subordinate to a Captain of Engineers,

---

[47] Thomas U. Walter to Secretary of the Interior James Harlan, May 26, 1865, RG 42, NARA. Walter did not submit the drawings to the Commissioner of Public Buildings and Grounds as he promised in his letter. The government purchased many of Walter's drawings of the Capitol from his daughters Olivia and Ida Walter in 1917. Architectural historian William Allen interprets Walter's resignation as a bluff since Walter was genuinely surprised when it was accepted. He kept the drawings so that he might be considered indispensable.

who the reports show devoted the greater part of his time to the business management and discussions on heating, ventilation, and acoustics.

In the selection of Thomas U. Walter to design and supervise the United States Capitol extension, Millard Fillmore showed his appreciation of capacity already displayed in executed work. After a survey of the buildings of the period there can be no doubt that Walter was the man best fitted for this important and delicate addition. His love of refined and classical proportions and details, his good taste, and his rare restraint in reproducing the features of the old work and harmonizing the new with it, instead of endeavoring to destroy the old building for self-aggrandizement, showed a man of rare capacity. The working drawings which he made, a large proportion of them with his own hands, are evidence of his capacity in the practical execution of the work.[48] Plans, sections, and elevations were all carefully drawn, figured, and colored. The details for construction and ornamentation were all worked out with the minutest care. In the execution of the exterior the stories, orders, belts, and details of the old building as designed by Thornton were extended through the new work [Plates 202 and 203],

while the detailing of the doorways, where it would not conflict, was more elaborate than the entrances on the old work [Plate 204]. The drawings of the corridor extending through the south wing [Plate 205], the Senate retiring room in the north wing [Plate 206], and the main vestibule in the south wing [Plate 207] show the care with which the general scheme was evolved on paper. The details in most instances are refined and classical in their tendencies, as are shown in the columns and antae of the Senate retiring room and columns and pilasters of the vestibule [Plate 208]. The capitals shown in Plate 209 are reductions of full-size drawings. The ceiling and ironwork in the rooms devoted to the Congressional Library was more freely treated than the other portions of the building [Plate 210]. Plates 211 to 213 show detail drawings made for the principal stairways. Plates 190, 193, and 214 are reductions from detail drawings of the House and Senate chambers. The care and accuracy with which his constructional details are worked out is shown in the drawings of vaulting for the antechamber, north wing [Plate 215], and the arching of the vestibule in the south wing [Plate 216]. The designs of Walter for chimney pieces, one of which is given [Plate 217], furniture [Plate 218], and lamp-posts [Plate 219] are not as satisfactory as the work on the actual structure, being deficient in classical feeling and evidently being influenced by the fashion of the period in such designs, although they are drawn with the same minuteness of detail shown in other portions of his work.

---

[48] Draftsman August G. Schoenborn (1827–1902) assisted Walter in this work. See Allen, *The Dome of the United States Capitol,* 76. Walter's extensive drawings of the Capitol are located in the collections of the Architect of the Capitol, the Prints and Photographs Division at the Library of Congress, and the Athenaeum in Philadelphia, Pennsylvania.

PLATE 200

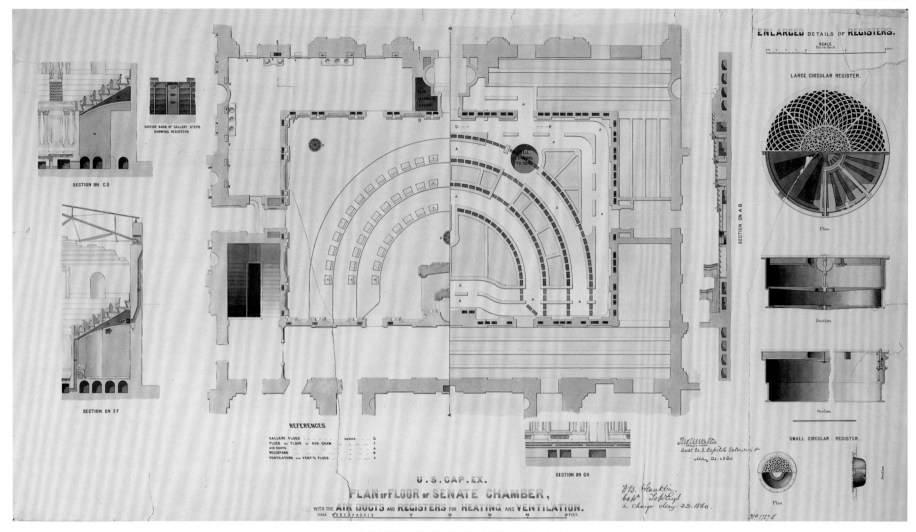

PLAN FOR HEATING AND VENTILATING.

PLATE 201

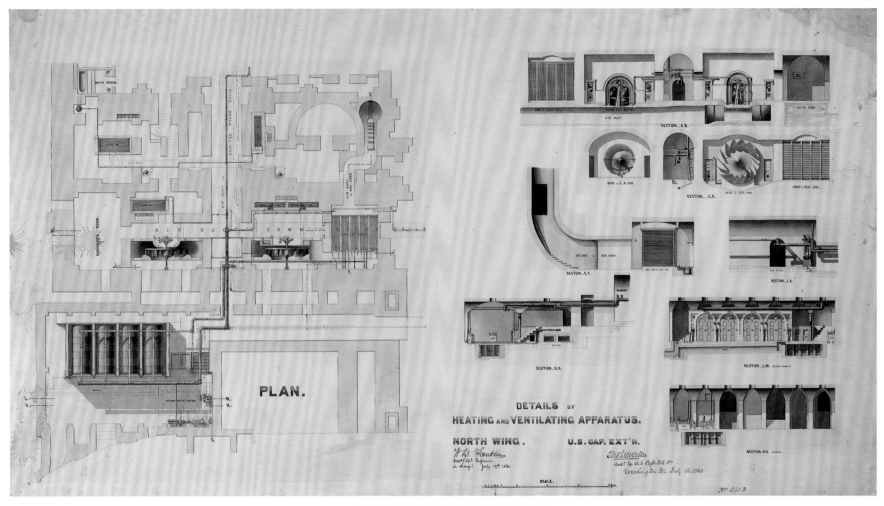

DETAILS OF HEATING AND VENTILATING.

PLATE 202

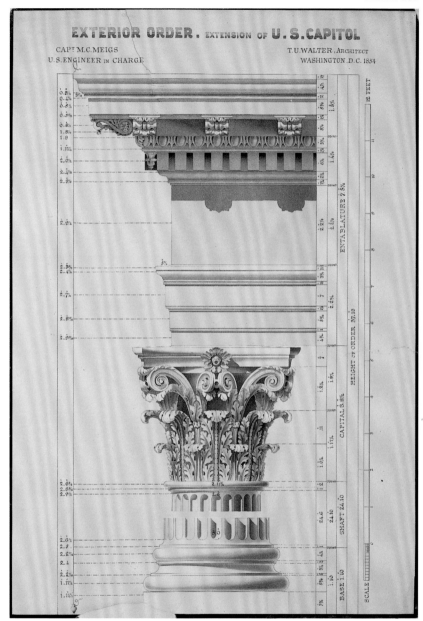

EXTERIOR ORDER OF THE CAPITOL EXTENSION—WALTER ARCHITECT.

PLATE 203

DESIGN SHOWING CORNER OF CAPITOL—WALTER ARCHITECT.

Dated 1851.

PLATE 204

ELEVATION

SECTION

DESIGN FOR EASTERN DOORS
EXTENSION OF U.S. CAPITOL

SCALE ¾ OF AN INCH
TO A FOOT

WROUGHT IRON HINGE

PLAN

PLAN OF HANGING OF DOORS FULL SIZE

DETAILS OF EASTERN DOORWAYS,—WALTER ARCHITECT.

PLATE 205

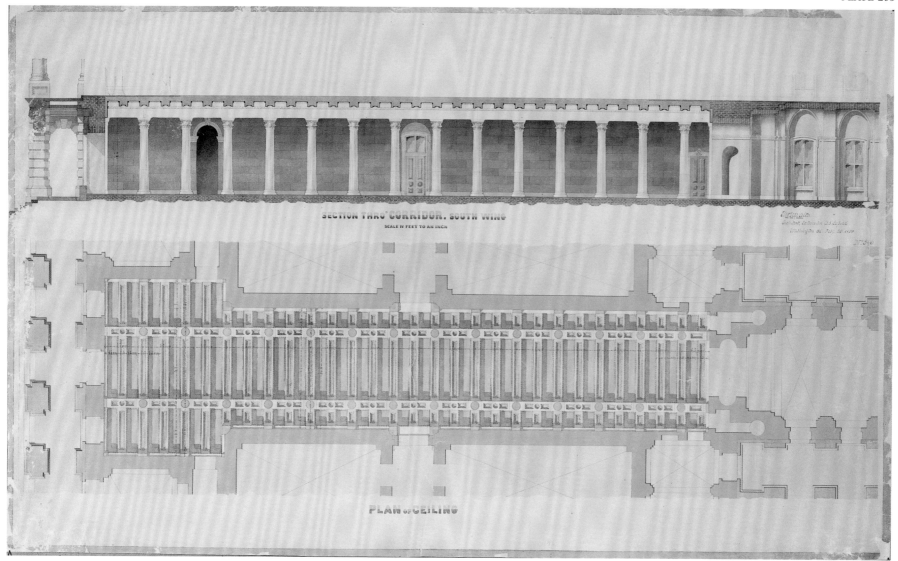

SECTION THRO' CORRIDOR, SOUTH WING
SCALE 1/2 FEET TO AN INCH

PLAN OF CEILING

CORRIDOR THROUGH BASEMENT SOUTH WING.—WALTER ARCHITECT.

This corridor is known today as the Hall of Columns (related drawing, plate 241).

PLATE 206

SECTIONS AND PLAN OF SENATE RETIRING ROOM—WALTER ARCHITECT.

Today the space is known as the Marble Room. This drawing also shows the Vice President's Room and the President's Room
at the left and right, respectively. Ca. 1856.

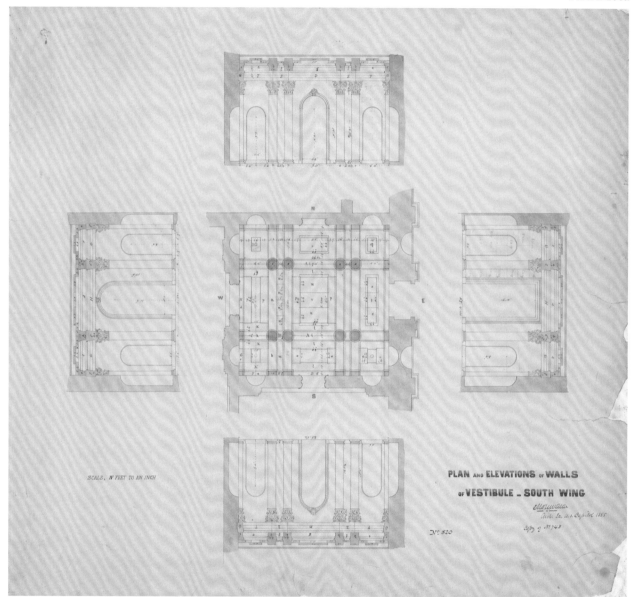

SCALE, IV FEET TO AN INCH

PLAN AND ELEVATIONS OF WALLS
OF VESTIBULE — SOUTH WING

PLAN AND ELEVATION OF WALLS, BASEMENT VESTIBULE, SOUTH WING,—T. U. WALTER, ARCHITECT.

The center bays of this space have been infilled with two elevators.
Brown's caption is mistaken: this vestibule is located on the second floor. September 11, 1855.

PLATE 207

VESTIBULE, SOUTH WING,—T. U. WALTER, ARCHITECT.

This drawing depicts the south end of the Hall of Columns.

PLATE 208

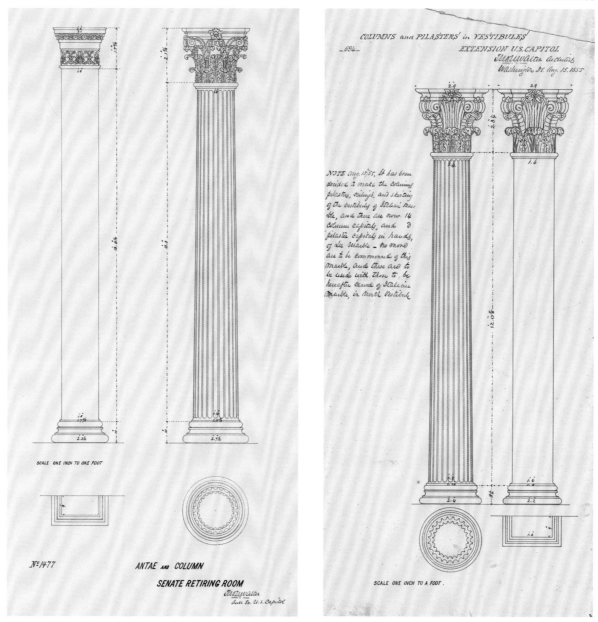

DETAILS OF COLUMNS,—WALTER, ARCHITECT.

Left: Marble Room columns, drawing dated July 14, 1857. Right: Walter's Corinthian capital with corn leaves, tobacco, and magnolias, drawing dated August 15, 1855.

PLATE 209

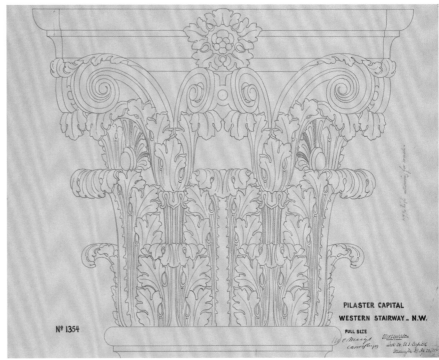

DETAILS OF CAPITALS, NORTH WING,—T. U. WALTER, ARCHITECT.

Left: Senate Retiring Room, April 17, 1857.

Right: Western Stairway, April 27, 1857.

PLATE 210

PERSPECTIVE OF CONSOLE, SUPPORTING CEILING. DETAILS OF CONGRESSIONAL LIBRARY.

DRAWING OF CONSOLE, OLD CONGRESSIONAL LIBRARY,—T. U. WALTER, ARCHITECT.
Related photograph, plate 253a.

PLATE 211

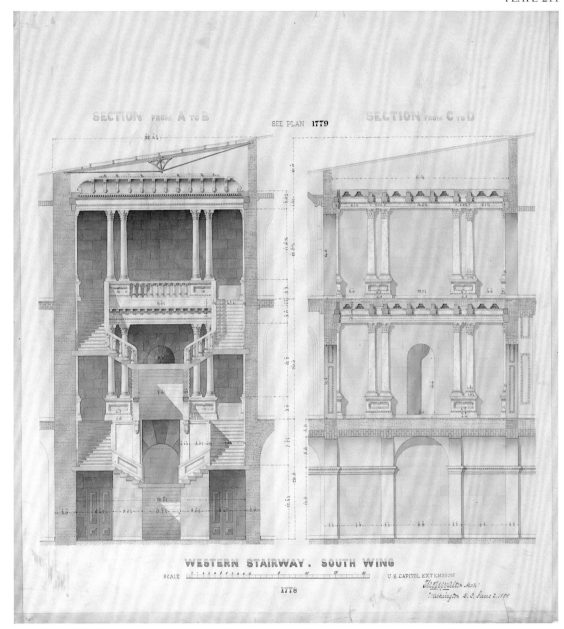

SECTION FROM A TO B   SEE PLAN 1779   SECTION FROM C TO D

WESTERN STAIRWAY. SOUTH WING

SCALE   U.S. CAPITOL EXTENSION

1778

WESTERN STAIRWAY—WALTER ARCHITECT.

PLATE 212

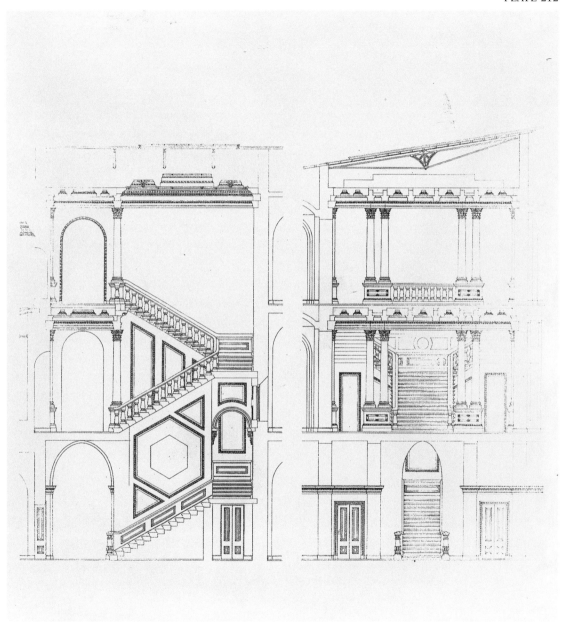

SECTION OF STAIRWAY.

June 2, 1858.

PLATE 213

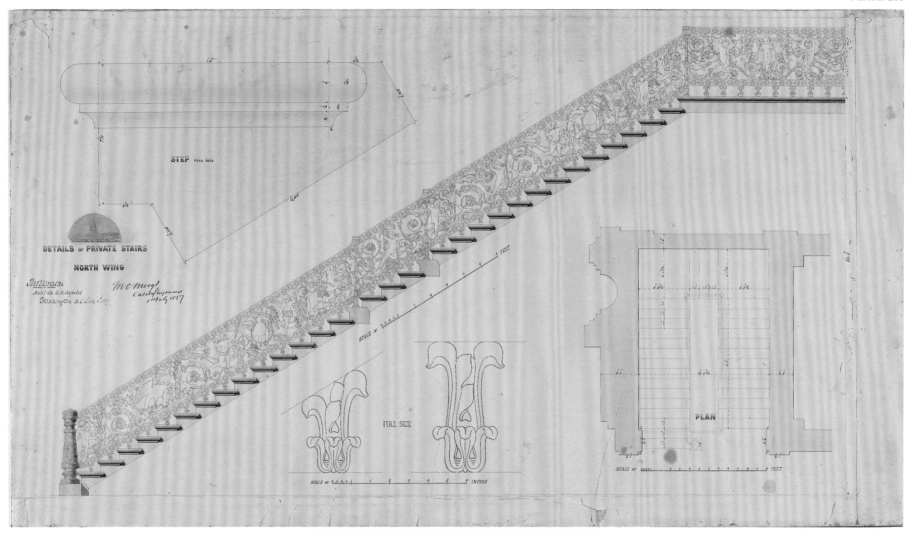

STEP FULL SIZE

DETAILS OF PRIVATE STAIRS

NORTH WING

FULL SIZE

PLAN

DETAILS OF BRONZE STAIRWAY—WALTER ARCHITECT.

PLATE 214

PERSPECTIVE OF SPEAKER'S DESK,—WALTER ARCHITECT.

Ca. 1857.

PLATE 215

DETAILS OF VAULTING ANTE CHAMBER, NORTH WING,—T. U. WALTER ARCHITECT.

Senate Reception Room (related photograph, plate 231).

PLATE 216

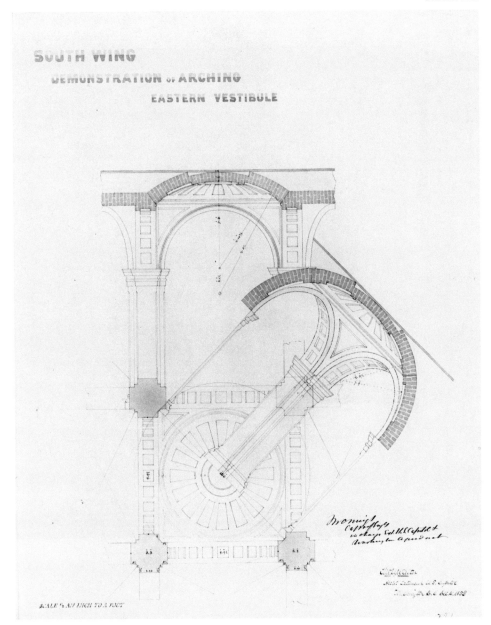

DETAIL OF CORRIDOR ARCHES,—T. U. WALTER, ARCHITECT.

This vestibule is located on the first floor of the House of Representatives' Wing.

PLATE 217

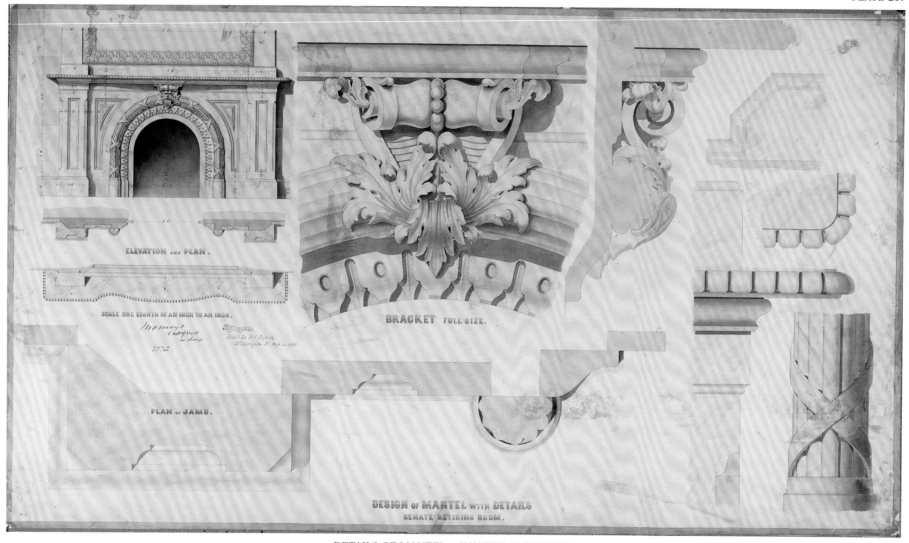

DETAILS OF MANTEL,—WALTER ARCHITECT.

This mantel is located in the Marble Room.

PLATE 218

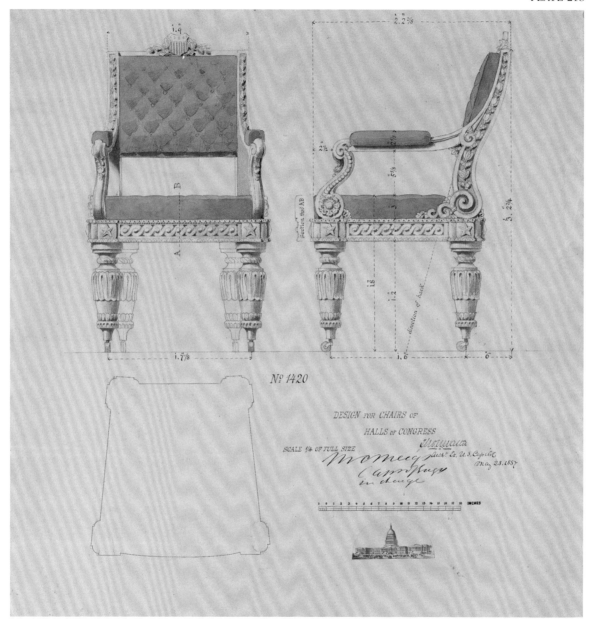

No 1420

DESIGN FOR CHAIRS OF HALLS OF CONGRESS,—T. U. WALTER, ARCHITECT.

PLATE 219

DESIGN FOR LAMP POST ON EAST ENTRANCE,—T. U. WALTER, ARCHITECT.

Ca. 1863.

CHAPTER XIII

THE WORK ON THE CAPITOL UNDER THE
SUPERVISION OF EDWARD CLARK, ARCHITECT

EDWARD CLARK, who was placed in charge of the Capitol after the retirement of Thomas U. Walter in 1865, carried on the work to completion in accordance with the designs of his predecessor. In 1865 the eastern portico of the south wing was completed with the exception of the capping stones for the cheek blocks. Work was commenced on the enlargement of the Congressional Library, so as to include the whole of the central west extension. Iron and brick work was substituted for the old wooden construction, and the hot-air furnaces which heated the remodeled portion of the building were replaced by steam. In 1866 the northern and western porticoes of the north wing were completed. In 1867 all the porticoes were completed.

By act of Congress March 30, 1867, the central portion of the building and all repair work were placed under the charge of the Architect of the Capitol. Previous to this date the old portion of the building and repairs were under the Commissioner of Public Buildings and Grounds.[1]

In 1867 hot-air furnaces were removed from the cellar of the old building and steam heating substituted in the Law Library, its office rooms and passages. The old vertical skylight over the Supreme Court room was removed and a new light of small glass in cast-iron frames substituted.[2] March 2, 1867, the gas for illuminating the Rotunda was ignited by an electric current.

During the year 1868 all the balustrades and exterior marble work were completed and chimneys topped out and capped. A water-closet system was placed in the upper story of the north wing. Grading was done on the grounds and terraces. Mr. Clark recommended treating the Capitol grounds, the Mall, and the President's grounds in one comprehensive plan.[3]

By act of Congress March 3, 1869, all repairs, improvements, and extensions to the heating apparatus were placed in the charge of the Architect of the Capitol. All stables and temporary building constructions were removed from the grounds and the grading progressed.[4]

During the year 1870 all the work of cleaning and pointing the stonework was finished and the extensions were completed on the exterior. At this time the stone stairway leading from the Supreme Court at the northeast corner of the central building was removed, the

---

[1] The office of Commissioner of Public Buildings and Grounds was abolished for practical and political reasons in 1867. The responsibilities were too extensive for one person to manage, and the incumbent Benjamin. B. French had stirred congressional animosity as a staunch supporter of President Andrew Johnson. The commissioner's duties for the Capitol were briefly transferred to the Army Corps of Engineers. "An Act to Provide in Part for Grading the Public Grounds, and for Other Purposes," 40th Cong., 1st sess., in *United States Statutes at Large*, vol. 15, 13. Within two weeks, the Corps of Engineers was relieved of its duties at the Capitol, which were transferred to the Architect of the Capitol Extension (15 stat. 13, March 30, 1867).

[2] The skylight was on the roof of the Capitol. See "Report of the Architect of the Capitol Extension," in *Report of the Secretary of the Interior, Part I*, H. ex. doc. 1 (40–2), Serial 1326, 524–530.

[3] Architect of the United States Capitol Extension, "Report of the Architect of the Capitol Extension," in *Report of the Secretary of the Interior*, H. ex. doc. 1 (40–3), Serial 1366, 889–894.

[4] "An Act Making Appropriations for the Legislative, Executive, and Judicial Expenses of the Government for the Year Ending the 30th of June, 1870," 40th Cong., 3rd sess., in *United States Statutes at Large*, vol. 15, 284.

space in the basement connected with the Law Library, the corresponding space on the principal story fitted up for the Attorney-General, and in the attic for a storeroom.[5] The painting and interior decoration by Brumidi was carried on from year to year in the halls and committee rooms of the House and Senate. Each year a few of the hot-air furnaces in the old building were removed and the steam heating apparatus extended.

The illustrations [Plates 220 to 223] show the subbasement, basement, and principal story and attic as the building was completed. Plates 224 to 253 show exterior and interior views of the completed building.

In 1871 the depressed floor between the Rotunda and old House of Representatives was raised to correspond with the other floor levels. It was found necessary at this period to relay the portico steps on the west. The foundations of these steps had been placed on made ground and the settlement required constant attention.[6] It was found necessary every few years to paint the Dome and stonework of the old building. Steam heating was extended year by year in the central building, as well as yearly changes made in the details of the heating apparatus of the new building.

Thomas U. Walter, before retiring from the position of Architect, had several times recommended an extension of the eastern front of the central building. Plates 274 to 277 gives the plan and perspective view of a proposed enlargement of this part of the building made by Walter in the latter part of 1874.

By act of Congress March 3, 1872, the squares numbered 687 and 688, bounded by First street east and B streets north and south, were purchased and the buildings on them removed during the year 1873.[7]

Edward Clark, in 1873, as he had done in previous reports, recommended the employment of a landscape architect to lay out and ornament the grounds. The recommendations were finally approved by Congress June 23, 1874, and the improvement of the grounds was placed in charge of Frederick Law Olmsted.[8] His first broad suggestions were for a plaza on the east and a marble terrace on the west of the building. From this period the grading of the grounds, setting curbing and dwarf walls around the grounds, ornamental flower beds, and lamp-posts, laying walks, and planting progressed from year to year, the north portion of the east park being completed in 1878. The greater part of all the stone boundary walls were finished in 1880 and work progressed on the walks on the west front.[9]

June 30, 1882, Mr. Olmsted reported all the entrances complete, together with the walls and coping; foundation walls for a parapet complete, and 24,000 feet of plain and 10,000 feet of mosaic artificial-stone flagging laid. In this report he makes a protest against the lack of appropriations for carrying on the marble terraces.[10] Plate 256 shows the plan of the grounds and terraces as designed by Mr. Olmsted.

The terraces, stairways, and other architectural features connected with the landscape were designed by Wisedell, while Mr. Clark

[5] "Report of the Architect of the Capitol Extension," in *Report of the Secretary of the Interior,* H. ex. doc. 1 (41–3), Serial 1449, 861–866.

[6] "Report of the Architect of the Capitol Extension," in *Report of the Secretary of the Interior,* H. ex. doc. 1 (42–2), Serial 1505, 1125–1129.

[7] "An Act Making Appropriations to Supply Deficiencies in the Appropriations for the Service of the Government for the Fiscal Year Ending June 30th, 1873," 42nd Cong., 3rd sess., in *United States Statutes at Large,* vol. 17, 537.

[8] "An Act Making Appropriations to Sundry Civil Expenses of the Government for the Fiscal Year Ending June 30th, 1875, and for Other Purposes," 43rd Cong., 1st sess., in *United States Statutes at Large,* vol. 18, pt. 3, 214.

[9] Olmsted outlined his plan in a letter to Clark, printed in "Report of the Architect of the Capitol Extension," in *Report of the Secretary of the Interior,* H. ex. doc. 1 (43–2), Serial 1639, 731–737. Progress reports were published in succeeding reports.

[10] "Annual Report of the Architect of the United States Capitol" [For the Fiscal Year Ended 30 June, 1882], in H. ex. doc. 1 (47–2), Serial 2100, 907–925.

represented the Government in the supervision of the work. The space under the terraces was divided up into committee and storage rooms [Plates 258 and 259]. The north approach and terrace were completed in 1886. In 1887 the contract for the construction of the principal terrace and grand stairways on the west front of the Capitol was awarded to the Vermont Marble Company. The foundations for this terrace consisted of 194 wells, averaging in depth 20 feet, sunk to the solid ground and filled with concrete. The report of 1890 shows that the principal part of the stonework and the committee rooms which were provided in this terrace were completed. This portion of the work was finally finished in 1892, although the work of surfacing the top and filling up the foundation was not finished until 1894.[11]

Modern innovations first made their appearance in the Capitol in 1874, by the introduction of a screw elevator in the Senate wing. This form of elevator caused so much noise that the contractor agreed at his own expense to alter it and have it run by cables, and in 1876 the elevator was changed to a hydraulic machine (see reports of 1876–77).[12] An elevator was built in the House wing and the one originally placed in the Senate was rebuilt in 1882. In 1883 a sidewalk lift was put in the Senate and a freight lift put in the north end of the western corridor. In 1888 an additional elevator was put in each wing of the Capitol by the Crane Elevator Company, and in 1890 a hydraulic one was placed in the east front, constructed so as to connect with the terrace rooms (see report of 1895).[13]

In 1878 a committee was appointed to investigate the question of lighting by electricity instead of gas. Experiments were conducted with different electric-light patents. Mr. J. H. Rogers reported in 1880 that he did not consider the light steady enough for legislative halls. Electric lights were introduced during this year on the piers at the Pennsylvania avenue entrance, but they were not considered satisfactory as late as October, 1881. During the year 1882 A. B. Talcott was made the electrician of the House. Mr. Clark reported in July, 1884, that the United States Electric Lighting Company had placed lights at the north, south, and west approaches of the Capitol at their own expense, and that the Brush-Swann Company were allowed to put experimental lights on the Dome, with the intention of illuminating the grounds and avenues from this point. Electric lighting was further extended in 1885, the Edison company being allowed to put incandescent lights in the cloak rooms, lobbies, and stairways. About this time the arc lamps on the approaches were found to be undesirable, as they caused a disagreeable accumulation of insects around the building.[14]

The incandescent lights were found so satisfactory that by act of Congress August 4, 1886, six hundred and fifty were installed in the Senate wing by Royce & Marean for the Sawyer Electric Company, and the same company put two hundred in the House, which were in satisfactory operation in 1888.[15] July, 1889, a committee was appointed

---

[13] "Annual Report of the Architect of the United States Capitol" [For the Fiscal Year Ended 30 June, 1882, 1883, 1888, 1890, and 1895], 3.

[14] Architect of the United States Capitol, "Annual Report of the Architect of the United States Capitol" [For the Fiscal Year Ended 30 June, 1878, 1881, 1882, 1884, and 1885], 3–5.

[15] "Annual Report of the Architect of the United States Capitol" [For the Fiscal Year Ended 30 June, 1888], 4–5. The lights were installed in 1888. See also "An Act Making Appropriations for Sundry Civil Expenses of the Government for the Fiscal Year Ending June 30, 1887, and for Other Purposes," 49th Cong., 1st sess., in United States Statutes at Large, vol. 24, 239.

---

[11] "Annual Report of the Architect of the United States Capitol" [For the Fiscal Year Ended 30 June, 1886, 1887, 1890, and 1894], 4–5. In 1991–1993, the Architect of the Capitol directed a major project that repaired the Olmsted terrace and added further space in the Capitol by infilling the original light courts. See RG 40, Subject Files, Curator's Office, AOC.

[12] "Annual Report of the Architect of the United States Capitol" [For the Fiscal Year Ended 30 June, 1877], 3.

to consider the question of enlarging the existing plant and putting in a modern one, and the lighting was extended during the years 1889, 1890, and 1891. The latter year new dynamos were put in place. At this period the elevator machinery was rented from the electric-light company at the rate of $200 per month.[16] Each year the electric lights were used in a greater number of rooms until in 1895, when under the acts of March 3, 1893, and March 2, 1895, arrangements were made to purchase the machinery, and contracts were made with the Westinghouse company, who agreed to take out all the engines and dynamos of the original plant and replace them with modern low-tension machinery.[17] They were to put in four direct-connecting engines and dynamos with a capacity of 1,250 16-candle-power lamps each. It was not until 1897 that electric lights were substituted for gas over the glass ceiling of the Senate and House of Representatives.[18] This substitution prevented a constant source of trouble with the glass skylights, which, during cold weather, frequently cracked from the unequal heat caused by the cold on the outside and the great heat produced by the gas in the space beneath the roof.

Electric bells were first introduced in 1891, when they were put in the committee rooms and the offices, to ring in the House within easy hearing of the Doorkeeper.[19] It was not until 1895 that electric bells were placed at each member's desk, with an annunciator in the cloakroom. Prior to this time pages were summoned by a member clapping his hands.[20]

Another modern innovation was a complete system of plumbing and drainage, which was installed in 1893. There is nothing to show the character of the plumbing which was placed in the center building or in the wings from 1850 to 1860. The character of the closets and piping used at that period must have been extremely crude and decidedly lacking in sanitary qualities. The simple statement is made in various reports that water-closets, basins, and bath tubs were put in various places and moved from time to time. The original bath tubs put in the wings were cut from the solid marble. These were afterwards replaced by copper tubs, but later the marble tubs were reinstalled.[21] These changes were made from time to time, whenever the committee thought it desirable to alter the location of the toilet rooms or when the space which they occupied was wanted for some other purpose.

Acting under instructions from the Committee on Public Buildings and Grounds, George E. Waring and John S. Billings made reports on the drainage system of the Capitol May 28 and June 28, 1892. The execution of the recommendations contained in these reports was authorized by the sundry civil act of August 5, 1892, and a contract was made with the Durham House Drainage Company, of New York, for

---

[16] "Annual Report of the Architect of the United States Capitol" [For the Fiscal Year Ended 30 June, 1889, 1890, and 1891], 3–4.

[17] "An Act Making Appropriations for Sundry Civil Expenses of the Government for the Fiscal Year Ending June 30, 1894, and for Other Purposes," 52nd Cong., 2d sess., in *United States Statutes at Large*, vol. 27, 591; and "An Act Making Appropriations for Sundry Civil Expenses of the Government for the Fiscal Year Ending June 30, 1896, and for Other Purposes," 52nd Cong., 2d sess., in *United States Statutes at Large*, vol. 28, 935–936.

[18] *Report of the Architect of the United States Capitol, together with Report of Prof. S. H. Woodbridge, relative to Improving Ventilation of Senate Wing of the Capitol, to the Secretary of the Interior, for the Fiscal Year Ended June 30, 1897* (Washington: Government Printing Office, 1897), 7–8.

[19] "Annual Report of the Architect of the United States Capitol" [For the Fiscal Year Ended 30 June, 1891], 3.

[20] "Annual Report of the Architect of the United States Capitol" [For the Fiscal Year Ended 30 June, 1895], 3–4.

[21] Marble tubs were installed only in the Senate wing (two of the tubs are still in place). See RG 40, Subject Files, Curator's Office, AOC.

drain, soil, and waste pipes for $27,984.50, with W. H. Quick, of New York, for plumbing fixtures and marble work for $36,475.01, and with H. I. Gregory, of Washington, for cooking fixtures for $1,966.41. The tiling was contracted for by the square foot. This work was commenced August, 1892. The Durham system of wrought iron with screw joints and special fittings was used throughout for the pipe work. Each wing and the center building were provided with 8-inch galvanized-steel pipes suspended by iron straps in the brick sewer. Additional support was given this main by the branch lines which passed through and rested upon the brickwork of the sewer. Each of the main lines ran to a point beyond the trap of the sewer, and had a running trap of its own, with a fresh-air inlet on its upper side. In the Senate wing the 8-inch pipe continues to a point inside the main west wall of the building, where it receives a 6-inch branch which drains a large number of fixtures; beyond this point the pipe is reduced to 6-inch and later to 5-inch pipe. The main pipe in the center building and south wing are reduced in the same manner, in proportion to the waste matter which they receive. All the piping below the floor or in the cellar is of steel galvanized, and all exposed or accessible above the basement floor, continuing to the open ends above the roof, is of brass with screw joints. Where these pipes are visible they are run in single lengths, nickel-plated, and polished. Below the cellar floor the pipes were tested by hydraulic pressure and above the floor by pneumatic pressure of 10 pounds to the inch. All pipes which receive foul matter are extended full size to the roof, at which point they are enlarged and carried through the roof. Siphon (Dececo) closets were used. Grease traps were put on all sinks and anti-siphon traps on all other fixtures. No back venting was used in connection with the system. The following number of fixtures were put in: Wash basins, 174; bidets, 2; water-closets, 87; sinks, 25; urinals, 41; corridor sinks, 20; bath tubs, 16; drinking fountains, 4; needle bath, 1; cellar-floor sinks, 41; vapor baths, 16; ice-box connections, 5. The work was completed October 1, 1893.[22]

Repairs to and alterations of the Capitol have been continuously made, and will be so long as the nation lives and grows. When such alterations cease the nation will be on the decline.

Among the first changes introduced was the substitution of hot-air furnaces in place of open fireplaces in the old building, before the extension was commenced. These furnaces were gradually replaced by a steam heating apparatus. When the Library on the west was remodeled steam was put in this portion.

B. B. French, Commissioner of Public Buildings and Grounds, suggested, October 13, 1863, the installation of steam coils in place of furnaces to heat the Rotunda. In 1865, when the old Congressional

---

[22] Information on the improvements made in reconstruction of the water, drainage, and sewer system of the Capitol may be found in a letter of July 1, 1893, by George E. Waring, sanitary engineer, reprinted in "Report of the Architect of the United States Capitol to the Secretary of the Interior, 1893" (Washington: Government Printing Office, 1893), 4–5. Waring and John Shaw Billings made reports on the drainage system of the Capitol on May 28 and June 28, 1892. Waring was an agriculturalist, public health official, and author of works on sanitary drainage, street cleaning, and waste disposal. Alexander Crever Abbott, a doctor of science and public health, was professor at the University of Pennsylvania and author of *The Principles of Bacteriology* (1892) and *The Hygiene of Transmissible Diseases* (1899). Waring and Abbott were assisted by John Shaw Billings, author of *Principles of Ventilation and Heating* (1886), who held various surgical posts in the United States Army from 1862 until his retirement in 1895. He was also a professor of hygiene at the University of Pennsylvania (1891), and was in charge of vital and social statistics for the Tenth Census (1890) and Eleventh Census (1900). Matthew C. Butler of South Carolina, Democratic senator, 1877–1895, submitted a resolution March 21, 1862, authorizing the Committee on Public Buildings and Grounds to select two expert architects to make a thorough examination of the sanitary condition of the Capitol. The resolution was agreed to on March 22, 1892. The committee's report was submitted July 5, 1892 by George G. Vest of Missouri, Democratic senator, 1879–1903, and chairman of the Committee on Public Buildings and Grounds in the Fifty-third Congress.

Library was enlarged on the north and south, the space was heated by steam. In 1867 the furnaces were removed from beneath the room occupied by the Court of Claims and the passages and halls of the sub-basement of the old building and steam introduced in their place. A similar change in the heating apparatus followed in the old Hall of Representatives and part of the Rotunda in 1869. In 1870 it was added to the northern half of the Rotunda and six committee rooms. Thus this gradual substitution of steam heat was carried on. Steam heating apparatus was placed in the galleries of the Supreme Court room in 1874. In 1876 the furnaces were all removed.

The roof of the old building, as well as of the extensions, was constantly causing trouble because of leakage in the covering, gutters, and skylights, necessitating almost yearly repairs from the beginning of the work to the present time. Another cause of constant change in the arrangement and fitting up of rooms in the Capitol has been the change of occupants and the increase of membership of the House, Senate, and Supreme Court, with the constant increase of committees, officials, and clerks. After the first session in the new House, the following resolution was passed: "The Superintendent of the Capitol Extension is directed, after the adjournment of the present session of Congress, to remove the desks from the House and make such a rearrangement of the seats of members as to bring them within the smallest convenient space." [23] To carry out this resolution it was necessary to reconstruct the floor and heat flues beneath the floor. New seats were arranged in concentric circles with aisles radiating from the Speaker's desk.

The report of John B. Blake, Commissioner of Public Buildings and Grounds, November 16, 1860, shows that the old Senate Chamber was converted into a court room for the Supreme Court, the principal features being preserved; at the same time the Supreme Court room was fitted for a Law Library, the two being connected by a private stairway. [24]

During this year two rooms were fitted up for the Court of Claims, and the naval monument was removed to Annapolis from its position at the head of the stairway on the west front of the Capitol.

In the years 1865 to 1867 the Library was extended so as to occupy all the west extension above the basement floor, and the old Hall of Representatives was retiled with marble. [25]

During the year 1870 the stone stairway at the northeast corner of the building was taken out, the space in the basement being connected with the Law Library and in the principal story fitted up for the Attorney-General. [26]

The depressed floor leading from the Rotunda to the old Hall of Representatives (Statuary Hall) was not raised to a level with the other floors until 1871. [27]

The roofs and many of the partitions of the old building were of wooden construction when the Library was remodeled after the fire in 1851. This portion of the building was rebuilt of noncombustible material, and on its further extension in 1865 the fireproofing was carried on with the improvement. With few exceptions Mr. Clark has

[23] Members complained that the House Chamber was too large and that they had to struggle to be heard. Benches replaced desks and chairs as a temporary measure in 1860. Some of this furniture is now in the Rotunda.

[24] See "Report of the Commissioner of Public Buildings," in *Report of the Secretary of the Interior,* S. ex. doc. 2 (36–1), Serial 1023, 840–49.

[25] The floor of the House of Representatives was retiled in 1864. See "Annual Report of the Architect of the United States Capitol" [For the Fiscal Year Ended 30 June, 1865, 1866, and 1867], 3–5.

[26] "Annual Report of the Architect of the United States Capitol Extension" [For the Fiscal Year Ended 30 June, 1870], 3.

[27] "Annual Report of the Architect of the United States Capitol" [For the Fiscal Year Ended 30 June, 1871], 3–4.

recommended in each of his reports since 1873 fireproofing the whole of the old central building, taking occasion whenever improvements are made to fireproof the portion which is undergoing change.[28]

By act of May 3, 1881, the gallery of the old House was made fireproof by removing the old wooden floor and joists and replacing them with brick and iron. The rooms beneath were fitted up as a document library.[29] During the same year the north part of the old building was reconstructed of noncombustible material as a document room for the Senate, and an iron stairway substituted for the wooden one. In the years 1883 and 1884 the roof of the colonnade in the old Hall of Representatives was made fireproof. The semicircular timber partition in the rear was removed and replaced by brick, and the timber ceiling was taken down and replaced by iron beams and brick arches, and the space fitted up with bookshelves. In the same years brick partitions were built in the crypt to accommodate the overflow from the Library.

In 1892 the Senate kitchen was extended under the pavement of the open court, and this, with the old apartment, was incased with glazed tile and brick and the whole supplied with an improved cooking outfit.[30] Coal vaults having a capacity of 800 tons were built under the pavement and the grass plat on the east of the building. The House restaurant was not enlarged until 1896.[31]

On September 18, 1893, one hundred years after the corner stone of the original building was laid by George Washington, the centennial anniversary of that event was commemorated. The event was ushered in by all the bells of the city ringing centennial chimes. The procession moved from the Executive Mansion, with President Grover Cleveland escorted by orators, committees, distinguished guests, and United States and National Guard cavalry. Having the place of honor, next in line came Alexandria-Washington Lodge, No. 22, of Masons, from Alexandria, the lodge which had performed the Masonic ceremonies one hundred years before. Other Masonic and secret orders followed. Then came the different societies of the Revolution and Colonial Wars. These were followed by United States, District of Columbia, and Virginia troops and the procession of firemen from Washington and other cities.

A few minutes before 2 o'clock the United States Senate, preceded by its President, Sergeant-at-Arms, Secretary, and Doorkeeper, passed through the Rotunda to the grand stand on the east central portico. They were followed by the House of Representatives, preceded by the Speaker, Clerk, Sergeant-at-Arms, and Doorkeeper. When the members of the House had been seated President Cleveland was escorted to the platform by the Joint Committee of Congress.

The Right Rev. William Pinkney, bishop of Maryland, invoked the blessing of God upon the United States, after which a chorus of 1,500 voices, accompanied by the Marine Band, sang the "Te Deum." President Cleveland made a short address and William Wirt Henry made an elaborate oration. After this oration the chorus sang "The Star Spangled Banner."

Vice-President Stevenson, on behalf of the Senate, Speaker C. F. Crisp, on behalf of the House of Representatives, and Justice

[28] "Annual Report of the Architect of the United States Capitol" [For the Fiscal Year Ended 30 June, 1873], 3–4.

[29] "An Act Making Appropriations for Sundry Civil Expenses of the Government, for the Fiscal Year Ending June 30th, 1882, and for Other Purposes," 46th Cong., 3rd sess., in United States Statutes at Large, vol. 21, 449.

[30] Report of the Architect of the United States Capitol to the Secretary of the Interior, 1893 (Washington: Government Printing Office, 1893), 3.

[31] Report of the Architect of the United States Capitol to the Secretary of the Interior, 1896 (Washington: Government Printing Office, 1896), 3–4.

Henry Billings Brown, on behalf of the Supreme Court, made addresses. After addresses made by members of the committee the ceremonies closed by the singing of "America" by the chorus and thousands of the spectators.[32]

A bronze tablet was placed on the southeast corner of the old Senate wing to commemorate this event, being above the point where the original corner stone was laid.[33] The following inscription was placed upon the tablet:

Beneath this tablet the corner stone of
the Capitol of the United States of America
was laid by

GEORGE WASHINGTON,

First President, September 8, 1793.
On the Hundredth Anniversary,
In the year 1893,
In the presence of Congress, the Executive and the Judiciary,
and a vast concourse of grateful people of
the District of Columbia commemorated the event.
Grover Cleveland, President of the United States.
Adlai Ewing Stevenson, Vice-President.
Charles Frederick Crisp, Speaker of the House of Representatives.
Daniel Wolsey Voorhees, Chairman of Committee of Congress.
Lawrence Gardner, Chairman Citizens' Committee.

By virtue of an act approved June 11, 1896, S. H. Woodbridge designed alterations in the heating and ventilating apparatus of the Senate wing of the Capitol.[34] This work was carried into execution during the year 1897. The entire woodwork of the Senate Chamber floor and gallery was removed and replaced by light iron framework, which was covered with an air-tight wooden floor. The space beneath the Senate and gallery floors was made into a plenum chamber. From these chambers the air was forced out at high velocities near the occupant of each desk, at points around the perimeter of the chamber, near the President's desk, and through the chair supports in the galleries. The high velocity of the air was reduced where it entered the chamber by large diffusing surfaces, 100 square inches being allowed for each.

---

[32] For contemporary newspaper accounts of the centennial celebrations, see "A Century: The Capitol's Celebration Today," *The Evening Star* [Washington, D.C.], September 18, 1893, 1–2; "One Century Gone: The Capitol's Centennial Fittingly Celebrated," *The Washington Post*, September 19, 1893, 1–2; and "Reviewing a Century Past: Much Oratory and Music at the Capitol Building," *The Washington Post*, September 19, 1893, 1; 5; 7.

[33] "Joint Resolution Providing for the Placing of a Tablet Upon the Capitol to Commemorate the Laying of the Corner Stone of the Building September 18, 1793," 53rd Cong., 2nd sess., in "An Act Making Appropriations for Sundry Civil Expenses of the Government for the Fiscal Year Ending June 30, 1895, and for Other Purposes," in *United States Statutes at Large,* vol. 28, 581–582. A stone believed to be the cornerstone has recently been found located on the southeast corner of the South wing (Old House of Representatives, now Statuary Hall), which would be the southeast corner of the Old Capitol building.

[34] "An Act Making Appropriations for Sundry Civil Expenses of the Government for the Fiscal Year Ending June 30, 1897, and for Other Purposes," 54th Cong., 1st sess., in *United States Statutes at Large,* vol. 29, 432.

CHAPTER XIV

THE HEATING AND VENTILATING OF THE CAPITOL

ANY members of Congress, as might be expected of so many men of different temperaments and in such different physical conditions, found the warming and ventilating apparatus as first devised unsatisfactory.

As early as 1854, because of complaints of overheating in some portions of the building and drafts in other portions, Captain Meigs made an effort to rectify the trouble in this respect.[1] With this purpose in view the register under each desk was supplied with diffusing boxes and valves so that each member could regulate the heat according to his personal feeling. Deflectors were put in front of all wall registers in the Senate, openings in the risers of steps were removed, and a small circular register was put under each Senator's desk. Mr. Walter, after his duties ceased as Architect, made a report, May 6, 1866, upon the heating of the building.[2] In this report a brief account of the heating apparatus is given, with a clear description of the method adopted in heating and ventilating the Capitol wings. The fresh air was drawn in by large fans and forced into chambers and through steam coils, whence it was carried by ducts to the Halls of Congress, passageways, and committee rooms. Four fans were used, one for each Hall of Congress and one for the committee rooms and hallways in each wing. The supply was drawn from the side wings on the west of the corridors connecting with the old building and at the level of the terraces; this entrance, being shut out from the street, was supposed to be free from dust. The registers in the Halls of Congress were located in the floor and distributed over the surface.

The objections raised to the effectiveness of the ventilating system were first put in concrete form by a joint committee of the two Houses on ventilation, February 20, 1865.[3] Mr. Buckalew, who was chairman of this committee, stated that under the appropriation act of July 2, 1864, plans had been obtained for proposed changes in heating and ventilation. These plans were made by Charles F. Anderson, who has been mentioned before as one of the competitors for the extension of the Capitol.[4] His report named as defects in the existing arrangements the location of the air inlets near the ground and street level, where dust and dirt were taken into the circulation, the overheating of the air by the steam, the deficiency of moisture, the registers in floors and dust rising from them, the inequality of temperature, the imperfect removal of air because of the method of outlet in the roofs, and the presence of unnecessary quantities of gas in the Chambers. The committee approved of the suggestions and made the report a part of the committee report. The changes suggested were as follows: The air should be brought in through vertical stacks with inlets at a high elevation, from which it was to be conducted, after being warmed, to air spaces in the

---

[1] In 1853 scientists A. D. Bache and Joseph Henry were commissioned to study the heating, ventilating, and acoustics of the Capitol. Meigs accompanied Bache and Henry on their study of major public buildings in northeastern cities and collaborated in the development of modifications to the Capitol. *DHC*, 587–588.

[2] Secretary James Harlan, *Report on Warming and Ventilating the Capitol* (Washington: Government Printing Office, 1866).

[3] *Report of the Joint Select Committee on Warming and Ventilating the Capitol*, S. report 128 (38–2), Serial 1211.

[4] Charles F. Anderson, *Architect's Report and Plans for the Improvement of the Lighting, Heating, Ventilation, and Acoustics of the Senate Chamber and Hall of the House of Representatives* (Washington: Government Printing Office, 1864).

roof. Anderson's idea was to force the air into the roof chamber and exhaust it at the floor level. The coils were to be heated by hot water instead of steam, so as to prevent overheating, and the air was to be hydrated by jets of water located in the ducts. To accomplish this proposed modification it was necessary to elevate the ceilings about 15 feet, make the roof double, and insert windows around the upper part of the Halls, making a clerestory. Anderson calls attention to the fact that Meigs adopted the down-draft system in 1853 and then abandoned the measure. Anderson accompanied his report with twenty drawings and estimates for the proposed changes.

Thomas U. Walter, in the above-mentioned report to James Harlan, Secretary of the Interior, includes reports from Prof. Joseph Henry and Dr. Charles M. Wetherell, of the Smithsonian Institution. The latter gives an exhaustive review of the chemical condition of air, temperature, hygrometric condition, air currents, and a bibliography, with extracts bearing upon the subject of ventilation. Mr. Walter describes the plan of heating as given previously in these pages. The examination of the scientists led them to report that the means provided for a supply of warm and pure air were ample, and they agreed that the principal cause of complaint was a deficiency of moisture.[5]

After a careful investigation Mr. Buckalew's committee reported everything in a satisfactory condition, with the exception of the absence of any method of charging the air with moisture, which Professor Henry considered of great importance and probably the cause of the disagreeable effects of which the members complained. He recommended steps to be taken to rectify this fault. The dissatisfaction of the Congressmen continued, and various schemes and plans have been submitted from that period to the present time, some for simple devices to overcome special defects, as well as plans for a complete revision of the system.

June 20, 1868, Mr. Covode, chairman of the Committee on Public Buildings and Grounds, made a report under the following resolution of Congress:

"Whereas the confined and poisonous air of the Hall and corridors of the Representatives' wing of the Capitol has caused much sickness and even deaths among the members of the House, and under present arrangements must continue to remain in a poisonous condition:

"*Resolved*, That the Committee on Public Buildings and Grounds be directed to examine at once and report to the House by what means a sufficient supply of pure air may be obtained for said Hall, and that the committee be empowered to use the present means of ventilation to the best advantage at present, and that they report by bill or otherwise."[6]

This committee authorized an investigation by Gen. Hermann Haupt, chief engineer of the Pennsylvania Railroad, and Lewis W. Leeds, a specialist in heating and ventilating, and ended with a recommendation that someone of ability and experience be employed to further examine and report upon the subject. General Haupt proposed an inlet for fresh air at the level of the gallery, with a forced ventilation, and no outlets at the ceiling, but outlets in the floor, thus making a plenum chamber of the Hall, with the necessary exit of foul air at the floor level. He contended that the heated air which was let into the Chamber at the floor simply passed through the Hall and out at the ceiling without carrying the carbonic-acid gas with it, but leaving this product at or near the floor level or point of breathing. Mr. Leeds agreed with the idea of having the outlet for vitiated air at the floor, but thought a certain amount of radiant heat was necessary, and proposed open fires in connection with the apparatus for supplying heated air. He called attention to the fact that the inlets in the floor were more or less contaminated by the refuse tobacco and spittle which had accumulated in them, and the

---

[5] Harlan, *Report on Warming and Ventilating the Capitol.*

[6] Committee on Public Buildings and Grounds, H. report 65 (39–3), Serial 1358.

air which came into the room was offensive from that cause; therefore he made this a plea for abolishing the inlets in the floor.[7]

Among suggested changes may be mentioned one of A. J. Marshall, July 28, 1868, who proposed to take the air in through high towers, keep it under compression in an air chamber in the roof, and this pressure was to force it out of the Hall at registers in the floors. He commends this system as being part of the scheme which was advocated by C. F. Anderson.[8]

William Loughbridge, June 23, 1870, proposed to have a plenum chamber under the Speaker's desk, and from this point by radial ducts to conduct the heated air to each desk, and have registers in the faces of the desks, with open glass panels in the ceiling for hot air. Each desk was to be provided with deflectors, so that the members could deflect the hot air along the floor or on their person at will.

March 3, 1871, Mr. Jenckes, chairman of a select committee, made a report stating that several committees had investigated the subject and that many reports had been made, "but their investigations and the elaborate reports which followed them have led to nothing substantial in the way of improving the condition of the two Halls. The evils were felt and admitted, but the plans which were proposed for removing them did not meet the approbation of either House." [9] This report makes a careful review of the whole subject. Chairman Jenckes expresses his surprise at the conflicting views of the many engineers, experts, and committees, as well as the oddities which had been submitted to Congress for approval. Among the many suggestions presented, the following is worthy of mention: The plan suggested by Lavan C. Stiners required the remodeling of the building from foundation to roof, and in case a new building was to

---

[7] Ibid.

[8] *Memorial on Ventilation of the Halls of Congress*, S. doc. 110 (40–2), Serial 1319.

[9] See *Report on Lighting of the Capitol*, H. report 48 (41–3), Serial 1464.

be constructed the committee thought it probable that his scheme might receive favorable consideration. They did not think it could be installed for a less sum than $1,100,000.

This committee found that the greatest obstacle to an even temperature was the construction of the roof. The roof had an area of over 17,000 square feet. About 4,000 square feet of this area was glass, while the remaining portions were of copper three-sixteenths of an inch, corrugated, and fitted loosely together where they lapped; the expansion and contraction of these plates left open fissures for nearly the whole area of the roof, through which streams of cold air had access to the space between the roof and the ceiling. This cold air chilled the Chamber into and from which the hot air was expected to pass and caused down currents to the floor of the House.

The committee caused a fireproof ceiling to be placed a few inches below the roof, and the effects of the downward currents were almost, if not completely, stopped. By using grate fires in the cloakrooms in connection with the changes suggested below the committee felt that the heating would be all that could be desired.

The defects in ventilation they found consisted in the difference between the theory that the air forced in at the registers would pass out through the roof, heating and carrying with it all the foul air of the room, and the fact that the currents of warm air passed up directly to the roof, leaving the foul air. At the same time the downward currents from the cold roof also prevented the foul air from passing off. These down currents were particularly perceptible in the central portion under the glass ceiling and over the heads of the members. The registers were in the floors in a horizontal position, across the Hall, scattered between the desks and under the feet of the members, and unavoidably became the receptacle for the dust and dirt which was driven out into the Chamber as soon as the fans were operated. This dust caused much irritation and coughing among the members.

No means were employed to moisten the overheated air from the coils. The cloakrooms with no ventilation, the great difference in the audiences of the Hall, and the effect of sun and cold on the roof are mentioned as disturbing elements in securing proper ventilation. The committee would not recommend radical changes, as it seemed by no means certain that the plans suggested would be successful when applied to halls of such magnitude as those under consideration. They recommended that the foul air be drawn from the space between the roof and ceiling, thus causing a vacuum and drawing out the foul air at the ceiling. A flue, already in existence, they thought could be utilized, which, with an additional flue which could be built, would give a sufficient area for the purpose. A similar plan had been adopted for the Senate Chamber with marked success. Ducts were to be arranged under the floors, and registers to be inserted in the steps in a vertical position. This plan had also been introduced in the Senate with successful results. Open fires were recommended for cloakrooms, and ventilating ducts for the gas, while exhaust ducts were to be placed in the cloakroom chimneys from the galleries. Similar ducts were recommended for the Senate Chamber. The suggested changes were made, with a marked improvement in the effect.

To improve the fresh-air supply of the House of Representatives, two large air flues were constructed, during the year 1876, leading to the men's gallery and opening into boxes under the seats. The fronts and sides of the seats in the gallery were perforated so as to distribute the air evenly over the total area.[10] During this year Joseph Henry, Thomas Lincoln Casey, Edward Clark, F. Schumann, and John S. Billings were appointed as a Commission to consider the subject of ventilation. The report of this Commission, printed in connection with the report of the Architect of the Capitol, October, 1877, makes the following recommendations: They do not think it desirable to change the present upward system of ventilation, and do not consider it possible to obtain natural ventilation by means of windows. While they consider the fresh-air supply sufficient for ordinary conditions, they think that it should be increased so as to be ample for extraordinary conditions. They recommend a large increase of fresh air to the galleries and the substitution of galvanized-iron flues for the brick flues under the floor, as well as a duct leading to a tower in the grounds which should be 30 feet high, through which the fresh-air supply should be taken. They urgently recommend a method of moistening and cooling the air before it is introduced into the Hall, as well as an additional supply of air for the upper lobbies. They also recommend that outlets in the roof should be arranged so that the wind would not affect the outflow of air; that electric signals be placed between floor and engine room; that the heating and ventilation be placed under one man, and that the person who is to have charge of construction and the work after completion should be one of the above Commission.[11]

To carry out the suggestions of the Commission, Robert Briggs was employed, and during the years 1877 to 1879 the following changes were made in the heating and ventilating system:

A fresh-air inlet or duct was built running to the principal fan from the inlet tower, located at a point 200 feet west of the Capitol.[12] The ducts leading from the fan were changed, and a large delivery main was constructed from the fan to a point near the center of the wing, where one of the central rooms was changed into a heating chamber. The air, after passing through the heating coils, was forced into a moistening and dust-cleansing chamber. Two ducts led upward through the

---

[10] "Annual Report of the Architect of the United States Capitol" [For the Fiscal Year Ended 30 June, 1876], 755.

[11] "Annual Report of the Architect of the United States Capitol" [For the Fiscal Year Ended 30 June, 1877], 3–5.

[12] Two inlet towers for ventilating the Capitol were built and remain on the west front grounds.

basement story to different parts of the hall on each side of the central Hall, where they ended in inclosed chambers. From these chambers the air passed into circular ducts directly under the desks, while others led into the space behind the desks. Separate ducts took the air to the galleries. The distributing branches to the space beneath the seats were made of sheet iron and controlled by dampers.

The ducts were increased to the following dimensions:

	Square feet
Principal supply duct	120
Delivery duct	80
Main duct to Hall	40
South gallery duct	14
North gallery duct	7

The area for the exit of the foul air in the attic was increased by the construction of a large louver with an area of 140 square feet.

The old steam coils were reconstructed and made into four sections, containing 45,000 feet of radiating surface and made of 1-inch pipe. The sections were placed in the lower part of the heating chamber and inclosed by sheet-iron coverings, separating them from the upper portion. The entrance of the air into this chamber was controlled by a louver partition; by opening the lower slats and closing the upper ones, the air passed through the coils and by opening the upper slats and closing the lower ones, the air passed over the coils without being heated, except to a very moderate degree.

In the moistening and cleansing chamber both steam and water jets were placed, through which the air could be forced. Around this chamber a passageway was arranged, so that the air, when desired, could be passed directly to the points of distribution without being charged with moisture.

The air entered the Hall as it formerly did through perforations in the risers of steps, various registers being placed around the Speaker's desk and large registers retained in the corners of the Hall, in the space beyond the desks. During the year 1880 the registers were enlarged.[13]

In the report of the Architect of October 1, 1881, he states that the result of the changes in the heating and ventilating system had proved very satisfactory with the exception of a deficiency in the moisture of the air. The changes left no perceptible drafts, and only a variation of 1° was noticed in different portions of the Hall. The conditions remained satisfactory throughout the year 1883.[14]

Additions were made to the inlets and outlets of the Senate in 1885. In 1889 the heating apparatus was reported as still working satisfactorily. In 1890 a tower for the fresh-air inlet to the Senate was built 400 feet west of the Senate wing.[15]

The Senators in 1896 determined to completely remodel the heating and ventilating system of the Senate wing, and by act approved June 11, 1896, authorized alterations of the apparatus according to plans made by S. H. Woodbridge. The changes were made during the years 1896 and 1897.[16]

---

[13] "Annual Report of the Architect of the United States Capitol" [For the Fiscal Year Ended 30 June, 1880], 3.

[14] "Annual Report of the Architect of the United States Capitol" [For the Fiscal Year Ended 30 June, 1881 and 1883], 4–5.

[15] "Annual Report of the Architect of the United States Capitol" [For the Fiscal Year Ended 30 June, 1885 and 1890], 3–4.

[16] "An Act Making Appropriations for Sundry Civil Expenses of the Government for the Fiscal Year Ending June 30, 1897, and for Other Purposes," 54th Cong., 1st sess., in *United States Statutes At Large,* vol. 29, 433. See also "Annual Report of the Architect of the United States Capitol" [For the Fiscal Year Ended 30 June, 1897], 3–6, especially the appendix by Professor S. H. Woodbridge, "Report Rendered on the Material Furnished for and Labor Performed in Improving the Ventilation of the Senate Wing of the United States Capitol, Under the Appropriation Made Therefor June, 1887," 25–26. Improvement of the ventilation of the Capitol remained a recurrent issue with the members of Congress until the introduction of modern air-conditioning systems in 1935–36. For a discussion of the effects of summer heat on the deliberations of Congress before and after the introduction

The entire woodwork of the Senate Chamber and gallery floors was removed, and replaced by an iron framework on which were laid substantial wooden floors with air and dust proof joints.

These floors were made tight enough to make two plenum chambers, one in the space beneath the Senate Chamber floor and another under the gallery floor. The air is forced into the Chamber through registers at a high velocity near the seat of each Senator, at various points on the perimeter of the Chamber, near the President's desk, and in the galleries. The velocity of the incoming air is reduced where it enters the Chamber by large diffusing surfaces, the area of the openings being 100 square inches for each Senator's desk, 120 square inches for each desk-leg diffuser, and the same for the chair-leg diffusers in the galleries. These openings are all placed in a vertical position, so that it is difficult for them to become receptacles for dust and dirt. The total area of the openings is 169 square feet for the floor of the Senate and 600 square feet for the gallery.

The openings in the central portion of the ceiling were closed, and openings were made in the perimeter of the Senate Chamber, near the ceiling, with the object of preventing downward drafts in the center of the Chamber. The air passes out over the galleries through areas smaller than the areas of the inlets. The old iron and wood fan was replaced by a light steel fan, which delivers 35,000 cubic feet of air per minute when making 125 revolutions a minute, and 48,000 cubic feet per minute when making 150 revolutions a minute. The old battery of steam coils was replaced by four batteries containing 23,000 square feet

of surface each. Two of these coils are intended for steam only, one for steam in winter and refrigerating brine in summer, and one for refrigerating brine exclusively.

The air is led to the Senate Chamber and to the galleries by separate ducts or channels, from different coils, so that the air to the galleries may be heated to a greater temperature than that to the Chamber floor; this provision is intended to prevent a downward draft.

In the attic space above the ceiling steam coils have been located in sections to equalize the temperature in this space. This is intended particularly for night use, when the Chamber is usually cool and has a tendency to downward currents. A thermophone gives the engineer in the basement the temperature of the attic. The air is removed from the roof space by an 8-foot inverted Blackman wheel fan run by a direct-connected electric motor with 130 revolutions a minute. The Senate coat rooms, which were supposed to be ventilated by registers in the ceilings with ducts terminating under the galleries, were found to contain an inadequate amount of fresh air. The ducts were extended to the space above the corridors, where they were connected with fans which are capable of withdrawing 800 to 1,000 cubic feet of air per minute from each room.

Arrangements were made to heat and ventilate the corridors and committee rooms, with 35,000 feet of cubic air per minute, by installing a new 10-foot fan and tempering coils to heat the air to 65°. The air is then forced to the stacks at the base of flues which were intended to run to one direct outlet, but in many cases it was found upon investigation that the coils were connected with the flues of several rooms. In the new arrangement the ducts were so arranged that the air could be forced through these coils or be allowed to pass around them, in all cases depending upon the temperature desired in the rooms.

The old apparatus in the Supreme Court room was also completely remodeled. A new fan was put in capable of supplying 15,000 cubic feet

of air conditioning, see "Cooler Air and Longer Sessions: Air Conditioning Keeps Congress on Job," *Heating, Piping & Air Conditioning* 18 (October 1946): 76–77; for a description of the project, see "Cooling Congress: Capitol, Senate, and House Office Buildings Air Conditioned," *Architectural Forum* 67 (July 1937): 82.

of air per minute, the air entering the room at various points through diffusing and baffling surfaces so as to prevent unpleasant drafts.

The kitchen and toilet rooms were also rearranged so as to obtain better ventilation.

Pneumatic steam valves were placed so as to govern the temperature in different portions of the Senate wing and Supreme Court section, by the automatic operation of thermostats which were placed in different parts of the Senate rooms and halls.

By means of a thermophone the temperature is indicated in the corridor tunnel, committee-room and Senate fan chambers, plenum chamber beneath the Senate on both the north and south sides, plenum chamber of the north and south galleries, also in the north and south galleries and Senate Chamber attic. Pneumatic steam valves are operated automatically from all these points, controlling the heat according to the adjustment of the apparatus.

In the engineer's room are placed rheostats for starting and stopping the various fans, as well as meters to indicate the power and rate of current on each fan. Charts show the speed and volume of air delivered by the various fans.

Mr. Woodbridge recommends, in his report of 1897, that all flues from corridors be run in galvanized-iron ducts to an exhaust chamber, where the air would be withdrawn by an exhaust fan.

CHAPTER XV

ELEVATORS AND LIGHTING

THE addition of and experiments with such modern appliances as elevators and electric lights, so as to add to the convenience of occupants of the Capitol, form an interesting part of the history of this structure. A "noiseless" screw elevator was the first form adopted. It was so noisy that the contractor changed it in 1874 to an ordinary cable elevator. In 1876 this was taken out and a hydraulic elevator substituted, and in 1877 a hydraulic elevator was placed in the Senate wing.[1] Judging from the reports the first elevators were simply for freight purposes, as the first passenger elevator (hydraulic) was put in the south wing in 1882, at the end of the east corridor, as provided for in the act of May 3, 1881.[2] During the same year a warehouse lift was placed in the Senate wing for the purpose of conveying documents to the folding room in the basement. In 1883 a sidewalk lift was put in to carry documents to the cellar, and a freight lift was put at the north end of the west corridor, both in the Senate wing.[3] In 1887 a contract was made with the Crane Elevator Company

for two additional elevators. In the year 1895 a hydraulic passenger elevator was constructed in the vestibule leading to the Supreme Court room, the eastern elevator in the House wing was changed from a gravity machine to one operated by a pressure tank, and the western elevator in the same wing was extended to the cellar. In 1898 the elevator to the Supreme Court room was destroyed by an explosion and fire and the system was changed to an electric elevator.[4]

During construction gas pipes were laid throughout the wings for the House and Senate chambers, corridors, and many of the committee rooms. A 10-inch main was laid, with two 8-inch branches for each wing, and two large meters were placed under each connecting corridor. Captain Meigs, in his report of November, 1857, says that the gas company were not able to supply the gas without a new gasometer and advocates the Government making its own gas.[5]

---

[1] "Annual Report of the Architect of the United States Capitol" [For the Fiscal Year Ended 30 June, 1874 and 1876], 753 and 755. A passenger elevator was installed for the senators in 1873. For a discussion of the historical development of elevator service in the Capitol, see *Report of the Architect of the Capitol: Letter from the Architect of the Capitol Transmitting the Annual Report of the Office of the Architect of the Capitol for the Fiscal Year Ended June 30, 1934*, S. doc. 42 (74–1), Serial 9909.

[2] "An Act Making Appropriations for Sundry Civil Expenses of the Government for the Fiscal Year Ending June 30, 1882, and for Other Purposes," 47th Cong., 1st sess., in *United States Statutes at Large*, vol. 21, 449.

[3] The lift was actually installed on the west end of the north corridor, not the north end of the west corridor. "Annual Report of the Architect of the United States Capitol" [For the Fiscal Year Ended 30 June, 1883 and 1887], 3–4.

[4] "Annual Report of the Architect of the United States Capitol" [For the Fiscal Year Ended 30 June, 1895], 3. The explosion and fire occurred on November 6, 1898. See the reports of Glenn Brown and Charles Munroe, in *Annual Report of the Architect of the United States Capitol to the Secretary of the Interior, for the Fiscal Year Ended June 30, 1899* (Washington: Government Printing Office, 1899), 24–40. For contemporary news accounts, see "Wreck and Ruin: The National Capitol Building Damaged by an Explosion," *The Evening Star,* November 7, 1898, 3; "The Capitol Fire: Assistant Architect Woods Investigating Extent of Disaster," *The Evening Star,* November 8, 1898, 3; "Explosion at the Capitol: Vast Damage Caused in the Center of the Nation's Great Structure," *Washington Post,* November 6, 1898, 1; and "Counting Up the Cost: Extent of the Damage Caused by the Capitol Fire," *Washington Post,* November 8, 1898, 2.

[5] Captain of Engineers in Charge of the U.S. Capitol Extension, "Report on Capitol Extension, Reconstruction of Dome, and Post Office Extension," in *Message of the President of the United States to the Two Houses of Congress at the Commencement of the First Session of the Thirty-fifth Congress* (Washington: Government Printing Office, 1858), 40–47.

In 1864 arrangements were made for introducing Garden's magnetic gas-lighting apparatus, which was installed in 1865, and March 2, 1867, the Rotunda was lighted by gas ignited by electric current.[6]

In the year 1878 a Commission was appointed to investigate the question of lighting the building by electricity. In 1880 I. H. Rogers, who had charge of the electric gas lighting in the Capitol, made experiments on the different patented electric lights and reported that he did not consider them steady enough for lighting a legislative hall. The report of 1881 shows the electric lights still unsatisfactory. A. B. Talcott was appointed electrician of the House in 1882. In the year 1884 the United States Electric Lighting Company, at their own cost, were allowed to install arc lamps at the top of the steps of the north, south, and west approaches; and the Brush-Swann Company were allowed to place in the Dome experimental lamps which they thought would illuminate the grounds and avenues around the Capitol. The Edison Company were allowed, in 1885, to place incandescent lamps in the cloak rooms and lobbies and on the stairways. The arc lamps were found objectionable because they attracted such a large number of insects around the building. In 1886 the incandescent lamps placed in the cloak rooms and lobbies were found to be very much superior to gas, which had been previously used for lighting these apartments. In the year 1888 the Sawyer-Man Electric Company, through Royce & Marean, were given permission to install, at their own expense, 200 lamps in the House wing and 650 lamps in the Senate wing, by act of August 4, 1886.[7] Many of these lights were in use during the year 1888 and proved so satisfactory that the Committee on Public Buildings and Grounds was authorized to investigate the subject of lighting the building by electricity. The use of electric lighting proved so satisfactory that arrangements were made in 1895 to purchase the electric plants in the Capitol, as authorized by the acts of March 3, 1893, and March 2, 1895.[8] A contract was made with the Westinghouse Company in which they agreed to take out all engines and dynamos of the original plant and replace them with modern low-tension machines, consisting of four direct-connected engines and dynamos, with a capacity of 1,250 16-candlepower lamps each. Electric lights replaced gas in the space over the ceilings of the House and the Senate in 1897. The heat caused by the gas lighting in the Senate Chamber was so great that in cold weather the difference in temperature between the inside and outside caused the glass in the skylights to crack. The use of electric lights was found to remedy this defect. During this year a contract to light the grounds by electricity was carried out, and electric fans were installed in the kitchen and toilet rooms to carry off disagreeable odors.[9]

---

[6] Gardnier's (not Garden) apparatus was installed, tested, and lit in 1865–66. "Report of the Commissioner of Public Buildings," in *Report of the Secretary of the Interior,* H. ex. doc. 1 (39–2), Serial 1284; "Report of the Architect of the Capitol Extension," in *Report of the Secretary of the Interior,* H. ex. doc. 1 (39–1), Serial 1248.

[7] An Act Making Appropriations for Sundry Civil Expenses of the Government for the Fiscal Year Ending June 30, 1887, and for Other Purposes," 49th Cong., 1st sess., in *United States Statutes at Large,* vol. 24, 239.

[8] An Act Making Appropriations for Sundry Civil Expenses of the Government for the Fiscal Year Ending June 30, 1894, and for Other Purposes," 52nd Cong., 2nd sess., in *United States Statutes at Large,* vol. 27, 591; "An Act Making Appropriations for Sundry Civil Expenses of the Government for the Fiscal Year Ending June 30, 1896, and for Other Purposes," 53rd Cong., 3rd sess., in *United States Statutes at Large,* vol. 28, 935.

[9] "Annual Report of the Architect of the United States Capitol" [For the Fiscal Year Ended 30 June, 1897], 7–8.

PLATE 220

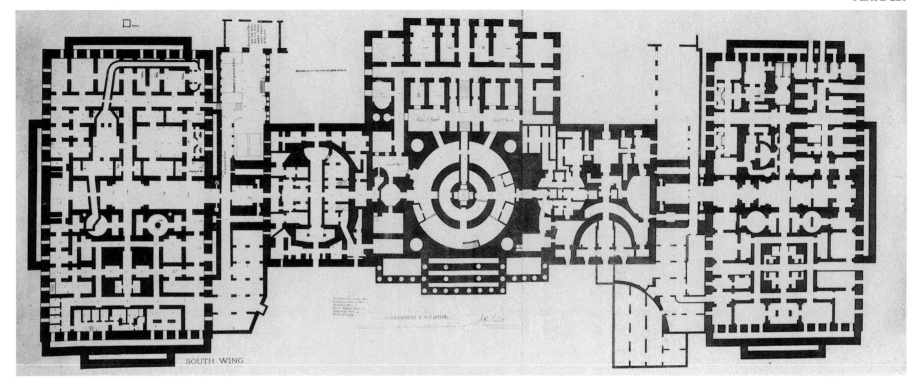

THE BUILDING AS COMPLETED, CELLAR PLAN.

Plan of the current basement level produced under the direction of J. E. Powell, electrical engineer, Treasury Department, 1888. *Location unknown.*

PLATE 221

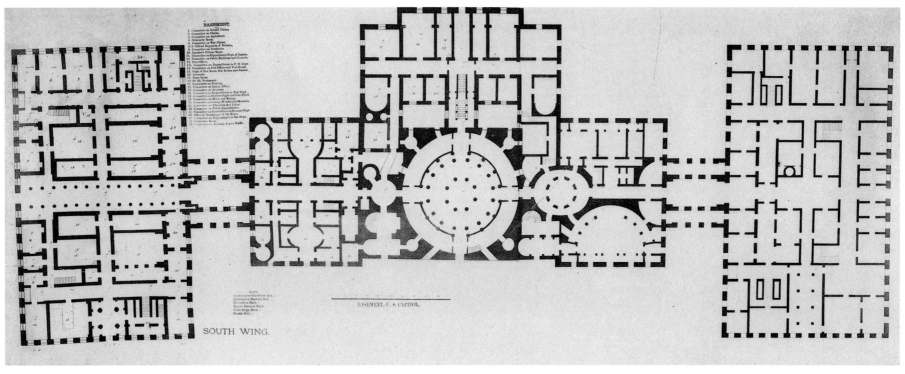

THE BUILDING AS COMPLETED, BASEMENT PLAN.

Plan of the current first floor produced under the direction of J. E. Powell, electrical engineer, Treasury Department, 1888. *Location unknown.*

PLATE 222

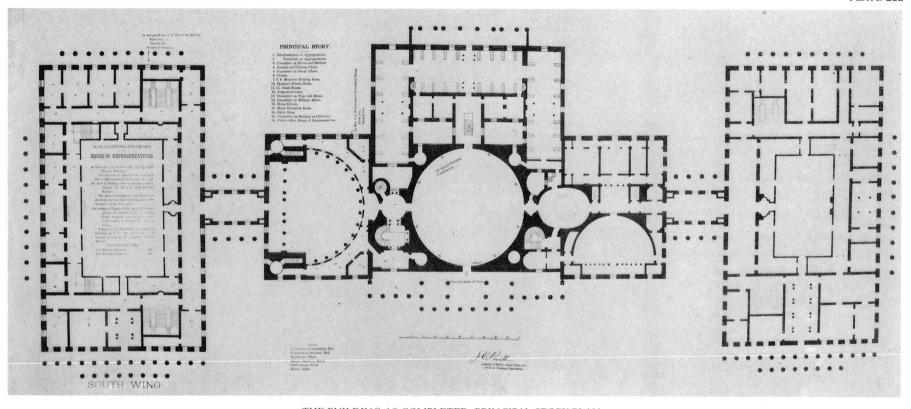

THE BUILDING AS COMPLETED, PRINCIPAL STORY PLAN.

Plan of the second floor produced under the direction of J. E. Powell, electrical engineer, Treasury Department, 1888. *Location unknown.*

PLATE 223

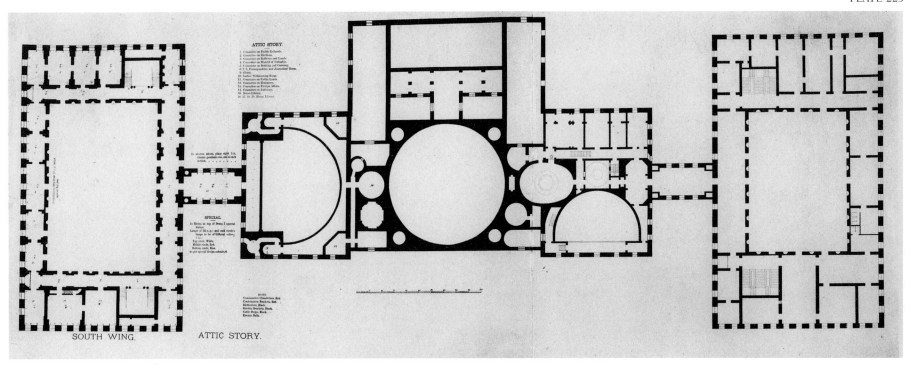

THE BUILDING AS COMPLETED, ATTIC PLAN.

Plan of the third floor produced under the direction of J. E. Powell, electrical engineer, Treasury Department, 1888. *Location unknown.*

PLATE 224

EAST FRONT, AS COMPLETED.

PLATE 225

NORTHEAST VIEW, AS COMPLETED.

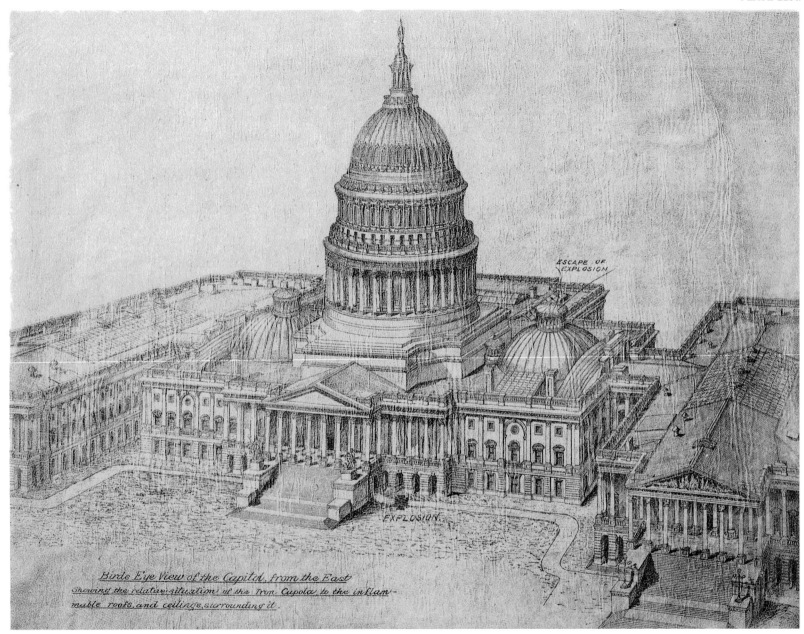

Birds Eye View of the Capital from the East
Showing the relative situation of the Iron Cupola to the inflammable roofs and ceilings surrounding it.

BIRD'S EYE VIEW SHOWING ROOF OF CAPITOL.

Drawing illustrating the area of the Capitol damaged in the 1898 gas explosion. *Location unknown.*

Chapter XVI

The Building as Completed, From Walter's Designs

EDWARD CLARK supervised the completion of the Capitol from the designs of Thomas U. Walter, leaving the building as it stands to-day. The terraces on the west, north, and south are a part of the general landscape scheme of Frederick Law Olmsted. The building consists of the central or old building, and two wings, or the Capitol extension, with the new Dome on the old building.

The cellar [Plate 220] contained space on the central western extension available for office and committee rooms. Other portions of the cellar are given up to the heating and ventilating apparatus, or are used for storage. Beneath the center of the Dome a vault was built in the cellar to contain the remains of George Washington, but because of the objection of the family to his burial in the Capitol his body never rested in the contemplated spot.

The basement story [Plate 221] is above the surface of the ground. The space in this story is utilized by the Supreme Court library, under the old Senate Chamber, the other rooms being divided between the House of Representatives, the Senate, and the Supreme Court, and used by these branches of the Government for committee, office, or storage purposes.

The principal floor [Plate 222] contains the two Halls of Congress, in the center of each wing, with their necessary corridors and approaches, surrounded by lobbies and committee rooms. The Congressional Library was located in the central western extension of the old building. The south wing of the old building, in which was located the old House of Representatives, is thrown into a public hall for the display of statuary, and the north wing is given to the Supreme Court,

the old Senate Chamber being devoted to the court room and the west front being used by the court officials for office and robing rooms.[1]

The attic story [Plate 223] is so arranged in each wing that the public has access from its corridors to the galleries of the House and Senate Chambers, with provision for the press and committee rooms facing the exterior walls of the building. Document rooms are also provided on this floor.

Plates 224, 225, 225a show the eastern front of the building as completed, the principal new features being the porticoes on the wings, which are similar to the central portico designed by Latrobe. Although the original design of Thornton contemplated a central portico he did not contemplate the broad flight of steps which extends to the ground from the principal story, and it is a question of taste whether the original design would not have been more satisfactory, the broad flight of steps leading to a single doorway seeming a useless feature.

The character of the western front has been changed by the marble terrace and steps which replaced the old earth terrace, but the building remains as it was completed [Plates 261–262].

Entrance is obtained to the Senate wing by doorways on the basement story from the north and east. There was formerly an entrance from the west, which has been closed, the end of the hall being utilized as a room. The entrance on the east is into a vestibule [Plate 226] with square

---

[1] The Congressional Library was demolished and committee rooms were created in 1900–01. The old Supreme Court was restored to its historic appearance for the Nation's 1976 bicentennial and is now used as a museum space to interpret the history of the Capitol Building.

white-marble columns, from which spring arches surmounted by domical ceilings. The side walls of this vestibule are paneled in marble.[2] This vestibule opens on the north into a reception room, on the south to the public stairway, and on the west into the principal corridor running east and west. The reception or public room has both side walls and vaulted ceiling painted in oil fresco by Brumidi [Plate 227]. The private hallway of the Senators is a dignified vaulted corridor with walls and ceiling painted in oil fresco by Brumidi.[3] The illustration of this hallway [Plate 228] shows clearly the character of the design adopted in the corridors and hallways, as well as the character of decoration adopted for the wall surface in the basement of the Senate wing of the Capitol.

At the east and west ends of the Senate Chamber are private stairways, with marble steps and elaborate, well modeled, and effective bronze railings, for the use of Senators [Plate 229]. On the south of the basement vestibule is an entrance to one of the principal public stairways. The design of this stairway is similar to the one used on the east and west of the House wing (see Plate 244), and there is a corresponding stairway on the east side of the Senate. In the Senate wing white marble is used in the steps, balustrades, columns, and cornices, as well as in the ceilings over the landings, while on the House side Tennessee marble is used, with bronze capitals to the columns. On the principal floor corridors with arched and vaulted ceilings surround the Senate Chamber on the south, east, and west; these corridors have simply

tinted wall and ceiling surfaces [Plate 230]. On the north of the Senate Chamber is located the Senators' retiring room [Plate 231]. This is an impressive room with paneled walls, a colonnade and pilasters supporting a ceiling, all in white marble. To this room the Senators retire for conversation and the reception of special visitors. On the west of the Senate Chamber is another marble hall with a classical colonnade [Plate 232]. North of the public corridor and west of the Senator's retiring room is the public reception room.[4] This room has a flat domical ceiling resting upon flat elliptical arches [Plate 233]. The frescoing in this room was never completed. Brumidi has painted groups depicting Peace, War, Freedom, Agriculture, and in the corners of the room the virtues Prudence, Justice, Temperance, and Fortitude are represented. The group on the south of the room shows Washington in consultation with two of his first Cabinet officers—Thomas Jefferson, Secretary of State, and Alexander Hamilton, Secretary of the Treasury.

At the west end of the Senators' retiring room is located a room known as the President's room [Plate 234]. This is used by the President upon occasions when his services are required at the Capitol. It is more elaborately furnished and decorated than any room in the Capitol building. On the ceiling corners are fresco portraits of Columbus in the southeast, Americus Vespucius in the northwest, Benjamin Franklin in the southwest, and William Brewster, an elder of Plymouth Colony, in the northeast. The ceiling is decorated by groups representing Religion, Liberty, Executive Authority, and Legislation on the north, south, east, and west, respectively. On the walls are portraits of Washington and his first cabinet—Jefferson, Hamilton, Knox, Randolph, and Osgood.[5]

[2] The east vestibule walls are not marble panels; they have a scagliola finish. RG 40, Subject Files, Curator's Office, AOC.

[3] Brumidi's medium actually was true fresco for the corridor lunettes and room vaults, various mixtures for the walls, and tempera for the corridor ceilings. For information on Brumidi's technique and the recent conservation of his frescoes in the Capitol, see RG 40, Subject Files, Curator's Office, AOC. See also Barbara A. Wolanin, "Constantino Brumidi's Frescoes in the United States Capitol," in Irma B. Jaffe, ed., *The Italian Presence in the United States Capitol, 1760–1860* (New York: Fordham University Press, 1989), 150–164.

[4] In the Senate wing the white marble was from Italy. The Senators' retiring room was finished in Tennessee marble, which has a brownish-red hue. The marble hall and public reception room are located on the east rather than west side of the building. RG 40, Subject Files, Curator's Office, AOC.

[5] This room was also painted by Brumidi. RG 40, Subject Files, Curator's Office, AOC.

PLATE 226

CORRIDOR, BASEMENT NORTH WING.

Today this space is the east elevator lobby (related drawing, plate 216).

PLATE 227

PUBLIC ROOM, NORTH WING, BASEMENT.

The Patent Corridor, one of the Brumidi Corridors, outside the entrance to S–116.

PLATE 228

CORRIDOR BASEMENT, NORTH WING, FRESCOES BY BRUMIDI, PAINTER.

The North Corridor, one of the Brumidi Corridors, looking east toward S–116.

PLATE 229

SENATORS PRIVATE BRONZE STAIRWAY, NORTH WING,—T. U. WALTER ARCHITECT.

Designed by Constantino Brumidi, modeled by Edmond Baudin, and cast by Archer, Warner,
Miskey and Co. of Philadelphia, 1857–59 (related drawing, plate 213).

PLATE 230

SENATE CORRIDOR, PRINCIPAL FLOOR.
View to the west toward S–224.

PLATE 231

SENATE LOBBY OR RECEPTION ROOM.

S–215, the Senators' Retiring Room, also called the Marble Room.

PLATE 232

SENATE CORRIDOR, PRINCIPAL STORY.

View to the west, Senate Chamber doors. The space behind the screen of columns has been infilled with elevators (related drawing, plate 208).

PLATE 233

PUBLIC RECEPTION ROOM, PRINCIPAL STORY, NORTH WING

S–213, the Senate Reception Room.

PLATE 234

THE PRESIDENT'S ROOM, NORTH WING.

S–216. The room's appearance is largely unaltered; the original chandelier and furniture have been retained.

PLATE 235

THE VICE PRESIDENT'S ROOM, NORTH WING.

S–214, now the formal Office of the Vice President. The painting of Washington has been moved
to the restored Old Senate Chamber.

446

PLATE 236

ROOM OF THE SENATE COMMITTEE OF THE DISTRICT OF COLUMBIA.

S–211, now the Lyndon Baines Johnson Room, under the jurisdiction of the Secretary of the Senate.

PLATE 237

NAVAL AND PHILIPPINE COMMITTEES ROOM, SENATE WING.

S–127, now used by the Senate Committee on Appropriations.

FIGURE 24

S–127, Senate Committee on Appropriations.

PLATE 238

ROOM OF THE SENATE MILITARY COMMITTEE.

S–128, part of the suite now occupied by the Senate Committee on Appropriations.

PLATE 239

JUDICIARY COMMITTEE ROOM, SENATE.

S–126, now part of the suite occupied by the Senate Committee on Appropriations.
The ceiling murals were later covered with other designs.

451

PLATE 240

UNITED STATES SENATE CHAMBER.

Photograph illustrating the room's ambient skylight and rich decorative character prior to its remodeling in 1949.

FIGURE 25

The Senate Chamber at the end of the twentieth century.

PLATE 241

BASEMENT HALL, SOUTH WING.

The Hall of Columns (related drawings, plates 205 and 207).
The Mindon tiles have been replaced with marble.

PLATE 242

NORTH CORRIDOR, HOUSE OF REPRESENTATIVES.

View west toward H–323 on the third floor.

PLATE 243

LOBBY OR CORRIDOR, SOUTH OF HOUSE OF REPRESENTATIVES.
H–212, 213, and 214, Member's Retiring Room. The center space was the original Speaker's office.

PLATE 244

FOUR PRINCIPAL STAIRWAYS, SIMILAR IN DESIGN ON HOUSE AND SENATE WING.

This marble staircase is located on the east side of the House wing between the second and third floors.

PLATE 245

ROOM OF SPEAKER OF THE HOUSE OF REPRESENTATIVES.

H–211, now the Parliamentarian's office.

PLATE 246

WAYS AND MEANS COMMITTEE ROOM, HOUSE OF REPRESENTATIVES.
H–209, now shared by the Speaker's office and the House Parliamentarian.

PLATE 247

NAVAL COMMITTEE ROOM, HOUSE OF REPRESENTATIVES.

H–219, now used by the House Majority Leader.

PLATE 248

COMMITTEE ON AGRICULTURE, HOUSE OF REPRESENTATIVES.

H–144, now used by the House Committee on Appropriations. This was the first room frescoed by Constantino Brumidi.

FIGURE 26

H–144, the House Committee on Appropriations.

PLATE 249

MACE OF SARGENT-AT-ARMS. UNITED STATES HOUSE OF REPRESENTATIVES.

This mace is still used today in the modern chamber.

PLATE 250

HOUSE OF REPRESENTATIVES.

A view from the House floor toward the Speaker's rostrum before 1901 remodeling.

FIGURE 27

The House of Representatives Chamber at the end of the twentieth century.

PLATE 251

OLD CONGRESSIONAL LIBRARY.

Photograph taken during the Library's demolition in 1900.

PLATE 252

NORTH AND SOUTH HALLS, OLD CONGRESSIONAL LIBRARY,—T. U. WALTER, ARCHITECT.

These sections of the library space, photographed during the Library's demolition in
1900, were originally built under the direction of Edward Clark in 1865–66.

PLATE 253

DETAIL OF IRON WORK IN OLD CONGRESSIONAL LIBRARY,—T. U. WALTER, ARCHITECT.

Photograph taken to record this work before demolition in 1900.

CEILING OF WEST HALL, OLD CONGRESSIONAL LIBRARY,—T. U. WALTER, ARCHITECT.

This photograph was taken to record the design of the ceiling and consoles, but it also shows the
empty bookshelves in the abandoned library just before demolition in 1900 (related drawing, plate 210).

The room of the Vice-President [Plate 235] is on the east of the Senators' private room. This room has a domical ceiling resting upon flat elliptical arches, and in it hangs the noted painting of Washington by Rembrandt Peale.[6] The walls and ceilings are simply tinted.

The Senate Committee on the District of Columbia occupies a room north of the marble corridor [Plate 236]. This room has been elaborately frescoed by Brumidi, the principal groups representing History, Geography, Physics, and the Telegraph.[7]

Three of the most important committee rooms in the Senate wing are those of the committees on Agriculture, Military Affairs, and Naval Affairs. In the room of the Committee on Agriculture are frescoes of agricultural subjects, while the walls and ceilings of the room of the Committee on Naval Affairs [Plate 237] are decorated by frescoes suggested by work in Pompeii, which are neither pleasing in effect nor in keeping with the architecture of the Capitol. The room of the Committee on Military Affairs [Plate 238] is decorated by historical frescoes by Brumidi—the Consultation of Washington and Lafayette at Valley Forge, the Storming of Stony Point by Anthony Wayne, the Death of Wooster at Danbury, Connecticut, the Massacre at Boston, 1770, and Major Pitcairn at the Battle of Lexington.[8]

The Committee on the Judiciary occupies the room in the northwest corner of the Senate wing [Plate 239]. This is more simply decorated than the other Senate committee rooms, the corners and ceilings being treated with scroll and line decoration.

The Senate Chamber [Plates 179, 240] is a rectangular room, 113 feet 6 inches in length, 80 feet 3 inches in width, and 36 feet in height. It is surrounded by a gallery which will seat 690 people. Under the galleries are private lobbies and rooms for the use of Senators. The Vice-President, acting as presiding officer, has his desk located on the south side of the hall. On the right is the seat of the Sergeant-at-Arms and on the left that of the Doorkeeper. In front of the Vice-President's desk is the table for the Reading Clerks, the Chief Clerk, and the Journal Clerk; below this are tables for the Official Stenographers. The seats and desks for the Senators are arranged in a semicircle, radiating from and facing the presiding officer, the different political parties being grouped together. The wall surfaces are treated with pilasters and panels enriched with ornaments in relief, decorated and gilded. The ceiling consists of glass panels resting upon heavy beams. The panels contain symbolic decorations of War, Peace, Union, and Progress. In the rear of the gallery of the Senate have been placed from time to time busts of the various Vice-Presidents who have presided over the Senate.[9]

The south wing of the Capitol is occupied by the House of Representatives, with its various corridors, reception, committee, and work rooms. The general arrangement is similar to the arrangement of the Senate wing, but the space occupied by the Hall is much larger and the space devoted to halls and lobbies much smaller.

The principal difference in the basement story of the House wing consists in the colonnaded hallway running through this wing from north to south [Plate 241]. This hall has a long colonnade of columns

---

[6] This painting has been relocated to the restored Old Senate Chamber. RG 40, Subject Files, Curator's Office, AOC.

[7] Brumidi painted these frescoes when the room was used as the Senate Post Office. Today S–211 is called the Lyndon Baines Johnson Room. RG 40, Subject Files, Curator's Office, AOC.

[8] The former room of the Committee on Agriculture is in the House wing (H–144). The rooms for the Committees on Naval and Military Affairs are now used by the Senate Committee on Appropriations. RG 40, Subject Files, Curator's Office, AOC.

[9] The legislative chambers were extensively remodeled in 1949–50. The Vice-President's desk is located on the north, not the south, side of the hall. The original desks and busts of the Vice Presidents were retained. RG 40, Subject Files, Curator's Office, AOC.

with marble side walls and ceiling in the form of lintels and panels.[10] The capitals are modeled from the capitals of the Temple of the Winds, Athens, the tobacco plant being utilized in the second row of leaves. The entrances to the basement of the south wing are on the east, west, and south, as well as one from the Rotunda on the north. North of the east and west entrances are located the principal stairways, similar in design to those in the Senate wing, which give the public access to the principal corridors. The private stairways [Plate 229] of the members are located in the south corridor.

The principal floor has simply tinted corridors. A public corridor surrounds the House on the north, east, and west. Plate 242 gives a clear idea of the character of these corridors. On the south of the House of Representatives is located the lobby, or retiring room of the members [Plate 243]. The public stairways from the principal story to the attic have steps of white marble, and balustrade columns and cornice of Tennessee marble with bronze Corinthian capitals [Plate 244].[11] The Speaker's room [Plate 245], on the south of the Representatives' room, is quite unpretentious and simply furnished, with plainly tinted wall and ceiling surfaces. The committee rooms of the House of Representatives are not as elaborately decorated as similar committee rooms in the Senate wing. The most effective rooms of this character are the ones occupied by the Ways and Means Committee [Plate 246], the Committee on Naval Affairs [Plate 247], and the Committee on Agriculture [Plate 248].

Plate 249 shows the mace used by the Sergeant-at-Arms, which ordinarily rests upon a stand on the right of the Speaker's desk.[12]

The Hall of the House of Representatives [Plate 250] occupies the central portion of the south wing, being surrounded by a gallery—three sides being used by the public and the south side for private and press galleries. The room is 139 feet in length, 93 feet in width, and 36 feet in height. The ceiling is paneled with glass similar to the ceiling [Plate 192] of the Senate Chamber, the decorations consisting of stained-glass medallions depicting the coats of arms of the various States and Territories of the Union.[13] The cloakrooms are under the gallery, with doors opening into the Hall of the House of Representatives. The Speaker's desk [Plate 214] is on the south side of the room and below it is the desk for the reading clerk and official stenographers. The Members' desks are placed in semicircular rows, of which the Speaker's desk forms the center. The space beneath the galleries is utilized for private retiring rooms. The attic story of this portion of the building contains committee rooms, press rooms, and, to the north, the House document room.

The western central projection of the old building contained the area on the western front designed by Bulfinch for the Congressional Library. The interior of this portion of the building was destroyed by fire, together with three-fifths of its contents, December 24, 1851, when, as related in other portions of this work, Thomas U. Walter made designs for refitting the room, making the work, together with the shelving, of iron, so that the construction would be noninflammable.[14] The work as completed made an effective room, with central corridors

---

[10] The side walls of the hall have a scagliola finish, and the ceiling is iron. RG 40, Subject Files, Curator's Office, AOC.

[11] The cornice is actually white Lee or Italian marble and the capitals are zinc painted to look like bronze. RG 40, Subject Files, Curator's Office, AOC.

[12] The mace is still brought out every time the House meets. RG 40, Subject Files, Curator's Office, AOC.

[13] During the 1949–50 remodeling of the House Chamber, the original state seals were copied on the new ceiling.

[14] For further discussion of the damage sustained by the Congressional Library in the 1851 fire, see *For Congress and the Nation: A Chronological History of the Library of Congress* (Washington: Library of Congress, 1979), 58; Charles A. Goodman and Helen W. Dalrymple, *The Library of Congress* (Boulder, Colo.: Westview Press, 1982), 26.

and two tiers of galleries from which opened book alcoves. The western hall of the Library, which was first completed [Plate 251], was 34 feet in width and 92 feet in length. The north and south sections were completed at a later date [Plate 252]. The detailing shows clearly the character and method of construction [Plates 253, 253a]. The books were removed from the Capitol July 31, 1897, when the new Congressional Library building was completed and ready to receive them.

---

[15] Removal of the book stacks and ironwork began on June 11 and was completed July 25, 1900. See *Annual Report of the Architect of the United States Capitol to the Secretary of the Interior for the Fiscal Year Ended June 30, 1901* (Washington: Government Printing Office, 1901), 5.

During the year 1900 the alcoves, shelves, and library fittings were removed and the space divided into two stories of committee rooms.[15]

The architectural features of other portions of the old building has been but slightly changed. The Senate Chamber has been changed for the use of the Supreme Court [Plate 103]; the old Hall of Representatives has become a Statuary Hall [Plate 101], and the old Supreme Court room is now a law library [Plate 94]. The lower portion of the Rotunda is unchanged, while the Dome has been added to the upper portion [Plates 97, 186]. The lobbies, halls, and stairways, as they appear at the present time, are shown in connection with the history of the old portion of the building [Plates 92, 96, 100, 101a, 102, 104].

Chapter XVII

The Terraces and Landscape Work

Frederick Law Olmsted, *Landscape Architect*

THE first scheme for landscape work to surround the new building was a drawing [Plate 254] submitted by Thomas U. Walter in his report of 1864.[1] This plan necessitated the purchase of additional ground on the north and south of the Capitol. Plate 255 gives the area, with the certificate of Randolph Coyle, surveyor; the chairman of the Senate Committee on Public Buildings and Grounds, J. A. Bayard, and the chairman of the House committee, Edward Ball. The bill for this purchase passed the Senate in 1866, but it was not until 1873, under the act of March 3, 1872, that the grading was commenced.[2]

In his report of November, 1873, Edward Clark recommended the employment of a landscape architect to lay out the grounds.

By act of June 23, 1874, the improvement of the grounds was placed in charge of Frederick Law Olmsted, of Brookline, Mass.[3] His first recommendation was for a broad plaza east of the Capitol, with marble terraces and a grand stairway on the west to replace the earth

terraces and the old stairway which were in existence at this period. The scheme, with the walks, terraces, retaining walls, and entrance ways, is shown in Plate 256. The work of grading, making walks, low boundary walls, ornamental piers for lamps, and entrance ways continued through the years 1875 to 1881, when the work which related to the grounds was completed, but no appropriation had been made to build the marble terraces and stairway. In the report of F. L. Olmsted, October, 1881, he urges an appropriation for these items of the scheme as approved by the act of 1874.[4] The designs for the architectural features of the grounds and terraces were made by Thomas Wisedell, an architect working under Mr. Olmsted's instruction. The active work on the terraces was commenced in 1883. The work on the western terrace and principal stairway was awarded to the Vermont Marble Company in 1887. The foundations for this portion of the terrace consisted of 194 wells sunk to solid ground and filled with concrete, with an average depth of 20 feet. In Mr. Olmsted's report of July 1, 1885, he states that

---

[1] "Report of the Architect of the Capitol Extension," in *Report of the Secretary of the Interior* (Washington: Government Printing Office, 1864), 689–696.

[2] "An Act Making Appropriations for the Legislative, Executive, and Judicial Expenses of the Government for the Year Ending June 30, 1873, and for Other Purposes," 42nd Cong., 2nd sess., in *United States Statutes at Large,* vol. 17, 83.

[3] "An Act Making Appropriations for Sundry Civil Expenses of the Government for the Fiscal Year Ending June 30, 1875, and for Other Purposes," contains the following passage: "For improvement of the Capitol Grounds, according to the plans and under the general direction of Fred. Law Olmsted, to be expended by the Architect of the Capitol, $200,000." Act of March 21, 1874, entitled "An Act Making an Appropriation for a Topographical Survey of the Capitol Grounds and Plans for Improving the Same," 43rd

Cong., 1st sess., *United States Statutes at Large,* vol. 18, pt. 3, 23 and 214, states: "Be it enacted by the Senate and House of Representatives of the United States of America in Congress assembled, That the sum of $3,000 or so much thereof as may be necessary be and the same is hereby appropriated out of any money in the Treasury not otherwise appropriated, to be expended under the direction of the Committees on Public Buildings and Grounds of the Senate and House of Representatives in procuring a topographical survey of the Capitol grounds and the employment of Fred. Law Olmstead [sic], of New York, in furnishing plans for laying out, improving and enclosing the same."

[4] See *Annual Report of the Architect of the United States Capitol. Including Capitol Grounds, Court-house, Public Printing Office, and Plans for School-houses for the District of Columbia for the Fiscal Year Ending June 30, 1881* (Washington: Government Printing Office, 1881), 14–15.

because of the purely architectural character of the terraces they should be constructed under the sole responsibility of the Architect of the Capitol, and therefore he retires from the supervision of the construction of this portion of the work.[5] The marble and granite work on the terraces is mentioned in the report of July 1, 1890, as being completed, but the balustrade of the stairways and the connection of the terraces with the main building were not finished until 1892.[6] Plate 257 gives an enlarged view, showing the top of the terraces with the open area ways between the terrace rooms and the building. The area under the terraces was divided into 93 rooms [Plate 258]. The rooms were lighted either by windows facing the areas or by pavement lights on the walks of the terrace above. The arrangement of these rooms in the central portion of the west terrace was modified so as to provide a greater number of rooms with exterior windows on the court, which could be utilized as committee rooms [Plate 259]. The marble terrace, with its solid wall surface which makes it legitimately a part of the building, is vastly more impressive and justifies the sacrifice of direct windows in the rooms overlooking the grounds. This was accomplished only by a determined effort on the part of Mr. Olmsted, who insisted on the artistic being superior to the utilitarian in this imposing structure.

The stairways, open court, and plaza are very effective in the simple and dignified treatment adopted [Plate 260] and shown in the perspective drawing submitted by Mr. Olmsted. The western views of the building [Plates 261, 262] have been remarkably improved by this work. Where formerly the building apparently rested on a steep earth embankment, the stonework now reaches the level ground, and while it adds to the apparent height of the building it also gives the appearance of a more stable foundation. While the effect of the landscape work in detail and as a whole is to be highly commended, giving many pleasing views of planting both in shrubbery and trees, as well as broad and effective lawns and imposing walks and plazas, the designs of the walls, lamp-posts at the entrances [Plates 263, 264], and other architectural details, though in many cases interesting in themselves, are not in harmony with the Capitol. They were designed at an unfortunate period in our architectural history, when there was a tendency among architects to discard the classical motives which are so necessary to the effect of any work around the Capitol. The fountain on the west of the grounds [Plate 265] shows one of the most curious and objectionable combinations, both in form and detail.

The remarkable effectiveness of the lawns in connection with the planting and distant views is shown in Plate 266. The broad lawn on the west of the building [Plate 267], unbroken, with the stairway, terraces, and Capitol at its east end, is truly imposing. The broad paved plaza on the east of the Capitol [Plate 268] illustrates what pleasing and dignified effects may be produced by a proper proportion of simple lines with a judicious placing of architectural objects and the planting of fine trees. The drinking fountain on the west of the Senate wing [Plate 269] is a picturesque feature of the grounds when seen in connection with the beautiful group of trees, shrubs, and vines which surround it.[7] The wisdom shown in the selection of Frederick Law Olmsted has been proved by the broad, imposing, as well as pleasing effects recognized by all who view the finished results. The dignity and effectiveness of the Capitol might so easily have been spoiled by a man of moderate capacity that it is a cause for congratulation that the one

[5] See *Annual Report of the Architect of the United States Capitol.* [For the Fiscal Year Ending June 30, 1885.] (Washington: Government Printing Office, 1885), 5–6.

[6] *Report of the Architect of the United States Capitol to the Secretary of the Interior, 1890* (Washington: Government Printing Office, 1892), 4.

[7] This structure is known as the "Summer House" or "Grotto" today. RG 40, Subject Files, Curator's Office, AOC.

capable man, probably, in the country at that date was chosen for this important work. The selection of Thornton for the original design, Walter for the extension, and Olmsted for the final landscape work has produced most happy results. A comparison of the private work of these men with that done by their contemporaries in architecture and landscape gardening proves that they were the most capable men in their professions at the time the selections were made. And, further, the sense of artistic effects, fitness, harmony, and refinement of detail on the Capitol will entitle them to a place at the head of their professions in the history of the country. The selection of artists who have proved their fitness in executed work is a precedent that may well be followed in future work of importance.

PLATE 254

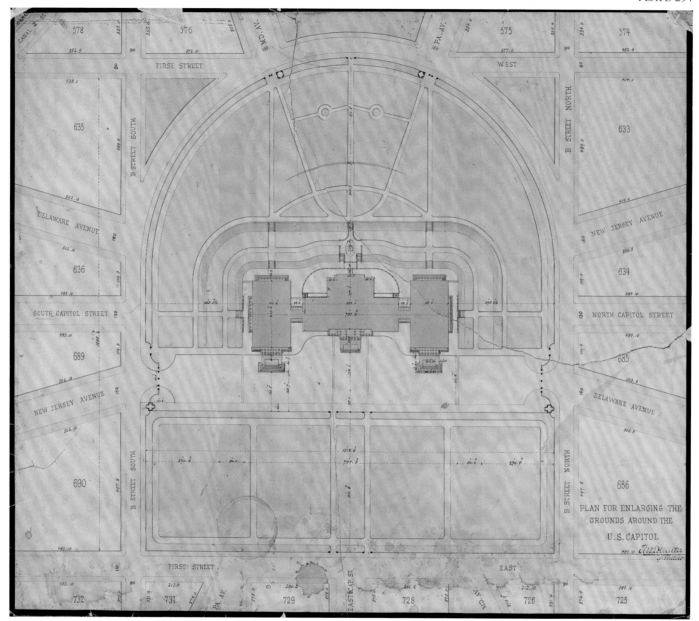

LANDSCAPE TREATMENT, BY T. U. WALTER, ARCHITECT.

Plan for the enlargement of the Capitol grounds, ca. 1864.

PLATE 255

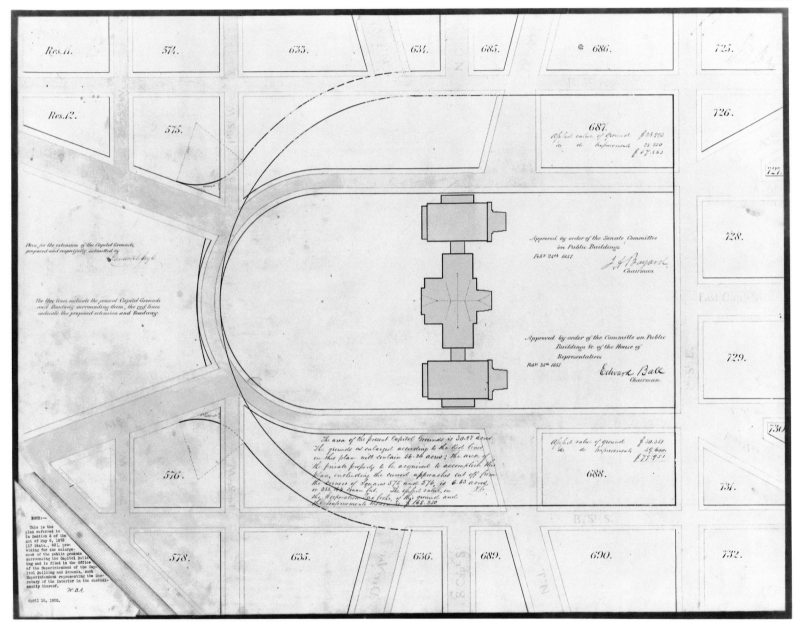

PLAT MADE FOR PURCHASE OF ADDITIONAL GROUND.

Dated February 24, 1857.

PLATE 256

PLAN OF FREDERICK LAW OLMSTED, FOR TERRACES AND GROUNDS.

Terraces and naturalistic landscape design for the Capitol grounds, 1874.

PLATE 257

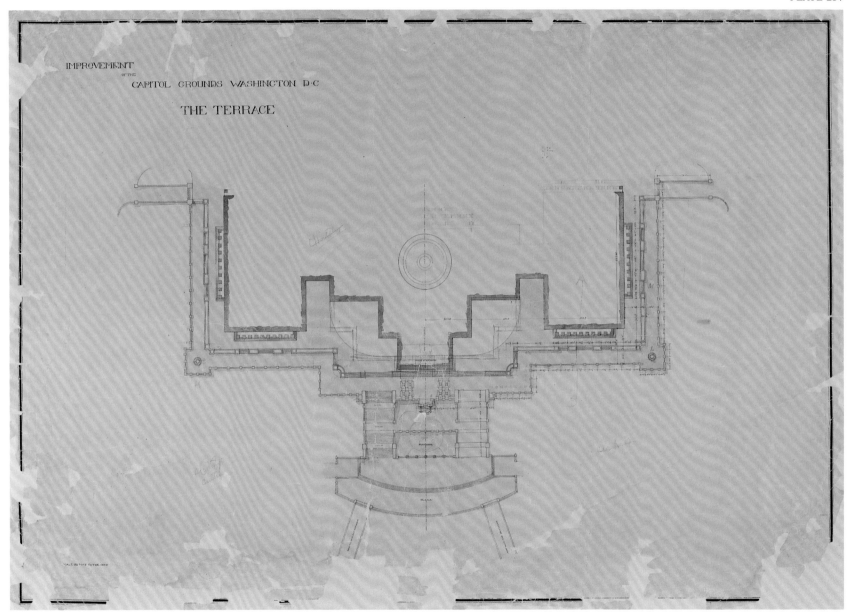

PLAN OF TERRACES AND WESTERN STAIRWAY,—F. L. OLMSTED, LANDSCAPE ARCHITECT.

Preliminary plan of the terraces and west stairway, 1874. The design of the area around the central staircase would be substantially revised in the mid-1880s.

PLATE 258

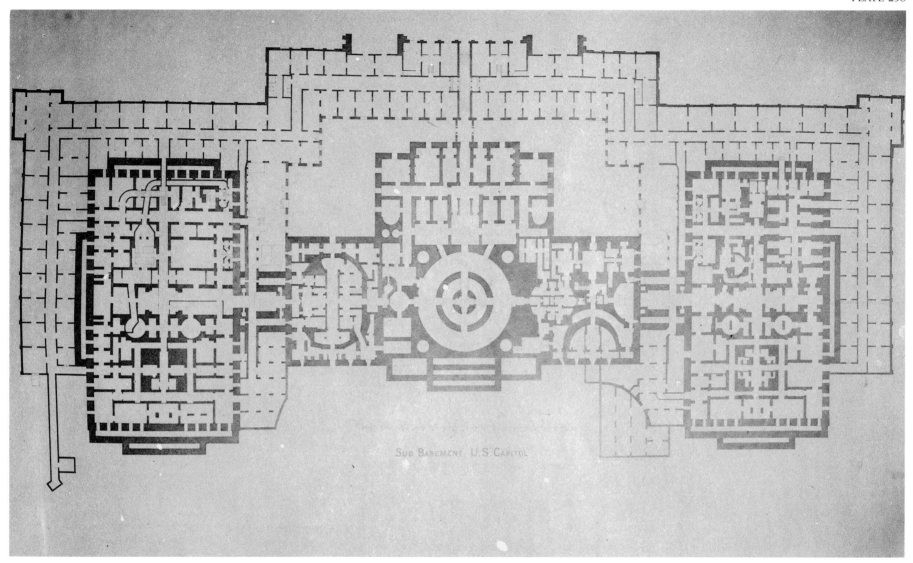

SUB BASEMENT. U.S. CAPITOL

PLAN OF BASEMENT, SHOWING ROOMS BENEATH THE MARBLE TERRACE.

The plan as built ca. 1895. *Location unknown.*

PLATE 259

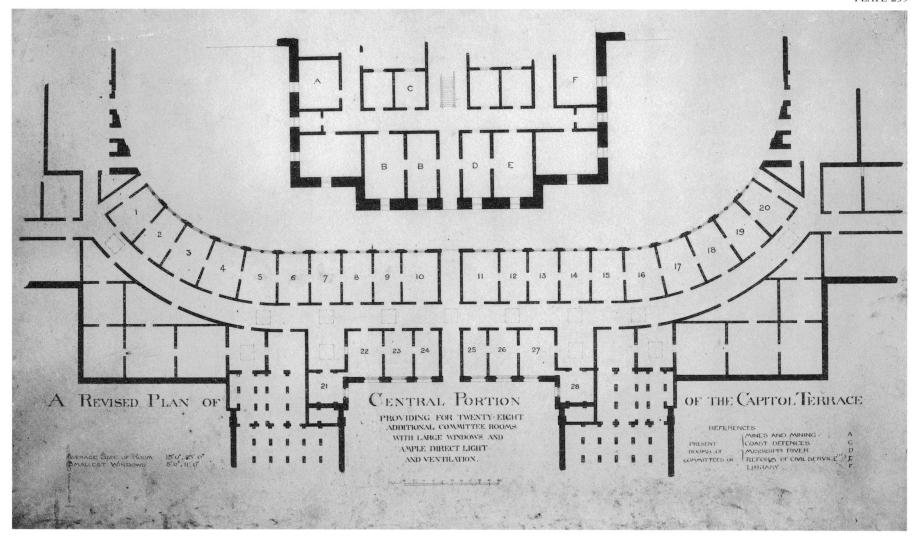

REVISED PLAN OF ROOMS UNDER THE TERRACE.

Proposal indicating the retention of parts of the Bulfinch Terrace, ca. 1886. *Location unknown.*

PLATE 260

PERSPECTIVE OF EXTERIOR STAIRWAYS, FREDERICK LAW OLMSTED, LANDSCAPE ARCHITECT.

West terrace design before 1886.

PLATE 261

NORTHWEST VIEW OF CAPITOL, SHOWING MARBLE TERRACE.

PLATE 262

SOUTHWEST VIEW OF CAPITOL, SHOWING MARBLE TERRACE.

PLATE 263

BALUSTRADE AND LANTERN,—F. L. OLMSTED, LANDSCAPE ARCHITECT.

PLATE 264

LAMP POST AND PLANTING,—F. L. OLMSTED, LANDSCAPE ARCHITECT.

PLATE 265

FOUNTAIN, EAST END OF GROUNDS.

Fountain located on the west end of the Capitol grounds. The drinking fountain, Summer House, and stone lamps reflect the ornate Victorian style of the architectural additions to Olmsted's naturalistic landscape design.

PLATE 266

SOUTH LAWN AND TERRACE,—F. L. OLMSTED, LANDSCAPE ARCHITECT.

PLATE 267

WESTERN LAWN,—F. L. OLMSTED, LANDSCAPE ARCHITECT.

PLATE 268

PLAZA EAST OF CAPITOL,—F. L. OLMSTED, LANDSCAPE ARCHITECT.

With the exception of the removal of the statue of George Washington, the east plaza changed little throughout the twentieth century
(related photograph, plate 118).

PLATE 269

GROTTO AND GROVE ON WEST OF CAPITOL,—F. L. OLMSTED, LANDSCAPE ARCHITECT.

The Summer House is on the northwest grounds.

BRONZE TABLET ERECTED ON THE ONE HUNDREDTH ANNIVERSARY, OF LAYING THE CORNER STONE.

This plaque is located on the first floor of the Capitol near the entrance to the Old Supreme Court Chamber.

Chapter XVIII

The Recent Alterations and Proposed Additions to the Capitol

B Y JOINT RESOLUTION of Congress June 6, 1900, the portion of the Capitol embraced by the central projection on the west, which was vacated by the Congressional Library when it removed into its new building, was ordered to be divided into committee rooms for the use of the Senate and House of Representatives. The resolution did not put a limit on the cost of the alteration, simply stating "And such sum as is necessary to make the construction herein provided for is hereby appropriated out of any money in the Treasury not otherwise appropriated."[1] Immediately upon the adjournment of Congress the old alcoves, shelves, and ceilings of the Library were removed and the work of alteration commenced.

The plan of the committee rooms is simple and direct [Plates 270, 271, 272]. All partitions are of brick and the ceilings are of brick vaulting, carrying out the same style of construction as that adopted in the old parts of the building. The principal hall [Plates 273, 273a] is cased with marble, with the stairway from the west entrance running between marble colonnades. An elaborate marble and bronze stairway was erected leading from the principal to the attic story during this improvement. As it interfered to a certain extent with the doorway leading to the west central portico it has been removed. This alteration of the old Library gives two stories of committee rooms, and a space under the roof which it is proposed to make into a reference library for Senators and Representatives. The changes in this portion of the building necessitated a change in the heating apparatus. The principal lines were carried through a duct beneath the floor and a single-pipe system used for the radiators. This alteration gave Congress a much-needed addition to its committee-room space.

The need for additional room has been the cause of several proposed additions to the Capitol, the most interesting of which are two designs by Thomas U. Walter in 1874 and one design by Smithmeyer & Pelz, presented January 15, 1881. In one of the plans submitted by Walter [Plate 274] he proposes to extend the east front of the old building 275 feet east and to build a portico similar to the porticoes on the extensions. From this proposed central portico a long corridor with a colonnade on each side was to lead to the central Rotunda. Two large open courts were placed on either side of this corridor. Around these courts were grouped the committee and other rooms for the use of Congress.

The perspective [Plate 275] shows how this extension in ordinary views of the building would throw all of the completed portions of the Capitol out of balance. The Dome would not be in the center from any view of the building from the east, except in the case of a direct front view, nor in any view from the north or the south. The central portion would overshadow the wings to such an extent as to belittle them.

The second scheme submitted by Walter was very much more satisfactory. The plan [Plate 276] contemplated an addition on both the east and the west of the old building, having only a slight projection beyond the wings on either side.

In this plan a colonnade extended in a broken line along the full width of the east front, with a portico similar to the porticoes on the wings. On the west front he placed a similar central portico without the

[1] "Joint Resolution Relating to the Use of the Rooms Lately Occupied by the Congressional Library in the Capitol," 56th Cong., 1st sess., in *United States Statutes at Large*, vol. 31, 719.

long and broad flights of steps which are such prominent features of the eastern entrances.

The perspective [Plate 277] shows a very dignified and well-balanced structure, with the Dome as a central feature, the building having a harmonious appearance from all directions. The central portion and the wings group well together and appear as legitimate parts of one structure. The slight recess between the wings and the main building gives very little depth of shadow and obliterates the fore court, which is one of the effective features of the present structure. These designs were hastily prepared at the request of the Committee on the Library and were only preliminary studies, which would have been matured and altered by Walter in the preparation of the working drawings.[2]

The plans of Walter did not contemplate a change in the rooms of the old building, but left intact the old Hall of Representatives and the Supreme Court room, as well as the committee rooms. The east and west fronts of the old building were thus made to front on interior courts instead of looking into the Capitol grounds.

J. L. Smithmeyer and Paul J. Pelz submitted a design [Plate 278] for alterations in the central building in which the old Hall of Representatives and Senate Chamber (Supreme Court room) were obliterated. New apartments were planned for the Supreme Court, the Attorney-General, and the Court of Claims, as well as a caucus room. Four grand stairways were provided in the space between the main building and the wings. The only portions of the old building left were the Rotunda and the Dome. The perspective of this design [Plate 279] shows a well-balanced structure with the Dome in the center. The front

of the central extensions is divided into three portions—a central portico with two corner pavilions. Each corner pavilion has two corner towers, forming turrets capped by small domes. In this way eight small domes extend above the roof line and are subordinate to the principal central Dome. The exterior dignity and repose of the building would be more or less marred by this addition of small domes, and the front is broken up by too great a variety of treatment.

The erection of an independent office structure for the House of Representatives, now in process of accomplishment under the act of March 3, 1903, will provide additional room for the use of Congress, and it seems probable that a Senate office building will be erected and the Supreme Court will be located in a separate structure.

On the afternoon of Sunday, November 6, 1898, the portion of the Capitol occupied by the Supreme Court (the old Senate wing) was damaged by an explosion, which was followed by a fire of considerable magnitude. The character of the construction of the old building, which was of solid masonry piers and brick vaulting, the form of construction best adapted to resist both explosion and fire, prevented this portion of the building with its contents from being completely destroyed on this occasion. On the morning after the explosion Edward Clark, Architect of the Capitol, requested Glenn Brown, architect, and Charles Munroe, expert on explosives, to make an investigation as to the cause and effects of the explosion and fire.

The reports on the explosion by these gentlemen, together with that of the Architect of the Capitol, were published in the latter's report of June 30, 1899.[3] They contain, besides a carefully prepared description of damages and recommendations for reconstruction, 6 sheets of diagrams and 44 reproductions of photographs illustrating the effects

---

[2] During the period Walter prepared these drawings he had suffered financial setbacks and needed the work. He was also pursuing a claim for compensation for architectural services above and beyond his duties as Architect of the Capitol Extension. See William C. Allen, *The Dome of the United States Capitol: An Architectural History* (Washington: Government Printing Office, 1992), 75.

[3] *Annual Report of the Architect of the United States Capitol to the Secretary of the Interior, for the Fiscal Year Ended June 30, 1899* (Washington: Government Printing Office, 1899), 20–44.

of the explosion and the fire which followed. On all material points the reports show an agreement as to the cause, effects, and necessary repairs, although the investigations were made independently.

The explosion took place in one or more of the compartments in the cellar under the small rotunda north of the central building. From this space the effects produced by the explosion could be seen radiating north as far as the end of the old building, south beyond the center line of the principal Rotunda, west to the west front of the old building, and east to the east front of the old building. The space in the cellar where the explosion took place was approximately 47,000 cubic feet. Of this area 37,000 cubic feet, although divided into numerous rooms and compartments, was practically one chamber, as all the compartments communicated directly by open doorways. Ten thousand cubic feet of space was separated from the above by lightly built walls or doors which were not a part of the construction and therefore easily overthrown. The explosion exerted its greatest energy in the small rotunda, in the vestibule east of this rotunda, and in the rooms just west of it, where the massive brick vaulting and the stone flagging were blown up, leaving large areas open to the cellar. The fire resulting from the explosion destroyed many papers in the cellar, as well as the furniture and fittings in the rooms adjoining the Supreme Court room on the south, and in the rooms on the principal and second stories occupied by the court officers on the west side of the building. The fire passed through the roof in the stairway hall, burning the wooden skylights and the woodwork at the base of the Dome.

This explosion occurred so near the time for Congress to assemble that it required great expedition to make the necessary repairs before it met. Elliott Woods, assistant to Mr. Clark, by employing workmen day and night succeeded in having all the débris removed, the vaulting and floors relaid, and the plastering done, so that the building was in condition to receive Congress at its regular time of meeting.

PLATE 270

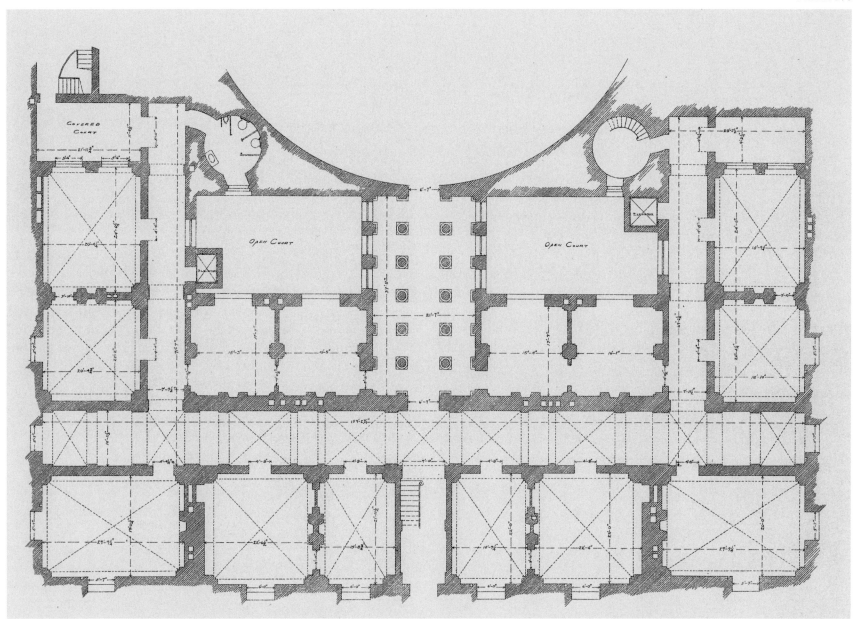

COMMITTEE ROOMS IN SPACE FORMERLY OCCUPIED BY CONGRESSIONAL LIBRARY,—PRINCIPAL STORY PLAN.

1900 drawing prepared under the direction of Elliott Woods, Acting Architect of the Capitol.

PLATE 271

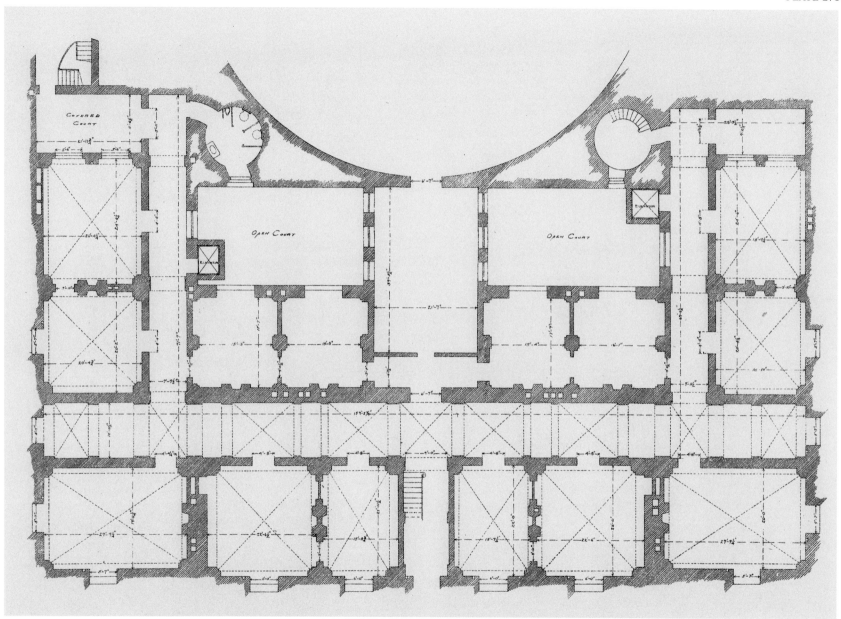

COMMITTEE ROOMS IN SPACE FORMERLY OCCUPIED BY CONGRESSIONAL LIBRARY,—ATTIC STORY PLAN.

1900 drawing prepared under the direction of Elliott Woods, Acting Architect of the Capitol.

PLATE 272

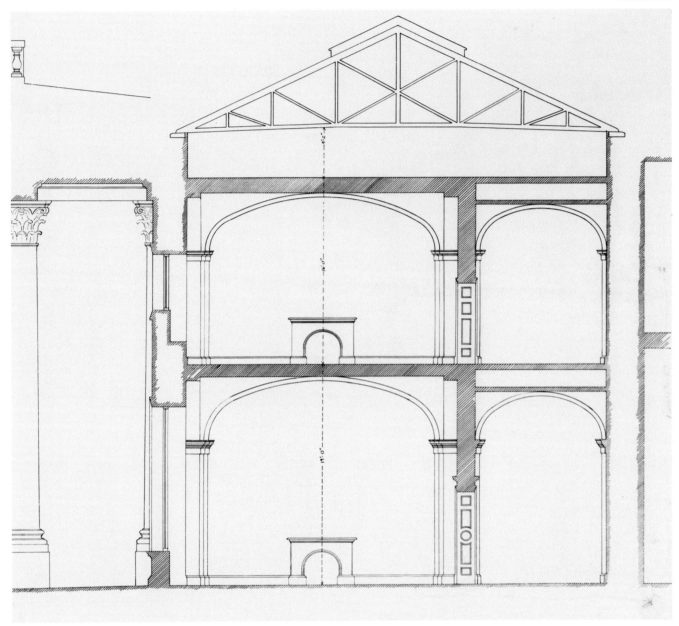

COMMITTEE ROOMS IN SPACE FORMERLY OCCUPIED BY CONGRESSIONAL LIBRARY,—SECTION.

1900 drawing prepared under the direction of Elliott Woods, Acting Architect of the Capitol.

PLATE 273

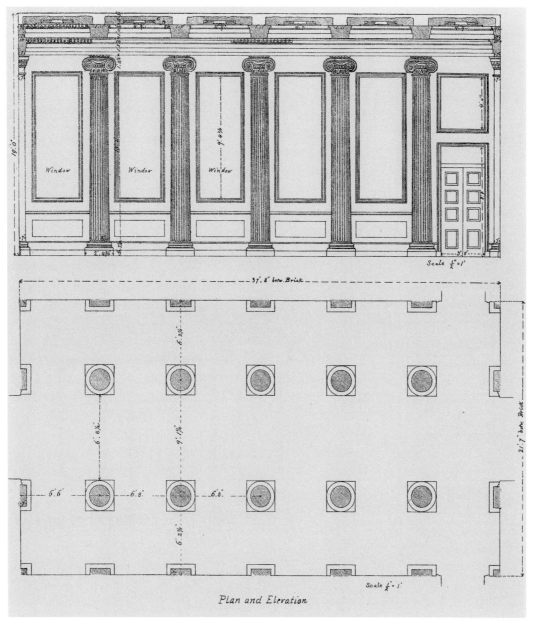

Plan and Elevation

COLONNADE FROM ROTUNDA TO NEW COMMITTEE ROOMS.

1900 drawing prepared under the direction of Elliott Woods, Acting Architect of the Capitol.

499

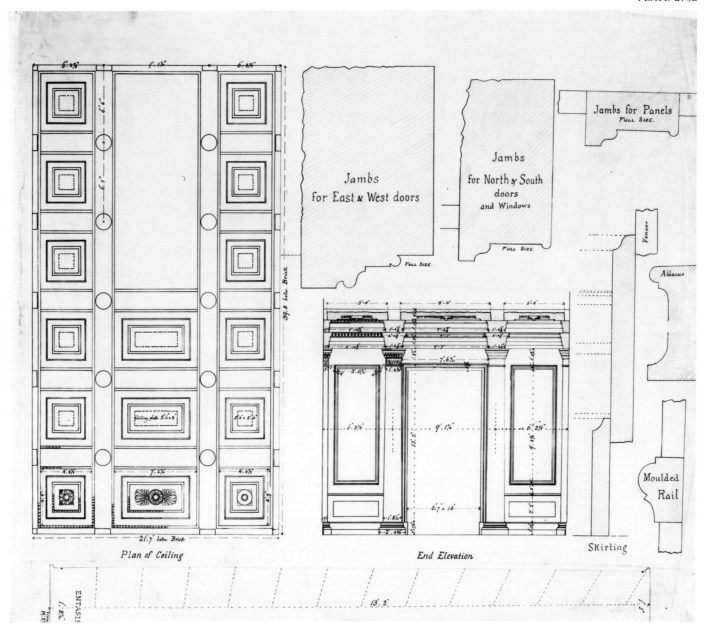

Jambs for Panels
FULL SIZE.

Jambs
for East & West doors

Jambs
for North & South
doors
and Windows

FULL SIZE.

FULL SIZE.

Veneer

Abbacus

Moulded
Rail

Plan of Ceiling

End Elevation

Skirting

ENTASIS

CEILING AND WALL PANELLING IN CORRIDOR LEADING TO NEW COMMITTEE ROOMS.

1900 drawing prepared under the direction of Elliott Woods, Acting Architect of the Capitol.

500

PLATE 274

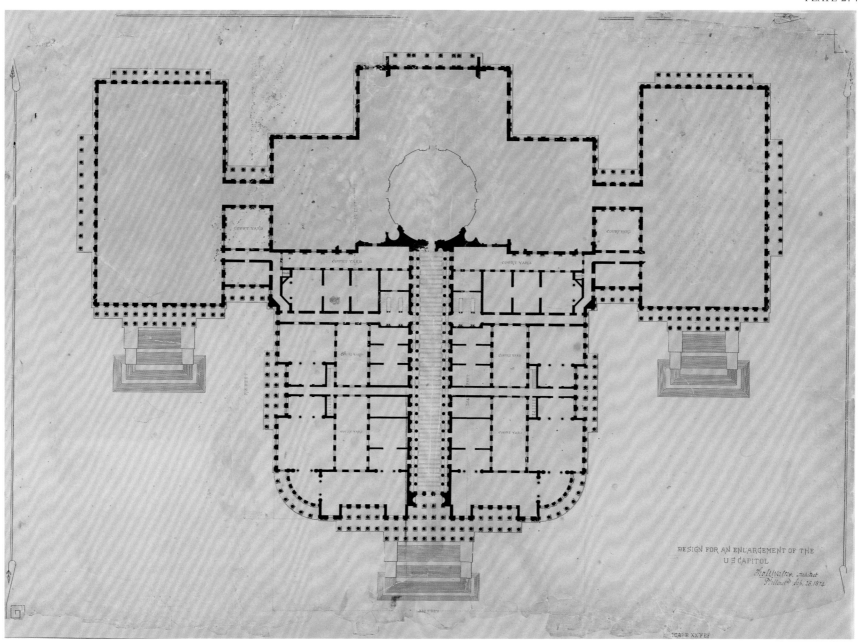

DESIGN FOR ENLARGEMENT OF THE CAPITOL 1874, PLAN OF PRINCIPAL STORY—T. U. WALTER ARCHITECT.

Walter's proposed design was never implemented.

501

PLATE 275

PLAN FOR ENLARGEMENT OF THE CAPITOL 1874, PERSPECTIVE VIEW—T. U. WALTER ARCHITECT.

Persepctive drawing illustrating Walter's proposed extension to the east (related drawing, plate 274).

PLATE 276

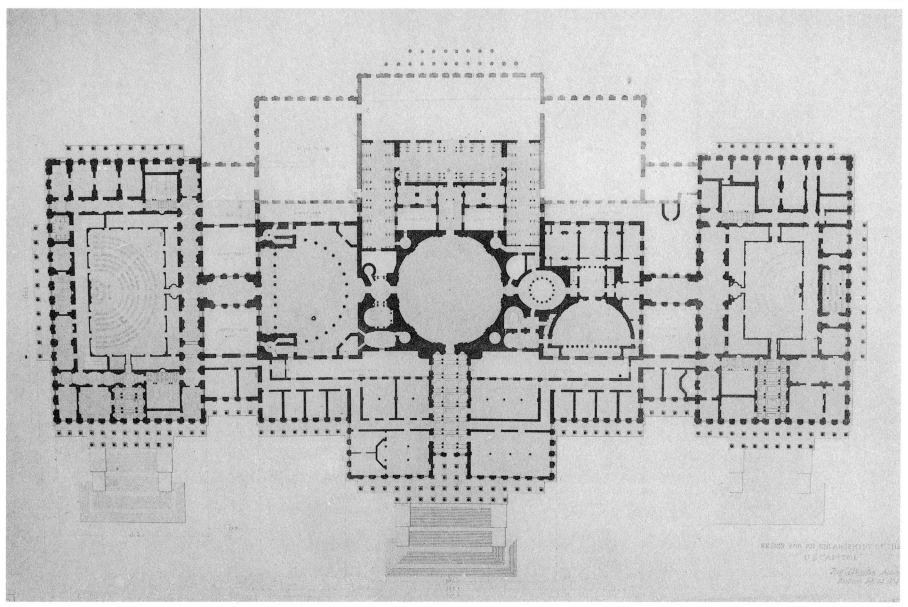

DESIGN FOR THE EXTENSION OF THE CENTER OF THE CAPITOL,—T. U. WALTER, ARCHITECT, 1874.

Walter's proposed design was never implemented.

PLATE 277

DESIGN FOR THE EXTENSION OF THE CENTRAL PORTION OF THE CAPITOL, PERSPECTIVE VIEW,—T. U. WALTER, ARCHITECT, 1874.

Perspective drawing illustrating Walter's proposed extension of the center of the Capitol to the east

(related drawing, plate 276). *Location unknown.*

PLATE 278

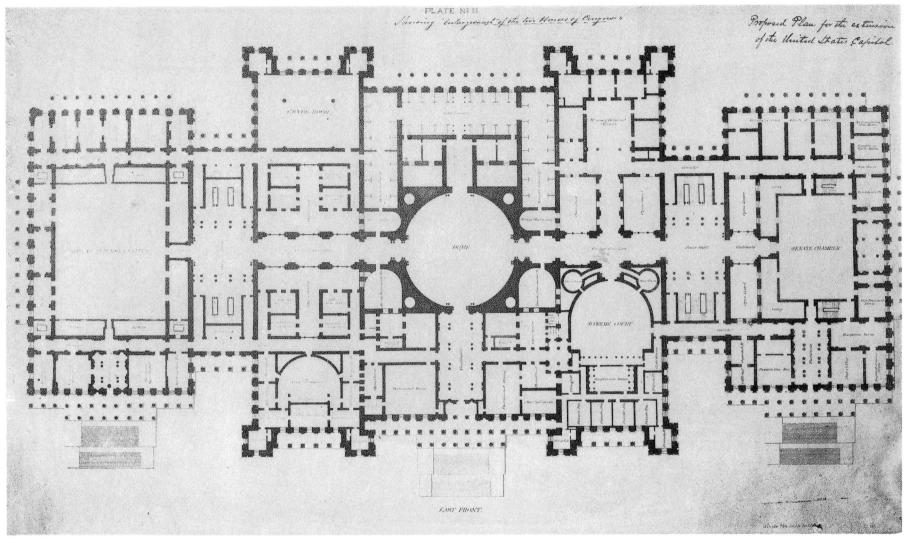

PROPOSED PLAN FOR EXTENDING CENTER OF THE CAPITOL,—SMITHMEYER & PELZ, ARCHITECTS.

This plan accompanied the perspective illustrated in plate 279. Brown noted in the text that the design was prepared in 1881. *Location unknown.*

PLATE 279

PLAN FOR THE EXTENSION OF THE U.S.CAPITOL.
(WITH INTRODUCTION OF TURRETS)

SUBMITTED BY
J.L.SMITHMEYER, ARCHITECT.

DESIGN FOR THE EXTENSION OF THE CENTRAL PORTION OF THE CAPITOL, PERSPECTIVE,—J. L. SMITHMEYER & P. J. PELZ, ARCHITECTS.

Brown may have obtained a copy of this drawing from Paul J. Pelz. *Prints and Photographs Division, LC.*

Chapter XIX

Decoration

THE principle or system inaugurated by the early Congresses of acquiring statuary and paintings of historic interest as decorations for the Capitol has continued to the present day. When the new wings of the Capitol extension approached completion, their decorative treatment was carefully considered by Thomas U. Walter, the Architect, and M. C. Meigs, the Superintendent.[1] The group ordered from Horatio Greenough before the wings were begun was not placed in position until the extension was well advanced. The determination at this period in our history appears to have been to obtain the work from the most noted sculptors of the country. The selection fell upon Thomas Crawford, of New York, a student of Thorwaldsen who had made a reputation by his work in Italy; Randolph Rogers, of New York, a student of Bartolini, of Italy; and, later, upon Hiram Powers, of Vermont, who had established his reputation while residing in Florence. With paintings framed or paneled the same principle was maintained, William Henry Powell, of New York, and James Walker being selected. For the purpose of fresco painting it was apparently thought that no American could be secured, and Constantino Brumidi was employed from 1855 until the date of his death in 1880. Not very long after the extension of the Capitol was in readiness for decoration, many Congressmen who had little confidence in Captain Meigs's artistic capacity moved to appoint a commission of artists to select and supervise the character and installation of paintings and statuary. This movement resulted in the acts of Congress of June 12, 1858, and March 3, 1859, which authorized the President to appoint an art commission.[2]

The act provided that no more of the appropriations should be expended in embellishing any part of the Capitol with sculpture or paintings, unless the design for the same had undergone the examination of a Commission of distinguished artists, not to exceed three in number, to be selected by the President, and that the designs which the said Commission accepted should also receive the subsequent approval of the Joint Committee on the Library of Congress; but this provision was not to be construed to apply to the execution of designs heretofore made and accepted from Crawford and Rogers. May 15, 1859, President Buchanan appointed Henry K. Brown, sculptor, and James R. Lambdin and John F. Kensett, painters.

This Commission organized June 1, 1859, and submitted their only report February 22, 1860.[3] The report is interesting and valuable, being presented by the only Art Commission ever appointed by the

---

[1] Brown assumed that Meigs and Walter together made decisions concerning the art and sculpture for the Capitol. However, Meigs made most of the decisions. See Russell Weigley, "Captain Meigs and the Artists of the Capitol: Federal Patronage of Art in the 1850's," *Records of the Columbia Historical Society of Washington, D.C.* (1971): 285–305.

[2] "An Act Making Appropriations for Sundry Civil Expenses of the Government for the Year Ending the 30th of June, 1859," in *Statutes at Large and Treaties of the United States of America*, vol. 11, 323; and "Act Authorizing the President to Appoint an Art Commission to Select and Supervise the Character and Installation of Paintings and Statuary," in *United States Statutes at Large*, vol. 11, 428.

[3] "Report of the United States Art Commission," in *Art Commission: Letter of the Secretary of War, Communicating in Compliance with a Resolution of the House, the Report of the Art Commission*, H. ex. doc. 43 (36–1), Serial 1048. The recommendations of this commission were ignored. Brown nevertheless appreciated the report and promoted it as a historical precedent for the appointment of a federal fine arts commission.

Government. They recommended the employment of American artists and the selection of subjects from American history for decorative purposes, and criticised the work of Brumidi in painting rooms in the style of the loggias of Raphael, the baths of Titus and Pompeii, as well as his foreign treatment of American subjects. The detailed recommendations of this Commission are interesting, although little intelligent consideration has been shown to their report. First they recommended that the frieze in the Rotunda, where T. U. Walter suggested bas-relief, should depict civil and religious Freedom. Below the frieze they suggested subjects illustrating colonial and Revolutionary history, the same to continue in the halls leading from the Rotunda to the Senate and to the House of Representatives. The Commission thought the Halls of Congress the proper place for decorations that would illustrate the legislative history of the States and the Nation. Strange as it may seem, no statue or painting of Madison, who took such a prominent and useful part in the making of the Constitution of the United States, has been placed in the Capitol.[4] The Art Commission noticed this failure to honor one who had done so much in the formation of the basis of the Government, and therefore recommended that a prominent place be given to Madison in the decoration of the House of Representatives. It was the opinion of the Commission "that far greater sobriety should be given to these Halls in their general effect, so as to render them less distracting to the eye. Few are aware how disturbing to thought the display of gaudy, inharmonious colors can be made. This very quality renders such combination of colors unsuited to halls of deliberation, where calm thought and unimpassioned reason are supposed to reside." It was not thought desirable to paint permanent decorations on the grand stairway. It was considered a mistake to employ Horace Vernet, with whom the Committee on the Library were in communication, to paint one of these panels. "No matter how valuable a piece of his work might be in a gallery, he would not have the proper feeling to produce an American historical painting." They believed that the Supreme Court room would be most appropriately decorated with subjects relating to the judicial history of the country. The lobbies of the Senate and House of Representatives were thought the proper places for portraying incidents in pioneer life and scenes illustrating the manners and customs of different sections of the country. The committee rooms should be decorated according to the purposes to which they were applied. For the pediment of the south wing the Commission recommended alto-rilievo instead of detached figures, such as were used in the pediment of the north wing, figures in high relief being more appropriate for architectural treatment than detached pieces of sculpture.

The opinion of the Art Commission as to the effectiveness or good results obtained from competition is of interest and of sufficient value to be heeded to-day. They say: "The well-known repugnance of artists of the first rank, who have achieved a national reputation, to compete with each other would render this method a doubtful policy to pursue with them. It is therefore deemed but respectful and proper to award to such artists commissions for works for which their talents and requirements have fitted them. The commissioners are sustained in their position by the experience and practice of all nations in similar cases."

This interesting report ends with the following extract from a memorial of artists to Congress in 1858: "The advancement of art in the United States may be most surely and completely attained by the establishment of an art commission, composed of those designated by the united voice of American artists as competent to the office, who shall be accepted as the exponents of the authority and influence of American

---

[4] There is still no statue of Madison in the Capitol. A painting depicting Madison was placed near the House Chamber in 2003. The James Madison Memorial Building of the Library of Congress (1978) was named in his honor, and a statue is located in a memorial hall off the lobby.

art; who shall be the channels for the distribution of all appropriations to be made by Congress for art purposes, and who shall secure to artists an intelligent and unbiased adjudication upon the designs they may present for the embellishment of the national buildings."

The lack of intelligent and continuous supervision in the selection, installation, harmony of color with surroundings, scale in relation to the building and with each other of the decorations is immediately felt in passing through the Capitol. The few artistic results are marred or ruined by their surroundings or location; and, strange to say, this lack of art feeling has been growing more and more manifest as the years pass.[5]

In early years, when we had few artists of capacity, those who were most famous were selected. Now, when we have such sculptors and painters as St. Gaudens, French, MacMonnies, La Farge, Abbey, and Sargent, who are recognized as great in all parts of the world, they are ignored in the decorations of our greatest building, and the Capitol is being filled with decorations, paintings, and sculpture by men and women comparatively unknown. And, added to the unhappy selection, there is no attention paid to the scale of the building, the scale of the various objects, the harmony of color, or the treatment in their installation. It might be thought that the business instinct, if not the artistic sense, of our people would lead their representatives in Congress to delegate such questions to those of artistic training. It is to be hoped that the positive deterioration shown by the results in the Capitol may lead to an awakening of intelligent interest in this matter and more careful forethought.

[5] Brown was a major critic of government policy toward the fine arts and believed that many paintings in the Capitol and White House "would not be allowed hanging space in a third class art gallery." See Glenn Brown, "Art and the Federal Government," *Appleton's Magazine* 7 (February 1906): 243. Brown interpreted the formation of the Capitol art commission in 1860 as a major precedent for legislation promoted by the Public Art League in 1897 that called for a board of experts to administer the government's selection of works of art and architecture. See Glenn Brown, *Memories, 1860–1930: A Winning Crusade to Revive George Washington's Vision of a Capital City* (Washington: W. F. Roberts, 1931), 357–365. Brown exaggerated the importance of the Capitol art commission and its report, but he did recognize and publicize the emergence of a curatorial responsibility for the Office of the Architect of the Capitol. In 1909 Charles E. Fairman was employed, and he became the first professional art curator for the Capitol.

CHAPTER XX

SCULPTURE

STATUARY being more intimately connected with the structure of the building, this branch of artistic expression was first used as a decorative feature in the Capitol extension.[1] The two groups of statuary which were intended as a capping for the blocking courses on the eastern central portico were ordered from Luigi Persico, an Italian, and Horatio Greenough, the first native American to receive a commission of this kind on the Capitol. The group by Persico, The Discovery, was completed and placed in position before the Capitol extension was authorized. It was moved from the navy-yard, where it landed, and placed in the position which it now occupies in 1846. This group consists of a figure of Columbus holding aloft a sphere, while at his feet cowers an Indian maiden [Plate 280]. The group by Greenough, called The Rescue [Plate 281], although ordered at the same time, was not installed until 1854. It represents an American frontiersman, with shrinking wife on one side, overpowering an Indian. These groups are more or less theatrical in their composition and poses. They are not sufficiently architectural in their lines to flank the entrance portico of a classical building. The figures by Greenough are strong in their modeling and interesting as typifying the early struggles of our forefathers. Little can be said in praise of the group by Persico.[2]

As soon as the extension of the Capitol was well advanced Thomas Crawford was employed to do the figure work on the additions to the building. The various pieces of sculpture considered necessary were ordered during the years 1853 to 1854. The group in the pediment for the east portico of the north or Senate wing was the first to receive consideration [Plate 283]. As early as 1855 models were received from Italy for the figure of the Mechanic and the group of Instruction, while all the models were received and many of the figures were cut in marble by the year 1857. Crawford died in London October 16, 1857. According to the report of Captain Meigs the work which had been intrusted to Crawford was so far advanced that it could be easily given to others for completion in bronze or marble. The pieces in addition to the figures in the pediment for which he furnished models were the bronze doors for the north and south wings, the figures of Justice and History, over the doorway of the Senate wing, and the figure of Freedom, the crowning feature of the Dome.[3]

---

[1] Brown created the tables that accompany this chapter probably after surveying the Capitol and recording the location of each piece of sculpture in 1900. He compiled the table by using data obtained from Capitol guidebooks and from the *Statutes at Large*. The legislation authorizing expenditures typically included the name of the sculptor and his or her rate of remuneration. It was also likely that Brown consulted nineteenth-century reports submitted to Congress on the cost of artwork in the Capitol, such as *Expenditures in the District of Columbia: Report,* H. Rept. 515 (28–1), Serial 446, and Secretary Orville H. Browning's March 1869 report regarding various accounts paid for works of art in the Capitol. To determine the date the pieces entered the Capitol's collection, Brown probably consulted the congressional journals, which usually contain an account of an unveiling ceremony.

[2] For biographical information on Persico and Greenough and a study of the controversy these works created in their day, see Vivian Green Fryd, "Two Sculptures for the Capitol: Horatio Greenough's *Rescue* and Luigi Persico's *Discovery of America,*" *American Art Journal* 19 (1987): 16–39. Both groups were placed in storage in 1958.

[3] For a biographical sketch and discussion of Crawford's work on the sculpture for the Capitol, see Sylvia E. Crane, *White Silence: Greenough, Powers, and Crawford: American Sculptors in Nineteenth-Century Italy* (Coral Gables: University of Miami Press, 1972). Crawford died on September 10, 1857. RG 40, Subject Files, Curator's Office, AOC.

The group in the pediment of the east portico of the north wing [Plate 283] represents the progress of civilization in America and the decadence of the original American before this progress. The center of the group is a figure of America. On the right of this figure are the elements of strength on which our country relies—the Soldier, Merchant, Schoolmaster, Youth, and Mechanic, ending with a wheat sheaf and anchor as emblems of prosperity and stability. Placed on the left of America are the forerunners of civilization, the Pioneer, the Hunter, the Indian Warrior, Mother and Child, and finally the Indian grave. These pieces of sculpture are in full relief, chiseled in marble from Lee, Mass., and made from the models of Crawford in the shops on the Capitol grounds. The execution of the marble work on these figures was performed by skilled Italians. Casoni cut the figures of America and the Indian family. G. Butti cut the figures of the soldier, merchant, Indian chief, pioneer, and hunter. G. Caspero executed the Indian grave, and T. Gagliardi the wheat sheaf and anchor. The figures were placed in the pediment between the years 1860 and 1864.[4]

The statue of Freedom [Plate 199], modeled by Thomas Crawford, was cast at the foundry of Clark Mills, near Bladensburg, Md. Crawford forwarded to Jefferson Davis, Secretary of War, photographs from the model of the statue, and Davis objected to the liberty cap as being an emblem of emancipated slaves, while Americans were freeborn. He also thought that the bundle of rods which suggested the functions of a Roman lictor had lost its symbolic character. In March, 1856, Crawford, because of the criticisms of the Secretary, dispensed with the cap and used a helmet with a crest composed of an eagle's head and an arrangement of feathers suggested by the costume of Indian tribes.

Crawford named the group Armed Liberty, but its official title from its reception at the Capitol has been the figure of Freedom.

Photographs of this modified model were accepted by Jefferson Davis. The statue as completed stands upon a tholus. The right hand rests upon a sword, while the left holds an olive branch. The drapery is held in place by a brooch with "U.S." on the face. The head is crowned, as mentioned in Crawford's letter, with a freely treated helmet encircled with stars. A full-size plaster model of this statue occupies the central position in the National Museum.[5]

Thomas Crawford also made models for bronze doors for the two wings, those of the south wing being completed by W. H. Rinehart, of Maryland. The doors for the Senate wing [Plate 287] were cast at Chicopee, Mass., by James T. Ames, in 1868.[6] Each leaf of the doorway is divided into four panels and a medallion. The top of each leaf is treated with a star encircled by a wreath. The sculptured panels on the north leaf, beginning at the top, depict the death of Warren at Bunker Hill, General Washington rebuking General Lee at the battle of Monmouth, and Alexander Hamilton storming the redoubt at Yorktown. The medallion shows a conflict between a Hessian soldier and a farmer. The panels on the south leaf show the laying of the corner stone of the Capitol by Washington, Washington taking the oath of office, and Washington passing through New Jersey on his way to be inaugurated President. The medallion represents peace and agriculture. These doors weigh 14,000 pounds and cost $56,495.11, Crawford receiving $6,000 of the amount. Plate 288 shows the model for the bronze doors for the House wing. These models, for which $8,940 was paid, are now stored

---

[5]The plaster model is now on display in the basement of the Rotunda of the Russell Senate Office Building. The United States Capitol Preservation Commission funded the restoration of the bronze statue of *Freedom* in 1993.

[6]William H. Rinehart completed the models for the bronze doors of the east entrance of the Senate wing. RG 40, Subject Files, Curator's Office, AOC.

---

[4]The sculptural group was set in place in 1863. RG 40, Subject Files, Curator's Office, AOC.

in the Capitol, never having been cast in bronze.[7] The scenes depicted upon these doors represent important events in our Indian and Revolutionary wars and civil events in our history. The figures of Justice and History, by Crawford, were placed over the eastern doorway of the Senate wing.

December 24, 1851. The fire which occurred in the Congressional Library destroyed a number of pieces of sculpture. The minutes of the Library Committee mention a number which were placed in the library at this date, and the newspapers and guidebooks of the period make note of a number of others as having been destroyed by the fire. From all sources there were apparently destroyed statues of Jefferson and Apollo, the latter by Clark Mills; bust in marble of Columbus, Vespucius, George Washington, and Thomas Jefferson, by Ceracci; Lafayette, by David, and of Hassler, Judge Marshall, General Taylor, John Quincy Adams, and Van Buren. There were plaster busts of Jackson, Moultrie, and Ogdall, a medallion of Madison, and a bronze likeness of Washington.[8]

Randolph Rogers made but one contribution to the sculptural work of the Capitol, the bronze doors now at the eastern entrance of the central portico [Plate 286]. These were ordered in 1853 or 1854, and were cast in bronze by Von Muller, of Munich, during the years 1859–1861. The doors were received in this country in 1863 and placed by Captain Meigs in the doorway between the old Hall of Representatives and the new south wing.[9] Thomas U. Walter made a protest against this location, and in the year 1871 they were taken down and put in their present position at the principal eastern doorway. The bronze work consists of a frame, two doors, and a semicircular tympanum. Each leaf of the doorway is divided into four square panels, and the tympanum contains one semicircular panel. All the panels contain sculptured scenes in relief, depicting events in the life of Columbus. The leaf on the south, beginning at the bottom, shows Columbus before the Council of Salamanca, the setting forth for the court of Spain, the interview with Ferdinand and Isabella, and the departure from Palos. The semicircular tympanum represents the landing of Columbus in the New World, October 12, 1492, on the island of Guanahani. The leaf on the north, beginning at the top, depicts further events in the life of Columbus—the embarkation for home, the landing and reception at Barcelona, the recall and arrest, and his death. In the stiles of the doors are niches in which are placed sixteen statuettes, representing historical characters connected with the early history of the New World, as follows: Alexander VI of Rome, Ferdinand and Isabella of Spain, Charles VIII of France, John II of Portugal, Henry VII of England, Mendoza, Lady Beatriz de Bobadilla, Perez, Pinzon, Bartholomew Columbus, Ojeda, Vespucci, Cortez, Balboa, and Pizarro. On the rails of the doors are figures of Irving, Prescott, and other historians. The bronze frame contains emblematic figures of Asia, Europe, America, and Africa, while at the crown is a head of Columbus. The architectural effect of these doors is pleasing and the composition and sculptural work is skillfully handled.

Probably the most interesting piece of statuary which has been placed in the Capitol since the completion of the building is the bronze statue of Thomas Jefferson [Plate 290] by a noted French sculptor,

---

[7]Rinehart's models for these House wing doors were cast at the Chicopee, Mass., foundry and installed in 1905. The models were subsequently lost. RG 40, Subject Files, Curator's Office, AOC.

[8]For a contemporary newspaper account of the fire, see "The National Library Destroyed by Fire," *National Intelligencer,* December 25, 1851.

[9]Superintendent Montgomery Meigs ordered the doors to be cast in 1859. He did not supervise their installation in the Capitol in 1863 because he was then Quartermaster

---

General of the United States Army. Brown misspells Ferdinand von Miller's name. The doors were moved 32 feet east in 1961 from the Rotunda to the central portico of the east front extension. RG 40, Subject Files, Curator's Office, AOC.

P. T. David d'Anvers.[10] This statue was presented to the Government by Lieut. Uriah P. Levy. On the 27th of March, 1834, the Committee on the Library voted to accept this statue, and recommended that it be "placed in the front garden of the Capitol." May 30 the Committee agreed to present a joint resolution to place the statue in the eastern garden of the Capitol. There appears to be no further record showing the disposition of this statue, but it was located in the north garden of the White House in the early fifties, where it remained until the fountain was put in the center of the grounds during Grant's Administration in 1874, when the statue was moved to the Capitol and placed in the Hall of Sculpture. In 1900 it was moved to the Rotunda.

Hiram Powers, one of the most noted sculptors of our country, was authorized March 3, 1855, to make statues of Thomas Jefferson and Benjamin Franklin [Plates 285, 284]. These statues were executed and placed in the Capitol in 1863.[11] Horatio Stone, another prominent sculptor, was employed August 5, 1856, to make a model for a statue of John Hancock, from which the Committee on the Library promised to have one of marble made if they considered it satisfactory. The statue in marble, together with one of Alexander Hamilton [Plate 291], was ordered June 11, 1866. They were finished and placed in the Capitol in 1871. The same committee gave Stone an order for a statue of Senator E. D. Baker February 9, 1874.[12]

The plaster cast of George Washington [Plate 282], from the statue by the noted French sculptor Jean Antoine Houdon, was apparently placed in the Capitol of the United States without record. From the fact that the cast is not mentioned in a list of statuary made in 1869, and that an appropriation was made for it in 1870, it was most probably placed in the Capitol at that date. The original marble of this cast is in Richmond, Va., and its execution was authorized by the State legislature in a resolution of January 22, 1784. Acting under authority of Governor Harrison, Jefferson and Franklin selected Houdon, who was the most famous French sculptor of the day. Upon the acceptance of the commission Houdon came to this country in 1785 and visited Mount Vernon October 2. Here he had an opportunity to study the American hero and statesman, as well as to actually measure and make models from life of the face, head, and chest. Washington was 54 years old at this time. In addition to the merits of the statue as a piece of sculpture, a peculiar interest attaches to it as the only one modeled from life. The costume, which was modeled from the uniform worn by Washington as Commander in Chief of the American Army, adds to the historic interest of the figure, which has grace and dignity in the pose as well as accuracy of feature. In the opinion of Chief Justice John Marshall, it "represented the original as perfectly as a living man could be represented in marble."

The fact that the statue in the Capitol is a cast causes it to lose a large part of the delicacy and beauty of the original, and this delicacy has been further destroyed by probable efforts at cleaning and more than one coat of paint.

This statue was made life size (6 feet 2 inches high), and arrived in this country May 4, 1796. On January 14, 1853, the sculptor W. J. Hubard, of Richmond, Va., was accorded the exclusive right for seven years to make three casts of this statue. He made two casts, but for fear of injuring the statue did not make a third one. From the plaster bronze

---

[10] The correct spelling is P. J. (Pierre Jean) David d'Angers. For a sketch of his career and his work at the Capitol, see Mary T. Christian, "The Capitol Sculpture of David d'Angers: Portraits of American Heroes Influence Path of American Public Sculpture," *Capitol Dome* 25 (August 1990): 4–5. RG 40, Subject Files, Curator's Office, AOC.

[11] For a modern study of Powers's career, see Crane, *White Silence,* 169–251.

[12] For a biography of Stone and a discussion of his works in the Capitol, see Charles E. Fairman, *Art and Artists of the Capitol of the United States of America* (Washington: Government Printing Office, 1927), 147–148, 309–310, and 372; and RG 40, Subject Files, Curator's Office, AOC. Hancock was placed in 1861, Hamilton in 1868.

castings were made. The first one was purchased by the State of Virginia for the Virginia Military Institute, at Lexington, Va., in March, 1856, for $10,000. The following States have purchased bronze replicas: North Carolina, South Carolina, New York (recently in Central Park Museum), and Missouri. The United States purchased one of the plaster casts, paying the widow of W. J. Hubard, who was killed during the civil war, $2,000 for it in April, 1870.

Another statue ordered by the Government, under the act of Congress of March 2, 1867, was one of Abraham Lincoln, by Vinnie Ream, sculptor. This statue was completed in 1870.

During remodelling the building a poetic bronze fountain was taken from the front of the Post Office Building and removed to the Capitol, where it is now stored. It is a reclining Indian by W. H. Rinehart. When Rinehart came to this country in 1857 from Italy, where he had established his studio, he made the figures of the Indian and Pioneer which were cast in bronze for the clock in the House of Representatives.

An important step was taken by Congress in a section of the sundry civil bill of July 2, 1864, with the intention of acquiring statues to commemorate the great men of the United States. This law set apart the old Hall of Representatives as a National Hall of Statuary, and the President was authorized to invite each State to contribute for its adornment two statues, in either bronze or marble, of deceased citizens of the State whom "for historic renown or from civic or military services" the State should consider worthy of national commemoration. If there had been a wise provision for a competent artistic selection and installation this law might have been the means of a far-reaching good. The unhappy selection of sculptors for many of the statues, the difference in scale, and the variety of installation produce an effect totally lacking in dignity and artistic results [Plates 292, 293]. As a means of procuring works of art to adorn and enhance the building the method of purchasing, accepting, mounting, and placing the statues has been a failure. There has been no

effort to obtain either uniformity or harmony in material, size, pose, or pedestal. They harmonize neither with each other nor with the architecture of the building. Many of the statues are copies of existing works by inferior artists. The character of the building and the surroundings have apparently never been taken into consideration. A large majority of the statues are but poor examples of art, and the result, taken as a whole, is very unsatisfactory, marring instead of enhancing the beauty of the old Hall of Representatives.[13] The statue of Lewis Cass [Plate 294], by Daniel C. French, is one of the interesting exceptions, this piece of sculpture having much dignity and strength.

The States which have taken advantage of this opportunity to commemorate their distinguished men are Rhode Island, Nathanael Greene and Roger Williams; Connecticut, Roger Sherman and Jonathan Trumbull; New York, George Clinton and Robert Livingston; Massachusetts, Samuel Adams and John Winthrop; Maine, William King; Ohio, James A. Garfield and William Allen; New Jersey, Richard Stockton and Philip Kearny; Michigan, Lewis Cass; Illinois, James Shields; New Hampshire, Daniel Webster and John Stark; West Virginia, John W. Kenna; Wisconsin, Jacques Marquette; Indiana, O. P. Morton; Vermont, Ethan Allen and Jacob Collamer; Missouri, Frank P. Blair and George H. Benton; Pennsylvania, Robert Fulton and J. P. G. Muhlenberg; Maryland, Charles Carroll and John Hanson. The dates when these statues were acquired and when they were installed in the Capitol, the name of the sculptor, and the price, wherever it has been possible to obtain the facts, have been placed in a table accompanying this chapter.

[13] The statuary has been extensively rearranged for greater harmony with the building. The most recent additions to the collection are the statues of Sarah Winnemucca, Nevada, and Po'pay, New Mexico, 2005, bringing the total number to 100.

By Senate resolution of May 13, 1886, busts of the deceased Vice-Presidents have been purchased and placed in the galleries of the Senate. Busts were also purchased of Chief Justices of the Supreme Court. A list of these busts will be found in the accompanying table (No. VI).

Before the extension of the Capitol an effort was made to beautify the grounds by the Greenough statue of Washington [Plate 118], located in the east grounds, and the Tripoli Naval Monument [Plate 89], which was placed on the west terrace.

Since the completion of the building three pieces of statuary have been erected as an adornment of the grounds and one of the old groups of sculpture has been removed from its place west of the Capitol.

The Tripoli Naval Monument was erected in 1806, by naval officers to their comrades who fell at Tripoli, in the navy-yard at Washington. It was mutilated by the British in 1814, placed on the west terrace of the Capitol in 1831, and finally moved from the Capitol grounds to Annapolis, Md., in 1860.

Members of the Philadelphia Bar tendered a statue of Chief Justice John Marshall [Plate 296], by W. W. Story, which was accepted December 22, 1882, and unveiled May 14, 1884. The monument consists of a base on which are emblematic groups in outline, one representing Minerva dictating the Constitution to young America, and the other Victory leading young America to swear fidelity on the Altar of the Union. A seated figure which crowns the pedestal well typifies the calm dignity of a broad-minded jurist. Its location in the center of the west plaza, with the terrace in the background, adds materially to its impressiveness.[14]

The Peace Monument [Plate 297] at the intersection of Pennsylvania avenue and First street west, makes a part of the Capitol grounds, although it is not a satisfactory piece of work for so important a position. A satisfactory result could not be expected from this group when its history is told. Admiral Porter received $16,000 with which he was instructed to have made an ideal group representing Grief and History, which was to be erected on a simple pedestal in Annapolis. It was afterwards decided to place the work in Washington upon a promise from Congress of an increase in the amount to be expended upon the group. Congress appropriated $6,500, which was not sufficient to materially alter what had been done, but Admiral Porter insisted against the judgment of the sculptor, Mr. Franklin Simmons, on a higher pedestal with additional groups on the front and rear. The architectural portion was designed by Bonanni Brothers, of Carrara, Italy. The monument was transported to this country by a United States ship of war, and erected in 1877.[15]

The monument to James A. Garfield [Plate 298], by J. Q. A. Ward, is placed at the intersection of First street west and Maryland avenue, in a position south of the east and west axis of the Capitol, similar to the location of the Peace Monument on the north. This work consists of a figure of Garfield on a high pedestal, with three sitting figures on the base, typifying the youth, the warrior, and the statesman. This monument was ordered in 1882 and unveiled May 12, 1887. It is a dignified work of art.[16]

---

[14] William Wetmore Story's statue of John Marshall was moved into the Supreme Court Building and the bas-reliefs were recently put on display. RG 40, Subject Files, Curator's Office, AOC.

[15] The Peace Monument was restored in 1991. For a historical sketch and description of the restoration, see Barbara A. Wolanin, "The Peace Monument and its Restoration," *Capitol Dome* 26 (July 1991): 6. The additional groups Brown mentioned, bronze dolphins and lanterns, were not funded by Congress. RG 40, Subject Files, Curator's Office, AOC. See also James M. Goode, *The Outdoor Sculpture of Washington, D.C.* (Washington: Smithsonian Institution Press, 1974), 242.

[16] The Garfield monument underwent restoration in 1992. For a historical sketch of the monument and description of the restoration, see Barbara A. Wolanin, "Restoration of the Garfield Monument," *Capitol Dome* 27 (November 1992): 6–7; and RG 40, Subject Files, Curator's Office, AOC.

The clock [Plate 295] in the House of Representatives has two well-modeled bronze figures, one of an Indian and the other of a pioneer.[17] These figures, together with the wreaths and eagle surmounting the composition, make an effective and pleasing group of sculpture. The castings were made by Cornelius and Baker. The eagle, which was the final piece of the composition, cast by Archer, Warner, and Miskey, cost $150. The cost of the other portions of the clock was, apparently, taken from the general appropriations and does not appear as an individual item. The Senate clock, which has little merit, was purchased by act of Congress under a special appropriation of $2,000.

The private bronze stairways [Plates 213–229] which were erected during the construction of the building are well worthy to be classified with the sculpture of the Capitol. These stairways were designed by T. U. Walter, modeled by Baudin, 1859, and cast by Warner, Miskey, and Merrill, at a cost of $22,498.[18]

[17]This clock is on display in the Capitol's crypt. RG 40, Subject Files, Curator's Office, AOC.

[18]The four cast-bronze railings were designed by Constantino Brumidi, modeled by Edmond Baudin, and fabricated by the Philadelphia firm of Archer, Warner, Miskey & Co. (the company underwent reorganization and became Warner, Miskey, and Merrill in 1858). The railings were restored in 1989. See Pamela A. Violante, "Railings Returned to 19th Century Splendor," *Capitol Dome* 24 (May 1989): 3, 8.

PLATE 280

THE DISCOVERY,—PERSICO SCULPTOR.

Luigi Persico, *The Discovery*, marble, placed on the south cheek block of the Capitol in 1844.
The work was removed during the east front extension project and is in storage.

PLATE 281

PLATE 281.—Greenough's Group of "The Rescue," not having been printed with the other plates, has been omitted, as it would require a resolution of Congress to print the plate at the present time.

Horatio Greenough, *The Rescue*, marble, erected on the north cheek block of the Capitol in 1853.
This photograph was taken before the sculpture was placed in storage in 1958. It is not known why Brown omitted a photograph of the statue, nor why he stated that a resolution of Congress would be needed to print the plate. It is possible the book had already gone to press.

PLATE 282

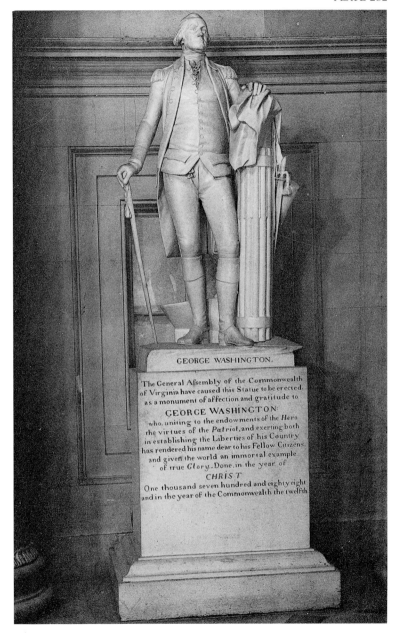

CAST OF STATUE OF GEO. WASHINGTON, JEAN ANTOINE HOUDON, SCULPTOR.

A 1909 bronze cast from the original 1788 marble now stands in the Rotunda to replace this plaster version.

PLATE 283

SCULPTURE, EASTERN PEDIMENT, NORTH WING,—THOMAS CRAWFORD, SCULPTOR.

Drawing by T.U. Walter. *Progress of Civilization*, marble, 1863.

PLATE 284

STATUE OF BENJ. FRANKLIN, HIRAM POWERS SCULPTOR.

Marble, placed in 1862, located in the east corridor of the Senate wing on the second floor.

PLATE 285

THOMAS JEFFERSON, HIRAM POWERS, SCULPTOR.

Marble, placed in 1863, located on the second floor in the east corridor of the House of Representatives wing.

PLATE 286

BRONZE DOORS, CENTRAL WEST PORTICO,—RANDOLPH ROGERS, SCULPTOR.

Brown mistakenly located these doors. They were initially installed between the old Hall of the House and the new House extension in 1863;
in 1871 they were moved to the eastern entrance to the Rotunda. In 1961, when the east front of the Capitol was extended,
they were moved 32 feet east to the new east portico.

PLATE 287

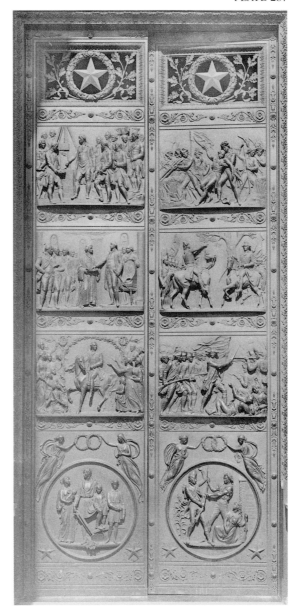

BRONZE DOORS, SENATE WING,—THOMAS CRAWFORD, SCULPTOR.

The doors were installed in 1868. Executed by William A. Rinehart from Crawford's designs after his
death and cast by the Ames Foundry in Chicopee, Massachusetts, between 1864 and 1868.

PLATE 288

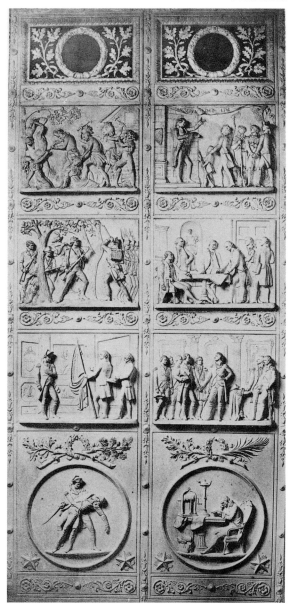

CAST FOR BRONZE DOORS, SOUTH WING,—THOMAS CRAWFORD, SCULPTOR.

Plaster model for the bronze doors to the House of Representatives that were installed in 1905. William A. Rinehart executed the models from Crawford's designs after the sculptor's death. They were cast in 1903 by Melzar H. Mosman of Chicopee, Massachusetts, and installed in 1905.

PLATE 289

GROUP OF JUSTICES, U. S. SUPREME COURT

Augustus St. Gaudens, *Roger B. Taney*, marble, 1877.
Thomas P. Jones, *Salmon P. Chase*, marble, 1875.
Augustus St. Gaudens, *Morrison R. Waite*, marble, 1875.

The bust of Taney is now located in the Robing Room adjacent to the Old Supreme Court Chamber, S–141;
the busts of Chase and Waite were moved to the Supreme Court Building in 1973.

PLATE 290

THOMAS JEFFERSON, P. T. DAVID D'ANGERS, SCULPTOR.
Bronze, 1833, located in the Rotunda.

PLATE 291

ALEXANDER HAMILTON, HORATIO STONE SCULPTOR.

Marble, 1868, located in the Rotunda.

PLATE 292

| O. P. MORTON, | JOHN WINTHROP, | JOHN STARK, | DANIEL WEBSTER, |
| CHAS. H. NIEHAUS, SCULPTOR | R. S. GREENOUGH, SCULPTOR | CARL CONRADS, SCULPTOR | COPY BY CARL CONRADS, SCULPTOR |

Oliver P. Morton, marble, 1900. *John Winthrop,* marble, 1876. *John Stark,* marble, 1894. *Daniel Webster,* marble, 1894.

The statues in the Capitol have been relocated at various times for aesthetic and practical reasons,
and many are no longer where they appear in Brown's photographs.

PLATE 293

FRANCIS BLAIR.   ROGER SHERMAN.   JONATHAN TRUMBULL.   JACOB COLLAMER.   ETHAN ALLEN.   LEWIS CASS.   J. A. GARFIELD.
GROUP OF STATUES IN STATUARY HALL.

Alexander Doyle, *Francis P. Blair, Jr.*, marble, 1899. Chauncey B. Ives, *Roger Sherman*, marble, 1872. Chauncey B. Ives, *Jonathan Trumbull*, marble, 1872. Preston Powers, *Jacob Collamer*, marble, 1881. Larkin G. Mead, *Ethan Allen*, marble, 1876. Daniel Chester French, *Lewis Cass*, marble, 1889. Charles H. Niehaus, *James A. Garfield*, marble, 1886.

The statues in the Capitol have been relocated at various times for aesthetic and practical reasons, and many are no longer where they appear in Brown's photographs.

PLATE 294

LEWIS CASS, DANIEL C. FRENCH, SCULPTOR.

Marble, 1889, Statuary Hall. Brown used a photograph of the plaster model for the marble statue.

PLATE 295

BRONZE CLOCK, HOUSE OF REPRESENTATIVES.

William A. Rinehart and others, 1857; currently on exhibition in the Crypt.

PLATE 296

CHIEF JUSTICE JOHN MARTHALL,—W. W. STORY, SCULPTOR.

Bronze, 1883, placed on the Capitol grounds, west front in 1884. Transferred to the Supreme Court in 1985.
The Chief Justice's surname, Marshall, is misspelled in Brown's caption.

PLATE 297

THE PEACE MONUMENT.

Franklin S. Simmons, marble, 1877, located in the traffic circle at the intersection of Pennsylvania Avenue and 1st Street, N.W.

PLATE 298

STATUE OF JAMES A. GARFIELD, J. Q. A. WARD. SCULPTOR.

President James A. Garfield Memorial, bronze and marble, 1887, located in the traffic circle at the intersection of Maryland Avenue and 1st Street, S.W.

NOTE: This table contains the information published by Glenn Brown, which has not been corrected or updated.

Table V.   Sculpture in the Capitol.

Title.	Ordered, purchased, or accepted.	Placed in Capitol.	Name of sculptor.	Cost.	If donated, by whom presented.	Location in Capitol in 1900.
Liberty.	1807	1807	Giuseppe Franzoni.	$5 per day		Originally placed between columns in old House of Representatives, destroyed by British 1814.
Car of History (clock).	1815	1819	Giuseppe Franzoni. Francesco Iardella.	$5 per day		Statuary Hall.
Justice (group—low relief).	1820	1820	Giuseppe Franzoni.	$5 per day		Supreme Court library.
Preservation of Captain Smith (relief).	1823	1826	Antoni Capallano.	$3,500.00		Bas-relief in Rotunda.
Landing of the Pilgrims (relief).	1823	1826	Enrico Causici.	3,500.00		Do.
Conflict with Boone (relief).	1823	1826	Do.	3,500.00		Do.
Treaty with Indians (relief).	1823	1826	Nicholas Gevelot.	3,500.00		Do.
Liberty and Eagle (cast).	1823	1829	Enrico Causici.	1,850.00		In tympanum over cornice Statuary Hall.
Eagle.	1829	1829	Valaperti.	500.00		Cornice Statuary Hall.
Wreath and relief portraits.	1827	1827	Causici. Capallano.	9,000.00		Rotunda, and east portico.
War.	1829	1837	Luigi Persico.	12,000.00		Niche, central east portico.
Peace.	1829	1837	Do.	12,000.00		Do.
America, Justice, and Hope (group).	1829	1830	Do.	15,000.00		Pediment of east central portico.
Tripoli naval monument.	Mar. 2, 1831	1831	Chas. Micali.		Naval officers.	Navy-yard 1806, west terrace 1831 to 1860, removed to Annapolis, Md.
George Washington.	Feb. 13, 1832	1843 [1] 1847 [2]	Horatio Greenough.	42,170.74		Plaza, east grounds.
The Discovery (group).	Mar. 3, 1837	1846	Luigi Persico.	27,796.74		East central portico.
Jefferson.						Destroyed by fire in Congressional Library, Dec. 24, 1851.
Apollo (bronze).			Mills.			Do.
The Rescue (group).	Mar. 3, 1837	1854	Horatio Greenough.	27,796.74		East central portico.
Group in pediment.	1853–54	1860–1864	Thomas Crawford.	20,000.00 [3] 20,600.00 [4]		East pediment, north or Senate wing.
Justice and History.	1853–54	1863	Do.	3,000.00		Over doorway, east front, Senate wing.
Bronze doors, Senate wing.	1853–54	1868	Do.	6,000.00 [3] 50,495.11 [5]		Entrance from east portico, North wing.
Cast for bronze doors, south wing. Plaster.	1854		Do. W. H. Rinehart.	8,940.00 [3]		Stored.

[1] In Rotunda.   [2] East grounds.   [3] Model.   [4] Cutting.   [5] Casting.

NOTE: *This table contains the information published by Glenn Brown, which has not been corrected or updated.*

Table V.   Sculpture in the Capitol. *(Continued)*

Title.	Ordered, purchased, or accepted.	Placed in Capitol.	Name of sculptor.	Cost.	If donated, by whom presented.	Location in Capitol in 1900.
Bronze doors.	1853–54	1863	Randolph Rogers.	$8,000.00 [3] 17,000.00 [5]		Designed for passageway leading from old Hall of Representatives, 1871 placed in entrance on central east portico.
Freedom (bronze).	1853–54	1863	Thomas Crawford.	3,000.00 [3] 9,800.00 [5] 10,996.83 [6]		Surmounting the Dome.
Thomas Jefferson.	Mar. 3, 1855	1863	Hiram Powers.	10,000.00		Foot of staircase, House corridor, east side.
Benjamin Franklin.	Mar. 3, 1855	1863	Do.	10,000.00		Foot of staircase, Senate corridor, east side.
John Hancock.	Aug. 5, 1856 [3] June 11, 1866 [7]	1871	Horatio Stone.	10,000.00		Foot of staircase, Senate corridor, west side.
Bronze stairways.	1858	1866	Baudin.	22,958.00 [5]		Private stairways, House and Senate.
Bronze clock, figure of Indian, Pioneer (bronze).	1857		W. H. Rinehart.			Gallery, House of Representatives.
Eagle over clock (bronze).		1866	G. Butti.	150.00 [5]		Over clock in House gallery.
Bronze ornaments.	1858	1866	Cornelius & Baker.	6,196.00		House and Senate wing.
Alexander Hamilton.	June 11, 1866	1871	Horatio Stone.	10,000.00		Rotunda.
George Washington (cast).	1870	1870	Jean Antoine Houdon (cast by W. J. Hubard).	2,000.00		Statuary Hall.
Sitting Indian and Fountain (bronze).	Mar. 1, 1887	1887	W. H. Rinehart.			Stored. Brought from Post Office when steps were changed in grading F street.
Abraham Lincoln.	Mar. 2, 1867	1870	Vinnie Ream.	15,000.00		Rotunda.
Nathanael Greene.	Mar. 29, 1867	1870	H. K. Brown.	8,000.00 [8]	State of Rhode Island.	Statuary Hall.
Roger Williams.	1868	1871	Franklin Simmons.	11,000.00	Do.	Do.
Thomas Jefferson (bronze).	Mar. 27, 1834	1874	P. T. David d'Anvers.		Capt. Uriah P. Levy.	Rotunda. In north garden of White House, 1850 to 1874.
E. D. Baker.	Feb. 9, 1874	1876	Horatio Stone.	10,000.00		Rotunda.
George Clinton (bronze).	1872	1874	H. K. Brown.	13,500.00	State of New York.	Statuary Hall.
Robert Livingston (bronze).	1872	1874	E. D. Palmer.	12,950.00	Do.	Do.
Samuel Adams.	1873	1876	Anne Whitney.	10,500.00	State of Massachusetts.	Do.
John Winthrop.	1872	1876	R. S. Greenough.	10,000.00	Do.	Do.
William King.	1875	1878	Franklin Simmons.	4,000.00	State of Maine.	Do.

[3] Model.   [5] Casting.   [6] Erecting.   [7] Marble.   [8] In gold.

NOTE: This table contains the information published by Glenn Brown, which has not been corrected or updated.

Table V.   Sculpture in the Capitol. *(Continued)*

Title.	Ordered, purchased, or accepted.	Placed in Capitol.	Name of sculptor.	Cost.	If donated, by whom presented.	Location in Capitol in 1900.
James A. Garfield.	1882	1884	C. H. Niehaus.	$10,000.00	State of Ohio.	Statuary Hall.
William Allen.	1884	1885	Do.	9,500.00	Do.	Do.
Richard Stockton.	Feb. 27, 1873	1888	H. K. Brown.	8,088.00	State of New Jersey.	Do.
Philip Kearny.	Feb. 27, 1873	1888	Do.	8,088.00	Do.	Do.
Lewis Cass.	1887	1889	Daniel C. French.	10,000.00	State of Michigan.	Do.
James Shields (bronze).	June 15, 1893	1893	L. W. Volk.	9,000.00	State of Illinois.	Do.
Daniel Webster.	1894	1895	Copy by Conrad from Thomas Ball.	4,484.00	State of New Hampshire.	Do.
John Stark.	1887	1895	Carl Conrad.	4,484.00	Do.	Do.
John W. Kenna.	1893	1901	Alex Doyle.	5,000.00	State of West Virginia.	Do.
Jacques Marquette.	1895	1896	G. Trentanove.	8,000.00	State of Wisconsin.	Do.
Oliver P. Morton.	1898	1900	C. H. Niehaus.	5,000.00	State of Indiana.	Do.
U. S. Grant.	Aug. 14, 1890	Feb. 5, 1900	Franklin Simmons.	10,000.00	Grand Army of the Republic.	Rotunda.
Johathan Trumbull.	1868	1872	C. B. Ives.	7,386.00	State of Connecticut.	Statuary Hall.
Roger Sherman.	1868	1872	Do.	7,386.00	Do.	Do.
Ethan Allen.	1872	1875	L. C. Mead.	5,300.00	State of Vermont.	Do.
Jacob Collamer.	1874	1880	Preston Powers.	6,081.25	Do.	Do.
Frank P. Blair.	Apr. 18, 1877	1899	Alex Doyle.	6,000.00	State of Missouri.	Do.
Thomas H. Benton.	Apr. 18, 1877	1899	Do.	6,000.00	Do.	Do.
Robert Fulton.	1877	1884	Howard Roberts.	7,500.00	State of Pennsylvania.	Do.
J. P. G. Muhlenberg.	1877	1884	Blanche Nevin.	7,500.00	Do.	Do.
Charles Carroll (bronze).		1901	R. E. Brooks.	12,000.00	State of Maryland.	Do.
John Hanson (bronze).		1901	Do.	12,000.00	Do.	Do.
John Marshall.	Dec. 21, 1882	May 14, 1884	W .W. Story.	40,000.00	Members of the Philadelphia bar paid $20,000.	West plaza, west grounds.
Peace Monument.		1877	Franklin Simmons.	22,500.00	$16,000 contributed through Admiral Porter.	Intersection of Pennsylvania avenue and Capitol grounds, west side.
James A. Garfield.	1882	Mar. 12, 1887	J. Q. A. Ward.	65,000.00	Army of the Cumberland paid $35,000.	Intersection of Maryland avenue and Capitol grounds, west side.

NOTE: *This table contains the information published by Glenn Brown, which has not been corrected or updated.*

Table VI.   Sculptured busts in the Capitol.

Title.	Ordered, purchased, or accepted.	Placed in Capitol.	Name of sculptor.	If donated, by whom presented.	Cost.	Location in Capitol in 1900.
Lafayette.	Feb. 28, 1829	1829	P. T. David d'Anvers.	Sculptor.		Destroyed by fire in the Congressional Library, Dec. 24, 1851.
General Taylor.			Italian artist.			Do.
Columbus.	Feb. 9, 1831	1831	Guiseppe Ceracci.		$500.00	Do.
Vespucius.	Do.	1831	Do.		500.00	
George Washington.	Do.	1831	Do.		500.00	
Thomas Jefferson.	Jan. 4, 1834	1834	Do.		4,000.00	
John Quincy Adams.	1838	1838	L. Persico.	Sculptor.		
Ferdinand R. Hassler.	May 1, 1844	1844		F. E. Hassler.		
Judge Marshall.						Do.
Van Buren.						
Jackson (plaster).						
Moultrie (plaster).						
Ogdall (plaster?).						
Madison (medallion).						
Washington (bronze).						
Chief Justice John Jay.	Mar. 2, 1831	1831	John Frazee.		400.00	Supreme Court room.
Chief Justice Oliver Ellsworth.	June 4, 1834	1840	Auger.		865.25	Do.
Chief Justice John Marshall.	Jan. 30, 1836	1840	Hiram Powers.		500.00	Do.
Kosciusko.	Feb. 27, 1857	1857	H. D. Saunders.		500.00	North lobby Senate gallery.
Justice John Rutledge.	Jan. 27, 1856	1858	A. Galt.		800.00	Supreme Court room.
Abraham Lincoln.	Jan. 1, 1866	1868	Mrs. S. F. Ames.		2,000.00	North lobby Senate gallery.
Thomas Crawford.	Feb. 9, 1871	1871	Gagliardi.		100.00	Do.
Abraham Lincoln (bronze).	Dec. 18, 1871	1871		Col. A. De Groot.		Marble room Senate wing.
Chief Justice Salmon P. Chase.	May 6, 1874	1876	T. Jones.		1,000.00	Supreme Court room.
Chief Justice R. B. Taney.	Jan. 19, 1876	1877	Copy from Rinehart.		1,000.00	Do.
Henry Clay.	Feb. 21, 1881	1881	A. P. Henry.		200.00	Senate Committee on Library.
Pulaski.	Mar. 6, 1882	1882	H. Dmochowski.		1,500.00	North lobby Senate gallery.
L. S. Foster.	Jan. 25, 1885	1885	C. Caverley.	Mrs. Foster.		Vice-President's room.
Vice-President Henry Wilson.	Jan. 25, 1885	1886	Daniel C. French.		1,000.00	Do.
Garibaldi.	Mar.—, 1888	1888	Guiseppe Martegana.	Dr. Verdi.		North lobby Senate gallery.
Vice-President Hannibal Hamlin.	Jan. 2, 1886	1890	Franklin Simmons.		800.00	Senate gallery.
Vice-President William A. Wheeler.	Do.		Edw. C. Potter.		800.00	Do.
Vice-President Chester A. Arthur.	Do.		Augustus St. Gaudens.		800.00	Do.
Vice-President John Adams.	Do.	1890	Daniel C. French.		800.00	Do.

NOTE: This table contains the information published by Glenn Brown, which has not been corrected or updated.

Table VI. Sculptured busts in the Capitol. (*Continued*)

Title.	Ordered, purchased, or accepted.	Placed in Capitol.	Name of sculptor.	If donated, by whom presented.	Cost.	Location in Capitol in 1900.
Vice-President Thomas Jefferson.	Jan. 2, 1886	1890	M. Ezekiel.		$800.00	Senate gallery.
Vice-President John C. Calhoun.	Feb. 23, 1887	1896	Copy by Theo. A. Mills.		800.00	Do.
Vice-President T. A. Hendricks.		1890	U. S. J. Dunbar.		800.00	Do.
Vice-President Daniel Tompkins.		1891	C. H. Niehaus.		800.00	Do.
Vice-President Levi P. Morton.		1891	Edwin Elwell.		800.00	Do.
Vice-President Elbridge Gerry.		1892	Herbert Adams.		800.00	Do.
Vice-President Aaron Burr.		1894	J. Jouvenal.		800.00	Do.
Vice-President Martin Van Buren.		1894	U. S. J. Dunbar.		800.00	Do.
Vice-President G. M. Dallas.		1894	H. K. Ellicott.		800.00	Do.
Vice-President A. E. Stevenson.		1894	Franklin Simmons.		800.00	Do.
Vice-President George Clinton.		1894	V. A. Crane.		800.00	Do.
Vice-President R. M. Johnson.		1894	J. P. Voorhees.		800.00	Do.
Vice-President William R. King.		1896	W. E. McCauslin.		800.00	Do.
Vice-President Schuyler Colfax.		1897	F. M. Goodwin.		800.00	Do.
Vice-President J. C. Breckinridge.		1897	J. P. Voorhees.		800.00	Do.
Vice-President John Tyler.	Feb. 5, 1898	1898	W. E. McCauslin.		800.00	North vestibule main floor Senate.
Vice-President Andrew Johnson.		1900	Do.		800.00	Do.
Chief Justice Morrison R. Waite.	Mar. 6, 1889	1892	Augustus St. Gaudens.		1,500.00	Supreme Court room.
Vice-President Millard Fillmore.		1895	R. Cushing.		800.00	Senate gallery.
Vice-President Garret A. Hobart.		1900	F. E. Elwell.		800.00	Do.
William McKinley.	Mar. 3, 1903	1903	Emma C. Guild.		2,000.00	President's room, Senate wing.
John Q. Adams.		1868	J. C. King.			Clerk's room, House of Representatives.
Charles Sumner.			Martin Millmore.			North lobby Senate gallery.
Indian chief, bronze.						House corridor, foot of staircase.
Chippewa chief.		1858	Copy by Jos. Lasalle from F. Vincenti.			North lobby Senate gallery.

NOTE: *This table contains the information published by Glenn Brown, which has not been corrected or updated.*

Table VII. Medals formerly in the Capitol.

Title.	Received.	If donated, by whom presented.	Cost when purchased.	Remarks.
Napoleon medals.		Mr. Erving.		This collection consisted of 142 medals. The larger were struck under the authority of Napoleon between the years 1796 and 1815, and were commemorative of himself, his family, generals, battles, victories, foundations of various schools, and treaties of peace.
American medals.		Do.		The American medals were of Washington, Columbus, Franklin, Kosciusko, Paul Jones, William Washington, Colonel Howard, General Gates, and Captain Hull.
Distinguished Americans.	1830	Owned by Adam Eckfeldt.	$2 each	No list of these medals.
Collection of medals of war of 1812.	1830			No further data concerning these medals.
Medal in honor of Sir John Soane.	June 4, 1836	Struck by architects of London—presented.		
Medal commemorating the battle of the Cowpens.	Jan. 9, 1840	Gen. Dan Morgan.		
Commemorating centennial of New Haven, Conn.	Jan. 4, 1841	Wm. M. Boardman.		
Four medals.	Jan. 14, 1842	Chas. Serruys, chargé d'affaires Belgium.		
Kosciusko.	Feb.—, 1842	Presented.		
Napoleonic medals.	Do.	Do.		No list of these medals given.
James Fenimore Cooper.	Jan. 8, 1845	Commodore J. D. Elliott.		
Historical medals struck from the mint of France.	July 31, 1850	Presented.		Do.

Between 1,100 and 1,200 medals were damaged by the fire in the Congressional Library December 24, 1851.

Extracts from minutes of the Committee on the Library.

January 8, 1852.—"That all books, maps, statuary, paintings, and medals in the Library were entirely destroyed."

July 19, 1861.—The Library Committee authorized the Librarian to present the medals damaged by fire to the Smithsonian Institution.

CHAPTER XXI

PAINTINGS AND FRESCOES

BEFORE the commencement of the Capitol extension, the large paintings for the panels in the Rotunda were completed, with one exception. Henry Inman, one of the four artists with whom contracts were made for the historical panels, died January 17, 1846, without having commenced the painting, although he had received $6,000 on account for the work. March 3, 1847, a contract was made with W. H. Powell to paint the vacant panel. It was not placed in the Rotunda until 1855. This panel, The Discovery of the Mississippi [Plate 299], is intended to depict De Soto and his small band of followers, the first Caucasians to see our mighty Mississippi. It is a spirited composition, in no sense realistic, idealizing both Spaniards and Indians.

The fire which occurred in 1851 in the Congressional Library destroyed portraits of the first five Presidents by Gilbert Stuart, which were for sale but had not been purchased by the Government. There were also destroyed by this fire two portraits of Columbus, one of Peyton Randolph, Bolivar, Steuben, De Kalb, Cortez, and Hanson.[1]

The Battle of Chapultepec [Plate 307], by James Walker, was ordered in 1858 and completed in 1862. Walker was present at the battle, and the painting gives a historical representation of the occurrence without being a great artistic production. The uniforms of the soldiers correspond to those worn by our soldiers during the Mexican war. This picture was painted with the intention of having it placed in the room of the Committee on Military Affairs, a much more suitable location than its present one on the landing of the staircase.[2]

Westward the Course of Empire takes its Way [Plate 302], by Emmanuel Leutze, a German artist of prominence, was ordered by General Meigs July 9, 1861, and completed in 1862. The representation of pioneers with their wagons and camping outfits, the mountain scenery, and Daniel Boone, always attracts the attention of visitors. The method of applying the paint to the wall adopted in this painting has been used only in this one instance in the Capitol. The basis is a thin layer of cement of powdered marble, quartz, dolomite, and air-worn lime. The water colors are applied on this cement and fixed by a spray of water-glass solution. By the method employed it is much easier to make corrections in the painting than with ordinary fresco work.

The Battle on Lake Erie [Plate 301], by W. H. Powell, was ordered in 1865 and completed in 1871. It represents Commodore Oliver Hazard Perry passing from the disabled flagship Lawrence in the midst of the battle in a rowboat to the Niagara. While dramatic, the painting has few artistic qualities. The Grand Canyon of the Yellowstone [Plate 303] and The Chasm of the Colorado [Plate 304], by Thomas Moran, were placed in the Capitol in 1873.[3] These paintings give a vivid representation of western scenery and are interesting examples of the work of Moran, one of the most noted of American artists. The Discovery of the Hudson

---

[2] Walker's *The Battle of Chapultepec* has been on loan and is no longer displayed at the Capitol. See Senate Curator file. Note that Brown's completion dates for works of art often reflect the date that the works were placed in the Capitol rather than the date that the artist finished or dated them.

[3] Both paintings were transferred to the Department of the Interior in 1950 and are now on display at the Smithsonian American Art Museum. RG 40, Subject Files, Curator's Office, AOC.

---

[1] For a contemporary account of the fire, see "The National Library Destroyed by Fire!" *National Intelligencer,* December 25, 1851.

[Plate 308] and A California Landscape [Plate 309], both by Albert Bierstadt, are careful studies of eastern and western views in the United States. For his studies on the Hudson Bierstadt, according to Tuckerman, set up his studio on the river and made accurate sketches from nature.[4]

The Emancipation Proclamation, by Frank Carpenter, was presented in 1878 by Mrs. Elizabeth Thompson.[5] It is a poor artistic representation of a great event. The Electoral Commission, by Cornelia Adèle Fassett [Plate 313], was purchased in 1885, and is interesting as a collection of portraits of distinguished men and women of the period impossibly seated and grouped.[6] The Recall of Columbus, by A. G. Heaton [Plate 314], represents Columbus, after fruitless endeavors, leaving the court despondent being recalled at the bridge of Pinos to undertake his voyage of discovery.[7]

Among the great number of portraits which have been purchased or presented very few are valuable or interesting from an art standpoint. Among them may be mentioned those of Chief Justice John Marshall by Rembrandt Peale, George Washington by Gilbert Stuart [Plate 305] and by Rembrandt Peale [Plate 128], Benjamin West by himself, George Washington by Charles Wilson Peale, Henry Laurens by J. S. Copley, Thomas Jefferson by Thomas Sully, and Thomas B. Reed by John S. Sargent. Henry Clay by Fagnani, and of Joseph Varnum unsigned by the artist.[8]

As the interior of the Capitol extension approached completion the necessity for wall decoration became apparent, and it was thought necessary to obtain a fresco painter from abroad. Constantino Brumidi was employed from 1855 to 1880, and did all of the frescoing between those periods.[9] The greater part of this work was performed at the rate of $10 a day, but contracts were made for a limited number of the larger pieces [Plates 300, 310, 311, 311a, 311b]. Many of these frescoes are shown in the views of the halls and committee rooms.

A list of paintings giving the dates of purchase and of installation in the Capitol, the cost, and the artists' names, as far as it has been possible to ascertain the facts, follows.[10]

[8] Rembrandt Peale's portrait of *George Washington* (1828), purchased by the Senate in 1832, now hangs in the Old Senate Chamber. Charles Willson Peale's *George Washington at Princeton* (1779), purchased in 1882, is located in the Senate wing, third floor, west corridor. (Note that Brown misspelled Charles Willson Peale's middle name.) The portrait of *Henry Laurens* (1784), purchased in 1886, is no longer thought to be by John Singleton Copley and is now attributed to Lemuel Francis Abbott. See Senate Curator's files. Thomas Sully's portrait *Thomas Jefferson* (1856) hangs in S–211, while a portrait of *Andrew Jackson* (1845) attributed to Sully is in a private office in the Senate wing. John Singer Sargent's *Thomas B. Reed* is located in the Speaker's lobby on the second floor of the House wing, as is Guiseppe Fagnani's portrait *Henry Clay*, a gift of the artist. RG 40, Subject Files, Curator's Office, AOC.

[9] Brumidi painted all of the scenes in true fresco, but many other artists were employed in the decoration of the Capitol, including James Leslie, Emmerich Carstens, and Joseph Rakemann. See RG 40, Subject Files, Curator's Office, AOC.

[10] Brown derived data for his tables on the paintings in the Capitol from the *United States Statutes at Large,* which reprinted both public and private laws enacted by Congress relative to the artwork in the Capitol. Treasury Department records also contain warrants drawn for payment to certain individuals who worked on the Capitol. Brown probably consulted two nineteenth-century reports submitted to Congress on the artwork in the Capitol: the United States Art Commission (May 1860) and Secretary Orville H. Browning's March 1869 report regarding various accounts paid for works of art in the Capitol. To determine the date the pieces entered the Capitol's collection, Brown probably consulted the congressional journals, which usually contain accounts of unveiling ceremonies. Brown's tables cannot be relied upon for accuracy, and his figures, dates, and names should be double-checked.

[4] *Discovery of the Hudson River* and *Entrance Into Monterey* are now in storage. RG 40, Subject Files, Curator's Office, AOC.

[5] *First Reading of the Emancipation Proclamation* is now located in the west staircase of the Senate wing. RG 40, Subject Files, Curator's Office, AOC.

[6] *The Florida Case before the Electoral Commission,* painted in 1879, now hangs in the Senate wing, third floor, east corridor.

[7] *Recall of Columbus* currently hangs in the Senate wing, third floor, east corridor.

NOTE: *This table contains the information published by Glenn Brown, which has not been corrected or updated.*

Table VIII. Paintings in the Capitol.

Title.	Ordered, purchased, or accepted.	Placed in Capitol.	Name of painter.	Cost.	By whom presented.	Location in Capitol in 1900.
Declaration of Independence.	Feb. 6, 1817	1822–23	John Trumbull.	$8,000.00		Rotunda.
Surrender of Burgoyne.	Do.	1822–23	Do.	8,000.00		Do.
Surrender of Cornwallis.	Do.	1822–23	Do.	8,000.00		Do.
Resignation of General Washington.	Do.	1822–23	Do.	8,000.00		Do.
Lafayette.	1824	1824	Ary Scheffer.		Lafayette.	House of Representatives.
Washington.	June 23, 1832	1832	Rembrandt Peale.	2,000.00		Vice-President's room, Senate wing.
Baptism of Pocahontas.	Feb. 28, 1837	1842	John G. Chapman.	10,000.00		Rotunda.
Landing of Columbus.	Do.	1844–45	John Vanderlyn.	10,000.00		Do.
Embarkation of the Pilgrims.	Do.	1846–47	Robert Weir.	10,000.00		Do.
George Washington.	1834	1834	John Vanderlyn.	2,500.00		House of Representatives.
Judge Johnson.	May 28, 1836	1836			John S. Cogdell.	
Hernando Cortez.	Jan. 9, 1840	1840			George G. Barrell, U.S. consul, Malaga.	
Columbus.	(1)	1842			Do.	
Columbus.	July 22, 1842	1842			Arthur Middleton.	
John Hanson.	Feb. 15, 1841	1841			Judge Hanson.	Destroyed by the fire in the Congressional Library, 1851.
Baron De Kalb.	June 2, 1848	1848			De Kalb family.	
Washington.	(2)	1851	Gilbert Stuart.	(3)		
Adams.	(2)	1851	Do.	(3)		
Jefferson.	(2)	1851	Do.	(3)		
Madison.	(2)	1851	Do.	(3)		
Monroe.	(2)	1851	Do.	(3)		
Peyton Randolph.		1851				
Bolivar.		1851				
Baron Steuben.		1851	Pyne.			
Discovery of the Mississippi.	Mar. 3, 1847	1855	W. H. Powell.	12,000.00		Rotunda.
Westward the Course of Empire takes its Way.	July 9, 1861	1862	Emmanuel Leutze.	20,000.00		West stairway, House of Representatives wing.
Battle on Lake Erie.	Mar. 2, 1865	1871	W. H. Powell.	25,000.00		East stairway, Senate wing.
Battle of Chapultepec.	1858	1862	James Walker.	6,137.37		West stairway, Senate wing.

[1] Mentioned by Watterson.
[2] On probation for purchase from 1840 to 1851.
[3] Valued by owner (Mr. Phelps) at $1,000 each.

NOTE: This table contains the information published by Glenn Brown, which has not been corrected or updated.

Table VIII.   Paintings in the Capitol. *(Continued)*

Title.	Ordered, purchased, or accepted.	Placed in Capitol.	Name of painter.	Cost.	By whom presented.	Location in Capitol in 1900.
Joshua Giddings.	June 26, 1867	1867	Miss. C. L. Ransom.	$1,000.00		Statuary Hall.
Henry Clay.	Mar. 1, 1871	1871	John Neagle.	1,500.00		East stairway hall, House of Representatives wing.
Gunning Bedford.			Charles Wilson Peale.[5]			East stairway hall, House of Representatives.
Chas. Carroll.	Apr. 23, 1870	1870	Thomas Sully.[5]	500.00		Do.
Grand Canyon of the Yellowstone.	June 10, 1872	1873	Thomas Moran.	10,000.00		Senate lobby.
Chasm of the Colorado.	Do.	1873	Do.	10,000.00		Do.
Discovery of the Hudson.	Mar. 3, 1875	1875	Albert Bierstadt.	10,000.00		House of Representatives.
California Landscape.		1875	Do.	10,000.00		Do.
Joseph Henry.	Mar. 20, 1872	1875	Henry Ulke.	600.00		Sergeant-at-Arms's room, Senate wing.
Benjamin West.	Jan. 8, 1876	1876	Benjamin West.	500.00		Senate Committee on the Library.
George Washington [6]	Jan. 7, 1876	1876	Gilbert Stuart.	1,200.00		Main Senate corridor.
Do.[7]	Dec. 12, 1886		Do.	1,200.00		Room Senate Committee on Finance.
Agassiz.	Feb. 7, 1877	1877	Henry Ulke.	(4)		Not located.
Emancipation Proclamation.	Jan. 25, 1878	1878	Frank Carpenter.	25,000.00 [5]	Mrs. Elizabeth Thompson.	East stairway, House of Representatives wing.
John Adams.	Mar. 31, 1881	1881	Copy from Gilbert Stuart by Andrews.	150.00		Main Senate corridor.
John Marshall.	Jan.—, 1881	1881	Copy from William D. Washington by R. Brookes.	650.00		West stairway hall, House of Representatives wing.
Henry Clay.	Feb. 23, 1881	1881	H. F. Darby.	1,333.33		East stairway hall, Senate wing.
John C. Calhoun.	Do.	1881	Do.	1,333.33		Do.
Daniel Webster.	Do.	1881	M. R. Brady, from sketches by J. Neagle.	1,333.33		Do.
George Washington.	Apr. 10, 1882	1882	Charles Wilson Peale.	5,000.00		West stairway hall, Senate wing.
Chief Justice Coleridge, England (engraving).	1883	1883			Chief Justice Coleridge.	Supreme Court robing room.
Recall of Columbus.	Apr. 25, 1884	1884	A. G. Heaton.	3,000.00		Room of Senate Committee on Public Lands.

[4] Purchase price not given.
[5] Indicates not from thoroughly reliable data.
[6] Called the Thomas Chestnut painting.
[7] Painted for Edw. Pennington, Pres. Phil. Acad. Fine Arts.

NOTE: This table contains the information published by Glenn Brown, which has not been corrected or updated.

Table VIII. Paintings in the Capitol. (Continued)

Title.	Ordered, purchased, or accepted.	Placed in Capitol.	Name of painter.	Cost.	By whom presented.	Location in Capitol in 1900.
Electoral Commission.	Feb. 25, 1885	1885	Cornelia Adèle Fassett.	$7,500.00		Senate lobby, gallery floor.
Henry Laurens.	May 20, 1886	1886	John Singleton Copley.	1,200.00		Senate Committee on Finance.
U. S. Grant.	July 22, 1886	1886	W. Cogswell.	750.00		Room of Senate Committee on Rules.
Farming in Dakota.	Mar. 3, 1887	1888	Carl Guthers.	3,000.00		Transferred to the agricultural department about 1889.
Salmon P. Chase.	Feb. 23, 1887	1887	W. Cogswell.	750.00		Supreme Court room.
Pocahontas.		1893			Owner; not yet accepted.	Room of Senate Committee on Rules.
John Marshall.	1873	1873	Rembrandt Peale.		Salmon P. Chase	Supreme Court robing room.
Oliver Ellsworth.	Oct. 2, 1888	1889	Copy from R. Earle by Elliott.	500.00		Do.
Justice Waite.	Do.	1889	Cornelia Adèle Fassett.	500.00		Do.
Justice Rutledge.	Do.	1889	Copy of miniature by John Trumbull, by Robert Hinckley.	500.00		Do.
Justice Marshall.	Apr. 3, 1890	1890	Martin.	1,000.00		Do.
Justice John Jay.		1870–1875	Gray, after Gilbert Stuart..		John Jay, minister to Austria.	Do.
Justice Taney.			Healy.		Washington Bar Association.	Do.
Justice Marshall.			Copy of St. Mémin by Rice.			Do.
Thomas Jefferson.	May 6, 1874	1874	Thomas Sully.			Senate corridor.
Patrick Henry.			G. B. Mathews.			Do.
Battle of Monitor and Merrimac.	Jan. 6, 1887	1887	Wm. F. Halsall.	5,000.00		Senate lobby.
Abraham Lincoln (mosaic).	1866	1866	Salviati.		Salviati	Do.
James A. Garfield (mosaic).	1882	1882	Do.		Do.	Do.
John Adams Dix.	Jan. 29, 1883	1883	I. R. Morrell.	600.00		Do.
Charles Sumner.	July 22, 1886	1886	W. Ingalls.	500.00		Do.
Table Rock, Niagara.			Regis Gignoux.		Mrs. Carroll	Do.
Life among the Sioux, 8 paintings.	1863	1863–1875	Lieut. Col. Seth Eastman.	(1)		Room of House Committee on Indian Affairs.
Life among the Sioux, one painting.	Do.		Do.	(1)		Office of Superintendent of the Capitol.
To Dislodge the British.	Feb. 17, 1890	Feb. 17, 1899	John Blake White.		Octavius A. White	Senate lobby, gallery floor.
Marion Inviting British Officer to Dinner.	Do.	Do.	Do.		Do.	Do.

[1] Retired on full pay in consideration of making paintings.

Table VIII.   Paintings in the Capitol. *(Continued)*

Title.	Ordered, purchased, or accepted.	Placed in Capitol.	Name of painter.	Cost.	By whom presented.	Location in Capitol in 1900.
Sergeant Jasper and Newton Rescuing Prisoners.	Feb. 17, 1890	Feb. 17, 1890	John Blake White.		Octavius A. White.	Senate lobby, gallery floor.
Battle of Fort Moultrie.	Do.	Do.	Do.		Do.	Do.
Portraits of Speakers House of Representatives:						
Thomas B. Reed, Maine.	1891	1891	John S. Sargent.		Henry C. Lodge and others.	Lobby, House of Representatives.
Henry Clay.	Jan. 14, 1852	1852	Giuseppe Fagnani.		G. Fagnani.	House lobby.
Robert C. Winthrop, Massachusetts.	1884	1885	D. Huntington.		Citizens of Massachusetts.	Do.
Frederick Muhlenberg, Pennsylvania.	1881	1881	Copy by Waugh.			Do.
*John W. Jones, Virginia.	1880	1880	Louis Wieser.	$60.00		Do.
*James L. Orr, South Carolina.	1880	1880	Do.	60.00		Do.
*William Pennington, New Jersey.	1880	1880	Do.			Do.
Joseph P. Varnum, Massachusetts.	1886	1888	Chas. L. Elliott.		State of Massachusetts.	Do.
*R. M. T. Hunter, Virginia.	1880	1880	Louis Wieser.	60.00		Do.
*Andrew Stevenson, Virginia.	1880	1880	Do.	60.00		Do.
Theodore Sedgwick, Massachusetts.	1886	1888	Copy G. Stuart by Edgar Parke.		State of Massachusetts.	Do.
*Schuyler Colfax, Indiana.	1880	1880	Louis Wieser.	60.00		Do.
Jonathan Trumbull, Connecticut.		1880	H. I. Thompson.			Do.
Nathaniel P. Banks, Massachusetts.	1886	1888	R. W. Vonnoh.		State of Massachusetts.	Do.
*Jonathan Dayton, New Jersey.	1880	1880	Louis Wieser.	60.00		Do.
John W. Taylor, New York.			Miss C. L. Ransom.			Do.
*Philip P. Barbour, Virginia.	1880	1880	Louis Wieser.	60.00		Do.
*John Bell, Tennessee.	1880	1880	Do.	60.00		Do.
*Linn Boyd, Kentucky.	1880	1880	Do.	60.00		Do.
*Michael Kerr, Indiana.	1880	1880	Do.	60.00		Do.
Samuel Randall, Pennsylvania.	1891		W. A. Greaves.			Do.
*James G. Blaine, Maine.	1880	1880	Louis Wieser.	60.00		Do.

*Asterisk indicates crayon portraits. Those drawn by Wieser the cost included a gold frame.
Portraits without asterisk preceding them are in oil.

NOTE: *This table contains the information published by Glenn Brown, which has not been corrected or updated.*

Table VIII.   Paintings in the Capitol. *(Continued)*

Title.	Ordered, purchased, or accepted.	Placed in Capitol.	Name of painter.	Cost.	By whom presented.	Location in Capitol in 1900.
Portraits of Speakers House of Representatives: *continued*						
Charles F. Crisp, Georgia.	1894		Robt. Hinckley.			House lobby.
*James G. Carlisle, Kentucky.	1888		A. J. Frey.			Do.
Galusha A. Grow, Pennsylvania.	1891		W. A. Greaves.			Do.
*J. Warren Keifer, Ohio.	1882	1882	Louis Wieser.	$50.00		Do.
*John W. Davis, Indiana.	1880	1880	Do.	60.00		Do.
*Howell Cobb, Georgia.	1880	1880	Do.	60.00		Do.
*James K. Polk, Tennessee.	1880	1880	Do.	60.00		Do.
*Landon Cheves, South Carolina.	1880	1880	Do.	60.00		Do.
*John White, Kentucky.	1880	1880	Do.	60.00		Do.
John W. Taylor.						Speaker's room, House.
Forts Knox, Tyler, Snelling, Scammel, George, Defiance, Sumter, Mackinac, Mifflin, Lafayette, Tompkins, Wadsworth, West Point, Delaware, Jefferson, Trumbull, Rice.						Room of Committee on Military Affairs, House of Representatives.
James A. Garfield.	Jan. 9, 1885	1885				House Committee on Appropriations.
A. G. Thurman.	Jan. 7, 1896	1896	J. H. Witt.	250.00		Senate Committee on Judiciary.
Gen. Geo. H. Thomas.	May 10, 1888	1888	S. W. Price.	2,500.00		Senate Committee on Arid Lands.
John Paul Jones.	Apr. 3, 1890	1892	G. B. Mathews.	500.00		Do.
Winfield Scott.	Mar. 3, 1891	1892	Edward Troye.	3,000.00		Stored.[1]
Reporters United States Supreme Court:						
Dallas.	1891	1891	Copy by Robert Hinckley.		Placed in Capitol by J. C. Bancroft Davis. Not formally presented or accepted.	Anteroom of United States Supreme Court—formerly room of Reporters of the United States Supreme Court.
Cranch.	1891	1891	Do.		Do.	
Wheaton.	1891	1891	Do.		Do.	
Peters.	1891	1891	Do.		Do.	
Howard.	1891	1891	Do.		Do.	
Black.	1891	1891	Do.		Do.	
Wallace.	1891	1891	Do.		Do.	
Otto.	1891	1891	Do.		Do.	

*Asterisk indicates crayon portraits. Crayons by Weiser cost includes a gold frame.
Portraits without asterisk preceding them are in oil.
[1] This painting was first offered to the Government May 12, 1862.

Table VIII.   Paintings in the Capitol. *(Continued)*

Title.	Ordered, purchased, or accepted.	Placed in Capitol.	Name of painter.	Cost.	By whom presented.	Location in Capitol in 1900.
Justice Samuel F. Miller.						Clerk's room of United States Supreme Court.
Clerks of Supreme Court:						
John Tucker.			Copy by C. H. Armor.			Do.
Samuel Bayard.					Presented by family.	Do.
E. B. Caldwell.			Copy by Armor.			Do.
William Griffith.			H. McDonald.			Do.
William T. Carroll.						Do.
D. W. Middleton.			Thomas Hicks.		Supreme Court bar.	Do.

Portraits without asterisk preceding them are in oil.

Table IX.   Frescoes in the Capitol.

Location and description.	Approximate date of completion.	Cost.	Artist.
HOUSE OF REPRESENTATIVES WING.			

Committee on Agriculture:
    Ceiling—The four seasons, Spring, Summer, Autumn, Winter.
    East wall—Cincinnatus called from the Plow to Defend Rome.
    West wall—Putnam called from the Plow to the American Army.
    South wall—
        Head of Washington on panel.
        Cutting Grain with a Sickle.
    North wall—
        Head of Jefferson on a panel.
        Harvesting with a Reaper.
	1855		Constantino Brumidi.

Committee on Elections: Fresco designs.			Leslie.
House of Representatives—Surrender of Cornwallis.			
SENATE WING.			

The President's room:
    Ceiling—
        Northeast—William Brewster, elder, Plymouth colony.
        Southeast—Christopher Columbus.
        Southwest—Benjamin Franklin.
        Northwest—Americus Vespucius.
    Groups—
        North—Religion.
        East—Executive Authority.
        South—Liberty.
        West—Legislation.
	1855–1864	Amount paid for various committee rooms from Apr. 7, 1855, to Dec. 3, 1864, $19,485.51, at rate of $10 per day.	Constantino Brumidi.

NOTE: *This table contains the information published by Glenn Brown, which has not been corrected or updated.*

Table IX.   Frescoes in the Capitol. *(Continued)*

Location and description.	Approximate date of completion.	Cost.	Artist.
SENATE WING. *(Continued)*			

Walls—Portraits of Washington, Jefferson, Hamilton, Knox, Randolph, Osgood.
Public reception room:
   Ceiling—
      Groups—Peace, Freedom, War, Agriculture.
      Figures—Prudence, Justice, Temperance, Fortitude.
   Wall—Washington in Consultation with Hamilton.
Sergeant-at-Arms's room: Dissolution of Union, Prosperity, Welcome of Erring Daughter.
Ground-floor corridor:
   Franklin in Laboratory.
   John Fitch working on Model of Steamboat.
   Signing Articles of Peace, 1782, with portraits of Richard Oswald for Great Britain, John
      Adams, Benjamin Franklin, John Jay, and Henry Laurens for the United States.
   The Cession of Louisiana.
Committee on Military Affairs:
   Washington and Lafayette in Consultation at Valley Forge.
   Storming of Stony Point.
   Death of General Wooster.
   The Boston Massacre.
Committee on Naval Affairs: Thetis, Venus, Amphitrite, and America.
Committee on Foreign Affairs, Signing Treaty.
Committee on Indian Affairs (decorated for Committee on Agriculture):
   Vines, fruit pieces, and Cupids.
   Columbus and Indian maiden.
Committee on the District of Columbia: Ceiling—History, Physics, Geography, Telegraph.
	1855–1864	Amount paid for various committee rooms from Apr. 7, 1855, to Dec. 3, 1864, $19,485.51, at rate of $10 per day.	Constantino Brumidi.
			
			Brumidi (from sketches by Benj. West).

Senate post-office: Three panels and four ceiling groups.	1869	$4,989.00	Constantino Brumidi.
ROTUNDA.			

Canopy in Rotunda:
   Center—Washington, with Freedom on the right and Victory on the left, with a circle of thirteen
      female figures representing the original States; on a banneret the motto "E Pluribus Unum."
   Base—Groups, The Spirit of Revolution; Liberty conquering Royalty; Minerva, the Goddess of
      Arts and Sciences; Mercury, representing Commerce; Vulcan the God of Mechanics, and
      Neptune, the God of the Sea.
	1865–1869	$39,500.00	Do.

Frieze in Rotunda:
   Landing of Columbus.
   Cortez entering the Hall of the Montezumas.
   Pizarro's Conquest of Peru.
   Burial of De Soto.
   Landing of the Pilgrims.
   Penn's Treaty with the Indians.
	1869–1880	From 1869 to 1880, approximately $25,000 was expended.	Do.

Plymouth Colony. Oglethorpe and the Indians. The Battle of Lexington. The Declaration of Independence. Surrender of Cornwallis. The Death of Tecumseh. General Scott's Entry into the City of Mexico. Discovery of Gold in California.	1889	$10,084.00	Filippo Costaggani (from sketches by Brumidi).

DE SOTO'S DISCOVERY OF THE MISSISSIPPI

A.D. 1541

1. DE SOTO 2. MOORISH SERVANT. 3. CONFESSOR. 4. YOUNG SPANISH CAVALIER. 5. *Cannon dragged up by Artillerymen.*
6. *Company of stalwart men planting a cross.* 7. *Ecclesiastic bearing the censer.* 8. *Old Priest blessing the cross.*
9. *Soldier dressing his wounded leg.* 10. *Camp-chest with arms, helmets and other implements of war.* 11. *Group of standard-bearers and helmeted men.*
12. *Two young Indian maidens* 13. INDIAN CHIEFS *bearing the pipe of peace.*
In the distance is seen the Mississippi Its waters are broken by glancing canoes, magical islands and purple shores.

PLATE 299

THE DISCOVERY OF THE MISSISSIPPI, WM. H. POWELL, PAINTER.

Oil on canvas, 1853, located in the Capitol Rotunda.

PLATE 300

WASHINGTON'S HEADQUARTERS IN YORKTOWN,—FRESCO BY BRUMIDI.

Cornwallis Sues for Cessation of Hostilities Under the Flag of Truce, 1857.
Originally in House Chamber; removed and placed in Members' dining room, H–117, in 1962.

PLATE 301

PERRY'S VICTORY ON LAKE ERIE, W. H. POWELL, PAINTER.

Battle of Lake Erie, oil on canvas, 1873, located in the Senate wing, east staircase.

PLATE 302

WESTWARD, THE COURSE OF EMPIRE TAKES ITS WAY, EMANUEL LEUTZE, PAINTER.

Stereochromy, 1862, located in the House wing, west stairway.

PLATE 303

THE CHASM OF THE COLORADO BY THOMAS MORAN.

Oil on canvas, 1874, transferred to the Department of the Interior in 1950. On loan to the Smithsonian American Art Museum, Smithsonian Institution.

PLATE 304

THE GRAND CANYON OF THE YELLOWSTONE, THOS. MORAN, PAINTER.

Oil on canvas, 1872, transferred to the Department of the Interior in 1950. On loan to the Smithsonian American Art Museum, Smithsonian Institution.

PLATE 305

GEORGE WASHINGTON,—BY GILBERT STUART.

Oil on canvas, purchased 1876, located in S–207.

PLATE 306

HENRY CLAY,—BY H. F. DARBY.

Oil on canvas, purchased in 1881, located in the Senate wing, second floor, main corridor.

THE BATTLE OF CHAPULTEPEC,—BY JAMES WALKER.

Oil on canvas, purchased in 1862; now on loan outside the Capitol.

PLATE 307

PLATE 308

DISCOVERY OF THE HUDSON, ALBERT BIERSTADT, PAINTER.

Discovery of the Hudson River, oil on canvas, purchased in 1875, currently in storage.

PLATE 309

CALIFORNIA LANDSCAPE, ALBERT BIERSTADT, PAINTER.

Entrance Into Monterey, oil on canvas, purchased 1878, currently in storage.

PLATE 310

VIEW OF ROTUNDA FROM FLOOR, FRESCO BY BRUMIDI.

Apotheosis of George Washington, fresco, 1865, canopy of the dome.

PLATE 311

ERECTING THE FIRST HOUSE IN PLYMOUTH, FRESCO ON FRIEZE OF ROTUNDA,—BRUMIDI & COSTAGGINI, PAINTERS.

Photograph showing the extensive damage caused by leaks in the late nineteenth century.

THE DECLARATION OF INDEPENDENCE, FRESCO ON FRIEZE OF ROTUNDA,—BRUMIDI & COSTAGGINI, PAINTERS.

Modern photograph showing the painting after restoration.

FRESCO ON FRIEZE OF ROTUNDA, THE BATTLE OF LEXINGTON, BRUMIDI & COSTAGGINI, PAINTERS.

Modern photograph showing the painting after restoration.

PLATE 312

JOHN JAY, COPY BY GRAY AFTER GILBERT STUART.

Henry Peters Gray, oil on canvas, 1853. The painting is in the collection of the Supreme Court of the United States.

THE ELECTORAL COMMISSION.

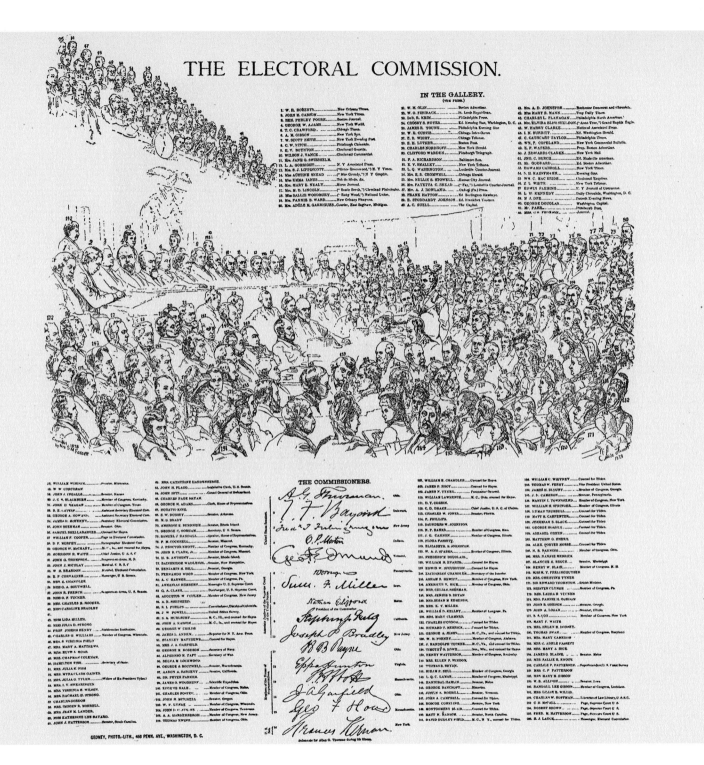

PLATE 313

THE ELECTORAL COMMISSION, ADELE FASSETT, PAINTER.

The Florida Case before the Electoral Commission, oil on canvas, 1879, located in the Senate wing, third floor, east corridor.

PLATE 314

THE RECALL OF COLUMBUS, A. G. HEATON, PAINTER.

Oil on canvas, 1882, located in Senate wing, third floor, east corridor.

Chapter XXII
Architects of the Capitol Extension

THOMAS USTICK WALTER.

[Plates 315, 316.]

MR. WALTER was born in Philadelphia September 4, 1804, of Joseph S. and Deborah Walter, and was named after Rev. Thomas Ustick, a well-known divine in the early part of the past century. He had a good education and showed proficiency in mathematics. In 1819 he entered the office of William Strickland, a prominent architect of that day. After the study of mechanical drawing he left Strickland, and for seven years studied mathematics, physics, drawing, painting, construction, and landscape painting, the latter branch under an artist named Mason. In the year 1828 he again entered the office of Strickland and devoted himself exclusively to the study of architecture for two years. He commenced the practice of architecture in 1830 and was appointed architect of the Philadelphia County Prison October 14, 1831. His design for the Girard College for Orphans was adopted in 1833. This work was carried out under his supervision, being finished in 1847. Upon the completion of the building he was elected one of the directors of the college and served three years. During the year 1838 he was sent abroad by the Girard trustees to study the various European seats of learning. On this trip he visited England, Scotland, Ireland, Germany, France, and Italy.

Mr. Walter was a pioneer and active promoter in starting an association entitled "The American Institution of Architecture," being elected secretary at its organization March 22, 1837. The good-fellowship of the profession at this period was not sufficient to keep this association together for any length of time.

In the year 1843 Mr. Walter was invited by the Government of Venezuela to examine the port of La Guaira, with a view to constructing a breakwater to protect the harbor and facilitate the discharge of cargoes. After visiting the country he prepared drawings and specifications for the work, which was completed October 24, 1845.

His connection with the Capitol building has been described in other portions of this book. While acting as Architect of the Capitol he designed the east and west wings of the Patent Office, the extension of the General Post-Office, the north, south, and west fronts of the United States Treasury building, the marine barracks at Brooklyn and Pensacola, and the Government Hospital for the Insane, at Washington. Upon his appointment as Architect of the Capitol in 1851 he moved his family to Washington, where they remained until 1865, when his connection with the building ceased and he returned to Philadelphia. Before coming to Washington he had a large private practice in Philadelphia, designing many public and private buildings in that city and other parts of the country. In 1849 he received the honorary degree of master of arts from Madison University, New York; in 1853 that of doctor of philosophy from the University of Lewisburg, Pa.; and that of doctor of laws from Harvard in 1857. Mr. Walter held the professorship of architecture in the Franklin Institute, of which he was a member from 1829 until his death, and delivered many lectures on architecture in Philadelphia and Washington. Among the notable articles by him which appeared in the Journal of the Franklin Institute may be mentioned "Architecture in the Middle Ages," "Formation of an Artificial Spectrum," "Orders of Architecture," and descriptions of the county

PLATE 315

THOMAS U. WALTER, ARCHITECT.
Portrait of Walter, ca. 1857. *AIA Archives.*

PLATE 316

THOMAS U. WALTER, ARCHITECT.
Photograph of Walter, ca. 1885. *AIA Archives.*

prison and Girard College. He was a member of the American Philosophical Society for a period of thirty years. He was one of the founders of the American Institute of Architects, in 1857, and was elected its second president upon the death of Richard Upjohn, serving from 1877 to 1887. Upon leaving Washington Mr. Walter assisted John MacArthur on the new city hall in Philadelphia, holding the position until his death, October 30, 1887.[1]

Mr. Walter, in his architectural designs, followed classical models, and his work showed well-studied plans, a dignity in mass, and a refinement in detail which give his buildings a quality that will be appreciated by the refined and cultured of the future. He was an indefatigable student and industrious worker until his death. He lent a willing hand and gave with zeal his time to any matter which tended to advance the profession of architecture, and endeared himself to all who came in contact with him by his genial social qualities.

As I remember him, his personal appearance was most striking— a large frame, with a strong and impressive face and head crowned with bushy white hair.

The principles upon which he acted during life are well expressed in the following extract with which he closed an address to the American Institute of Architects:

"We owe to our country, to the age in which we live, to our families, to ourselves, to devote the rapidly fleeting hours of our lives to the accomplishment of the greatest possible good in our vocation, ever seeking to discharge our duties in all good conscience toward those whose interests are intrusted to our care, toward coworkers in the realm of art, and toward Him in whom we live and move and have our being." [2]

EDWARD CLARK.
[Plate 317.]

Edward Clark was born in Philadelphia August 15, 1822. He was the son of James Clark, an architect of that city, and his mother was a daughter of Capt. John Cottman, of the Revolutionary Army. He was educated at the public schools and academies of Philadelphia, but chiefly under the direction of his uncle, Thomas Clark, who was an engineer in the Army. He was instructed in mechanical and free-hand drawing by his father, and at an early age entered the office of Thomas U. Walter, being made superintendent of the construction of the extension of the Patent Office and General Post-Office when Mr. Walter was placed in charge of these buildings in 1851. In 1865, upon the resignation of Mr. Walter, he was appointed Architect of the Capitol.

During his long service in Washington Mr. Clark devoted himself almost exclusively to the special work in his charge, declining to enter into competition with architects in private practice, but giving his services freely to the many charitable and eleemosynary institutions of the District and elsewhere. He was invited by the board of commissioners to revise the plans of the State capitol of Iowa, which he did to their entire satisfaction.

At the time of his death Mr. Clark was the oldest member of the board of trustees of the Corcoran Gallery of Art, having served for many years as chairman of the committee on works of art, and having also been appointed chairman of a special committee to superintend the construction of the new gallery.

He was a Fellow of the American Institute of Architects from 1888 to the time of his death, a member of the Clarendon Historical Society

[1] Brown's major sources for his biographical sketch of Walter included James Q. Howard, "The Architects of the American Capitol," *International Review* 1 (November–December, 1874): 736–753; "T. U. Walter," *Building News* [London] 24 (1883): 785; and George C. Mason, Jr., "Biographical Memoirs of Thomas U. Walter," *Proceedings of the Twenty-second Annual Convention of the American Institute of Architects* (New York: Oberhauser and Company, Printers, 1889), 101–108.

[2] Proceedings of the *Annual Convention of the American Institute of Architects, 1889.*

of Edinburgh, and also a member of many scientific, musical, and literary societies.

Possessed of a remarkably retentive memory, a lover of books and music from his childhood, Mr. Clark was a most delightful companion. A collector of music for more than sixty years, he left what was probably the largest private collection in Washington.

He died in Washington on January 6, 1902, having been continuously employed on the architectural work of the Government for fifty-one years.[3]

FREDERICK LAW OLMSTED.
[Plate 318.]

Mr. Olmsted was born in Hartford, Conn., April 26, 1822. He studied civil engineering three years, and later pursued scientific studies at Yale College. After this he was for two years a working student of agriculture, and then spent seven years as a farmer and horticulturist upon his own land. At this early period he was an ardent lover of natural scenery, and for the enjoyment of it made many journeys both in the saddle and on foot.

He made four trips to Europe, in each case giving special study to parks and pleasure grounds, public forests, zoological and botanical gardens, and the plans and manner of enlargement of towns and suburbs. Letters from and the advice of Prof. Asa Gray, A. J. Downing, and Sir William Hooker gave him special facilities for such study.

In 1853 and 1854 he was engaged in the study of the economical conditions of the slave States. In order to make close observations of rural details he traveled a distance of more than 4,000 miles in these States on horseback.

During the spring of 1857 he was appointed superintendent of the preparatory work of the projected Central Park of New York. The following fall, in association with Calvert Vaux, he devised a plan for this park which was selected as the most satisfactory of thirty-three plans submitted in competition, and the firm was employed to execute the work.

At the outbreak of the civil war in 1861 Mr. Olmsted was appointed by the President a member of the National Sanitary Commission, and was asked by his associates to take the duty of organizing and managing its executive business. In the fall of 1863, the work of the Commission having been fully developed and the successful accomplishment of its objects assured, he resigned the position and passed the next two years on the Pacific slope. He there served as chairman of the California State commission, taking the custody of the Yosemite and Mariposa reservations, ceded to the State by Congress as public parks. In 1865 he returned to New York and entered into partnership with Vaux & Withers upon the general practice of landscape architecture. In 1872 this partnership was dissolved, and he served for a time as president and treasurer of the park commission of New York, being afterwards their landscape architect for nearly six years. In 1878 he moved to Boston, and in 1884 took into partnership his son, John Charles Olmsted, and in 1889 Henry Sargent Codman, both of whom had received their professional training in his office, and had afterwards pursued studies in Europe under his advice.

Mr. Olmsted was employed upon upward of eighty public recreation grounds. He also had a large practice in the laying out of towns, suburban villa districts, and private grounds, and in the pursuit of this practice he visited every State in the Union. His work in connection with the Capitol has been described in other portions of this volume. He was the designer of the general scheme for the restoration and preservation of the natural scenery of Niagara Falls and, in association with Mr. Vaux, of the plan now being carried out by the State of New York for this purpose.

---

[3] "Obituary of Edward Clark," *Proceedings of the Thirtieth Annual Convention of the American Institute of Architects* (Washington: Gibson Brothers, 1903), 249.

PLATE 317

EDWARD CLARK, ARCHITECT.
Photograph of Edward Clark, ca. 1895.

PLATE 318

FREDERICK LAW OLMSTED, LANDSCAPE ARCHITECT.

Photograph of Olmsted, ca. 1885. *National Park Service, Olmsted National Historic Site.*

Mr. Olmsted was the author of the following works: Walks and Talks of an American Farmer in England, first published in 1852, and several times reprinted, one edition having been prepared especially for the common school libraries of the State of Ohio; A Journey in the Seaboard Slave States, 1856; A Journey in Texas, 1857; A Journey in the Back Country, 1861. Translations of A Journey in Texas have been published in Paris and Leipzig. At the outbreak of the civil war a compilation of the last three works was published in London under the title of The Cotton Kingdom, and was much quoted by those leaders of English public opinion who favored the northern view of the conflict.

In addition to the above books Mr. Olmsted wrote much on special problems of his profession, which is to be found in various periodicals and in printed reports of park commissions and other bodies.

Mr. Olmsted received the honorary degree of A.M. from Amherst College, and both A.M. and LL.D. from Harvard and Yale universities. He was an honorary member of the American Institute of Architects, the Boston Society of Architects, the London Metropolitan Public Gardens Association, the Military Order of the Loyal Legion, and the Harvard Phi Beta Kappa. He was one of the founders and an honorary member of the Metropolitan Art Museum and the Union League, and an active member of the Century Club of New York and the St. Botolph Club of Boston, as well as many scientific and benevolent societies. He died August 28, 1903.[4]

---

[4] In his bibliography Brown did not cite any secondary sources for his biographical sketch of Olmsted. Frederick Law Olmsted, Jr., probably provided Brown with the information appearing here and in the discussion of Olmsted's design of the Capitol grounds. The younger Olmsted worked closely with Brown as a featured speaker at the American Institute of Architect's 1900 convention in Washington. Brown was well known to Olmsted as a key supporter of the Senate Park Commission after Olmsted was appointed to the board with Charles McKim, Daniel Burnham, and Augustus St. Gaudens in 1901.

LIST OF THE MORE NOTABLE PUBLIC OR SEMIPUBLIC GROUNDS FORMED OR FORMING MAINLY AFTER PLANS DEVISED BY FREDERICK LAW OLMSTED, AND GENERALLY IN PARTNERSHIP WITH ONE OR ANOTHER OF THE FOLLOWING GENTLEMEN: CALVERT VAUX, JOHN C. OLMSTED, HENRY S. CODMAN, CHARLES ELIOT.

Public Parks: Central Park, Mount Morris Park, Riverside Park, and Morningside Park, New York; Prospect Park, Washington Park, Ocean Park, and Eastern Parkway, Brooklyn; Washington Park and Jackson Park, Chicago; North Park, South Park, and Cazenovia Park, Buffalo; Seaside Park and Beardsley Park, Bridgeport, Conn.; Mount Royal, Montreal; The Fens, Muddy River Improvement, Jamaica Park, Arnold Arboretum, Franklin Park, Marine Park, Charlesbank, Beacon Parkway, Boston; Genesee Park, Seneca Park, Highland Park, Rochester; Belle Isle Park, Detroit; Cherokee Park, Shawnee Park, Iroquois Park, Louisville; Lake Park, West Side Park, River Park, Milwaukee; Washington Square, Baltimore.

Grounds of public and semipublic buildings: World's Columbian Exposition grounds, Chicago, Ill.; United States Capitol grounds, Washington; Statehouse grounds, Hartford, Conn.; capitol and city hall grounds, Buffalo, N.Y.; town hall, North Easton, Mass.; Schuylkill Arsenal grounds, Philadelphia, Pa.; grounds of insane hospital at Hartford, Conn., and at Buffalo, Poughkeepsie, and White Plains, N.Y.; Leake & Watts Orphan House, Yonkers, N.Y.; Columbia Institution for the Deaf and Dumb, Washington.

Colleges: Amherst College, Amherst, Mass.; Yale University, New Haven, Conn.; Hamilton College, Clinton, N.Y.; College of New Jersey, Princeton, N.J.; Trinity College, Hartford, Conn.; University of Vermont, Burlington, Vt.; Williams College, Williamstown, Mass.; Massachusetts Agricultural College, Amherst, Mass.; Smith College, Northampton, Mass.; University of California, Berkeley, Cal.; Stanford University, Palo Alto, Cal.; Columbia University, New York, N.Y.; Dartmouth College, Hanover, N.H.; Cornell University, Ithaca, N.Y.

Grounds of railroad stations: Palmer, Auburndale, Chestnut Hill, and North Easton, Mass.

Schools: Lawrenceville School, Lawrenceville, N.J.; Phillips Academy, Andover, Mass.; Groton School, Groton, Mass.; Bryn Mawr School, Baltimore, Md.

Private places: Estates of George W. Vanderbilt, Biltmore, N.C.; J. C. Phillips, Beverly, Mass.; B. Schlesinger, J. H. White, Charles Storrow, and J. Randolph Coolidge, Brookline, Mass.; R. H. I. Goddard and H. G. Russell, Providence, R.I.; Wirt D. Walker, Pittsfield, Mass.; Whitelaw Reid, White Plains, N.Y.; J. J. Albright, Buffalo, N.Y.; J. M. Longyear, Marquette, Mich., and many others.

Suburban land divisions: Aspinwall Hill and Fisher Hill, Brookline, Mass.; Swampscott Land Trust, Swampscott, Mass.; Rocky Farm, etc., Newport, R.I.; Riverside, Chicago, Ill.; Berkeley, Cal.; Sudbrook Land Company, Baltimore, Md.; Depew, Buffalo, N.Y.; Log Cabin Farm, Detroit, Mich.

THOMAS WISEDELL.
[Plate 321.]

Mr. Wisedell was born in London September 28, 1846, and in early life became a pupil of Robert J. Withers, an architect. While still with Mr. Withers, his ability attracted the attention of Calvert Vaux, of the firm of Vaux & Withers, of New York City, the latter of whom was a brother of the London architect. Mr. Vaux induced him to come to this country in 1868. For many years thereafter he was an assistant to Vaux & Withers, and in 1879 became a member of the firm of Kimball & Wisedell. Mr. Wisedell designed many public works and places of amusement. For eight or ten years he, under the direction of Frederick Law Olmsted, designed the architectural features of the improvements of the Capitol grounds at Washington. Among them was the terrace around the Capitol. He also designed the architectural work with Mr. Olmsted as the landscape architect of many other parks at various places in this country. The architectural work of Prospect Park, Brooklyn, is an example in point. In connection with Mr. Kimball, he designed and built many well-known theaters. Among these are the Madison Square Theater, Harrigan & Hart's Theater, and the Casino, at Broadway and Thirty-ninth street, in New York City; the Springfield Opera House at Springfield, Mass., and the Yonkers Opera House, Yonkers, N.Y. He died September 30, 1884.[5]

[5] Brown probably derived his information on Thomas Wisedell from interviews with Frederick Law Olmsted, Jr. and Edward Clark.

CHAPTER XXIII

SUPERINTENDENTS OF THE CAPITOL EXTENSION

MONTGOMERY C. MEIGS [Plate 319] was born at Augusta, Ga., May 13, 1816, and was the son of Charles D. Meigs and Mary Montgomery. He was a lineal descendant of Vincent Meigs, who emigrated to America in 1634 and settled in Connecticut. He was educated at Franklin Institute and the University of Pennsylvania, and at the age of 16 entered the Military Academy at West Point, from which he was graduated in 1836.

He entered the Engineer Corps, and was made captain in 1853. He assisted Robert E. Lee in the surveys of the harbor of St. Louis and the rapids of the Mississippi. He was employed in the Engineer Bureau in Washington, D.C., from 1849 to 1850, making the surveys and plans for the Washington Aqueduct. These plans were adopted by Congress in 1853 to 1861 and he was made chief engineer, and the work, including Cabin John Bridge, the most imposing stone arch in the world, was executed under his direction.[1] His work in connection with the Capitol has already been described in this volume. In 1861 he was ordered to Florida to the relief of Fort Pickens, which he was instrumental in saving, thus securing to the United States the important harbor of Pensacola. He was commissioned colonel May 14, 1861, Quartermaster-General May 15, 1861, with the rank of brigadier-general, which rank he retained until he was retired, February 6, 1882. His duties as Quartermaster-General, in charge of the business of equipment and supplies, kept him principally confined to Washington. He was present at the first battle of Bull Run and during the siege of Chattanooga, and visited the armies of McClellan, Butler, and Grant during their operations on the James and the Potomac, at times taking personal charge of the base of supplies. In 1876 he was a member of the Commission for the Reform and Reorganization of the Army. He was a member of the boards to prepare plans for the National Museum and War Department buildings. After his retirement, by special act of Congress, he was made architect and superintendent of the Pension building, which was executed from his designs. He died in Washington, D.C., January 2, 1892.[2]

WILLIAM BUEL FRANKLIN [Plate 320] was born in York, Pa., February 27, 1823, and was graduated from West Point in 1843 at the head of his class. He served in the Topographical Engineers until the beginning of the civil war, being appointed captain July 1, 1857. In 1861 he was stationed in Washington and acted as superintendent of the Capitol extension and the Treasury and Post-Office Department buildings.[3] He became a colonel May 14, 1861; brigadier-general June 30, 1862, for meritorious conduct in the battles before Richmond, and major-general March 13, 1865, for signal services during the civil war. He took part in the battles of Bull Run, Yorktown, West Point, White Oak Bridge, Savage Station, Malvern Hill, and Harrisons Landing. He

---

[1] Meigs was superintendent of the Capitol extension from 1853 to 1859 and again from February 1861 to April 1861.

[2] Brown made two errors in his sketch of Meigs's life. Meigs was born on May 8, 1816, and his plan for the Washington Aqueduct was adopted in 1852. Brown's sources were Samuel P. Langley, "Montgomery C. Meigs," *Bulletin of the Philosophical Society of Washington* 12 (1892–1894): 471–476; W. Rhees, "Montgomery C. Meigs Sketch," in George Brown Goode, ed., *Annual Report of the Board of Regents, Smithsonian Institution, 1846–1896* (Washington: Smithsonian Institution, 1897), 103.

[3] Franklin was stationed in Washington in 1859 before the outbreak of the Civil War.

was at Cramptons Gap, South Mountain, September 14, and at Antietam September 17, 1862. At the battle of Fredericksburg, December 13, 1862, he commanded the left grand division. He was badly wounded at the battle of Sabine Crossroads April 8, 1864. He resigned from the Army March 15, 1866, and was for some time president of the Colt's Firearms Company, Hartford, Conn. He was State commissioner of Connecticut at the Centennial Exposition, Philadelphia, Presidential elector in 1876, adjutant-general of Connecticut 1877–78, and president of the Board of Managers of the National Home for Disabled Volunteer Soldiers from 1880 to 1887. He died March 8, 1903.

CONSTANTINO BRUMIDI [Plate 322] was born in Rome, Italy, June 10, 1805. His father was a Greek and his mother an Italian. He studied in the Academia di San Luca. He painted frescoes in several palaces in Rome, and worked three years in the Vatican under Gregory XVI. Brumidi was a captain in the Papal Guards during the Italian revolution. Just before Rossi was assassinated, refusing to execute commands to turn the guns of his company upon the oppressed, he was arrested and thrown into prison. He was released at the intervention of the Pope, upon condition that he immediately leave Italy. He landed in New York in 1849 and was naturalized in 1852. He could not secure satisfactory employment, and went to Mexico, where he stayed three years, when he came to Washington and spent the rest of his life working upon the frescoes of the Capitol. He died February 19, 1880.[4]

---

[4] Brumidi was actually born on July 26, 1805, landed in New York in 1852, and became a naturalized citizen in 1857. He was in Mexico for part of 1854. Brown probably obtained his information on Brumidi from Edward Clark.

PLATE 319

GENERAL M. C. MEIGGS, SUPERINTENDENT.

Brown's plate is a detail of the original photograph taken ca. 1865. Brown misspelled Meigs's name in his caption. *Brady Collection, NARA.*

PLATE 320

GENERAL W. B. FRANKLIN, SUPERINTENDENT.

Photograph taken ca. 1865. *Location unknown.*

PLATE 321

THOMAS WISEDELL, ASSISTANT TO F. L. OLMSTED.

Photograph taken ca. 1880. *Location unknown.*

PLATE 322

CONSTANTINO BRUMIDI, FRESCO PAINTER.

Photograph taken by Meigs in 1859.

Chapter XXIV

Miscellaneous Data of the Capitol Extension

WHEN the Capitol extension was commenced the work was placed in charge of the Secretary of the Interior, under whom it remained from June 11, 1851, to March 28, 1853, when the authority was transferred to the Secretary of War, remaining under this branch of the Government until April 16, 1862. At the latter date it was again transferred to the Interior Department, under the jurisdiction of which it remains at the present time. The old Capitol building when the extension was authorized was under the Commissioner of Public Buildings and Grounds, an officer of the Interior Department, but when the new work was commenced the extension of the building was placed under the architect, he being made responsible only to the Secretary of the Interior. The Commissioner of Public Buildings and Grounds retained jurisdiction over the old portion of the building and had charge of its maintenance and repairs until March 30, 1867, when the building and grounds were put in charge of the Architect of the Capitol. When the work was placed in charge of the War Department, a captain of the Engineer Corps was made superintendent and disbursing officer.

Previous to March 3, 1869, repairs and improvements of the heating apparatus were in charge of officers appointed by each house; after that date they were placed under the Architect of the Capitol.

It was the policy of Edward Clark whenever improvements of magnitude were contemplated to seek the advice of the most prominent experts. In this way Dr. John S. Billings, Robert Briggs, and S. H. Woodbridge were consulted on heating and ventilation, George E. Waring on plumbing, and Frederick Law Olmsted on landscape architecture.

The high quality of the work shown in the old structure, the extension, and the Dome must be largely attributed to the jealous care with which the Presidents of the United States, who by law appoint the architects, have avoided the appointment of incompetent men, and the zeal with which they sought and secured the men who had proved themselves by their artistic work the most competent to undertake the designing and supervision of the principal architectural structure in the United States.

Large portions of the work on the extension were done by the day, the brick, lime, sand, rubblestone, and lumber being purchased in the open market and the labor being employed on day's wages at the prevailing rates. Contracts were made for granite, iron, marble, and the heating apparatus. The price of brick ranged from $6.37 to $8 per thousand. Ironwork varied according to its character, sash weights costing $44.80 per ton; bolts, washers, and rods $89.60 per ton; window frames $201.60 per ton, and skylight frames as high as $268.80 per ton—the average being about $90 per ton. Rubblestone was furnished for $2.25 per perch. Rice, Baird & Heebner, Philadelphia, made contracts to furnish marble from Lee, Berkshire County, Mass., for blocks over 30 cubic feet at $1.98 per cubic foot, and all under 30 cubic feet at 65 cents per cubic foot in the rough. This contract was changed February 20, 1854, so as to read: "The price for all blocks exceeding 18-inch bed or containing over 30 cubic feet and not over 120 cubic feet, $1.98 per cubic foot; all under 30 cubic feet and 18-inch bed or less, 65 cents. Column shafts for the corridor of the south basement, $200 each. Tennessee marble, $5 per cubic foot; green serpentine, $7; breccia from the Potomac, $4; levant from north coast of Africa, $5; Italian statuary, $7.95; ordinary Italian, $2.75." Rice, Baird & Heebner furnished the columnar shafts for the various porticoes, 100 in number, from the Conolly quarries, Cockeysville, Md., in monolithic blocks, at $1,400 each. The shafts contain 262.5 cubic feet and cost $5.33 per cubic foot. Cement cost $1.39½ per barrel, lime 97 cents per barrel, and sand 18 cents per barrel. The cost of brickwork laid was $22.10¹⁰⁄₁₀ per thousand. Marble cutting varied in price from 75 cents to $4 per cubic foot, according to the character of the moldings or stone.

Lumber was obtained for the following prices: Spruce, $1.50 to $2.50 per hundred feet; North Carolina pine, from $2.50 to $3.50; white pine, $3 to $4; ash, $3.50; oak, $3.50. Shingles cost from $8.75 to $10 per thousand.

The prices paid to workmen previous to 1860, when most of the work was done on the building, varied as follows: Laborers, from $1.25 to $1.50 per day; masons, $2.25 to $2.50; foremen, $4 to $5; modeler, $6; bronze founder, $6; brass molder, $2.75; plasterers, $2; carpenters, $2.

The principal contractors, with character of the labor or material which they supplied on the Capitol, were as follows: James S. Piper, Baltimore, Md., rubblestone; Samuel Seely, New York, and Henry Hoover, Washington, lime; Aloysius N. Clements, Washington, sand; George Schafer, Funktown, D.C., and Alex. R. Boteler, Shepherdstown, W. Va., cement; Christopher Adams and Cornelius Wendell, brick-makers, Washington; John Purdy and John Libbey & Sons, lumber, Washington; Henry Exall, Richmond, Va., and Mathew G. Emery, Washington, contracted to furnish, cut, and lay granite in basement.

Rice, Baird & Heebner, Philadelphia, contracted to deliver all marble in the rough, while Provost, Winter & Co., Washington, made an agreement for cutting and laying all marble work.

Poole & Hunt, Baltimore, Md., and Janes, Beebe & Co., New York, Cooper, Hewitt & Co., New York, made contracts for cast iron; Janes, Fowler, and Kirtland, New York, for ornamental ironwork.

Morris & Tanner (The Tredeger Iron Works), Richmond, Va., and the Phoenix Iron Works, Philadelphia, supplied the wrought-iron work.

The heating and ventilating was done by Nason & Dodge, Philadelphia, with Robert Briggs in charge of the work; J. H. & J. C. Schneider, Washington, furnished the bronze registers.

Warner, Miskey, and Merrill, afterwards Archer, Warner & Miskey, Philadelphia, made bronze work for private stairways in House and Senate wings, and the eagle and probably the clock in the House of Representatives; and Cornelius & Baker, Philadelphia, made the bronze caps for columns and pilasters and the bronze arms to the gallery seats in the House of Representatives and the bronze figures of the Pioneer and Indian for the clock in the House of Representatives.

Miller & Coates, New York, supplied the encaustic tiles for the floors throughout the halls and corridors.

The Vermont Marble Company, Proctor, Vt., were the contractors for the terraces and the steps.

Appended hereto are five tables, the first giving a list of the principal men who have worked on the Capitol, with date of service and salary (Table No. X); the second giving the general dimensions (Table No. XI); the third a list of the trees and shrubs planted in the Capitol grounds by Frederick Law Olmsted (Table No. XII); the fourth a statement of appropriations and disbursements on the Capitol from 1850 to 1900 (Table No. XIII), and the fifth giving a summary of the cost of the building (Table No. XIV)[1].

---

[1] The tables in Brown's volumes have been reprinted in this edition with his original foot-notes. Brown obtained the data for his tables from a variety of sources, including statutes enacted by Congress establishing the names, salaries, and duties of the principal individuals in charge of the Capitol prior to the design and construction of the Capitol Extension.

The *U.S. Statutes at Large* reprinted both public and private laws enacted by Congress relative to the construction, repair, furniture, lighting, and artwork in the Capitol over the time period covered in the first volume. Treasury Department records also contained records for warrants drawn for payment to certain individuals who worked on the Capitol. Most of the information gathered here was a matter of public record, such as salary information contained in the reports of the Architect of the Capitol.

NOTE: *This table contains the information published by Glenn Brown, which has not been corrected or updated.*

Table X. Names, salaries, and duties of the principal men connected with the Capitol extension, 1850–1900.

[See Vol. I for similar table for the period 1793 to 1850.]

Office.	Name.	Date of service.	Salary.	Remarks.
Secretary of Interior.	A. H. H. Stuart.	June 11, 1851, to Mar. 23, 1853	Part of duties as Secretary; no additional salary.	Cabinet officers directly responsible to the President for work on the Capitol, and to whom architects, superintendents, and contractors were responsible.
Secretary of War.	Jefferson Davis.	Mar. 23, 1853, to Mar. 3, 1857	Do.	
	Samuel Cooper (ad interim).	Mar. 3, 1857, to Mar. 7, 1857	Do.	
	John B. Floyd.	Mar. 7, 1857, to Dec. 31, 1860	Do.	
	Joseph Holt.	Jan. 1, 1861, to Mar. 10, 1861	Do.	
	Simon Cameron.	Mar. 11, 1861, to Jan. 19, 1862	Do.	
	Edwin M. Stanton.	Jan. 20, 1862, to Apr. 16, 1862	Do.	
Secretary of Interior.	Caleb B. Smith.	Apr. 16, 1862, to Jan. 8, 1863	Do.	
	J. P. Usher.	Jan. 8, 1863, to May 15, 1865	Do.	
	James Harlan.	May 15, 1865, to July 27, 1866	Do.	
	Orville H. Browning.	July 27, 1866, to Mar. 5, 1869	Do.	
	Jacob D. Cox.	Mar. 5, 1869, to Nov. 1, 1870	Do.	
	Columbus Delano.	Nov. 1, 1870, to Oct. 19, 1875	Do.	
	Zachariah Chandler.	Oct. 19, 1875, to Mar. 12, 1877	Do.	
	Carl Schurz.	Mar. 12, 1877, to Mar. 5, 1881	Do.	
	S. J. Kirkwood.	Mar. 5, 1881, to Apr. 6, 1882	Do.	
	H. M. Teller.	Apr. 6, 1882, to Mar. 6, 1885	Do.	
	L. Q. C. Lamar.	Mar. 6, 1885, to Jan. 16, 1888	Do.	
	W. F. Vilas.	Jan. 16, 1888, to Mar. 6, 1889	Do.	
	John W. Noble.	Mar. 6, 1889, to Mar. 6, 1893	Do.	
	Hoke Smith.	Mar. 6, 1893, to Sept. 1, 1896	Do.	
	David R. Francis.	Sept. 1, 1896, to Mar. 5, 1897	Do.	
	Cornelius N. Bliss.	Mar. 5, 1897, to Dec. 21, 1898	Do.	
	Ethan A. Hitchcock.	Dec. 21, 1898, in office 1903	Do.	
	Robert McClellan.	Mar. 7, 1853, to Mar. 6, 1857	Do.	In charge of grounds and completed portion of building while the Secretary of War was in control of construction.
	Jacob Thompson.	Mar. 6, 1857, to Jan. 8, 1861	Do.	
	Caleb B. Smith.	Mar. 5, 1861, to Jan. 8, 1863	Do.	
Commissioner of Public Buildings and Grounds.	William Easby.	Mar. 14, 1851, to July 1, 1853	$2,000.00	In charge of maintenance and repairs on the old or central portion of the Capitol, never in charge of construction on the Capitol extension, but in charge of portions of the building as completed. In 1867 all jurisdiction over Capitol taken from them and placed under the Architect.
	B. B. French.	July 1, 1853, to July 28, 1855	2,000.00	
	John B. Blake.	July 28, 1855, to July 12, 1861	2,000.00	
	Wm. S. Wood.[1]	July 12, 1861, to Sept. 7, 1861	2,000.00	
	B. B. French.[2]	Sept. 7, 1861, to Mar. 13, 1867	2,000.00	
Architect.	Thomas Ustick Walter.	June 11, 1851, to May 26, 1865	4,500.00	Make all drawings and specifications and supervise the work. Part of the time acting also as disbursing officer.
	Edward Clark.	May 27, 1865, to Jan. 6, 1902	4,500.00	
	Frederick Law Olmsted.	June 23, 1874, to —, 1892	23,275.83[3]	Make drawings, lay out and supervise the grounds, terraces, walls, lamps, and other matter pertaining to the landscape.
	Thomas Wisedell.	Do.	9,729.91[3]	Designs for architectural features of the landscape under F. L. Olmsted.
Superintendent.	Montgomery C. Meigs.	Mar. 23, 1853, to Nov. 1, 1859	(4)	In charge of questions of engineering and construction and letting of contracts and acting as disbursing officer.
	W. B. Franklin.	Nov. 1, 1859, to Feb. 27, 1861	(4)	
	J. N. Macomb.	Feb. 27, 1861, to Apr. 16, 1862	(4)	Acting for M. C. Meigs, who had the legal appointment but was ordered south for service.
	Samuel Strong.	1851 to 1852	2,000.00	Superintendent of construction under Mr. Walter's direction.

[1] Was not confirmed.
[2] Second term.
[3] Personal service for the whole work.
[4] Salary of $1,800 as captain of engineers; no additional salary as superintendent.

NOTE: This table contains the information published by Glenn Brown, which has not been corrected or updated.

Table X. Names, salaries, and duties of the principal men connected with the Capitol extension, 1850–1900. (*Continued*)
[See Vol. I for similar table for the period 1793 to 1850.]

Office.	Name.	Date of service.	Salary.	Remarks.
Fresco artist.	Constantino Brumidi. Filippo Costaggini.	1855 to 1880 1880 to 1900	$10.00 [5] (6)	All of the frescoing.
Heating and ventilating engineer.	Robert Briggs.	Aug. 16, 1855, to Apr. 2, 1859 1877 to 1879	(7)	Making the designs and drawings for arrangement of whole heating apparatus under inspection of and consultation with Captain Meigs.
	S. H. Woodbridge.	June 11, 1896, to Dec.—, 1897	2,325.25 [3]	New heating and ventilating plant under Edward Clark.
Sanitary engineer.	Geo. E. Waring. F. W. Farquhar.	Aug. 5, 1892, to Oct. 1, 1893 Aug. 5, 1892, to Oct. 1, 1893	1,931.47 [3] 3,521.35 [3]	Design and superintend new plumbing system. Principal assistant to Geo. E. Waring.
Civil engineer.	Albert L. Rives.	1855 to 1860	3.00 [5]	Assisting Captain Meigs on construction.
	C. H. Cobb.	1879 to 1883	1,800.00	Assisting F. L. Olmsted on grounds.
Draftsman.	Clement N. West. August Schoenborn. Henry Schoenborn. William Luce. E. Carstens. Franklin Ober. William Hambucher. P. Scragg. F. W. Howard. G. C. Humphrey. Charles Zolicoffer. J. de La Camp. Richard M. Hunt. Nepo Haug. Albert De Zeyk. Joe Heindl. Emil Frederick. John Wood. Ed. W. Donn.	1851 to 1853 1851 to 1902 1853 to ——[9] 1853 to 1854 1854 to 1860 1854 to 1855 1855 to 1860 1855 to ——[9] 1855 to 1860 1855 to 1860 1855 to 1860 1855 to 1860 1856 to 1858 1856 to 1858 1855 to 1860 1855 to 1860 1855 to ——[9] 1856 to 1860 1856 to ——[9]	3.00 [5] (8) 2.50 to 3.00 [5] 2.50 [5] 4.00 [5] 2.50 [5] 3.00 [5] 3.00 [5] 2.00 [5] 3.00 [5] 2.50 [5] 3.00 [5] 4.50 [5] 2.50 [5] 2.50 [5] 2.50 [5] 3.00 [5] 3.50 [5] 2.00 [5]	Making and copying drawings.
Clerk.	Z. W. Denham. William J. Fitzpatrick. James Bryan. E. H. Weightman. Bernard Sears. F. W. Clemons William McPyncheon. Henry S. Sherwood. Wm. Elliott Woods. George Williams.	1852 to ——[9] 1853 to 1860 1854 to 1855 1856 to 1860 1869 to 1879 1869 to 1889 1869 to 1893 1879 to 1883. 1889 to 1900 1897 to 1900	1,200.00 to 1,500.00 2.25 to 3.00 [6] 3.33 [5] 4.00 [5] 1,800.00 1,800.00 to 2,000.00 1,800.00 1,800.00 1,200.00 to 1,800.00 [10] 1,200.00	Bookkeeping, accounting, and other clerical duties.

[5] Per day.
[6] $10 per day when working.
[7] Paid by contractor.

[8] 1853 to 1857, $1.50 to $4.25 per day; 1857 to 1869, $1,800 per year; 1869 to 1875, $2,000 per year; 1875 to 1901, $1,800 per year.
[9] Date of discharge not noted, probably between 1860 and 1862.
[10] 1885, subforeman, $60 per month; 1887, $75 per month.

NOTE: This table contains the information published by Glenn Brown, which has not been corrected or updated.

Table XI. General dimensions of the Capitol.

[All dimensions of length and breadth taken at line of subbase.]

Dimensions of Building as a Whole.	Ft.	In.
Length from north to south outside of terrace balustrade	849	7½
Length from north to south extreme projection of portico steps	756	2½
Length from north to south at face of portico subbasement	746	6½
Length from north to south at face of building subbasement	725	7½
Width in center from east to west, taking extreme projections of east portico and west terrace steps	480	4
Width in center from face of west upper terrace to extreme step projection on east	374	9
Width in center from face of west portico to face of east portico	229	5
Width of building at center from east to west, excluding porticoes, recessed at center	184	6½
Width of old wing from face of building east to west	122	0
Width of connecting corridor from east to west, including colonnades	56	7
Width east to west from extreme projection of east steps to outside of terrace balustrade through north and south wings	389	11
Width east to west through north and south wings from extreme projection of steps on west to extreme projection of steps on east	343	8½
Width east to west of north and south wings from face of east to face of west portico	270	10
Width east to west of north and south wings of the building, exclusive of porticoes	239	7

Dimension of Wings and Center Building.	Ft.	In.
The Capitol extension:		
North and south wings of Capitol extension, exclusive of porticoes—		
North and south axis	142	10
East and west axis	239	7
North and south porticoes—		
North and south axis	10	5½
East and west axis	121	4
West porticoes—		
East and west axis	10	5½
North and south axis	105	8
East porticoes, first projection—		
East and west axis	10	5½
North and south axis	139	7
Center projection of east portico—		
East and west axis	10	4
North and south axis	77	9
Extreme projection of east portico, including steps	88	10
Corridors connecting extension with old building:		
North and south axis	44	1
East and west axis	56	7
Center or old building:		
Center, exclusive of porticoes—		
North and south axis	351	9
East and west axis at old wings	122	0
Projecting wing on west of center building—		
East and west axis	70	10
North and south axis	170	9
Portico on west—		
East and west axis	12	½
North and south axis	102	3
Portico on east, including recess in front—		
East and west axis	22	7
North and south axis	162	9
Central projection from portico—		
East and west axis	10	5½
North and south axis	79	0
Extreme projection of steps and central portico from face of old wings east and west axis	75	0

Marble Terraces.	Ft.	In.
Terraces to outside of balustrade, north and south of Capitol:		
North and south axis	62	0
East and west axis	269	6
Terraces west of Capitol, total length, north and south axis	849	7½
Terraces west of wings:		
East and west axis	61	6
North and south axis	226	11
Terraces west of center, including interior court:		
East and west axis	169	3½
North and south axis	395	10
Projection of west terrace opposite western projection in center building:		
East and west axis	9	4
North and south axis	284	9½
Lower terrace, between stairways, with circular recess:		
East and west axis	54	3
North and south axis	284	9½
Steps in western terraces:		
North and south axis	55	6
East and west axis	50	6
Height of terrace on the west:		
At stairway	28	0
At north and south corners	20	0

Orders of the Capitol.	Ft.	In.
Subbase variable in height according to grades. East front from 1 foot 11 inches to 3 feet 10 inches; west front wings 3 feet 10 inches; west court yard 19 feet 5 inches.		
Basement	20	7
Blocking course	3	0
Columns, including capital and base	30	5
Entablature	7	3½
Balustrade	6	6½
From center to center of columns and pilasters on north and south fronts of wings	12	10⅓
From center to center of columns and pilasters on west front of wings	11	1½
From center to center of columns on east front of wings	10	3½
Order on first circular colonnade of Dome:		
Columns (height)	27	½
Entablature (height)	6	8½
Center to center of columns	10	6
Order on lantern:		
Columns (height)	15	1
Entablature (height)	4	1
Size of window openings in Capitol extension:		
Basement windows—		
Width	4	9
Height	9	9
Principal story windows—		
Width	4	9
Height	10	0
Attic windows—		
Width	4	9
Height	4	9
Heights of stories in Capitol:		
Basement, floor to floor	20	0
Principal story, floor to floor	20	0
Attic story, floor to floor	20	0

NOTE: *This table contains the information published by Glenn Brown, which has not been corrected or updated.*

Table XI. General dimensions of the Capitol. (*Continued*)
[All dimensions of length and breadth taken at line of subbase.]

Dome and Rotunda.	Ft.	In.
The old Dome, 1830 to 1855:		
Height of old Dome	145	0
Height of old Rotunda	96	0
The new Dome:		
Octagonal base of Dome	135	5
Diameter at circular colonnade	123	8
Diameter at wall line in Rotunda	94	9
Diameter at panel line	96	9
Height from balustrade of building to top	216	3
Height from ground to top, at east portico	287	6
Height from ground in court to top, at west portico	307	6
Lantern, diameter	24	4
Lantern, height	50	0
Rotunda from balustrade under canopy to the floor	152	3
Rotunda from top of canopy to floor	180	3
Statue of Freedom	19	6

House of Representatives.	Ft.	In.
Room occupied in 1800:		
East and west axis	35	0
North and south axis	86	0
Height	36	0
Temporary House Chamber, 1801 to 1807 (the Oven):		
East and west axis	94	0
North and south axis	70	0
Height	18	0
Old House of Representatives (Statuary Hall):		
Before destruction by British, colonnade with semicircular ends radius reaching to center of columns	31	11
Total length east and west of inclosing colonnades, center of columns	88	10
Width, north and south axis, to center of columns	63	10
House after destruction by British (in present form, minor changes of floor levels and partitions producing minor differences in measurement):		
Radius to interior face of semicircular colonnade	46	8
Rectangular space south of amphitheater—		
North and south axis	30	4
East and west axis	75	3
Height to spring of ceiling	34	4
Highest point of domical ceiling	55	0
Radius of domical ceiling	59	2½
House of Representatives in Capitol extension:		
Length, east and west axis	139	0
Width, north and south axis	93	0
Height	36	0
Floor of the House—		
East and west axis	115	0
North and south axis	67	0

Senate Chamber.	Ft.	In.
Senate Chamber, before fire, 1814, 48 feet wide, 88 feet long, 41 feet high.		
Old Senate Chamber (Supreme Court):		
Radius of semicircle (center 8 inches north of south wall)	37	6
Rectangular area on west—		
East and west axis	10	1½
North and south axis	52	5
Height to spring of arch	24	7⅜
Radius of domical ceiling	46	11½
Highest point of ceiling	43	7½
Senate Chamber in Capitol extension:		
Floor of Senate—		
East and west axis	84	0
North and south axis	51	0
Length from east to west, including galleries	113	3
Width from north to south	80	3
Height	36	0

Congressional Library.	Ft.	In.
First Library room, opposite old Senate Chamber:		
East and west axis	35	0
North and south axis	86	0
Height	36	0
Second Library room, west central projection:		
East and west axis	34	0
North and south axis	92	0
Height	36	0
Library after fire of 1851 to removal from Capitol:		
West hall—		
East and west axis	34	0
North and south axis	92	0
Height	36	0
South hall—		
East and west axis	67	0
North and south axis	28	3
Height	36	0
North hall—		
East and west axis	67	0
North and south axis	28	3
Height	36	0

NOTE: This table contains the information published by Glenn Brown, which has not been corrected or updated.

Table XII. List of trees and shrubs in the Capitol grounds. As given by F. L. Olmsted.

Habitat.	Habitat.	Habitat.
Abelia rupestris . . . . China.	Catalpa bignonioides . . . . South Atlantic States.	Diospyros virginiana. Persimmon . . . . Atlantic States.
Acer campestre. English field maple . . . . Europe.	aurea. Golden catalpa . . . . . Hort.	Eleagnus hortensis . . . . Southern Europe.
dasycarpum. Silver maple . . . . Atlantic States.	bungei, var. nana. Dwarf catalpa . . . . Hort.	Erica carnea . . . . Europe.
laetum . . . . Caucasus.	Cedrella sinensis . . . . Northern China.	polifolia . . . . Europe.
palmatum . . . . Japan.	Celastrus scandens. Bittersweet . . . . Atlantic States.	Euonymus americanus. Strawberry bush . . . . Atlantic States.
atropurpureum . . . . Japan.	Cercis canadensis. Red bud . . . . Atlantic States.	atropurpureus. Burning bush . . . . Atlantic States.
versicolor . . . . Japan.	chinensis . . . . Eastern Asia.	japonicus . . . . Japan.
laciniata variegata . . . . Japan.	Chamaecyparis obtusa. (Retinospora) . . . . Japan.	variegatus . . . . Hort.
rosea marginata . . . . Japan.	nana. (Retinospora) . . . . . . Japan.	radicans . . . . Japan.
reticulatum . . . . Japan.	plumosa. (Retinospora) . . . Japan.	Fagus ferruginea. American beech . . . . Atlantic States.
micranthum . . . . Japan.	squarrosa. (Retinospora) . . Japan.	sylvatica. European beech . . . . Europe.
polycristata . . . . Japan.	pisifera. (Retinospora) . . . . Japan.	purpurea. Purple beech . . . . Europe.
Aesculus glabra. Ohio buckeye . . . . Western States.	aurea. (Retinospora) . . . . . Japan.	incisa. Cut-leaved beech . . . . Europe.
hippocastanum. Horse-chestnut . . . . . . Persia.	Chionanthus virginica. Fringe tree . . . . South Atlantic States.	Forsythia fortunei . . . . China.
Aralia chinensis . . . . Eastern Asia.	Cladrastis tinctoria. Yellowwood . . . . Kentucky and Tennessee.	suspensa . . . . China.
spinosa. Hercules's club . . . . Atlantic States.	Clerodendron trichotomum . . . . Japan.	viridissima . . . . China.
Amorpha fruticosa. False indigo . . . . Atlantic States.	Clethra alnifolia. White alder . . . . Atlantic States.	Fraxinus americana. White ash . . . . Atlantic States.
Aucuba japonica . . . . Japan.	Colutea arborescens. Bladder senna . . . . Europe.	excelsior. European ash . . . . Europe.
Azalea amoena . . . . China.	Cornus florida. Flowering dogwood . . . . Atlantic States.	Gymnocladus canadensis. Kentucky coffee tree . . Western States.
mollis . . . . Japan.	mas. Cornel. . . . . Europe.	Halesia tetraptera. Silver bell . . . . South Atlantic States.
nudiflora . . . . Atlantic States.	variegata . . . . Hort.	Hedera helix hibernica. Irish ivy . . . . Europe.
Benzoin odoriferum. Spice bush . . . . Atlantic States.	paniculata . . . . North Atlantic States.	Hibiscus syriacus. Althea . . . . Syria.
Berberis aquifolium. Oregon grape . . . . North Pacific States.	stolonifera. Red osier . . . . Atlantic States.	Hippophae rhamnoides. Sea buckthorn . . . . Europe.
fortuni . . . . China.	stricta. Stiff cornel . . . . Southern States.	Hydrangea hortensis . . . . Japan.
japonica. Japan mahonia . . . . Japan.	Corylus americana. American hazel . . . . Atlantic States.	paniculata grandiflora . . . . Japan.
thunbergii . . . . Japan.	tubulosa atropurpurea. Purple hazel . . . . Europe.	Hypericum prolificum. St. John's wort . . . . Atlantic States.
vulgaris. Barberry . . . . Europe.	Cotoneaster acuminata simonsii . . . . Himalayas.	Idesia polycarpa . . . . Japan.
atropurpurena. Purple barberry . . . . . Hort.	microphylla . . . . Siberia.	Ilex aquifolium.English holly . . . . Europe.
Betula alba. White birch . . . . North Europe.	Crataegus crus-galli, var. Newcastle thorn . . . . . Atlantic States.	augustifolium . . . . Hort.
lenta. Black birch . . . . Atlantic States.	oxyacantha. Hawthorn. . . . . Europe.	ferox. Hedgehog holly . . . . Hort.
Buxus japonica . . . . Japan.	var. Hawthorn . . . . Europe.	argenteum . . . . Hort.
sempervirens, var. tree box . . . . Europe.	Daphne cneorum . . . . Europe.	aureum . . . . Hort.
round-leaved box . . . . Hort.	Deutzia gracilis . . . . Japan.	opaca. American holly . . . . Atlantic States.
golden variegated box . . . . . Hort.	scabra . . . . Japan.	Jasminum nudiflorum. Yellow jessamine . . . . China.
narrow-leaved box . . . . Hort.	flore pleno . . . . Hort.	Juniperus recurva squamata . . . . Nepaul.
Callicarpa americana . . . . South Atlantic States.	purpurea . . . . Hort.	sabina. Juniper . . . . Northern Hemisphere.
Calycanthus floridus. Sweet-scented shrub . . . . . South Atlantic States.	Diervilla hortensis . . . . Japan.	nana. Prostrate juniper . . . . . . Northern States.
Caragana arborescens. Siberian pea . . . . Siberia.	alba . . . . Hort.	tamariscifolia . . . . Europe.
Carpinus caroliniana. Water beech . . . . Atlantic States.	nivea . . . . Hort.	Koelreuteria paniculata . . . . China.
duinensis . . . . Caucasus.	grandiflora variegata . . . . Hort.	Laburnum vulgare. Golden chain . . . . Europe.
Carya olivaeformis. Pecan nut . . . . Western States.	rosea . . . . China.	Lagerstroemia indica rubra. Crepe myrtle . . . . . . India.
Castanea pumila. Chinquapin . . . . Southern States.	amabilis . . . . Hort.	
vesca. Sweet chestnut . . . . Europe.	foliis variegata . . . . Hort.	
	grandiflora, var. vanhouttei . . . . Hort.	

592

NOTE: *This table contains the information published by Glenn Brown, which has not been corrected or updated.*

Table XII. List of trees and shrubs in the Capitol grounds. As given by F. L. Olmsted. *(Continued)*

Habitat.	Habitat.	Habitat.
Ligustrum ovalifolium . . . . Japan.	Quercus imbricaria. Shingle oak . . . . Europe.	Tilia americana. Basswood . . . . Atlantic States.
vulgare. Privet . . . . Europe.	macrocarpa. Bur oak . . . . Atlantic States.	europaea. Linden. . . . . Europe.
Liquidambar styraciflua. Sweet gum . . . . Atlantic States.	palustris. Pin oak . . . . Atlantic States.	heterophylla. White basswood . . . . Atlantic States.
Liriodendron tulipifera. Tulip tree . . . . Atlantic States.	phellos. Willow oak . . . . South Atlantic States.	Ulmus americana. American elm . . . . Atlantic States.
Lonicera brachypoda. Honeysuckle . . . . Japan.	prinus. Chestnut oak . . . . Atlantic States.	alata. Whahoo . . . . Southern States.
aurea reticulata . . . . Japan.	prinoides. Chinquapin oak . . . . Atlantic States.	campestris. English elm . . . . Europe.
fragrantissima. Bush honeysuckle . . . . . China.	robur. English oak . . . . Europe.	fastigiata. Fastigiate elm . . . . . Hort.
tartarica. Tartarian honeysuckle . . . . Siberia.	concordia . . . . Hort.	microphylla . . . . Hort.
Maclura aurantiaca. Osage orange . . . . Arkansas.	nigricans . . . . Hort.	pendule. Weeping elm . . . . . . Hort.
Magnolia acuminata. Cucumber tree . . . . Atlantic States.	Rhamnus carolinianus . . . . South Atlantic States.	purpurea. Purple elm . . . . Hort.
conspicua. Yulan . . . . China.	catharticus. Buckthorn . . . . Europe.	var. Huntingdon elm . . . . Hort.
cordata. Yellow cucumber tree . . . . South Atlantic States.	Rhus cotinus. Smoke bush . . . . Southern Europe.	montana. Dutch elm . . . . Europe.
glauca. Sweet bay. . . . . Atlantic States.	glabra laciniata. Cut-leaved sumac . . . . . . Pennsylvania.	Viburnum opulus. Guelder rose . . . . Europe.
grandiflora. Bull bay . . . . South Atlantic States.	Rosa rubiginosa. Sweet brier . . . . Europe.	plicatum . . . . Japan.
purpurea. Purple magnolia . . . . Japan.	rugosa . . . . Japan.	prunifolium . . . . Atlantic States.
tripetala. Umbrella tree . . . . South Atlantic States.	Rubus leucodermis . . . . Japan.	Zizyphus vulgaris. Christ's thorn . . . . Southern Europe.
Morus alba. White mulberry . . . . Europe.	Salisburia biloba. Gingko . . . . China.	
rubra. Red mulberry . . . . Atlantic States.	Sambucus canadensis variegata.	
Neillia opulifolia . . . . Atlantic States.	Variegated elder . . . . Atlantic States.	
aurea . . . . Hort.	Sassafras officinale . . . . Atlantic States.	
Nyssa sylvatica. Sour gum . . . . Atlantic States.	Shepherdia argentea. Buffalo berry . . . . Western	
Ostrya virginica. Hop hornbeam . . . . Atlantic States.	North America.	
Paulownia imperialis . . . . Japan.	Sophora japonica . . . . Japan.	
Phillodendron amurense . . . . Manchuria.	Spiraea cantoniensis . . . . China.	
Philadelphus coronarius. Mock-orange . . . . China.	chamaedrifolia . . . . Siberia.	
grandiflorus. Syringa . . . . South Atlantic States.	japonica alba . . . . Japan.	
inodorus . . . . South Atlantic States.	rubra . . . . Japan.	
Planera aquatica. Water elm . . . . South Atlantic States.	lindleyana . . . . Himalayas.	
Platanus occidentalis. Sycamore . . . . Atlantic States.	douglassii, var . . . . California.	
orientalis. Oriental plane . . . . Western Europe.	prunifolia . . . . Japan.	
Podocarpus taxifolius . . . . Japan.	thunbergii . . . . Japan.	
Populus angustifolia. Willow-leaved poplar . . . . Rocky Mountains.	Staphylea trifolia. Bladder nut . . . . Atlantic States.	
Prunus japonica . . . . Japan.	Styrax japonicum . . . . Japan.	
japonica flore pleno . . . . Japan.	officinale . . . . Europe.	
sinensis. Sand pear . . . . China.	Symphoricarpus racemosus. Snowberry . . . . North America.	
padus. Bird cherry . . . . Europe.	vulgaris. Indian currant . . . . . . Northern States.	
serotina. Rum cherry . . . . Atlantic States.	Syringa josikaea . . . . Central Europe.	
spinosa. Sloe . . . . Europe.	persica. Persian lilac . . . . Western Asia.	
triloba . . . . China.	vulgaris. Lilac . . . . Europe.	
Pyrus coronaria . . . . South Atlantic States.	alba. White lilac . . . . Europe.	
japonica. Japan quince . . . . Japan.	Tamarix africana. Tamarisk . . . . Southern Europe.	
Quercus alba. White oak . . . . Atlantic States.	Taxus adpressa . . . . Japan.	
cerris. Turkey oak . . . . Europe.	baccata. Yew . . . . Europe.	
	aurea. Golden yew . . . . Hort.	

NOTE: *This table contains the information published by Glenn Brown, which has not been corrected or updated.*

Table XIII. Statement of appropriations from the National Treasury for the Capitol from 1850 to 1900.
[This table is continuous with similar table in Volume I, and totals where they relate to both periods are calculated from the beginning.]

General object (title of appropriation), and details and explanations.	Date of act making the appropriation.	References to the Statutes at Large. Volume.	Page.	Section.	Amount of annual appropriation.	Year of expenditure.	Expenditure by warrants.	Repayments.	Amount carried to the surplus fund.	Net expenditures.
Extension of the Capitol.										
For the extension of the Capitol, according to such plan as may be approved by the President, to be expended under his direction by such architect as he may appoint to execute the same.	Sept. 30, 1850	9	538	I	$100,000.00					
For the continuance of the work on the two wings of the Capitol.	Apr. 14, 1852	10	146		500,000.00	1852	$175,000.00			$175,000.00
For the extension of the United States Capitol.	Mar. 3, 1853	10	181	I	400,000.00	1853	515,000.00			515,000.00
	Do.	10	206	I	600,000.00[1]	1854	465,000.00[1]			465,000.00
For the Capitol extension.	Aug. 4, 1854	10	569	I	750,000.00[1]	1855	630,000.00[1]			630,000.00
	Mar. 3, 1855	10	638	I	325,000.00[1]	1856	770,000.00[1]			770,000.00
For continuing the Capitol extension.	Aug. 18, 1856	11	86	I	750,000.00[1]					
For United States Capitol extension.	Mar. 3, 1857	11	226	I	900,000.00[1]	1857	880,000.00[1]			880,000.00
						1858	890,000.00[1]			890,000.00
	June 12, 1858	11	323	I			750,000.00[1]			
	Mar. 3, 1859	11	428	I	400,000.00[1]	1859	940,000.00[1]			940,000.00
For payment of the unpaid expenses incurred in altering the arrangements of the Hall of the House of Representatives, under the order of the House.	May 24, 1860	12	18		3,700.00[1]	1860	213,700.00[1]			213,700.00
To pay for labor on and materials furnished for the Capitol extension.	June 25, 1860	12	105	I	153,601.74[1]					
For the prosecution of the work on the Capitol extension during the fiscal year ending June 30, 1861.	Do.	12	105	I	300,000.00[1]					
To enable the superintendent to take care of the marble which has been delivered, and of the shops occupied, and to lay the marble flooring of the porticos, and to pay for the bronze doors.	Do.	12	105	I	48,920.00[1]					
For contingencies of the Capitol extension.	Do.	12	105	I	2,300.00[1]					
To enable the superintendent of the Capitol extension to purchase from Rice & Heebner thirty-four monolithic columns of American marble at the price specified in their supplemental contract of Mar. 30, 1854.	Do.	12	105	I	47,600.00[1]					
To enable the superintendent of the Capitol extension to pay for labor and materials used, to carry out the resolution of the House of Representatives of Feb. 21, 1860.	Feb. 19, 1861	12	132		2,500.00[1]	1861	434,500.00[1]	$151.90[1]		434,348.10

[1]Expended under the direction of the War Department.

NOTE: *This table contains the information published by Glenn Brown, which has not been corrected or updated.*

Table XIII. Statement of appropriations from the National Treasury for the Capitol from 1850 to 1900. *(Continued)*

General object (title of appropriation), and details and explanations.	Date of act making the appropriation.	References to the Statutes at Large. Volume.	Page.	Section.	Amount of annual appropriation.	Year of expenditure.	Expenditure by warrants.	Repayments.	Amount carried to the surplus fund.	Net expenditures.
Extension of the Capitol. *(Continued)*										
For the Capitol extension.	Mar. 2, 1861	12	219	I	$25,971.40[1]	1862	$26,000.00[1]	$782.69[1]		$25,217.31
Do.	Do.	12	219	I	224,028.60[1]	1862	30,000.00			30,000.00
						1863	288,500.00			288,500.00
For continuing the work on the Capitol extension.	Mar. 3, 1863	12	748	I	150,000.00					
For the Capitol extension.	Mar. 14, 1864	13	25	I	150,000.00	1864	306,511.97	7,204.12		299,307.85
For continuing the work on the Capitol extension.	July 2, 1864	13	350	I	300,000.00	1865	292,500.00	18,056.87		274,443.13
	Apr. 7, 1866	14	19	I	175,000.00	1866	266,663.84	38,558.49		228,105.35
For the Capitol extension.	July 28, 1866	14	314	I	200,000.00					
For ventilating.	Mar. 2, 1867	14	468	I	9,000.00					
For supplying deficiency in appropriation for work on the Capitol extension.	Do.	14	468	I	29,800.00					
For eight additional monolithic columns.	Do.	14	468	I	11,200.00	1867	254,500.00	5,290.99		249,209.01
For continuing the work on the Capitol extension.	Do.	14	461	I	250,000.00	1868	249,696.57			249,696.57
For repairing and finishing the Capitol extension.	July 20, 1868	15	115	I	100,000.00	1869	109,129.12	8,034.70		101,094.42
For finishing and repairing the work of the United States Capitol extension.	Mar. 3, 1869	15	306	I	75,000.00					
For continuing the work on the Capitol grounds and repairing the Capitol building.	Apr. 20, 1870	16	86	I	20,000.00	1870	95,000.00			95,000.00
For finishing and repairing the work on the Capitol extension and for curbing and flagging upper terraces.	July 15, 1870	16	302	I	100,000.00	1871	100,000.00			100,00.00
	Mar. 3, 1871	16	501	I	65,000.00					
For the purpose of buying and putting in place a new boiler, water tank, and steam pump in the south wing.	May 18, 1872	17	131	I	10,000.00	1872	77,072.37	2,072.37		75,000.00
For finishing and repairing the work on the Capitol extension and for completing the flagging of the upper terraces.	June 10, 1872	17	361	I	50,000.00	1873	50,000.00	645.35	$645.35	49,354.65
For continuing the work on the Capitol and for general care and repairs thereof.	Mar. 3, 1873	17	518	I	65,000.00	1873	12,000.00			12,000.00
For extending the inlets to the Senate Chamber for fresh air to the lower terrace near the western park.	Do.	17	518	I	10,000.00					

[1] Expended under the direction of the War Department.

Table XIII. Statement of appropriations from the National Treasury for the Capitol from 1850 to 1900. (*Continued*)

General object (title of appropriation), and details and explanations.	Date of act making the appropriation.	References to the Statutes at Large.			Amount of annual appropriation.	Year of expenditure.	Expenditure by warrants.	Repayments.	Amount carried to the surplus fund.	Net expenditures.
		Volume.	Page.	Section.						
Extension of the Capitol. (*Continued*)										
For constructing coal vaults within the open space at the east front of the Capitol between the wings and the old building.	Mar. 3, 1873	17	518	I	$16,000.00	1874	$79,000.00			$79,000.00
Transferred from repairs.					6,322.65	1875	6,322.65			6,322.65
Total.					8,075,944.39		8,156,096.52	$80,797.48	$645.35	8,075,299.04
New Dome.										
For removing the present Dome over the central portion of the Capitol and the construction of one upon the plan as designed by Thomas U. Walter, architect of the Capitol extension, under the direction of the President.	Mar. 3, 1855	10	663	I	100,000.00[1]	1855 1856	20,000.00[1] 35,000.00[1]			20,000.00 35,000.00
For continuing the construction of the new Dome of the Capitol.	Aug. 18, 1856	11	86	I	100,000.00[1]	1857	50,000.00[1]			50,000.00
For continuing the work of the new Dome.	Mar. 3, 1857	11	226	I	500,000.00[1]	1858 1859 1860 1861 1862 1862 1863	130,000.00[1] 40,000.00[1] 140,000.00[1] 165,000.00[1] 10,000.00[1] 35,000.00 103,859.21	20,000.00[1] .70[1] 8,858.51[1]		110,000.00 40,000.00 140,000.00 164,999.30 1,141.49 35,000.00 103,859.21
For continuing the work on the new Dome of the Capitol.	Mar. 3, 1863	12	748	I	200,000.00	1864 1865	122,000.00 79,540.39	1,540.39		120,459.61 79,540.39
For completing the Dome of the Capitol.	Apr. 7, 1866	14	19	I	50,000.00	1866 1867	40,621.38 12,904.91	3,621.38		37,000.00 12,904.91
For the Dome of the Capitol.	Mar. 2, 1867	14	461	I	15,000.00	1868		14,970.86		14,970.86
For repairing and finishing the work on the new Dome of the Capitol.	July 20, 1868	15	115	I	5,000.00	1869	5,330.83	206.60		5,124.23
The Secretary of the Treasury authorized to pay to Janes, Fowler, Kirtland & Co., of New York, contractors for building the Dome of the Capitol at Washington, in full satisfaction of all claim for losses or damages arising from the action of the Government in stopping, ordering, and directing the construction of said work.	Feb. 9, 1871	16	681	I	60,000.00	1871	60,000.00			60,000.00

[1] Expended under the direction of the War Department.

NOTE: *This table contains the information published by Glenn Brown, which has not been corrected or updated.*

Table XIII. Statement of appropriations from the National Treasury for the Capitol from 1850 to 1900. (*Continued*)

General object (title of appropriation), and details and explanations.	Date of act making the appropriation.	References to the Statutes at Large.			Amount of annual appropriation.	Year of expenditure.	Expenditure by warrants.	Repayments.	Amount carried to the surplus fund.	Net expenditures.
		Volume.	Page.	Section.						
New Dome. (*Continued*)										
For finishing and repairing the work on the new Dome of the Capitol.	Mar. 3, 1869	15	306	I	$5,000.00	1870	$5,000.00			$5,000.00
	July 15, 1870	16	302	I	4,000.00	1871 1872	4,000.00	$683.30	$683.30	3,316.70
	Mar. 3, 1871	16	501	I	5,000.00	1872	9,410.33	4,410.33		5,000.00
	June 10, 1872	17	361	I	4,000.00	1873 1875	4,000.00	24.81	24.81	3,975.19
Total.					1,048,000.00		1,086,637.91	39,346.02	708.11	1,047,291.89
Repairs.										
To supply the deficiency in the appropriation for the casual repairs of the Capitol.	July 21, 1852	10	18	I	1,500.00					
For the annual repairs of the Capitol, water-closets, public stables, pavements and other walks within and around the Capitol square, the flagging in the crypt, the doors of the wood vaults, etc.	Aug. 31, 1852	10	91	I	7,000.00	1853	8,500.00			8,500.00
For taking up, repairing, and relaying the steps of the east portico of the Capitol, and for taking up, dressing, supplying new flagging, and relaying the same in the arcade under the portico.	Do.	10	93	I	1,500.00	1853	1,500.00			1,500.00
For supplying a deficiency in the appropriation for completing the room under the Senate post-office.	Mar. 3, 1853	10	207	I	451.31	1853	451.31			451.31
For annual repairs of the Capitol, water-closets, public stables, water pipes, pavements and other walks within and around the Capitol square, painting the interior of all the committee rooms, cleaning out and paving the vaults under the crypt, extending gas pipes, etc.	Do.	10	207	I	6,800.00					
For repairs of the Capitol and improving the grounds around it.	May 31, 1854	10	293	I	6,500.00	1854	13,300.00			13,300.00
For repair and renewal of the gas pipes through the Capitol.	Aug. 4, 1854	10	568	I	3,500.00	1855 1856 1859	3,500.00 75.40	75.40 11.53	11.53	3,488.47
For painting and repairs inside of the Capitol and new furnaces under the Senate Chamber and Supreme Court room.	Aug. 4, 1854	10	568	I	5,000.00	1855 1856	3,000.00 2,338.87	338.87		3,000.00 2,000.00

Table XIII. Statement of appropriations from the National Treasury for the Capitol from 1850 to 1900. (*Continued*)

General object (title of appropriation), and details and explanations.	Date of act making the appropriation.	References to the Statutes at Large.			Amount of annual appropriation.	Year of expenditure.	Expenditure by warrants.	Repayments.	Amount carried to the surplus fund.	Net expenditures.
		Volume.	Page.	Section.						
Repairs. (*Continued*)										
For permanent repair of the roof of the Capitol with copper.	Aug. 4, 1854	10	569	I	$2,000.00	1855	$1,844.27			$1,844.27
						1856	162.38		137.28	
						1862	6.65			
							18.45	$18.45		
For annual repairs of the Capitol, water-closets, public stables, water pipes, pavements and other walks within the Capitol square, broken glass, and locks.	Aug. 4, 1854	10	569	I	5,000.00	1855	5,000.00			5,000.00
	Mar. 3, 1855	10	663	I	5,000.00	1856	5,000.00			5,000.00
	Aug. 18, 1856	11	88	I	8,000.00	1857	8,000.00			8,000.00
	Mar. 3, 1857	11	225	I	6,000.00	1858	6,000.00			6,000.00
For repairs of the furnaces under the Senate Chamber and Supreme Court room.	Do.	11	226	I	500.00	1858	500.00			500.00
For annual repairs of the Capitol, water-closets, public stables, water pipes, pavements and other walks within the Capitol square, broken glass, and locks.	June 12, 1858	11	322	I	6,000.00	1859	6,000.00			6,000.00
For repairs of furnaces under the Senate Chamber and Supreme Court room.	Do.	11	322	I	1,000.00	1859	1,000.00			1,000.00
For annual repairs of the Capitol, water-closets, public stables, water pipes, pavements, etc.	Mar. 3, 1859	11	427	I	5,000.00	1860	5,000.00			5,000.00
	June 25, 1860	12	107	I	5,000.00	1861	5,000.00			5,000.00
For converting the Senate Chamber into a court room, the old court room into a law library, and for fitting up the rooms in connection with them for the use of the Supreme Court.	Do.	12	110	2	25,000.00	1861	25,000.00			24,960.00
						1862	1,232.38	1,272.38	40.00	
For annual repairs of the Capitol, water-closets, public stables, water pipes, pavements and other walks, broken glass, etc.	Mar. 2, 1861	12	216	I	5,000.00	1862	5,000.00			5,000.00
For repairs of furnaces under the Senate Chamber and Supreme Court room.	Do.	12	217	I	500.00	1862	500.00	1.30	1.30	498.70
For annual repairs of the Capitol, water-closets, public stables, water pipes, broken glass, and locks.	July 24, 1861	12	272	I	1,000.00	1862	1,000.00			1,000.00
To enable the Commissioner of Public Buildings to pay for painting in the interior of the Capitol, and for general repairs.	Mar. 1, 1862	12	352	2	3,200.00	1862	3,200.00			3,200.00
To enable the Commissioner of Public Buildings to replace the thin glass in the roof of the Library of Congress with glass of proper thickness, and to ventilate the Library.	Mar. 14, 1862	12	368	2	900.00	1862	900.00			900.00
For annual repairs of the Capitol, water-closets, public stables, water pipes, pavements, and other walks within the Capitol square, broken glass, locks, etc.	Mar. 1, 1862	12	349	I	6,000.00					

Table XIII. Statement of appropriations from the National Treasury for the Capitol from 1850 to 1900. (*Continued*)

General object (title of appropriation), and details and explanations.	Date of act making the appropriation.	References to the Statutes at Large.			Amount of annual appropriation.	Year of expenditure.	Expenditure by warrants.	Repayments.	Amount carried to the surplus fund.	Net expenditures.
		Volume.	Page.	Section.						
Repairs. (*Continued*)										
To supply a deficiency of appropriation for repairs of the Capitol made by W. S. Wood, late Commissioner of Public Buildings.	Mar. 3, 1862	12	351	I	$934.78	1863	$6,784.78			$6,784.78
For painting the outside of the old portion of the Capitol.	July 11, 1862	12	533	I	8,000.00	1863	8,000.00			8,000.00
To supply a deficiency in the appropriation for the contingent fund of the Senate for furniture, fitting of rooms, gas-fitting, repairing, painting, etc.	Do.	12	535	3	10,000.00	1863 1867	10,000.00	$986.10	$986.10	9,013.90
For annual repairs of the Capitol, water-closets, public stables, water pipes, pavements and other walks within the Capitol square, broken glass, and locks, and for the protection of the building and keeping the main approaches to it unencumbered.	Mar. 3, 1863 July 2, 1864	12 13	746 346	I I	8,000.00 8,000.00	1864 1865	8,467.00 8,000.00	317.00		8,150.00 8,000.00
For cleaning and painting the crypt and passages under the Rotunda.	Do.	13	348	2	2,000.00	1865	2,000.00			2,000.00
To pay expenses incurred by the Commissioner of Public Buildings in enlarging bench in Supreme Court room.	Do.	13	348	2	1,214.00	1865 1870	1,214.00	26.53	26.53	1,187.47
For completing the tiling of the floor of the old Hall of Representatives under the same authority that the work has already been done.	Mar. 2, 1865	13	447	I	3,875.00	1866 1870	3,875.00	326.29	326.29	3,548.71
For fitting up rooms in the basement, under the court room of the Supreme Court, for a consultation room for the court.	Apr. 7, 1866	14	18	I	6,500.00	1866	6,500.00			6,500.00
For annual repairs of the Capitol, water-closets, public stables, water pipes, pavements and other walks within the Capitol square, broken glass, etc.	Do.	14	18	I	8,000.00	1866	8,000.00			8,000.00
For casing with stone and erecting a wall in front of the north basement of the old part of the Capitol so as to correspond with the south basement, already completed.	Do.	14	18	I	4,300.00	1866 1870	4,300.00	6.85	6.85	4,293.15
For repairing roof of the old portion of the Capitol.	Do.	14	19	I	5,450.00	1866	5,450.00			5,450.00
To cause to be painted in the square panels of glass in the ceiling of the House of Representatives the escutcheons of the States of West Virginia and Nevada.	July 28, 1866	14	314	I	130.00	1867	130.00			130.00
To enable the Commissioner of Public Buildings to reconstruct the lower water-closets of the Supreme Court room, to place marble around the furnace register, by way of protection, and to make such other improvements as the Chief Justice of the court may desire.	Do.	14	325	I	1,500.00	1867 1870	1,500.00	2.86	2.86	1,497.14

NOTE: *This table contains the information published by Glenn Brown, which has not been corrected or updated.*

Table XIII. Statement of appropriations from the National Treasury for the Capitol from 1850 to 1900. *(Continued)*

General object (title of appropriation), and details and explanations.	Date of act making the appropriation.	References to the Statutes at Large.			Amount of annual appropriation.	Year of expenditure.	Expenditure by warrants.	Repayments.	Amount carried to the surplus fund.	Net expenditures.
		Volume.	Page.	Section.						
Repairs. *(Continued)*										
For annual repairs of the Capitol, water-closets, and to put the proper number of water-closets in the upper stories, public stables, water pipes, pavements and other walks within the Capitol square, broken glass, etc.	July 18, 1866	14	314	I	$12,000.00					
To replace the bruised and worn copper water pipes or roof gutters of the Capitol building with iron pipes.	Mar. 2, 1867	14	469	I	3,000.00	1867	$15,402.52	$402.52		$15,000.00
For annual repairs of the Capitol, water-closets, public stables, water pipes, pavements, etc.	Do.	14	462	I	12,000.00	1868	12,500.00			12,424.71
For casual repairs of all the furnaces under the Capitol.	Do.	14	462	I	500.00	1870		75.29	$75.29	
For plumbing, gas fitting, and labor.	July 20, 1868	15	93	I	5,000.00	1869 1871 1872	5,000.00	1,448.03	1,448.03	3,551.97
For annual repairs, such as painting, glazing, keeping roofs in order, also water pipes, pavements, and approaches to public buildings.	July 20, 1868	15	115	I	15,000.00					
For the payment of outstanding liabilities incurred by the late Commissioner of Public Buildings for materials furnished and labor done in repairing the old portion of the Capitol building prior to and during fiscal year ending June 30, 1867.	July 25, 1868	15	172	I	5,484.22	1869	25,691.28	5,207.06		20,484.22
For additional labor, cleaning the center building of the Capitol, repairing the Washington statue on the east grounds of the Capitol, cleaning and repairing columns in the building, laying a new brick pavement on the west front, and repairing fountains.	Do.	15	176	I	1,500.00	1869 1871 1872	1,500.00	213.18	213.18	1,286.82
For plumbing, gas fitting, and labor.	Mar. 3, 1869	15	284	I	5,000.00	1872			5,000.00	
For the annual repairs of the old portion of the Capitol, such as painting, glazing, keeping roof in order, etc.	Do.	15	307	I	10,000.00	1870	10,000.00			10,000.00
To enable the Secretary of the Treasury to close the accounts of B. B. French, late Commissioner of Public Buildings.	Apr. 20, 1870	16	88	I	108.90	1870	108.90			108.90
For taking out private stairway leading to law library to Supreme Court room and fitting the room thus made with shelving for library.	July 15, 1870	16	301	I	2,000.00	1871	2,000.00			2,000.00
For widening the passageways between the Senate and House wings of the Capitol.	Mar. 3, 1871	16	501	I	10,000.00	1871 1872	5,000.00 7,490.16	2,490.16		5,000.00 5,000.00

NOTE: *This table contains the information published by Glenn Brown, which has not been corrected or updated.*

Table XIII. Statement of appropriations from the National Treasury for the Capitol from 1850 to 1900. *(Continued)*

General object (title of appropriation), and details and explanations.	Date of act making the appropriation.	References to the Statutes at Large.			Amount of annual appropriation.	Year of expenditure.	Expenditure by warrants.	Repayments.	Amount carried to the surplus fund.	Net expenditures.
		Volume.	Page.	Section.						
Repairs. *(Continued)*										
For annual repairs of the old portion of the Capitol building, painting, glazing, etc.	July 15, 1870	16	302	I	$10,000.00	1871	$15,000.00	$.37		$14,999.63
	Mar. 3, 1871	16	501	I	10,000.00	1872	6,852.88	1,852.88		5,000.00
	June 10, 1872	17	361	I	10,000.00	1873	10,000.00			10,000.00
					1875		$.37			
For alteration and refitting the Hall of the House of Representatives for accommodation of the increased number of members and better ventilation and lighting thereof, to be extended under the supervision of the Architect of the Capitol extension, according to a plan to be established by resolution of the House.	Mar. 3, 1873	17	519		40,000.00	1873	10,000.00			10,000.00
						1874	30,000.00			23,677.35
						1875		6,322.65	6,322.65[1]	
For an elevator in the Senate wing of the Capitol.	Mar. 3, 1873	17	538		10,000.00	1874	10,000.00			10,000.00
For work on the Capitol and for general care and repairs thereof.	June 23, 1874	18	214	I	50,000.00					
For lathing and plastering the under surface of the roof above the ceiling of the Senate Chamber.	Do.	18	214		4,000.00					
For a new steam pump to supply the tanks located in the attic of the Senate wing of the Capitol.	Do.	18	214		800.00					
For such portion of replacing the defective portion of the roof on the Capitol near the Dome, by a copper roofing of fireproof construction, and for erecting fire walls.	Do.	18	214		15,000.00	1875	69,800.00			69,800.00
For the purchase of a noiseless steam pump for the heating and ventilating department of the House of Representatives.	Mar. 3, 1875	18	375		1,000					
For repairing steam boilers and for steam traps for Senate wing.	Mar. 3, 1875	18	385		3,500.00					
For work on the Capitol and for general care and repairs thereof.	Do.	18	384		50,000.00	1876	54,500.00			54,500.00
For work on the Capitol, and for general care and repair thereof.	July 31, 1876	19	115	I	78,000.00	1877	78,000.00			78,000.00
	Mar. 3, 1877	19	348	I	64,000.00	1878	64,000.00			64,000.00
	Apr. 30, 1878	20	44	I	64,000.00	1878	64,000.00			64,000.00
	June 20, 1878	20	226	I	55,000.00	1879	55,000.00			55,000.00
	Mar. 3, 1879	20	391	I	50,000.00	1880	50,000.00			50,000.00
	June 16, 1880	21	272	I	57,000.00	1881	48,500.00			48,500.00
	Mar. 3, 1881	21	449	I	53,000.00	1882	54,500.00			54,500.00
	Aug. 7, 1882	22	325	I	44,400.00	1883	44,400.00		7,000.00	44,400.00
	Mar. 3, 1883	22	593	I	2,500.00	1883	2,500.00			2,500.00
	Aug. 5, 1882	22	270	I	4,000.00	1883	3,997.45			3,997.45
	Mar. 3, 1883	22	621	I	54,400.00	1884	54,331.57		2.55	54,331.57

[1] Transferred to "Extension of the Capitol."

NOTE: *This table contains the information published by Glenn Brown, which has not been corrected or updated.*

Table XIII. Statement of appropriations from the National Treasury for the Capitol from 1850 to 1900. *(Continued)*

General object (title of appropriation), and details and explanations.	Date of act making the appropriation.	References to the Statutes at Large.			Amount of annual appropriation.	Year of expenditure.	Expenditure by warrants.	Repayments.	Amount carried to the surplus fund.	Net expenditures.
		Volume.	Page.	Section.						
Repairs. *(Continued)*										
For work on the Capitol, and for general care and repair thereof. *(Continued)*	July 7, 1884	23	208	I	$43,000.00	1885	$43,000.00		$68.43	$43,000.00
	Mar. 3, 1885	23	497	I	38,000.00	1886	38,000.00			38,000.00
	Aug. 4, 1886	24	239	I	38,000.00	1887	37,966.25			37,966.25
	Mar. 3, 1887	24	525	I	35,000.00	1888	35,000.00		33.75	35,000.00
	Oct. 2, 1888	25	522	I	35,000.00	1889	34,999.05			34,999.05
	Mar. 2, 1889	25	958	I	39,000.00	1890	38,633.58			38,633.58
	Aug. 30, 1890	26	388	I	31,000.00	1891	29,942.51		367.37	29,942.51
	Mar. 3, 1891	26	970	I	30,000.00					
	Mar. 18, 1892	27	8	I	9,000.00	1892	39,978.43		57.49	39,978.43
	Aug. 5, 1892	27	367	I	20,000.00					
	Mar. 3, 1893	27	657	I	10,000.00	1893	19,969.14		21.57	19,969.14
	Do.	27	591	I	20,000.00					
	Apr. 21, 1894	28	59	I	8,000.00	1894	37,000.00		30.86	37,000.00
	Aug. 18, 1894	28	393	I	36,475.00	1895	33,000.00			33,000.00
	Mar. 2, 1895	28	935	I	25,000.00					
	Feb. 26, 1896	29	22	I	9,000.00	1896	38,475.00			38,475.00
	June 11, 1896	29	432	I	30,000.00	1897	29,999.40			29,999.40
	June 4, 1897	30	31	I	30,000.00	1898	29,999.64		.60	29,999.64
	July 1, 1898	30	617	I	40,500.00					
	Mar. 3, 1899	30	1231	I	28,000.00	1899	68,495.02		.36	68,495.02
	Do.	30	1094	I	30,000.00					
	Mar. 30, 1900	31	56	I	7,200.00					
	June 6, 1900	31	298	I	3,500.00	1900	39,971.95		4.45	39,971.95
	Do.	31	612	I	49,090.86	1901	49,777.49		39.80	49,777.49
	Mar. 3, 1901	31	1035	I	49,090.86	1901	49,777.49		39.80	49,777.49
Elevators and steam machinery, Senate.	Aug. 7, 1882	22	338	I	10,500.00	1883	10,000.00			10,000.00
						1884	494.67			494.67
						1885			5.33	
Elevator, Senate.	Mar. 3, 1887	24	526	I	15,000.00	1887	5,000.00			5,000.00
						1888	3,500.00			3,500.00
						1889		$385.05	6,885.05	
						1901			7.49	
West elevator, Senate.	Aug. 30, 1890	26	388	I	3,500.00	1891	3,452.00			3,452.00
						1892	48.00			48.00
Elevator, Senate.	July 19, 1897	30	127	I	6,500.00	1898				6,499.89
	July 7, 1898	30	672	I	20,000.00	1899	19,992.51			19,992.51
						1900			.11	

NOTE: *This table contains the information published by Glenn Brown, which has not been corrected or updated.*

Table XIII. Statement of appropriations from the National Treasury for the Capitol from 1850 to 1900. *(Continued)*

General object (title of appropriation), and details and explanations.	Date of act making the appropriation.	References to the Statutes at Large.			Amount of annual appropriation.	Year of expenditure.	Expenditure by warrants.	Repayments.	Amount carried to the surplus fund.	Net expenditures.
		Volume.	Page.	Section.						
Repairs. *(Continued)*										
Elevator, House of Representatives.	Mar. 3, 1881	21	449	I	$7,000.00	1882	$7,000.00			$7,000.00
Mar. 3, 1887		24	526	I	12,000.00	1887	5,000.00			5,000.00
						1888	3,449.34			3,499.34
						1889	500.00			500.00
						1890	1,854.80			1,854.80
						1891	391.54			391.54
						1892	750.30			750.30
						1893		$3.79	$7.81	
Flags for the Capitol.	Aug. 18, 1894	28	393	I	100.00	1895	22.10			22.10
	Mar. 2, 1895	28	935	I	100.00	1896	54.60			54.60
	June 11, 1896	29	432	I	100.00	1897	147.50		27.90	147.50
	June 4, 1897	30	31	I	100.00	1898	80.25		31.40	80.25
	July 1, 1898	30	917	I	100.00	1899	76.50			76.50
	Mar. 3, 1899	30	1094	I	100.00	1900	157.50		2.25	157.50
	June 6, 1900	31	612	I	100.00	1901	80.50		19.00	80.50
Special repairs, Senate.	Mar. 2, 1895	28	935	I	3,580.00	1896	3,575.26			3,575.26
						1897	4.74			4.74
	July 7, 1898	30	685	I	1,414.43	1899	1,414.43			1,414.43
Special repairs, House of Representatives.	June 4, 1897	30	32	I	8,500.00	1898	8,372.81			8,372.81
						1899	124.64			124.64
						1900			2.55	
Refurnishing Hall and rooms, House of Representatives.	Mar. 3, 1901	31	1157	I	61,000.00	1901	10,000.00			10,000.00
Reconstructing central portion of the Capitol.	Do.	31	1156	I	153,500.00	1901	5,000.00			5,000.00
Doors for the Senate.	June 8, 1896	29	300	I	2,035.00	1897	2,035.00			2,035.00
	June 6, 1900	31	298	I	949.00	1901	949.00			949.00
Plans for Capitol extension.	Mar. 3, 1901	31	1156 1157	I	1,500.00					
Arranging Court of Claims rooms.	July 1, 1879	21	55	I	2,000.00	1880	2,000.00			2,000.00
Private stairway, Supreme Court.								2.60	2.60	

NOTE: *This table contains the information published by Glenn Brown, which has not been corrected or updated.*

Table XIII. Statement of appropriations from the National Treasury for the Capitol from 1850 to 1900. (*Continued*)

General object (title of appropriation), and details and explanations.	Date of act making the appropriation.	References to the Statutes at Large.			Amount of annual appropriation.	Year of expenditure.	Expenditure by warrants.	Repayments.	Amount carried to the surplus fund.	Net expenditures.
		Volume.	Page.	Section.						
Repairs. (*Continued*)										
Reservoirs for drinking water.	Oct. 2, 1888	25	523	I	$1,500.00	1889 1891 1893	$1,500.00	$187.13	$187.13	$1,500.00
Sanitary improvements of the Capitol.	Aug. 5, 1892	27	367	I	97,496.06	1893 1894 1895 1896	69,000.00 28,345.63 148.40 2.03			69,000.00 28,345.63 148.40 2.03
Repairs to pipe line that supplies the Capitol.	Mar. 2, 1895	28	944	I	10,000.00	1896	10,000.00			10,000.00
Additional cases for the law library.	June 4, 1897	30	31	I	400.00	1898 1900	399.34		.66	399.34
Fireproof shelving, Senate.	Mar. 3, 1901	31	1157	I	25,000.00					
Reconstructing rooms, old Congressional Library.	June 6, 1900	31	719	I	288,021.93	1901	288,021.93			288,021.93
Total.					2,561,700.63		2,330,921.74	29,112.82	33,889.06	2,302,387.49
Balance.									226,002.65	
Lighting.										
For lighting Pennsylvania avenue, from Capitol square to the Treasury Department, and compensation of two lamplighters for the same, and for lighting the Capitol and Capitol grounds and President's House: *Provided*, That no contract shall be made for a longer term than one year, and that the Commissioner of Public Buildings advertise for proposals for furnishing gas to light the Capitol, President's House, Pennsylvania avenue, and other public grounds, after March 1, 1852, and that a contract be made with the person offering the best terms, under the direction of the Committee on Public Buildings.	Mar. 3, 1851	9	613	I	12,000.00	1852	13,451.65			13,451.65
For extending the gas pipes and providing lamp-posts, lamps, and burners in front of the Executive buildings on Fifteenth and Seventeenth streets and the north front of the President's grounds.	Mar. 3, 1851	9	613	I	6,500.00	1852 1853 1854	4,000.00 123.54 1,215.65		1,160.81	4,000.00 123.54 1,215.65
For lighting Pennsylvania avenue, from the Capitol grounds to the President's House, the Capitol grounds, the President's House and grounds, and the streets around the Executive offices.	Aug. 31, 1852 Mar. 3, 1853	10 10	93 207	I I	16,000.00 22,000.00	1853 1854	12,516.25 14,905.18			12,516.25 14,905.18

NOTE: *This table contains the information published by Glenn Brown, which has not been corrected or updated.*

Table XIII. Statement of appropriations from the National Treasury for the Capitol from 1850 to 1900. *(Continued)*

General object (title of appropriation), and details and explanations.	Date of act making the appropriation.	References to the Statutes at Large.			Amount of annual appropriation.	Year of expenditure.	Expenditure by warrants.	Repayments.	Amount carried to the surplus fund.	Net expenditures.
		Volume.	Page.	Section.						
Lighting. *(Continued)*										
For erecting lamp-posts and lamps on both sides of Pennsylvania avenue, from Seventeenth street to Georgetown and from the Capitol to the navy-yard.	Do. May 31, 1854	10 10	207 293	I I	$3,700.00 1,200.00	1854	$5,415.00	$515.00		$4,900.00
For furnishing lamps and lamp-posts, from Sixteenth to Seventeenth streets, on Pennsylvania avenue.	Aug. 4, 1854	10	569	I	500.00	1855 1856 1862	414.00 86.00	86.00	$86.00	414.00
For lighting Pennsylvania avenue, from the Capitol grounds to the President's House, the Capitol grounds, the President's House and grounds, and the streets around the Executive offices.	Aug. 4, 1854	10	569	I	22,000.00	1855	20,629.84			20,629.84
For lighting the President's House and Capitol, the public grounds around them, around the Executive offices, Pennsylvania avenue, and East Capitol street to Second street.	Mar. 3, 1855 Aug. 18, 1856	10 11	664 88	I I	25,000.00 27,000.00	1856 1857	32,769.98 20,000.00		3,203.99[1] 974.76[2]	32,769.98 20,000.00
For lighting the President's House and Capitol, the public grounds around them and around the Executive offices, and Pennsylvania avenue.	Mar. 3, 1857	11	225	I	27,000.00					
For erecting cast-iron lamp-posts and lighting the same with gas, from the western terminus of Pennsylvania avenue through Bridge and High streets, Georgetown.	Mar. 3, 1857	11	225	I	4,000.00	1858	4,000.00			4,000.00
For lighting the President's House and Capitol, the public grounds around them and around the Executive offices, and Pennsylvania avenue and Bridge and High streets in Georgetown.	May 4, 1858 June 12, 1858 Mar. 3, 1859	11 11 11	268 322 427	I I I	5,000.00 43,000.00 43,000.00	1858 1859 1860	33,000.00 39,000.00 43,000.00			33,000.00 39,000.00 43,000.00
For erecting 30 additional lamp-posts in Bridge and High streets, Georgetown.	June 12, 1858	11	322	I	810.00	1859	810.00			810.00
For laying down gas pipes and erecting gas lamps on Four-and-a-half, Seventh, and Twelfth streets, across the plat of earth described in the plan of the city as reservation numbers two and three, commonly known as the Mall, to be expended under the direction of the Commissioner of Public Buildings.	Feb. 2, 1859	11	378	I	6,400.00	1860 1862	6,400.00	781.45	781.45	5,618.55
For lighting with gas Four-and-a-half, Seventh, and Twelfth streets across the public Mall.	Mar. 3, 1859	11	427	I	4,000.00	1860	4,000.00			4,000.00
For lighting the Capitol and President's House, the public grounds around them and around the Executive offices, and Pennsylvania avenue, Bridge and High streets in Georgetown, Four-and-a-half, Seventh, and Twelfth streets across the Mall.	June 25, 1860 Mar. 2, 1861	12 12	107 216	I I	42,000.00 42,000.00	1861	47,057.60			47,057.60
For lighting the Capitol and President's House, the public grounds around them and around the Executive offices.	July 24, 1861	12	272	3	8,000.00	1862	56,652.31	1,709.91		54,942.40

[1]Transferred to "Lafayette Square."　　　[2]Transferred to "Insane asylum maintenance," etc.

Table XIII. Statement of appropriations from the National Treasury for the Capitol from 1850 to 1900. (*Continued*)

General object (title of appropriation), and details and explanations.	Date of act making the appropriation.	References to the Statutes at Large.			Amount of annual appropriation.	Year of expenditure.	Expenditure by warrants.	Repayments.	Amount carried to the surplus fund.	Net expenditures.
		Volume.	Page.	Section.						
Lighting. (*Continued*)										
For lighting the Capitol and President's House, etc., Pennsylvania avenue, Bridge and High streets in Georgetown, Four-and-a-half street, and Seventh and Twelfth streets across the Mall.	Mar. 1, 1862	12	350	I	$50,000.00					
To supply the deficiency in the appropriation for lighting the Capitol and public grounds.	July 11, 1862	12	534	3	12,000.00	1863	$62,000.00	$1,922.83		$60,077.17
For lighting the Capitol and President's House, the public grounds around them, around the Executive offices, and Pennsylvania avenue, Bridge and High streets in Georgetown, and Four-and-a-half, Seventh, and Twelfth streets across the Mall.	Mar. 3, 1863	12	746	I	62,000.00	1864	63,922.83			63,922.83
For lighting Maryland avenue west, and Sixth street south.	Do.	12	750	4	15,000.00	1864	15,000.00			15,000.00
For lighting the Capitol and President's House, the public grounds around them, Pennsylvania avenue, Bridge and High streets in Georgetown, Four-and-a-half, Seventh, and Twelfth streets across the Mall, Maryland avenue west, and Sixth street south.	July 2, 1864 Apr. 7, 1866	13 14	347 18	I I	63,500.00 85,000.00	1865	63,500.00			63,500.00
For supplying deficiency in appropriation for lighting President's House, Capitol, public grounds, and streets.	Do.	14	19	I	13,000.00	1866	98,000.00			98,000.00
For lighting the Capitol, President's House, the public grounds around them, and Pennsylvania avenue.	July 28, 1866	14	314	I	60,000.00					
For lighting Four-and-a-half street across the Mall, and Maryland avenue west and Sixth street south: *Provided*, That the corporation of Washington City shall light their street lamps with 7-foot burners, twenty-one nights in each month, from dark until daylight, and that no part of this appropriation shall be disbursed until it is proved to the satisfaction of the Commissioner of Public Buildings that said corporation have so lighted their street lamps.	Do.	14	315	I	15,000.00					
To meet a deficiency in lighting Bridge and High streets, Georgetown, for the three months of the last fiscal year.	Do.	14	325	I	1,100.00					
For pay of lamplighters, gas fitting, plumbing, lamp-posts, lanterns, glass, paints, matches, materials and repairs of all sorts.	Do.	14	315	I	20,000.00	1867	96,085.99			96,085.99
For lighting the Capitol and President's House and public grounds around them, around the Executive offices, and Pennsylvania avenue.	Mar. 2, 1867	14	462	I	55,000.00	1868	55,014.01			55,014.01
For lighting Four-and-a-half street across the Mall and Maryland avenue west and Sixth street south.	Do.	14	462		15,000.00	1870			15,000.00	

Table XIII. Statement of appropriations from the National Treasury for the Capitol from 1850 to 1900. (*Continued*)

General object (title of appropriation), and details and explanations.	Date of act making the appropriation.	References to the Statutes at Large.			Amount of annual appropriation.	Year of expenditure.	Expenditure by warrants.	Repayments.	Amount carried to the surplus fund.	Net expenditures.
		Volume.	Page.	Section.						
Lighting. (*Continued*) For lighting the Rotunda of the Capitol with gas, by a branch from the electric battery which lights the Dome.	Mar. 2, 1867	14	464	I	$3,000.00	1868	$3,000.00			$3,000.00
For lighting the Capitol and President's House and public grounds around them, around the Executive offices, and Pennsylvania avenue.	July 20, 1868	15	118	I	30,000.00					
To supply the deficiency in the appropriation for lighting the Capitol and President's House, the public grounds around them and around the Executive offices.	Mar. 3, 1869	15	314	I	12,000.00	1869	41,990.00			41,990.00
For lighting the Capitol and President's House, the public grounds around them and around the Executive offices.	Mar. 29, 1869 Apr. 20, 1870	16 16	52 90	I	30,000.00 8,000.00					
To enable the Secretary of the Treasury to close the accounts of B. B. French, late Commissioner of Public Buildings.	Do.	16	88	I	7,758.14	1870	45,758.14			45,758.14
For lighting President's House, Capitol, and public grounds.	July 15, 1870	16	301	I	40,000.00	1871	40,000.00	$1.71		39,998.29
For materials and putting up Wilson's electric gas lighter in the Senate Chamber: *Provided,* That the same can be done under the control of the Architect of the Capitol extension during the recess, and at an expense not exceeding the amount herein appropriated.	Do.	16	314	I	4,500.00	1871 1872	4,500.00 4,500.00	4,500.00		4,500.00
For lighting President's House, Capitol, and public grounds.	Mar. 3, 1871	16	504	I	40,000.00					
For pay of lamplighters, plumbing, gas fitting, lamps, lamp-posts, matches, and repairs of all sorts.	Do.	16	504	I	10,000.00	1872	50,000.00		11.71	50,000.00
For lighting Capitol and Executive Mansion and public grounds.	June 10, 1872	17	364	I	45,000.00					
For lamps and lamp-posts for center and south walk, west Capitol grounds.	Do.	17	364	I	500.00					
For pay of lamplighters, gas fitting, plumbing, lamps, posts, and repairs of all sorts.	Do.	17	364	I	15,000.00					
For fuel for propagating garden and lodges in public grounds.	Do.	17	364	I	500.00	1873	61,000.00			61,000.00
For lighting the Capitol, Executive Mansion, and grounds.	Mar. 3, 1873	17	527		45,000.00					
For pay of lamplighters, gas fitting, plumbing, lamps, posts, and repairs of all sorts.	Do.	17	527		15,000.00					
For fuel for propagating garden and watchmen's lodges.	Do.	17	527		800.00	1874	60,800.00			60,800.00
For gas for Capitol, Executive Mansion, and grounds.	June 23, 1874	18	225		35,000.00					

NOTE: *This table contains the information published by Glenn Brown, which has not been corrected or updated.*

Table XIII. Statement of appropriations from the National Treasury for the Capitol from 1850 to 1900. *(Continued)*

General object (title of appropriation), and details and explanations.	Date of act making the appropriation.	References to the Statutes at Large.			Amount of annual appropriation.	Year of expenditure.	Expenditure by warrants.	Repayments.	Amount carried to the surplus fund.	Net expenditures.
		Volume.	Page.	Section.						
Lighting. *(Continued)*										
For pay of lamplighters, gas fitting, plumbing, etc.	June 23, 1874	18	225		$15,000.00					
For fuel for watchmen's lodges and for the greenhouses at propagating gardens.	Do.	18	225		1,000.00	1875	$51,000.00	$10,257.62		$40,742.38
For gas for lighting the Capitol and Executive Mansion.	Mar. 3, 1875	18	393		35,000.00					
For pay of lamplighters, plumbers, etc., and for material for the electrical battery.	Do.	18	393		15,000.00					
For new chandeliers for the corridors and passages of the House of Representatives to correspond with those in the Senate.	Do.	18	393		5,000.00					
For fuel for the watchmen's lodges and for the greenhouse.	Do.	18	393		1,000.00	1876	56,000.00		$10,257.62	56,000.00
Gas Fitting, etc.										
For pay for lamplighters, gas fitting, plumbing, lamp-posts, lanterns, glass, paints, matches, materials, and repairs of all sorts.	Mar. 2, 1867	14	462	I	25,000.00					
	July 20, 1868	15	118	I	5,000.00	1868	22,000.00			22,000.00
	Mar. 3, 1869	15	309	I	5,000.00	1869	8,000.00			8,000.00
	Apr. 20, 1870	16	90	I	1,000.00	1870	6,000.00			6,000.00
	July 15, 1870	16	301	I	5,000.00	1871	5,000.00	.22		4,999.78
						1872			.22	
Gas and Electric Lighting.										
Purchase of dynamos, House of Representatives and Rotunda.	Mar. 3, 1879	20	391	I	2,400.00	1880	2,400.00			2,400.00
Electric-light plant, House of Representatives.	Do.	27	657	I	15,392.63	1895	15,392.63			15,392.63
	Mar. 2, 1895	28	935	I	20,000.00	1896	20,000.00			20,000.00
Electric-light plant, Senate.	Aug. 4, 1886	24	239	I	20,000.00	1888	9,000.00			9,000.00
	Feb. 1, 1888	25	17	I	5,350.00	1890	1,651.85			1,651.85
	Mar. 2, 1895	28	935	I	10,000.00	1891	2,256.42			2,256.42
						1892	1,096.01			1,096.01
						1893	1,044.79			1,044.79
						1894	1,223.17			1,223.17
						1895	812.21			812.21
						1896	17,021.61			17,021.61
						1897	824.34			824.34
						1898	419.60			419.60
						1899		1.67	1.67	

NOTE: This table contains the information published by Glenn Brown, which has not been corrected or updated.

Table XIII. Statement of appropriations from the National Treasury for the Capitol from 1850 to 1900. (*Continued*)

General object (title of appropriation), and details and explanations.	Date of act making the appropriation.	References to the Statutes at Large.			Amount of annual appropriation.	Year of expenditure.	Expenditure by warrants.	Repayments.	Amount carried to the surplus fund.	Net expenditures.
		Volume.	Page.	Section.						
Gas and Electric Lighting. (*Continued*)										
Electric-light plants, Capitol and grounds.	June 11, 1896	29	433	I	$45,000.00	1897 1898 1899	$43,728.00 1,271.59	$.90	$1.31	$43,728.00 1,271.59
For additions to dynamo rooms and for chandeliers.	June 6, 1900	31	298	I	3,216.24	1900	2,000.00			$2,000.00
Total					1,529,676.29		1,516,757.82	19,860.69	31,562.92	1,516,899.70
Balance									1,216.24	
Heating and Ventilating.										
For furnishing and putting up new furnaces and repairing old furnaces, rebuilding and ventilating air chambers for the House of Representatives.	Aug. 4, 1854	10	568	I	4,500.00	1855	4,500.00			4,500.00
For expenses of heating and ventilating apparatus.	Feb. 20, 1861	12	134	I	12,000.00	1862	12,000.00			12,000.00
For repairs to all furnaces under the Capitol.	Mar. 1, 1862	12	350	I	500.00	1863	500.00			500.00
To enable the Commissioner of Public Buildings to have the old furnace under the Library of Congress removed, and a new one erected in its place.	Do.	12	352	I	325.00	1862	325.00			325.00
For expenses of heating and ventilating apparatus.	Mar. 14, 1862	12	356	I	14,000.00	1863	14,000.00	41.33		13,958.67
For a deficiency for the present fiscal year for keeping furnaces nine months.	Do.	12	367	2	400.00	1862	400.00			400.00
For casual repairs of all the furnaces under the Capitol.	Mar. 3, 1863	12	746	I	500.00	1864	500.00			500.00
For expenses of heating and ventilating apparatus.	Feb. 25, 1863	12	683	I	14,000.00	1864	14,041.33			14,041.33
To enable the Commissioner of Public Buildings to erect two new furnaces under the Rotunda of the Capitol, two under the old Hall of the House, and two under the Supreme Court room and vestibule to the same.	Mar. 3, 1863	12	746	I	5,500.00	1864	5,500.00			5,500.00
For expenses of heating and ventilating apparatus.	June 25, 1864	13	146	I	16,000.00	1865	16,000.00			16,000.00
To enable the Commissioner of Public Buildings to reconstruct five of the old burnt-out furnaces now under the old portion of the Capitol.	July 2, 1864	13	346	I	5,000.00	1865 1869	4,858.30		141.70	4,858.30
For casual repairs of all the furnaces under the Capitol.	July 2, 1864	13	347	2	500.00	1865	500.00			500.00
For expenses of heating and ventilating apparatus.	Mar. 2, 1865	13	446	I	16,000.00					

NOTE: *This table contains the information published by Glenn Brown, which has not been corrected or updated.*

Table XIII. Statement of appropriations from the National Treasury for the Capitol from 1850 to 1900. (*Continued*)

General object (title of appropriation), and details and explanations.	Date of act making the appropriation.	References to the Statutes at Large.			Amount of annual appropriation.	Year of expenditure.	Expenditure by warrants.	Repayments.	Amount carried to the surplus fund.	Net expenditures.
		Volume.	Page.	Section.						
Heating and Ventilating. (*Continued*)										
For fuel and repairs of heating and ventilating apparatus, to be provided under the charge of the Sergeant-at-Arms.	Apr. 7, 1866	14	24	I	$16,250.00	1866	$20,000.00			$20,000.00
For casual repairs of all the furnaces under the Capitol.	Do.	14	18	I	500.00	1866	500.00			500.00
For expenses of heating and ventilating apparatus.	July 23, 1866 Mar. 2, 1867	14 14	192 441	I I	20,500.00 25,000.00	1867 1868	32,475.00 26,221.91	$946.91		31,528.09 26,221.91
For casual repairs of all the furnaces under the Capitol.	July 28, 1866	14	315	I	500.00	1867	500.00			500.00
To ventilate the bathroom of the House of Representatives.	Do.	14	325	I	200.00	1868	200.00			200.00
For heating with steam the Supreme Court room, law library, and the passages and stairways adjacent to the court room, and for other repairs and improvements of said room.	Mar. 2, 1867	14	462	I	15,000.00	1868 1869	14,997.20		$2.80	14,997.20
To pay the expenses incurred under the resolution of the Senate directing the hydration of the atmosphere of the Senate Chamber.	Mar. 29, 1867	15	7	I	7,500.00	1867	7,500.00			7,500.00
For deficiency in the appropriation for defraying the expense of hydration of the Senate Chamber.	June 8, 1868	15	64	I	3,000.00	1869	1,061.59			1,061.59
For expenses of heating and ventilating apparatus, including coal, wood, and labor.	July 20, 1868	15	93	I	20,000.00					
Deficiency for heating and ventilating.	Mar. 3, 1869	15	312	I	5,000.00	1869	24,000.85	4,000.85		20,000.00
For expenses of heating and ventilating apparatus, including coal, wood, and labor.	Do.	15	284	I	25,000.00	1870	20,151.33			20,151.33
The Sergeant-at-Arms of the Senate authorized to purchase two exhaust fans, one engine, exhaust pipes, etc., for the removal of the impure air of the Senate Chamber.	July 15, 1870	16	309	7	5,000.00	1871	5,000.00			5,000.00
For fuel for the heating apparatus.	July 12, 1870	16	231	I	6,000.00					
Deficiency for fuel.	Mar. 3, 1871	16	515	I	2,000.00	1871	8,000.00	2,979.55		5,020.45
For expenses of heating and ventilating apparatus for fiscal year ending June 30, 1871.	May 18, 1872	17	122	I	400.00	1872 1872	400.00		1,938.22 12,828.22	400.00
For enlarging the shafts of escape for the impure air of the Senate Chamber.	July 15, 1870	16	300	I	2,500.00					

Table XIII. Statement of appropriations from the National Treasury for the Capitol from 1850 to 1900. (*Continued*)

General object (title of appropriation), and details and explanations.	Date of act making the appropriation.	References to the Statutes at Large.			Amount of annual appropriation.	Year of expenditure.	Expenditure by warrants.	Repayments.	Amount carried to the surplus fund.	Net expenditures.
		Volume.	Page.	Section.						
Heating and Ventilating. (*Continued*)										
For improving the heating and ventilating of the Senate.	Mar. 3, 1871	16	500	I	$3,000.00	1871	$4,000.00			$4,000.00
						1872	1,500.00			1,286.00
						1873		$214.00		
						1875			$214.00	
For ceiling with iron laths under the copper roof of the Hall of the House of Representatives, and for additional glass panels, flues, doors, and apparatus for improving the lighting and ventilating of said Hall.	July 15, 1870	16	312	I	15,000.00					
For enlarging air shaft, plastering ceiling of corridors, readjustment of flues under the floor, new registers, and for new floor in the Hall of House of Representatives; for additional fans for the exhaustion of vitiated air from the Hall, etc.	Mar. 3, 1871	16	501	I	20,000.00	1871	25,000.00			25,000.00
						1872	12,724.95	2,724.95		10,000.00
For covering the steam pipes in the Capitol with fireproof nonconducting felting.	Apr. 20, 1871	17	12	27	8,000.00	1871	8,000.00			7,891.70
						1872	637.17	637.67	.50	
						1873		107.80		
						1875			107.80	
Heating apparatus, Senate.	June 29, 1878	20	237	I	4,250.00	1879	4,250.00			4,250.00
	Mar. 3, 1879	20	391	I	4,000.00	1880	4,000.00			4,000.00
	June 16, 1880	21	279	I	10,000.00	1881	9,500.00			9,500.00
						1882	500.00			500.00
						1883		.01	.01	
Boiler vaults and boilers, Senate.	Aug. 4, 1886	24	239	I	10,500.00	1887	3,500.00			3,500.00
						1888	6,999.13			6,999.13
						1889			.87	
Steam boilers, Senate.	Aug. 30, 1890	26	388	I	15,000.00	1891	500.00			500.00
						1892	14,465.88			14,465.88
						1893	34.04		.08	34.04
Steam heating and machinery, Senate.	Aug. 5, 1882	27	367	I	2,375.00	1893	1,000.00			1,000.00
						1894	1,326.48			1,326.48
						1895	48.22			48.22
						1896	.30			.30
	June 11, 1896	29	432	I	4,600.00	1897	4,557.21			4,557.21
	June 4, 1897	30	32	I	3,165.00	1898	3,115.06			3,115.06
	July 1, 1898	30	617	I	4,859.00	1899	4,882.59		23.49	4,882.59
	Mar. 3, 1899	30	1094	I	4,751.00					
	June 6, 1900	31	298	I	202.00	1900	4,644.03		49	4,644.03
	Do.	31	613	I	3,285.00	1901	3,637.09		1.13	3,637.09

Table XIII. Statement of appropriations from the National Treasury for the Capitol from 1850 to 1900. (*Continued*)

General object (title of appropriation), and details and explanations.	Date of act making the appropriation.	References to the Statutes at Large.			Amount of annual appropriation.	Year of expenditure.	Expenditure by warrants.	Repayments.	Amount carried to the surplus fund.	Net expenditures.
		Volume.	Page.	Section.						
Heating and Ventilating. (*Continued*)										
Heating apparatus, House of Representatives.	June 16, 1880	21	280	I	$1,000.00	1881	$1,000.00			$1,000.00
Steam boilers, House of Representatives.	Oct. 2, 1888	25	522	I	12,000.00	1889	11,000.00			11,000.00
						1890	1,000.00			1,000.00
Ventilation, Senate.	July 7, 1884	23	209	I	6,000.00	1885	6,000.00			6,000.00
	Aug. 4, 1886	24	239	I	1,500.00	1887	1,500.00			1,500.00
	Mar. 2, 1889	25	958	I	8,000.00	1890	8,000.00			8,000.00
	June 11, 1896	29	433	I	55,000.00	1897	48,365.38			48,365.38
						1898	4,648.33			4,648.33
						1899	1,620.61			1,620.61
						1900	319.97			319.97
	June 6, 1900	31	613	I	500.00	1901	545.71			545.71
Ventilation, House of Representatives.	Mar. 3, 1879	20	402	I	30,000.00	1879	5,000.00			5,000.00
						1880	25,000.00			25,000.00
	Feb. 1, 1888	25	17	I	800.00	1888	800.00			800.00
						1891		$187.40		
						1893			$187.40	
	Mar. 3, 1901	31	1157	I	51,200.00	1901	5,222.75			5,222.75
Ventilation, Supreme Court rooms.	Mar. 2, 1889	25	958	I	2,500.00	1890	2,189.72			2,189.72
						1891	308.37		1.91	308.37
Fire-extinguishing apparatus, etc.	June 20, 1878	20	237	I	3,750.00	1879	3,750.00			3,750.00
	June 16, 1880	21	272	I	1,200.00	1881	1,200.00			1,200.00
Total					554,754.82		504,668.32	11,840.47	15,948.81	493,015.26
Balance									45,978.16	
Improving the Grounds.										
For improving public grounds north, south, and west of the Capitol.	Mar. 3, 1851	9	612	I	2,500.00	1851	2,500.00			2,500.00
For removing fences, grading streets, etc., preparatory to the extension of the Capitol grounds.	Mar. 3, 1855	10	662	I	15,000.00	1855	3,000.00			3,000.00
						1856	12,000.00			
						1859		.35	.35	11,999.65
For painting the iron railing around the Capitol grounds.	July 2, 1864	13	348	2	1,500.00	1865	1,500.00			1,500.00
Improvement of grounds, purchase of plants for garden, and contingent expenses incident thereto.	Apr. 7, 1866	14	18	I	2,000.00	1866	2,000.00			2,000.00

NOTE: *This table contains the information published by Glenn Brown, which has not been corrected or updated.*

Table XIII. Statement of appropriations from the National Treasury for the Capitol from 1850 to 1900. *(Continued)*

General object (title of appropriation), and details and explanations.	Date of act making the appropriation.	References to the Statutes at Large.			Amount of annual appropriation.	Year of expenditure.	Expenditure by warrants.	Repayments.	Amount carried to the surplus fund.	Net expenditures.
		Volume.	Page.	Section.						
Improving the Grounds. *(Continued)*										
For grading, filling up, removing buildings, and improving the public grounds and streets around the Capitol.	Mar. 30, 1868	15	13	I	$20,000.00	1867	$20,000.00			$20,000.00
Improving Capitol grounds.	July 20, 1868	15	118	I	2,000.00	1869 1870	2,000.00	$.11	$.11	1,999.89
For continuing the grading and filling up of the Capitol grounds.	July 25, 1868	15	176	I	10,000.00	1869	10,000.00			10,000.00
For continuing the grading and filling up of the Capitol grounds.	Mar. 3, 1869	15	309	I	15,000.00	1870	15,000.00			15,000.00
For improvement, care, protection, and repair of seats and fountains in Capitol grounds.	Mar. 3, 1869	15	309	I	1,000.00	1870	1,000.00			1,000.00
For improvements and care of seats and fountains.	July 15, 1870	16	301	I	1,000.00	1871 1872	1,000.00	401.47 1.19	402.66	597.34
For continuing the grading and filling up of the Capitol grounds.	July 15, 1870	16	302	I	25,000.00					
For additional lamps and service pipe in the east and west parks, Capitol grounds.	Mar. 3, 1871 May 18, 1872	16 17	501 132	I I	20,000.00 4,000.00	1871 1872	35,000.00 4,000.00			35,000.00 4,000.00
For continuing the work of grading and filling, and for planting the grounds around the Capitol, paving B street north, from Delaware to New Jersey avenues and the quadrant, thence to Pennsylvania avenue, and for curbing and paving the footways around the Capitol grounds, $35,000, which shall be available immediately.	June 10, 1872	17	361		35,000.00	1872	22,552.56	2,552.56		20,000.00
For grading and paving the streets and footways around the Capitol, and running from Pennsylvania avenue to B street north and south to the line of the east front of the Capitol, and for improving the grounds within that area.	Mar. 3, 1873	17	519		125,000.00	1873 1874 1875	40,000.00 125,000.00 282.45	15,000.00 282.45		40,000.00 110,000.00
To enlarge the public grounds surrounding the Capitol, including in such extension the two squares designated on the plan of the city of Washington as Nos. 687 and 688, respectively, and to purchase such private property as may be necessary for carrying this act into effect.	May 8, 1872		84	6, 7	400,000.00					
To purchase all the remaining estate and improvements in square No. 688.	Mar. 3, 1873	17	537	I	284,199.15	1873	684,199.15			684,199.15
For the examination of titles, plats, surveys, and appraisement forming the basis of the purchase by the United States of squares Nos. 687 and 688.	Do.	17	538	I	7,000.00	1873	7,000.00			7,000.00
For 10,844 square feet of land on South Capitol and South B streets, with the building standing thereon, to be paid to the trustees of Israel African Methodist Episcopal Church.	Do.	17	519		15,000.00	1874 1875	15,000.00	50.00	50.00	14,950.00

NOTE: This table contains the information published by Glenn Brown, which has not been corrected or updated.

Table XIII. Statement of appropriations from the National Treasury for the Capitol from 1850 to 1900. (*Continued*)

General object (title of appropriation), and details and explanations.	Date of act making the appropriation.	References to the Statutes at Large.			Amount of annual appropriation.	Year of expenditure.	Expenditure by warrants.	Repayments.	Amount carried to the surplus fund.	Net expenditures.
		Volume.	Page.	Section.						
Improving the Grounds. (*Continued*)										
To procure a topographical survey of the Capitol grounds and the employment of Fred. Law Olmsted, of New York, in furnishing plans for laying out the grounds.	Mar. 21, 1874	18	23		$3,000.00		$3,000.00			$3,000.00
For improving Capitol grounds and for sewers and street lights for the same: *Provided*, That so much of said sum as is necessary shall be expended by the Architect of the Capitol in forthwith removing from the Capitol grounds the engine building south of the Capitol.	June 21, 1874	18	146		20,000.00	1874				
For improvement of Capitol grounds according to the plans and under the general direction of Fred. Law Olmsted, to be expended by the Architect of the Capitol.	June 23, 1874	18	214		200,000.00	1875 1876	220,681.64 .38	$681.64 .76		219,999.62
For improvement of the Capitol grounds according to the plans and under the general direction of Fred. Law Olmsted, to be expended by the Architect of the Capitol.	Mar. 3, 1875	18	384		200,000.00					
For continuing the work of the improvement of the Capitol grounds.	Apr. 21, 1876	19	35		20,000.00	1876	220,000.00			220,000.00
Landscape and Terraces.										
Improving the Capitol grounds.	July 31, 1876	19	115	I	125,000.00	1877	125,000.00		$.38	125,000.00
	Mar. 3, 1877	19	348	I	173,000.00	1877	30,000.00			30,000.00
	Apr. 30, 1878	20	44	I	9,000.00	1878	152,000.00			152,000.00
	June 20, 1878	20	226	I	100,000.00	1879	80,000.00			80,000.00
	Mar. 3, 1879	20	391	I	60,000.00	1880	80,000.00			80,000.00
	June 16, 1880	21	272	I	60,000.00	1881	55,500.00			55,500.00
	Mar. 3, 1881	21	449	I	60,000.00	1882	64,392.50			64,392.50
	Aug. 7, 1882	22	325	I	65,000.00	1883	63,474.53		107.50	63,474.53
	Mar. 3, 1883	22	621	I	65,000.00	1884	64,999.31		1,525.47	64,999.31
	July 7, 1884	23	208	I	52,000.00	1885	39,999.31		.69	39,999.31
	Mar. 3, 1885	23	497	I	35,000.00	1886	28,682.31		.69	28,682.31
	Aug. 4, 1886	24	239	I	25,000.00	1887	29,748.99		13,317.69	29,748.99
	Mar. 3, 1887	24	525	I	20,000.00	1888	20,000.00		251.01	20,000.00
	Oct. 2, 1888	25	522	I	20,000.00	1889	19,905.87			19,905.87
	Mar. 2, 1889	25	958	I	30,000.00	1890	30,068.02			30,068.02
	Aug. 30, 1890	26	388	I	20,000.00	1891	18,998.28		25.11	18,998.28
	Mar. 3, 1891	26	970	I	16,000.00	1892	16,000.00		2.72	16,000.00
	Aug. 5, 1892	27	368	I	15,000.00	1893	13,000.00			13,000.00
	Mar. 3, 1893	27	591	I	12,000.00					
	Apr. 21, 1894	28	59	I	1,000.00	1894	15,000.00			15,000.00
	Aug. 18, 1894	28	393	I	12,000.00					
	Mar. 2, 1895	28	857	I	3,000.00	1895	14,990.00			14,990.00
	Do.	28	935	I	12,000.00					

Table XIII. Statement of appropriations from the National Treasury for the Capitol from 1850 to 1900. *(Continued)*

General object (title of appropriation), and details and explanations.	Date of act making the appropriation.	Volume.	Page.	Section.	Amount of annual appropriation.	Year of expenditure.	Expenditure by warrants.	Repayments.	Amount carried to the surplus fund.	Net expenditures.
Landscape and Terraces. *(Continued)*										
Improving the Capitol grounds.	June 11, 1896	29	457	I	$900.00	1896	$13,510.00			$13,510.00
	Do.	29	433	I	12,000.00	1897	12,400.00			12,400.00
	June 4, 1897	30	31	I	12,000.00	1898	11,991.27			11,991.27
	July 1, 1898	30	617	I	20,000.00					
	Mar. 3, 1899	30	1231	I	4,800.00	1899	24,795.21		$8.73	24,795.21
	Do.	30	1094	I	16,000.00					
	June 6, 1900	31	298	I	850.00	1900	16,751.00		4.79	16,751.00
	Do.	31	613	I	16,782.15	1901	16,781.07		100.00	16,781.07
	Mar. 3, 1901	31	1035	I	16,782.15	1901	16,781.07		100.00	16,781.07
Payment to G.W. Cook for improving the Capitol grounds.	June 20,1878	20	226	I	5,000.00	1879 1881	4,200.74		799.26	4,200.74
	Aug. 5, 1882	22	267	I	4,530.57	1883	4,530.57			4,530.57
	Mar. 3, 1885	23	498	I	2,404.88	1886	2,404.88			2,404.88
Retained percentages, improving the Capitol grounds.	Mar. 3, 1879	20	391	I	2,217.94	1880	2,117.31		100.63	2,117.31
	June 16, 1880	21	272	I	6,246.72	1881	6,246.72			6,246.72
						1882		$35.52		
						1883			35.52	
Capitol terraces.	July 7, 1884	23	208	I	60,000.00					
	Mar. 3, 1885	23	497	I	200,000.00	1885	53,000.00			53,000.00
						1886	149,999.80			149,999.80
	Aug. 4, 1886	24	237 271	I	177,833.48	1887	143,000.00			143,000.00
	Mar. 3, 1887	24	525	I	330,000.00	1888	239,908.88			239,908.88
	Oct. 2, 1888	25	523	I	15,000.00	1889	124,984.75			124,984.75
	Mar. 2, 1889	25	958	I	14,000.00					
	Apr. 4, 1890	26	43	I	7,500.00	1890	73,000.00			73,000.00
	Aug. 30, 1890	26	388	I	27,000.00					
	Mar. 3, 1891	26	970	I	14,000.00					
	Do.	26	878	I	7,500.00	1891	49,000.00			49,000.00
	Aug. 5, 1892	27	368	I	8,000.00	1892	19,310.98			19,310.98
						1893	2,400.00			2,400.00
						1894	3,575.35			3,575.35
						1895	2,651.34			2,651.34
						1896	2.38			2.38
Pavement, Capitol grounds.	Mar. 3, 1891	26	970	I	40,000.00	1892	38,453.60			38,453.60
						1893	734.69			734.69
						1894	140.52			140.52
						1895	277.15			277.15
						1896	394.04			394.04

Table XIII. Statement of appropriations from the National Treasury for the Capitol from 1850 to 1900. (*Continued*)

General object (title of appropriation), and details and explanations.	Date of act making the appropriation.	References to the Statutes at Large.			Amount of annual appropriation.	Year of expenditure.	Expenditure by warrants.	Repayments.	Amount carried to the surplus fund.	Net expenditures.
		Volume.	Page.	Section.						
Landscape and Terraces. (*Continued*)										
Pavement, Capitol grounds. (*Continued*)	July 19, 1897	30	127	I	$14,000.00	1898	$10,658.82			$10,658.82
						1899	3,341.13			3,341.13
						1900			$.05	
Total					3,643,278.13		3,645,550.36	$19,006.05	16,733.36	3,626,579.83
Balance									.08	
Works of Art. *Painting by William H. Powell.*										
Transferred from "Paintings by Vanderlyn," etc.					4,000.00					
For the execution of an historical painting for the Rotunda of the Capitol by William H. Powell, in place of the one contracted for with Henry Inman, deceased, under the joint resolution of June 23, 1836 (5 Stats., 133), and the Library Committee are hereby directed to contract with the said William H. Powell to execute the said painting, on the same terms as were made with the said Inman.	Mar. 3, 1847	9	164	I	6,000.00	1848	2,000.00			2,000.00
						1849	2,000.00			2,000.00
						1850	2,000.00			2,000.00
						1852	2,000.00			2,000.00
To enable the Committee on the Library to pay to William H. Powell, in full for the picture painted by him for the United States, in addition to the sum heretofore appropriated by law.	Mar. 3, 1855	10	668	2	2,000.00	1855	4,000.00			4,000.00
Total					12,000.00		12,000.00			12,000.00
Perry's Victory on Lake Erie.										
The Joint Committee on the Library are directed to enter into a contract with William H. Powell, of the State of Ohio, to paint a picture for the United States, to be placed at the head of one of the grand staircases in the Capitol, illustrative of some naval victory, the particular subject of the painting to be agreed on by the committee and the artist: *Provided,* That the entire expense of said picture shall not exceed $25,000; and $2,000 shall be paid to said William H. Powell in advance, to enable him to prepare for the work, the remainder of said installments at intervals of not less than one year, the last installment to be retained until the picture is completed and put up.	Mar. 2, 1865	13	570		25,000.00					
To enable the Joint Committee on the Library to pay the first installment due on a contract made with William H. Powell for a naval picture to be placed in the Capitol, in pursuance of a joint resolution approved March 2, 1865 (as above).	Apr. 7, 1866	14	21	I	2,000.00	1866	2,000.00			2,000.00
						1867	5,000.00		2,000.00 [1]	5,000.00
						1868	1,000.00	1,000.00		
						1870	12,000.00			12,000.00
						1871	2,095.00			2,095.00
						1872	3,000.00		905.00	3,000.00

[1] Transferred to "Purchase of books for the Library of Congress."

NOTE: *This table contains the information published by Glenn Brown, which has not been corrected or updated.*

Table XIII. Statement of appropriations from the National Treasury for the Capitol from 1850 to 1900. *(Continued)*

General object (title of appropriation), and details and explanations.	Date of act making the appropriation.	References to the Statutes at Large.			Amount of annual appropriation.	Year of expenditure.	Expenditure by warrants.	Repayments.	Amount carried to the surplus fund.	Net expenditures.
		Volume.	Page.	Section.						
Works of Art. *(Continued)*										
To pay the last installment due W. H. Powell for picture illustrative of Perry's victory.	Mar. 3, 1873	17	540	I	$905.00	1874	$905.00			$905.00
Total					27,905.00		26,000.00	$1,000.00	$2,905.00	25,000.00
Hubard's cast of the Houdon statue of Washington.										
To compensate the widow of the late W. J. Hubard for the cast of the Houdon statue of Washington executed by him, said sum to be in full of all demands for said statue.	July 15, 1870	16	315	I	2,000.00	1871	2,000.00			2,000.00
Canyon of the Yellowstone.										
To enable the Joint Committee on the Library to purchase Moran's large painting of the Canyon of the Yellowstone.	June 10, 1872	17	362	I	10,000.00	1873	10,000.00			10,000.00
Works of Hiram Powers.										
To enable the President of the United States to contract with Hiram Powers for some work of art executed or to be executed by him and suitable for the ornamentation of the Capitol.	Mar. 3, 1855	10	674	28	25,000.00	1859 1861 1863 1864 1865	5,000.00 5,000.00 5,000.00 5,018.00		4,982.00	5,000.00 5,000.00 5,000.00 5,018.00
Total					25,000.00		20,018.00		4,982.00	20,018.00
Ornamenting the Capitol.										
For furnishing and ornamenting the Capitol with such works of art as may be ordered and approved by the Joint Committee on the Library, to be placed in either wing of the extension when ready for their reception.	Aug. 18, 1856	11	88	I	20,000.00	1857 1858 1860 1861 1866	1,750.00 1,500.00 1,700.00 1,050.00 2,500.00			1,750.00 1,500.00 1,700.00 1,050.00 2,500.00
For an additional appropriation, to be expended under the direction of the Joint Committee on the Library, to decorate the Capitol with such works of art as may be ordered and approved by said committee, as provided by act approved August 18, 1856.	July 28, 1886	14	317	I	5,000.00	1867 1868 1869 1870 1871 1872	3,000.00 6,905.00 2,604.11 500.00 5,000.00	1,905.00	395.89	3,000.00 5,000.00 2,604.11 500.00 5,000.00
For an additional appropriation—and said committee, whenever, in their judgment, it shall be expedient, are authorized to accept any work of the fine arts, on behalf of Congress, which may be offered, and to assign the same such place in the Capitol as they may deem suitable, and shall have the supervision of all works of art that may be placed in the Capitol.	June 10, 1872	17	362	I	15,000.00	1874 1875	2,500.00 12,500.00			2,500.00 12,500.00

NOTE: *This table contains the information published by Glenn Brown, which has not been corrected or updated.*

Table XIII. Statement of appropriations from the National Treasury for the Capitol from 1850 to 1900. (*Continued*)

General object (title of appropriation), and details and explanations.	Date of act making the appropriation.	Volume.	Page.	Section.	Amount of annual appropriation.	Year of expenditure.	Expenditure by warrants.	Repayments.	Amount carried to the surplus fund.	Net expenditures.
Works of Art. (*Continued*)										
To enable the Joint Committee on the Library to purchase such works of art for ornamenting the Capitol as may be ordered and approved.	June 23, 1874	18	209	I	$10,000.00	1875	$10,000.00			$10,000.00
	Mar. 3, 1875	18	376	I	15,000.00	1876	11,700.00	$1,000.00		10,700.00
Works of art in the Capitol.						1877	2,000.00			2,000.00
						1878			$2,300.00	
	June 20, 1878	20	239	I	15,000.00	1879	14,305.43			14,305.43
	June 21, 1879	21	26	I	5,000.00	1880	5,000.00		694.57	5,000.00
	June 16, 1880	21	281	I	10,000.00	1881	10,000.00			10,000.00
	Mar. 3, 1881	21	449	I	10,000.00	1882	10,000.00			10,000.00
	Aug. 7, 1882	22	238	I	10,000.00	1883		100.00	100.00	
						1884	8,000.00			8,000.00
	July 7, 1884	23	125	I	12,000.00	1885	8,000.00			8,000.00
	Mar. 3, 1885	23	394	I	5,000.00	1886	11,000.00			11,000.00
	Aug. 4, 1886	24	254	I	10,000.00	1887	8,500.00			8,500.00
						1893		14.22	1,514.22	
Protecting paintings in the Rotunda.	Oct. 2, 1888	25	547	I	500.00	1889	400.00			400.00
						1891		10.00	110.00	
Repairing frames in Rotunda.	Mar. 2, 1889	25	958	I	1,000.00	1890	600.00			600.00
						1891		2.88	402.88	
Repairs of paintings in the Capitol.	Aug. 18, 1894	28	393	I	1,000.00	1895	1,000.00			1,000.00
	Mar. 2, 1895	28	935	I	1,500.00	1896	750.00			750.00
	June 11, 1896	29	432	I	1,500.00	1897	2,250.00			2,250.00
	June 4, 1897	30	31	I	1,500.00	1898	1,493.86		6.14	1,493.86
	July 1, 1898	30	617	I	1,500.00	1899	1,500.00			1,500.00
	Mar. 3, 1899	30	1094	I	1,500.00	1900	1,500.00			1,500.00
	June 6, 1900	31	613	I	1,500.00	1901	1,500.00			1,500.00
Busts of Chief Justices Taney and Chase.						1877	550.00		450.00	550.00
Portraits of the Presidents.	June 20, 1878	20	239	I	3,000.00	1879	2,150.00		850.00	2,150.00
						1885		4.50		
						1886			4.50	
Purchase of painting "Farming in Dakota."	Mar. 3, 1887	24	535	I	3,000.00	1888	3,000.00			3,000.00
Oil portraits of Chief Justices Rutledge, Ellsworth, and Waite.	Oct. 2, 1888	25	547	I	1,500.00	1889	1,500.00			1,500.00
						1891		270.00		
						1893			270.00	

Table XIII. Statement of appropriations from the National Treasury for the Capitol from 1850 to 1900. *(Continued)*

General object (title of appropriation), and details and explanations.	Date of act making the appropriation.	References to the Statutes at Large.			Amount of annual appropriation.	Year of expenditure.	Expenditure by warrants.	Repayments.	Amount carried to the surplus fund.	Net expenditures.
		Volume.	Page.	Section.						
Works of Art. *(Continued)*										
Bust of the late Chief Justice Waite.	Mar. 2, 1889	25	927	I	$1,500.00	1892	$1,500.00			$1,500.00
Portrait of John Paul Jones.	Mar. 3, 1891	26	988	I	750.00	1892	750.00			750.00
Portrait of Gen. Winfield Scott.	Do.	26	988	I	3,000.00	1892	3,000.00			3,000.00
Portrait of Chief Justice Marshall.	Aug. 30, 1890	26	410	I	1,000.00					
Payment to C. Brumidi for frescoing the Rotunda.	June 20, 1878 Mar. 3, 1879	20 20	226 391	I I	500.00 700.00	1879 1881	500.00 700.00			500.00 700.00
Total					169,450.00		164,658.40	3,306.60	7,098.20	161,753.40
Balance									1,000.00	

Table XIV. Cost of the Capitol.

Cost of the old building:
    Wings of old Senate and House $788,077.98
    Rebuilding old wings after mutilation by British 687,126.00
    Center portion 957,647.36
        Total cost of the old or center building $2,432,851.34
Capitol extension (new Senate and House wings) 8,075,299.04
New Dome 1,047,291.89
Landscape work and marble terraces 3,626,579.83
Heating and ventilating 493,015.26
Lighting (approximated from expenditures on streets, Executive Mansion, etc.) 250,000.00
        Total original cost of building and grounds $15,925,037.36
Repairs from 1827 to 1901 . . . . 2,302,387.49
        Total cost of building and grounds, including repairs, to 1901 . . . . 18,227,424.85
Cost of statuary, painting, and decorative work 867,824.21
Estimated cost of works of art in building and grounds presented to the Government 400,000.00
        Total cost of works of art 1,267,824.21
Deduct—
    Amount paid for statuary, paintings, and decorative work, included in construction appropriations . 440,281.34
    Estimated cost of works of art in building and grounds presented to the Government 400,000.00
                                                                   840,281.34
Amount actually paid by Government for works of art, exclusive of those paid for from construction appropriations 427,542.87
    Total expenditure on building and grounds and works of art 18,654,967.72

Bibliography, United States Capitol, 1794–1900

To produce his *History of the United States Capitol*, Glenn Brown used a variety of source materials, including correspondence, drawings, guide books, scholarly and popular literature, congressional statutes, and government records. At the time of its publication in 1902, this bibliography contained the most comprehensive list of primary and secondary sources then available on the Capitol. However, omission of key facts of publication in many of Brown's citations have left them inadequate for modern readers. Likewise, changes in the location of government records over the years have rendered Brown's section on manuscript materials obsolete.

A revised version of Brown's bibliography is therefore presented here with modernized citations and with a summary of the types of manuscript materials Brown consulted. Brown's original subject headings and his arrangement of entries have been retained in chronological order by date of publication. His annotations of government documents have been deleted since they have been superseded by more useful abstracts in John R. Kerwood's *The United States Capitol: An Annotated Bibliography* (Norman, OK: University of Oklahoma, 1973). Multiple editions of works have been cited as one entry and duplicate or unidentifiable entries have been omitted. Following Brown's bibliography is a selected bibliography of works published since he completed the *History*.

Manuscript Material

Owned by Private Individuals

In this category, Brown cited the correspondence of Benjamin Henry Latrobe to John Lenthall, Superintendent of the Capitol between 1803 and 1807. This correspondence dealt with execution of Latrobe's plans and administration of the construction of the Capitol. In 1900 this material was in the possession of Lenthall's grandson, William S. Abert, who had commissioned a house and office building designed by Brown in 1896. It is now deposited at the Manuscript Division of the Library of Congress and has been reproduced in Edward C. Carter II, editor in chief, and Thomas E. Jeffrey, microfiche editor, *The Papers of Benjamin Henry Latrobe*, microtext edition (Clifton, N.J.: James T. White & Company, 1976) and John C. Van Horne and Lee W. Formalt, eds., *The Correspondence and Miscellaneous Papers of Benjamin Henry Latrobe*, 3 vols. (New Haven: Yale University Press, 1984). Brown also cited a collection of letters, notes, and essays by William Thornton that are now deposited at the Manuscript Division.

In the State Department

Between 1890 and 1900 the State Department was located in the building known today as the Old Executive Office Building. In this category, Brown cited the correspondence of George Washington, Thomas Jefferson, James Madison, and James Monroe on the selection of sites for the Capitol and other federal buildings and on administrative and design issues related to the Capitol and its environs. Included are letters to and from Benjamin H. Latrobe, William Thornton, and the Commissioners of the District of Columbia. Some of these letters have been reprinted in the American State Papers series, while others can be found at the Manuscript Division of the Library of Congress and the National Archives and Records Administration.

In the Capitol Building

In this category, Brown cited official journals of the Senate and House Committees on the Library from 1829 to 1903. He probably examined these journals at one of the libraries then located in the Capitol. Today these journals are part of the Records of the U.S. Senate (Record Group 46), and the Records of the House of Representatives (Record Group 233), located in the Center for Legislative Archives at the National Archives and Records Administration in Washington, D.C. In addition, Brown cited miscellaneous letters and accounts in the Office of the Superintendent of Capitol Buildings and Grounds, which are now part of the Records of the Office of Public Buildings and Public Parks of the National Capital (Record Group 42) housed in the Civil Reference Branch of the National Archives.

In the War Department

In this category, Brown cited three groups of manuscripts then stored at the War Department: correspondence and accounts dated from 1853 to 1862 in the Office of the Chief of Engineers; correspondence, ledgers, and journals of the Commissioners of Public Buildings and Grounds dated from 1791 to 1867 pertaining to the Capitol design, construction, and contracts; and official proceedings of the Commissioners of the District of Columbia dated from 1791 to 1816. These manuscripts are now part of Record Group 42 at the National Archives. Brown also cited numerous congressional statutes governing the Commissioners of Public Buildings and Grounds between 1790 and 1833. These statutes are reprinted in the *United States Statutes at Large*. Presidential correspondence dated from 1791 to 1869 pertaining to the old Capitol Building and a journal of proceedings of a commission on the Capitol composed of the Secretaries of State, Treasury, and War, dated from 1838 to 1841, are now in Record Group 42.

In the Interior Department

In this category, Brown cited a series of file boxes numbered 116 to 121, which contained the correspondence of various officials, such as Thomas U. Walter, Benjamin B. French, and Edward Clark. The dates of this correspondence, 1851 to 1866, coincided with the design and construction of the Capitol extension. Also included were contracts and applications for employment, as well as documents pertaining to Capitol artwork and the purchase and condemnation of lots near the Capitol. Today these documents are stored at the National Archives.

In the Treasury Department

In this category, Brown cited a variety of financial records. From the office of the first auditor, he identified 20 volumes of indices describing settled government accounts for the period 1803 to 1894 relating to the construction and repair of the Capitol. These volumes also recorded expenditures on furniture and works of art in the building. From the office of the fifth auditor, which maintained a record of executive department expenditures, Brown consulted a series of volumes containing quarterly treasury accounts paid by warrants. These 36 volumes, dating from 1853 to 1862, contained warrants drawn in favor of Montgomery C. Meigs, William Buel Franklin, and John N. Macomb for payments on the Capitol extension and the new dome. Today, the various auditors' records are located at the National Archives.

Books and Pamphlets Relating to or Containing Matter on the Capitol

In this category, Brown cited government documents containing useful information on the Capitol available in pamphlet form and other works of general interest on the building's design and construction. Many of these items are now available in the Rare Books and Special Collections Division at the Library of Congress.

Jefferson, Thomas. *Message from the President of the United States (to the House of Representatives transmitting accounts stating the several sums that have been expended on the Capitol, the President's House (etc.), within the City of Washington)*. December 23, 1803. Washington: A. and G. Way, 1803.

Thornton, William. *Statement of B. H. Latrobe Corrected Regarding the Architecture of the Capitol*. Washington: 1803.

———. *To the Members of the House of Representatives of the United States (replying to criticisms of Benjamin H. Latrobe on the Capitol)*. Washington: 1805.

Latrobe, Benjamin. *Letter from the Surveyor of the Public Buildings at the City of Washington to the Chairman of the Committee Appointed 17th ultimo, on a message from the President of the United States, on the subject of said buildings.* (n.p., n.d.)

———. *Report of the Surveyor of Public Buildings.* November 25, 1806. Washington: A. and G. Way, 1806.

———. *A Private Letter to the Individual Members of Congress on the Subject of the Public Buildings of the United States at Washington.* Washington: Samuel H. Smith, 1806.

Dunlap, William. *History of the Rise and Progress of the Arts of Design in the United States.* Edited by Alexander Wyckoff. 3 Vols. New York: G. P. Scott and Co., 1834.

Tuthill, Louisa Caroline Higgins. *History of Architecture from the Earliest Times, its Present Condition in Europe and the United States, With a Biography of Eminent Architects.* Philadelphia: Lindsay and Blakiston, 1848.

Anderson, Charles Frederick. *Enlargement of the Capitol of the United States.* Washington: Gideon and Company, 1851.

Wyeth, Samuel Douglas. *Diagrams of the Floor of the Senate and House of Representatives After a New and Improved Plan.* Washington: Gibson Brothers, 1864.

———. *The Rotunda and the Dome of the United States Capitol.* Washington: Gibson Brothers, 1869.

The National Capital Explained and Illustrated: A Convenient Guide to All Points of Interest in the City of Washington. Washington: Devlin and Company, 1871.

Speech of Nathaniel P. Chipman on the Extension of the Capitol Grounds. Delivered in the House of Representatives March 16, 1872. [In a bound collection of speeches by Chipman, 1871–1873, at the Library of Congress, n.d., n.p.]

Fergusson, James. *History of the Modern Renaissance Styles,* Vol. 3 of *A History of Architecture in All Countries from the Earliest Times to the Present Day.* London: J. Murray, 1862–73.

Townsend, Alfred C. *Washington: Outside and Inside.* Hartford: J. Betts and Company, 1873.

Long, Francis C. *A Mystery of the Dome: A Poem in Two Cantos.* Washington: Beardsley and Snodgrass, 1875.

American Cyclopedia. New York: Ripley and Dana, 1876.

Hughes, William D. *The Capitol and Its Grounds: Their Defects, Plan for Improvement.* Washington: R. Beresford, 1876.

Johnston, Elizabeth B. *Original Portraits of Washington, Including Statues, Monuments and Medals.* Boston: James R. Osgood and Company, 1882.

Porter, John Addison. "The City of Washington, Its Origin, and Administration." In *Johns Hopkins University Studies in Historical and Political Science,* edited by Herbert B. Adams. 3d ser., vol. 3. Baltimore: Johns Hopkins University, 1885.

Capitol Centennial Committee. *Centennial Anniversary of the Laying of the Cornerstone of the National Capitol.* Washington: Capitol Centennial Committee, 1893.

Walker, Duncan S., ed. *Celebration of the 100th Anniversary of the Laying of the Original Cornerstone in 1793 and of the Cornerstone of the Extension in 1851.* Washington: Government Printing Office, 1896.

Hazelton, George C. *The National Capitol: Its Architecture, Art, and History.* New York: J. F. Taylor and Company, 1897.

Guide Books with Data on the Capitol

All of the guide books Brown cited were and remain in the collections of the Library of Congress.

Elliot, Jonathan. *Elliot's Washington Pocket Almanac or Stranger's Manual for the Year of Our Lord 1826.* Washington: S. A. Elliot, 1826, 1828, and 1829.

———. *Historical Sketches of the Ten-Miles Square Forming the District of Columbia.* Washington: J. Elliot, Jr., 1830.

Mills, Robert. *Guide to the Capitol and Architectural Buildings.* Washington: Privately printed, 1834.

Elliot, William. *The Washington Guide.* Washington: Franck Taylor, 1837.

Mills, Robert. *Guide to the National Executive Offices and the Capitol of the United States.* Washington: Peter Force, Printer, 1841.

Force, William Q. *Pictures of Washington and Its Vicinity.* Washington: William A. Force, 1845.

Watterson, George. *A New Guide to Washington.* Washington: William H. Morrison, 1842, 1847, 1848.

Mills, Robert. *Guide to the Capitol and National Executive Offices of the United States.* Washington: William Greer, Printer, 1847–48, 1850, and 1854.

Bohn, Casimir. *Bohn's Handbook of Washington.* Washington: C. Bohn, 1852, 1854, 1856, 1859, 1860, and 1861.

Morrison, W. H. and O. M. *Morrison's Stranger's Guide for Washington City.* Washington: W. H. and O. H. Morrison, 1860, 1862, 1868, 1872, 1875, and 1876.

Wyeth, Samuel D. *The Federal City: Or Ins and Abouts of Washington.* 3rd ed. Washington: Gibson Brothers, 1868.

———. *The Rotunda and the Dome of the United States Capitol.* Washington: Gibson Brothers, 1869.

Keim, De Benneville Randolph. *Keim's Capitol Interior and Diagrams: A Complete Guide to All Parts of the Capitol.* Washington: For the compiler, 1874, 1875, 1884.

Wyeth, Samuel D. *Roose's Companion and Guide to Washington and Vicinity.* Washington: Gibson Brothers, 1876, 1878, 1881, 1882, 1884, 1885, 1887, 1888, and 1889.

Articles in Magazines and Society Publications

Many of the popular magazines Brown consulted were located at the Library of Congress. He started building a reference library of major American and British professional journals immediately after the American Institute of Architects moved its headquarters to the Octagon in Washington, D.C., in 1898.

"Chamber of Representatives at Washington." *Penny Magazine of the Society of the Diffusion of Useful Knowledge* (October 10, 1835): 399–400.

"The Capitol at Washington." *Burton's Gentleman's Magazine* 5 (November 1839): 231–235.

"Remarks on Antient [sic] and Modern Porticoes." *Civil Engineer and Architect's Journal* 3 (1840): 293–296.

Greeley, Horace. "Capitol." *United States Illustrated*, edited by Charles A. Dana. New York: H. J. Meyer, 1854.

———. "Capitol and Hall of Representatives." *United States Illustrated* (1854).

Furness, William H. "New Capitol." *United States Illustrated* (1854).

"Bronzing Cast Iron Doors." *The Builder* [London] 21 (January 10, 1863): 26.

"Our National Capitol." *Beadle's Monthly* (April 1867): 293–307.

Spofford, Harriet P. "A Public Building." *Harper's New Monthly Magazine* 38 (January 1869): 204–10.

"The Capitol at Washington." *Building News* [London] 16 (January 29, 1869): 83–84, 92–94.

"Movement of the Dome of the Capitol at Washington, during the Gale of December 10–12, 1869." *American Journal of Science* 99 (1870): 384–385.

Wight, Peter B. "Government Architecture and Government Architects." *American Architect and Building News* 1 (March 18, 1876): 83–85.

Cluss, Adolph. "Architects and Architecture of the United States." *Proceedings of the Tenth Annual Proceedings of the American Institute of Architects*. Boston: Franklin Press, 1876.

"The United States Capitol, Washington." *American Architect and Building News* 4 (December 21, 1878): 205.

Lathrop, George B. "The Nation in a Nutshell." *Harper's Magazine* 62 (March 1881): 541–555.

Latrobe, John H. B. "The Capitol and Washington at the Beginning of the Present Century." *An Address Delivered by John H. B. Latrobe Before the American Institute of Architects*. Baltimore: William K. Boyle, 1881.

"Painting the Capitol Dome." *American Architect and Building News* 12 (December 1882): 271.

Poore, Benjamin Perley. "The Capitol at Washington." *Century Magazine* 25 (April 1883): 803–819.

Ralph, Julian. "Our National Capital." *Harper's New Monthly Magazine* 40 (April 1895): 657–674.

Brown, Glenn. "History of the United States Capitol." *American Architect and Building News* 52–55 (May 9, 1896): 51–54; (May 23, 1896): 75–77; (June 13, 1896): 99–102; (July 4, 1896): 3–5; (July 25, 1896): 27–30; (September 5, 1896): 75–78; (October 3, 1896): 3–6; (October 24, 1896): 27–29; (December 5, 1896): 81–83; (January 2, 1897): 3–6; (February 20, 1897): 59–60.

Biographies of Architects and Superintendents

Most of the monographs Brown cited were and are located at the Library of Congress.

Hoban, James. *Eulogy Pronounced March 6, 1846*. Washington: J. E. Norris, 1846.

The Architectural Dictionary. London: Architectural Publication Society, 1852–1892. 8 vols. Articles on Thornton, Latrobe, Bulfinch, Walter, and Washington City.

Howard, James Q. "The Architects of the American Capitol." *International Review* 1 (November–December 1874): 736–753.

"Walter, T. U." *Building News* [London] 24 (1883): 785.

Coote, C. T. "Discourse Delivered at the Second Presbyterian Church, December 27, 1832, on the Decease of Peter Lenox." Washington: n.p., 1883.

Mason, George C., Jr. "Biographical Memoirs of Thomas U. Walter." *Proceedings of the Twenty-second Annual Convention of the American Institute of Architects*. New York: Oberhauser and Company, Printers, 1889: 101–108.

Willard, Ashton R. "Charles Bulfinch, the Architect." *New England Magazine* 3 (November 1890): 27.

Langley, Samuel P. "Montgomery C. Meigs." *Bulletin of the Philosophical Society of Washington* 12 (1892–1894): 471–476.

Brown, Glenn. "Dr. William Thornton, Architect." *Architectural Record* 6 (July 1896): 53–70.

Bulfinch, Charles. *The Life and Letters of Charles Bulfinch, Architect*. Edited by Ellen S. Bulfinch. Boston: Houghton Mifflin, 1896.

"Obituary of Edward Clark." *Proceedings of the Thirty-sixth Annual Convention of the American Institute of Architects*. Washington: Gibson Brothers, 1903: 249.

Rhees, W. J. "Montgomery C. Meigs Sketch." In *Annual Report of the Board of Regents, Smithsonian Institution, 1846–1896*. Edited by George Browne Goode: 103.

Government Documents Relating to the Capitol

In this category Brown provided a comprehensive listing of public documents then available pertaining to the design, construction, and cost of the Capitol Building. Beginning with the fifteenth Congress (1817–1819) publications of the House and Senate can be found in the congressional serial set. Most of the pre-serial-set items cited by Brown relating to the Capitol's construction can be found in two locations. The first is a compilation at the Library of Congress Rare Books and Special Collections Division (LC RBSC), entitled *Public Documents of the First Fourteen Congresses, 1789–1817* (Washington: Government Printing Office, 1900), prepared by General A. W. Greeley, and its supplement (Washington: Government Printing Office, 1904). Pre-serial-set entries with an "LC" notation are from an annotated Greeley compilation at RBSC, and the retrieval numbers are cited to facilitate use of these original rare public documents. Other items can be found at the National Archives and Records Administration. They have been microfilmed as part of the National Archives Microfilm Publication M 371, *Records of the District of Columbia Commissioners and of the Offices Concerned with Public Buildings, 1791–1867.* The Center for Legislative Archives at the National Archives holds copies of many of these same documents within three record groups: RG 46, Records of the U.S. Senate; RG 233, Records of the U.S. House of Representatives; and RG 287, Publications of the U.S. Government. Those entries with a "Z4" notation are from the latter record group.

Most of the records cited by Brown in the congressional serial set either originated in Congress or were transmitted to Congress by the executive branch. In the latter instance many items are part of a larger document, usually an annual report of the operations of the Cabinet departments, submitted by the president for the consideration of Congress. To locate them a researcher must supplement the serial set citation provided below with the page number listed in the index of the corresponding volume of published congressional documents.

Citations for public records cited by Brown where the originating body (House or Senate) is unclear in the serial set are preceded by the term "U.S. Congress." Some of Brown's original citations in this category could not be located and have been omitted from this bibliography.

Documents Relating to Progress, Construction, and Expenditures on the Building

U.S. Congress. House. 5th Congress, 2nd Session. *State of Accounts and Progress of Public Buildings.* Commissioners Scott, Thornton, and White. Dec. 14, 1797. LC RBSC, 5S2D7.

———. 5th Congress, 2nd Session. *State of Accounts and Progress of Public Buildings.* Commissioners Scott, Thornton, and White. May 29, 1798. LC RBSC, 5S2D36.

———. 6th Congress, 1st Session. *State of Accounts and Progress of Public Buildings.* Commissioners Scott, Thornton, and White. Dec. 5, 1798. LC RBSC, 6H1D3.

Jefferson, Thomas. *Message from the President of the United States (to the Senate and Representatives), transmitting sundry documents relative to the affairs of the city of Washington.* Jan. 25, 1803. CLA/NARA (RG 287). Z4.7/2: HP17.

U.S. Congress. 8th Congress, 1st Session. *Report of Surveyor of Public Buildings.* B. Henry Latrobe. Feb. 22, 1804. LC RBSC, 8S1D36.

U.S. House. 8th Congress, 2nd Session. *Letter from the Surveyor of Public Buildings on Estimates for Completing South Wing of Capitol.* B. Henry Latrobe. Feb. 28, 1804. LC RBSC, 8S1D36.

Report on the Buildings at Washington. Rep. P. R. Thompson. March 6, 1804. CLA/NARA (RG 287). Z4.8/1: HR.

U.S. Congress. 8th Congress, 2nd Session. *Report of Surveyor of Public Buildings.* B. Henry Latrobe. Dec. 6, 1804. LC RBSC, 8S2D8.

Estimate for Finishing South Wing of Capitol. Benjamin H. Latrobe. Jan. 9, 1805. CLA/NARA (RG 287).Z4.8/2: HR.

U.S. Congress. 9th Congress, 1st Session. *Report of Surveyor of Public Buildings.* B. Henry Latrobe. Dec. 27, 1805. LC RBSC, 9S1D16.

———. 9th Congress, 1st Session. *Report of Surveyor of Public Buildings.* B. Henry Latrobe. Dec. 15, 1806. LC RBSC, 9H2D8.

Jefferson, Thomas. *Message Transmitting Account Stating the Several Sums That Have Been Expended on the Capitol, the President's House, etc.* Dec. 23, 1806. CLA/NARA (RG 287).Z4.9/2: HR10.

U.S. Congress. 10th Congress, 1st Session. *Letter and Report from Surveyor of Public Buildings.* B. Henry Latrobe. Oct. 28, 1807. LC RBSC, 10H1D4.

———. 10th Congress, 1st Session. *Report of Surveyor of Public Buildings.* B. Henry Latrobe. March 25, 1808. LC RBSC, 10H1D108.

———. 10th Congress, 2nd Session. *Report of Surveyor of Public Buildings.* B. Henry Latrobe. March 25, 1808. LC RBSC, 10S2D7.

Report on the Capitol. Senator B. Thurston. Feb. 18, 1809. Ex. Doc. (10–2). CA/NARA File #Sen 11A–F8 RG 46 (S).

Report on the Public Buildings. Benjamin H. Latrobe. June 13, 1809. Ex. Doc. (11–2). CA/NARA File #Sen 11A–F8 RG46 (S).

Report on the Public Buildings. Benjamin H. Latrobe. Dec. 21, 1809. Ex. Doc. (11–2). CA/NARA File #Sen 11A–E2 RG 46 (S).

U.S. Congress. 11th Congress, 3rd Session. *Report of Surveyor of Public Buildings.* B. Henry Latrobe. Jan. 15, 1811. LC RBSC, 11H3D40.

U.S. House. 11th Congress, 3rd Session. *Reports of Superintendent of the City and Surveyor of Public Buildings.* Thomas Munroe and B. Henry Latrobe. Feb. 26, 1811. LC RBSC, 11H3D95.

U.S. Congress. Senate. 14th Congress, 2nd Session. *Reports of Surveyor of the Capitol and Superintendent of the White House.* B. Henry Latrobe and James Hoban. Feb. 14, 1817. LC RBSC, 14S2D63.

U.S. House. 14th Congress, 2nd Session. *Memorial of B. Henry Latrobe, Surveyor of the Capitol of the United States.* Feb. 26, 1817. LC RBSC, 14H2D99.

———. 15th Congress, 2nd Session. *Message on Public Buildings.* (H. Doc. 8). Washington, 1818. (Serial Set 17).

U.S. Senate. 15th Congress, 2nd Session. *Memorial of Surveyor.* (S. Doc. 53). Washington, 1818. (Serial Set 14).

U.S. House. 17th Congress, 1st Session. *Message on Public Buildings.* (H. Doc. 9). Washington, 1822. (Serial Set 76).

———. 17th Congress, 1st Session. *Report on Public Buildings.* (H. Committee Rpt. 76). Washington, 1822. (Serial Set 71).

———. 17th Congress, 1st Session. *Report on the Capitol.* (H. Committee Rpt. 79). Washington, 1822. (Serial Set 71).

———. 17th Congress, 2nd Session. *Report on Alterations in the Hall of Representatives.* (H. Committee Rpt. 90). Washington, 1823. (Serial Set 87).

U.S. Congress. 17th Congress, 2nd Session. *Report on Work Done in the Capitol.* (Committee Rpt. 91). Washington, 1823. (Serial Set 87).

———. 17th Congress, 2nd Session. *Report on the Public Buildings.* (Committee Rpt. 93). Washington, 1823. (Serial Set 87).

———. 18th Congress, 1st Session. *Report on the Public Buildings.* (Committee Rpt. 60). Washington, 1824. (Serial Set 105).

———. 18th Congress, 1st Session. *Public Buildings.* (Committee Rpt. 106). Washington, 1824. (Serial Set 106).

U.S. House. 19th Congress, 2nd Session. *Appropriations for the Capitol.* (H. Ex. Doc. 51). Washington, 1827. (Serial Set 150).

———. 20th Congress, 1st Session. *Estimates for Public Buildings.* (H. Ex. Doc. 180). Washington, 1828. (Serial Set 173).

———. *The Hall of the House of Representatives.* (H. Rpt. 123). Washington, 1830. (Serial Set 199).

———. 24th Congress, 1st Session. *Letter Relating to Hall of Representatives.* (Ex. Doc. 266). Washington, 1836. (Serial Set 291).

———. 24th Congress, 1st Session. *Report on Public Buildings.* (H. Rpt. 350). Washington, 1836. (Serial Set 294).

———. 24th Congress, 2nd Session. *Estimates for Public Buildings and Grounds.* (H. Ex. Doc. 109). Washington, 1837. (Serial Set 303).

———. 24th Congress, 2nd Session. *Report on Expenditures for Public Buildings.* (H. Rpt. 312). Washington, 1837. (Serial Set 306).

U.S. Congress. 25th Congress, 3rd Session. *Report on Public Buildings.* (Ex. Doc. 20). Washington, 1838. (Serial Set 345).

U.S. House. 28th Congress, 1st Session. *Letter on Contracts for Public Buildings.* (H. Doc. 17). Washington, 1843. (Serial Set 441).

———. 28th Congress, 1st Session. *Report on Adapting Library Room for Chamber of Representatives.* (H. Rpt. 516). Washington, 1844. (Serial Set 447).

U.S. Senate. 29th Congress, 1st Session. *Report on Increasing Senate Chamber Accommodation.* (S. Doc. 251). Washington, 1846. (Serial Set 474).

U.S. House. 29th Congress, 2nd Session. *Report on Public Buildings.* (H. Doc. 14). Washington, 1846. (Serial Set 499).

U.S. Senate. 31st Congress, 1st Session. *Memorial of Robert Mills.* (S. Rpt. 145). Washington, 1850. (Serial Set 565).

———. 31st Congress, 2nd Session. *Report on the Enlargement of the Capitol Building.* (S. Rpt. 273). Washington, 1850. (Serial Set 593).

U.S. House. 31st Congress, 2nd Session. *Commissioners of Public Buildings: Contracts.* (H. Ex. Doc. 15). Washington, 1851. (Serial Set 598).

U.S. Senate. 32nd Congress, 1st Session. *Report of the Architect of the Capitol.* (S. Ex. Doc. 52). Washington, 1851. (Serial Set 619).

U.S. House. 32nd Congress, 1st Session. *Report on the Interior Department.* (H. Ex. Doc. 2). Washington, 1851. (Serial Set 635).

U.S. Congress. 32nd Congress, 1st Session. *Report of Architect on Congressional Library.* (S. Rpt. 63). Washington, 1852. (Serial Set 630).

U.S. Senate. 32nd Congress, 1st Session. *Message on Capitol Extension and Patent Office.* (S. Ex. Doc. 33). Washington, 1852. (Serial Set 618).

U.S. House. 32nd Congress, 1st Session. *Message of the President on Extension of the Capitol.* (H. Ex. Doc. 60). Washington, 1852. (Serial Set 641).

———. 32nd Congress, 1st Session. *Annual Report of the Commissioner of Public Buildings.* (H. Ex. Doc. 79). Washington, 1852. (Serial Set 641).

U.S. Senate. 32nd Congress, 1st Session. *Message of President Giving Information Relative to Extension of Capitol.* (S. Ex. Doc. 52). Washington, 1852. (Serial Set 619).

———. 32nd Congress, 1st Session. *Report of the Architect on Congressional Library.* (S. Committee Rpt. 163). Washington, 1852. (Serial Set 630).

U.S. House. 32nd Congress, 1st Session. *Letter of Commissioner of Public Buildings on Contracts.* (H. Misc. Doc. 66). Washington, 1852. (Serial Set 652).

———. 32nd Congress, 2nd Session. *Report on Public Buildings.* (H. Ex. Doc. 1). Washington, 1852. (Serial Set 673).

———. 32nd Congress, 2nd Session. *Report on Public Buildings and Grounds.* (H. Misc. Doc. 20). Washington, 1853. (Serial Set 685).

———. 32nd Congress, 2nd Session. *Contracts.* (H. Misc. Doc. 23). Washington, 1853. (Serial Set 685).

———. 33rd Congress, 1st Session. *Annual Report.* (H. Ex. Doc. 2). Washington, 1853. (Serial Set 675).

U.S. Senate. 33rd Congress, 1st Session. *Report on Capitol Extension.* (S. Ex. Doc. 1). Washington, 1853. (Serial Set 691).

U.S. House. 33rd Congress, 1st Session. *Report on Capitol Extension Stone-Cutters.* (H. Rpt. 306). Washington, 1853. (Serial Set 744).

———. 33rd Congress, 1st Session. *Report on Capitol Extension.* (H. Ex. Doc. 1), Washington, 1854. (Serial Set 777).

———. 34th Congress, 1st Session. *Report on Public Buildings and Grounds.* (H. Ex. Doc. 1). Washington, 1854. (Serial Set 840).

———. 34th Congress, 1st Session. *Report on Capitol and Post Office Extensions.* (H. Doc. 1). Washington, 1855. (Serial Set 841).

———. 34th Congress, 1st Session. *Message on Capitol Extension.* (H. Ex. Doc. 138). Washington, 1856. (Serial Set 864).

———. 34th Congress, 1st Session. *Reports on Capitol Dome.* (H. Misc. Doc. 65). Washington, 1856. (Serial Set 866).

———. 34th Congress, 1st Session. *Capitol and Post Office Extensions.* (H. Ex. Doc. 139). Washington, 1856. (Serial Set 864).

———. 34th Congress, 3rd Session. *Report on Public Buildings.* (H. Ex. Doc. 1). Washington, 1856. (Serial Set 893).

U.S. Senate. 34th Congress, 2nd Session. *Report on the Public Buildings.* (S. Ex. Doc. 11). Washington, 1858. (Serial Set 919).

U.S. House. 35th Congress, 1st Session. *Annual Report on Capitol Extension.* (H. Ex. Doc. 11). Washington, 1858. (Serial Set 920).

U.S. Senate. 36th Congress, 1st Session. *Letter from the Superintendent of the Capitol Extension.* (S. Misc. Doc. 29). Washington, 1860. (Serial Set 1038).

———. 36th Congress, 1st Session. *Report on Contracts for Marble.* (S. Ex. Doc. 22). Washington, 1860. (Serial Set 1031).

———. 36th Congress, 1st Session. *Message of President Buchanan.* (S. Ex. Doc. 20). Washington, 1860. (Serial Set 1031).

———. 36th Congress, 1st Session. *Letter of Superintendent of the Capitol of the New Chairman of the Committee on Public Buildings and Grounds.* (S. Misc. Doc. 29). Washington, 1860. (Serial Set 1038).

———. 36th Congress, 1st Session. *Report of Captain Franklin.* (S. Ex. Doc. 1). Washington, 1860. (Serial Set 1078).

———. 37th Congress, 2nd Session. *Annual Report of the Commissioner of Public Buildings.* (S. Doc. 1). Washington, Government Printing Office, 1861. (Serial Set 1117).

———. 37th Congress, 2nd Session. *Report on the Capitol Extension.* (S. Misc. Doc. 97). Washington, Government Printing Office, 1862. (Serial Set 1124).

U.S. House. 37th Congress, 2nd Session. *Report on Extension of Public Buildings.* (H. Rpt. 137). Washington, Government Printing Office, 1862. (Serial Set 1145).

———. 37th Congress, 3rd Session. *Report of the Architect of the Capitol Extension.* (H. Ex. Doc. 1). Washington: Government Printing Office, 1862. (Serial Set 1157).

———. 38th Congress, 1st Session. *Report of the Architect of the Capitol Extension.* (H. Ex. Doc. 1). Washington: Government Printing Office, 1863. (Serial Set 1182).

———. 38th Congress, 1st Session. *Report on the Public Buildings.* (H. Ex. Doc. 1). Washington: Government Printing Office, 1863. (Serial Set 1182).

U.S. Senate. 38th Congress, 1st Session. *Report on the Capitol Extension.* (S. Misc. Doc. 15). Washington: Government Printing Office, 1864. (Serial Set 1177).

U.S. House. 40th Congress, 2nd Session. *Report on Repairs to the Capitol.* (H. Ex. Doc. 21). Washington: Government Printing Office, 1867. (Serial Set 1330).

———. 42nd Congress, 3rd Session. *Letter on Extension of the Capitol Grounds.* (H. Ex. Doc. 46). Washington: Government Printing Office, 1872. (Serial Set 1565).

———. 44th Congress, 1st Session. *Report on Improvement of the Capitol Grounds.* (H. Rpt. 357). Washington: Government Printing Office, 1876. (Serial Set 1709).

———. 46th Congress, 2nd Session. *Report of the Architect of the Capitol.* (H. Ex. Doc. 1). Washington: Government Printing Office, 1879. (Serial Set 1911).

U.S. Senate. 46th Congress, 2nd Session. *Improvement of the Grounds South of Capitol.* (S. Misc. Doc. 102). Washington: Government Printing Office, 1880. (Serial Set 1891).

U.S. House. 46th Congress, 3rd Session. *Annual Report of the Architect of the Capitol.* (H. Ex. Doc. 1). Washington: Government Printing Office, 1880. (Serial Set 1960).

———. 47th Congress, 1st Session. *The Grounds South of the Capitol.* (H. Ex. Doc. 699). Washington: Government Printing Office, 1882. (Serial Set 2067).

——. 48th Congress, 1st Session. *Letter from the Secretary of the Treasury, transmitting estimates for proposed terraces and approaches for the United States Capitol, Washington, D.C.* (H. Ex. Doc. 9). Washington: Government Printing Office, 1883. (Serial Set 2193).

——. 49th Congress, 1st Session. *Pay for Work on the Capitol Terraces.* (H. Ex. Doc. 1). Washington: Government Printing Office, 1886. (Serial Set 2378).

——. 54th Congress, 2nd Session. *Statement as to the Filtration of Water Used in Capitol.* (H. Doc. 14). Washington: Government Printing Office, 1896. (Serial Set 3505).

——. 56th Congress, 1st Session. *Architect of the Capitol Report for 1899.* (H. Doc. 5). Washington: Government Printing Office, 1899. (Serial Set 3917).

——. 56th Congress, 1st Session. *Alterations in Rooms Lately Occupied by Library of Congress.* (H. Rpt. 23). Washington: Government Printing Office, 1891. (Serial Set 4021).

Documents Relating to the Painting and Sculpture

U.S. House. 19th Congress, 2nd Session. *Report on Designs for Paintings.* (H. Rpt. 8). Washington: 1826. (Serial Set 159).

——. 20th Congress, 2nd Session. *Letter Relative to National Paintings.* (H. Ex. Doc. 10). Washington: 1828. (Serial Set 184).

——. 24th Congress, 2nd Session. *Report on Paintings for the Capitol Rotunda.* (H. Rpt. 294). Washington: 1837. (Serial Set 306).

——. 26th Congress, 1st Session. *Letter Regarding Statues of Washington in Rotunda.* (H. Doc. 124). Washington: 1840. (Serial Set 365).

U.S. Senate. 34th Congress, 1st Session. *Report on Bust of Chief Justice John Rutledge.* (S. Rpt. 205). Washington: 1856. (Serial Set 837).

U.S. House. 36th Congress, 1st Session. *Report on the United States Art Commission.* (H. Ex. Doc. 43). Washington: 1860. (Serial Set 1048).

——. 40th Congress, 3rd Session. *Report on Decorations at the United States Capitol.* (H. Ex. Doc. 100). Washington: Government Printing Office, 1869. (Serial Set 1381).

——. 41st Congress, 2nd Session. *Letter on the Statue of General Greene.* (H. Misc. Doc. 23). Washington: Government Printing Office, 1870. (Serial Set 1431).

——. 41st Congress, 2nd Session. *Special Report of the Commissioner of Education, with Paper on Art in the District of Columbia.* (H. Ex. Doc. 315). Washington: Government Printing Office, 1871. (Serial Set 1427).

——. 41st Congress, 2nd Session. *Letter on the Bronze Doors in the Capitol.* (H. Misc. Doc. 28). Washington: Government Printing Office, 1870. (Serial Set 1433).

U.S. Senate. 48th Congress, 1st Session. *Report Submitted by Senator Sherman, from the Library Committee, May 14, 1884, on the Ceremonies of Unveiling the Statue of John Marshall.* (S. Rpt. 544). Washington: Government Printing Office, 1884. (Serial Set 2176).

U.S. Senate. 55th Congress, 2nd Session. *Capitol.* (S. Rpt. 631). Washington: Government Printing Office, 1898. (Serial Set 3622).

U.S. House. 55th Congress, 2nd Session. *Capitol.* (H. Rpt. 884). Washington: Government Printing Office, 1898. (Serial Set 3720).

U.S. Senate. 57th Congress, 2nd Session. *Marble Bust of General Lafayette.* (S. Rpt. 2544). Washington: Government Printing Office, 1903. (Serial Set 4410).

Heating and Ventilation

U.S. Senate. 35th Congress, 2nd Session. *Report on Heating the Capitol.* (S. Rpt. 388). Washington, 1859. (Serial Set 994).

——. 36th Congress, 1st Session. *Message of the President, in Compliance With a Resolution of the Senate, for Information in Relation to the Heating and Ventilation of the Capitol Extension, etc.* (S. Ex. Doc. 20). Washington, 1860. (Serial Set 1031).

——. 38th Congress, 2nd Session. *Report of the Joint Select Committee on Warming and Ventilating the Capitol.* (S. Rpt. 128). Washington: Government Printing Office, 1865. (Serial Set 1211).

U.S. Senate. 39th Congress, 1st Session. *Report.* (S. Rpt. 137). Washington: Government Printing Office, 1866. (Serial Set 1240).

U.S. House. 39th Congress, 1st Session. *Report on Warming and Ventilating the Capitol.* (H. Ex. Doc. 100). Washington: Government Printing Office, 1866. (Serial Set 1263).

U.S. Senate. 40th Congress, 2nd Session. *Memorial on Ventilation of the Halls of Congress.* (S. Misc. Doc. 110). Washington: Government Printing Office, 1868. (Serial Set 1319).

U.S. House. 40th Congress, 3rd Session. *Report on Ventilation of the House.* (H. Rpt. 19). Washington: Government Printing Office, 1869. (Serial Set 1388).

U.S. Congress. House and Senate. House. 41st Congress, 3rd Session. *Reports of Joint Committee on the Ventilation of the Capitol.* (H. Rpts. 48–49). Washington: Government Printing Office, 1871. (Serial Set 1464).

U.S. House. 46th Congress, 2nd Session. *Report on Ventilation of the House.* (H. Rpt. 22). Washington: Government Printing Office, 1879. (Serial Set 1934).

——. 53rd Congress, 2nd Session. *Ventilation of House of Representatives.* (H. Rpt. 853). Washington: Government Printing Office, 1894. (Serial Set 3271).

——. 53rd Congress, 3rd Session. *Report of Minority on Sanitary Condition of Capitol and Administration of Architect of Capitol.* (H. Rpt. 1980). Washington: Government Printing Office, 1895. (Serial Set 3346).

U.S. Senate. 54th Congress, 1st Session. *Ventilation, etc.* (S. Rpt. 713). Washington: Government Printing Office, 1896. (Serial Set 3365).

U.S. House. 54th Congress, 1st Session. *Ventilation and Acoustics Committee Reports.* (H. Rpt. 1825). Washington: Government Printing Office, 1896. (Serial Set 3464).

Water Supply and Sanitation

U.S. House. 21st Congress, 1st Session. *Water Supply of Capitol*. (H. Rpt. 145). Washington, 1830. (Serial Set 199).

———. 21st Congress, 1st Session. *Water for Public Buildings at Washington*. (H. Rpt. 281). Washington, 1830. (Serial Set 200).

———. 21st Congress, 1st Session. *Water for Capitol*. (H. Rpt. 344). Washington, 1830. (Serial Set 201).

U.S. Senate. 52nd Congress, 1st Session. *Letter Relative to Sanitary Condition of Senate Wing of Capitol*. (S. Misc. Doc. 42). Washington: Government Printing Office, 1892. (Serial Set 2904).

———. 52nd Congress, 1st Session. *Resolution Providing for Examination of Sanitary Condition of Capitol*. (S. Misc. Doc. 98). Washington: Government Printing Office, 1892. (Serial Set 2907).

U.S. House. 53rd Congress, 3rd Session. *Report on the Sanitary Condition of Capitol and Administration of Architect of the Capitol*. (H. Rpt. 1980). Washington: Government Printing Office, 1895. (Serial Set 3346).

———. 55th Congress, 3rd Session. *Report from Committee on Public Buildings and Grounds, Amending House Bill 4756, for Filtration of Water Supply of Capitol*. (H. Rpt. 1999). Washington: Government Printing Office, 1899. (Serial Set 3840).

Lighting the Capitol

U.S. Senate. 26th Congress, 1st Session. *Documents Relative to Lighting Capitol, etc.* (S. Doc. 434). Washington, 1840. (Serial Set 359).

U.S. House. 27th Congress, 1st Session. *Report on Gas Lights*. (H. Rpt. 6). Washington, 1841. (Serial Set 393).

———. 41st Congress, 3rd Session. *Report on Lighting of Capitol*. (H. Rpts. 48–49). Washington: Government Printing Office, 1871. (Serial Set 1464).

———. 50th Congress, 2nd Session. *Lighting the Capitol and Grounds*. (H. Ex. Doc. 101). Washington: Government Printing Office, 1889. (Serial Set 2651).

U.S. Senate. 51st Congress, 1st Session. *Lighting of Capitol*. (S. Misc. Doc. 27). Washington: Government Printing Office, 1889. (Serial Set 2698).

———. 54th Congress, 1st Session. *Lighting the Capitol*. (S. Rpt. 714). Washington: Government Printing Office, 1896. (Serial Set 3365).

Elevators

U.S. Senate. 46th Congress, 1st Session. *Letters on Elevators in Public Buildings*. (S. Ex. Doc. 27). Washington: Government Printing Office, 1879. (Serial Set 1869).

U.S. House. 51st Congress, 1st Session. *Resolution of Inquiry as to Elevator at Main Entrance to Capitol*. (H. Misc. Doc. 107). Washington: Government Printing Office, 1890. (Serial Set 2768).

———. 51st Congress, 1st Session. *Erection of Additional Elevator in Capitol Recommended*. (H. Rpt. 210). Washington: Government Printing Office, 1890. (Serial Set 2807).

Miscellaneous Matter

U.S. Senate. 15th Congress, 2nd Session. *Memorial of the Surveyor of Public Buildings*. (S. Doc. 53). Washington, 1818. (Serial Set 14).

———. 17th Congress, 1st Session. *Message on the Temporary Capitol*. (S. Doc. 21). Washington, 1822. (Serial Set 59).

———. 18th Congress, 1st Session. *Message on the Longtitude of the Capitol*. (S. Doc. 53). Washington, 1822. (Serial Set 91).

U.S. House. 21st Congress, 1st Session. *Memorial Relating to Hall of Representatives*. (H. Rpt. 83). Washington, 1830. (Serial Set 199).

———. 21st Congress, 1st Session. *Memorial on Defects in Representatives Hall*. (H. Rpt. 123). Washington, 1830. (Serial Set 199).

———. 23rd Congress, 1st Session. *Report on Claim of Robert Mills*. (H. Rpt. 275). Washington, 1834. (Serial Set 261).

U.S. Senate. 27th Congress, 2nd Session. *Report on Petition of Littleton Denis Treakle*. (S. Doc. 293). Washington, 1842. (Serial Set 398).

U.S. House. 27th Congress, 2nd Session. *Memorial on Construction of Public Buildings*. (H. Rpt. 460). Washington, 1842. (Serial Set 408).

———. 27th Congress, 2nd Session. *Report on Establishing the Longitude of the Capitol*. (H. Rpt. 683). Washington, 1842. (Serial Set 409).

———. 30th Congress, 1st Session. *Report on Injury to Capitol*. (H. Rpt. 61). Washington, 1842. (Serial Set 521).

———. 32nd Congress, 1st Session. *Report on Public Grounds*. (H. Ex. Doc. 69). Washington, 1852. (Serial Set 641).

U.S. Senate. 32nd Congress, 2nd Session. *On Frauds in Construction of Capitol*. (S. Select Com. Rpt. 1). Washington, 1853. (Serial Set 688).

———. 37th Congress, 2nd Session. *Report on Public Buildings*. (S. Misc. Doc. 8). Washington: Government Printing Office, 1861. (Serial Set 1124).

———. 38th Congress, 1st Session. *Committee on Public Buildings Favorable to Prayer of Commissioners for Services Rendered as Architect in Improvement of Capitol Building*. (S. Doc. 39). Washington: Government Printing Office, 1864. (Serial Set 1178).

U.S. House. 41st Congress, 3rd Session. *Memorial for Removal of Capitol*. (H. Misc. Doc. 105). Washington: Government Printing Office, 1871. (Serial Set 1463).

———. 41st Congress, 3rd Session. *Moving to Mississippi Valley.* (H. Rpt. 52). Washington: Government Printing Office, 1871. (Serial Set 1464).

———. 41st Congress, 3rd Session. *Report on Public Property.* (H. Misc. Doc. 67). Washington: Government Printing Office, 1871. (Serial Set 1463).

———. 42nd Congress, 2nd Session. *Report on Public Property.* (H. Misc. Doc. 20). Washington: Government Printing Office, 1871. (Serial Set 1524).

———. 42nd Congress, 3rd Session. *Report on Public Property.* (H. Misc. Doc. 45). Washington: Government Printing Office, 1873. (Serial Set 1572).

———. 43rd Congress, 1st Session. *Report on Telegraph Offices in the Capitol.* (H. Misc. Doc. 269). Washington: Government Printing Office, 1874. (Serial Set 1621).

———. 44th Congress, 1st Session. *Report on Public Property.* (H. Misc. Doc. 39). Washington: Government Printing Office, 1876. (Serial Set 1698).

U.S. Senate. 45th Congress, 2nd Session. *Statement of Appropriations and Expenditures from the National Treasury in the District of Columbia from July 16, 1790 to June 30, 1876.* Washington: Government Printing Office, 1876. (S. Ex. Doc. 84) (Serial Set 1782).

U.S. House. 46th Congress, 3rd Session. *Additional Accommodations for the Library of Congress.* (H. Rpt. 85). Washington: Government Printing Office, 1881. (Serial Set 1982).

U.S. Senate. 52nd Congress, 1st Session. *Examination of Capitol Under Senate Resolutions of March 22 and April 12, 1892.* (S. Rpt. 880). Washington: Government Printing Office, 1892. (Serial Set 2915).

———. 53rd Congress, 2nd Session. *Report Submitting S.R. 51, as Substitute for S. 1137, to Print Proceedings of Centennial Celebration of Laying of Cornerstone of Capitol. Senator Arthur P. Gorman.* (S. Rpt. 160). Washington: Government Printing Office, 1894. (Serial Set 3179).

———. 53rd Congress, 2nd Session. *Report Amending and Favoring S. 409 for Relief of Olivia and Ida Walter, Heirs of Thomas U. Walter.* (S. Rpt. 178). Washington: Government Printing Office, 1894. (Serial Set 3179).

U.S. House. 53rd Congress, 2nd Session. *Report Amending and Favoring H.R. 1326, for Relief of Olivia and Ida Walter, heirs of Thomas U. Walter.* (H. Rpt. 732). Washington: Government Printing Office, 1894. (Serial Set 3270).

———. 54th Congress, 1st Session. *Report from Committee on Claims, Favoring House Bill 154, for Relief of Olivia and Ida Walter, Heirs of Thomas U. Walter.* (H. Rpt. 342). Washington: Government Printing Office, 1894. (Serial Set 3458).

U.S. Senate. 54th Congress, 1st Session. *Report from Committee of Claims, Amending Senate Bill 278, for Relief of Olivia and Ida Walter, Heirs of Thomas U. Walter.* (S. Rpt. 309). Washington: Government Printing Office, 1896. (Serial Set 3363).

———. 54th Congress, 1st Session. *Report from Committee of Claims, Favoring Senate Bill 278, for Relief of Olivia and Ida Walter, Heirs of Thomas U. Walter as Substitute for Identical House Bill 154.* (S. Rpt. 1686). Washington: Government Printing Office, 1896. (Serial Set 3463).

———. 55th Congress, 1st Session. *Report from Committee of Claims, Favoring S. 1269, for Relief of Olivia and Ida Walter, Heirs of Thomas U. Walter.* (S. Rpt. 69). Washington: Government Printing Office, 1897. (Serial Set 3569).

———. 55th Congress, 2nd Session. *(History of Claim of) Heirs of Walter.* (S. Rpt. 544). Washington: Government Printing Office, 1898. (Serial Set 3620).

Brown, Glenn. "Report on the Effects of an Explosion in the United States Capitol, November 8, 1898." In *Annual Report of the Architect of the Capitol* (Washington: Government Printing Office, 1899): 29–46.

Munroe, Charles. "Report on the Effects of an Explosion in the United States Capitol, November 8, 1898." In *Annual Report of the Architect of the Capitol* (Washington: Government Printing Office, 1899): 1–28.

Selected Bibliography, United States Capitol, Since 1902

A detailed collection of information on the Capitol artists, architects, builders, room histories, and artwork is located in the Curator's Files, Office of the Architect of the Capitol.

Allen, William C. *The United States Capitol: A Brief Architectural History.* Washington: Government Printing Office, 1991.

———. *The Dome of the United States Capitol: An Architectural History.* Washington: Government Printing Office, 1992.

———. *"In the Greatest Solemn Dignity": The Capitol's Four Cornerstones.* Washington: Government Printing Office, 1994.

———. *History of the United States Capitol: A Chronicle of Design, Construction, and Politics.* Washington: Government Printing Office, 2001.

Architect of the Capitol. *Toward a Master Plan for the U.S. Capitol.* Washington: Government Printing Office, 1977.

———. *Art in the United States Capitol.* Washington: Government Printing Office, 1978.

Arnebeck, Bob. *Through a Fiery Trial: Building Washington, 1790–1800.* Lanham: Madison Books, 1991.

Bannister, Turpin C. "The Genealogy of the Dome of the United States Capitol," *Journal of the Society of Architectural Historians,* vol. 7 (January/June, 1948): 1–31.

Bennett, Wells. "Stephen Hallet and His Designs for the National Capitol, 1791–1794," *Journal of the American Institute of Architects* 4 (July/October, 1916): 1–31.

Bowling, Kenneth R. *Creating the Federal City, 1774–1800: Potomac Fever.* Washington: American Institute of Architects Press, 1988.

———. *The Creation of Washington, D.C.: The Idea and Location of the American Capital.* Fairfax, Va.: George Mason University Press, 1991.

Brown, Glenn. *1860–1930 Memories: A Winning Crusade to Revive George Washington's Vision of a Capital City.* Washington: W.F. Roberts, 1931.

Brownell, Charles E. and Jeffrey Cohen, *The Architectural Drawings of Benjamin Henry Latrobe.* New Haven: Yale University Press, 1994.

Bryan, John M., ed. *The Drawings of Robert Mills.* Washington: American Architectural Foundation, 1989.

Bushong, William. *Uncle Sam's Architects: Builders of the Capitol.* Washington: U.S. Capitol Historical Society, 1994.

Butler, Jeanne F. "Competition 1792: Designing a Nation's Capitol." *Capitol Studies,* vol. 4, No. 1, 1977.

Caemmerer, Hans Paul. *Washington: The National Capital.* Washington: Government Printing Office, 1932.

———. *A Manual on the Origin and Development of Washington.* Washington: Government Printing Office, 1939.

———. "The Sesquicentennial of the Laying of the Cornerstone of the United States Capitol by George Washington." *Records of the Columbia Historical Society,* 1944: 161–189.

———. "Architects of the United States Capitol," *Records of the Columbia Historical Society,* 1948–1949: 1–28.

———. *The Life of Pierre Charles L'Enfant, Planner of the City Beautiful, the City of Washington.* Washington: National Republic Publishing Co., 1950.

———. *Historic Washington: Capital of the Nation.* Washington: Government Printing Office, 1954.

Campioli, Mario. "An Historic Review and Current Proposals for the Nation's Capitol." *Journal of the American Institute of Architects* 39 (January 1963): 49–52.

———. "The Proposed Extension of the West Front of the Capitol," *Records of the Columbia Historical Society,* 1969–70: 212–236.

———. "The Capitol's Old Senate, House, and Supreme Court Chambers." *Capitol Dome* 4 (April 1969): 2–4.

———. "Building the Capitol." In Charles Peterson, ed., *Building Early America.* Radnor, Pa.: Chilton, 1976.

Carter, Edward C. "Benjamin Henry Latrobe and the Growth and Development of Washington, 1798–1818." *Records of the Columbia Historical Society,* 1971–1972: 128–49.

———. "The Engineer as Agent of Technological Transfer: The American Career of Benjamin Henry Latrobe." In Barbara E. Benson, ed. *Benjamin Henry Latrobe and Moncure Robinson.* Wilmington, Delaware: Eleutherian Mills—Hagley Foundation, 1975.

———. *Benjamin Henry Latrobe and Public Works: Professionalism, Private Interest, and Public Policy in the Age of Jefferson.* Washington: Public Works Historical Society, 1976.

———, ed. *The Journals of Benjamin Henry Latrobe, 1799–1820: From Philadelphia to New Orleans.* Ser. I, vol. 3. New Haven: Yale University Press, 1981.

Carter, Edward C. et al. *The Papers of Benjamin Henry Latrobe.* Microfiche ed. Clifton, N.J.: James T. White, 1976.

Carter, Edward C., John C. Van Horne, and Charles Brownell. *Latrobe's View of America, 1795–1820.* New Haven: Yale University Press, 1985.

Clark, Allen C. "Doctor and Mrs. Thornton." *Records of the Columbia Historical Society,* 1915: 144–208.

Commission for Enlarging the Capitol Grounds. Washington: Government Printing Office, 1928.

Cosentino, Andrew J. and Henry H. Glassie. *The Capital Image: Painters in Washington, 1890–1915.* Washington: Smithsonian Institution Press, 1983.

di Giacomantino, William C. "All the President's Men: George Washington's Federal City Commissioners." *Washington History* 3 (Spring/Summer, 1991): 53–75.

Dickinson, William C., Dean A. Herrin, and Donald R. Kennon, eds. *Montgomery C. Meigs and the Building of the National's Capital.* Athens: Ohio University Press, published for the United States Capitol Historical Society, 2001.

Documentary History of the Construction and Development of the United States Capitol Building and Grounds. Washington: Government Printing Office, 1904.

Dowd, Mary Jane, comp. *Records of the Office of Public Buildings and Public Parks of the National Capital: Record Group 42, Inventory 16.* Washington: National Archives and Records Administration, 1992.

Ennis, Robert B. "Thomas U. Walter." *Nineteenth Century* 5 (Autumn 1979): 59–60.

———. "Thomas U. Walter." *Macmillan Encyclopedia of Architects.* New York: The Free Press, 1982.

Fairman, Charles E. *Art and Artists of the Capitol of the United States of America.* Washington: Government Printing Office, 1927.

Fein, Albert. *Frederick Law Olmsted and the American Environmental Tradition.* New York: Brazilier, 1972.

Frary, Ihna T. *They Built the Capitol.* New York: Arno Press, 1940.

Fryd, Vivien Green. "Two Sculptures for the Capitol: Horatio Greenough's *Rescue* and Luigi Persico's *Discovery of America.*" *The American Art Journal* 19 (1987): 16–39.

———. *Art and Empire: The Politics of Ethnicity in the United States Capitol, 1815–1860.* New Haven: Yale University Press, 1992.

Gallagher, H. M. Pierce. *Robert Mills, Architect of the Washington Monument.* New York: Columbia University Press, 1935.

Goode, James M. *The Outdoor Sculpture of Washington, D.C.* Washington: Smithsonian Institution Press, 1974.

———. *Capital Losses*. Washington: Smithsonian Institution Press, 1979.

———. "Architecture and Politics: Thomas U. Walter and the Enlargement of the United States Capitol, 1850–1865." Ph.D. Dissertation, George Washington University, 1995.

Gutheim, Frederick. *Worthy of the Nation: The Planning and Development of the National Capital City*. Washington: Smithsonian Institution Press, 1977.

Gutheim, Frederick and Wilcomb Washburn. *The Federal City, Plans and Realities*. Washington: Smithsonian Institution Press, 1976.

Hamlin, Talbot F. "The Birth of American Architecture." *Parnussus* 10 (November 1938): 8–12.

———. "The Greek Revival in America and Some of Its Critics." *Art Bulletin* 24 (1942): 244–58.

———. "Benjamin Henry Latrobe: The Man and the Architect." *Maryland Historical Magazine* 37 (1942): 339–360.

———. *Greek Revival Architecture in America*. New York: Dover Press, 1944 (reprint 1966).

———. "Benjamin Henry Latrobe, 1764–1820." *Magazine of Art* 41 (1948): 89–95.

———. "Federal Architecture in Washington: The First Fifty Years." *Magazine of Art* 43 (1950): 223–29.

———. *Benjamin Henry Latrobe*. New York: Oxford University Press, 1955.

———. "A Previously Unpublished Perspective of the United States by B. H. Latrobe, 1764–1820." *Journal of the Society of Architectural Historians* 15 (May 1956): 26–27.

Hawkins, Don Alexander. "William Thornton's Lost Design of the United States Capitol." Unpublished manuscript, Curator's Office, Architect of the Capitol, Washington, D.C.

Hazelton, George C. *The National Capitol: Its Architecture, Art, and History*. New York: J. F. Taylor & Co., 1902.

Holzer, Harold and Joseph Farber. "Sculpture of the United States Capitol." *Antiques* 116 (July 1979): 146–159.

Howard, Alexandra M. "Stephen Hallet and William Thornton at the U.S. Capitol, 1791–1797." M.A. Thesis, University of Virginia, 1974.

Howells, John Mead. "Charles Bulfinch, Architect." *American Architect and Building News* 93 (1908): 194–200.

Huxtable, Ada Louise. "Architecture." In *Washington: The New York Times Guide to the Nation's Capital*. Washington: Robert B. Luce, 1967: 197–216.

Jaffe, Irma B, ed. *The Italian Presence in American Art, 1760–1860*. New York: Fordham University Press, 1989.

Jennings, J. L. Sibley, Jr. "Artistry as Design: L'Enfant's Extraordinary City." *Quarterly Journal of the Library of Congress"* 36 (Summer 1979): 225–278.

Kennon, Donald R., ed. *A Republic for the Ages: The United States Capitol and the Political Culture of the Early Republic*. Charlottesville: The University Press of Virginia, published for the United States Capitol Historical Society, 1999.

Kennon, Donald R., ed. *The United States Capitol: Designing and Deccorating a National Icon*, Athens: Ohio University Press, published for the United States Capitol Historical Society, 2000.

Kennon, Donald R., and Thomas P. Somma, eds. *American Pantheon: Sculptural and Artistic Decoration of the United States Capitol*. Athens: Ohio University Press, published for the U.S. Capitol Historical Society, 2004.

Kerwood, John R. *The United States Capitol: An Annotated Bibliography*. Norman, OK: University of Oklahoma Press, 1973.

Kimball, Fiske. "Thomas Jefferson and the First Monument of the Classical Revival in America." *Journal of the American Institute of Architects* 3 (1915): 473–491.

———. "Thomas Jefferson and the Origins of the Classical Revival in America." *Art and Archeology* 1 (1915): 219–227.

———. *Thomas Jefferson, Architect*. 1916. Reprint. New York: Da Capo, 1968.

———. "Benjamin Henry Latrobe and the Beginnings of Architectural and Engineering Practice in America." *Michigan Technic* 30 (1917): 218–223.

———. "Charles Bulfinch." *Dictionary of American Biography*. Vol. 3. New York: Scribner's Sons, 1933: 245–247.

———. "William Thornton." *Dictionary of American Biography*. Vol. 18 (New York: Scribner, 1936: 504–507.

Kirker, Harold. *The Architecture of Charles Bulfinch*. Cambridge: Harvard University Press, 1969.

Kirker, Harold, and James Kirker. *Charles Bulfinch's Boston, 1787–1817*. New York: Oxford University Press, 1964.

Klapthor, Margaret B. "Furniture in the Capitol: Desks and Chairs Used in the Chamber of the House of Representatives, 1819–1857." *Records of the Columbia Historical Society*, 1969–70: 190–211.

Kloss, William, and Diane K. Skvarla. *United States Senate Catalogue of Fine Art*. Edited by Jane R. McGoldrick. Washington: Government Printing Office, 2002.

Latrobe, Ferdinand C., II. "Benjamin Henry Latrobe: Descent and Works." *Maryland Historical Society Magazine* 33 (1938): 247–261.

Latrobe, John H. B. "Construction of the Public Buildings in Washington." *Maryland Historical Magazine* 4 (1909): 221–228.

"Latrobe Postscripts: Death of Lenthall." *Journal of the Society of Architectural Historians* 16 (October 1957): 31–32.

Longstreth, Richard, ed. *The Mall in Washington, 1791–1991*. Washington: National Gallery of Art, 1991.

Lowry, Bates, ed. *The Architecture of Washington, D.C.* New York: Dunlap, 1978.

———. *Building a National Image: Architectural Drawings for the American Democracy, 1789–1912*. Washington: National Building Museum, 1985.

Maroon, Fred J., and Suzy Maroon. *The United States Capitol*. New York: Stewart, Tabori & Chang, 1993.

McLaughlin, Charles C. "The Capitol in Peril?: The West Front Controversy from Walter to Stewart." *Records of the Columbia Historical Society*, 1969–70: 237–265.

Murdock, Myrtle. *Constantino Brumidi, Michelangelo of the United States Capitol*. Washington: Monumental Press, 1950.

Nichols, Frederick D. *Thomas Jefferson's Architectural Drawings with Commentary and a Check List*. 5th ed. Charlottesville: University Press of Virginia, 1984.

Norton, Paul F. "Latrobe's Ceiling for the Hall of Representatives." *Journal of the Society of Architectural Historians* 10 (May 1951): 5–10.

———. *Latrobe, Jefferson, and the National Capitol*. New York: Garland Publishers, 1977.

Padover, Saul. *Thomas Jefferson and the National Capital*. Washington: Government Printing Office, 1946.

Place, Charles A. *Charles Bulfinch, Architect and Citizen*. Boston and New York: Houghton, Mifflin Co., 1925.

Reed, Henry Hope. *The United States Capitol: Its Architecture and Decoration*. New York: W.W. Norton & Company, 2005.

Reiff, Daniel D. *Washington Architecture, 1791–1861: Problems in Development*. Washington: U.S. Commission of Fine Arts, 1971.

Reps, John W. *Monumental Washington: The Planning and Development of the Capital Center*. Princeton, N.J.: Princeton University Press, 1967.

———. *Washington on View*. Chapel Hill: University of North Carolina Press, 1991.

Ridout, Orlando. *Building the Octagon*. Washington: American Institute of Architects Press, 1989.

Roper, Laura Wood. *FLO: A Biography of Frederick Law Olmsted*. Baltimore: Johns Hopkins University, 1973.

Rosenberger, Homer T. "Thomas U. Walter and the Completion of the United States Capitol," *Records of the Columbia Historical Society*, 1948–1950: 273–322.

Rusk, William Sener. "Thomas U. Walter." *Dictionary of American Biography*. Vol. 19. New York: Charles Scribner's Sons, 1936: 397–398.

———. "Thomas U. Walter and His Works." *Americana* 33 (1939): 151–179.

———. *William Thornton, Benjamin H. Latrobe, Thomas U. Walter, and the Classical Influence in Their Works*. Baltimore: Johns Hopkins University, 1939.

Scott, Pamela. "Stephen Hallet's Designs for the United States Capitol." *Winterthur Portfolio* 27 (Summer/Autumn 1992): 145–170.

———. " 'This Vast Empire': Development of the Mall from 1791 to 1848." In *The Mall in Washington 1791–1991*, ed. Richard Longstreth, 37–58. Washington: National Gallery of Art, 1991.

———. *Temple of Liberty: Building the Capitol for a New Nation*. New York: Oxford University Press, 1995.

Shannon, Martha A. S. "The Architecture of Charles Bulfinch." *American Magazine of Art* 16 (1925): 431–437.

Skramstad, Harold K. "The Engineer as Architect in Washington: The Contribution of Montgomery Meigs." *Records of the Columbia Historical Society*, 1969–70: 266–284.

Somma, Thomas P. *The Apotheosis of Democracy, 1908–1916: The Pediment for the House Wing of the United States Capitol*. Newark: University of Delaware Press, 1995.

Stearns, Elinor and David Yerkes. *William Thornton*. Washington: American Institute of Architects Foundation, 1976.

Stephenson, Richard W. "The Delineation of a Grand Plan." *Quarterly Journal of the Library of Congress* 36 (Summer 1979): 207–24.

Stern, Philip Van Doren. "The Capitol." *Records of the Columbia Historical Society*, 1969–70: 178–189.

Stevenson, Elizabeth. *Park Maker: A Life of Frederick Law Olmsted*. New York: Macmillan, 1977.

Thorndike, Joseph J., Jr., ed. *Three Centuries of Notable American Architects*. New York: American Heritage Publishing Company, 1981.

Van Horne, John C. and Lee Formwalt, eds. *The Correspondence and Miscellaneous Papers of Benjamin Henry Latrobe*. Ser. IV, vol. 1. New Haven, Conn.: Yale University Press, 1984.

Van Horne, John C., ed. *The Correspondence and Miscellaneous Papers of Benjamin Henry Latrobe*. Ser. IV, vols. 2 and 3. New Haven, Conn.: Yale University Press, 1986 and 1988.

Weigley, Russell. *Quartermaster General of the Union Army: A Biography of M. C. Meigs*. New York: Columbia University Press, 1959.

———. "Captain Meigs and the Artists of the Capitol: Federal Patronage of Art in the 1850's." *Records of the Columbia Historical Society*, 1969–70: 285–305.

Wolanin, Barbara. *Constantino Brumidi: Artist of the Capitol*. Washington: Government Printing Office, 1998.

Wolff, Wendy, ed. *Captiol Builder: The Shorthand Journals of Montgomery C. Meigs, 1853–1859, 1861*. Washington, D.C.: U.S. Government Printing Office, 2001.

Young, James Sterling. *The Washington Community, 1800–1828*. New York: Columbia University Press, 1966.

INDEX TO THE ANNOTATED EDITION

cized, 9; design of dome over portico, 131; discharged, 78; early life of, 266; first plan of lost, 60; lays foundations of Capitol, 77; modification of Thornton's plan, 63; objections to Thornton plan, 62; plan of preferred by commissioners, 58; plans for Capitol, 64; reasons for discharge of, 91; salary of, 103; Thornton's plan and, 60–64

Hamilton, Alexander, 513; painting of, 436

Hancock, John, 249, 513

Hanson, John, 514

Harbaugh, Leonard, 45, 58, 94

Harlan, James, 387, 420

Hart, Philip, 45

Haskin, J. A., 386

Haupt, Hermann, 420

Hazelhurst, Isaac, 259

Heaton, A. G., 543

Henry, Joseph: commission on marble and, 340; commission on heating, ventilation, and acoustics and, 343, 372, 374; commission on ventilation and, 422; report on heating and ventilating Capitol, 420

Henry, William Wirt, 417

Hill, David J., 27

History, 510

Hoban, James, 58, 63, 76, 91, 94, 104, 105, 123; appointed superintendent of Capitol, 68, 77; as superintendent, 103, 123; authority over Capitol and President's House, 78; awarded premium for design of President's House, 266; design for President's House selected, 45; early work in Charleston, 266; on rooms of Senate Chamber, 98; on Thornton's plan, 61–62; prefers copper covering, 141; reports on Capitol, 97–101, 102; resumes superintendence of Capitol, 93; salary of, 103; services end as superintendent, 92

Hoffman, Charles, 253

Holt, Joseph, 375

Hood, James F., 27

Hoover, Andrew, 319

Hoover, Henry, 587

Hotel Kenmore, 257

Houdon, Jean Antoine, 513

House Chamber, 304; condition of in 1857, 354

House Library, 302

House of Representatives: accommodations enlarged (1801), 102; antechamber, 101; appoints committee to investigate condition of Chamber, 354; arrangement of described ca. 1900, 470; art work in, 34; clock of, 516, 587; committee rooms, 412; described in 1799, 98, 101; gallery, 101, 417; investigates Capitol extension, 342; Latrobe's modifications to Thornton's plan, 108–111; meets in new Chamber (1807), 121; new Hall occupied, 355; new office building (1903), 494; seats replaced, 416; semicircular room recommended for, 140; skylights, 121; space needed for, 114. See also Hall of Representatives.

House restaurant, 417

Howard, J. Q., 78, 104

Hubard, W. J., 513

Hubner, Charles, 319

Hull, Commodore, 292

Hunter, R. M. T., 33, 303

Iardella, Francisco, 215, 276, 297; succeeds Andrei, 175

Inman, Henry, 250, 296, 542

Instruction, 510

Interior Department, 341

J. H. & J. C. Schneider, 587

Jackson, Andrew, 174; appoints Mills architect, 212

Janes, Beebe & Co., 341, 355, 587

Janes, Fowler, and Kirtland, 587

Jay, John: bust of, 217, 293

Jefferson, Thomas, 43, 45, 63, 103, 104, 115, 154; appoints Thornton clerk of patents, 258; bust of, 217, 294; calls for advertising competition for Capitol and President's House, 44; calls for Corinthian columns, 121; consulted on painting, 249; design of capitals and, 130; elected President, 102; letter to Latrobe re Thornton, 107; letters to Latrobe, 105; on floors of Senate Chamber, 98; on Thornton's plan, 59; opinion sought on Thornton's plan, 62; painting of, 436; portrait of, 543; Robert Mills and, 269; statue of by d'Anvers, 512–513; statue of by Powers, 513; suggestions for Capitol, 108, 114; suggestions for skylight, 121; Thornton's plan and, 30, 31, 179; tiles and windows for Capitol, 120